UNLOCKING
CONTRACT
LAW

UNLOCKING THE LAW

4th edition

Chris Turner

Routledge
Taylor & Francis Group

LONDON AND NEW YORK

Fourth edition published 2014
by Routledge
2 Park Square, Milton Park, Abingdon, Oxon OX14 4RN

Simultaneously published in the USA and Canada
by Routledge
711 Third Avenue, New York, NY 10017

Routledge is an imprint of the Taylor & Francis Group, an informa business

First edition published by Hodder Education in 2004
Third edition published by Hodder Education in 2010

British Library Cataloguing in Publication Data
A catalogue record for this book is available from the British Library

Library of Congress Cataloging-in-Publication Data
Turner, Chris (Barrister)
   Unlocking contract law / Chris Turner. — Fourth edition.
      pages cm. — (Unlocking the law)
   1. Contracts—England 2. Contracts—Wales.   I. Title.
   KD1554.T875 2014
   346.4202'2—dc23
                                                           2013020813
ISBN: 978-1-4441-7417-5 (pbk)
ISBN: 978-0-203-77941-5 (ebk)

Typeset in Palatino LT-Roman
Project Managed and Typeset by: diacriTech

Contents

11 VITIATING FACTORS: DURESS AND UNDUE INFLUENCE

12 VITIATING FACTORS: ILLEGALITY AND UNENFORCEABLE CONTRACTS

Acknowledgements

The books in the Unlocking the Law series are a departure from traditional law texts and represent one view of a type of learning resource that the editors always felt is particularly useful to students. The success of the series and the fact that many of its features have been subsequently emulated in other publications must surely vindicate that view. The series editors would therefore like to thank the original publishers, Hodder Education, for their support in making the original project a successful reality. In particular we would like to thank Alexia Chan for showing great faith in the project and for her help in getting the series off the ground. We would also like to thank the current publisher, Routledge for the warm enthusiasm it has shown in taking over the series. In this respect we must also thank Fiona Briden, Commissioning Editor for the series for her commitment and enthusiasm towards the series and for her support.

Guide to the book

In the *Unlocking the Law* books all the essential elements that make up the law are clearly defined to bring the law alive and make it memorable. In addition, the books are enhanced with learning features to reinforce learning and test your knowledge as you study. Follow this guide to make sure you get the most from reading this book.

AIMS AND OBJECTIVES

Defines what you will learn in each chapter.

SECTION

definition
Find key legal terminology at-a-glance.

Highlights sections from Acts.

ARTICLE

Defines Articles of the EC Treaty or of the European Convention on Human Rights or other Treaty.

tutor tip
Provides key ideas on how to get ahead from lecturers.

CLAUSE

Shows a Bill going through Parliament or a draft Bill proposed by the Law Commission.

CASE EXAMPLE

Illustrates the law in action.

JUDGMENT

Provides extracts from judgments on cases.

QUOTATION

Encourages you to engage with primary sources.

ACTIVITY

Enables you to test yourself as you progress through the chapter.

student mentor tip

Offers advice from law graduates on the best way to achieve the results you want.

SAMPLE ESSAY QUESTIONS

Provide you with real-life sample essays and show you the best way to plan your answer.

SUMMARY

Concludes each chapter to reinforce learning.

Preface

The 'Unlocking the Law' series on its creation was hailed as an entirely new style of undergraduate law textbooks and many of its ground-breaking features have subsequently been emulated in other publications. However, many student texts are still very prose dense and have little in the way of interactive materials to help a student feel his or her way through the course of study on a given module.

The purpose of the series has always been to try to make learning each subject area more accessible by focusing on actual learning needs, and by providing a range of different supporting materials and features.

All topic areas are broken up into manageable sections with a logical progression and extensive use of headings and numerous sub-headings as well as an extensive contents list and index. Each book in the series also contains a variety of flow charts, diagrams, key facts charts and summaries to reinforce the information in the body of the text. Diagrams and flow charts are particularly useful because they can provide a quick and easy understanding of the key points, especially when revising for examinations. Key facts charts not only provide a quick visual guide through the subject but are also useful for revision.

Many cases are separated out for easy access and all cases have full citation in the text as well as the table of cases for easy reference. The emphasis of the series is on depth of understanding much more than breadth of detail. For this reason each text also includes key extracts from judgments where appropriate. Extracts from academic comment from journal articles and leading texts are also included to give some insight into the academic debate on complex or controversial areas. In both cases these are highlighted and removed from the body of the text.

Finally the books also include much formative 'self-testing', with a variety of activities ranging through subject specific comprehension, application of the law and a range of other activities to help the student gain a good idea of his or her progress in the course. Appendices with guides on completing essay style questions and legal problem solving supplement and support this interactivity. Besides this a sample essay plan is added at the end of most chapters.

A feature of the most recent editions is the inclusion of some case extracts from the actual law reports which not only provide more detail on some of the important cases but also help to support students in their use of law reports by providing a simple commentary and also activities to cement understanding.

Contract law is actually a very relevant and useful area of law. We are all constantly forming different contractual relationships even though we might not think about them in that manner. An understanding of the basic rules of contract in any case is essential for a full understanding of other areas such as commercial law and employment law. Since Contract Law is also in the main a common law area much of this book is devoted to cases and case notes, and these are separated out in the text for easy reference.

The book is designed to cover all of the main topic areas on undergraduate, degree-equivalent and professional contract syllabuses and help provide a full understanding of each.

I hope that you will gain as much enjoyment in reading about the Contract Law, and testing your understanding with the various activities in the book as I have had in writing it, and that you gain much enjoyment and interest from your study of the law.

The law is stated as I believe it to be on 1st August 2013.

Chris Turner

List of figures

Table of cases

Table of legislation and other instruments

TABLE OF LEGISLATION AND OTHER INSTRUMENTS

1

The origins and character of contract law

1.1 The origins and functions of the law of contract

1.1.1 Development of the law of contract

Much of the modern law of contract developed in the nineteenth century and derives from the *laissez-faire* principles of economics that characterised the Industrial Revolution.

Nevertheless, the origins of contract law are much more ancient than that and are to be found in the early common law of the Middle Ages. The main preoccupation of society at that time was land ownership and law developed very quickly in relation to the protection of ownership of land or of interests in land. As a result, the law of that time was also mainly concerned with property rights.

The distinction that the law drew in terms of identifying the enforceability of rights was between formal agreements and informal ones. A formal agreement was one made in writing and which was authenticated by the practice of 'sealing'. This is the origin of the deed, which was the method accepted for transfer of land and interests in land up to 1989, when the requirement to complete the document by the process of sealing was relaxed in favour of the already common practice of witnessing the document.

Two principal types of formal **agreement**, which were required to be under seal to be enforceable, developed during the twelfth century:

- A covenant – such an agreement was usually to do something, for example an agreement to build a house. The available remedy that developed in relation to such agreements was specific performance.
- A formal debt – this was again an agreement under seal, but to pay a sum of money. This agreement was actionable as an 'obligation' and the available remedy was the payment of the debt.

agreement

The first requirement for a validly formed contract which involves a valid offer by one party being followed by a valid acceptance by the other

detinue

In early contract law an action for delivery of a chattel

assumpsit

An old form of enforcing an undertaking to carry out a promise

consideration

The thing (or promise) given by a party to a contract in exchange for what the other party gives (promises to give)

Informal agreements also gradually gained the recognition of the law. These became known as 'parol' agreements, following the simple meaning of the word at the time: 'by word of honour'. The clear problem with informal agreements was the availability of proof of their actual existence in order for the parties to be able to enforce their provisions.

Two particular actions developed for informal agreements:

- An action for debt – this was usually an oral agreement for the sale of the goods, and the remedy sought was usually the price of the goods
- **Detinue** – this was a claim in respect of a chattel due to the person bringing the action, for instance for delivery of a horse or other livestock.

The more modern law of contract begins with the law of '**assumpsit**' in the fourteenth century. This had its origins in the tort of trespass, and was an action in respect of the breach of an informal promise. The *assumpsit* was the undertaking to carry out the promise.

Moving even further forward in time, one of the most essential requirements of modern contract law, the doctrine of **consideration**, was also established. The consideration was the reason for the promise being given, and was based on the assumption that nobody does anything for nothing.

1.1.2 The purposes of contract law

People make contracts all the time, whether individually or within the framework of a business activity. In this way there are inevitably many different types of contracts and the contracts may satisfy different purposes. However, it is possible to identify an overriding purpose as identified in the following quote:

QUOTATION

'… contract law has many "purposes", but the central one is to support and to control the millions of agreements that collectively make up the "market economy".'

H G Beale, W D Bishop and M P Furmston, Contract Cases and Materials
(4th edn, Butterworths, 2001)

In a market economy, everything depends on an exchange of resources, whether that means the sale and purchase of goods or services or the payment of a wage in return for labour. In some instances, the exchange takes place immediately but more often the exchange is based on a set of promises, for example the promise to deliver goods in return for the promise to pay for them after they are delivered.

term

An obligation under a contract

Contract law tends to be the means of supporting the bargain and of ensuring that there will be a remedy if the agreement is not carried out according to the **terms** laid down by the parties. By developing a body of rules to deal with specific situations it also gives parties who contract a set of guidelines by which they can safely contract in the future without having to negotiate each separate aspect of the contract. The rules, then, not only identify how the parties must behave in order to say that they have formed a valid and enforceable contract; they also identify things that the parties must not do in order to achieve the contract, such as misrepresenting the truth of the agreement being reached. In essence, then, the law of contract gives contracting parties a framework to operate within and a means of finding a remedy when things go wrong.

However, the function of the law of contract is to balance out the interests of a free market and the protection of the weaker parties to contracts. Generally, this would be through consumer protection of one sort or another.

Adams and Brownsword identify that

QUOTATION

'... market-individualism enshrines the landmark principles of "freedom of contract" and "sanctity of contract", the essential thrust of which is to give the parties the maximum licence in setting their own terms, and to hold parties to their freely made bargains.'

In pursuit of this aim they suggest that judges 'should offer no succour to parties who are simply trying to escape from a bad bargain [as this] results in an economically efficient use of resources'. On the other hand, they identify that the need to protect consumers also means that judges must ensure that

QUOTATION

'... contracting parties should not mislead each other, that they should act in good faith, that a stronger party should not exploit the weakness of another's bargaining position, that no party should profit from his own wrong or be unjustly enriched, that remedies should be proportionate to the breach, [and] that contracting parties who are at fault should not be able to dodge their responsibilities.'

R Brownsword and J N Adams, Understanding Contract Law
(Fontana, 1987) pp 52–53

Inevitably, what this also means is that judges will also engage in policy decisions with the following result, as identified by Beale, Bishop and Furmston:

QUOTATION

'In some cases the control takes the form of frustrating the parties for the good of the rest of society.'

H G Beale, W D Bishop and M P Furmston, Contract Cases and Materials
(4th edn, Butterworths, 2001)

There are many areas of contract law where we can identify underlying policy.

1.1.3 The character of modern contracts

It is quite usual for non-lawyers to assume that a contract is an official agreement of some kind that is written down, and that has probably even been prepared by a lawyer. This, of course, is not the case. We all make many contracts every day, even though we rarely put them into writing or contemplate the consequences of making them. In fact, we generally take the situation for granted and it is not until such time as we realise that we have not got what we bargained for that we begin to think in terms of any rights attaching to the transaction.

For instance, this morning I had to go to London. I parked my car in the multi-storey car park at Wolverhampton station, taking the ticket from the machine at the entrance.

Inside the station, I bought a newspaper. On the train, I bought a cup of coffee in a sealed container and a packet of crisps.

There is nothing exceptional about any of these events. I gave no thought to contract law in relation to any one of them, but I was making a contract in every case.

However, the implications of the various transactions and the significance of contract law become apparent if in each case I do not get what I bargained for. If, for instance, on opening the newspaper I discovered that only the cover pages were printed on, or on drinking it that the coffee was in fact tea, or on eating them that the crisps were mouldy, or finally that on returning from London I found my car had been badly damaged in the car park, I would want at least my money back, and probably some other form of remedy. At that point I would be very eager to know about the contractual nature of the arrangements that I had made in each case.

The thing that distinguishes a contract in the modern day, then, is not necessarily whether it is in a written agreement, even though this may have been absolutely critical in former times. The significant point is that there is in fact an agreement made between two parties, by which they are both bound, and which if necessary can be enforced in the courts. Of course, many agreements will be in written form. However, many more will merely be made orally, and of course some may even be made by conduct, as is often the case in auctions. Such contracts are called simple contracts.

Some contracts, because of their nature, have to be in writing or in other cases there should at least be evidence of the existence of the contract in writing. These contracts we call speciality contracts, and the most common is a contract for the transfer of land, but these are beyond the scope of this book.

A contract is essentially a commercial agreement, an agreement between two parties which is enforceable in law. It is based on the promises that the two parties make to each other. However, while the law rightly protects many of the promises that we make to one another, not all promises are contractual. For instance, a beneficiary under a will has in effect been promised that inheritance and has a legal right to receive it. The will is not, however, covered by contract law. The heir has promised nothing in return for the inheritance.

A contract can alternatively be described as a bargain. One party makes a promise in return for the promise of the other and the promises are mutually enforceable because of the price that one party has paid for the promise of the other.

Many of the rules of contract law came about in the nineteenth century. At that time, people believed very much in the idea that there was freedom of contract. This is a nice idea, that we are all free to make whatever contracts we want, on whatever terms we want.

It does not, of course, bear much relationship with reality. Commonly, the two parties to a contract have unequal bargaining strength. A prospective employee at interview is rarely telling the prospective employer what conditions he is prepared to work for, but is trying to impress to get the job.

Consumers too, even though they may have a choice of where to buy from, will rarely negotiate the terms of the transaction they are making. More often than not, in the present day, contracts with businesses will be done on the latter's 'standard forms'.

As a result of this, Parliament in the twentieth and early twenty-first centuries has produced many laws inserting, or implying, terms into contracts which the parties themselves have not chosen but by which they both are bound.

So the notion of freedom of contract is not as straightforward as it seems, and a party to a contract has to be aware of the numerous contractual obligations by which he will be bound other than those which he has personally negotiated.

1.1.4 The reasons that contracts are enforced

As we have seen, then, a contract is an enforceable agreement between two parties. The rules regarding enforceability of agreements obviously grew out of the need for certainty in relationships, whether between businesses or between private individuals. We can none of us safely conduct ourselves without knowing that we are able to rely on arrangements that we have made.

The enforceability of contracts is based on three significant factors:

- An agreement made between two parties creates legitimate expectations in both that the terms of the arrangement will be carried out and that they will receive whatever benefit that is expected from the agreement.
- Parties will commonly risk expenditure or do work in reliance on a promise that a particular agreement will be carried out.
- It is simply unfair that if one party is ready to perform, or indeed has performed, their part of the bargain, the other party should escape or avoid his obligations without some means of redress for the injured party.

1.2 The concept of freedom of contract

Freedom of contract is not just something that we expect – the right to contract with whomever we want and on the terms that we want – it is also at the heart of contract law. In the nineteenth century, when many of the rules of contract law were devised, Britain was subject to what was known as *laissez-faire* economics. In modern times, politicians as well as economists refer to this as 'the market' and there is a prevailing theory that market forces rather than government intervention should dictate the economic relations between people.

The basic proposition in any case is that the parties to a contract should be free to include in a contract whatever terms they choose. In this way the courts will not interfere in contracts by trying to make a bad bargain good. They will merely ensure that there is a bargain and that it has been properly created. Treitel identified this point clearly when he said:

QUOTATION

'In its most obvious sense, the expression "freedom of contract" is used to refer to the general principle that the law does not restrict the terms on which the parties may contract: it will not give relief merely because the terms of the contract are harsh or unfair to one party.'

G H Treitel, An Outline of the Law of Contracts
(5th edn, Butterworths, 1995)

The idea of freedom of contract is central to enforcement of contracts and it runs through many of the individual rules of contract law:

consensus ad idem

The agreement between the parties– literally a meeting of minds

- An agreement (offer and acceptance) is said not to exist unless there is a *consensus ad idem*, the so-called mutuality of the parties. So even though the parties think that they have agreed on something, there will not be an enforceable contract between them unless this mutuality can be shown. The law prevents one party from forcing goods and services on another party without an actual agreement to take them. This is apparent in the common law rules on acceptance as well as in statutes such as the Unsolicited Goods and Services Act 1971.
- Contract law only concerns itself with the enforcement of bargains. The rules on consideration, including the most modern case law such as *Williams v Roffey Bros &*

Nicholls Contractors Ltd [1990] 1 All ER 512, demonstrate that the courts are not interested in the quality of the bargain that parties freely reach. They are merely concerned with the existence of a bargain that is then enforceable.

- The requirement that an enforceable agreement must also include within it the intention that the parties are legally bound is another example of freedom of contract. Many agreements are reached between parties where they would not consider that they had brought themselves within the law. We are free to make contracts where we agree to be bound. We will not be bound by agreements that we never intend should carry any legal weight. Even if it is wrong that we break these agreements, it is equally wrong that we should be hauled before the courts for a promise that has no legal basis which for some reason we cannot keep, and the law sensibly recognises this.
- Freedom of contract is recognised also in the fact that many of the terms or obligations of the contract by which the parties are then bound are decided upon by the parties themselves. Where bargaining strength is equal, the law will even allow terms that are clearly disadvantageous to a party if he freely agreed to be bound by it. A very extreme example of this can be seen in the so-called '*Securicor* cases' in exclusion clauses (see section 7.2.2).
- Even though the court can be seen to be operating in a protectionist manner towards one party, the rules relating to the various **vitiating factors** are in effect another example of freedom of contract. This relates back to the idea of a *consensus ad idem*. If a party is entering a contract only because of false information, or being mistaken as to material facts, or is in any way coerced to enter the contract, then the law will declare the contract void or will set it aside. This will happen because the basis of contracting must be that a party enters the arrangement with free will and by exercising choice.
- Freedom can even be seen in one sense in the rules on **discharge**. For instance, where a party has failed to perform all obligations under the contract precisely, it may still be possible for the other party to accept part-performance, and inevitably to pay only for the part done or given. In the same way, the rules on **breach** of contract allow a party who is the victim of the breach of a central term to choose between giving up his own obligations or continuing with the contract, if it would be advantageous, and merely gaining compensation for the breach in question.

As the law of contract has developed, however, it has also been recognised that the parties to a contract cannot be given unlimited freedom and the law has in many instances intervened to give greater protection to the parties. There are a number of reasons for this:

- It is recognised that very often the parties are of unequal bargaining strength and therefore one party would be able to dictate the terms of the contract, possibly at the expense of the weaker party.
- Particularly since the middle of the twentieth century, judges, Parliament and, more recently, the European Union have all been concerned to give greater protection to consumers to avoid them being taken advantage of by unscrupulous businessmen in contracts that are driven more by the profit motive of business rather than the individual needs of consumers.
- It would be unfair to allow one party to take advantage of the other party's **mistake** or to take advantage of a falsehood, or to allow one party to coerce the other party to enter the contract against his will.
- In certain instances either the courts or Parliament have recognised that it is unacceptable or inadvisable to allow parties to enter specific types of contracts.

vitiating factor

A defect that renders an otherwise validly formed contract void or voidable

discharge

How a contract comes to an end

breach

A failure to honour the obligations under the contract

mistake

A wrong assumption made by one or more parties to a contract on entering the contract

There are many examples of this protectionism. An obvious example from the common law would be the rules on undue influence that have been developed by the courts in relation to wives who have agreed to allow property jointly owned with their husbands to be used as security for loans. There are many examples of protectionism in statute, usually falling under the general classification of consumer protection (see section 1.4).

1.3 Contract law compared with other areas of law

1.3.1 Contract law compared with tort

Sometimes both the law of contract and the law of torts are seen as a general law of 'obligations'. Certainly, both branches of the law compensate victims for the harm done to them. Both branches of the law are also ultimately based on duties owed by one party to another.

The traditional distinction between the two is the character of the duty owed. In the case of torts, specific duties are imposed by law and apply to everyone. In contract law, the duties are imposed by the parties themselves and operate only to the extent agreed upon before the contract was formed. Similarly, in the case of tort the duty is usually owed generally to all persons likely to be affected by the tort. In contract law, on the other hand, the duty is only to the other party to the contract.

1.3.2 The interrelationship between contract law and tort

Nevertheless, the distinction is not always so clear and there are many complications and overlaps. In the law of contract many duties are now imposed on parties by statute and as a result of EU law, irrespective of the actual wishes of the parties to the contract. This has been particularly the case in the area of consumer contracts. In the law of torts, in those situations where the law does allow recovery for a pure economic loss, the distinction between the two again is somewhat blurred.

There can be overlap too in areas such as product liability where there can be claims for negligence and also for breach of implied statutory conditions under the contract. In such circumstances a choice is sometimes made whether to sue a manufacturer in tort or a supplier under contract law.

Similar complications have arisen in the field of medicine. Normally, we would expect legal actions to be brought in medical negligence in tort. However, where a patient has taken advantage of private medicine the rules of contract law can be invoked if they may have a more satisfactory answer – if, for instance, the contractual duty is higher than the duty in tort.

Difficulties can also arise because of the doctrine of privity in contract law and the exceptions to it, although legislation has removed some of the hardships here. However, the absence of a contractual relationship again may not prevent an action being brought for a breach of a duty in tort if such a duty exists.

1.3.3 Contract law compared with criminal law

Contract law is very obviously different from criminal law in the same senses that all areas of civil law differ from the criminal law. The differences can be used as an example generally of the differences between criminal law and civil law.

- The whole context of the case is different – the criminal law involves the regulation of behaviour that is unacceptable to the state, while civil law involves the resolution of disputes between two parties (in the case of contract law, a dispute over a contract).
- The purpose of the action is different. In criminal law the purpose is to preserve order in the community. Civil law seeks to regulate relationships and settle disputes (eg, a breach of contract).
- The parties are completely different. In criminal law the state prosecutes a defendant. In civil law, as in a contract action, a defendant answers a claim from a claimant.
- The standard of proof is also different. In criminal law, because a defendant's liberty may be at stake, the prosecution must prove the case beyond a reasonable doubt. In contract actions, on the other hand, as in civil actions in general, the claimant has to prove his case only on a balance of probabilities.
- The potential resolution of the action differs also. A successful criminal trial results in a conviction and subsequent punishment with whatever appropriate sentence. In contract law, as in other civil law actions, a successful claimant will have proved the defendant liable and the defendant must then provide a remedy, often **damages**.
- Besides this, of course, the range of courts in which actions may be heard also varies. Criminal trials will be in either the Magistrates' Court or the Crown Court, depending on the seriousness of the offence. A contract claim could, if seeking under £5,000 worth of damages, be sought under the small claims procedure in the County Court by the claimant himself. Alternatively, depending on the value and complexity of the action, it could be sought under the fast-track procedure in the County Court or the multi-track procedure in either the County Court or the High Court.

> **damages**
>
> A common remedy for a breach of contract – a sum of money compensation aiming to put the injured party in the position he would have been in had the contract been properly performed

Nevertheless, this is not to say that the criminal law has absolutely no relevance for problems arising out of contractual relationships. Particularly in the protection of consumers, the criminal law can be used for the regulation of contracts and the ultimate protection of the consumer. A number of statutes, as well as certain statutory instruments, employ the criminal law as an enforcement mechanism. These include the Consumer Credit Act 1974, the Consumer Protection Act 1987, the Food Safety Act 1990, the Package Travel, Package Holidays and Package Tours Regulations 1992, the Trade Descriptions Act 1968, the Weights and Measures Act 1985 and the Consumer Protection (Distance Selling) Regulations 2000, to name but a few.

The use of the criminal law in this way in the context of consumer contracts is very significant. This is because it gives bodies such as Trading Standards Departments the power and the opportunity to take a more proactive as well as a deterrent role in enforcing appropriate standards of contracting in a consumer context. This is so significant because the consumer in most instances is at a disadvantage, being the weaker party in the bargain.

1.4 Contract law and the protection of consumers

> *caveat emptor*
>
> means 'let the buyer beware' – so is a principle of freedom of contract

The law of contract was traditionally concerned only with the existence of and the simple regulation of bargains made between individuals. In the nineteenth century this meant that the maxim *caveat emptor* was influential throughout the law.

During previous centuries, this might have been appropriate. Communities were for the most part rural, the master/servant relationship mirrored the realities of economic activity, and there was little in the way of a consumer society. However, in the twentieth century there was a great increase in spending power, the traditional economic relationships changed and the nature of society made a lot of the traditional rules unfair or unworkable.

In the last third of the twentieth century, consumer groups began to emerge to press for fairer treatment and protections. Judicial attitudes to certain contractual rules developed towards the protection of consumers and Parliament also introduced legislation to give greater consumer protection. Finally, membership of the EU has also led to the introduction of a number of significant protections.

Consumer protection (consumer law) is a significant area of law in its own right. As well as contract law, statutory and EU interventions and other common law developments have meant that the area as a whole must be seen to include both tort and criminal law. Nevertheless, there have been significant developments for the protection of the consumer that relate specifically to contract law. These include:

- The rebuttable presumption of an intention to create legal relations in a commercial contract.
- The attitude of the courts towards expert opinions when incorporating terms into contracts (compare *Oscar Chess Ltd v Williams* [1957] 1 WLR 370 and *Dick Bentley Productions Ltd v Harold Smith (Motors) Ltd* [1965] 1 WLR 623).
- The common law protection against excessively unfair terms in *Interfoto Picture Library v Stiletto Visual Programmes Ltd* [1988] 2 WLR 615.
- The implied terms in statutes such as the Sale of Goods Act 1979 and the Supply of Goods and Services Act 1982 and also in the more recent Consumer Protection (Distance Selling) Regulations 2000.
- The controls on **exclusion clauses** provided by the common law, by Parliament through the Unfair Contract Terms Act 1977, and ultimately as a result of membership of the European Union through the Unfair Terms in Consumer Contracts Regulations 1999.
- The common law and statutory rules protecting minors by declaring certain contracts void or allowing the **minor** to avoid the consequences of certain other contracts.

1.5 The effects on contract law of membership of the EU

It would be difficult to overemphasise the significance of membership of the EU to any area of English law concerned with economics. Students of employment law, company law, commercial law and general consumer law all need a good appreciation of the effects of EU law and of the influence of treaty articles, directives and regulations on English law, in order to have a good understanding of their subjects.

Contract law is no exception. Since the UK first became a member on 1st January 1973, after signing the treaties and passing the European Communities Act 1972, there have been a number of initiatives leading to changes and developments within English contract law.

Not all of these developments, but certainly many of them, have had particular impact on consumer protection. Not every individual aspect of contract law has been affected but in various chapters the significant influences of EU law will become apparent.

- In the case of agreement (offer and acceptance), the Consumer Protection (Distance Selling) Regulations 2000 have been introduced, affecting the way that we form contracts through modern electronic means. The regulations were introduced to implement provisions of the EU Directive 97/7, the Distance Selling Directive. The Electronic Commerce Directive 2000/31 also demands a specific form of acknowledgement in electronic selling.

- The same regulations have an impact also on the terms of contracts made through electronic means, by implying terms into such agreements.
- In the case of exclusion clauses the Unfair Terms in Consumer Contracts Regulations 1999, first introduced as the Unfair Terms in Consumer Contracts Regulations 1994, regulate consumer contracts to prevent unfair advantage being taken of the consumer. The effect of the regulations is that the party dealing with the consumer cannot insert advantageous terms into contracts where there is no comparable term in favour of the consumer. The regulations implemented EU Directive 93/13, the Unfair Terms in Consumer Contracts Directive.
- In the case of illegal contracts Article 101 and Article 102 of the TFEU regulate and prevent unfair competition.
- In the case of third-party rights, particularly those associated with agency relationships, the Commercial Agents (Council Directive) Regulations 1993 have also introduced specific rules relating to commercial agents.

Inevitably, one of the problems confronting absolute harmonisation of the laws of the European Union is the major differences between the English common law system and the civil systems adopted in most continental nations. An attempt has been made to create a framework for a standard European-wide contract law. This came in the form of the Lando Commission which in 2000 published *Principles of European Contract Law* covering all areas of contract law.

1.6 Contract law and other jurisdictions

English contract law clearly originally developed within a fairly insular framework.

Inevitably, as international trade developed, this created a number of problems in matching the different common law and civil law systems. As a result, various treaties were entered into; for instance there is an international agreement on regulating the carriage of goods by sea: the Hague–Visby Rules.

Although similar attempts to create international agreements for the sale of goods have failed to achieve universal application, the existence of the Internet, among other things, has led to the need to have certainty in the way that various disputes are handled.

In commercial relationships it is possible for the parties to adopt standard forms and agree to abide by them.

One of the significant differences in approaches to contract law is in the application of the idea of 'good faith' in contracting. English judges traditionally rejected such an approach because of its possible effects on the notion of freedom of contract. However, the influence of EU law particularly has meant the introduction of the idea, at least to a limited degree. It can be seen in both the Unfair Terms in Consumer Contracts Regulations 1999 and the Commercial Agents (Council Directive) Regulations 1993. Further developments may well mean an increase in the application of the concept.

ACTIVITY

Self-assessment questions

1. How were the courts originally certain that there was an enforceable contract?
2. What was the difference between 'covenants' and 'debts'?
3. What was 'detinue'?
4. What is *'assumpsit'* and what does it have in common with modern contract law?
5. What are the major features of modern contracts?
6. Why are many of the original rules of contract law impractical in modern times?

7. What are the main reasons for contracts being enforced?
8. What features does contract law have in common with tort?
9. What are the major differences between contract law and tort?
10. In what ways has English contract law changed and developed in order to provide for consumer protection?
11. What effects has membership of the EU had on contract law?

A simple contract completed by performance

A contract is perfectly formed:
- a mutual agreement
- supported by consideration by both parties
- with an intention to create legal relations.

The contract contains obligations (terms):
- expressed by the parties
- implied from the presumed intention of the parties
- implied by statute.

The contract is discharged:
- by performance
- by agreement of the parties
- because it is frustrated by an intervening event.

There is nothing to vitiate the contract and render it void or voidable by one party.

A simple contract rendered void or voidable because of a vitiating factor

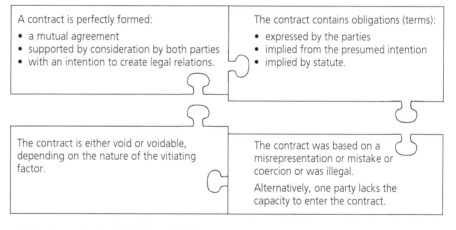

A contract is perfectly formed:
- a mutual agreement
- supported by consideration by both parties
- with an intention to create legal relations.

The contract contains obligations (terms):
- expressed by the parties
- implied from the presumed intention
- implied by statute.

The contract is either void or voidable, depending on the nature of the vitiating factor.

The contract was based on a misrepresentation or mistake or coercion or was illegal.

Alternatively, one party lacks the capacity to enter the contract.

A simple contract which is breached

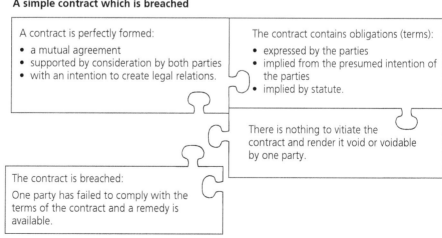

A contract is perfectly formed:
- a mutual agreement
- supported by consideration by both parties
- with an intention to create legal relations.

The contract contains obligations (terms):
- expressed by the parties
- implied from the presumed intention of the parties
- implied by statute.

There is nothing to vitiate the contract and render it void or voidable by one party.

The contract is breached:

One party has failed to comply with the terms of the contract and a remedy is available.

Figure 1.1 How the various elements of a contract fit together

SUMMARY

- Originally most agreements had to be in writing – this included covenant (a written agreement to do something) and formal debt (an agreement under seal to pay money).
- Informal agreements gradually gained recognition in the courts – this included an action for debt (oral rather than formal) and detinue (an action for delivery of a chattel) and later *assumpsit* (an undertaking to carry out a promise).
- The major purpose of contract law is to support agreements and ensure the availability of remedies for agreements that are not carried out or not carried out according to the terms laid down by the parties.
- Modern contracts divide into simple contracts (can be made in any form) and speciality contracts (usually for transfers of land or interests in land and required to be in specific form).
- Freedom of contract allows parties to determine their own arrangements – but the law often regulates contracts for the protection of parties with weaker bargaining strength, eg, consumers.
- Membership of the EU and EU law have had a major impact in introducing more extensive consumer protection.

2

Formation of a contract: Offer and acceptance

AIMS AND OBJECTIVES

After reading this chapter you should be able to:

- Understand the essential requirements for valid formation of a contract
- Understand the basic character of an offer
- Distinguish between an offer and an invitation to treat
- Understand the need for communication
- Understand how offers can be withdrawn and in what circumstances
- Understand how an offer can be terminated
- Understand the basic character of acceptance
- Distinguish between a counter-offer and a mere enquiry
- Understand the significance of different methods of communication
- Understand the circumstances in which unilateral contracts are made
- Critically analyse the area
- Apply the law to factual situations and reach conclusions

2.1 Formation of contracts and the concept of agreement

We know from our introduction to the law of contract that the law concerns 'bargains' that are made between parties. The major significance of the word 'bargain' is that it involves an agreement that is binding on both parties. In contract law, then, it is insufficient merely that an agreement exists between two parties but rather that it involves that specific type of agreement which is enforceable by both parties in a court of law.

A contract is completed when both sides honour an agreement by carrying out their particular side of the bargain. It is a breach of contract when a party fails to do so.

However, because of the special nature of contractual agreements, we cannot identify a breach of contract where we may feel that we have not got what we paid for or 'bargained' for, without first showing that the agreement was indeed a contract.

So the first thing that may need to be determined in any contract case is that there is proof that a contract actually exists, as opposed to some less formal, and thus unenforceable, arrangement between the parties. It is possible to tell if the arrangement is a contract because to be so it must have been formed according to certain standard rules. These are the rules of **formation of contract**.

A contract is only formed in law where the following can be shown to exist:

- an **agreement** – which is based on mutuality between the parties – the so-called *consensus ad idem*
- **consideration** – which means that both sides are bound to give something to each other – the *quid pro quo* or proof that a bargain exists, and
- **intention** – it must be the intention of both parties to be legally bound by the terms of the agreement that they have reached.

These three elements are considered individually in Chapters 2, 3 and 4.

Agreement is the first and most basic of these requirements. A contractual agreement is said to exist when a valid offer is followed by a valid acceptance. This seems straightforward enough, and where one person offers to sell something to another party who accepts the price and agrees to buy, then there will normally be no difficulty.

In practice, though, negotiations can be much more complex than this and on the other hand agreements can be identified which appear to have no formal negotiating steps, purchasing goods from a vending machine being a classic example of that.

Butler Machine Tool Co v Ex-Cell-O Corporation [1979] 1 WLR 401 is a case involving the so-called 'battle of the forms', ie, an argument over which of standard form terms should apply. In his judgment Lord Denning MR suggested that judges should decide whether a contract existed by examining the evidence in its totality rather than trying to apply a strict test of offer and acceptance.

JUDGMENT

'In many of these cases our traditional analysis of offer, counter offer, rejection, acceptance and so-forth is out of date. The better way is to look at all the documents passing between the parties and glean from them, or from the conduct of the parties, whether they have reached agreement on all material points, even though there may be differences between the forms and conditions printed on the back of them.'

Even if other judges sympathised with the logic of Lord Denning's assertion, it is unlikely that they would publicly admit it, so in all cases it is still necessary to return to and apply the traditional test of offer and acceptance.

2.2 Offer

2.2.1 The character of an offer

An **offer** has been described as an unconditional statement of a person's intention to be bound by the terms of the offer made and thus the intention to contract with the other person.

On face value this seems to be a fairly obvious and straightforward principle. The **offeror** will have made plain in the offer the **conditions** to which he is prepared to

offeror

The person making an offer

condition

An important term of a contract which is said to 'go to the root of the contract' allowing the victim of the breach of the term to repudiate his own obligations under the contract as well as to sue for damages

offeree

A person to whom an offer is made

be bound in the event of acceptance of the offer. Inevitably, the contract will not be formed without the **offeree** accepting those terms also.

However, this sort of definition of offer is still important in describing how the process works because what it in effect also means is that the offeror must not in any way impair the ability of the offeree to accept the offer. This could occur, for instance, if the offeror were to impose extra obligations which were external to the terms of the offer itself. In this instance the offeror might in effect actually be preventing the offeree from accepting the offer and reaching an agreement and in this case whatever the proposition made, it could not in law be classed as a legitimate offer.

A simply stated offer, for example 'I offer to sell you my *Unlocking Contract Law* book for £15', would present no problems at all. This may still be the case even though the word 'offer ' is not used by the party making it, for example 'Would you like to buy my *Unlocking Contract Law* book for £15?'.

An offer is very often phrased as a question and in any case demands a response: either an acceptance or a rejection of the offer. However, there are many situations in which things that look as though they may in some way include an offer nevertheless do not have the same outcome. These are generally categorised as invitations to treat and must be distinguished from offers.

2.2.2 Distinguishing offer from invitation to treat

As we have seen, a person making an offer is called an **offeror** and the person to whom the offer is made, and who thus can accept it, is called the **offeree**.

The offer is a statement of intent by the offeror to be legally bound by the terms of the offer if it is accepted, and the contract exists once acceptance has taken place. If the offer is plainly stated, for example 'Would you like to buy my car for £8,000?',

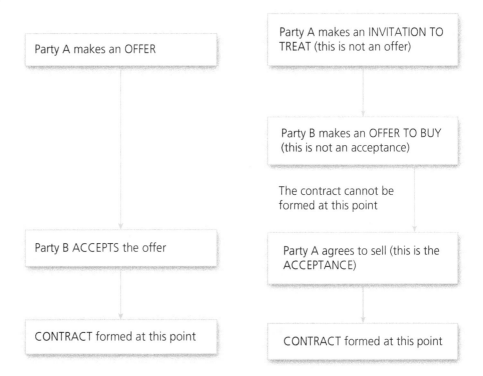

Figure 2.1 The point at which a contract is made in a standard offer and acceptance, and where there is firstly an invitation to treat

....

invitation to treat

An invitation to a party to make an offer to buy as distinct from an offer

....

then the question is easily identified as an offer, and you only have to say 'Yes, I will buy your car for £8,000' for there to be an easily identifiable acceptance too.

It is not always the case, however, that the first stage in negotiations is an offer. Often the first step is an entirely passive state and is not therefore open to acceptance, for example a tin of beans placed on display on a supermarket shelf. This is not an offer and is an example of an **invitation to treat**, in other words an invitation to the other party to make an offer, usually an offer to buy. The contract is then formed by the agreement to sell, which is the acceptance in this case.

2.2.3 Examples of invitation to treat

a) *Goods displayed on shelves in a self-service shop*

Goods displayed in a self-service shop are not an offer that is then accepted when the customer picks the goods from the shelves. They are an invitation to treat, an invitation to the buyer to make an offer to buy. *Pharmaceutical Society of GB v Boots Cash Chemists Ltd* [1953] 1 All ER 482 identifies that this is done by the customer taking them to the cash desk where the contract is formed when the sale is agreed.

CASE EXTRACT

Pharmaceutical Society of GB v Boots Cash Chemists Ltd
[1953] 1 All ER 482

In the case extract below a significant section of the judgment has been reproduced in the left-hand column. Individual points arising from the judgment are briefly explained in the right-hand column. Read the extract including the commentary in the right-hand column and complete the exercise that follows.

LORD JUSTICE SOMERVELL: This is an appeal from the Lord Chief Justice ... raising a question under section 18(1)(a)(iii) of the Pharmacy and Poisons Act, 1933. The [claimant is] the Pharmaceutical Society [which was] incorporated by Royal Charter. One of [its] duties is to take all reasonable steps to enforce the provisions of the Act. The provision in question is:	*Shows the case involves breach of a regulatory offence*
"... it shall not be lawful for a person to sell any poison included in Part I of the Poisons List, unless ... the sale is effected by, or under the supervision of, a registered pharmacist".	*Identifies the duty of the Pharmaceutical Society* *The actual regulatory offence*
The Defendants, Messrs Boots Cash Chemists (Southern) Limited have recently introduced into one or more of their premises ... a self-service system. We have a number of photographs and one can see a number of articles such as toilet articles, laxatives, ointments and tonics, the kind of articles which one normally finds in one of Messrs Boots' shops, laid out on shelves. The customer when he comes in is invited to take a receptacle and goes round and can choose the articles which he wants. He then goes to one of two desks at the end of the room, and there, admittedly, there is a registered pharmacist, able to carry out, subject to the point which I will mention in a moment, such duties as are involved in his position. It is not disputed that in a chemist's shop where this system does not prevail a man may go in and ask a young lady, who will not herself be a registered pharmacist, for one of these articles on the List and the transaction may be completed and the article paid for,	*The basic facts – a new style of self-service shopping had been introduced*

although the registered pharmacist, who will no doubt be on the premises, will not know anything himself of the transaction unless the assistant serving the customer, or the customer, requires to put a question to him.

... I should emphasise, as the Lord Chief Justice did, that these are not dangerous drugs. They are things which contain very small proportions of poison and I imagine many of them are the type of drug which has a warning as to what doses are to be taken. They are drugs which can be obtained under the law without a doctor's prescription.

The point which is taken by the [claimant] is this: It is said that the purchase is complete if and when a customer going round the shelves takes an article and puts it in the receptacle which he or she is carrying, and therefore if that is right when the customer comes to the pay desk, having completed the tour of the premises, the registered pharmacist, if so minded, has no power to say: "This drug ought not to be sold to this customer". Whether and in what circumstances he would have that power we need not enquire, but one can, of course, see that there is a difference if supervision can only be exercised at a time when the contract is completed.

I agree with the Lord Chief Justice in everything he says, but I will put it shortly in my own words. Whether that is a right view depends on what are the legal implications of this layout, the invitation to the customer. Is it to be regarded as an offer which is completed and both sides bound when the article is put into the receptacle, or is it to be regarded as a more organised way of doing what is done already in many types of shops — and a bookseller is perhaps the best example — namely, enabling customers to have free access to what is in the shop to look at the different articles and then, ultimately, having got the ones which they wish to buy, coming up to the assistant and saying "I want this"? The assistant in 999 times out of 1,000 says "That is all right", and the money passes and the transaction is completed. I agree entirely with what the Lord Chief Justice says and the reasons he gives for his conclusion that in the case of the ordinary shop, although goods are displayed and it is intended that customers should go and choose what they want, the contract is not completed until, the customer having indicated the articles which he needs, the shop-keeper or someone on his behalf accepts that offer. Then the contract is completed. I can see no reason at all, that being I think clearly the normal position, for drawing any different implication as a result of this layout. The Lord Chief Justice, I think, expressed one of the most formidable difficulties in the way of the suggestion when he pointed out that, if the [claimant is] right, once an article has been placed in the receptacle the customer himself is bound and he would have no right without paying for the first article to substitute an article which he saw later of the same kind and which he perhaps preferred. I can see no reason for implying from this arrangement which the Defendants have referred to any implication other than that which the Lord Chief Justice found in it, namely, that it is a convenient method of enabling customers to see what there is and choose and

The problem things under the poisons list might be sold without the pharmacist knowing

But such a transaction would only be for non-prescription drugs

The legal problem – when is the contract made: when the buyer selects the goods or at the pay desk

The problem of when the contract is made is repeated here

Identifies that when the contract is made might not be a problem in another type of shop

The ratio of the case – the contract is not made until the customer takes the goods to the pay desk – the customer offers to buy and the contract is made when the shop accept

Practical difficulty of the shopper not being able to change his mind

possibly put back and substitute articles which they wish to have and then go up to the cashier and offer to buy what they have so far chosen. On that conclusion the case fails, because it is admitted that then there was supervision in the sense required by the Act and at the appropriate moment of time. For these reasons ... the appeal should be dismissed.

So there is supervision when the contract for sale of prescription drugs is made
And there is no offence

Key Points from the case of *Pharmaceutical Society of GB v Boots Cash Chemists Ltd* [1953] 1 All ER 482 above:

- The basis of the problem – Under s18 of the Pharmacy and Poisons Act certain drugs and poisons could not be sold unless this was 'under the supervision' of a registered pharmacist'. Boots had altered one of its shops to self-service, which is the common style of shopping today but at the time was novel. The problem was the point at which the contract was formed when the customer selected the goods or when they were actually presented at the cash desk, if the first then it would be a breach of s18.
- It was identified that the contract is in fact made at the cash desk – the customer in presenting the goods is making an offer to buy and if the shop assistant agrees the sale this would represent the acceptance and the contract is formed at that point (the self-service display of the goods only represents an invitation to the customer to make an offer to buy – an invitation to treat)
- If the rule was otherwise it would mean that the customer would be instantly bound as soon as he selected the goods from the shelf and would not legally be able to change his mind after if he saw another product which he preferred.
- It would also deny freedom of contract to the shop keeper as well as the customer.
- The rule as it was applied in the case ensured that at the point at which the contract was in fact made it could always be under the supervision of the pharmacist.

ACTIVITY

In the following situations suggest how the rule from the case above would operate and whether a contract has been formed or not.

1. An eight-year-old boy, Andy, has gone into an off license, selected a litre bottle of rum from the shelf and taken it to the counter. The sales assistant, Brenda, has told him that she cannot serve him because he is under the age of eighteen.
2. A customer, Connie, has been wheeling her shopping trolley through Madsavings Supermarket. She has picked up several items and when she has found a different brand of the same product which is cheaper further down the aisle she has selected that product and abandoned the one she had earlier picked but in the wrong place. This has now happened with seven different items and the manager, Dave, is very annoyed that Connie is causing his staff extra work and tells Connie that she has to buy all of the items that she has selected and then put down again.
3. Euan, who is twenty-four but very young looking enters a newsagents and asks to purchase twenty cigarettes. Francesca, the assistant, asks Euan for identity for proof of his age since cigarettes cannot be sold to someone under the age of sixteen. Euan explains that he has no identity with him and Francesca refuses to serve him as a result.

2.2.4 Situations which are not invitation to treat

There are clearly certain situations in which, while we would normally associate them with invitation to treat, the circumstances involved or the nature of the words used mean that there has in fact been an offer rather than an invitation to treat. In this way the choice of words may be of particular significance. For instance, the words 'Special Offer' attached to a display of goods would ordinarily not alter the fact of the display being an invitation to treat. To signify that an offer is in fact being made would depend on other words that may be added. So 'Special Offer: 10p only to first 10 customers' would represent a specific offer that could only be accepted by the first 10 customers, as indicated by the words used.

Examples of situations that are complicated in this way include:

a) *Advertisements involving a unilateral offer*

If the advertisement indicates a course of action in return for which the advertiser makes a promise to pay, then he is bound by this promise. The promise forms the basis of an offer and it is irrelevant that it is made in the context of an advertisement which would normally be regarded only as an invitation to treat.

CASE EXAMPLE

Carlill v The Carbolic Smoke Ball Co Ltd [1893] 1 QB 256

The company advertised a patent medicine, the smoke ball, with the promise that if a purchaser used it correctly it would provide them with immunity from a range of illnesses including influenza. Besides this, the Smoke Ball Company indicated in the advertisement that if a person used the product and still got flu, then the company would pay them £100. Mrs Carlill did get flu after using the smoke ball in the correct fashion. The advertisement would normally be seen as no more than an invitation to treat, with the hope that a person reading the advertisement might be persuaded to offer to purchase the product, after which a contract could be formed.

However, the precise wording was held to indicate a contractual relationship quite separate to the contract for the sale and purchase of the smoke ball itself. The court enforced Mrs Carlill's claim for the £100. The promise amounted to an offer that could be accepted by anyone who used the smoke ball correctly and still got the flu. The company was contractually bound by the offer to pay the sum which was accepted when Mrs Carlill purchased the smoke ball. In fact, the Smoke Ball Company raised any number of defences in arguing the claim. Such possible defences included, as above, that the advertisement was a mere puff; that there was no offer made to a particular person (see section 2.2.5); that there was no notification of acceptance (see section 2.3.3 (d)); and also that even if there was a contract, that it would be illegal under the Gaming Acts. The court rejected all the various defences. The offer was a unilateral offer, meaning that, unlike a **bilateral contract**, where both offer and acceptance are stated, here performance and acceptance were the same (see section 2.2.7).

bilateral contract

A contract where both parties have negotiated the terms

JUDGMENT

Bowen LJ explained the position in his judgment: 'Was it intended that the £100 should, if the conditions be fulfilled, be paid? The advertisement says that £1,000 is lodged at the bank for that purpose. Therefore it cannot be said that the statement that £100 would be paid was intended to be a mere puff. I think it was intended to be understood by the public as an offer which was to be acted upon.'

b) *A statement of price where an offer is also intended*

As we have seen, a mere statement of price is not binding on the party making it. However, sometimes other factors indicate that the statement in fact is also intended as an offer. In these cases then it will be binding if the other party acts on the statement.

CASE EXAMPLE

Biggs v Boyd Gibbins [1971] 1 WLR 913

This involved the negotiations for the sale of a house. In response to the offer of a lower price than he had paid for the house himself, the seller wrote, 'For a quick sale I will accept £26,000'. The purchaser replied, 'I accept your offer'. In response, the seller then wrote, 'I thank you for accepting my price of £26,000. My wife and I are both pleased that you are purchasing the property'. Because of its place in the negotiations and because of the response to the alleged acceptance, the court held that the seller's first letter was indeed an offer that the seller had accepted.

c) *Competitive tendering*

Normally, an invitation to tender for the supply of goods or services is no more than an invitation to treat. For instance, a company wants its office painted. It invites tenders and various decorators will respond with different prices for the work. The company is free to choose any of the decorators, not necessarily the cheapest. If, however, the company has in its advertisement agreed that the work will go to the tenderer with the lowest price, then it is bound to give the work to that person.

CASE EXAMPLE

Harvela Investments Ltd v Royal Trust Co of Canada Ltd [1986] AC 207

The Trust Company wanted to sell a large quantity of land that it owned, in a single transaction. To achieve this it had invited tenders from two interested parties for the purchase of all of the land. It indicated to both prospective purchasers that the sale of the land would go to the party making the higher bid. The party making the lower bid had tendered a price of $2,100,000 but had also included in the bid an alternative bid of $101,000 in excess of any other offer (a so-called 'referential bid'). The Trust Company accepted this referential bid and Harvela, the party that in fact had made the higher bid, found out and then sued the Trust Company successfully. It was for the court to determine whether the invitation to tender was, as would usually be the case in tenders, only an invitation to treat. It also needed to decide which of the bids was in fact the higher. In answer to the first issue, the court held that the wording of the invitation to tender made it an offer that could only be accepted by the highest bidder. In answer to the second question, the court held that the referential bid could not be accepted as binding in law. As the court explained, if both parties had entered such a bid then no contract could emerge from the tender since each referential bid in turn would be higher than the other one, which in turn would invoke the other referential bid, and so on without end. The contract in those circumstances could never be complete and the court could not accept the referential bid as a valid bid.

The contractual stages in a standard auction situation

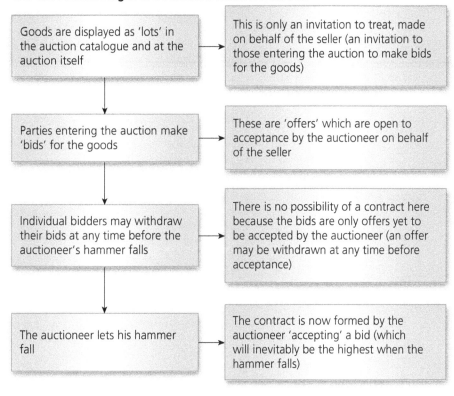

The contractual stages in a competitive tender

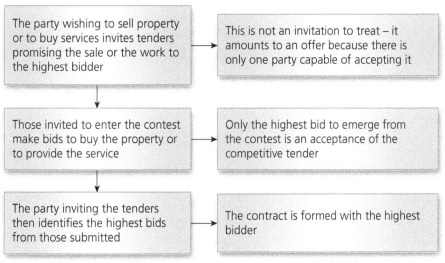

Figure 2.2 The differences between a standard auction situation and a competitive tender

Another problem with competitive tendering has also come to light in the case law. Irrespective of whether a tender is accepted, there may still be an obligation on the party inviting tenders to consider all tenders, and this in itself has legal consequences.

CASE EXAMPLE

Blackpool and Fylde Aero Club Ltd v Blackpool Borough Council [1990] 1 WLR 1195

For many years the club had held the concession to run pleasure flights from the council's airport. When the concession was due for renewal the council put it out to competitive tender, and invited tenders from the club and six other parties. Under the terms of the tender all tenders were to be submitted in unmarked envelopes in a particular box in the council premises by twelve noon on a specific date. The council stated that it would not be bound to accept any bid. The club placed its bid in the box at 11.00 am on the due date but by accident the box was not emptied after this time and the club's bid was therefore not considered by the council. Following the receipt of tenders the concession was given to another group, RR Helicopters. When officers of the council later discovered the club's tender they at first decided to repeat the exercise but they were then threatened with legal action by RR Helicopters. The club claimed breach of a contract to consider all tenders delivered by the due time. Its claim was upheld. The court felt that there was an implied undertaking to operate by the rules that the council had already set, despite the fact that the invitation to tender for the concession was only an invitation to treat.

d) Auctions advertised as 'without reserve'

Traditionally, auctions were of two distinct forms. The first is where a 'reserve price' for each lot is included. A reserve price is the minimum price that will be acceptable to the seller. In this situation, if the bidding fails to reach the reserve price then no sale can take place, and in consequence no contract is formed. See *McManus v Fortescue* [1907] 2 KB 1.

In the case of an auction held by reserve then there is only one possible outcome: the goods will become the property of the highest *bona fide* bidder. It had, however, been held in *obiter* that no contract of sale can materialise between the owner of the goods and the highest bidder where the auctioneer refuses the sale or for any reason fails to accept the bid of the highest *bona fide* bidder. In this instance it was said that a collateral contract is created between the highest *bona fide* bidder and the auctioneer himself, so that the auctioneer may then be sued for breach of contract. See *Warlow v Harrison* (1859) 1 E&E 309. This point has been examined more recently.

CASE EXAMPLE

Barry v Heathcote Ball & Co (Commercial Auctions) Ltd [2001] 1 All ER 994; 1 WLR 1962

Here, in an auction advertised as 'without reserve' the auctioneer withdrew from the auction two lots, machinery worth £14,251. In doing so he refused bids of £200 for each machine made by the claimant and which were the highest bids. The auctioneer then sold them on privately at £750 each. The claimant bidder sued, arguing that the 'highest bid' rule should apply. The court, approving *Warlow v Harrison*, accepted the existence of a collateral contract between the bidder and the auctioneer and awarded the claimant £27,600 damages.

ACTIVITY

Quick quiz

Explain whether the following situations involve offers or mere invitations to treat:

1. A sign in a shop window reading:

> SPECIAL OFFER
> BETTA BAKE CAKES
> ONLY 25p EACH

2. An advertisement in a newspaper which reads:

> Tenders are invited for the internal painting and refurbishment
> of all ten campus buildings of the University of Midhampton.
> All tenders to be submitted to the General Manager (Estates),
> University of Midhampton, Central Road, Midhampton MH1
> 7HM by 12.00 noon on 14th November 2010.

3. My friend has an old Austin Healey sports car that I particularly like. When I ask him how much he would sell it for he replies, 'You could not buy a car like that for less than £20,000 these days'.

4. An advertisement in a local newspaper which reads:

> YOU MUST NOT MISS
> MEDIAMART
> SPECIAL OPENING BONANZA.
> DVD PLAYERS RRP £199
> ONLY 99P
> TO OUR FIRST 10 CUSTOMERS.

5. A sign in a DIY store window which reads:

> BUDGET HAMMER DRILLS – ONLY £19.99.
> IF YOU CAN BUY CHEAPER ELSEWHERE
> WE WILL REFUND THE DIFFERENCE

Quick quiz

Now do the same in a simpler form and suggest whether or not an offer exists in the following examples:

1. I tell you that I have a thousand copies of my new *Unlocking Contract Law* text, the price of which is only £19.99.
2. My new *Unlocking Contract Law* text is advertised in the Student Handbook at only £19.99.
3. I write you a letter in which I say, 'Would you like a copy of my new *Unlocking Contract Law* textbook? It is only £19.99.'
4. I write a letter to all students to whom I teach contract law, saying, 'Why not buy my book *Unlocking Contract Law* from me for only £19.99?'.
5. A group of students approach me, all wanting a copy of *Unlocking Contract Law*. I tell them that I only have one copy left and I will sell it to whoever will pay me most.

2.2.5 Communicating the offer

Once we know whether a party is making an offer, and is then intending to contract, we must be satisfied that the offer conforms to the rules to show whether it is a valid offer or not. One of these is that the offer must be communicated to the offeree. Without knowledge of the offer there is nothing of substance for the offeree to accept. To hold otherwise would of course be not only difficult for the courts to enforce but would offend the basic principle of freedom of contract.

The offer must be communicated to the offeree

As has already been said, it is impossible to accept something of which you have no knowledge. In turn, this means that however prepared the offeror is to contract with another party, he is unable to turn this willingness to contract into a legally enforceable arrangement without making the other party aware of that willingness and of the terms on which he is willing to be bound.

CASE EXAMPLE

Taylor v Laird (1856) 25 LJ Ex 329

Taylor was the commander of Laird's ship. During a voyage he decided to give up the captaincy of the ship but then worked his passage back to Britain as an ordinary crew member. He then tried to claim wages from the owner but failed. As the court identified, the ship owner was unaware of Taylor's decision to quit as captain and moreover he had received no offer from Taylor to work in an alternative capacity which he could have then accepted or otherwise. The fairness of the rule can be seen if it is remembered that had the arrangement been enforced it would have been without any actual agreement on Laird's part.

An offer can be made to one person but it can also be made to the whole world

It is common for offers to be made to individuals but case law shows that negotiation between a single offeror and a single offeree is not a requirement of contract law. On the contrary, the offer can be made to a number of people and indeed even to the whole world. Anyone who has then had actual notice of the offer can be classed as an offeree and is entitled to accept.

CASE EXAMPLE

Carlill v The Carbolic Smoke Ball Co [1893] 1 QB 256

The company raised a number of arguments in trying to dismiss Mrs Carlill's claim. One such argument was that there could have been no contract formed with Mrs Carlill because she was not a genuine offeree. It argued that even if the court were prepared to see the advertisement as an offer, no offer had been made to Mrs Carlill personally. This argument also failed. The court held that it had made an offer generally and that she had accepted by buying the smoke ball, using it and by still getting flu. As can be seen from the judgments in the case, the situation was no different to any situation where a reward is offered. There was a 'unilateral offer' (see section 2.2.7).

JUDGMENT

Lord Justice Lindley identified the legal reasoning: 'it is said that [the offer] is not made to anyone in particular. Now that point is common to the words of this advertisement and to the words of all other advertisements offering rewards. They are offers to anyone who performs the conditions named in the advertisement, and anybody who does perform the conditions accepts the offer.'

The offeree must have clear knowledge of the existence of the offer for it to be valid and enforceable

It almost goes without saying that, if the offeree is unaware of the existence of the offer, then he cannot be said to have accepted. The fact that the offer is unilateral makes no difference to the principle.

CASE EXAMPLE

Inland Revenue Commissioners v Fry (2001) NLJ, 7th December

The IRC claimed that Fry owed them £113,000. She sent a cheque for £10,000 to the IRC with a letter stating that the cheque was 'in full settlement' and that if presented for payment this would be acceptance of her offer. IRC procedure was for cashiers to bank cheques received before accompanying correspondence was then sent on to a case worker. The case worker here immediately phoned the defendant to say that the £10,000 could be treated as part-payment or she could have the money back. Fry insisted that the Revenue were bound to accept the offer, having cashed the cheque. The court held that while an offeree could accept a unilateral offer which prescribed its manner of acceptance, by acting in accordance with that manner there had to be knowledge of the offer when the act was done. IRC were actually ignorant of the offer here so there was no acceptance.

The rule develops out of the older reward cases *R v Clarke* (1927) 40 CLR 227 and *Williams v Cawardine* (1833) 5 C & P 566. In the first case the High Court of Australia rejected the claim to a reward for information leading to the arrest and conviction of the murderers of police officers. Here, an accomplice claiming the reward after the event had been motivated only by the chance of a pardon, not by knowledge of the offer. In the latter case the King's Bench accepted the claim to the reward even though information had been given to ease the claimant's conscience, since it was also given in full knowledge of the existence of the reward.

2.2.6 Certainty

Since an offer must demonstrate willingness on the part of the offeror to be bound by the terms of the offer, then the terms on which it is intended that the contract will be formed must be certain. If there was any doubt as to the terms on which the parties were contracting, then the offeree would not know exactly what he was accepting and the contract would be impossible to perform. On this basis it is said that the terms of the offer must be certain. Where the words of an offer are too vague then the parties cannot be certain of the precise character of the agreement, which will be unenforceable as a result.

CASE EXAMPLE

Guthing v Lynn (1831) 2 B & Ad 232

This concerned an agreement for the sale and purchase of a horse. A promise was also made to pay an extra £5 'if the horse is lucky'. It was held that this could not be an offer. It was too vague. There was no way of determining what exactly 'lucky' meant and therefore the parties could not be bound by the promise.

Where there is uncertainty as to terms and the contract is yet to be performed then the courts generally have no difficulty in declaring that the contract is unenforceable.

CASE EXAMPLE

White v Bluett (1853) LJ Ex 36

A son owed his father money on a promissory note. The father then died and his executors were trying to recover the money. The son claimed that he had an agreement with his father that the debt would be forgotten in return for the son's promise not to complain about the distribution of the father's assets in his will. The court rejected this argument since the alleged promise was too vague to form an enforceable agreement between them.

However, where performance of the contract has already begun then the courts may be more willing to enforce the agreement.

CASE EXAMPLE

Foley v Classique Coaches Ltd [1934] 2 KB 1

Here, the claimant sold petrol. He contracted with the defendants to supply them with petrol for their coach business 'at a price to be agreed by the parties in writing from time to time'. In fact, the parties never produced any written agreement as to price. When the coach company later tried to repudiate the contract the court held that it could not. Despite the vagueness of the term, the court held that there would be an implied term that a reasonable price should be paid for the petrol. The defendants were unable to back out of the agreement for vagueness in this instance because both sides had performed for three years.

A more dramatic example of this can be seen in *British Steel Corporation v Cleveland Bridge and Engineering Co* [1984] 1 All ER 504 (see section 2.4) where the judge in the case ordered that a payment be enforced because what was required under the contract had been eventually supplied. He did so despite feeling unable to find evidence that a contract actually existed since there was no indication of anything on which the two parties had ever agreed.

Inevitably, certainty is a problem in modern contracting since many contracts are based on more complex negotiations than a simple offer and acceptance. This is particularly true of business and commercial dealings where in any case there is the added complication that the parties will probably be dealing on standard business forms where the terms contained in each may in fact conflict (see section 2.4). One way round this problem in a modern context is the use of arbitration where reaching sensible compromises between the parties may be more important than purely technical principles of law.

ACTIVITY

Quick quiz

In the following examples, using cases examined above, consider whether the terms of the offer are certain enough for a contract to be formed if they are accepted.

Sukhy agrees to sell an important book on contract law to Chris for:

1. a fair price
2. a good price
3. a bargain price
4. a price which is to be fixed by Sukhy's friend Dalvinder when Sukhy next sees him
5. a price that is 10 per cent below normal retail price
6. a price that will stop Chris from moaning
7. a price to be agreed between Sukhy and Chris at a later date
8. a price of £15.

2.2.7 Revocation of offers

Inevitably, a person making an offer may wish at some point to withdraw the offer. This in itself is merely another demonstration of freedom of contract. Besides this, it would be unfair if the offeror, having made an offer, was bound to wait for an indefinite period of time before the offer was accepted. Particularly in business arrangements, the offeror must have the opportunity to move on and find an alternative offeree in order to sell his goods or services. For these reasons it is possible to withdraw or revoke the offer if certain requirements are met.

It is possible to withdraw an offer, at any time before the offer is accepted

The basic rule allows the offeror to withdraw his offer but this revocation can only occur if the offer has not already been accepted. Once acceptance occurs, the contract is formed and revocation is not possible.

CASE EXAMPLE

Routledge v Grant (1828) 4 Bing 653

Grant had offered his house for sale on the understanding that the offer would remain open for six weeks only. Grant in fact took the house off the market before the six-week period ended. The court held that his actions were legitimate because at the time of his revocation there had been no acceptance.

One possible exception to this basic rule is where the offeree pays money to the offeror in order to keep the offer open. In this instance there is a quite separate agreement for which the payment is consideration in return for the offer remaining open and the offeror is then bound to keep it open.

The offeror must communicate the withdrawal of the offer to the offeree

Communication is a critical factor throughout the whole process of offer and acceptance, for the reasons already stated. While the offeror is entitled to withdraw the offer before acceptance of it, the fact of this withdrawal must be communicated to the offeree who otherwise would be unfairly treated. Any withdrawal of the offer that is not communicated is inevitably invalid.

CASE EXAMPLE

Byrne v Van Tienhoven (1880) 5 CPD 344

A series of negotiations took place between the two parties as follows:

- On 1st October Van Tienhoven wrote and posted from Cardiff a letter to Byrne, who was in New York, offering to sell certain specific goods.
- On 8th October, however, Van Tienhoven changed his mind and then sent a letter withdrawing the offer made on 1st October.
- On 11th October Byrne, having received the letter of 1st October, accepted the offer made in it in a telegram.
- On 15th October Byrne also posted a letter confirming this in writing.
- On 20th October Byrne then received Van Tienhoven's second letter withdrawing the offer. This second letter, and the revocation of the offer, was invalid because it had not been received until after Byrne's acceptance of the offer in the telegram of 11th October. This is because where the post is used as an accepted method of communication, a letter of acceptance generally becomes valid on posting rather than when it is received (see the 'postal rule' in section 2.3 below)

The case is interesting as it is laid out above because it shows just how important it is to keep a track of dates as well as other information during contractual negotiations in determining when, if at all, the contract is actually formed. The dates also become important when considering application of the 'postal rule' (see section 2.3).

Communication of the withdrawal of the offer can be made by any reliable third party

While the offeror must communicate any revocation of the offer prior to acceptance, he need not necessarily do this in person. Very often in any case there are third parties or agents involved in the formation of contracts. On this basis the revocation can be communicated through a third party. However, for the revocation to be valid, the third party must be a reliable source of information, and one on whom both parties can rely.

CASE EXAMPLE

Dickinson v Dodds (1876) 2 ChD 463

Dodds had offered to sell houses to Dickinson and the offer was to remain open until 9 am on 12th June, having been made on 10th June. Dickinson did in fact intend to accept the offer but did not do so immediately. When Berry, an apparently reliable mutual acquaintance of both parties, notified Dickinson that Dodds had withdrawn the offer, Dickinson then sent an acceptance, but by the time this was received the house was already sold. Dickinson claimed an unlawful revocation and a breach of contract. The court held that the revocation was acceptable and valid. Berry was shown to be a mutual acquaintance on whom both could rely.

A unilateral offer cannot be withdrawn while the offeree is performing

There is one major example where the basic rule allowing revocation of an offer prior to acceptance will not apply. This is the so-called **'unilateral contract'**. Thus,

unilateral contract

A contract formed where one party performs as required by the other party's unilateral offer

wherever a continuing act amounts to the acceptance then the offeror is unable to withdraw the offer until such time as either:

- the act of acceptance is complete – at which time the contract itself is also complete, or
- there is a failure to perform by the offeree.

Thus, in a unilateral contract the offeree actually accepts the offer by performing his side of the bargain. This is particularly common where rewards are offered and the offeree complies with the terms of the offer by returning whatever it is that the reward is offered for. It would clearly be unfair to prevent this once the other party had begun.

CASE EXAMPLE

Carlill v The Carbolic Smoke Ball Co [1893] 1 QB 256

The case operates in the classical way in the same way as rewards. In answer to Mrs Carlill's claims the company argued two lines of defence. Firstly, it argued that a unilateral contract could not be formed with the whole world as there could be no idea with whom the contract was made. Secondly, it argued that no contract existed because no notice of acceptance had been received. As seen already (see section 2.2.5), the court rejected the first argument on the basis that the contract could be made with anyone who came forward and performed the act of acceptance. To the second argument the court answered that in the conventional sense of agreement that notification of acceptance was synonymous with purchasing the smoke ball, and that the contract was complete when, after purchasing it, Mrs Carlill still contracted flu.

The principle has been well explained in more orthodox circumstances for demonstrating the rule.

CASE EXAMPLE

Errington v Errington & Woods [1952] 1 KB 290

A father bought a house and mortgaged it in his own name for his son and daughter-in-law to live in. He then promised his son and daughter-in-law that he would transfer title in the property to them when they had paid off the mortgage. When the father died and other members of the family wanted possession of the house, their action failed. The father's promise could not be withdrawn so long as the couple kept up the mortgage repayments, after which the house would be theirs.

JUDGMENT

Lord Denning, in ordering that the other members of the family were denied possession, explained the principle of law, which has become known as the 'Errington principle': 'the father's promise was a unilateral contract – a promise of the house in return for their act of paying the instalments. It could not be revoked by him once the couple entered on performance of the act, but it would cease to bind him if they left it incomplete and unperformed, which they have not done.'

In the case of rewards the principle is quite simply demonstrated. The offer is straightforwardly the offer of a reward. Acceptance occurs not merely on the finding of the lost object but when the offeror is actually notified of its safe return.

2.2.8 Termination of offer

As we have already seen, an agreement only occurs where a valid offer is made which is then validly accepted. This cannot occur if the offer is withdrawn or ceases to exist. Inevitably, an offer need not stay open forever. There are a number of ways in which the offer can be said to have terminated.

Acceptance of the offer by the offeree

This is the most obvious and straightforward way in which the offer comes to an end. If the offeree unconditionally agrees to be bound by the terms of the offer then a contract is formed.

Rejection of the offer by the offeree

Alternatives to this of course are where the offer is refused (in which case there is no contract) or met with a counter-offer (in which case negotiations may still be in process – see section 2.3).

Revocation of the offer by the offeror

As we have already seen in section 2.2.7, if the offeror decides to withdraw the offer and communicates this effectively to the offeree before acceptance, then the offer will also terminate.

This is relatively straightforward in the case of bilateral contracts. However, as we have also seen in section 2.2.7 in the case of unilateral contracts, the offer cannot generally be withdrawn if the offeree is still in the act of performance.

Lapse of time

- If the offer is stated to terminate at a particular date then it can no longer be accepted after that date has expired.
- Where no specific date for the offer to terminate has been indicated then the offer can be said to have lapsed after a reasonable time has passed.

CASE EXAMPLE

Ramsgate Victoria Hotel Co Ltd v Montefiore (1866) LR 1 Ex 109

Montefiore had offered to buy shares in June but the company only issued the shares in November. It was held that his offer to buy had lapsed. The court recognised that no offer could stay open indefinitely and that after a reasonable time an offer would lapse. In the case of a transaction where the value of the goods or services could change rapidly, as in the case here, then a reasonable time is likely to be short.

Death of one of the parties

If one of the parties dies then the effect on the offer and any potential acceptance may be different, depending on which party dies:

- If the offeree dies then this will cause the offer to lapse and his representatives will be unable to accept on his behalf: see *Reynolds v Atherton* (1921) 125 LT 690.
- If an offeror dies, however, his representatives may still be bound by an acceptance that is made in ignorance of the offeror 's death: see *Bradbury v Morgan* (1862) 1 H & C 249.
- Although if the offeror dies and the offeree knows of this, then it is unlikely that he could still claim to accept the offer.

Non-fulfilment of a condition precedent

If the parties have agreed to meet certain conditions before the contract can validly be formed then a failure to meet such a condition means that the offer has lapsed and is no longer open to acceptance.

CASE EXAMPLE

Financings Ltd v Stimson [1962] 3 All ER 386

This involved an agreement for the purchase of a car under a hire purchase agreement. A condition implied by law into such agreements was that the car would remain in the same condition from the time of the offer up to the point of acceptance. The car was actually stolen from the car showroom before the contract was concluded. As a result, the court held that the purchaser was not bound by his agreement to buy it.

ACTIVITY

Self-assessment questions

1. What is an offer?
2. What is the major difference between an offer and an invitation to treat?
3. What would happen if a customer in a supermarket took tins of beans from a shelf but changed her mind and discarded them before reaching the cash desk?
4. What would happen if I ordered goods advertised in a magazine and the seller wrote back to say that supplies were exhausted?
5. What makes a unilateral offer different from an invitation to treat?
6. Is it possible for an offer to be made to more than one person?
7. Why is it important to notify an offeree before withdrawing the offer?
8. Is it true to say that it is better for an offeree that negotiations prior to a contract are all carried out by letter, and if so why is that so?
9. What factors would you take into account in determining whether a reasonable time for an offer to stay open had lapsed?
10. If you find my lost dog and return it to me and later see an advertisement in the newspaper offering a reward for return of the dog, can you claim it?

KEY FACTS

Rules of offer	Case/statute
A contract is made where there is an agreement between two parties.	
An agreement is a valid offer followed by a valid acceptance.	
Offer must be distinguished from:	
• an 'invitation to treat' and	*Boots v Pharmaceutical Society of GB*
• a mere statement of price.	*Harvey v Facey*
Competitive tendering is different.	*Royal Trust Co of Canada v Harvela Investments*
An offer must be communicated.	*Taylor v Laird*
The offeree must be aware of the existence of the offer.	*IRC v Fry*
An offer can be made to the whole world.	*Carlill v Carbolic Smoke Ball Co*
The terms of the offer must be certain.	*Guthing v Lynn*

Rules of offer	Case/statute
An offer can be withdrawn at any time up to acceptance.	*Routledge v Grant*
But the withdrawal must be communicated to the offeree.	*Byrne v van Tienhoven*
This can be by a reliable third party.	*Dickinson v Dodds*
Unilateral offers do not require acceptance, only performance.	*Errington v Errington and Woods*
An offer ends: • on acceptance • on proper withdrawal • on lapse of time • on death of one of the parties.	

2.3 Acceptance

2.3.1 The role of acceptance in agreement

We have already seen in section 2.1 that an agreement is not complete and a contract cannot then be formed until such time as the offer has been validly accepted. In this way **acceptance** is of critical importance in the enforcement of contracts because generally rights and obligations begin from the time of acceptance. Indeed, in sale of goods contracts the risk in the goods generally passes at this point also.

It is clearly very important, then, to identify that whatever response is made to the offer is in fact a valid acceptance. Just as with an offer, where there are other situations that look familiar to an offer but are not, there are many possible responses to the offer not all of which amount to an acceptance. Not all negotiations conform absolutely into clearly defined and identifiable offer and acceptance and this is particularly so of modern commercial contracting where the negotiation stage is much more drawn out and complex. In order to identify acceptance for the purpose of establishing the existence of a contract, therefore, we need to analyse the response to the offer and be satisfied of two things:

- that the response is in fact an acceptance, rather than any other response, and that it corresponds absolutely with the rules of acceptance
- that this acceptance has been communicated properly to the offeror.

2.3.2 The basic rules of acceptance

A valid acceptance is a statement of intention to be bound absolutely and unconditionally by the terms of the offer, just as the offer is a statement of willingness to be bound by the terms of the offer unconditionally.

For the acceptance to be unequivocal and unconditional it follows, then, that the acceptance must correspond exactly and in every detail with the offer made. If this is not the case then no contract is formed and the parties cannot be bound by terms on which in effect they have not agreed.

This is the so-called 'mirror image' rule. It probably applies quite simply and straightforwardly in the case of simple consumer contracts, a simple purchase of goods for a set price, for instance. However, as we have already seen, it is unlikely in any commercial dealing that such a simple pattern ever occurs without the presence of much more complex and protracted negotiating stages. Inevitably, in such contractual negotiations there will be an element of disagreement or contradiction between the parties until an eventual compromise is reached. The use of standard

acceptance
An unconditional positive response to an offer

forms also complicates the process still further, where the parties have not necessarily freely negotiated in person but are expecting to contract on their own usual terms, unchallenged by the other party who also has a similar misconception.

a) The acceptance must be unconditional

In operating the 'mirror image' rule the acceptance must conform exactly to the terms of the offer or it is invalid and no contract will have been formed. It follows that any attempt to vary the terms of the offer is not an acceptance but what is commonly referred to as a counter-offer. The effect of a counter-offer is to terminate the original offer, which is then no longer open to be accepted by the offeree.

CASE EXAMPLE

Hyde v Wrench [1840] 49 ER 132

Wrench offered to sell his farm to Hyde for £1,000. Hyde, instead of accepting the offer, unconditionally rejected the price and offered to pay £950 as an alternative. Wrench rejected this price. Hyde then tried to accept the original price and claim breach of contract when he realised that Wrench was selling to another party. In the Rolls Court Lord Langdale rejected Hyde's claim and held that since the counter-offer amounted to a rejection of the offer, the original offer was no longer open for Hyde to accept.

JUDGMENT

Lord Langdale's reasoning is simple and straightforward: 'if [the offer] had at once been unconditionally accepted, there would undoubtedly have been a perfect binding contract; instead of that, the plaintiff made an offer of his own, to purchase the property for £950, and he thereby rejected the offer previously made by the defendant. I think that it was not afterwards competent for him to revive the proposal of the defendant, by tendering an acceptance of it; and that, therefore, there exists no obligation of any sort between the parties.'

b) Even ancillary terms should be accepted

It is still possible to see the offeree's response as a counter-offer rejecting the offer rather than an acceptance where the offeree is in disagreement over ancillary terms rather than central terms which the offeree is agreeing to.

CASE EXAMPLE

Jones v Daniel [1894] 2 Ch 332

Here, the defendant had offered to buy land from the claimant for a price of £1,450. The claimant wrote in response to the offer, accepting it and including a document of sale requiring the defendant's signature and also containing a number of additional terms on method of payment, proof of title and final performance. The court held that these ancillary terms could not be contractual until such time as the defendant had agreed to them and accepted them himself. They were counter-offers and, even though they concerned ancillary matters, they amounted to a counter-offer and a rejection of the original offer by the defendant.

c) Mere enquiries do not count as rejection

Not everything said by the offeree during the negotiations amounts to a counter-offer, even though it may appear to run contrary to the terms of the offer. It will depend on how these statements are phrased as to the effect they will have on the forming of the contract. In this way something that is a mere enquiry about the contract, which does not in fact seek to vary the terms of the offer, is not a counter-offer, as it does not reject the terms of the offer. This means that the offer is still open to acceptance by the offeree. The offeror is not entitled to consider the offer closed and contract elsewhere.

CASE EXAMPLE

Stevenson v McLean (1880) 5 QBD 346

In a response to an offer to sell iron, the price and quantity were accepted but the offeree wished to know whether delivery could be staggered, as he would have to make arrangements otherwise to accept delivery of the total. Having heard nothing further, the claimant then sent a letter of acceptance. He sued on discovering that the iron had been sold to a third party. The defendant's claim that there had been a counter-offer failed. The court held that it was not a rejection of the offer; it was merely an enquiry about details, and the offer was still open to acceptance. The claimant was successful in his action for breach of contract.

d) A counter-offer can become a term of the agreement if it is accepted

Negotiations leading up to a contract being formed can include a number of counter-offers from both sides. This is in the nature of negotiation, each side trying to secure the best possible bargain and the most advantageous contract. Wherever a counter-offer is accepted and the contract continues after this then it is the terms of the counter-offer rather than those of the original offer that form the basis of the eventual agreement.

CASE EXAMPLE

Davies & Co v William Old (1969) 67 LGR 395

Sub-contracted shopfitters had contracted with the architects in a building contract on the basis of their tender to sub-contract to the main contractors, the defendants in the case. The main contractors, under instruction from the architects, issued the order for the work. The contractors did so on their own standard forms which included a clause that the contractors would not be bound to pay sub-contractors until the contractors themselves were paid. The work order was accepted by the sub-contractors who commenced work on the project. When the sub-contractors were then not paid for some work that they had done under the contract they sued for breach of contract. Their action failed. The court identified that the clause in the work order amounted to a counter-offer which had then been in effect accepted by the sub-contractors when they commenced the work under those terms.

e) Technical counter-offers will not always count as a rejection of the offer if they are of no importance to the parties

Where there is a counter-offer relating to a central term of the offer this straightforwardly counts as a rejection of the offer which is then not open to acceptance, as we have seen. The situation is more complex and the consequences are less obvious when ancillary terms of the offer are involved; the parties do not express a clear concern over these ancillary terms; and the discrepancy between the original offer and the flawed 'acceptance' was not immediately noticed. In such situations the court may well ignore the counteroffer if the parties have gone on to contract successfully.

CASE EXAMPLE

Brogden v Metropolitan Railway Co (1877) 2 App Cas 666

The parties to the contract had a long-standing informal arrangement over the supply of coal. The parties then decided to make the arrangement more formal and a draft contract was sent to Brogden by the Railway Company. Brogden inserted the name of an arbitrator into a section of the form left blank specifically for that purpose, signed the agreement and returned it to the Railway Company. The company secretary for the Railway Company then signed the returned contract without looking at it. Brogden then continued to supply coal and was paid for deliveries. The two parties then got into conflict over other matters and Brogden tried to avoid his obligations, claiming that there was no contract between the parties because of a counter-offer by the Railway Company. The House of Lords accepted that technically the insertion of the arbitrator's name amounted to a counter-offer. Nevertheless, the court held that this had no immediate effect on the two parties who had continued to supply coal on the one hand and accept it and pay for it on the other. The parties had accepted the counter-offer as part of the agreement and could not claim that the contract did not in fact exist.

f) *The courts will not allow a party to benefit from both the counter-offer and the original offer*

A simple rejection of the offer or any attempt to vary its substantive meaning is a counter-offer and means that the offer is no longer open to acceptance. However, the courts are prepared to look at the true nature of the negotiations and will require that a meaningful agreement has been reached. They will not, in this respect, allow parties to introduce relatively meaningless counter-offers that are unlikely to be challenged in order to get the best of both worlds and be able to rely on either the original offer or the counter-offer as suits them best.

CASE EXAMPLE

Pars Technology Ltd v City Link Transport Holdings Ltd
[1999] EWCA Civ 1822

The parties were already in dispute with one another concerning an earlier agreement. The parties negotiated a settlement under which the defendant offered to pay £13,500 plus a refund of carriage charges of £7.50 and including VAT on this amount. The claimant then accepted this settlement in a letter. The defendant later claimed that the acceptance was invalid because the claimant's letter of acceptance stated that VAT should be paid on the whole amount owed and therefore was a counter-offer. The Court of Appeal decided that the whole correspondence between the parties should be considered in determining whether or not there was a contractual agreement. In the event it found that the claimant had clearly accepted the defendant's offer in its letter and that a binding contract thus resulted from the defendant's offer which was binding on both parties. The defendant could not escape its own clearly accepted obligations merely because the claimant had restated the position in a different and contrary way.

g) The acceptance may be in any form but if there is a required form then it must be in that form to be valid

Usually, it does not matter how the acceptance is made, as long as it is effectively communicated to the offeror. However, in certain circumstances the offeror has stated in the offer that only a particular type of acceptance is appropriate and there may be many obvious reasons for this. In such circumstances, if the offeree fails to respond in the prescribed manner then the response cannot be considered as an acceptance even though it is unconditional and conforms to the 'mirror image' rule.

CASE EXAMPLE

Compagnie de Commerce et Commissions SARL v Parkinson Stove Co [1953] 2 Lloyd's Rep 487

Parkinson Stove made an offer to the claimant company and in it stipulated that any acceptance should be made on a particular form supplied with the offer, and also stated firmly that no other form of acceptance would be considered valid or acted on. In the event, the company tried to claim that it had accepted in writing. Even though this was strong evidence of acceptance, the Court of Appeal would not class it as valid since the terms of the offer itself had identified that it would not and had indicated quite clearly the appropriate and only method of acceptance.

2.3.3 Communication of the acceptance

Just as in the case of offer, in acceptance one of the most critical factors is that the acceptance is communicated. It would be foolish and unworkable to say that an agreement can be formed without communication by the parties involved. Nevertheless, communication can be more loosely defined within the area of acceptance and there are, therefore, some significant exceptions to the basic rule.

a) The acceptance must be communicated to the offeror

Only a genuine offeree, one to whom the offer has been made, can actually accept the offer. It follows, then, that only a genuine offeree can communicate acceptance and that any supposed acceptance that is made by a party not authorised under the terms of the offer to make it cannot be classed as an acceptance.

CASE EXAMPLE

Powell v Lee (1908) 99 LT 284

The claimant here had applied for a position as headmaster of a school and had attended an interview. The interviewing committee decided to appoint him but did not officially tell him at that point. One of the panel, who was clearly not authorised to do so, then told Powell what the decision of the committee had been. The committee later changed its views and Powell was not appointed. He sued, claiming that the committee had already in effect accepted his offer of work. The court rejected this claim. He was not in a contractual position until the official notification of the committee was given to him.

Of course, acceptance could be construed from the conduct of the parties. This is illustrated in *Brogden v Metropolitan Railway Co* (1877) 2 App Cas 666 where the parties continued to supply coal on the one hand and pay for it on the other despite their disagreement (see section 2.3.2). However, conduct would only be accepted as amounting to acceptance when this can be objectively demonstrated to have been the intention of the offeree: *Day Morris Associates v Voyce* [2003] EWCA Civ 189; [2003] All ER (D) 368.

b) Silence can never amount to acceptance

Communication of an acceptance is an almost inevitable requirement. Without this rule, unscrupulous parties might always try to hold people to offers of which they were totally unaware. This in itself is the basis of the Unsolicited Goods and Services Act 1971 which prevents businesses from sending people goods through the post and then claiming payment despite the fact that the parties receiving those goods have never requested them in the first place. It goes without saying, then, that the acceptance must be a positive act, and that no indication of acceptance can ever be taken from silence.

CASE EXAMPLE

Felthouse v Bindley [1863] 142 ER 1037

An uncle and nephew had negotiated over the sale of the nephew's horse. The uncle had said, 'If I hear no more from you I shall consider the horse mine at £30 15s'. The nephew's stock was then put up for auction. At the sale the auctioneer failed to withdraw the horse from the sale as he had been instructed to do by the nephew, and the horse was sold to another party. In order to claim conversion in tort against the auctioneer, the uncle needed to prove that a contract existed with his nephew for the sale and purchase of the horse. The uncle's action against the auctioneer failed. He was unable to prove that the horse was his. The nephew had not actually accepted his offer to buy. The court would not accept the nephew's silence on the matter as any indication of acceptance.

There is a further provision that confirms in a more recent form the basic rule that silence cannot amount to acceptance. The Unsolicited Goods and Services Act 1971 prevented sellers from enforcing contract obligations on the recipients of goods that were sent to them without them being requested. The Act even allowed that party to keep the goods after six months if the seller had done nothing to retrieve them. The Consumer Protection (Distance Selling) Regulations 2000 has in effect replaced that provision and again the recipient of the goods is not bound to accept the goods. Regulation 24(4) also makes it an offence to seek payment for the goods.

c) The acceptance can be in any form

Unless the offeror has indicated a particular method of acceptance, which is the only valid method, then there are no specific rules on how acceptance can be communicated. It can be in writing, by words, or indeed even by conduct ('Do you want to buy my car for £10,000?' followed by a simple nod of the head is an obvious example of this). Of course, if the offeror requires it to be in a specific form then it must be in that form or it will be invalid.

CASE EXAMPLE

Yates v Pulleyn (1975) 119 SJ 370

One party was given an option to purchase land. According to the terms of the offer, this option was required to be exercised by notice in writing 'sent by registered or recorded delivery post'. While ordinary post was accepted as a suitable alternative, the court did acknowledge the importance of responding by a stipulated method.

d) *A unilateral offer requires no acceptance other than performance*

In a unilateral contract such as a reward situation, acceptance and performance are in effect one and the same thing. So where there is a reward offered for safe return of a lost dog there is no need for a party to reply to the person offering the reward, saying 'I am looking for and hoping to find your lost dog'. It is sufficient that, if that party finds the dog, he returns it to the owner at which point he can then claim the reward provided always of course that the party was aware of the existence of the reward. Otherwise the party could not be said to be accepting the offer of the reward by returning the dog.

CASE EXAMPLE

Carlill v The Carbolic Smoke Ball Co Ltd [1893] 1 QB 256

Mrs Carlill's situation is very much like the reward situation and, as we have seen, it was accepted by the court as a unilateral offer. Mrs Carlill had done everything that might have been expected of her under the unilateral offer. She had bought the smoke ball expecting that it would prevent cold and flu-type illnesses. She had used it according to the instructions supplied and she had still caught flu. The Smoke Ball Company had made an offer that anybody who used the smoke ball according to the methods indicated and still caught one of the named illnesses was entitled to £100. Among its many arguments, the company claimed that it could not be in a contractual relationship with Mrs Carlill and bound by its promise since no communication of acceptance had occurred. The court identified that in the case of unilateral contracts a formal acceptance was not only unnecessary but also irrelevant since performing according to the terms of the offer was acceptance in itself.

e) *The 'postal rule'*

In the ordinary sense where an offer has been made some direct communication of acceptance is required. Unilateral contracts are an exception to this basic rule. Another exception in a sense is the 'postal rule'. It is an exception because, where the post is used, it is possible for the contract to be formed even if the letter of acceptance is in fact never received.

The basic rule is quite old and simply stated. Where use of the ordinary postal system is the normal, anticipated or agreed means of accepting the offer then the contract is formed at the time that the letter of acceptance is posted, and not when it is actually received.

CASE EXAMPLE

Adams v Lindsell [1818] 106 ER 250

The rule actually began with this case. It involved an offer for the sale of wool. Because the parties were not in close contact, the seller asked for an acceptance by post. The prospective purchaser replied on the same day that the offer was received and sent the acceptance in a letter, as required. However, the letter of acceptance was not received until long afterwards, by which time the seller had sold the wool. The purchaser sued, claiming a breach of contract. The court examined the reality of contracting at a distance at the time. The court developed the rule because of the possible injustices that could be caused by delays in the postal system in its early days. It was held that the letter of acceptance was effective from its time of posting and that a binding contract existed at that point rather than at any later point when the letter may or may not be received.

It has been stated that the letter of acceptance would need to be properly stamped and addressed for the rule to apply: *Re London and Northern Bank, ex parte Jones* [1900] 1 Ch 220. In any case, for the rule to apply, the letter must be fully within the control of the post office, which it would not be if the letter was given to a postman while delivering, as this would not be authorised.

The logical consequence of the rule is that the acceptance may be effective and the contract may be formed even though the actual notification of acceptance is received at a point later than a revocation of the original offer has been made.

CASE EXAMPLE

Henthorn v Fraser [1892] 2 Ch 27

Fraser, representing a building society for whom he worked, made offers in writing to sell houses to Henthorn, the offer to remain open for 14 days. The day after the offer was made, the building society then posted another letter, revoking the original offer from noon on that day. When Henthorn received the offers he posted to the building society a letter of acceptance that was postmarked 3.50 pm. On the same day at 5 pm Henthorn then received the letter of revocation from the building society.

Even more remarkably, the rule will inevitably apply as a result where the letter of acceptance is in fact never received by the offeror, rather than merely delayed in the post.

CASE EXAMPLE

Household Fire Insurance v Grant (1879) 4 Ex D 216

Grant made a written offer to purchase shares. The insurance company then posted a letter of allotment to Grant, the normal method of notification of acceptance. This letter was posted but never received by Grant. At a later stage, the insurance company went into liquidation. Because Grant was identified as a shareholder, he would be liable to creditors of the company for the face value of the shares that he had been allotted. Grant's claim that he was not a shareholder and should not be liable for the value of the shares failed. The court held that he had become a shareholder even though unaware of it because the letter of allotment never arrived with him. The contract had been formed at the moment of posting and it was irrelevant to Grant's liability that he had never received the letter. His name and shareholding would have been registered in the company's name and his liability as a shareholder was evident from this.

It is, nevertheless, possible to avoid the effects of the postal rule by the offeror stating in the offer that there will be no contract until the acceptance is actually received by him. In this case the contract is only complete on communication of the acceptance.

CASE EXAMPLE

Holwell Securities v Hughes [1974] 1 WLR 155

Hughes sent the firm the option to purchase certain land. The option was exercisable by notice in writing, to be received by Hughes by a certain date. The firm posted its acceptance but this never in fact reached Hughes. The firm's attempt to make use of the postal rule failed because under the terms of Hughes' offer the acceptance was required to be 'by notice in writing'. The court held that the fact that actual communication of acceptance was required meant that the postal rule could not apply in the circumstances. The firm could not claim that a contract existed with Hughes as a result.

Similarly, the offeror may prevent the rule from applying by prescribing the method of acceptance.

JUDGMENT

It was identified by Buckley J in *Manchester Diocesan Council for Education v Commercial and General Investments Ltd* [1969] 3 All ER 159 that 'an offeror, who by the terms of his offer insists on acceptance in a particular way is entitled to insist that he is not bound unless acceptance is effected or communicated in that precise way'.

f) *The problem of modern methods of communicating acceptance*

In modern times the development of new technologies and different methods of communication have made the postal rule irrelevant in many circumstances. The telephone, for instance, is an instantaneous means of communicating information and therefore appears to be the same as a face-to-face dealing.

CASE EXAMPLE

Entores Ltd v Miles Far East Corporation [1955] 2 QB 327

Here, Dutch agents of an American company accepted an offer for the sale and purchase of equipment made by a British company by telex. In a later dispute between the parties, the claimant would have been unable to sue the defendant unless the contract was made in England. The Court of Appeal held that, because of the method of communicating, the contract was actually made in England when the telex was received, not when it was transmitted in Holland.

JUDGMENT

In identifying that the postal rule could not be applied to communication by either telex or telephone, Lord Denning gave an interesting explanation: 'Suppose, for instance, that I shout an offer to a man across a river or a courtyard but I do not hear his reply because it is drowned by an aircraft flying overhead. There is no contract at that moment. If he wishes to make a contract he must wait till the aircraft is gone and then shout back his acceptance so that I can hear what he says. Not till I have the answer am I bound.'

However, telephone answering machines mean that a party may leave a message which is not then listened to for a few days at least. This obviously creates problems in determining when an acceptance delivered in this way is valid. Both telex machines and the fax system transmit messages almost instantaneously but if a party is away from the machine then the same problems apply. The use of e-mail is of course yet another complication.

As a result, the answer as to when the acceptance is valid and the contract is formed in more modern methods of communication is not absolutely clear, and other circumstances may have to be taken into account rather than just the method of responding itself. The important factor does seem to be how instantaneous the method is, but this cannot be relied on absolutely.

CASE EXAMPLE

Brinkibon Ltd v Stahag Stahl [1983] AC 34

The previous case law had stated that an acceptance by telex, like telephone, was sufficiently immediate communication to be effective straightaway, and therefore the normal rules of communication applied, and the postal rule could not apply. However, this case concerned an acceptance by telex that had been received out of office hours. The House of Lords considered all of the circumstances of the case and held that the acceptance could only be effective and the contract formed once the office was re-opened.

JUDGMENT

Lord Wilberforce recognised the difficulties inherent in modern methods of communication and concluded that, 'No universal rule can cover all such cases; they must be resolved by reference to the intention of the parties, by sound business practice and in some cases by a judgment where the risk should lie'.

Faxes, e-mail, and other use of the internet are even more modern forms of communication and the same problems and the same principles will very often apply.

More recently, as a result of having to implement EU Directive 97/7, the Distance Selling Directive, the Consumer Protection (Distance Selling) Regulations 2000 have also been introduced.

- The Regulations apply to contracts for the sale of goods and for the provisions of services made by a variety of modern methods, for example: telephone; fax; Internet shopping; mail order; e-mail; television shopping.
- The Regulations do not apply in certain identified contracts: transfers of land; building contracts; financial services; purchases from vending machines; auctions.
- Under reg 7, the seller/supplier is bound to provide the purchaser with certain minimum information, including:
  - the right to cancel the contract within seven days
  - description
  - price
  - arrangements for payment and delivery (and how long all of these remain open for)
  - the identity of the supplier.
- Written confirmation must also be given, according to reg 8.
- Inevitably, if these rules are not complied with then the contract is not formed.

The Electronic Commerce Directive 2000/31 has an impact also on offer and acceptance by electronic means.

- Article 11 says that, 'where [a purchaser] in accepting [a seller's] offer is required to give his consent through technological means, such as clicking on an icon, the contract is concluded when the recipient of the service has received from the service provider, electronically, an acknowledgement of receipt of the recipient's acceptance'.
- So this would appear to clear up some of the problems formerly encountered in determining when such agreements are actually complete and a contract is formed.

The Directive has been implemented through the Electronic Commerce (EC Directive) Regulations 2002.

ACTIVITY

Self-assessment questions

1. Why is the 'mirror image' rule necessary?
2. What are the different consequences of a counter-offer and a mere enquiry?
3. How does the judge decide whether a response to an offer is a counter-offer or a mere enquiry?
4. In what way can a counter-offer operate to influence the formation of a contract?
5. In what possible situations might a silent response nevertheless lead on to a contractual relationship?
6. Is there any justification for the postal rule in the modern day?
7. What problems result from modern-day rapid or instantaneous forms of communication and how have they been resolved?

2.4 The 'battle of the forms' and associated problems

Problems associated with offer and acceptance

Many contracts in a modern commercial context are not formed as the result of one party simply accepting the straightforward offer of the other. This would be too restrictive and rigid on business. Commercial enterprises contract in a variety of ways and negotiations may include disagreements, rejections, compromises and even threats before a final agreement is ever reached.

Sometimes people will also negotiate to try to get something different than that which is first offered. We have already seen the effect that a counter-offer can have on the parties. The question for the court is often when a mere enquiry ends and a counter-offer begins. This requires precise construction of the negotiations by judges and an awareness of the true intention of the parties.

One added complication is the common use of 'standard forms' by businesses. These are used in order for the business to be sure of always dealing on terms that are advantageous to it. This may not cause massive problems in a consumer sale. However, when two businesses are contracting it can create enormous problems. This type of situation is commonly referred to as the 'battle of the forms'. One business makes an offer on its standard forms. The customer then accepts on its own forms. The result may be an entirely contradictory situation. The question to be answered by the court is which terms should be taken as being the actual contractual ones in the case of a conflict between the two businesses.

As we have already seen, the general rule in the modern day is to take the last counter-offer as having been accepted, and give effect to its terms in the contract.

CASE EXAMPLE

Davies & Co Ltd v William Old (1969) 67 LGR 395

Shopfitters, following their successful tender, contracted with the architects in a building contract to sub-contract to the builders. The builders, under instruction from the architects, issued an order for work to the shopfitters. They did this on their own standard form that included a clause that they would not pay for work until they themselves had been paid. When the shopfitters later sued for some work that had not been paid for, their action failed. The builders' standard form was a counter-offer that the shopfitters had accepted by carrying on with the work.

The problem is further compounded because often the services or goods are provided before any settled agreement is reached. In any later conflict, the courts may find a contract does exist provided there has been no major disagreement between the parties. Sometimes, however, this proves impossible for the court to achieve and an alternative method of settling the dispute must be found.

CASE EXAMPLE

British Steel Corporation v Cleveland Bridge and Engineering Co [1984] 1 All ER 504

Cleveland Bridge and Engineering were sub-contracted to build the steel framework of a bank in Saudi Arabia. The work required four steel nodes that they asked BSC to manufacture. BSC wanted a disclaimer of liability for any loss caused by late delivery. The parties were never able to agree on this and so no written agreement was ever made. BSC, however, did make and deliver three of the nodes, but the last was delayed because of a strike. Cleveland Bridge refused to pay for the three nodes and claimed that BSC was in breach of contract for late delivery of the fourth. Because there was a total disagreement over a major term, the judge in the case found it impossible to recognise that a contract existed. He did order that BSC be paid for what they had supplied.

Where the parties negotiate an agreement subject to contract and one in fact begins performance before any agreement is apparently reached judges will not automatically find that a contract exists merely because performance by one party has commenced but rather because of unequivocal conduct by the parties.

CASE EXAMPLE

RTS Flexible Systems Ltd v Molkerei Alois Muller Gmbh & Co (UK Production) [2010] UKSC14

RTS, a supplier of automated packaging machines for the food industry, and Molkerei, a supplier of dairy products, had initially intended to enter into a detailed written contract for RTS to design and install two production lines in Molkerei's factory. Quotes were sent out for the work and then Molkerei sent RTS a letter of intent identifying that it wished to contract. The written contract, referred to as the MF/1 contract, would be subject to a series of complex terms and Molkerei wished to renegotiate these and did. However, as often happens they never agreed the final terms before work was begun with the agreement of both parties, although the actual work to be done and the price were never in dispute They continued to negotiate while work was undertaken and did eventually agree on the amended MF/1 contract but it was never signed. RTS received 70% of the payment due but after completion of the work a dispute arose over the quality of certain of the equipment provided and Molkerei refused to pay the remaining money owed and RTS sued. The issue was whether the parties were in a contract and if so which contract. The judge in the High court held that there was a contract but that it did not include the MF/1 terms. RTS appealed and the Court of Appeal held that no contract came into existence after the letter of intent. Molkerei appealed and the Supreme Court held that the critical factor was the unequivocal communications of the parties and it is this that should determine what the contract was. The parties had agreed to waive the subject to contract provisions and the appeal was allowed. The case is interesting because it takes a different approach to that of Lord Denning in Cleveland Bridge although the Supreme Court felt that the two different approaches were not incompatible.

Inevitably, one party will still see the result as unacceptable or disadvantageous. The courts are faced with a difficult dilemma in such circumstances and have proved relatively reluctant to move away from the traditional mechanics of offer and acceptance. However, this is not to say that alternative approaches have not been suggested.

JUDGMENT

In *Butler Machine Tool Co Ltd v Ex-Cell-O Corporation* [1979] 1 WLR 401 Lord Denning concluded that where the standard forms differ widely then, 'The terms and conditions of both parties are to be construed together. If they can be reconciled so as to give harmonious result, all well and good. If the differences are irreconcilable, so that they are mutually contradictory, then the conflicting terms may have to be scrapped and replaced by a reasonable implication'.

This proposition is probably too radical for most judges to accept, even though the judges have recognised a growing disparity between the simple rules of contract law and the needs of businesses when contracting.

JUDGMENT

In *New Zealand Shipping Co Ltd v A M Satterthwaite & Co Ltd (The Eurymedon)* [1975] AC 154 Lord Wilberforce made the following revealing statement: 'It is only the precise analysis of this complex of relations into the classical offer and acceptance, with identifiable consideration, that seems to present difficulty [but] English law, having committed itself to a rather technical and schematic doctrine of contract, in application takes a practical approach, often at the cost of forcing the facts to fit uneasily into the marked slots of offer and acceptance.'

It is quite easy to see the difficulties faced by the judges in using the very mechanical process of offer and acceptance. It is also easy to see how they might react to difficult situations when they are trying to balance the need to stick to the mechanical rules and the justice of the case. As P S Atiyah writes:

QUOTATION

It is of course questionable just how far judges will go down the road of enforcing purely beneficial agreements, as they did in effect in *Blackpool and Fylde Aero Club Ltd v Blackpool Borough Council* [1990] 1 WLR 1195. Judges are far more likely to retain an observance of the traditional technicalities of offer and acceptance.

CASE EXAMPLE

Walford v Miles [1992] 2 AC 128

Here, an offer was made for the sale of a photography business and the vendor then agreed to continue negotiations and not to withdraw from the sale or to sell to anyone else until the negotiations were concluded one way or another. The purchaser issued a comfort letter in response. The House of Lords, however, would recognise no enforceable contractual basis in the comfort letter and held that this provisional agreement between the two parties was too vague to be contractual.

Nevertheless, in contrast it has been held that a contract can still run despite the fact that certain terms under it still need to be agreed by the parties (see *Pagnan SpA v Feed Products Ltd* [1987] 2 Lloyd's Rep 601). The precise terms to be negotiated were, however, ancillary to the major purpose of the contract.

ACTIVITY

Self-assessment questions

1. Is there a satisfactory method of resolving a 'battle of forms'?
2. Is there any logic to the outcome of *Cleveland Bridge*?

SUMMARY

- A contract is formed only where there is an agreement between two parties.
- An agreement is a valid offer followed by a valid acceptance.
- Invitations to treat and mere statements of price are not offers.
- Offers have to be communicated to the other party, but can be made to the whole world.
- The terms of the offer must be certain.
- Offers can be withdrawn any time up to acceptance as long as this is communicated to the offeree which can be through a reliable third party.

- Unilateral offers do not require acceptance, only performance.
- An offer ends on acceptance, or on proper withdrawal, or on lapse of time, or on the death of one of the parties.
- Acceptance must be unconditional to be valid.
- But mere enquiries are not rejections of the offer.
- Like offers, acceptance has to be communicated to the other party.
- Where use of the post is the normal, anticipated method of acceptance, the contract is formed on posting (the postal rule) even if the acceptance is never received.
- There are slightly different rules for modern methods of communicating, eg, fax, e-mail.

SAMPLE ESSAY QUESTION

'Offer and acceptance, while an apparently simple concept, is in fact quite complex, and it is often difficult for judges to decide whether particular negotiations in fact involve either offer or acceptance.' Discuss whether the statement above accurately describes the development of rules on offer and acceptance.

Explain the basic principle of acceptance:

- Need for a *consensus ad idem*
- A valid offer followed by a valid acceptance

Explain the basic rules of offer:

- An offer is a statement of willingness to be bound by the terms of the offer
- It must be distinguished from 'invitation to treat' and a mere statement of price
- An offer must be communicated to the offeree – but can be made to the whole world
- Its terms must be certain
- An offer can be withdrawn any time up to acceptance – can be by a reliable third party
- A unilateral offer only requires performance
- Offer ends on acceptance, proper withdrawal, lapse of time, death of one of the parties

Explain the basic rules of acceptance:
- Acceptance must be unconditional – but mere enquiries are not rejections of the offer
- Acceptance must be communicated and if use of the post is the normal, anticipated method of acceptance the contract is formed on posting
- Modern methods of communicating such as fax, e-mail, internet are now governed by statutory provisions

Discuss whether offer and acceptance are complex:
- Non-standard transactions, eg, invitation to treat, including display, advertising, catalogues, self-service arrangements in shops, auction and tenders, rewards
- Problems associated with communication – including modern methods
- counter-offers – particularly in negotiations involving standard form contracts
- where there is no actual negotiation between the parties, eg vending machines

Discuss how judges have developed rules:
- judges developed the notion of invitation to treat
- judges created the concept of unilateral offer and
- identified that it cannot be revoked while the offeree is still performing
- judges have identified that the final counter-offer forms the basis of the contract
- judges created the postal rule
- judges differentiated between instantaneous communication and delayed communication

Rules of acceptance	Case/statute
Acceptance must be unconditional	*Hyde v Wrench*
• so a counter-offer counts as a rejection and the offer is no longer open to acceptance	*Hyde v Wrench*
• but mere enquiries are not rejections of the offer	*Stevenson v McLean*
• a counter-offer if accepted forms the basis of the agreement	*Davies & Co v William Old*
• but not if they are of no importance to the parties.	*Brogden v Metropolitan Railway Co*
Acceptance must be communicated	*Felthouse v Bindley*
• so silence is not acceptance	*Felthouse v Bindley*
• a unilateral offer is accepted by performance and the offer cannot be withdrawn while the offeree is still performing	*Carlill v Carbolic Smoke Ball Co*
• if use of the post is the normal, anticipated method of acceptance, the contract is formed on posting (the postal rule)	*Adams v Lindsell*
• this applies even if the acceptance is never received	*Household Fire Insurance v Grant*
• modern methods of communicating such as fax, e-mail and the internet cause problems in determining when a contract is formed – generally, it depends on how instant the communication is	*Brinkibon v Stahag Stahl*
• Some of these problems have now been resolved by the Electronic Commerce Directive and the Consumer Protection (Distance Selling) Regulations.	

Further reading

Cheshire, G, Fifoot, C and Furmston, M, *Law of Contract* (15th edn, Oxford University Press, 2006/Chapter 3.

Lewis, R 'Contracts between Businessmen: Reform of the Law of Firm Offers' (1982) J Law & Soc 153.

Stone, R, 'The Postal Rule in the Electronic Age' (1992) 15 SL Rev, Spring.

3

Formation of a contract: Consideration

AIMS AND OBJECTIVES

After reading this chapter you should be able to:

- Understand the origins and purposes of consideration
- Define consideration
- Distinguish between executory and executed consideration
- Understand the basic rules on consideration
- Critically analyse the area
- Apply the law to factual situations and reach conclusions

3.1 The origins and character of consideration

3.1.1 The origins, nature and purpose of consideration

As we have already seen, the law of contract deals with bargains. The rules of contract seek to differentiate between agreements where there is something to be gained by both parties, as is the case in a contract, and agreements which are purely gratuitous, as are gifts. Consideration developed as the 'proof' that a contract existed rather than a merely gratuitous promise.

Originally, contracts were only recognised if they were contained in a deed. This was absolutely logical in the case of transfers of land but was inconvenient in the case of other types of agreement. By the seventeenth century, in the case of agreements other than for land, the courts would demand evidence of the 'proof' that a bargain in fact existed. The giving of 'consideration' by both sides became the traditional method of ensuring that other types of agreement were contractual. It was the *quid pro quo*, the proof that a bargain in fact existed, and if no consideration could be found then the agreement could not be enforced. The exception is an agreement made by deed.

Initially, consideration was an essential procedural element, but was ill defined because it could involve almost anything that showed some movement of benefit and detriment. This is inevitably why there was no real attempt at clear definition before the nineteenth century and why it remains a problematic area even now.

3.1.2 Defining 'consideration'

Originally, it proved impossible to give a simple, single definition of 'consideration', and the pragmatic view was often taken that it was no more than the reason why the promise should be binding in law. Often in any case it was taken as being no more than a rule of evidence.

Many nineteenth-century cases looked for definitions based on benefit gained and detriment suffered. So, for instance, consideration was variously defined as:

- 'loss or inconvenience suffered by one party at the request of the other' – *Bunn v Guy* (1803) 4 East 190
- 'some detriment to the plaintiff or some benefit to the defendant' – *Thomas v Thomas* [1842] 2 QB 851.

A simple, early way of defining consideration came in *Currie v Misa* (1875) 1 App Cas 554 where it was described in terms of benefit and detriment: 'some right, interest, profit or benefit accruing to one party, or some forbearance, detriment, loss or responsibility given, suffered or undertaken by the other'. So if I contract with you for the sale and purchase of my *Unlocking Contract Law* textbook for £15, I am gaining the benefit of the £15 but I have the detriment of giving up the book. For you, it is the other way round: you gain the book and give up the money.

privity of contract

The requirement that to be capable of suing or being sued under a contract a person must actually be a party (privy) to th at contract

A more sophisticated definition was later provided in *Dunlop v Selfridge* [1915] AC 847. The case involved issues of both absence of consideration and lack of **privity of contract** by the party seeking to enforce the contractual provisions. Here, the House of Lords approved Sir Frederick Pollock's definition contained in his *Principles of Contract*, that 'an act of forbearance or the promise thereof is the price for which the promise of the other is bought, and the promise thus given for value is enforceable'.

In fact, although the judges are saying that they will not in contract law enforce a promise which has not been paid for in some way, in modern cases they have been shown to be willing to see almost any promise made in a commercial context as contractual. Therefore consideration can be surprisingly little, and it can seem difficult to fit the theory to real situations.

However it is defined, it is of course also important to see consideration in the overall context of formation. The separate elements are all equally essential to demonstrating that a contract in fact exists. Harmson stressed this point:

QUOTATION

'Consideration, offer and acceptance are an indivisible trinity, facets of one identical notion which is that of bargain. Indeed, consideration may conveniently be explained as merely the acceptance viewed from the offeror's side. We can no doubt separate offer, acceptance and consideration for our convenience … but they are logical and interdependent entities abstracted from the one entire reality which is bargain. We can no more abolish one without destroying the others than we can think of a circle without a circumference.'

C J Harmson, 'The Reform of Consideration' (1938) 54 Law Quarterly Review, p 234

3.1.3 Executed and executory consideration

Contract law would have no meaning unless it enforced promises as well as actual acts. Executory consideration is simply the exchange of promises to carry out acts or pass property at a later stage. If one party breaks their promise and fails to do what they are supposed to do under it, then they are in breach of contract and may be sued.

In unilateral contracts, however, the party making the unilateral offer is under no obligations until the other party performs (executes) their side of the bargain. This is called executed consideration, and a common example is a reward. We have already seen this principle in operation in *Carlill*'s case (*Carlill v The Carbolic Smoke Ball Co Ltd* [1893] 1 QB 256).

3.2 The basic rules of consideration

3.2.1 Adequacy and sufficiency of consideration

One of the most basic rules of consideration is that consideration need not be adequate but it must be sufficient. This seems to be a very confusing statement because in general terms we would expect adequacy and sufficiency to be the same thing. However, in the context of consideration the two words have very different meanings, 'adequacy' being used in its normal everyday sense and 'sufficiency' having a very precise legal meaning.

Adequacy

In fact, lawyers are using '**adequacy**' in its everyday form, ie, whether the parties are promising things of fairly equal value. Adequacy will be decided by the parties themselves. Freedom of contract would be badly affected if we could not decide ourselves whether we are satisfied with the bargain we have made. In certain circumstances, in any case, it may actually work to our ultimate advantage to make a bargain that on the face of it appears to be a bad one.

The courts, then, are not interested in whether there has been a good or a bad bargain made, only that a bargain exists, and they will seek to enforce the bargain that is actually agreed upon by the parties.

CASE EXAMPLE

Thomas v Thomas [1842] 2 QB 851

Before his death a man expressed the wish that his wife be allowed to remain in the house although this was not in his will. The executors carried out this wish and charged the widow a nominal ground rent of £1 per year. When they later tried to dispossess her, they failed. The moral obligation to carry out the man's wishes was not consideration, but the payment of ground rent, however small and apparently inadequate, was.

JUDGMENT

Patteson J in *Thomas v Thomas* explained as follows: 'Consideration means some thing which is of some value in the eye of the law, moving from the plaintiff: it may be of some benefit to the plaintiff, or some detriment to the defendant; but at all events it must be moving from the plaintiff. Now that which is suggested as the consideration here, a pious respect for the wishes of the testator, does not in any way move from the plaintiff; it moves from the testator; therefore, legally speaking, it forms no part of the consideration.'

Sufficiency

On the other hand, '**sufficiency**' is used here as a legal term, and it means that what is promised must:

- be real
- be tangible
- have some actual value.

CASE EXAMPLE

White v Bluett (1853) LJ Ex 36

A son owed his father money on a promissory note. When the father died and his executors were trying to recover the money, the son tried to claim that he was not bound to pay. He claimed an agreement with his father that the debt would be forgotten in return for the son's promise not to complain about the distribution of the father's assets in his will. The son failed. The promise was too intangible to be consideration for the father's promise to forgo the debt.

JUDGMENT

Pollock CB explained the position in the following way: 'In reality, there was no consideration whatsoever. The son had no right to complain, for the father might make what distribution of his property he liked; and the son's abstaining from doing what he had no right to do can be no consideration.'

What is real, tangible and of value is not always easily distinguishable.

CASE EXAMPLE

Ward v Byham [1956] 1 WLR 496

A father of an illegitimate child promised the mother money towards its upkeep if she would keep the child 'well looked after and happy'. The mother would be doing nothing more than she was already bound by law to do in looking after the child. The court was prepared to enforce the agreement, however, since there is no obligation in law to keep a child happy, and the promise to do so was seen as good consideration.

In fact, even things of no apparent worth have been classed as amounting to valuable consideration. Even where the argument is over free gifts, courts may still find that consideration exists, the significant point being that the parties are actually gaining in some way from the arrangement.

CASE EXAMPLE

Chappell v Nestlé Co [1960] AC 87

Nestlé had offered a record, normally retailing at 6s 8d (not quite equivalent to 34p now), for 1s 6d (7.5p now) plus three chocolate bar wrappers, to promote their chocolate. On receipt, the wrappers were thrown away. They were still held to be good consideration when the holders of the copyright of the record sued to prevent the promotion because they would receive substantially fewer royalties from it.

JUDGMENT

Lord Somervell in *Chappell & Co Ltd v Nestlé Co Ltd* [1960] AC 87 commented on sufficiency: 'The question is whether the three wrappers were part of the consideration ... I think that they are part of the consideration. They are so described in the offer. "They", the wrappers, "will help you to get smash hit recordings" ... It is said that, when received, the wrappers are of no value to the respondents, the Nestlé Co Ltd. This I would have thought to be irrelevant. A contracting party can stipulate for what consideration he chooses. A peppercorn does not cease to be good consideration if it is established that the promisee does not like pepper and will throw away the corn'.

While the courts will inevitably consider whether there is an economic value to what is passed under an agreement, they fall short of actually defining 'economic value' too strictly or precisely.

CASE EXAMPLE

Edmonds v Lawson [2000] 2 WLR 1091

This case concerned the issue of whether or not trainee barristers should be paid during their pupillage and therefore whether a contractual relationship existed. The court considered the relationship between the pupil barrister and the pupil master and also the relationship between pupil barrister and chambers. Inevitably, the court considered what benefit, if any, would be gained from the pupil's association with both. In the case of the relationship with pupil masters, the pupils are in the main engaged in learning and in any case are paid for any actual work that they do during the second six months. As a result, the court did not believe that any particular benefit was gained by the pupil master and so there was no consideration and no contract between them. On the other hand, the court felt that chambers did gain by the relationship with pupils. It was in their own interest to attract talented pupils who might later take up vacant tenancies. So there was a benefit amounting to consideration and a contractual relationship could be identified in the case of chambers.

It would seem that the accusation that if a court wishes to enforce a promise in a commercial context it will always find something to act as consideration seems to be proved when set against the reasoning in certain cases (see, for instance, *Williams v Roffey Bros & Nicholls Contractors Ltd* [1990] 1 All ER 512).

CASE EXAMPLE

Alliance Bank Ltd v Broom (1864) 2 Drew & Sm 289

Broom owed the bank £22,000. The bank demanded security for the loan and Broom promised as security certain goods that he was due to receive under another contract. Normally it would have been practice for the bank at the time to give a promise not to sue in return for this offer of security. However, no such promise was offered here. When Broom failed to give up the security the bank sued for possession of the goods. The promise of security would only be enforceable if it was indeed a contractual arrangement with consideration moving from both sides. Here there was apparently no consideration given by the bank. Nevertheless, the court construed that waiting for repayment of the loan was in itself consideration. The presumption must be that the court wished to ensure that at all times a creditor in a creditor/debtor relationship was protected against default on the loan.

3.2.2 Consideration moving from the promisee: the connection with privity

Again, the rule sounds somewhat complex but in fact it simply means that a person cannot sue or indeed be sued under a contract unless he has provided consideration. (This rule is interchangeable with the rule requiring privity of contract where a person is not able to sue on a contract to which he is not a party.)

CASE EXAMPLE

Tweddle v Atkinson [1861] 121 ER 762

Fathers of a young couple who intended to marry agreed in writing that each would settle a sum of money on the couple. The young woman's father died before giving over the money and the young man then sued the executors to the estate when they refused to hand over the money. Even though he was named in the agreements he failed because he had given no consideration for the agreement himself.

In diagram form, the situation can be expressed as follows:

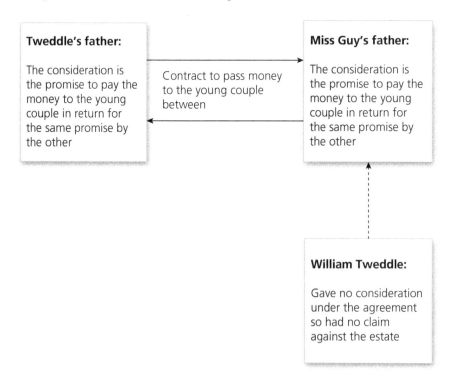

Figure 3.1 Using the agreement in *Tweddle v Atkinson* to illustrate the rule that consideration must move from the promisee

As with other rules of consideration, this rule is still subject to certain exceptions. One of the most obvious exceptions (which is also an exception to the basic doctrine of privity) is the collateral contract. This occurs when a promise is made of relevance to the contract by a person who is not a party to that contract but derives some benefit from it. In certain circumstances it may be possible for a party to the contract who has relied on this promise to sue on it even though it did not form part of the contract itself.

CASE EXAMPLE

Shanklin Pier Ltd v Detel Products Ltd [1951] 2 KB 854

The pier owners contracted with painting contractors to re-paint the pier. In doing so they demanded that the painters used a particular paint manufactured by the defendants. They had selected this paint because of representations made by the manufacturers about its resistance to weathering and sea erosion and the assurance that it would not peel. When the paint proved defective and the pier owners had to spend more than £4,000 to put the job right, they had no action against the painters who had used the paint as instructed. The pier owners were able to sue the manufacturers on the basis of the representation even though they had no contract with them.

3.2.3 Past consideration and the exception in *Lampleigh v Braithwaite*

Another rule of consideration is that it must not be past. This is another strange-sounding rule. It simply means that any consideration given cannot come before the agreement but must follow it. If a party has provided what he believes to be consideration but has done so before any agreement has been reached then there is no 'proof' that a bargain actually exists and therefore no proof either of the existence of a contract.

It is a sensible rule in that it can prevent the unscrupulous from forcing people into contracts on the basis of providing goods or services which they have not ordered. Quite simply, in any case it is a promise that has not been agreed to by both parties in their contract.

The basic rule

The rule will usually apply where one party has done a voluntary act and is trying to enforce the other party's later promise to pay.

CASE EXAMPLE

Re McArdle [1951] Ch 669

A son and his wife lived in his mother's house which, on her death, would be inherited by her son and her three other children. The son's wife paid for substantial repairs and improvements to the property. The mother then made her four children sign an agreement to reimburse the daughter-in-law out of her estate. When the mother died and the children refused to keep this promise, the daughter-in-law sued unsuccessfully. Her consideration for their promise was past. It came before they signed the agreement to repay her.

This is a modern restatement of a much older rule which in effect concerned guarantees about the subject-matter of a contract made after the actual agreement. Because the guarantee came after the agreement, it did not form part of the contract and could not be relied upon.

CASE EXAMPLE

Roscorla v Thomas (1842) 3 QBD 234

Here, an agreement was reached for the sale and purchase of a horse and a price of £30 agreed. After the deal was struck the seller was asked about the horse's character by the purchaser and the seller assured the purchaser that the horse was 'sound and free from vice'. In fact, the horse had a vicious temperament and bit people. The purchaser tried to sue on the basis of this later promise and failed. There was no consideration for the promise. The only possible consideration, the price paid for it, was past in relation to this later agreement.

JUDGMENT

Denman CJ explained the basic principle in the context of the case: 'It may be taken as a general rule, subject to exceptions, not applicable to this case, that the promise must be co-extensive with the consideration. In the present case, the only promise that would result from the consideration, as stated, and be co-extensive with it, would be to deliver the horse upon request. The precedent sale, without a warranty, though at the request of the defendant, imposes no other duty or obligation upon him. It is clear, therefore, that the consideration stated would not raise an implied promise by the defendant that the horse was sound or free from vice.'

In diagram form, it works this way:

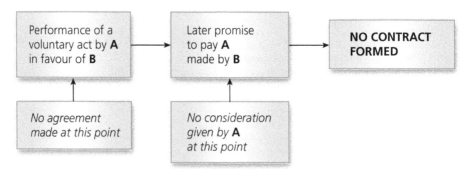

Figure 3.2 The operation of the past consideration rule

The exception to the rule

The rule will not always work justly, as the above case shows. In certain circumstances the rule will not apply. Where one of the parties has requested a service, the law sensibly concludes that he is prepared to pay for it. Even though that service is then carried out without any mention as to payment, or any apparent contractual agreement, a promise to pay coming after the service is performed will be enforced by the courts. This is known as the rule in *Lampleigh v Braithwaite* [1615] 80 ER 255, from the case of that name.

CASE EXAMPLE

Lampleigh v Braithwaite [1615] 80 ER 255

Braithwaite was accused of killing a man and asked Lampleigh to get him a King's pardon. This Lampleigh achieved at considerable expense to himself, and Braithwaite, in gratitude, promised to pay him £100, which he in fact never did. Lampleigh's claim that there was a contract succeeded. Because the service was requested, even though no price was mentioned at the time, it was clear that both parties would have contemplated a payment. The later promise to pay was clear evidence of this.

In diagram form, it works in the following way:

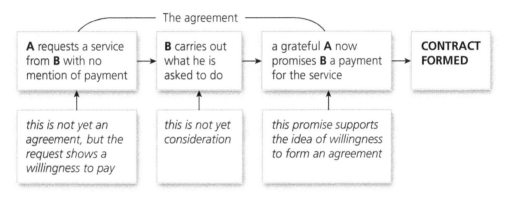

Figure 3.3 The exception in *Lampleigh v Braithwaite* in operation

The principle in *Lampleigh v Braithwaite* has subsequently been affirmed and restated by Lord Scarman in *Pao On v Lau Yiu Long* [1980] AC 614:

JUDGMENT

'An act done before the giving of a promise to make a payment or to confer some other benefit can sometimes be consideration for the promise. The act must have been done at the promisor's request, the parties must have understood that the act was to be remunerated further by a payment or the conferment of some other benefit and payment, or the conferment of a benefit must have been legally enforceable had it been promised in advance.'

There are in any case many more modern examples of the operation of the exception in *Lampleigh v Braithwaite* operating in a commercial context.

CASE EXAMPLE

Re Casey's Patent [1892] 1 Ch 104

Joint owners of a patent wrote to the claimant, agreeing to give him a one-third share of the patents in return for his services as manager of their patents. When the claimant wished to enforce this agreement they then claimed that the agreement was actually in respect of his past services and unenforceable for past consideration. He had in fact supplied no consideration following the agreement. Bowen LJ held that there was inevitably an implied promise that in managing the patents the claimant would be paid for his work. The later agreement to pay was therefore enforceable. It was an example of the exception in *Lampleigh v Braithwaite*.

ACTIVITY

Quick quiz

Consider the following events and decide whether an enforceable contract has been formed or whether consideration is only past.

1. While I was away on holiday abroad it was very hot at home too. My neighbour Alison noticed that some of my flowers were dying and so she watered them every day, saving them. I was very pleased when I returned and I told her that I would give her £20 for all her trouble. In fact, I have not given Alison the money and she wonders if she is actually entitled to it.

2. Last month I had to go to an exam board meeting in Birmingham. My car would not start so I asked one of my students, Neera, who has a car, if she would take me there. She quite happily agreed and gave me a lift there and even waited for the meeting to finish so that she could also give me a lift back. When we had returned I gave Neera the appropriate amount of money for the petrol that she had used but I also promised her that I would buy her a new copy of a law textbook costing £58.50 for which she had been saving hard. However, last week, when Neera asked when she could have the money for the book I told her that I no longer intend to buy the book for her.

3.3 Consideration and the performance of existing duties

3.3.1 The basic rule

It has long been accepted that where a party merely does something by which he is already legally bound this can never be sufficient to amount to consideration for an entirely fresh agreement.

The rule applies to any legal obligation firstly wherever there is a public duty created by law.

CASE EXAMPLE

Collins v Godefroy [1831] 109 ER 1040

A police officer was under a court order to attend and give evidence at a trial. It was important to the defendant that the officer attended so he promised to pay him a sum of money to ensure that he did so. The promise to pay was not contractual and was unenforceable. There was no consideration for it.

Inevitably, the rule has also been used to cover situations where the duty has arisen under an existing contract. The same principle will apply. Mere performance of the existing contractual duty cannot amount to sufficient consideration under a fresh contractual arrangement.

CASE EXAMPLE

Stilk v Myrick [1809] 170 ER 1168

Two members of a ship's crew of 11 deserted. The captain promised the remaining crew that they could share these two men's wages if they got the ship safely home. When the ship's owner refused to make the extra payments and was challenged in court, it was

58

FORMATION OF A CONTRACT: CONSIDERATION

held that the promise was not binding on him. The sailors were held to be bound by their contract to cope with the normal contingencies of the voyage, and these could include desertions, so there was no consideration for the captain's promise and no contract to enforce.

JUDGMENT

Lord Ellenborough in this case explained the reason behind the rule: 'There was no consideration for the ulterior pay promised to the mariners who remained with the ship. Before they sailed from London they had undertaken to do all that they could under all emergencies of the voyage. They had sold all their services till the voyage should be completed. If they had been at liberty to quit the vessel at Crondstadt, the case would have been quite different; or if the captain had capriciously discharged the two men … the others might not have been compellable to take the whole duty upon themselves, and their agreeing to do so might have been a sufficient consideration for the promise of an advance of wages. But the desertion of a part of the crew is to be considered an emergency of the voyage as much as their death; and those who remain are bound by the terms of their original contract to exert themselves to the utmost to bring the ship safely to her destined port.'

The basic principle that Lord Ellenborough identifies is simple enough: that merely giving all that was originally contracted for is insufficient to form the consideration for a fresh agreement. However, it has to be said that some of the finer points of his argument may well have been lost on the remaining crew.

In *Ward v Byham* [1956] 1 WLR 496 the agreement could be enforced because the court was able to construe that the mother was doing more than she was actually bound to do for the child.

3.3.2 The exceptions to the basic rule

The first major exception to the rule to be identified is that it will be consideration where what is given is more than could have been expected from performance of the existing duty, where in fact something extra is added to what the claimant is already bound to do. The extra element is the consideration for the new promise.

This principle will apply where a public duty is exceeded.

CASE EXAMPLE

Glassbrook Bros v Glamorgan County Council [1925] AC 270

During a strike a pit owner asked for extra protection from the police and promised a payment in return for this service. When the strike was over the pit owner refused to pay, claiming that the police were bound by their public duty to protect his pit. His argument failed. The court found that the police had provided more men than they would normally have done and so there was consideration for the promise.

JUDGMENT

Viscount Cave LC in the above case explained the rule as follows: 'The colliery owners repudiated liability on the grounds that there was no consideration for the promise to pay for the police protection and that such an agreement was against public policy. The case was tried by Bailhache J and he entered judgment for the plaintiffs saying: "There is an obligation on the police to afford efficient protection, but if an individual asks for special protection in a particular form, for the special protection so asked for in that particular form, the individual must pay. It appears … that there is nothing in the first point made for the colliery owners that there was no consideration made for the promise. It is clear that there was abundant consideration. The police authorities thought that it would be best to give protection by means of a flying column of police, but the colliery owners wanted the 'garrison' and promised to pay for it if it was sent".'

Interestingly, the exception to the basic rule has also been accepted in apparently social arrangements, where it is arguable whether it can in reality be considered that there is also an intention to create legal relations.

CASE EXAMPLE

Shadwell v Shadwell (1860) 9 CBNS 159

At a time when an action for breach of promise to marry was still available in law, a young man became engaged to marry. His uncle wrote to him, congratulating him and promising to pay him £150 per year until he reached an income of £600 per year as a Chancery barrister. The young man did in fact marry and claimed the money from his uncle when it remained unpaid. The court held that even though the claimant was legally bound to marry, doing so was good consideration for the uncle's promise and the promise was enforceable.

Inevitably, this principle has also been accepted where the existing duty is a contractual one and one party has given more than was identified as necessary in the contract.

CASE EXAMPLE

Hartley v Ponsonby (1857) 7 E & B 872

This case involved similar facts to *Stilk v Myrick* ([1809] 170 ER 1168) but only 19 members of a crew of 36 remained. A similar promise to pay more money to the remaining crew was enforced because the reduction in numbers made the voyage much more dangerous. The agreement to continue in these circumstances meant that the men had provided good consideration for the promise to pay them extra money.

The exception has been used even in situations where the consideration is not straightforwardly identifiable.

CASE EXAMPLE

Scotson v Pegg (1861) 6 H & N 295

Claimants contracted with one party to deliver coal to them or to their order. The contracting party then sold the coal to the defendants and instructed the claimants to deliver the coal to a third party, the defendants. The defendants then agreed with the claimants that in consideration of the claimants delivering the coal to them, the defendants would unload the coal at a fixed rate per day. The defendants failed to keep this arrangement and the claimants sued. The defendant argued that there was no consideration for the agreement with the claimants. The court rejected their argument and held that the performance of a duty owed to a third party could in fact provide consideration for a promise made by a third party.

Similarly, it has also been accepted, albeit by the Privy Council, that a promise to perform an existing obligation made to a third party can be valid consideration for a fresh agreement.

CASE EXAMPLE

Pao On v Lau Yiu Long [1980] AC 614

Both parties owned companies. The major asset in Pao's company was a building that Lau wished to purchase. An agreement was made whereby Lau's company would buy Pao's company in return for a large number of shares in Lau's company. To avoid the damage that sudden trading in this number of shares might cause, Lau inserted a clause in the contract that Pao should retain 60 per cent of the shares for at least one year. (We could call this Agreement 1.) Pao wanted a guarantee that the shares would not fall in value and a subsidiary agreement was made at the same time by which Lau would buy back 60 per cent of the shares at $2.50 each. Pao later realised that this might benefit Lau more if the shares rose in value and therefore refused to carry out the contract unless the subsidiary arrangement was scrapped and replaced with a straightforward indemnity by Lau against a fall in the value of the shares. Lau could have sued at this point for breach of contract but, fearing a loss of public confidence in his company as a result, agreed to the new terms. (We could call this Agreement 2.) When the value of the shares did then fall, Lau refused to honour the agreement and Pao then sought to enforce the indemnity. Lao offered two defences: Firstly, that the second agreement, the agreement to indemnify Pao, was past consideration and secondly that Pao had given no consideration for the second agreement since it only involved doing what he was bound to do under the first agreement – pass the company in return for the shares. In response to Lau's first defence, the Privy Council applied the rule in *Lampleigh v Braithwaite*. Lau's demand that Pao should not sell 60 per cent of the shares for one year was a request for a service that carried with it an implied promise to pay. This implied promise was later supported by the actual promise to indemnify Pao. The second of Lau's defences also failed. There was consideration. Pao, by continuing with the contract, was protecting the credibility and financial standing of Lau's company and the price payable in return for this was the indemnity.

JUDGMENT

Lord Scarman in this case accepted that, 'the consideration expressly stated in the written guarantee is sufficient in law to support Lau's promise of indemnity. An act done before the giving of a promise to make a payment or to confer some other benefit can sometimes be consideration for the promise … The parties understood at the time of the main agreement that the restriction on selling must be compensated for by the benefit of a guarantee against a drop in price: and such a guarantee would be legally enforceable. The agreed cancellation of the subsidiary agreement left, as the parties knew, the Paos unprotected in a respect in which at the time of the main agreement all were agreed they should be protected'.

In certain circumstances the principle has been accepted, again albeit by the Privy Council, where the agreement protects the commercial credibility of the contract. One significant feature in this instance is the existence of an agency relationship.

CASE EXAMPLE

New Zealand Shipping Co Ltd v A M Satterthwaite & Co Ltd (The Eurymedon) [1975] AC 154

This is a complex case demonstrating how far the courts are prepared to strain the simple meaning of 'consideration' in order to enforce an agreement that they believe must be enforced. Carriers contracted with the consignors of goods to ship drilling equipment. The carriers hired stevedores to unload the equipment, and these stevedores by their negligence caused substantial damage to it. The carriers' contract with the consignors contained a clause limiting their liability in the event of breach. The clause also identified that the protection offered by the limitation would extend to any servant or agent of the carriers. There were two questions for the court. Firstly, it had to decide whether there was a contractual relationship between the stevedores and the consignors. If so, the court was then required to determine whether the stevedores had provided any consideration for the promise by the consignors to be bound by the limitation clause. This was clearly questionable because the stevedores were doing nothing more than they were contractually bound to the carriers to do: unload the ship. The Privy Council accepted that there was a contractual relationship based on agency and that the promise made to the carriers by the stevedores could provide consideration in return for the promise made by the consignors to be bound by the limitation clause.

3.3.3 The exception in *Williams v Roffey*

The most recent, and in some ways the most significant, exception to the basic rule occurs where the party making the promise to pay extra is said to receive an extra benefit from the other party's agreement to complete what he was already bound to do under the existing arrangement.

CASE EXAMPLE

Williams v Roffey Bros & Nicholls Contractors Ltd [1990] 1 All ER 512

Roffey Bros builders sub-contracted the carpentry on a number of flats they were building to Williams for £20,000. Williams had under-quoted for the work and ran into financial difficulties. Because there was a delay clause in Roffey's building contract, meaning they would have to pay money to the client if the flats were not built on time, they promised to pay Williams another £10,300 if he would complete the carpentry on time. When Williams completed the work and Roffey's failed to pay extra, his claim to the money succeeded. Even though Williams was only doing what he was already contractually bound to do, Roffey's were gaining the extra benefit of not having to pay the money for delay to the client. Williams was providing consideration for their promise to pay him more for the work merely by completing his existing obligations on time. In answering the criticism that this proposition was incompatible with the rule in *Stilk v Myrick*, Lord Justice Glidewell, explaining that it was not, suggested rather that it 'refine[d] and limit[ed] the application of that principle, but [left] the principle unscathed' and commented that it was not surprising that 'a principle enunciated in relation to the rigours of seafaring life during the Napoleonic wars should be subjected during the succeeding 180 years to a process of refinement and limitation in its application in the present day'.

economic duress

Coercion or commercial pressure used by one party in an existing commercial contract to force a variation of the contract

It is important to remember that there was no attempt on Williams' part to extract the extra money by threats or coercion. The rules of **economic duress** would in any case have prevented him from succeeding and it is not surprising that the court made much reference to that doctrine.

What is clear from the case is that the courts do not want promises made in a business context to be broken. To prevent this it appears that they will find consideration even though it seems difficult to recognise anything real or tangible even if, in an indirect sense, there is a value.

JUDGMENT

Purchas LJ in his judgment (*Williams v Roffey Bros & Nicholls (Contractors) Ltd*) considered both issues. 'In the particular circumstances ... there was clearly a commercial advantage to both sides from a pragmatic point of view in reaching the agreement of 9th April. The defendants were on risk that as a result of the bargain that they had struck, the plaintiff would not or indeed possibly could not comply with his existing obligations without further finance. As a result of the agreement the defendants secured their position commercially. There was, however, no obligation added to the contractual duties imposed upon the plaintiff under the original contract. *Prima facie* this would appear to be a classic *Stilk v Myrick* case. It was, however, open to the plaintiff to be in deliberate breach of the contract in order to "cut his losses" commercially. In normal circumstances the suggestion that a contracting party can rely upon his own breach to establish consideration is distinctly unattractive. In many cases it obviously would be and if there was any element of duress brought upon the other contracting party under the modern development of this branch of the law, the proposed breaker of the contract would not benefit ... I consider that the modern approach to the question of consideration would be that where there were benefits derived by each party to a contract of variation, even though one party did not suffer a detriment, this would not be fatal to establishing sufficient consideration to support the agreement. If both parties benefit from an agreement it is not necessary that each also suffers a detriment ... on the facts ... the judge ... was entitled to reach the conclusion that consideration existed ...'

JUDGMENT

Russell LJ in his judgment succinctly identified the modern approach to consideration in such circumstances (*Williams v Roffey Bros & Nicholls (Contractors) Ltd*): 'While consideration remains a fundamental requirement before a contract not under seal can be enforced, the policy of the law in its search to do justice between the parties has developed considerably since the early nineteenth century when *Stilk v Myrick* ... was decided. In the late twentieth century I do not believe that the rigid approach to the concept of consideration to be found in *Stilk v Myrick* is either necessary or desirable. Consideration there must still be but in my judgment the courts nowadays should be more ready to find its existence so as to reflect the intention of the parties to the contract where the bargaining powers are not unequal and where the finding of consideration reflects the true intention of the parties.'

ACTIVITY

Multiple choice questions

In the following situations, select the appropriate statement from the choices which follow:
1. Mary, a student, asks Donald, her teacher, if he will give her good tuition for which she will pay him £100.
   a There is a contract. Mary will have to pay the £100 to Donald.
   b Mary will be able to sue Donald if his tuition is not good.
   c Donald cannot demand the £100 from Mary. He is only doing his duty.
   d Donald can sue for the £100 if Mary does not pay it.

2. Sid, the manager of a firm, promises Danny, a packer, £100 on top of his wages if he will stay at work late one evening to get out a rush order.
    a   There is no contract. Danny is only doing his job.
    b   Danny is entitled to the £100. He is doing extra to his normal job.
    c   Danny can only be paid the £100 if he does £100 worth of extra work.
    d   Sid can sue Danny if he refuses to stay late.

Always make sure you understand the over-ruling of cases, i.e. HOL over COA.

Holly, University of Southampton

3.3.4 The significance of *Williams v Roffey*

The principle from the case

All three judges in the Court of Appeal agreed that:

Wherever two parties, A and B, are engaged in a contract under which A is to supply goods or services to B and it becomes apparent to B that A will be unable actually to complete his contract, then if B promises A an additional payment to B for completing his contract, it will be enforceable providing that:

- this later promise is not gained as the result of economic duress by A; and
- B will gain an extra benefit by having the contract completed.

This means, in effect, that wherever the person making such a promise gains an extra "benefit in return for paying somebody to do what they are already bound to do under an existing contract, this promise will be enforced, notwithstanding an apparent lack of consideration for the second agreement. In this way *Stilk v Myrick* was being refined rather than overruled. Adams and Brownsword identify both the significance of the judgment and its potential problem:

QUOTATION

'*Williams v Roffey* represents an important staging post in the transformation of our conception of consideration. Judicial rhetoric still clings to the remnants of the exchange mode, of benefit being derived in return for the promise. However, the driving force behind the recent decisions on existing duty question quite clearly has been a mixture of consideration of fairness and commercial utility. In *Williams* … the court appreciated both that the defendants' promise was commercially necessary and that it would be unconscionable for them to go back on their word. The implications of the court's robust approach, however, extend beyond the doctrine of consideration.'

J Adams and R Brownsword, 'Contract, consideration and the critical path' (1990) 53 MLR 540

Analysis of the judgment

The case is achieving a significant purpose – it is ensuring that where a party freely and without undue pressure makes a promise in a commercial context, the party will be bound by the promise despite any apparent lack of consideration by the other party.

The clear justification for this proposition is that otherwise business is brought into disrepute.

The problem is that in order to achieve this objective, the judges appear to be straining the basic common law principle (the one contained in *Stilk v Myrick*) rather than distinguishing on the material facts (itself a sound way of developing the law).

However, it is possible to make a number of observations about the judgment:

- The only distinction the court was able to draw between the case and *Stilk v Myrick* was the apparent benefit gained by Roffey's in not paying penalties – but in law this would not be a problem to Roffey's as they would have an action against Williams for breach at the time he failed to complete on time, and indeed anticipatory breach and **repudiation** by Roffey's is not out of the question.
- The important distinction appears to be on a practical rather than a legal level – that suing Williams is unlikely to be advantageous to Roffey, because of his financial standing.
- Glidewell LJ refers to the case of *Ward v Byham* but he could of course have distinguished the case on the basis that in *Ward v Byham* there was good consideration since the mother was being asked to do more than she was already legally bound to do; in the present case, Williams was only being asked to perform his existing duties.
- Glidewell LJ also ignored the leading case of *Hartley v Ponsonby* (1857) E & B 872 which is of course distinguishable on exactly the same point – that the party was bringing something tangibly different to the new arrangement.
- The judgments contain many references to economic duress, or its absence, in the case but economic duress is plainly irrelevant on the facts, and if present would have resulted in the opposite decision and the principle in *Williams v Roffey* could not have been developed.
- The decision in *Pao On v Lau Yiu Long* is also referred to but, as a Privy Council case, it is only persuasive, and in any case is distinguishable on two grounds:

  (i) firstly that the case was decided on entirely different principles, ie, that Pao was supplying something central to the way in which Lau protected himself in the first agreement – the continued credibility of his company
  (ii) secondly that unfair pressure was applied in the former case.

- Taking into account the need for mutuality in contract, while there is arguably a benefit gained by Roffey's, there is no corresponding detriment to Williams – he is doing nothing more than he was already bound to do under the existing contract.
- The proper characteristics of good consideration are plainly absent in the second agreement between Williams and Roffey's and it is stretching the definition of consideration to try to make the agreement fit the usual legal concept.
- What is plainly more at issue is the fairness involved in Roffey's breaking an agreement with Williams that the latter clearly relied on in his course of action.
- This of course is the area where equity would be expected to intervene – to make fair the unfair in the common law.
- The principle developed in the case is not that far removed from estoppel – there are two potential difficulties:

  (i) estoppel operates in relation to agreements to accept part-payment of debts in discharge of the whole debt rather than in relation to offering the performance of existing duties as consideration for fresh agreements
  (ii) estoppel acts as a shield, not as a sword – and therefore cannot usually be the basis for founding an action.

Conclusions

- The case in effect introduces an entirely new principle of law, ie, that where a party voluntarily makes a bare promise in a commercial context on which the other party to the agreement relies, then the promisor should be bound by the promise.
- However, it does so by suggesting that the existing meaning of consideration in contracts is maintained.
- So the principle is one based primarily on reliance of the one party on the promise made by the other, rather than the strict rules on consideration.
- There are a number of potentially dangerous consequences to this reasoning:
  - It makes the rules too vague and uncertain to be followed easily in much simpler contractual relationships.
  - It has broader application in the wider context, ie, in any contract where an agreement is reached for one side to pay for the completion of an original agreement by the other party there is one obvious 'extra benefit' to be gained, namely not having to sue the other party in the event of their breach, and this is directly comparable to the extra benefit identified in the case.

Some of the difficulties raised by *Williams v Roffey* can be shown very simply by representing the two separate agreements in the case and those from the original precedent from *Stilk v Myrick* in diagram form (see page 60).

It is also interesting to note that the New Zealand Court of Appeal has adopted an entirely different, simpler and more sustainable approach than that in *Williams v Roffey* in *Antons Trawling Co Ltd v Smith* [2003] 2 NZLR 23: that the doctrine of consideration has no application to variations of contract. As the court identified:

JUDGMENT

'Where the parties who have already made such intention clear by entering legal relations have acted upon an agreement to a variation, in the absence of policy reasons to the contrary, they should be bound by their agreement.'

This approach would appear to have the effect of making both subsequent agreements in *Stilk v Myrick* and *Williams v Roffey* enforceable without the need to strain the meaning of consideration, as appears to be the result of the decision in the latter case.

ACTIVITY

Self-assessment questions

1. In what ways does the rule in *Stilk v Myrick* fit the standard definitions of consideration?
2. How did Lord Ellenborough justify the rule on the facts of the case?
3. What is the distinguishing feature, if any, between *Stilk v Myrick* and *Hartley v Ponsonby*?
4. How have the principles in these two cases been developed further by the courts?
5. Why exactly did Pao On succeed in the case of *Pao On v Lau Yiu Long*?
6. According to *Williams v Roffey Bros & Nicholls*, what exactly is an extra benefit?
7. What difficulties faced the court in *Williams v Roffey* in applying the traditional rule absolutely to the case?

8. Why is it difficult to see the distinction between the principles in *Stilk v Myrick* and *Williams v Roffey Bros & Nicholls*?
9. What difficulties does the principle in *Williams v Roffey* present for the rules on consideration?

Stilk v Myrick (*the principle represented by the two separate agreements*)

Agreement 1

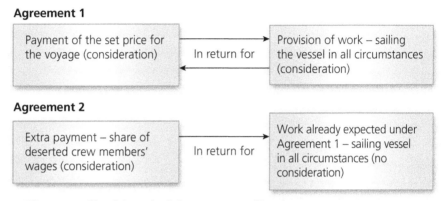

Agreement 2

Williams v Roffey (*the principle represented by the two separate agreements and expected by applying* Stilk v Myrick *strictly*)

Agreement 1

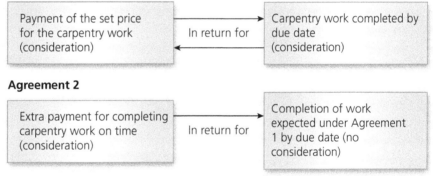

Agreement 2

Williams v Roffey (*the principle represented by the two separate agreements and distinguishing* Stilk v Myrick*)

Agreement 1

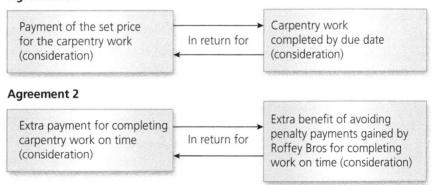

Agreement 2

Figure 3.4 The relationship between *Williams v Roffey* and *Stilk v Myrick*

Performance of existing duties as consideration	Case/statute
Merely performing an existing legal duty cannot be considered as consideration for a fresh promise.	*Collins v Godefroy*
Neither can merely carrying out an existing contractual obligation.	*Stilk v Myrick*
An exception to the rule is where something extra is added.	*Glassbrook Bros v Glamorgan County Council*
Applies also where something extra is added in contractual arrangements.	*Hartley v Ponsonby*
Third party interests may also provide an exception.	*Pao On v Lau Yiu Long*
As may preserving the integrity of a commercial relationship where there is an agency relationship.	*New Zealand Shipping Co v A M Satterthwaite (The Eurymedon)*
Where an extra benefit is to be gained by the one party and there is reliance on the promise by the other party, and in the absence of any economic duress then the extra benefit can amount to consideration.	*Willams v Roffey Bros & Nicholls*
Although this seems to conflict with general principles of consideration.	

3.4 Part-payment of a debt, pinnel's rule, and the doctrine of promissory estoppel

3.4.1 *The basic rule*

This was first stated in *Pinnel's Case* (1602) 5 Co Rep 117a; 77 ER 237. This held that payment of a smaller sum than the debt itself on the due date can never relieve the liability of the debtor to pay the whole debt, so the creditor can always sue for the balance of the debt which is unpaid.

JUDGMENT

The court explained the reasoning behind the rule in the case: 'Payment of a lesser sum on the day in satisfaction of a greater cannot be any satisfaction for the whole, because it appears to the judges that by no possibility a lesser sum can be a satisfaction to the plaintiff for a greater sum.'

The rule can operate fairly where the creditor is giving in to pressure by the debtor to accept less.

CASE EXAMPLE

D C Builders v Rees [1965] 3 All ER 837

Builders were owed £482 for the balance of work they had completed. After several months waiting for payment, and at a point where they were in danger of going out of business, they reluctantly accepted an offer by Rees to pay £300 in full satisfaction of the debt. When the builders then sued for the balance, they were successful. They were not prevented by the agreement to accept less, which in any case was extracted from them under pressure.

It can also sometimes seem to operate unfairly where the debtor genuinely relies on the promise of the creditor.

CASE EXAMPLE

Foakes v Beer (1884) 9 App Cas 605

Dr Foakes owed Mrs Beer £2,090 after a court judged against him. The two reached an agreement for Foakes to pay in instalments, with Mrs Beer agreeing that no further action would be taken if the debt was paid off by the agreed date. Later, Mrs Beer demanded interest, which is always payable on a judgment debt, and sued when Foakes refused to pay. She was successful as a result of *Pinnel's* rule.

3.4.2 *Exceptions to the rule*
There are two basic exceptions where the agreement to pay less than the full debt can be enforced.

....

accord and satisfaction

A method of replacing existing contractual terms with new ones

....

Accord and satisfaction
In other words, there is an agreement to accept something other than the money from the existing debt. This might take a number of forms:

- An agreement to accept an earlier payment of a smaller sum than the whole debt. (This was in fact what actually happened in *Pinnel's* case.) As an example, say I owe you £100 that I am due to pay on 1st March. You then agree to accept a payment of £80 made on 1st February. You will be unable to sue for the remaining £20. In effect, the earlier payment reflects consideration for the changed agreement.
- An agreement to accept something other than money instead of the debt. Say I owe you £1,000 and you accept instead my stereo hi-fi, worth about £800. You have the opportunity to place whatever value you wish on the goods. If you accept them in place of the money, the full debt is satisfied.
- An agreement to accept a part-payment together with something else, not to the value of the balance of the debt. Say I owe you £100 and you agree to accept £50 together with a law book worth £21.99. In cash value you have received only £71.99 but again the debt has been paid.

The doctrine of promissory estoppel
The doctrine acts as a defence to a claim by a creditor for the remainder of the debt where part-payment has been accepted.

The effect of the doctrine is to prevent (estop) the claimant from going back on the promise because it would be unfair and inequitable to do so.

Lord Denning developed the doctrine from the older doctrine of waiver *in obiter* statements.

CASE EXAMPLE

Central London Property Trust Ltd v High Trees House Ltd [1947] KB 130

From 1937 the defendants leased a block of flats in Wimbledon from the claimants to sub-let to tenants. When war started it was impossible to find tenants and so the defendants were unable to pay the rent. The claimants agreed to accept half rent, which the defendants continued to pay. By 1945 the flats were all let and the claimants wanted the rent returned to its former level and sued for the higher rent for the last two quarters.

They succeeded but Lord Denning stated *in obiter* that had they tried to sue for the extra rent for the whole period of the war they would have failed. Estoppel would prevent them from going back on the promise on which the defendants had relied so long as the circumstances persisted.

JUDGMENT

As Lord Denning stated: 'A promise was made which was intended to create legal relations and which to the knowledge of the person making the promise was going to be acted upon by the person to whom it was made, and which in fact was so acted upon. In such cases the courts have said that the promise must be honoured … the logical consequence, no doubt, is that a promise to accept a smaller sum in discharge of a larger debt if acted upon, is binding notwithstanding the absence of consideration.'

Unfortunately, Lord Denning's final statement here led some judges to the conclusion that the need for consideration to be proved in contracts had somehow been removed. Lord Denning was then called on to develop a more reliable explanation of the application of estoppel in a latter case.

CASE EXAMPLE

Combe v Combe [1951] 2 KB 215

A wife separated from her husband and sued him for a promise that he had quite gratuitously made to her that he would pay her £2 per week (ie, it was not under a legal maintenance order). The judge at first instance noted the lack of consideration but held that following *High Trees* this was irrelevant and found in the wife's favour.

JUDGMENT

In the Court of Appeal Lord Denning apologised for any confusion he had caused in *High Trees* and explained the doctrine further: 'Where one party has by his words or conduct made to the other party a promise or assurance which was intended to affect the legal conditions between them and be acted on accordingly, then once the other party has taken him at his word and acted on it, the one who gave the promise cannot afterwards be allowed to revert to the previous legal relations as if no such promise had been made.' Lord Birkett in the case made one further very significant comment in describing estoppel as 'a shield and not a sword'; in other words, it could only operate as a defence to a claim, not a means of bringing one.

The essential elements of the doctrine, then, as described in the case require the following to be used successfully:

- There must be an existing contractual relationship between the claimant and the defendant.
- The claimant must have agreed to waive (give up) some of his rights under that contract (the amount of the debt that has been unpaid).
- The claimant has waived these rights knowing that the defendant would rely on the promise in determining his future conduct.
- The defendant has in fact acted in reliance on the promise to forgo some of the debt.

The possible subsequent development of the doctrine is uncertain, particularly now that Lord Denning has died.

JUDGMENT

In *Brikom Investments Ltd v Carr* [1979] QB 467, for instance, Lord Justice Roskill stressed that 'it would be wrong to extend the doctrine of promissory estoppel, whatever its precise limits at the present day, to the extent of abolishing in this back-handed way the doctrine of consideration'.

Attempts to apply the principle in *Williams v Roffey* to situations involving promises to accept part-payment of debts in full satisfaction of the whole debt have been specifically rejected.

CASE EXAMPLE

Re Selectmove [1995] 2 All ER 531

Here, a company, which owed tax to the Inland Revenue, offered to pay its debt by instalments. The Collector of Taxes stated that he would contact the company if the arrangement was unsatisfactory and the company began to pay off its debt by instalments. The IRC then insisted that all arrears of tax be paid immediately or it would begin winding-up procedures against the company. The company tried to argue on the basis of *Williams v Roffey* that its promise to carry out an existing obligation was good consideration for the agreement to pay by instalments. The Court of Appeal distinguished *Williams v Roffey* as that case involved the provision of goods and services rather than payment of an existing debt. The court as a result felt itself bound rather by the basic precedent in *Foakes v Beer* and held that IRC was not bound by any agreement to accept payment by instalments. While the judgment appears to be inconsistent with the reasoning in *Williams v Roffey*, it may be seen as an attempt by the court to limit the scope of the principle so that the basic principles of part payments of debts remain unaffected.

The Court of Appeal more recently has taken quite a relaxed view in applying the doctrine of promissory estoppel to a statutory debt.

CASE EXAMPLE

Collier v P & M J Wright (Holdings) Ltd [2008] 1 WLR 643

Collier and two business partners took out a loan from Wright which they later defaulted on. Following County Court proceedings, the partners were ordered to pay back £46,800 in monthly instalments of £600, £200 each. Collier carried on paying for five years but the partnership later ended and the two other partners went into bankruptcy. Collier sought to have the debt set aside under insolvency rules on the basis of an agreement he said that he had made with Wright that if he continued paying his third share that Wright would not seek to get the balance from him but from his partners. The court held that there was no consideration for the agreement to accept part payment of the debt in satisfaction of the whole debt. However, the court held that Wright, following *High Trees* and *D C Builders v Rees*, was estopped from going back on the agreement to accept Collier's payments in satisfaction of the whole debt. It appears that the making of the part payment was the reliance and that having promised to accept it, it was inequitable for Wright to go back on the agreement.

QUOTATION

Robert Duxbury in "Promissory Estoppel and the part-payment of debts" Student Law Review Routledge-Cavendish Volume 57 Summer 2009 p20 argues that: "The difficulty with Collier v Wright is that it seems to treat the making of a part payment as the reliance. Thus once the creditor has accepted the part payment it will be inequitable for him to revert to his strict legal rights ... The effect of the decision is to reduce promissory estoppel – an equitable doctrine supposedly based on the conscionability or otherwise of the parties' conduct – to an automatic rule ... the effect ... will be to render Pinnel's case little more than a fall-back position where the minimal requirements for the operation of estoppel set by Collier v Wright itself are not satisfied."

ACTIVITY

Multiple choice question

In the following situation, select the appropriate statement from the choices which follow: Dave, a builder, owes his supplier £50,000 for materials. Dave has been unable to sell at a profit the house he has recently built, because of a slump in the property market, and has only £45,000. The supplier agrees to accept the £45,000 to prevent Dave from going out of business. Six months later, the supplier has learned that Dave has just gained a building contract worth £5 million.

a. Dave will have to pay the remaining £5,000 to the supplier immediately.
b. Dave can use the supplier's promise as a defence to a claim for the money.
c. The supplier can recover the materials used by Dave.
d. Dave can sue the supplier.

Self-assessment questions

1. Why did the law first develop the doctrine of consideration?
2. What, in simple terms, is consideration?
3. How do the nineteenth-century definitions based on detriment and benefit differ from the application of the doctrine in recent times?
4. Why is it unimportant whether the consideration is adequate or not?
5. What is the basic difference between something that is sufficient and something that is adequate?
6. How easy is it to accept cases such as *Chappell v Nestlé* in the light of the accepted legal meaning of 'sufficiency'?
7. Why is it impossible to form a contract with consideration that is past?
8. Exactly how does the exception in *Lampleigh v Braithwaite* operate?
9. What is the connection between the rule that consideration must move from the promisee and the rule requiring privity of contract?
10. How does the case of *Shanklin Pier v Detel Products* contradict or modify the basic rule?
11. In what ways could the rule that consideration must move from the promisee be said to be unfair?
12. What is the distinguishing feature, if any, between *Stilk v Myrick* and *Hartley v Ponsonby*?
13. Why is it difficult to see the distinction between the principles in *Stilk v Myrick* and *Williams v Roffey Bros & Nicholls*?
14. Why exactly did Pao On succeed in the case of *Pao On v Lau Yiu Long*?
15. Is there any relevance to promissory estoppel in the modern day?
16. Do the exceptions to *Pinnel* 's rule always cover every possible problem?
17. What is the effect of the judgment in *Re Selectmove*?

Definition and character	Case/statute	The basic rules	Case/statute
Consideration is 'the price for which the promise of the other is bought'.	Dunlop v Selfridge	Consideration need not be adequate.	Thomas v Thomas
Executory consideration is where the consideration is yet to change hands.		But it must be sufficient: that is it must be real, tangible and have value.	Chappell v Nestlé
Executed consideration is consideration that has already passed.		Consideration must not be past.	Re McArdle
		Except where it is a service that has been requested.	Lampleigh v Braithwaite
		A person seeking to sue on a contract must have given consideration under it.	Tweddle v Atkinson

Existing duties	Case/statute	Part-payment of a debt	Case/statute
Carrying out an existing contractual obligation cannot be consideration for a new promise.	Stilk v Myrick	Part-payment of a debt can never satisfy the whole debt.	Pinnel's rule
Unless something extra is added to the contract.	Hartley v Ponsonby	There are exceptions, eg, accord and satisfaction debt paid in a different form.	
Or a third party's interests are involved.	Pao On v Lau Yiu Long	And estoppel (where a party waiving rights is prevented from going back on the promise because of reliance by the other party).	Central London Property Trust v High Trees House
Or if an extra benefit is to be gained.	Williams v Roffey Bros & Nicholls	Williams v Roffey cannot be applied to agreements to accept part payment of a debt.	Re Selectmove

SUMMARY

- Consideration is 'the price for which the promise of the other is bought'.
- Consideration does not have to be adequate – but it must be sufficient, that is it must be real, tangible and have value.
- Consideration must not be past – except where a service has been requested or payment is implied.
- A person cannot sue or be sued under a contract unless they have given consideration.
- Performing existing contractual obligations or public duties cannot be consideration for a new promise – unless something extra is added to the contract or an extra benefit is to be gained.

■ Part payment of a debt can never satisfy the debt as a whole – although there are exceptions to the rule including accord and satisfaction (where the debt is paid in a different form), and estoppel (where a party waiving rights is prevented from going back on the promise because of reliance by the other party).

SAMPLE ESSAY QUESTION

Discuss the extent to which courts are prepared to accept that performance of an existing duty can provide consideration for an entirely fresh agreement.

Define consideration:
- The *quid pro quo* – the proof of the existence of a bargain enforceable in law
- *'An act of forbearance or the promise thereof is the price for which the promise of the other is bought, and the promise thus given for value is enforceable …'*

Explain the rule on performance of existing duties as consideration for fresh agreements:
- Not possible because there is in effect no consideration
- Applies not merely to contractual duties but also to statutory or other legal duties

Discuss the fact that the courts have created exceptions to the basic rule:
- Where something more is done or extra is provided
- Where the promise is made to a third party or where third party rights would inevitably be affected
- Where not to enforce the arrangement might threaten the integrity of a commercial agreement
- Where a party gains an extra benefit from the performance of the existing duty

Comment on the basic rule:
- The rule is necessary to avoid a party gaining more than he is entitled to without giving anything extra himself
- Before economic duress it would prevent a party from trying to extract more by threats

Discuss the exceptions created by the courts:

- It is logical that when something is added to the original consideration, this in effect is a new agreement supported by its own consideration
- But in, eg *Ward v Byham*, the agreement, being domestic, may lack intention to create a legal relationship
- Very often courts accept as consideration things difficult to identify as 'real, and tangible', eg *Williams v Roffey* – the case does not appear to be distinguishable from *Stilk v Myrick* and the solution provided by different jurisdictions appears more logical – the major purpose of the judgment seems to be preserving commercial integrity
- The problem of privity

Further reading

Denning, Lord, *The Discipline of Law* (Butterworths, 1979).
Hooley, R, 'Consideration and Existing Duty' [1991] JBL 19.
Noble, R, 'For your Consideration' (1991) 141 NLJ 1529.

4

Formation of a contract: Intention to create legal relations

AIMS AND OBJECTIVES

After reading this chapter you should be able to:

- Understand the purpose of the rule on intention
- Distinguish between social and domestic agreements and business arrangements
- Critically analyse the area
- Apply the law to factual situations and reach conclusions

4.1 The character and purpose of the rule

We all regularly make arrangements with each other, and we may even be doing things in return for something, and this seems as though there is consideration too and that the agreement may therefore be binding.

However, not every agreement that is made includes an intention that if we fail to keep to the agreement the other party should be able to sue us for breach of the agreement.

JUDGMENT

As Lord Stowell remarked in *Dalrymple v Dalrymple* (1811) 2 Hag Con 54 at 105: 'Contracts should not be ... the sports of an idle hour, mere matters of pleasantry and badinage, never intended by the parties to have any serious effect whatever.'

It would in any case not be sensible for the courts to be filled with actions on all of the broken promises that are ever made. Parents make promises of pocket money to their children who may expect the pocket money to be paid regularly. Husbands make promises to their wives that they never keep. Boyfriends and girlfriends make arrangements to meet that they fail to keep. It would fill the courts and hardly be sensible in each broken promise of this type to allow the disappointed parties to be able to sue even if it is upsetting and morally blameworthy when they are broken.

The law makes a sensible compromise by assuming that in certain situations we would usually not intend the agreement to be legally binding, while in others we usually would. This is the third major element of formation of contracts after agreement and consideration and is known as **intention to create legal relations**.

The courts have developed two key guidelines for determining whether or not an intention to create legal relations exists that would make an agreement enforceable. These are in the form of rebuttable presumptions:

- In the case of an agreement that is of a **social** or **domestic** nature it is presumed that there is **no** intention to create a legal relationship enforceable in law, unless the contrary can be proved.
- In the case of **commercial** or **business** arrangements it is presumed that there is an intention to create a legal relationship and that the agreement is legally enforceable, again, unless the contrary can be shown.

On this basis there are no hard and fast rules other than the application of the presumptions where they can apply. The area of intention, then, is very much decided on the facts in individual cases. The presumptions are generally followed unless there are any factors that allow them to be rebutted.

4.2 Social and domestic agreements

Families make arrangements among themselves on a daily basis, about who will do what work, who will pay for what and we could also include even promises that are made whereby one member of the family will buy a particular item for another family member. It is only logical that the courts will be unwilling to intervene and enforce such arrangements or the courts would be full of domestic disputes.

Nevertheless, the courts do have to have a coherent view of those arrangements in which judges can intervene and those in which they should not. This in itself creates its own difficulties. Hedley identifies both the problem and the effects of the presumption in domestic arrangements:

QUOTATION

'The judges wanted contract let into domestic contexts but only on their terms; and they found the perfect device for achieving this … The "legal relations" doctrine gave the judges carte blanche to impose or refuse contractual liability in unfamiliar contexts.'

Headley, 'Keeping Contract in its Place: Balfour v Balfour and the Enforceability of Informal Agreements' (1985) 5 OJLS 391

Generally, then, arrangements between family members will be left to the parties themselves to sort out and will thus not usually be held to be legally binding. This is obviously the case generally with husbands and wives.

CASE EXAMPLE

Balfour v Balfour [1919] 2 KB 571

A husband worked abroad on overseas service. His wife had to remain behind in England because of illness. The husband, as a result, promised her an allowance of £30 per month. The husband, however, failed to pay. At a later point in time the husband suggested that the two should separate; the wife later petitioned for divorce and her claim to payment of the allowance failed. The court held that the agreement had been reached at an amicable point in their relationship and not in contemplation of divorce. It was a purely domestic arrangement and the court felt that it was beyond its competence to interfere in what was a purely domestic arrangement and therefore that the agreement was not legally enforceable.

JUDGMENT

Atkin LJ explained the basic principle: 'It is necessary to remember that there are agreements between parties which do not result in contracts within the meaning of that term in our law [including] arrangements that are made between husband and wife ... they are not contracts because the parties did not intend that they should be attended by legal consequences. The small courts of this country would have to be multiplied one hundredfold if these arrangements did result in fact in legal obligations. They are not sued upon ... not because the parties are reluctant to enforce their legal rights when the agreement is broken, but ... because the parties in the inception of the arrangement never intended that they should be sued upon.'

However, where husband and wife are already estranged then an agreement between them may be taken as intended to be legally binding because the couple are at arm's length.

CASE EXAMPLE

Merritt v Merritt [1970] 1 WLR 1211

Here, the husband had deserted his wife for another woman. The marital home was in joint names. An agreement that the husband would pay the wife an income of £40 per month if she paid the outstanding mortgage was held by the court to be intended to create legally binding obligations between them. The court also identified that one further point in the wife's favour was that at the time of the arrangement she had got her husband to put in writing that he would transfer title in the property to her on completion of the mortgage. The wife had done what she was required to do under the agreement between them but the husband had nevertheless failed to transfer the title deeds. The wife's action for recognition of sole title rights was successful.

JUDGMENT

Lord Denning identified why the case was different to *Balfour v Balfour*: 'It is altogether different when the parties are not living in amity but are separated or about to separate. They then bargain keenly. They do not rely on honourable understandings. They want everything cut and dried. It may safely be presumed that they intend to create legal relations.'

Sometimes, of course, families make arrangements that appear to be business arrangements because of their character. In such cases the court will need to examine what the real purpose of the arrangement was and it is this purpose that will determine whether the agreement is enforceable or not.

CASE EXAMPLE

Jones v Padavatton [1969] 1 WLR 328

A mother provided an allowance for her daughter under an agreement for the daughter to give up her highly paid job in New York, study for the Bar in England and then return to practise in Trinidad where the mother lived. When the daughter was finding it difficult to manage on the allowance, the mother then bought a house for her to live in, part of which the daughter could let to supplement her income. They later quarrelled and the mother sought repossession of the house. The daughter's argument that the second agreement was contractual failed. The court could find no intent and held that it was too vague to be considered contractual.

If money has changed hands then it will not matter that the arrangement is made socially. It will be held as intended to be legally binding.

CASE EXAMPLE

Simpkins v Pays [1955] 1 WLR 975

A lodger and two members of the household with whom he lodged entered newspaper competitions in the lodger's name but paying equal shares of the entry money. They also did so on the clear understanding that they would share any winnings. When they did in fact win £750 the lodger refused to share the winnings. In defending the action he argued that the arrangement was not enforceable and did not give rise to a legal relationship, since it was purely domestic. The court would not accept this argument and the defence failed, possibly for policy reasons. He was bound by the agreement.

If parties put their financial security at risk in order to pursue a particular agreement, then it is generally accepted that it must have been intended that the agreement should be legally binding.

CASE EXAMPLE

Parker v Clarke [1960] 1 WLR 286

A young couple were persuaded by an older couple to sell their house in order to move in with the older couple, with the promise also that they would inherit property on the death of the old couple. When the two couples eventually fell out and the young couple were asked to leave, their action for damages succeeded. The judge held that giving up their security was an indication that the arrangement was intended to be legally binding and the presumption usually applied to domestic agreements was rebutted.

4.3 Commercial and business dealings

Businesses operate on an entirely different basis to private individuals. The whole purpose of the activities in which they engage is to make a profit. Businesses in any case operate within a legal framework and therefore it is presumed that agreements are contractual unless the facts involved prove otherwise.

An arrangement made within a business context is presumed to demonstrate an intention to be legally binding unless evidence can show a different intent. This principle may apply even though the agreement on the face of it appears to be gratuitous in character.

CASE EXAMPLE

Edwards v Skyways Ltd [1969] 1 WLR 349

An attempt to avoid making an agreed '*ex gratia*' payment (a so-called 'golden handshake') in a redundancy failed. Although '*ex gratia*' indicates no pre-existing liability to make the payment, the agreement to pay it, once made, was binding because of the context in which it was made.

It is commonplace in commercial situations to make offers of free gifts. The clear purpose of such arrangements is to promote the business. As a result, the arrangement can still be held to indicate a legal relationship and mean that the promise is legally binding.

CASE EXAMPLE

Esso Petroleum Co Ltd v Commissioners of Customs and Excise [1976] 1 All ER 117

Esso gave free World Cup coins with every four gallons of petrol purchased at the time of the World Cup. The Customs and Excise Department wanted to claim purchase tax from the transaction. To succeed it needed to show that the arrangement was contractual, the purchase of petrol being the consideration for the free coin, and also therefore that there was an intention to create a legal relationship. The House of Lords was actually divided on this issue. Those dissenting held that the transaction was too trivial to have any contractual base. However, the majority held that, since Esso was clearly trying to gain more business from the promotion, there was an intention to be bound by the arrangement.

JUDGMENT

Lord Simon of Glaisdale commented as follows: 'In the first place, Esso and the garage proprietors put the material out for their commercial advantage, and designed it to attract the custom of motorists. The whole transaction took place in a setting of business relations. In the second place, it seems to me in general undesirable to allow a commercial promoter to claim that what he has done is a mere puff, not intended to create legal relations. The coins may have been themselves of little intrinsic value, but all the evidence suggests that Esso contemplated that they would be attractive to motorists and that there would be a large commercial advantage to themselves from the scheme, an advantage in which the garage proprietors would also share.'

This principle has also been developed to cover those situations where prizes are offered in competitions. The purpose of such events is generally to promote the body offering the prize. As a result, there is generally presumed to be an intention to create a legal relationship which is then binding on the parties and can be relied on by members of the public who enter the competition.

CASE EXAMPLE

McGowan v Radio Buxton (2001) (unreported)

The claimant entered a radio competition for which the prize had been stated to be a Renault Clio car. She was told that she had won the competition but was given a four-inch scale model of a Clio. The defendants argued that there was no legally binding contract. The judge held that there was intention to create legal relations. The claimant entered the competition as a member of the public and that 'looking at the transcript of the broadcast, there was not even a hint that the car would be a toy'.

However, it is possible for a similar type of agreement not to contain an intention to be legally binding, where that is specifically stated in the agreement itself.

CASE EXAMPLE

Jones v Vernons' Pools Ltd [1938] 2 All ER 626

The pools company inserted a clause on all coupons, stating that 'the transaction should not give rise to any legal relationship ... but be binding in honour only'. The claimant alleged that he had completed and sent in a pools coupon but that the company had then lost his winning coupon, although the pools company claimed that they had never received it. The claimant sought payment of the appropriate winnings and failed. The clause was sufficiently precise and clear to prevent any legal claim.

The same type of principle applies and has operated with significant effect in the case of 'comfort letters'. Although such letters are worded so that they appear almost to amount to a guarantee that a transaction will be legally enforceable, they do not and will not give rise to legal obligations.

CASE EXAMPLE

Kleinwort Benson Ltd v Malaysian Mining Corporation [1989] 1 WLR 379

Kleinwort lent £10 million to Metals Ltd, which was a subsidiary company of the Malaysian Mining Corporation. The parent company (MMC) would not guarantee this loan but instead issued a comfort letter stating that its intention was to ensure that at all times Metals Ltd had sufficient funds available for repayment of the loan. When Metals Ltd went out of business without repaying Kleinwort, the latter then sued the parent company. Its action was based on the existence of the comfort letter, but failed. The court held that if it had actually required a guarantee of repayment then it should have insisted on one before engaging in the transaction, rather than accepting a mere comfort letter.

honour pledge clause

A clause in a contract stating that the contract is not legally enforceable

A similar principle, allowing a party in a commercial relationship to deny the consequences of an apparent contractual breach by means of a clause refuting that a legal relationship exists, has also succeeded through the use of a so-called '**honour pledge**' **clause**. The case in this sense is quite remarkable.

CASE EXAMPLE

Rose and Frank Co v J R Crompton & Bros [1923] 2 KB 261

Rose and Frank, a New York sales firm, continuously sold paper for Crompton, manufacturers of tissue, as their agents. Under the agreement, Rose and Frank had sales and distribution rights for a three-year period and there was an option to extend the time. A clause in the contract between them purported to oust the jurisdiction of the courts in the event of any dispute between the parties and to bind the parties instead by an 'honourable pledge'. This in effect stated that the agreement was not a formal agreement but a genuine statement of the purpose of the agreement between them and of the intention of the parties to pursue that purpose with mutual co-operation. The agreement was subsequently extended, but the manufacturers then terminated it too early and refused to process orders made before the termination. Rose and Frank then sued on the basis of the broken agency agreement and also for the failure to deliver the goods already ordered. The Court of Appeal, in a judgment which in effect extinguished the agency agreement as a legal relationship, upheld the termination as legitimate by virtue of the 'honour pledge' clause. On appeal to the House of Lords, the Law Lords did accept that this principle applied to the agreement between the parties as a whole, which could therefore be terminated without legal consequences, and therefore on that point upheld the decision of the Court of Appeal. Nevertheless, they would not accept that the principle could apply also to the specific transactions between the parties and on those specific transactions the decision of the Court of Appeal was reversed. This was on the basis that a separate contract could be inferred from the conduct of the parties and was enforceable without any reference to the original agreement.

JUDGMENT

Scrutton LJ explained the reasoning for the Court of Appeal accepting the 'honour pledge' clause as legitimate: 'It is quite possible for parties to come to an agreement by accepting a proposal with the result that the agreement does not give rise to legal relations. The reason for this is that the parties do not intend that their agreement shall give rise to legal relations. This intention may be implied from the subject-matter of the agreement, but it may also be expressed by the parties. In social and family relations such an intention is readily implied, while in business matters the opposite result would ordinarily follow. But I can see no reason why, even in business matters, the parties should not intend to rely on each other's good faith and honour, and to exclude all idea of settling disputes by any outside intervention, with the accompanying necessity of expressing themselves so precisely that outsiders may have no difficulty in understanding what they mean. If they clearly express such an intention I can see no reason in public policy why effect should not be given to their intention.'

Besides this, it is possible also that in certain circumstances where public bodies enter into informal arrangements, the courts may be unwilling to see those arrangements as contractual.

CASE EXAMPLE

Robinson v HM Customs and Excise (2000) *The Times*, 28 April

The claimant gave information to Customs and Excise as an informer. He later tried to claim that the agreement meant that he should be paid a fee and expenses for doing so. The court held that there was no intention to create legal relations in such circumstances. The decision was inevitably based on reasons of public policy.

Sometimes judges will find that parts of an agreement are intended to be legally binding, and other parts are not.

CASE EXAMPLE

Julian v Furby (1982) 132 NLJ 64

An experienced plasterer helped his daughter and son-in-law to alter and furnish their house. When the couple split up he sued the son-in-law for the price of the materials he had bought and also for his labour. The court agreed that there should be payment for the materials but not for the man's labour which was felt to be no more than any father would do for his daughter.

Sometimes also statutory provisions specifically indicate that a particular type of agreement is not one that leads to a legal relationship and enforceability. An example of this was under s 1 of the Law Reform (Miscellaneous Provisions) Act 1970. In this the former law was changed so that an engagement to marry was deemed not to be an agreement that could be enforced in law.

ACTIVITY

Self-assessment questions

1. How do courts decide if an agreement is intended to be legally binding?
2. Why do the courts feel that an agreement within a family should generally not be legally binding?
3. Why were the cases of *Balfour v Balfour* and *Merritt v Merritt* decided differently?
4. What were the peculiar circumstances of *Jones v Padavatton* that meant that the agreement could not be enforced?
5. Why should commercial agreements generally lead to a legal relationship?
6. What are some of the ways in which businesses try to get round the rules on intention and how successful are they?
7. What exactly is an 'honour pledge clause'?
8. What is the reasoning behind making free gifts, prizes in competitions and so on part of a legally enforceable agreement?

Quick quiz

Consider whether the courts would identify an intention to be legally bound in the following situations:
1. Trevor agrees that he will buy his son, Jason, a law book, in return for Jason mowing the lawns.
2. Trevor agrees that he will give his 16-year-old son, Jason, £10 per week pocket money.
3. Ricky agrees to take his secretary, Charlotte, out for a meal for getting an urgent job finished quickly and at very short notice.
4. Ricky agrees to take his friend, Charlotte, out for a meal.
5. Chris asks his daughter, Sally, to give up her part-time job for one week in order to proofread a draft of his latest *Contract Law* textbook and promises to pay her what she would normally earn.
6. Skinny & Co have always given their employees a £50 Christmas bonus but this year, because of falling orders, they have decided against doing it.
7. I agree to take my wife to the cinema but fail to turn up because I have had to stay longer at work.

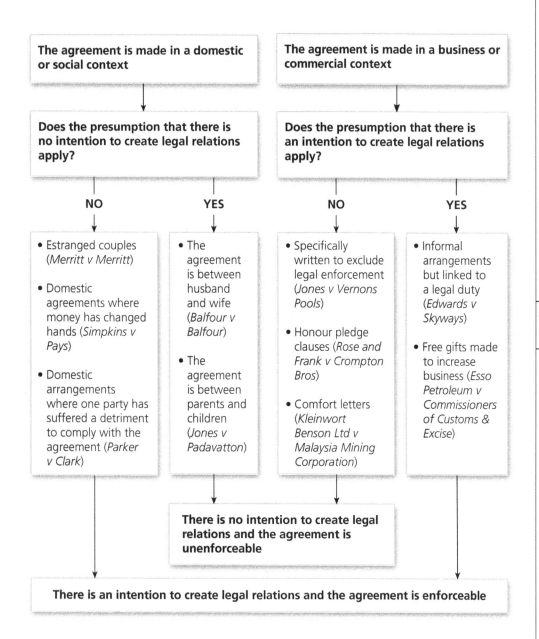

Figure 4.1 The uses of the presumptions in determining an intention to create legal relations

SUMMARY

- There are two rebuttable presumptions – that in social and domestic arrangements there is no intention to be legally bound, but that in commercial and business dealings there is such an intention.
- Arrangements between husband and wife are not usually legally binding – unless the couple is estranged and dealing 'at arm's length'.
- But agreements made in a social or domestic context are binding where the parties have spent money on it or have acted to their detriment.
- Agreements made in a business context are usually binding.

- This includes where free gifts are promised to promote sales and where prizes are offered in competitions.
- However, some agreements are binding in honour only and comfort letters create no legal obligations.

SAMPLE ESSAY QUESTION

Discuss the extent to which courts have taken a sensible approach in developing rules to determine whether the parties intend there to be a legally binding relationship between them.

Explain that intention to create legal relations is essential to the formation of a contract along with:
- Agreement (offer and acceptance)
- Consideration

Explain the approach taken by the courts in deciding whether there is an intention to create legal relations:
- Based on two rebuttable presumptions
- Social and domestic arrangements are not generally intended to give rise to legal relations
- Commercial relations usually are intended to create legal relations

Discuss why the presumption in domestic agreements has developed:
- Policy factors
- Not interfering in family life
- The trivial nature of many such agreements
- The potential waste of court time

Discuss why the presumption in commercial agreements has developed:
- Policy factors
- Consumer and commercial expectations
- Potential injustice to consumers etc
- Credibility of business arrangements

Discuss ways in which courts have been prepared to rebut the presumptions:

- Family members dealing at arm's length
- Domestic arrangements where parties act on reliance on the agreement or suffer a detriment by doing so
- Some commercial agreements are binding in honour only
- Comfort letters are not legally binding because there are no obligations
- Sometimes businesses without coercion agree to non-enforceable agreements – so rebutting the presumption protects freedom of contract

KEY FACTS

The two presumptions			
In social and domestic arrangements there is no intention to be legally bound.			
In commercial and business dealings there is an intention to be legally bound.			
Domestic agreements	Case/statute	**Commercial agreements**	Case/statute
Arrangements between husband and wife are not normally legally binding.	*Balfour v Balfour*	An agreement made in a business context is usually binding.	*Edwards v Skyways*
But are usually binding when the couple is estranged.	*Merritt v Merritt*	Even where free gifts are promised to promote sales.	*Esso v Commissioner of Customs & Excise*
An agreement is usually binding where the parties have spent money.	*Simpkin v Pays*	And with prizes offered in competitions.	*McGowan v Radio Buxton*
And where they have acted to their detriment.	*Parker v Clarke*	Some agreements are binding in honour only.	*Jones v Vernons Pools*
		And comfort letters are not legally binding.	*Kleinwort Benson v Malaysia Mining Corporation*

Further reading

Beale, H G, Bishop, W D and Furmston, M P, *Contract Cases and Materials* (5th edn, Oxford University Press 2007) Chapter 7.

Hedley, S, 'Keeping Contract in its Place: *Balfour v Balfour* and the Enforceability of Informal Agreements' (1985) 5 OJLS 391.

5

Form

AIMS AND OBJECTIVES

After reading this chapter you should be able to:

- Distinguish between simple contracts and speciality contracts
- Understand the requirements of contracts being in specific form
- Critically analyse the area
- Apply the law to factual situations and reach conclusions

5.1 Simple contracts, speciality contracts and the requirement for formalities

Form is not an aspect of contract law that many contract syllabuses now concern themselves with. However, it can in some instances be an important issue, and it is therefore worth knowing at least the basic rules. It is not, however, ever likely to be a major part of a contract law exam.

It is generally fair to say that with the majority of contracts the form in which they are made is not an issue. We make contracts every day, and probably all day long, without ever contemplating their legal significance and certainly without worrying about the specific form in which we have created them.

We can distinguish between 'simple' contracts and 'speciality' contracts.

In the case of **simple contracts** these can be made orally, in writing, or possibly even be implied by conduct. An example is where an auctioneer completes a contract at an auction by the fall of his hammer (although this might also be accompanied by words such as 'sold to the lady in the red dress').

- With contracts made in this way, there is no requirement for there to be any particular form.
- Evidence of compliance with the basic rules of formation will be sufficient to make such contracts enforceable in law.

However, with **speciality contracts** these need to have been created in a specific form to gain their validity.

- The 'form' in question will be to do with being written or evidenced in writing.
- This formal requirement indicates that a higher level of proof of the existence of the contract is required
- So speciality contracts are concerned with more significant property such as land or other transferable interests.

Speciality contracts come in one of three types:
- Agreements which must be created in the form of a deed.
- Agreements which must be made in writing
- Agreements which need only to be evidenced in writing, for example in a memorandum.

5.2 Agreements which must be in the form of a deed to be valid

Traditionally, any transaction that involved the conveyance of land or an interest in land had to be in a **deed** in order to be valid.

A deed was a document which was drafted on parchment, signed by the parties to the agreement, an impression made in sealing wax on the document, which was then delivered up by hand. In this way it was signed, sealed and delivered.

Under s 1(1) of the Law of Property (Miscellaneous Provisions) Act 1989 the requirement that the document be 'sealed' has been abolished. Now the document will be valid if it is made clear on the face of it that it is intended to act as a deed, and is validly executed. A new requirement is for the document to be formally witnessed, but this is no more than was already standard practice anyway.

A deed is also the standard means used for transferring of gifts that are thus unsupported by consideration. The classic example here is charitable gifts.

5.3 Contracts which must be in writing to be valid

A number of these exist. They are usually identified in a statute that will also outline the requirements.

They include cheques and other negotiable instruments and also credit agreements that must be in the prescribed form and conform to the requirements of the Consumer Credit Act 1974 as amended by Consumer Credit Act 2006.

Finally, they include sale or disposition of other interests in land. Section 40 of the Law of Property Act 1925 and the doctrine of part-performance formerly governed these. Now, however, such contracts come under s 2(1) of the Law of Property (Miscellaneous Provisions) Act 1989 which provides that:

'a contract for the sale or other disposition of an interest in land can only be made in writing and only by incorporating all the terms which the parties have expressly agreed in one document or, where contracts are exchanged, in each'.

The potential problem created by repeal of the doctrine of part-performance is that it makes it less easy for equity to intervene where there is a dispute over form.

5.4 Agreements needing evidence in writing to be valid

These are those contracts that were governed by the Statute of Frauds 1677.

Following the repeal of s 40 of the Law of Property Act 1925, the only contract requiring evidence in writing is a contract of guarantee. This is a promise made by one party to a second party to meet the debts of a third party in the event of the third party defaulting on the debt.

The basic rule is under s 4 that requires the agreement to be evidenced in a written note or memorandum. This memorandum must:

- be signed by the guarantor (or his agent)
- clearly be a signed admission of the existence of a contract, and
- contain all the material terms of the agreement, including the identities of all the parties involved and the precise subject-matter of the contract.

The guarantee is enforceable provided it is evidenced in writing in this way.

ACTIVITY

Self-assessment questions

1. In what circumstances will form be an issue in determining the contractual validity of an agreement?
2. What is the common thread that runs between agreements requiring specific form?
3. What is a deed? In what ways has the required form of a deed changed in recent years?
4. What is the common characteristic of contracts that must be created in written form?
5. What exactly is a guarantee?

KEY FACTS

Form
'Simple contracts' can be made orally, in writing or by conduct.
Speciality contracts will need to be created by the appropriate form or method. They mostly have to do with land or interests in land.
Under the Law Reform (Miscellaneous Provisions) Act 1989, transfers of land must be in the form of a deed, having been signed and witnessed.
Cheques and other negotiable instruments will need to be in writing.
Guarantees need to be in writing to be valid.

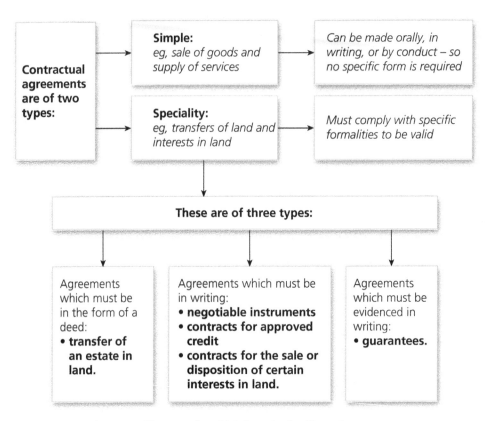

Figure 5.1 The ways in which form is significant in contracts

SUMMARY

....

- Simple contracts can generally be made in any form but speciality contracts require to be made in specific form.
- Some have to be made by deed to be valid, eg, transfers of land or interests in land.
- Some have to be in writing, eg, negotiable instruments.
- Some only require evidence in writing, eg, a guarantee of debts.

6

The obligations under a contract: Terms

AIMS AND OBJECTIVES

After reading this chapter you should be able to:

- Understand the significance of pre-contractual statements (representations)
- Understand how express terms are incorporated into contracts
- Understand the application of the parol evidence rule
- Understand when terms will be implied into contracts either by fact or by law
- Understand the different classifications of terms
- Understand how judges construe terms
- Critically analyse the area
- Apply the law to factual situations and reach conclusions

6.1 Pre-contractual statements and representations

6.1.1 The negotiation stage

We have so far looked at the methods of creating a contract between two parties and some other factors that may have a bearing on the making of a contract or the ability of the parties to enter into such an arrangement.

The terms of a contract are otherwise known as the contents of the contract and they represent what the parties have agreed to do or to give under the contract. In other words, they represent the obligations that the parties make to each other. Both sides will have obligations, as we have already seen. This is an inevitable consequence of both the *consensus ad idem* in offer and acceptance and also of the doctrine of consideration.

Under a contract, both sides will have to carry out their own side of the agreement for the contract to be completed. It is commonly a failure to honour a contractual obligation, and therefore a breach of a term of the contract, that leads to a dispute.

We would generally expect the terms of a contract to represent the outcome of the pre-contractual negotiations between the parties. In fact, the terms of a contract can be of two distinct types:

- whatever the parties have expressly agreed upon (otherwise known as the **express** terms), or
- what the law has decided should be included in the contract and therefore which are **implied** into the contract (see section 6.3).

However, not everything that the parties discuss during the pre-contractual stage or agree upon necessarily forms part of the contract.

Clearly, in the case of written agreements it ought to be a simple process to establish the **express terms** of the contract since they will be included in the written document and will usually be stated as being terms of the contract.

However, as we know, a large number of contracts are never produced in writing but are only made orally. In these contracts the major problem is an evidential one, identifying exactly which aspects of the oral negotiations represent the terms of the contract and which do not. The importance of these oral 'statements' is critical not only in determining the outcome of a particular dispute but also in identifying the remedies that are then available if a party wins his case.

The statements made by the parties in the pre-contractual stage are generally described in contract law as '**representations**'. It is the significance placed on these representations that determine how they will later be referred to and the impact that they may have on the outcome of a contractual dispute.

Any statement made at the time of contracting or before the contract is formed is referred to as a 'representation'. The representation may be as to current facts or as to intention of the parties. At this stage it is merely a statement that may or may not be relied upon once the contract is complete. The law then draws a sensible distinction between terms and representations.

- Any statement made by either party to the contract which may or may not have been intended to induce the other party to enter the contract but was not intended to form part of the contract is a representation. It may have certain legal consequences if certain circumstances are met but it never forms part of the contract. Even if the statement is false, therefore, it cannot amount to a breach of the contract itself.
- Any statement by which the parties to the contract do intend to be bound does also therefore form part of the contract and can be relied upon by the parties. These are the express **terms** of the contract and if they are not complied with there will be a breach of the contract. Even then, the type of remedy available will depend on the precise classification of the term.

express term

A term of the contract agreed by the parties in advance

representation

A statement made in the negotiating stages of a contract

6.1.2 Types of representation and their consequences

There are a number of statements made at the time the contract was formed or in the negotiations leading up to formation that will attach no liability and have no legal significance. They will be treated as such because the courts can find no reliance placed upon them by the parties, or indeed because no sensible person would believe that they would induce a party to enter a contract.

These types of representations can be broken down into three distinct categories:

- trade puffs
- mere opinions
- mere representations.

Trade puffs

Puffs are mere boasts or unsubstantiated claims. They are commonly made by, among others, advertisers of products or services. They are often nothing more than a catchy gimmick used in order to highlight the product that is being sold. 'Carlsberg – probably the best lager in the world' is an obvious example of such a boast. It is an exaggerated claim made to boost the saleability of the product. It is not intended to be taken seriously but to catch the attention. The law happily allows the producers some licence to make such statements since it is felt that nobody would actually take them seriously or be taken in by them. In this way the legal maxim *simplex commendatio non obligat* is applied. No obligations are created because no reliance can be placed upon them.

Inevitably, the closer the maker of the statement gets to making what appears to be a factually based statement, the more a risk is run of the puff achieving legal significance. Thus, a different legal view may be adopted when the statement, rather than being clearly identifiable as a mere boast, has included instead a specific promise or what amounts to an assertion of fact.

CASE EXAMPLE

Carlill v The Carbolic Smoke Ball Co Ltd [1893] 1 QB 256

Here, Mrs Carlill claimed on the promise that the company would pay £100 if the medicine failed to prevent a variety of cold-related illnesses. The Smoke Ball Company argued in its defence that the claim in the advertisement that the product would do as it suggested was a mere advertising gimmick, designed to sell more of the product. Its argument failed because of the promise it made to give £100 to anybody contracting one of the prescribed illnesses after using the smoke ball correctly. The fact that it had stated in its advertisement that a sum of money was deposited in a bank to cover such claims was even greater proof of its intention to be bound by its promise. In fact, the list of ailments that the advert promised could be cured or prevented was quite comprehensive. It included cough, catarrh, hoarseness, throat deafness, influenza, croup, cold in the head, asthma, loss of voice, snoring, hay fever, whooping cough, cold in the chest, bronchitis, sore eyes, headaches and neuralgia. This list in itself seems to be very precise and more than a mere boast which would have been surely stated in much more general terms.

JUDGMENT

Lord Justice Bowen explained why the statement could be taken seriously and relied upon rather than being dismissed as a mere puff: 'Was it intended that the £100 should, if the conditions be fulfilled, be paid? The advertisement says that £1,000 is lodged at the bank for that purpose. Therefore, it cannot be said that the statement that £100 would be paid was intended to be a mere puff. I think it was intended to be understood by the public as an offer which was to be acted upon … it was said there was no check on the part of the person who issued the advertisement, and that it would be an insensate thing to promise

£100 to a person who used the smoke ball unless you could check or superintend his manner of using it. The answer to that argument seems to be that if a person chooses to make extravagant promises of this kind, he probably does so because it pays him to make them … and there is no reason in law why he should not be bound by them.'

Mere opinions

Some statements made by a party to a contract attach little legal significance because they lack any weight and the other party ought not to rely on them. The obvious example of this is a mere opinion. An opinion does not carry any liability for the party making it because it is not based on fact.

CASE EXAMPLE

Bisset v Wilkinson [1927] AC 177

Here, a vendor was selling two blocks of land in New Zealand. The purchaser was intending to use the land for sheep farming, though it had not previously been used for that purpose, although sheep had formerly been kept on a small part of the land. The vendor, in response to a request by the purchaser, made a rough estimation that in his judgement the land could support 2,000 sheep. In fact, it could support nowhere near that number and did indeed prove impractical as a sheep farm. The purchaser sued and argued that the statement was an actionable misrepresentation. The Privy Council held that, because of the inexperience on which it was based, it was nothing more than an honest opinion, and was not actionable therefore because, as such, no reliance could be placed on it.

The outcome could, of course, be completely different if the statement of opinion were known to be untrue by the party expressing it. In this case the statement might well be actionable as a misrepresentation.

In contrast to a mere opinion, a party will be able to sue on the basis of a false opinion which has been stated by a party with specialist expertise in that field, and therefore who is in a superior bargaining position to the party to whom it is addressed. This is clearly the case because otherwise the party with expertise would be in a position to take an unfair advantage over the other party. Liability for the expert opinion may apply even though the opinion was expressed without actual knowledge of its falsehood at the time of making it.

CASE EXAMPLE

Esso Petroleum Co Ltd v Marden [1976] QB 801

Esso acquired a site on which it proposed to build a petrol station. On the basis of professional estimates it represented to Marden, a person intending to take on the franchise, that the filling station would have a throughput of 200,000 gallons per year. In fact, the local authority refused planning permission for the proposed layout of the petrol station. The result of this was that the pumps would be at the back of the site, and access to it would only be from side roads at the rear rather than from the main road at the front of the site. Marden queried the throughput figure but Esso assured him it would be possible. Despite Marden's best efforts, sales only ever reached 78,000 gallons; he lost money; and was unable to pay back a loan from Esso. Esso eventually sued for repossession of the site and Marden counter-claimed. One of Esso's arguments in defence was that the statement as to the likely throughput of petrol was a mere opinion. This argument failed to convince the court because of its extensive expertise in the area. Marden was able to rely on the estimate as though it were a factual statement.

**misrepresen-
tation**

A false statement
of fact made
by one party of
the contract to
the other at or
before the time of
contracting which
he intends should
induce the other
party to enter the
contract but which
is not intended to
form part of the
contract

Mere representations

Where a party to a contract has made a representation as to fact, which is intended to induce the other party to enter the contract, but which is not intended to form part of the contract, and it is in fact true, there can be no further contractual significance. What has been offered under the contract has been delivered and the contract is in fact complete. This is referred to as a 'mere representation'.

On the other hand, where a representation has been made so as to induce a party to enter a contract and they have done so, if the representation has been falsely made then there may well be further legal consequences. In this case, subject to other requirements (see section 9.2), the representation may amount to a **misrepresentation** which can be actionable and lead to a variety of remedies. This will be the case even though the representation has never actually become incorporated as a term of the contract.

The different significance attached to various types of pre-contractual statements can be expressed in the following table:

Type of statement (representation)	Contractual significance of the statement	Legal reasoning
Terms	These will attach liability (and if they are breached a range of remedies is available).	Because they are actually incorporated into the contract, and so they become the obligations under the contract by which the parties are bound.
Mere representations	These will attach NO liability.	Because, while they may induce a party to enter into the contract, they are not incorporated into the contract and were never intended to create binding obligations.
Misrepresentations	These will attach liability (and also a range of remedies depending on how deliberately the falsehood was made). Compare eg *Esso v Marden* and *Derry v Peek*.	Because even though they are not part of the contract, being false, they may have wrongly induced the other party to enter the contract, thus vitiating his free will.
Mere opinions	These will attach NO liability in themselves. *Bisset v Wilkinson*	Because neither party's opinion is any more valid than the other's, and therefore it cannot be relied upon.
Expert opinions	These will attach liability (possibly as terms if they are important enough to have been incorporated in the contract. If not, they may still amount to innocent misrepresentations). *Esso v Marden*	Because we do rely on expertise, and should be entitled to rely on the opinion of experts in making arrangements.
Trade puffs	These will attach NO liability, eg 'Carlsberg – probably the best lager in the world'.	Because the law credits us with more intelligence than to take advertisers' boasts too seriously.
Puffs with a specific promise attached	These will attach liability. *Carlill v Carbolic Smoke Ball Co*	Because the promise is quite specific and so we can rely on it rather than the puff, since it creates a separate contractual relationship.

Figure 6.1 The relationship between different types of representation and the legal consequences attaching to them

ACTIVITY

Self-assessment questions

1. In what ways does a term differ from a mere representation?
2. Why is it that some statements made before the contract attach no liability at all?
3. Why is there no liability attached to a trade puff?
4. Why do the courts attach no liability to a mere opinion?

6.1.3 The process of defining and distinguishing the express terms

Terms that have been expressly agreed upon by the parties will inevitably arise from the negotiations that have taken place prior to the contract being formed and the statements that each party makes to the other at that time. Such pre-contractual statements are generally known as 'representations'.

A pre-contractual statement may be made orally or in writing or indeed may be implied by conduct, as when a contract is formed on the fall of an auctioneer 's hammer. The impact that a pre-contractual statement will have on the contract will depend very much on the character of the statement and the context in which it is made.

In this way, certain statements made by the parties will have no significance at all in law, while some will actually form the obligations of the contract as terms, and will therefore be enforceable or their breach will lead to remedies. The significance of certain other pre-contractual statements may depend on whether they have been falsely stated or not, in which case they may be actionable.

Thus, in negotiations for the sale of my car I might make the following comments:

- It is a 1978 MGB GT.
- It is British Racing Green with gold stripes (in fact, the stripe on one side is missing).
- The price is only £7,000.
- It has had only two owners, including myself.
- The previous owner only used it to go shopping (in fact, it was a commercial traveller).
- It has done only 65,000 miles (in fact, the true mileage is 165,000).
- It is mechanically perfect.
- It has leather upholstery.
- It has been serviced 'quite often'.
- The petrol consumption is 'reasonable'.
- It is an ace little car.

Even a non-lawyer would see the point that the weight attached to these statements varies, as will also then the contractual significance. The fact that a car is mechanically perfect may be of critical importance to the buyer, but what exactly is an 'ace little car '?

Basically, any statement made at the time of the contract or in the period leading up to the contract is a representation. The effect of the statement is to represent that the information contained in the statement is true. One further aspect of the statement at this point is to represent the stated intention of the party making it.

ACTIVITY

Quick quiz

Try to work out which of the statements made about the car (above) may be significant enough to be classed as a term and which you think are not sufficiently important to be terms.

There are 11:

- make of car
- colour
- price
- number of owners
- previous use
- mechanical state
- upholstery
- mileage
- service record
- petrol consumption
- 'ace little car'.

ACTIVITY

Quick quiz

Which of the following situations do you think is likely to contain a term?

1. Jasvinder is a greengrocer. He puts a poster in his window, reading: 'The tastiest apples around'.
2. Andrew is selling his caravan. He describes it as a 'family caravan'. It has one double bed and two couches on which it would be possible for other people to sleep.
3. Annie has been given as a present a computer that she cannot use so she is selling it to Raj. Raj asks if it has a large memory and Annie says that she thinks it has.
4. Sid is selling his motorbike to Colin. He tells Colin that the bike is 'mechanically perfect'. In fact, the bike breaks down as Colin is leaving Sid's house.

KEY FACTS

Pre-contractual statements		
The express terms of a contract represent what the parties have agreed upon. These come from pre-contractual statements.		
The law distinguishes between	**Type of representation**	**Case/statute**
Those sufficiently significant to be incorporated into the contract as terms.	A trade puff has no effect on the contract – it is a mere boast, not to be taken seriously without another promise being attached.	*Carlill v The Carbolic Smoke Ball Co*
Those which, while not incorporated, nevertheless were intended to induce the other party to enter the contract (mere representations). If false, they are misrepresentations.		
Those intended to have no contractual significance at all, eg trade puffs and mere opinions.	An opinion carries no weight unless it is made by an expert.	*Bisset v Wilkinson*

6.2 Express terms

6.2.1 The nature of express terms

We have already explored the difference between representations and terms. In essence, they are distinguished by the legal consequences attached to them.

Quite simply, the terms of a contract are the obligations contained in it. Basically, then, a term is an expression of willingness by both parties to be bound by the obligation contained in it and if a term is breached, or not complied with, it will give the other party the right to sue.

Terms can be introduced by the parties themselves or implied by other means. Express terms are those which are agreed upon by the parties at the time the contract is formed. Since contracts can be formed in writing or orally or even by the conduct of the parties, then the terms may arise in many ways. They may form part of a written document. This in itself could be an individual expression of the agreement between the parties or indeed could be a standard method of contracting by a particular party, as in 'standard forms'. In contrast, they may be nothing more than a simple oral promise. They may arise after a single, simple agreement or after long, protracted negotiations. They may be critical to the performance of the contract or they may be purely descriptive. What they all have in common is that the parties themselves have agreed on them and they are all subject to some form of legal action if they are breached.

6.2.2 The process of incorporating express terms

Clearly, the dividing lines between some of the categories of statements in section 6.1.2 above are not always obvious. Where a contract is in writing then the process of distinguishing is generally simpler. The terms are as stated in the written contract. Where, however, negotiations leading up to the contract are oral, the courts have developed guidelines to determine whether a particular statement is a term of the contract or not.

In order to be a term of the contract, the statement must be incorporated and form part of the contract. Inevitably, since different parties may take a different view of the importance of particular pre-contractual statements, the courts have been called on to devise tests to determine whether or not a particular statement is incorporated as a term. In general, the courts adopt an objective analysis, basing their decision on what a reasonable man would consider was in the mind of the parties at the time they formed the contract.

6.2.3 Factors relevant to incorporating terms

Whether or not a statement is incorporated as a term can depend on a number of different factors. These have been developed by the judges in the case law in an attempt to produce a consistent approach.

The importance attached to the representation

The more importance is attached to the statement by either party then the more likely it is that it is a term. The logic of this is clear. Where a party relied on a statement to the extent that without it being incorporated into the contract as a term it is unlikely that the party would have entered the contract, then the provision identified in the statement is usually accepted as a term. To do otherwise would be to ignore the intention of that party.

CASE EXAMPLE

Birch v Paramount Estates (Liverpool) Ltd (1956) 16 EG 396

Here, a newly wed couple bought a new house from developers. They agreed to buy on the basis of a promise made to them that the house would be 'as good as the show house'. In fact, the house was not as good as the show house. The Court of Appeal concluded that the statement was so central to the agreement that it had been incorporated into the contract as a term. The couple would have been unlikely to contract but for the statement upon which they relied.

warranty

A minor term of a contract which only gives rise to an action for damages

In this way, the effect of the statement being so important may make it a **warranty** of the contract rather than a misrepresentation that it might otherwise have been. This demonstrates the difficult decisions courts may have to take.

CASE EXAMPLE

Couchman v Hill [1947] KB554

In a written agreement for the sale of a heifer (a young female cow, usually one that has not yet had a calf) the conditions of sale included a clause that lots were sold 'with all faults, imperfections and errors of description'. The sale catalogue actually described the heifer as 'unserved' (meaning not yet having been used for breeding). Prior to the making of the contract, the buyer asked both the auctioneer and the seller to confirm that the heifer was unserved, and they both assured him that it was. Relying on these assurances, he bought the heifer. However, not long afterwards he discovered that the heifer was having a calf, and it in fact died as a result of having a calf at too young an age. The Court of Appeal concluded that, despite the written terms in the contract, the representation was so crucial to the buyer in making the contract that it was incorporated as a term. It was more than a misrepresentation that would have induced him into entering the contract but not formed part of the obligations under it.

Where one party has requested specific details about the agreement then this can also be taken to indicate that importance is attached to the answer. Because of this, the courts will be willing to hold that they are incorporated into the contract as terms.

CASE EXAMPLE

Bannerman v White (1861) 10 CBNS 844

During negotiations for the purchase of hops, the defendant purchaser stated that 'if they have been treated with sulphur I am not interested in even knowing the price of them'. The seller gave assurances that they had not, which were also repeated when the same question was asked of samples that were produced. In fact, some of the crop had been treated with sulphur. When he discovered this, the defendant then repudiated the contract. The claimant argued that the discussions were only preliminary to the contract and not part of it. The court, however, accepted that the stipulations regarding sulphur amounted to a condition of the contract which was therefore breached. The repudiation was justifiable.

Special knowledge or skill affecting the equality of bargaining strength

As has been seen already, the courts are willing to accept that statements made by parties with specific expertise relevant to the contract can be relied upon. However, where the statement is made without any particular expertise or specialist knowledge to back it up, it is less likely to be construed as a term.

CASE EXAMPLE

Oscar Chess Ltd v Williams [1957] 1 WLR 370

The defendant, an ordinary motorist, sold his car to motor dealers for £290, describing it as a 1948 Morris 10. The defendant honestly believed this was the correct age of the car since that was the age given in the registration documents. When the car was later discovered to be a 1939 model, the motor dealers sued for breach of warranty, since the value of the car was obviously lower than the price that they had given. Their action failed. The defendant had no expertise or specialist skill, and was completely reliant on the registration documents in making the statement. The court held that it was no more than an innocent misrepresentation, at that time without a remedy, and hence the importance of the claimant trying to prove that the statement was incorporated as a term of the contract.

CASE EXAMPLE

Dick Bentley Productions Ltd v Harold Smith (Motors) Ltd [1965] 1 WLR 623

The claimant, a successful businessman, asked the defendants, who were car dealers, to find him a 'well vetted' Bentley car. In other words, he wanted one in good condition. The defendants found a car that they falsely stated had only done 20,000 miles since being fitted with a new engine and gearbox. In fact, it had done 100,000 miles. The claimant later found the car to be unsuitable, as well as discovering that the statement about the mileage was untrue, and sued for a breach of warranty. The Court of Appeal upheld the claim since the claimant relied on the specialist expertise of the car dealers in stating the mileage. The statement was a key issue in the claimant deciding to contract.

The time between making the statement and formation of the contract

Sometimes the court may assess the time lapse between the statement made in the negotiations and the creation of the contract itself, particularly if there is a major difference between the two. Generally, courts will hold that the longer the time difference between the two, the less possible it is to support any claim that the statement was in fact incorporated into the contract as a term. This is then particularly so where the substance of the statement is not repeated in the contract.

CASE EXAMPLE

Routledge v McKay [1954] 1 WLR 615

A motor cycle had actually first been registered in 1939. However, on a new registration book being issued this was wrongly stated as 1941. In 1949 the current owner, who was unaware of this inaccuracy, was selling the motor cycle and in response to a prospective buyer's enquiry as to the age gave the age in the registration documents. The prospective buyer then bought the motor cycle a week later, in a written contract that made no mention of the age. When he discovered the true age and tried to sue for breach of a term, he failed. The court held that the lapse of time was too wide to create a binding relationship based on the statement. The statement was not incorporated.

Reducing the agreement, including the statement, to writing

Inevitably, written evidence is more powerful and more immediately convincing than the spoken word. As a result, where a contract is made in a written document and a statement made orally between the parties is not then included in the written document, the court will generally infer that it was not intended to form part of the contract but is a mere representation.

CASE EXAMPLE

Routledge v McKay [1954] 1 WLR 615

Here, since the written agreement made no mention of the age of the motor cycle, the court held that it had not been considered important enough to be a term.

Furthermore, where a written agreement is signed this will generally make the contents of the agreement binding, irrespective of whether they have been read by the party signing. (There is a clear warning here that we should never be persuaded to sign any document without reading it first.)

CASE EXAMPLE

L'Estrange v Graucob [1934] 2 KB 394

The claimant bought a vending machine from the defendants on a written contract which in small print contained the clause 'any express or implied condition, statement or warranty, statutory or otherwise not stated herein is hereby excluded'. The machine turned out to be unsatisfactory and the claimant claimed for breach of an implied term as to fitness for purpose, under the Sale of Goods Act 1893. (Exclusions of liability for the implied terms were possible under the 1893 Act.) She also argued that she had not read the clause and had no knowledge of what it contained. Judgment was initially given to the claimant but on appeal she failed.

JUDGMENT

As Scrutton LJ put it: 'When a document containing contractual terms is signed, then, in the absence of fraud, or, I will add, misrepresentation, the party signing it is bound, and it is wholly immaterial whether he has read the document or not.' He also added 'the plaintiff, having put her signature to the document, and not having been induced to do so by any fraud or misrepresentation, cannot be heard to say that she is not bound by the terms of the document because she did not read them'.

(Of course, judgments such as the above would now be subject to the Unfair Contract Terms Act 1977 and the Unfair Terms in Consumer Contracts Regulations 1999.)

The rule clearly provides a great deal of certainty in forming contracts and is of obvious benefit in commercial transactions. Nevertheless, it has not escaped criticism, and the reasons for this are obvious. As Leslie Rutherford and Stephen Wilson point out:

QUOTATION

'… once a document is signed the parties are bound by its contents … the rule leaves no room for argument as to what was agreed by the parties. What the rule lacks in sophistication it makes up for in simplicity. But in terms of doing justice between parties it is less than ideal and it may be seen as lacking any firm theoretical foundation'.

L Rutherford and S Wilson 'Signature of a document',
New Law Journal, 13th March 1998

The extent to which the term is effectively drawn to the notice of the party subject to it

In general, a term will not be accepted as incorporated into the contract unless it is brought sufficiently to the attention of the party subject to it prior to or at the time the contract is made. This is one of the basic ways in which judges have developed protections for consumers in the case of exclusion clauses. Rules on incorporation of terms are interchangeable with the rules on incorporation of exclusion clauses, and cases such as *Olley v Marlborough Court Hotel* [1949] 1 KB 532, *Chapelton v Barry UDC* [1940] 1 KB 532 and *Thornton v Shoe Lane Parking Ltd* [1971] 2 QB 163 are all examples that could also be used to illustrate the basic point. So the party subject to an alleged term must have real knowledge of it before entering the contract or a court may not accept that it has been incorporated into the contract.

CASE EXAMPLE

O'Brien v MGN Ltd [2001] EWCA Civ 1279

The claimant bought a copy of the *Daily Mirror* containing a scratch card. On the card was printed 'For full rules and how to claim, see z'. The claimant bought another *Daily Mirror* containing a scratch card on a later day. The card and paper contained the words 'normal *Mirror* rules apply'. This second card showed a £50,000 prize but, because of a mistake, 1,472 other people were also told that they had won. The competition rules provided for a draw to take place in the event that there were more winners than prize money available. The paper organised a draw, with one prize of £50,000 and another £50,000 to be divided between all the others (£34 each). The contract included the phrase 'normal *Mirror* rules apply' and so it was held that this was sufficient to incorporate the terms. The newspaper had done just enough to bring the terms to the attention of the claimant since the rules were referred to on the back of each card and were available at the offices of the paper and in back issues of the paper.

The significance of standard forms

It is commonplace in a modern commercial context for parties to contract on their own standard terms and conditions. Very often this can lead to problems when the terms are mutually conflicting (see section 2.4). Where the contract has been formed orally, such terms can only be relied on if they have in fact been incorporated into the contract at the time of its formation.

CASE EXAMPLE

Lidl UK GmbH v Hertford Foods Ltd [2001] EWCA Civ 938 CA, 20th June

Here, in a contract for supply of corned beef, the seller was able to deliver only part of the order. He was unable to get further supplies because of circumstances beyond his control. The buyer then had to obtain supplies elsewhere at extra cost, for which the buyer then sued. Both parties then tried to rely on their own standard terms and conditions. The seller's terms included a '*force majeure*' clause which would make it not liable. Both parties had done business with each other before and so had seen and were aware of each other's terms, but the terms were actually inconsistent and had not been incorporated into earlier contracts. As the contract was made on the telephone and neither party had mentioned their standard terms at this time when the contract was actually formed, even though they had later sent them to the other, the Court of Appeal decided that neither set of terms was incorporated. The seller was in breach of contract and therefore liable.

It is important to remember that before the passing of the Misrepresentation Act 1967 it was crucial in most cases to prove that a particular representation was actually incorporated into the contract as a term. This was because the remedies available were very limited. A remedy was possible in only two cases:

- if fraud could be proved
- if it were possible to rescind the contract in equity.

Since the passing of the 1967 Act, many of the above claimants would not necessarily have to try to prove that the statement made to them amounted to a term of the contract. The 1967 Act allows a claimant an action even in respect of an innocent misrepresentation, such as that relating to the age of a vehicle found in its registration documents. Prior to this Act there were very limited circumstances in which a claim for misrepresentation could be made. So it was vital for a claimant to prove that a statement was a term, otherwise he may have had no remedy at all.

ACTIVITY

Quick quiz

Using the information in 6.2.3, consider whether a term has been incorporated into a contract in each of the following situations.

1. Bert and Ada, a retired couple, buy a bungalow on a new estate. When they saw the show house before the estate was built, it was surrounded by fields and woodland. They were promised that their bungalow would be in an equally peaceful setting. In fact, when they move into the bungalow it is on the edge of the estate across the road from a row of noisy factories.

2. Pablo, an art dealer, buys a painting from Robert who is selling off his mother's property after she dies, and who has no knowledge of art at all. Pablo asks Robert if he knows the origins of the painting. Robert says he thinks that his mother told him that it was by a 19th century landscape painter but is not sure. Pablo pays £500 for the painting thinking that it may be worth much more. Later Pablo discovers that the painting is 20th century and only worth about £50.

3. Ron saw an old Austin Healey Sprite sports car for sale outside a house on his way home from work. Ron had always wanted such a car when he was young. He inspected the car and asked the owner, Dave, how many owners the car had had. Dave replied 'only one or two'. Several weeks later when the car was still for sale Ron bought the car from Dave. In the brief written agreement there was only the make and age of car and agreed price, and no mention of the number of owners. Ron has now discovered that there have been 22 owners and wants Dave to take the car back.

6.2.4 The 'parol evidence' rule

parol evidence rule

A rule preventing the variation of a written contract by oral evidence

Historically, where a party to a written agreement was trying to show that the written document did not fully reflect the actual agreement that had been reached, he would come up against the '**parol evidence**' **rule**. The substance of this rule was that any oral or other evidence that the party was trying to introduce to show the actual agreement would not be accepted as admissible if it was to be used either to add to, or to vary or to contradict, the terms contained in the written contract.

The rule can easily be justified:

- Firstly, if the contract had been produced in written form then it was only logical for the court to suppose that anything omitted from the written document actually formed no part of the agreement.
- Secondly, the clear danger was that adding terms into the agreement after the written agreement was accepted would lead to uncertainty.

The problem with this very basic rule, however, is that many contracts are partly written and partly oral and therefore, in reality, both elements of the agreement would need to be considered in order to have an accurate picture of the contract in total. As a result of the shortcomings of the rule, over a long period of time a number of exceptions to the strict rule emerged and the effect of this was to render the rule generally unworkable.

Custom or trade usage

Terms can invariably be implied into a contract by trade custom (see implied terms, below). Particularly in business dealings, the parties may be used to a particular requirement, to the extent that they do not think to include it. Nevertheless the clear implication is that the parties would have expected to contract on the basis of these requirements. If a party could indeed produce evidence of an established trade practice and the expectation that this would be followed then the parol evidence rule might be overlooked.

Rectification

Where it can be shown that a written contract inaccurately represents the actual agreement reached by the two parties, then it is a basic principle of equity to allow rectification of the written document (to allow the inaccurate written document to be amended to represent the true agreement). Parol evidence can be introduced to show what the real agreement was. The inaccuracies are removed and replaced if necessary with the substance of the real agreement.

CASE EXAMPLE

Webster v Cecil [1861] 54 ER 812

Webster was trying to enforce his purchase of land where the written document identified the price as £1,250. Cecil was able to show that he had already refused an offer of £2,000, so that the accurate price must have been higher, and was in fact £2,250. The evidence was accepted by the court and the price in the written agreement was amended accordingly.

Invalidation by misrepresentation, mistake etc

Where a claimant is seeking to avoid the consequences of a contract having discovered that the contract has been made as the result of a mistake or a misrepresentation or other invalidating factor, he is clearly entitled to introduce evidence to that effect (see Chapters 9 and 10).

Where the written agreement represents only part of a larger agreement

Clearly, in some circumstances, as we have already seen, the court is prepared to accept that oral representations, because of their significance, are intended to be as much a part of the agreement as those included in the written document.

CASE EXAMPLE

J Evans & Son (Portsmouth) Ltd v Andrea Merzario Ltd [1976] 1 WLR 1078

The claimant regularly used the defendants as carriers to ship machinery from Italy and they did so on the defendants' standard forms. Originally the machines, which were liable to rust if left on deck, were always carried below decks. When the defendants started using containers, which would generally be kept on deck, the claimants expressed concern about rusting and were given an oral assurance that their machinery would still be stored below decks. One machine being carried for the claimants was put in a container and by error stored on deck. The container was not properly fastened and subsequently fell overboard. The Court of Appeal allowed the claimant to introduce evidence of the oral assurance; the standard forms did not represent the actual agreement; and the defendants were liable.

Where the contract depends on fulfilment of a specified event

Obviously, where the parties have a written agreement but have also agreed that the contract will come into effect only on fulfilment of some other condition, then evidence can be introduced to that effect. There is no attempt to vary the terms of the contract. The evidence of the oral agreement is introduced only to show that operation of the contract has been suspended until fulfilment of the condition.

CASE EXAMPLE

Pym v Campbell [1856] 119 ER 903

Here, there was a written agreement to buy a share of the patent of an invention. The claimant sued for a breach of this agreement. In fact, there was an oral agreement between the parties that the contract would not come into effect until the patent had been examined and verified by a third party. The court accepted that the defendant was allowed to introduce parol evidence of this.

Collateral contracts

The collateral contract is an exception to the basic rules on privity of contract (see section 13.2.10). The process of identifying the existence of a collateral agreement allows a party to sue the maker of a promise on which they have relied on entering a contract, even though that party is not a party to the actual contract.

A collateral agreement can also be relevant as an exception to the parol evidence rule in certain circumstances. For instance, where a promise is made which is dependent on the making of another contract, the promise is collateral, the making of the other contract is the consideration for the agreement between the two parties. Even though the promise may rank as only a representation in the major contract, it can be raised as evidence of the second or collateral contract.

CASE EXAMPLE

City and Westminster Properties (1934) Ltd v Mudd [1958] 2 All ER 733

The defendant rented a shop for six years, together with a small adjacent room in which he slept. The claimant landlords were fully aware of this arrangement. When the lease was up for renewal the landlords inserted a clause into the new lease restricting use of the premises to the 'showrooms, workrooms and offices only'. The inevitable effect of this would be to prevent the defendant from sleeping on the premises. The defendant then gained an oral assurance from the landlords that he could still sleep in the room, on the basis of which he then signed the new lease. The landlords then brought an action for forfeiture of the lease because of the defendant's breach of the new clause. The court accepted that the defendant had indeed broken the terms of the lease, but held that the landlords were unable to enforce its terms against him because of the collateral contract.

ACTIVITY

Self-assessment questions

1. In what ways can expertise or specialist knowledge be important in determining what the terms of a contract are?
2. What are the benefits of putting a contract in writing?
3. What is the effect of signing an agreement that you have not read?

KEY FACTS

Incorporation of terms	
Express oral terms must be incorporated into the contract – or the contract must be written.	
Factors to be considered in incorporating terms	**Case/statute**
The importance attached to them by the parties.	*Birch v Paramount Estates*
The relative bargaining strength of the parties.	*Oscar Chess v Williams*
The extent to which one party relied on the expertise of the other.	*Dick Bentley Productions v Harold Smith Motors*
Whether the term was sufficiently drawn to the other party's attention before the contract was formed.	*O'Brien v Mirror Group Newspapers*
Whether the representation was put in writing.	*Routledge v McKay*
A party is generally bound by anything that he has signed, whether or not he has read it.	*L'Estrange v Graucob*
Originally, the 'parol evidence' rule prevented a party from introducing evidence of oral agreements not actually in the written agreement – but there are now many exceptions to this rule.	

THE OBLIGATIONS UNDER A CONTRACT: TERMS

implied term

A term that is implied into a contract rather than being included by either party

6.3 Implied terms

6.3.1 The process of implying terms into a contract

Generally, the parties to a contract will be deemed to have included as express terms of the contract all of the various obligations by which they intend to be bound.

There are, however, occasions when terms will be implied into a contract, even though they do not appear in a written agreement or in the oral negotiations that have taken place leading up to the contract.

Terms will be implied into a contract for one of two reasons:

■ Because a court in a later dispute is trying to give effect to a presumed intention of the parties, even though these intentions have not been expressed (these are terms **implied by fact**).

Because the law demands that certain obligations are to be included in a contract irrespective of whether the parties have agreed on them or would naturally include them (these are terms **implied by law** – usually this will be as the result of some statutory provision aimed at redressing an imbalance in bargaining strength or seeking to protect a particular group, for instance consumers or employees, but it can also arise as a result of operation of the common law).

6.3.2 Terms implied by fact

Where terms are implied by fact, this is usually as a result of decisions in individual court cases. The courts have implied terms by fact in a variety of different circumstances. In all cases, what the court is trying to do is to give effect to the presumed intention of the parties at the time the contract was formed.

Terms implied by custom or habit

There is an old maxim that 'custom hardens into right'. In other words, if something has happened in a particular way over a long period of time then it is likely that it will be established that it has evolved into an actual and enforceable right. Much of the early common law was based on local custom. For instance, customary rights gained by long use, otherwise known as prescription, are common features in relation to the use of land. Bridle paths and public rights of way are an example of this. The same principle can be adopted where parties contract but are silent on features that may in any case be accepted as established custom.

CASE EXAMPLE

Hutton v Warren [1836] 150 ER 517

In this case a long-standing local custom was to the effect that on termination of an agricultural lease the tenant would be entitled to an allowance for seed and labour on the land. This was an important custom at a time when the majority of the population was engaged in subsistence agriculture. The court held that the lease made by the two parties must be viewed in the light of this custom.

JUDGMENT

Baron Parke explained the reasoning of the court in the Court of Exchequer: 'It has long been settled that in commercial transactions extrinsic evidence of custom and usage is admissible to annex incidents to written contracts, in matters with respect to which they are silent.'

Terms implied by trade or professional custom

The parties to a contract might be bound by an implied trade custom when it is accepted as their deemed intention, even though there are no express terms on the matter.

In marine insurance, for instance, it has long been a custom that there is an implied undertaking on the part of the broker that he will pay the premium to the insurer even where the party insured defaults on the payment.

Much of modern commercial law has its origins in custom. When the first Bills of Exchange Act 1882 was enacted, Parliament did little more than to incorporate the existing and long-standing practices of merchants in statutory form. The law was referred to for a long time as 'mercantile law'.

However, for the courts to be prepared to accept the custom as binding on the contracting parties by implication, the custom must be seen to operate so as to give effect to the contract by supporting the general purpose. It must not contradict the express terms, and therefore defeat the general purpose of the contract, or it will not be accepted as being implied into the contract.

CASE EXAMPLE

Les Affreteurs Reunis SA v Walford (Walford's Case) [1919] AC 801

In this case that also concerns an exception to the doctrine of privity of contract (see section 13.2.3), Walford was suing for a commission of 3 per cent that he had been promised as a result of negotiating a **charterparty** between Lubricating and Fuel Oils Co Ltd and the owners of the SS *Flore*. The commission had actually been mentioned in the contract between the two parties but since Walford was not a party to that contract he was unable to enforce it according to the privity rule. One argument of the defendants was that there was a custom that commission was payable only when the ship had actually been hired. In this instance the French Government had requisitioned the ship before the charterparty had actually occurred. If the custom was accepted then it would conflict with the clause in the contract requiring payment as soon as the hire agreement was signed, so it was held not to have been implied into the contract.

charterparty

A contract for the hire of a ship

Terms implied to give sense and meaning to the agreement

Sometimes a contract would be rendered meaningless or inoperable without the inclusion of a particular term, even though the parties to the contract have failed to include it expressly in their agreement. In such circumstances the court will be prepared to imply the term to give effect and sense to the agreement.

CASE EXAMPLE

Schawel v Reade [1913] 2 IR 64

The claimant wanted to buy a stallion for stud purposes. At the defendant's stables he was examining a horse advertised for sale when the defendant remarked, 'You need not look for anything: the horse is perfectly sound. If there was anything the matter with the horse I would tell you'. On this recommendation the claimant halted his inspection and later bought the horse. In fact, it turned out that the horse was unfit for stud purposes. Lord Moulton held that, even though the defendant's assurances did not amount to an express warranty as to the horse's fitness for stud, nevertheless they were an implied warranty to that effect. He was entitled to rely on the very general assurance made by the seller and by implication take it that the assurance covered the purpose for which he was buying the horse.

Terms implied to give business efficacy to a commercial contract

Exactly the same point applies in respect of business contracts. Parties would not freely enter a contract that had no benefit for them or indeed that might harm them or cause them some loss. So the courts will imply terms into a contract where they are not already included in express form in order to ensure business efficacy and sustain the agreement as a business-like arrangement.

CASE EXAMPLE

The Moorcock (1889) 14 PD 64

The defendants owned a wharf with a jetty on the Thames. They made an agreement with the claimant for him to dock his ship and unload cargoes at the wharf. Both parties were aware at the time of contracting that this could involve the vessel being at the jetty at low tide. In fact, the size of the vessel was too great for the depth of water in the wharf at low tide. As a result, the ship became grounded at the jetty and broke up on a ridge of rock. The claimant sued for the cost of the damage to the ship. The defendants argued that they had given no express undertaking as to the safety of the ship. The court held that there was an implied term that the owner of the wharf had taken reasonable steps to ascertain the state of the riverbed next to the jetty.

JUDGMENT

Bowen LJ explained that, 'In business transactions such as this, what the law desires to effect by the implication is to give such business efficacy … as must have been intended at all events by both parties who are businessmen'.

This basic principle is actually little more than common sense and difficult to argue against. As a result, the principle has been accepted and applied in subsequent cases.

Terms implied because of the prior conduct of the contracting parties

Quite simply, where the parties to a contract have a history of dealing on particular terms, if those terms are not included in a later contract they may be implied into it if the parties are dealing in otherwise essentially similar terms. Courts will accept that a party contracting after a course of similar dealings is entitled to expect that a later contract will be subject to similar terms, even if not expressly included in the agreement.

CASE EXAMPLE

Hillas v Arcos (1932) 147 LT 503

In an agreement made in 1931 the two parties contracted for the supply of standard-sized lengths of timber. The contract included an option clause allowing the claimants to buy a further 100,000 lengths during 1932. The agreement was otherwise quite vague as to the type of timber, the terms of shipment and many other features. Despite this, the contract was completed and the timber was supplied. In 1932 the claimants then wanted to order the further 100,000 lengths of timber, as indicated in the option, but the defendants refused to deliver them. Their argument was that since the 1931 agreement was vague in many major aspects, it was therefore no more than a basis for further negotiations. Nevertheless, the House of Lords held that, while the option clause lacked specific detail, it was drafted in the same terms as the contract of sale that had already been successfully completed. It was therefore implicit in the original contract that the option should be carried out in the same terms if the claimant wished to exercise it.

The test for implying a term by fact into a contract

Inevitably, if judges are prepared to imply terms by fact they must have a coherent and consistent means of doing so. The classic test for identifying whether or not a term will be implied into a contract by fact is that laid down in the judgment of MacKinnon LJ in *Shirlaw v Southern Foundries Ltd* [1939] 2 KB 206.

JUDGMENT

'*Prima facie* that which in any contract is left to be implied and need not be expressed is something so obvious that it goes without saying; so that if, while the parties were making their bargain, an officious bystander were to suggest some express provision for it in their agreement, they would testily suppress him with a common "Oh of course!"'

This is commonly known as the 'officious bystander' test. It is still the test used, and on the face of it is an adequate way of showing that what the court is doing is giving effect to the presumed intention of the parties. However, it does impose a very strict standard on the parties which in some senses can be regarded as an unrealistic one. The basic problem is that while one party will usually be all too willing to accept that the implied term at issue was what he actually intended to be part of the contract, the other party almost inevitably will be arguing the exact reverse, or there would be no dispute in the first place. In such circumstances it is perhaps somewhat artificial to say that the term implied actually does represent the true intention of the parties. Nevertheless it is a means of ensuring that one party does not take unfair advantage of the other party since the test is objective and the presumed intention is one that the reasonable man would have automatically expected to be included in the contract.

However, the natural consequence of these problems is that there will be circumstances in which courts will recognise that the 'officious bystander' rule cannot apply.

One example is where one party to the contract is totally unaware of the term that it is being suggested should be implied into the agreement. In this case it could never have been his intention that it be included, so the test is likely to fail.

CASE EXAMPLE

Spring v National Amalgamated Stevedores and Dockers Society
[1956] 1 WLR 585

This case involved an agreement between various trade unions, including the defendant union, which was known as the 'Bridlington Agreement', from the meeting of the TUC (Trade Union Congress) at which it was reached. The agreement was a means of regulating the transfer of members between different trade unions, principally to avoid 'poaching' of another union's members. The claimant joined the defendant union in breach of this rule on transfer but was actually totally unaware of the existence of the agreement. This breach was reported to the TUC Disputes Committee. The committee then demanded of the defendant union that it should expel the claimant. When it tried to do so, the claimant sued for breach of contract. The defendant union asked that a term should be implied into its agreement with Spring that it should follow the Bridlington Agreement. MacKinnon LJ's 'officious bystander' test was referred to but was rejected in the circumstances. As the court pointed out, if the claimant had been told about the Bridlington Agreement by an officious bystander, he would have had no idea what it was and therefore it could not be said to represent his true intention in entering the agreement.

The second example occurs where it is uncertain that both parties would have agreed to the term even if it had been included in the agreement. In such circumstances it is difficult to demonstrate that it was their presumed intention and therefore that it should be included by implication, in which case the test fails yet again.

CASE EXAMPLE

Shell (UK) Ltd v Lostock Garage Ltd [1977] 1 All ER 481

By an agreement between the two parties, Shell was to supply petrol and oil to Lostock who in return agreed to buy these products only from Shell. During a later 'price war', Shell supplied petrol to other garages at lower prices, forcing Lostock to sell at a loss. Lostock wanted inclusion of an implied term in the contract to the effect that Shell would not 'abnormally discriminate' against it. The Court of Appeal refused since Shell would never have agreed to it.

Lord Denning took a much more relaxed view to the process of implying terms by fact into a contract. He suggested that the process of implication need not be anything more than to include terms that are reasonable as between the parties in the circumstances of the case. There would appear to be some logic and at least fairness in this approach. Nevertheless the House of Lords rejected his approach.

CASE EXAMPLE

Liverpool City Council v Irwin [1976] 2 WLR 562; [1977] AC 239

Here, the council leased flats in a 15-floor tower block. There was no proper tenancy agreement though there was a list of tenants' obligations that were signed by the tenants. There were no express undertakings in the agreement on the part of the landlord. The council failed to maintain the common areas such as the stairs, lifts, corridors and rubbish chutes. These became badly vandalised over time, with no lighting and the lifts and rubbish chutes not working. The claimants were tenants who withheld the rent in protest. The council sued for repossession. The claimants counter-claimed and argued a breach of an implied term that the council should maintain the common areas. In the Court of Appeal Lord Denning felt that such a term could be implied because it was reasonable in the circumstances. The House of Lords, though, rejected this approach. In the event the House of Lords were not prepared to accept that the council had an absolute obligation to maintain the common areas. They did, however, accept that there was an implied term to take reasonable care to maintain the common areas, which they did not feel had been breached here by the council.

JUDGMENT

Lord Wilberforce said that to follow Lord Denning's approach would be to 'extend a long, and undesirable, way beyond sound authority'.

Lord Cross stated that, 'it is not enough for the court to say that the suggested term is a reasonable one, the presence of which would make the contract a better or fairer one' and identified that the 'officious bystander' test is the appropriate method for a term to be implied into a contract.

Nevertheless, the courts have recently been prepared to introduce the concept of 'reasonableness' into contractual terms. They have done so in circumstances where the express terms give the party who includes them a discretion in relation to the express terms. They have identified that what is known as '*Wednesbury* reasonableness' (a concept in administrative law from the case of *Associated Provincial Picture Houses Ltd v Wednesbury Corporation* [1948] 1 KB 223) should be applied to imply a term that such discretion is not used for an improper purpose.

CASE EXAMPLE

Paragon Finance v Nash [2001] EWCA Civ 1466

Here, mortgage lenders loaned money on variable interest rates, thus giving them the discretion to raise or lower the rates. Two different couples fell into arrears and then tried to challenge the mortgage agreements on the basis that the lenders' interest rates were a great deal higher than the rates of other lenders. The Court of Appeal held that a term should be implied into such contracts that the rates should not be set arbitrarily or dishonestly or for any improper purpose. On this basis, the court held that this would prevent the defendant from exercising the discretion to set the rates 'unreasonably', according to the *Wednesbury* principle. In other words, the rate should not be set in a way that no other mortgage lender, acting in a reasonable way, would do. However, the court also held that the loan agreement was not excessive even though the lender chose not to follow the bank rate or other lenders, and neither was it unlawful under the Consumer Credit Act 1974 or under the Unfair Contract Terms Act 1977. The implied term was not breached in the circumstances.

The 'officious bystander' test is clearly a strict test and the case above recognises that the courts in general are not prepared to imply terms into a contract by fact lightly. Judges have continued to apply the test strictly and avoid implying terms particularly where it is obvious that one party would definitely not have agreed to the term even if it had been suggested before the contract was formed.

CASE EXAMPLE

Wilson v Best Travel Ltd [1993] 1 All ER 353

The contract was between a tour operator and a holidaymaker, the claimant. While on holiday in Greece the claimant fell through a glass door and suffered quite severe injuries as a result. The glass door, while complying with Greek safety standards, was very thin and did not comply with British standards. The claimant sued the tour operator on the basis that it had breached its duty under s 13 of the Supply of Goods and Services Act 1982 to carry out its service with care and skill. The claimant also argued that a term should be implied into the contract with the tour operator that the hotel and its facilities would be safe. The court was not prepared to accept that such a term could be implied. The 'officious bystander' test could not apply because if asked MacKinnon LJ's question, the tour operator would clearly not have been prepared to accept that such a term existed when it concerned a matter that was entirely beyond its control.

Besides this, there are occasions when the courts feel that the situation is too complex to be resolved so simply. In other words, the 'officious bystander' might have insufficient understanding to put the question and the parties might not be able to answer with a simple 'but of course'.

CASE EXAMPLE

Ashmore v Corporation of Lloyd's (No 2) [1992] 2 Lloyd's Rep 620

This involved 'names' of Lloyd's, the claimants in the case. Lloyd's is a very large insurance company and much of its business involves very high-value insurance such as that on ships. Inevitably, if there is a claim on such insurance this will involve enormous losses. The 'names' are a large number of people who agree to underwrite potential losses in return for a share of the insurance premiums and the loss is then distributed and will not fall on the company itself which might possibly put it out of business. Some major problems and claims of the time had caused the 'names' to suffer substantial losses. The claimants were arguing that they had been let down by Lloyd's not informing them early enough of matters that might affect them and that a term should be implied into the contract to that effect. The judge considered that the nature of the information necessary to avoid the losses and the circumstances in which this should be released to the 'names' would have produced far too complex a question that would need to be asked if the 'officious bystander' test were to be applied. Besides this, the judge felt that the likely response of Lloyd's if it had been asked the question in this way would have been instead to consult its solicitors.

Nevertheless, the test is still in operation and the courts are still willing to employ it. They will do so when a strict application of the test will produce an answer that the court is satisfied represents the presumed intention of the parties. More recent case law appears to show a return to a more relaxed attitude by the courts.

CASE EXAMPLE

Equitable Life Assurance Society v Hyman [2000] 3 All ER 961

The Assurance Society proposed to reduce bonuses to certain policyholders. This was in contrast to its previous policy and was therefore contrary to the expectations of those policyholders. The rules of the Society did in fact give its officers quite a broad discretion on the issue of determining bonuses. Nevertheless the House of Lords held, applying the 'officious bystander' test, that a term should be implied into the agreement that the Society could not exercise its discretion contrary to the legitimate expectation of the policyholders and that such a term was inserted out of necessity.

Of course, it is also impossible to ignore the role of policy in the process of implying terms. Whatever the presumed intention of the parties is found to be, judges may also show other concerns. Elisabeth Peden identifies that:

QUOTATION

'The technique of implying terms in law provides courts with potential to regulate to some extent the behaviour of parties contracting within a particular type of relationship, in situations where parties do not specify requisite performance details.' She also suggests that the factors taken into account when implying terms are 'all policy concerns that the courts appear quietly to balance in coming to a decision whether or not to imply a term'. And that they do so to 'create a contractual relationship of a fair and reasonable type'.

E Peden, 'Policy concerns behind the implication of terms in law' (2001) 117 LQR 459 at 473

More recently, in determining what courts should take into account when deciding whether to imply terms into contracts, it has been suggested that they should 'recognise that … the existence and scope of standardised implied terms raise questions of reasonableness, fairness and the balancing of competing policy considerations'. In *Crossley v Faithful & Gould Holdings Ltd* [2004] EWCA Civ 293; [2004] IRLR 377, it was questioned whether a term could be implied into a contract of employment that the employer had an implied obligation to take care of the economic wellbeing of his employee. The Court of Appeal held that such an implied term would be too broad and would place an unreasonable burden on employers and that there were no policy reasons for implying such a general obligation on employers.

6.3.3 Terms implied by common law

Terms implied by fact into the contract by the courts are justified on the basis that they represent the presumed but unexpressed intentions of the parties. The simple logic behind the rule is that had the parties thought of the particular term at the time of contracting, they would have naturally included it.

In contrast, where a term is being implied into a contract by process of **law**, it is being inserted into the contract irrespective of the wishes of the parties. The justification here is that the law, whether the courts or Parliament itself, wishes to regulate such agreements, quite obviously for policy reasons and usually as a means of protecting the weaker of the parties.

Most often such terms will be implied because of a statutory provision. However, the courts might also imply a term by law because the judges feel that it is the type of term that should naturally be incorporated into a contract of the particular type and is an area not covered or not yet covered by statute. Once the term has been implied, the case will then stand as a precedent for future cases involving the same type of agreement.

CASE EXAMPLE

Liverpool City Council v Irwin [1977] AC 239

Here, the House of Lords could not imply as a matter of fact a term that the landlord was responsible for the common areas because it failed the 'officious bystander' test on the grounds discussed above in section 6.3.2. However, the court did accept that there should be a general obligation on a landlord in tenancy agreements to take reasonable care to maintain the common areas. On this basis the court was prepared to imply such a term into the tenancy agreement itself.

6.3.4 Terms implied by statute

In the nineteenth century the law of contract was most commonly governed by the maxim *caveat emptor* (let the buyer beware). The law was very much concerned with the actual process of contracting and little attention was paid to the fact that in many circumstances one party to the contract was in a significantly inferior bargaining position to the other party. Early statutes aimed at some form of consumer protection, such as the Sale of Goods Act 1893, did attempt to redress this imbalance. In the latter half of the twentieth century there was a much greater awareness of the needs of consumers, employees and other classes of people in contractual relationships who could easily be identified as the weaker of the two parties. The old maxim has been found wanting and unacceptable and Parliament, through Acts, has often given greater protection to the party with the weaker bargaining strength in certain types of contracts by the process of inserting or implying terms into the contracts irrespective of the express intentions of the parties.

Such a process is common in Acts governing consumer contracts, such as the Sale of Goods Act 1979 (as amended by the Sale and Supply of Goods Act 1994) and the Supply of Goods and Services Act 1982. One further and significant statute is the Unfair Contract Terms Act 1977 which is considered in detail in Chapter 7.

The process is also prominent in employment contracts. This occurs not only in the case of fundamental employment protections in the Employment Rights Act 1996, it also occurs in various more specific Acts outlawing discrimination, such as the Sex Discrimination Act 1975, the Race Relations Act 1976 now covered by the Equality Act 2010. These Acts, then, give a wide variety of protections to employees by the process of implying terms into the contract of employment. As such, any contractual terms indicated in the statement of particulars required to be given to each employee by s 1 of the 1996 Act represent only a small part of the overall contract enforceable by the employee.

The importance of terms implied in this way is that they provide a statutory protection that can be constantly relied upon because they will usually apply regardless of what is said in the contract.

Below are some examples of terms implied into contracts through statute or by other means which offer particular protections to consumers.

Sale of Goods Act 1979

The Act contains a number of implied terms which provide a very clear example of the process and its benefits.

Section 12 – the implied condition as to title

In any sale of goods contracts, a term s 12 automatically implies a term that the person selling the goods can pass on good title to them. In other words, he has the right to sell the goods.

CASE EXAMPLE

Niblett Ltd v Confectioners' Materials Co Ltd [1921] 3 KB 387

A seller sold 3,000 tins of condensed milk that were on consignment from America. The tins were marked 'Nissly' which Nestlé argued was too close to its brand name and therefore an infringement of its trademark. The goods were impounded as a result. The buyers then removed the labels as they were required to do and sold the goods on for whatever price they could get. The buyers successfully sued the sellers under s 12. The sellers had been unable to sell the goods in their original state legitimately. The court held that they were in breach of the implied condition under s 12.

The 1979 Act is aimed at consumer protection. This particular implied term can obviously protect a buyer in those circumstances where the seller does not own the goods and the original owner wants their return.

CASE EXAMPLE

Rowland v Divall [1923] 2 KB 500

The claimant bought a car that turned out to be stolen. When the proper owner took the car back, the claimant was able to recover the full price of the car from the seller. The seller had no rights of ownership over the car and the court held that s 12 applied.

Section 13 – the implied condition as to description

This section includes an implied term that the goods sold in a sale of goods contract must correspond to any description applied to them by the seller. Judges have interpreted this term in a narrow sense (see the case of *Arcos Ltd v E A Ronaasen & Son* [1933] AC 470 at section 16.2.1). They have also applied the term in a broader sense. In the latter sense, the term might even apply to things as apparently ancillary to the goods themselves as the packaging in which they are delivered.

CASE EXAMPLE

Re Moore & Co and Landauer & Co's Arbitration [1921] 2 KB 519

Two parties contracted for the sale and purchase of a consignment of tinned fruit. In the contract this was described as being in cartons of 30 tins. When, on delivery, half of the cartons were of 24 tins, there was a breach of s 13 even though the actual quantity of tins ordered was correct and despite the fact that the buyer intended to sell them and so would have been unaffected by the breach. The court, taking a narrow view, considered that the goods were not as they were described in the contract and the seller was liable.

Section 14(2) – the implied condition that the goods are of satisfactory quality

Unlike s 12 and s 13, this implied term, both s 14(2) and s 14(3), applies only where the goods are sold in the course of a business. Therefore the term cannot be implied in a contract involving a private sale. Nevertheless this statutory provision is one of the most powerful of the mechanisms of consumer protection.

The traditional requirement under the 1979 Act was that goods should be of 'merchantable' quality rather than of 'satisfactory' quality. 'Merchantability' was a legal term with a fairly narrow meaning, and which was not easily understood. 'Merchantable' was defined in s 14(6) as being fit for the purposes for which goods of the kind were commonly supplied. As a consequence of this, many parties could be left without a remedy.

CASE EXAMPLE

Bartlett v Sidney Marcus Ltd [1965] 1 WLR 1013

In this case a car was bought with a defective clutch. The sellers offered either to repair the clutch or to reduce the price by £25. The buyer initially accepted the price reduction but very soon had to replace the clutch at an extra cost of £45. Lord Denning nevertheless rejected the buyer's claim that because the defect was more costly this meant that the car was not merchantable and that he should be able to repudiate the contract. The goods were fit for their normal purposes and the buyer did not have the right to reject the goods.

In a similar fashion, the courts would accept that goods were of merchantable quality if they were fit for some of their usual purposes even though they were not necessarily fit for all of their purposes.

CASE EXAMPLE

Kendall (Henry) & Sons v William Lillico & Sons Ltd [1969] 2 AC 31

This involved a contract for the sale and purchase of groundnut extract that is normally used in cattle food. The buyer bred game birds and intended to feed it to the birds. The groundnut contained a toxin that actually killed many of the birds. The buyer sued. The court held that there could be no successful claim under s 14(2) since the goods were merchantable. They were fit for their normal purposes.

Nevertheless at times the courts were prepared to accept that even blemishes might amount to a breach of s 14(2). However, this would generally be the case because the goods had been described as 'luxury' goods or 'deluxe model' or something similar.

CASE EXAMPLE

Rogers v Parish (Scarborough) Ltd [1987] 2 All ER 232

Here, the contract was for the sale and purchase of a brand new Range Rover. The fact that the car misfired, had an oil leak, and there were scratches on the paintwork was enough to convince the court that the car was not of merchantable quality.

So, the higher the expectation of quality attached to the goods, the more likely it is that defects would allow the buyer to sue under s 14(2) if they fail to match up to the standards that might be expected of them.

CASE EXAMPLE

Shine v General Guarantee Corporation [1988] 1 All ER 911

Here, the claimant bought a second-hand sports car, a Fiat X-19. The car had actually been submerged in water for some time before the purchase, as a result of which the manufacturer's anti-corrosion guarantee had become invalid. The purchaser sued and succeeded in proving that the goods were unmerchantable because the court accepted that he was intent on buying an enthusiast's car and one from which he would have great expectations of quality.

In any case it is certainly true that considerations of safety would be taken into account when assessing standards of merchantability. The court would generally be prepared to take into account the consequences of any defects in relation to such considerations.

CASE EXAMPLE

Bernstein v Pamsons Motors (Golders Green) Ltd [1987] 2 All ER 220

Here, a new car was purchased under the contract. After it had only done 140 miles the engine seized because a drop of sealant was blocking the lubrication system. The sellers offered to repair the car free of charge but the buyer refused to take the car back. The court accepted that there was a breach of s 14(2) because of the possible later consequences of the defect and the dangers that it might cause.

The Sale and Supply of Goods Act 1994 amended s 14(2) of the 1979 Act, replacing the word 'merchantable' with the word 'satisfactory', a concept that was intended to be easily understood by consumers generally. 'Satisfactory' is explained in a new s 14(2A):

SECTION

'goods are of satisfactory quality if they meet the standard that a reasonable person would regard as satisfactory, taking account of any description of the goods, the price (if relevant) and all other relevant circumstances.'

The 1994 Act also inserted a new s 14(2b) explaining what factors can be taken into account in deciding whether or not the goods are of satisfactory quality. The definition would include:

SECTION

(a) fitness for all purposes for which goods of the kind in question are commonly supplied
(b) appearance and finish
(c) freedom from minor defects
(d) safety and
(e) durability

The new provisions should obviously make it much easier for consumers to bring claims in respect of defective goods.

Section 14(3) – the implied condition that the goods are fit for their purpose

Section 14(3) implies into sale of goods contracts a condition that the goods should be fit for the purposes for which they are required. The provision will apply where the buyer:

SECTION

'either expressly or impliedly makes known to the seller any particular purpose for which goods are being bought regardless of whether or not that is a purpose for which goods of that kind are commonly supplied.'

So the provision applies mainly where the buyer is relying on the skill and judgement of the seller in buying the goods and has expressed a particular purpose for which the goods are required. If the seller freely agrees to sell for that purpose then there is a clear breach if the goods are inadequate for the purpose.

CASE EXAMPLE

Baldry v Marshall [1925] 1 KB 260

Here, the buyer claimed that a Bugatti car was not fit for its purpose. He had asked the seller to supply him with a fast, flexible and easily managed car that would be comfortable and suitable for ordinary touring purposes. The Bugatti that he was sold did not conform to the requirements that he had set under the contract. The court accepted that he had stated his purpose and was entitled to rely on the skill and judgement of the seller. The seller had breached s 14(3) by failing to supply goods fit for the purpose actually described to him in the contract.

It may also apply, however, in respect of purposes that are implicit in the contract rather than actually stated. In other words, the courts will accept that some purposes should be obvious to the seller.

CASE EXAMPLE

Grant v Australian Knitting Mills Ltd [1936] AC 85

Here, the claimant purchased woollen underpants. The garments actually contained traces of chemicals which then caused the claimant to contract a painful skin disease. The court accepted that underpants have an obvious purpose and that the buyer would have impliedly made known the purpose for which he was buying the underpants even if he had not actually stated it to the seller. There was a clear breach of the implied term.

Section 15 – the implied condition that goods sold by sample should correspond with the sample

This provision is particularly appropriate when a seller is being sued by a customer for defective goods. If the seller is able to argue that the defect was not apparent in the sample on which he based the decision to buy the bulk for resale, then the seller is also able to use s 15 to claim against the original supplier.

CASE EXAMPLE

Godley v Perry [1960] 1 WLR 9, QBD

A boy was injured in the eye when the elastic snapped on a catapult that he had bought from a retailer. The retailer had taken on supplies of the toy after seeing a sample. The seller had tested the sample and was able to show that the bulk of the goods, and of course the catapult in question, did not match the quality of the sample and therefore the manufacturer was in breach.

Supply of Goods and Services Act 1982

Similar implied terms to those in the Sale of Goods Act 1979 are contained in the Supply of Goods and Services Act 1982. The 1982 Act obviously offers consumer protection in the case of the provision of services rather than for merely the sale of goods.

Since the 1982 Act covers situations where goods as well as services are provided, certain of the terms mirror those in the Sale of Goods Act 1979. These include an implied condition as to title (s 2); description (s 3); an implied condition of satisfactory quality and fitness for the purpose (s 4); and an implied condition in respect of sale by sample (s 5).

However, there are also three further significant implied terms that are of particular relevance to the supply of services.

Section 13 – in a contract for the supply of a service where the supplier is acting in the course of a business there is an implied term that the supplier will carry out the service with reasonable care and skill

So, a person paying for a service is entitled to expect that the person providing it is competent to undertake the work and will behave professionally. The work should be done with appropriate care and skill or there will be a breach of the implied term.

CASE EXAMPLE

Lawson v Supasink Ltd (1984) 3 TRL 37

Here, the defendant was contracted to design, supply and install a fitted kitchen for £1,200. Plans were drawn up but the defendant failed to follow them properly. The claimants then sued under s 13 and were able to recover their money. The court held that, since the work was shoddy, the defendant was not entitled to payment less the price of repairing defects.

Section 14 – here the time for the service to be carried out is not fixed, there is an implied term that the supplier will carry out the service within a reasonable time

Inevitably, in many contracts only an estimate can be given as to how long it will take to complete the service and therefore also what the eventual bill may be. Clearly, the provider of the service must have some leeway. Nevertheless the buyer is entitled to work carried out in a reasonable time or there will be a breach of s 14. It would be contrary to common sense to allow the provider of a service an unlimited time to carry out the contract.

CASE EXAMPLE

Charnock v Liverpool Corporation [1968] 1 WLR 1498

The defendant took eight weeks to repair a car when it was demonstrated to the court's satisfaction that a competent repair should have taken no more than five weeks. The defendant was held to be in breach of the implied term.

Section 15 – where the consideration for the service is not determined, there is an implied term that the party contracting with the supplier will pay a reasonable charge

Contract law, as we have already seen, does not tend to interfere with the actual bargain made by the parties. The parties are free to make their own bargain and if one party is prepared to pay an excessive price for goods or services then the courts accept this as the bargain. Nevertheless, if the specific price has not been set at the time of contracting then the purchaser would naturally be entitled to expect that the actual price was a reasonable figure. If the provider wants a price that is unreasonable then this should be indicated at the time of contracting, allowing the purchaser to consider the price and contract elsewhere if necessary.

Consumer Protection (Distance Selling) Regulations 2000

EU law has also been very important in developing consumer rights. The Unfair Terms in Consumer Contracts Regulations 1999, implementing EU Directive 93/13 (the Unfair Terms in Consumer Contracts Directive) are a classic example of this (see section 7.3.3).

As we have already seen in relation to offer and acceptance, the Directive, and therefore the Regulations introduced by statutory instrument, were a means of ensuring both clarity and protection of consumers in a whole range of modern methods of trading including telephone, fax, internet shopping, mail order, e-mail and television shopping (see section 2.3.3). Inevitably, because of the potentially international scope of these new means of contracting, one of the key purposes of the Directive was the harmonisation of rules within the member states of the European Union.

The Regulations also operate by including a number of implied terms in contracts entered into by such means, with which terms the seller will be expected to comply in order for that transaction to be binding. Implied terms stemming from the Regulations also offer the consumer other significant protections.

By reg 7, the seller must provide the consumer with a list of detailed information before the contract can be valid. These include:

- the identity of the supplier
- the description, price and delivery costs of the goods or services, including the arrangements for payment, delivery and performance
- the minimum period of the contract, for example in something like mobile phone rental
- the length of time the offer will remain open.

Significantly, reg 10 also offers the protection that the consumer must be informed of his right to cancel the contract within seven days. Regulation 7(4) also requires that in telephone communications the seller must make his identity and the purpose of the call known to the consumer at the start of the phone call.

Regulation 8 adds the requirement that the seller must present confirmation of all of this information also in writing, or by e-mail or fax.

There are more complex rules regarding cancellation in reg 11 for sale of goods contracts and reg 12 in the case of supply of goods and services contracts. Regulation 14 requires that where the consumer does cancel the contract his money must be returned within a maximum of 30 days from the date of cancellation.

The Regulations are also enforced by Trading Standards Departments through the means of criminal sanctions and are under the general control of the Director General of Fair Trading.

ACTIVITY

Self-assessment questions

1. What is the difference between an express term and an implied term?
2. In what ways are terms implied into a contract?
3. What is the difference between a term implied by fact and a term implied by law?
4. What difficulties exist in the application of the 'officious bystander' test?
5. For what reasons has Parliament chosen to imply terms into contracts through Acts of Parliament?

KEY FACTS

Implication of terms – three ways:			
By fact – because of the presumed intention of the parties			
By common law – because courts feel that such terms should always be present (*Liverpool City Council v Irwin*)			
By statute, eg, for consumer protection			
Terms implied by fact	**Case/statute**	**Statutory implied terms**	**Case/statute**
Custom or common	*Hutton v Warren*	goods should correspond with description	s 13 Sale of Goods Act 1979
Professional custom	*Walford's case*	and be of satisfactory quality	s 14(2) SGA
Business efficacy	*The Moorcock*	and fit for stated purposes	s 14(3) SGA
Past conduct of parties	*Hillas v Arcos*	if sold by sample, goods delivered must correspond to sample	s 15 SGA
All subject to 'officious bystander' test – if officious bystander had asked the parties about a term that was missing, would they have replied that it was obviously included.	*Shirlaw v Southern Foundrie*	services should be carried out with reasonable care and skill	s 13 Supply of Goods and Services Act 1982
		and be completed within a reasonable time	s 14 SGSA
		and if price not stated then must charge a reasonable price.	s 15 SGSA

6.4 The relative significance of terms

6.4.1 Introduction

We have already considered that where representations are made prior to the formation of the contract, some are inevitably considered to be more important than others (see section 6.1.2). As a result, some are incorporated in the contract and others are not.

In exactly the same way, the terms of a contract will have different weighting and are of differing significance to the contract. Some are of absolutely critical importance and without them the contract simply could not be completed. On the other hand, some terms will be descriptive or ancillary to the main purposes of the contract and are therefore seen as of lesser importance. This is because, even if they are breached, this will not mean that the contract cannot be carried out, even though the breach should still be compensated.

If terms are of different significance then the consequences of any breach of those terms will also vary in their significance and there are, of necessity, then, different remedies available to the parties, depending on the term that is breached.

The courts, then, have traditionally dealt with the issue by classifying terms into different categories. Broadly speaking, the courts have always distinguished between terms and determined their classification in two distinct ways:

- Firstly, the term can be categorised according to its importance to the completion of the contract.
- Secondly, the term can be categorised according to the remedies available to a party who is a victim of a breach of the term – a failure to honour the obligation.

As a result of these classifications the courts have determined that there are two separate types of term:

- conditions – those that are critical to the central purposes of the contract
- warranties – all other terms.

6.4.2 Conditions

Until fairly recently, judges recognised only two classes of term. The most important of these was the condition, which can be considered in two ways.

Firstly, a condition is a term of a contract which is so important to the contract that a failure to perform the condition would render the contract meaningless and destroy the whole purpose of the contract. As a result, anything that is accepted as being a condition is said to 'go to the root of' a contract.

Secondly, as a result of the significance of the term to the contract, the court allows the claimant who has suffered a breach of the term the fullest range of remedies available. When a condition is unfulfilled the claimant will not only be able to sue for damages but will also be entitled lawfully to repudiate his own obligations under the contract, or indeed do both. Repudiation used in this way, as a remedy, is the right of the victim of the breach to consider the contract ended as a result of the other party's breach of contract. This may be particularly appropriate as it may mean that the claimant can contract with an alternative party and treat himself as relieved of his obligations under the contract, without fear of the defendant successfully alleging a breach by the claimant instead.

CASE EXAMPLE

Poussard v Spiers and Pond (1876) 1 QBD 410

Here, an actress was contracted to appear in the lead role in an operetta for a season. The actress, who was taken ill, was unable to attend for the early performances, by which time the producers had given her role to the understudy. The actress sued for breach of contract but lost. The court held that she had in fact breached the contract by turning up after the first night. As the lead singer, her presence was crucial to the production and so was a condition entitling the producers to repudiate and terminate her contract for her non-attendance at the early performances.

6.4.3 Warranties

Warranties are regarded as minor terms of the contract or those where in general the contract might still continue despite their breach. Almost by default, then, a warranty is any other term in a contract and specifically one that does not go to the root of the contract.

Warranties are a residual category of terms dealing with obligations that are either ancillary or secondary to the major purpose of the contract.

As a result, the remedy for a breach of warranty is merely an action for damages. There is no right to repudiate for a breach of a warranty. If the party who is the victim of the breach of a warranty tries to repudiate his obligations then this itself is an unlawful and actionable repudiation.

CASE EXAMPLE

Bettini v Gye (1876) 1 QBD 183

This case involved fairly similar circumstances to the last. A singer was contracted to appear at a variety of theatres for a season of concerts. His contract included a term that he should attend rehearsals for six days prior to the beginning of the actual performances. In the event, he was absent for the first three days of rehearsals and on his return his role had been replaced. When the singer sued, the producers' claim that the obligation to attend rehearsals was a condition failed. The court held that the requirement was only ancillary to the main purpose of the contract which was appearing in the actual production. In consequence, the court held that the breach only entitled the producers to sue for damages and not to end the contract and replace the singer as they had done.

Thus, it can be seen that the way in which the terms are classified is critical in determining the outcome of the contract and the remedies available to the parties where there is a breach of the terms.

6.4.4 Innominate terms

innominate term

A term the remedy for breach of which depends on the consequences of the breach rather than on any prior classification

The problem of determining which category a term fits usually happens when the parties have been silent on the subject or where the contract is oral. The effect of the classification is to identify what the term was at the time of the formation of the contract, and therefore all later consequences depend on that classification.

During the latter half of the twentieth century the courts developed an approach by which they would describe terms as 'innominate'. This means that they do not give the term any specific classification but, in determining the outcome of a breach of the term, they will consider the consequence of the breach rather than how it is classified in deciding on what remedy should be awarded in the circumstances.

The central purpose of distinguishing between different classes of term is ultimately to determine what remedies are available to the victim of the breach of the term. The modern concept of the innominate term has developed out of a desire by judges that the right to repudiate a contract should only be available in the event of a breach when to grant such a remedy is fair to both sides.

The more traditional and rather simplistic process of classifying all terms as either conditions or warranties could lead to a number of problems of construction. Use of the innominate term as an alternative method of deciding the appropriate remedy in the event of a breach of a term was first considered in:

CASE EXAMPLE

Hong Kong Fir Shipping Co Ltd v Kawasaki Kisen Kaisha Ltd
(The Hong Kong Fir Case) [1962] 2 QB 26

The defendants chartered a ship from the claimants under a two-year charterparty. A term in the contract required that the ship should be 'in every way fitted for ordinary cargo service'. In fact, the ship broke down as a result of the incompetence of the engine room staff, and in any case was in a generally poor state of repair and not seaworthy, a fact admitted by the claimants. As a result, 18 weeks' use of the ship was lost by the defendants and they claimed to treat the contract as repudiated and at an end. The claimants sued, claiming that the term was only a warranty, only entitling the defendants to sue for damages. The Court of Appeal agreed. There were, however, some interesting points made in the judgments.

JUDGMENT

Lord Diplock felt that not all contracts could be simply divided into terms that are conditions and terms that are warranties, and that many contracts are of a more complex character. He considered that 'all that can be predicted is that some breaches will, and others will not, give rise to an event which will deprive the party not in default of substantially the whole benefit which it was intended that he should obtain from contract; and the legal consequences ... unless expressly provided for in the contract, depend on the nature of the event to which the breach gives rise and do not follow automatically from a prior classification ... as a "condition" or a "warranty".'

The process seems simple enough. The appropriate remedy is only determined after the consequences of the breach have first been identified. Only a breach of a term that was sufficiently serious would enable the contract to be repudiated by the victim of the breach. The innominate term in this way could be particularly useful in contracts such as charters where the results of the breach can vary all the way from rendering the contract impossible to relatively trivial effects.

Nevertheless, the clear difficulty with identifying terms as innominate is that it can leave the contractual relationship in a state of uncertainty. Nobody can be really sure what the outcome of a particular situation will be until the term has been breached and the judge in the case has construed the term and declared what remedy is appropriate. The doctrine suggested in the *Hong Kong Fir* case [1962] 2 QB 26 has, however, been accepted and applied in subsequent cases.

CASE EXAMPLE

Cehave NV v Bremer Handelsgesselschaft mbH (The Hansa Nord)
[1976] QB 44

A cargo of citrus pulp pellets to be used as cattle feed was rejected by the buyers because part of the consignment had suffered overheating and did not then conform to the term 'Shipment to be made in good condition'. As the sellers would not refund the price already paid, the buyers applied to the Rotterdam court which ordered its sale. Another party then bought the cargo and sold it on to the original buyers at a much lower price than they had paid the original sellers. The cargo was then used for its original purpose: cattle feed. The buyers argued that the goods were not merchantable within the meaning of the Sale of Goods Act 1893. Implied terms in the Sale of Goods Act are stated as being conditions, as we have already seen, and a breach would therefore justify repudiation. The action was at first successful. The Court of Appeal, however, applied the *Hong Kong Fir* approach, and accepted that, since the goods had been used for their original purpose, there was not a breach of the contract serious enough to justify repudiation. Only an action for damages was appropriate in the circumstances.

The use of the innominate term is particularly appropriate where there is unequal bargaining strength between the parties or where breaches of the contract are merely technical rather than material to the central purpose of the contract, and where therefore the traditional methods of classification would lead to an injustice.

CASE EXAMPLE

Reardon Smith Line Ltd v Hansen-Tangen [1976] 1 WLR 989

In a contract for the charter of a tanker the ship was described as 'Osaka 354', a reference to the shipyard at which the tanker would be built. In fact, because the shipyard had too many orders, the work was sub-contracted to another yard and the tanker became known as 'Oshima 004'. When the need for tankers lessened, the buyers tried to get out of the contract by claiming a breach of a condition that the tanker should correspond with the full description applied to in the documentation. The court held that since the breach was entirely technical and had no bearing on the outcome of the contract it could not justify repudiation.

However, the court may still classify a term as a condition, regardless of what the possible consequences of a breach might be, where it feels that the circumstances or the context in which the breach occurs demand it.

CASE EXAMPLE

Bunge Corporation v Tradax Export SA [1981] 1 WLR 711

In a contract for the sale of soya bean meal the buyers were required to give at least 15 days' notice of readiness to load the vessel. In the event, they gave only 13 days' notice. This would not necessarily prevent the sellers from completing their obligations. The first instance court held that since the consequences of the breach were minor it would not justify repudiation. The House of Lords, however, held that, since the sellers' obligation to ship was certainly a condition, the obligation to give notice to load in proper time should also be a condition, without regard to the consequences of the breach. Lord Wilberforce felt that stipulations as to time in mercantile contracts should usually be viewed as conditions.

6.5 The construction of terms

The remedies available to a party who has suffered a contractual breach depend on the classification given to the term that has been breached. The parties to a contract do not always think to outline prior to the contract the precise nature of the terms that they are incorporating into the contract or the precise remedies that they are contemplating will be available in the event of a breach. Where the parties are silent on the classification of terms or the classifications are vague, it will be for judges to construe what the terms are and their contractual significance.

Judges use a number of guiding principles:

- Where terms are implied into the contract by law then judges will apply the classification given to the terms in the statute; for example the implied terms in the Sale of Goods Act that we have already looked at are stated as conditions.
- Where the terms are implied by fact, the judges will construe them according to the presumed intention of the parties.
- Where the terms have been expressed by the parties who have identified how the terms are to be classified or what remedies attach to them, then the judges will generally try to give effect to the express wishes of the parties. To do otherwise would be to go against the idea of freedom of contract.
- Where the terms are expressed by the parties but the parties have failed to identify what type of term they are or what the appropriate remedy will be in the event of a breach, then the judges will construe those terms according to what they believe is the true intention of the parties. This in itself leads to problems and a number of different approaches by the courts.

It almost goes without saying that it is very advantageous if a term is a condition, since a greater range of remedies is available to the victim of the breach. The obvious consequence of this is that clever and unscrupulous parties to a contract will try to classify all of the terms of the contract as conditions. In view of the complexities of modern contracting, and particularly the use of the standard form contract, there may well be occasions when the judges feel that it is impossible to follow the express classification of the terms given by the parties. In any case, in fact, it will not usually be the classification chosen by both parties but rather by one party in standard forms. In this way, even though a term is stated as being a condition it may be construed in fact as a warranty by the court.

CASE EXAMPLE

Schuler (L) AG v Wickman Machine Tool Sales Ltd [1974] AC 235

In an agency contract, Wickman's were appointed sole distributors of Schuler's presses. It was stated as a condition of the contract that Wickman's representatives would make weekly visits to six large UK motor manufacturers to solicit orders for presses. A further term stated that the contract could be terminated for a breach of any condition in the contract that was not remedied within 60 days. The contract was to last more than four years, amounting to more than 1,400 visits. When, some way into the contract, Wickman's representatives failed to make a visit, Schuler sought to terminate the contract. In the House of Lords, Lord Reid felt that it was inevitable that during the length of the contract there would be occasions when maintaining weekly visits would be impossible. He also felt that the effect of accepting the term as a condition would be to entitle Schuler to terminate the contract even if there was only one failure to visit out of the 1,400. This would be an unreasonable burden on Wickman's and so the term could not stand as a condition.

In construing terms, judges may of course be aided in their construction by the guidance given in statutory definitions, and referring to the market in which the particular contract operates may also assist them.

CASE EXAMPLE

Maredelanto Cia Naviera SA v Bergbau-Handel GmbH (The Mihalis Angelos)
[1970] 3 All ER 125

A charterparty repudiated its contract with the ship-owners when the contract contained an 'expected readiness to load' clause and it was clear that the vessel would not be ready to load on time. There was a clear breach of a term but the court had to decide of which type in order to determine whether or not the repudiation was lawful. The House of Lords, using guidance from statutory terms as well as from the commercial character of the contract, decided that the term was in fact a condition and that the breach therefore justified the repudiation. The judges held that in commercial contracts predictability and certainty of relations must be the ultimate test of the significance of the term to the performance of the contract.

The result is that while in general a contract drafted by a lawyer should usually conform to the classification of terms given, nevertheless the courts may seek to preserve certainty in commercial contracts whatever the apparent intent of the parties.

CASE EXAMPLE

Harlingdon & Leinster Enterprises Ltd v Christopher Hull Fine Art Ltd
[1990] 3 WLR 13

Here, the defendants, who were art dealers, sold a painting, representing it as a Munter (a famous German expressionist painter). The sellers declared at the time of the contract that they had no expertise on such paintings whereas the buyers in fact did have. It was later discovered that the painting was a forgery. The buyers then tried to claim a breach of description by the sellers. The Court of Appeal held that the sale was not in fact a sale by description and therefore the buyers were not entitled to repudiate. There had been no reliance by the buyers on the description. On the contrary, they had relied on their own superior judgement in entering the contract.

Even the principles above have been subject to further modification or clarification by the judges. Lord Hoffmann, in *Investors Compensation Scheme Ltd v West Bromwich Building Society* [1998] 1 All ER 98, reconsidered the systems of construction of terms employed by judges and identified a number of principles that judges should take into account when construing terms:

- The process of construction should aim at a result that would be reached by a reasonable person having the benefit of the information available to the parties at the time the contract was formed.
- That such information might include absolutely anything that might affect the judgement of the reasonable person in construing the term.
- That any prior negotiations or expressions of subjective intent should only be used in an action for rectification of the document containing the term.
- That the meaning that might be conveyed to a reasonable person need not be the same as the words themselves since it would be possible for the reasonable man to conclude that, in context, the parties had actually chosen the wrong words.
- That it is possible to conclude from the context in which the agreement was reached that the parties had chosen the wrong words, otherwise the court might be attributing to the parties an intention which they plainly could not have had.

The overriding point is that the courts should be seeking to represent the actual intention of the parties when forming the contract.

JUDGMENT

The process has been described very effectively by Lord Steyn in *Sirius International Insurance Co (Publ) v FAI General Insurance Ltd* [2005] 1 All ER 191: 'The inquiry is objective: the question is what a reasonable person [in the circumstances of] the parties … would have understood the parties to have meant by the use of specific language. The answer to that question is to be gathered from the text under consideration and its relevant contextual scene.'

CASE EXAMPLE

Egan v Static Control Components (Europe) Ltd [2004] EWCA Civ 392

Egan was a director of a company which was supplied with components by the claimant. Before 1999 Egan signed three guarantees making him personally liable to the claimant for the company's debts up to a figure of £75,000. In 1999 the company owed the claimant £143,000, £68,000 of which was overdue. The claimant then asked Egan to repay in six weekly instalments and Egan then signed a new agreement guaranteeing the company's debts up to £150,000. The guarantee was in exactly the same form as the previous guarantees, and included the words 'goods you may supply'. In 2000 the company went into receivership owing the claimant £111,000. The claimant sought to recover the debt from Egan who counterclaimed that the 1999 guarantee applied only to goods supplied after it was signed. The Court of Appeal, applying the test from *Investors Compensation Scheme Ltd v West Bromwich Building Society*, held that a reasonable person would assume that the guarantee applied to both existing and future debts.

All of the above demonstrates that the process of construing terms is not an easy one and is one that is subject to broad judicial interpretation.

It is also possible that in seeking to represent what an ordinary person would objectively see as the true intentions of the parties the court might ignore what would amount to a literal interpretation of the words used and consider instead the context and background if it feels that something has gone wrong with the linguistic expression of the intention of the parties in the formal agreement.

CASE EXAMPLE

Chartbrook Ltd v Persimmon Homes Ltd [2009] UKHL 38

Chartbrook entered into an agreement with Persimmon Homes under which Persimmon would obtain planning permission, build houses on land owned by Chartbrook and sell them. Included in the price that Persimmon was bound to pay to Chartbrook for doing so was something called an 'Additional Residence Payment' which was based on a percentage of the price that it received for each property sold according to a formula set out in the contract. Eventually a dispute arose concerning the amount owed by Persimmon and this depended on construction of the words explaining the Additional Residence Payment in the written contract. Chartbrook felt that it owed £4,484,862 while Persimmon felt that it in fact only owed Chartbrook £897,051. Both the High Court and the Court of Appeal, applying a literal interpretation of the words in the agreement held that Chartbrook's view of the amount that it was owed was correct. Lord Justice Lawrence Collins dissented holding that an interpretation of the wording of the agreement based on the commercial background and 'business common sense' should be preferred to a pure literal interpretation of the agreement. Persimmon appealed to the House of Lords. Lord Hoffman, giving the leading judgment, agreed with this dissenting judgment. While he felt that it would require a strong case to persuade the court that something had gone wrong with the language used by the parties in the agreement so that it did not in fact represent their true intentions that this was such a case. The House held that the correction of such mistakes by construction of the contract was not separate branch of law but an essential part of the task of construction and also that where there was a clear mistake in the written expression of the agreement that the court should not read the agreement in isolation but should consider it in the context of the commercial background.

Type of term	Conditions	Warranties	Innominate terms
When identified	At the time that the contract was formed	At the time that the contract was formed	Following breach of the term
How identified	Can be identified: • When expressed by the parties – providing type of term conforms to character of a condition • If silent on type then judges will construe the intent of the parties • If implied usually construed according to how they are described	Can be identified: • When expressed by the parties – providing type of term conforms to character of a condition • If silent on type then judges will construe the intent of the parties • If implied usually construed according to how they are described	Can be identified: • By analysing the effect of the breach
Character of term	Goes to the root of the contract – breach of a condition renders proper performance of the contract impossible	A minor term – usually descriptive – performance of the contract is still possible	Depends on the effect of the breach: • If the breach renders proper performance impossible it acts like a condition • If breach has only minor effects, eg a technical breach, then acts as a warranty
Available remedy	Can repudiate obligations under the contract instead of or as well as suing for damage resulting from the breach	Can only sue for damages caused by the breach of the term	Depends on effect of breach: • If breach renders proper performance of the contract impossible then can repudiate and/or sue for damages • If effects of breach are only minor then can only sue for damages caused by breach of the term

Figure 6.2 Diagram illustrating the relative effects of terms

SUMMARY

- Terms are the obligations under a contract.
- Terms must be incorporated into the contract.
- In written contracts the terms are in written form but if the contract is oral, judges may consider different factors to determine whether the terms are incorporated, eg whether the term was sufficiently drawn to the other party's attention before the contract was formed.
- Although a party is generally bound by anything that he has signed, whether he has read it or not.
- Terms can also be implied into a contract in three ways: by fact – because of the presumed intention of the parties; by law – because the courts feel that such terms should always be present; and by statute – usually for consumer protection.
- There are different types of term – and which category a term falls into and which remedy is available are determined by how important it is to the contract.
- A condition is a term which 'goes to the root of the contract' – breach of a condition would render the contract meaningless, so that the party who is the victim of the breach can repudiate his obligations under the contract as well as or instead of suing for damages – but a warranty is a minor term with only damages available for breach.
- Judges sometimes also view terms as innominate: ie, the appropriate remedy is judged from the seriousness of the breach.
- If the parties are silent on what type the term is judges will construe it from the surrounding circumstances – while judges try to give effect to the express intentions of the parties, remedies for breach of a term will only be awarded if the term stated to be a condition operates like a condition.

SAMPLE ESSAY QUESTION

Discuss the extent to which it can be argued that the development of the innominate term in contracts merely adds to uncertainty.

Explain the traditional classification of terms in contracts:

- Traditionally two types of term – differing in character and the available remedy
- A condition goes to the root of the contract – so breach of a condition means the contract cannot be performed and the victim of the breach can repudiate and/or sue for damages
- A warranty is a minor term with only damages available for breach

Explain innominate terms:

- The nature of the terms is determined after the breach rather than looking at the term itself
- The appropriate remedy is judged from the seriousness of the breach

Discuss whether the traditional classification of terms leads to certainty:

- Breach of a condition gives a wider range of remedies to the party subject to the breach
- Breach of a warranty gives rise to only an action for damages
- So the descriptions and outcomes are fairly certain, allowing parties to plan in advance
- Consider though that parties do not always state in the contract whether the term is a condition or a warranty – which could lead to uncertainty

Discuss how judges construe terms:

- Where terms are implied by law, judges give the classification given in the statute
- If they are implied by fact, judges construe them according to the presumed intention of the parties
- With express terms, where the classification is identified, judges try to give effect to the express wishes of the parties
- If the parties have not identified the type of term, judges construe those terms according to what they believe is the true intention of the parties
- Judges will not enforce a term stated to be a condition unless it does go to the root of the contract
- So there is still some uncertainty with the two traditional classes

Consider whether the innominate term leads to greater uncertainty:

- Judges determine remedy from the seriousness of the breach
- Can be really useful for breaches which are purely technical in character
- But parties cannot guarantee outcome in advance – so there is uncertainty
- This may be a real problem in, for example, contracts where time is of the essence or where a party needs to repudiate

ACTIVITY

Self-assessment questions

1. What are the major differences between a 'condition' and a 'warranty'?
2. In what circumstances will the court ignore the classification given to a term by the parties themselves?
3. In what ways does a term classed as innominate differ from terms classified normally as conditions or warranties?
4. What are the advantages and disadvantages of defining terms as innominate?

KEY FACTS

Classification of terms	Case/statute
There are different types of terms – determined by how important they are to the contract – and type may determine available remedy.	
A condition is a term which 'goes to the root of' the contract – breach would render the contract meaningless, so the party who is the victim of the breach can repudiate and/or sue for damages.	*Poussard v Spiers*
A warranty is any other term – only damages are available.	*Bettini v Gye*
Judges sometimes also view terms as innominate: ie, the appropriate remedy is judged from the seriousness of the breach.	*The Hong Kong Fir Shipping case*
Remedies for breach will be awarded only if the condition operates like a condition. Where parties are silent on what type the term is, judges must construe it from the surrounding circumstances – while judges try to give effect to the express intentions of the parties.	*Schuler v Wickman Machine Tool Sales*
This can prevent the wrong remedy being given for breaches which are purely technical in character.	*Reardon Smith Line v Hansen Tangen*
Even statutory terms are sometimes judged according to the consequences of the breach.	*Cehave NV v Bremer Handelsgesselschaft MbH (The Hansa Nord)*

Further reading

Denning, Lord, *The Discipline of Law* (Butterworths, 1979), Part 1, Chapter 4.
Law Commission, *Law of Contract: The Parole Evidence Rule*, Report No 154, Cm 9700 (1986).
Peden, E, 'Policy concerns behind the implications of terms in law' (2001) 117 LQR 459.

7

The obligations under a contract: Exclusion and limitation clauses

AIMS AND OBJECTIVES

After reading this chapter you should be able to:

▨ Define exclusion and limitation clauses
▨ Understand judicial controls on use of exclusion or limitation clauses
▨ Understand the statutory controls under the Unfair Contract Terms Act 1977 and the Unfair Terms in Consumer Contracts Regulations 1999
▨ Critically analyse the area
▨ Apply the law to factual situations and reach conclusions

7.1 Definition and scope of exclusion clauses and limitation clauses

A clause in a contract that seeks to either limit or exclude liability for breaches of the contract is itself a term of the contract. It is therefore subject to all of the normal rules regarding terms, particularly those concerning incorporation of the term.

Such terms are often referred to in general terms as **exemption** clauses. Since they act as contractual defences they can be particularly harsh on the party subject to them and they often highlight the inequality of bargaining strength that can exist between different parties, notably providers of goods and services and consumers. Historically, the principle of *caveat emptor* (meaning 'buyer beware') gave a great deal of leeway to a seller and very little protection to a consumer. Even where statute intervened to create protections for the consumer, as in the Sale of Goods Act 1893, the sellers' superior position was generally preserved. A good example of this is s 55 of the 1893 Act that allowed sellers to exclude liability for breaches of the implied conditions in the Act, thus rendering it relatively ineffective.

As a result of the potential for unfairness, judges gradually developed common law rules to prevent sellers from having an unfettered discretion to avoid liability for their contractual breaches. During the latter half of the twentieth century a general trend towards consumer protection saw the introduction of more effective statutory controls and the UK has also had to implement controls created in European Community law.

7.2 Judicial control of exemption clauses

limitation clause

A clause in a contract limiting the amount payable in damages to a set sum

Although statutory and EU-led regulations are a modern and often straightforward means of controlling the use of exclusion clauses, judicial controls may still be effective in limiting the use of exclusion and **limitation clauses**.

By the principles that have been developed in the courts there is then potentially a three-stage process in considering the extent to which a party having inserted an exemption clause into a contract may rely on the clause:

- Firstly, it must be shown that the exclusion/limitation is actually a term of the contract otherwise it could not be relied upon anyway.
- Secondly, a proper construction of the clause will determine whether it actually seeks to protect the party inserting it into the contract in relation to the actual damage suffered or whether it is irrelevant or extraneous.
- Thirdly, a number of other tests designed to restrict the use of such clauses will also need to be considered and applied if necessary.

Coote summed up the interesting position taken by judges by saying:

QUOTATION

'To the observer coming to the subject from the outside, the attitudes of the English courts to exception clauses must seem a strange mixture of contradictions. In principle the common law has allowed freedom of exclusion to an extent greater than in most judicial systems. In practice English judges have for the most part viewed the exception clauses themselves with disfavour, and by and large have accorded to them the narrowest effect possible.'

B Coote, Exception Clauses *(Sweet & Maxwell, 1964), p 137*

student mentor tip

"Know your cases by reading them frequently and understanding them."

Anthony, London South Bank University

7.2.1 Incorporation of exemption clauses

Judges have shown a willingness to redress the imbalance to which exclusion clauses can give rise. They have done so initially by insisting on strict rules of incorporation of such clauses. Of course, exclusion/limitation clauses are in themselves terms of the contract. In this way the rules on incorporation are generally interchangeable with rules regarding incorporation of other terms, although the ones identified below are most specifically appropriate to exclusion clauses and were developed in cases where such terms were in question.

Signed agreements

As with terms in general, the initial proposition is that where a party has signed a written agreement then he is *prima facie* bound by that agreement. This will apply generally even though the party caught by the exclusion clause has not read the contract.

CASE EXAMPLE

L'Estrange v Graucob [1934] 2 KB 394

Here, as has already been seen (see section 6.2.3), the purchaser of a vending machine was subject to an exclusion clause in the signed agreement: 'any express or implied condition, statement or warranty, statutory or otherwise not stated herein is hereby excluded'. The court held that the purchaser was bound by the exclusion clause in the contract regardless of the fact that she had not read it and because of s 55 of the Sale of Goods Act 1893 was prevented from enforcing the implied terms in the 1893 Act.

Express knowledge of the clause

The first principle adopted by the courts is that an exemption clause will only be incorporated into a contract where the party subject to the clause has actual knowledge of the clause at the time the contract was made. If a party has no knowledge of the clause at the time of entering the contract then the other party cannot rely on the clause to avoid liability for contractual or other breaches.

CASE EXAMPLE

Olley v Marlborough Court Hotel [1949] 1 KB 532

Mr and Mrs Olley booked into the hotel and at this point the contract was formed. When they later went out they left the key at reception, as required by the rules of the hotel. In their absence a third party took the key, entered their room and stole Mrs Olley's fur coat. When Mrs Olley sought compensation from the hotel the owners argued that they were not liable because of an exclusion clause in the contract that 'the proprietors will not hold themselves liable for articles lost or stolen unless handed to the manageress for safe custody'. Mrs Olley sued. The Court of Appeal rejected the hotelier's defence. The court held that the clause had not been incorporated in the contract since it was on a notice on a wall inside the Olleys' room. At the material time when the contract was formed, the Olleys were unaware of the clause and therefore had been given no chance of negotiating different terms. The court was not prepared to allow the hotel to rely on a clause that was not a part of the contract.

On the other hand, where the parties have dealt on the same terms in the past it may be possible to imply knowledge of the clause from those past dealings. In this case it may be possible to argue that the clause has been incorporated into the contract as a term and can therefore be relied upon.

CASE EXAMPLE

Spurling (J) Ltd v Bradshaw [1956] 1 WLR 561

The defendant had contracted to store goods in the claimant's warehouse over many years. On the occasion in question he had stored a consignment of eight barrels of orange juice. When the claimant came to recover the orange juice he found it missing. The defendant refused to pay for the cost of storage and the claimant then sued and the defendant counter-claimed, alleging the claimant's negligence for the loss. The claimant pointed to their clause that excluded liability for any 'loss or damage occasioned by the negligence, wrongful act or default' of them or their servants contained in a receipt sent to the defendants. The defendants in turn argued that this was only sent out after the contract was actually formed. The court nevertheless accepted the validity of the exclusion since the parties had dealt on the same terms in the past. The court held that the defendant was bound by the clause since he was aware of it from past dealings and the clause had been consistently used in all prior dealings between the parties. The clause was incorporated in the present contract if only by implication.

However, the courts will not allow a party to rely on past dealings to imply knowledge of an exemption clause in order to incorporate it into the contract unless the previous dealings represent a consistent course of action.

CASE EXAMPLE

McCutcheon v David MacBrayne Ltd [1964] 1 WLR 125

The case of *McCutcheon v David MacBrayne Ltd* [1964] 1 WLR 125 (which follows) actually modifies the law in the two cases above.

JUDGMENT

As Lord Devlin put it, 'previous dealings are only relevant if they prove knowledge of the terms actual and not constructive and assent to them'.

CASE EXTRACT

In the case extract below a significant section of the judgment has been reproduced in the left-hand column. Individual points arising from the judgment are briefly explained in the right-hand column. Read the extract including the commentary in the right-hand column and complete the exercise that follows.

McCutcheon v David Brayne Ltd **[1964] 1 WLR 125**	*The basic facts*
LORD REID: The appellant [from Islay] while on the mainland … asked his brother-in-law, Mr M'Sporran, a farmer in Islay, to have his car sent by the respondents to West Loch Tarbert. Mr M'Sporran took the car to Port Askaig … in the respondents' office … the purser of … "Lochiel," … quoted the freight for a return journey for the car. He paid the money, obtained a receipt and delivered the car to the respondents. It was shipped on the "Lochiel," but the vessel … sank, owing to negligent navigation by the respondents' servants, and the car was a total loss. The appellant sues for its value, agreed at £480.	
The question is, what was the contract between the parties? The contract was an oral one. No document was signed or changed hands until the contract was completed. I agree with the unanimous view of the learned Judges of the Court of Session that the terms of the receipt which was made out by the purser and handed to Mr M'Sporran after he paid the freight cannot be regarded as terms of the contract. So the case is not one of the familiar ticket cases where the question is whether conditions endorsed on, or	*The contract was oral since no document was exchanged until after the contract was formed* *It is not like the 'ticket cases' where terms on the ticket are brought to the purchaser's notice in advance of contracting*

referred to in, a ticket or other document handed to the consignor in making the contract are binding on the consignor. If conditions not mentioned when this contract was made are to be added to, or regarded as part of, this contract, it must be for some reason different from those principles which are now well settled in ticket cases. If this oral contract stands unqualified, there can be no doubt that the respondents are liable for the damage caused by the negligence of their servants.

The respondents' case is that their elaborate printed conditions form part of this contract. If they do, then … they exclude liability in this case … The respondents exhibit copies of these conditions in their office, but neither the appellant nor his agent Mr M'Sporran had read [them] and … they can play no part in the decision of this case. Their practice was to require consignors to sign "risk notes," which included these conditions, before accepting any goods for carriage, but on this occasion no risk note was signed. The respondents' clerkess, knowing that Mr M'Sporran was bringing the car for shipment, made out a risk note for his signature, but when he arrived she was not there and he dealt with the purser of the "Lochiel," …. He asked for a return passage for the car. The purser quoted a charge of some six pounds. He paid that sum, and then the purser made out and gave him a receipt which he put in his pocket without looking at it. He then delivered the car. The purser forgot to ask him to sign the risk note.

Respondents are trying to rely on an exclusion clause in printed conditions to avoid liability

The Lord Ordinary believed the evidence of Mr M'Sporran and the appellant. Mr M'Sporran had consigned goods of various kinds on a number of previous occasions. He said that sometimes he had signed a note, sometimes he had not. On one occasion he had sent his own car. A risk note for that consignment was produced, signed by him. He had never read the risk notes signed by him. He says:

But appellant and his agent had not read the conditions

"I sort of just signed it at the time as a matter of form."

Usually they would be in a risk note which required a signature so should have been read but this did not occur on this occasion

He admitted that he knew he was signing in connexion with some conditions, but he did not know what they were. In particular, he did not know that he was agreeing to send the goods at owner's risk. The appellant had consigned goods on four previous occasions. On three of them he was acting on behalf of his employer. On the other occasion he had sent his own car. Each time he had signed a risk note. He also admitted that he knew there were conditions, but said that he did not know what they were.

There had been previous dealings between the respondent and the appellant's agent

The respondents contend that, by reason of the knowledge thus gained by the appellant and his agent in these previous transactions, the appellant is bound by their conditions. But this case differs essentially from the ticket cases. There the carrier in making the contract hands over a document containing or referring to conditions which he intends to be part of the contract. So if the consignor or passenger, when accepting the document, knows, or ought as a reasonable man to know, that that is the carrier's intention, he can hardly deny that the conditions are part of the contract, or claim, in the absence of special circumstances, to be in a better position than he would be if he had read the document. But here, … neither party referred to, or indeed had in mind, any additional terms, and the contract was complete and fully effective without any additional terms. If it could be said that, when making the contract, Mr M'Sporran knew that the respondents always required a risk note to be signed and knew that the purser was simply forgetting to put it before him for signature, then it might be said that neither he nor his principal could take advantage of the error of the other party of which he was aware. But counsel frankly admitted that he could not put his case as high as that.

And the appellant's agent was aware of the practice

The only other ground on which it would seem possible to import these conditions is that based on a course of dealing. If two parties have made a series of similar contracts each containing certain conditions, and then they make another without expressly referring to those conditions, it may be that those conditions ought to be implied. If the officious bystander had asked them whether they had intended to leave out the conditions this time, both must, as honest men, have said "Of course not." But again the facts here will not support that ground. According to Mr M'Sporran, there had been no consistent course of dealing; sometimes he was asked to sign and sometimes not. And, moreover, he did not know what the conditions were. This time he was offered an oral contract without any reference to conditions, and he accepted the offer in good faith.

But did not know what the conditions were

The respondents also rely on the appellant's previous knowledge. I doubt whether it is possible to spell out a course of dealing in his case. In all but one of the previous cases he had been acting on behalf of his employer in sending a different kind of goods and he did not know that the respondents always sought to … exclude[e] liability for their own negligence. So it cannot be said that, when he asked his agent to make a contract for him, he knew that

And the respondent argued that this meant that there was implied knowledge of the conditions

And this could bind a party who knew that a risk note was always required

Application of the officious bystander test to a consistent course of dealing

this or, indeed, any other special term would be included in it. He left his agent a free hand to contract, and I see nothing to prevent him from taking advantage of the contract which his agent in fact made. ...In this case, I do not think that either party was reasonably bound or entitled to conclude from the attitude of the other as known to him that these conditions were intended by the other party to be part of this contract. I would therefore allow the appeal ....

But there was no consistent course of dealing here

And there was no actual knowledge of the conditions

Neither party was bound by the conditions so the respondent could not rely on them

Key Points from the case of *McCutcheon v David Brayne Ltd* [1964] 1 WLR 125 above:

- The basis of the problem – A contract was made which was oral because no document was produced until after the contract was formed – to avoid liability for the destruction of the appellant's car the respondent sought to rely on an exclusion clause posted in its office and printed on risk notes that were usually signed at the time of contracting – in this case the appellant's agent had seen the risk notes on former occasions but was unaware of the conditions
- On this basis the case was different to the 'ticket cases' where the party is bound by the conditions on the ticket because they have been brought to his attention at the time of contracting
- Where there was a consistent course of dealings on the conditions a party contracting would be subject to those conditions because of implied knowledge of the conditions
- This would be because of the officious bystander test and the presumed intention of the parties
- But there was no consistent course of dealings and there was no actual knowledge of the conditions so the appellant could not be bound by the exclusion clause and the respondent could not avoid liability for the destruction of the appellant's car

ACTIVITY

Using the key points from the case extract above and the principles from the two case examples above the case extract produce a brief revision aid distinguishing the principles in *Olley v Marlborough Court Hotel* [1949]; *Spurling v Bradshaw* [1956] and *McCutcheon v David Brayne Ltd* [1964].

Sufficiency of notice of the exemption clause

In general, the courts will not accept that an exemption clause has been incorporated into a contract unless the party who is subject to the clause has been made sufficiently aware of the existence of the clause in the contract. Again, this must be before or at the time that the contract was formed.

The obligation, then, is firmly on the party inserting the clause into the contract to bring it to the attention of the other party before it can be relied on, so that the party who wishes to rely on the exclusion clause is relieved of liability for their contractual breach.

CASE EXAMPLE

Parker v South Eastern Railway Co (1877) 2 CPD 416

The claimant left his luggage in the cloakroom of the station and was given a ticket on paying a fee. On the back of the ticket was a clause stating that the railway company would not be liable for any luggage that exceeded £10 in value. Mr Parker's luggage was worth more than that amount and when it was stolen he claimed compensation from the railway company. The defendants' attempt to rely on the exclusion clause failed at trial since the defendants could not show that they had instructed the claimant to read the clause or had otherwise brought the claimant's attention to the existence of the exclusion clause. The trial judge put two questions to the jury. Was the claimant aware of the special condition attached to leaving the parcel? Was the claimant under any obligation to make himself aware of the conditions? The jury answered 'no' to both questions. In the Court of Appeal, Mellish LJ identified that the real questions for the jury to answer (the so-called 'Mellish test') were as below.

JUDGMENT

As Mellish LJ put it: 'the proper direction to leave to the jury in these cases is, that if the person receiving the ticket did not see or know that there was any writing on the ticket, he is not bound by the conditions; that if he knew there was writing, and knew or believed that the writing contained conditions, then he is bound by the conditions; that if he knew there was writing on the ticket, but did not know or believe that the writing contained conditions, nevertheless he would be bound, if the delivering of the ticket to him in such a manner that he could see that there was writing upon it, was, in the opinion of the jury, reasonable notice that the writing contained conditions'. A re-trial was ordered but did not take place.

Clearly, one of the key issues in the *Parker* case would have been whether or not the claimant could have been legitimately expected to contemplate that the cloakroom ticket in fact formed the basis of a written contract. An exclusion/limitation clause will not be incorporated into the contract when, on an objective analysis, it is not contained in a document that would ordinarily be perceived as being a contractual document or having contractual significance. In this respect the so-called 'ticket cases' are significant since the principle affects so much of modern contracting methods.

CASE EXAMPLE

Chapelton v Barry Urban District Council [1940] 1 KB 532

Here, the claimant hired deckchairs on the beach at Barry, and received two tickets from the council's beach attendant on paying the cost of hiring the chairs. On the back of these small tickets were the words 'The council will not be liable for any accident or damage arising from the hire of the chair', though the claimant did not read it, believing it to be only a receipt. The canvas on one chair was defective and it collapsed, injuring the claimant as a result. He claimed compensation and the council then tried to rely on its exclusion clause. The court would not accept the legitimacy of the clause and the defence failed since the existence of the clause was not effectively bought to the attention of the claimant. The court held that it was unreasonable to assume that the claimant would automatically understand that the ticket was a contractual document. The council was therefore liable for the claimant's injuries.

The exemption clause might not be incorporated either where reference to it is contained in another document given to the claimant prior to the formation of the contract but where insufficient is done to bring the claimant's attention to the existence of the clause.

CASE EXAMPLE

Dillon v Baltic Shipping Co Ltd (The Mikhail Lermontov) [1991] 2 Lloyd's Rep 155, NSW

A woman booked to go on a cruise with her daughter. In the booking form there was a clause that the contract of carriage was 'subject to conditions and regulations printed on the tickets'. In fact, the contract of carriage would only then be issued some time later, at the same time as the tickets. During the cruise the ship sank and the claimant was injured as a result. When the woman claimed for compensation the defendant shipping company sought to rely on the exclusion clause in the contract of carriage. This defence failed. The court held that there was insufficient notice given in the booking form actually to draw the claimant's attention to the existence of the exclusion clause and it could not be relied upon to avoid liability for the negligence.

One further question concerns the precise extent to which parties inserting exemption clauses in contracts must go in order to claim that they are brought sufficiently to the attention of the other party and therefore incorporated in the contract. Judges at different times have shown that a party seeking to rely on an exclusion clause in order to avoid liability has a very high duty to achieve this end. This is graphically illustrated in more than one judgment of Lord Denning. The case considered below is also relevant to the requirement that the party subject to the clause must be aware of the clause at the time of contracting. Finally, the case also puts into perspective some of the problems of modern forms of contracting. These inevitably include dealing with vending machines, ticket machines or other situations where there is no actual contact with the party seeking to insert the clause or his agents at the time when the contract is formed.

CASE EXAMPLE

Thornton v Shoe Lane Parking Ltd [1971] 2 QB 163

The claimant was injured in a car park owned by the defendants. At the entrance to the car park there was a notice that, as well as identifying the charges for parking, also stated that parking was at the owner's risk. On entering the car park a motorist was required to stop at a barrier and take a ticket from a machine, at which point the barrier would lift, allowing entry to the car park. On each ticket was printed the words: 'This ticket is issued subject to the conditions of issue as displayed on the premises'. Notices inside the car park then listed the conditions of the contract and these included a clause excluding liability for both damage to property and for personal injury. When the claimant sued for compensation for his injuries, the defendants argued that he was bound by the exclusion clause but the court rejected their argument. It was held that there was insufficient attempt made to draw the claimant's attention to the existence of the clause for the defendant to be able to rely on it to avoid liability.

JUDGMENT

Lord Denning identified that the customer in such situations has no chance of nego-tiating. He 'pays his money and gets a ticket. He cannot refuse it. He cannot get his money back. He may protest to the machine, even swear at it. But it will remain un-moved. He is committed beyond recall ... The contract was concluded at that time'. In consequence, Lord Denning says the customer is bound by the terms of the contract 'as long as they are sufficiently brought to his notice before-hand, but not otherwise'. In other words, for the party including the clause in the contract, a very high degree of notice is required for it to be effective. As he had previously stated, in *Spurling v Bradshaw* [1956] 1 WLR 561 when looking at what needs to be done to draw a clause to the attention of the party subject to it: 'Some clauses which I have seen would need to be printed in red ink with a red hand pointing to it before the notice could be held to be sufficient.'

As has already been mentioned, the rules on incorporation of terms apply both to the usual terms and to exemption clauses, since these are a very specific type of term with very particular consequences. Case law has also demonstrated that the courts are prepared to apply this strict approach not only to exemption clauses but also to other terms that could be disadvantageous to a party subjected to them. In certain instances then the courts have adopted the same position in contracts containing clauses that are particularly burden-some to the other party regardless of the clause not being an exclusion clause.

CASE EXAMPLE

Interfoto Picture Library Ltd v Stiletto Visual Programmes Ltd
[1988] 2 WLR 615

Here, the defendants hired photographic transparencies for a visual aid in a presentation, from a party with whom they had no previous dealings. In the claimants' delivery note, which the defendants did not read, was a clause referring to a holding fee and VAT for each day when the transparencies were not returned past a set deadline, 19th March. When the defendants returned the transparencies on 2nd April they were presented with a bill for £3,783.50 in respect of the holding charge for late return. The claimants sued when the defendants refused to pay, and succeeded in their claim.

JUDGMENT

Dillon LJ in the Court of Appeal held that: 'if one condition in a set of printed condi-tions is particularly onerous or unusual, the party seeking to enforce it must show that that condition was fairly brought to the attention of the other party in the most explicit way'.

7.2.2 Construction of the contract

Even though an exemption clause satisfies the above tests and therefore appears to have been successfully incorporated into a contract, this does not necessarily mean that it will operate successfully in all cases to avoid liability on the part of the party inserting it into the contract. The clause might still fail on a construction of the contract as a whole and this might be for a number of reasons.

The contra preferentem rule

The *contra preferentem* rule is a device that can be applied whenever a contract contains ambiguities. The basic principle is that if a party wishes to secure an exclusion from liability for contractual breaches by means of incorporation of an exemption clause into the contract, then the clause must be specific as to the circumstances in which the exemption is claimed. If the clause is in fact in any way ambiguous then the ambiguity is said to work in favour of the other party so that the clause will fail.

CASE EXAMPLE

Andrews Bros (Bournemouth) Ltd v Singer & Co [1934] 1 KB 17

Here, the contract was for the sale and purchase of what were described in the contract as 'new Singer cars'. The contract contained a clause excluding 'all conditions, warranties and liabilities implied by statute, common law or otherwise'. One car delivered under the contract was, technically speaking, a used car because a prospective purchaser had used it. The dealer was then sued for damages and tried to rely on the clause in defending the claim. The Court of Appeal held that the supply of 'new Singer cars' was an express term of the contract. Since the exclusion clause actually applied to 'implied terms', the *contra preferentem* rule would prevent it being used in relation to express terms. The exclusion clause could not be relied on and the defence failed.

The effect of the *contra preferentem* rule as applied to exemption clauses then is that, where there is any ambiguity in the contract, ambiguity will work against the party seeking to rely on the clause rather than the party subject to it. The party inserting the clause into the contract cannot rely upon it to avoid liability unless it clearly and precisely covers the circumstances on which the claim is based.

CASE EXAMPLE

Hollier v Rambler Motors (AMC) Ltd [1972] QB 71

Hollier left his car with the garage for repair as he had done on occasions in the past. The normal conditions of the contract were contained in a form that Hollier had signed on previous occasions but not on the occasion in question. This form included a term that: 'The company is not responsible for damage caused by fire to customers' cars on the premises'. The car was damaged in a fire that was caused by the defendants' negligence. The car owner sued for compensation and the garage owner tried to rely on the clause excluding liability for fire. The Court of Appeal held firstly that the form was not incorporated into the contract in this case merely because of the previous course of dealings. It also concluded that for the garage to rely on the exclusion clause it must have stated in it without any ambiguity that it would not be liable in the event of its own negligence. In the absence of such precise wording the customer might rightly conclude when making the contract that the garage owners would not generally be liable except where the fire damage was caused by their own negligence when they would naturally be liable.

Traditionally the courts were prepared to accept an exclusion clause exempting liability for negligence provided that it was expressly indicated in the agreement that liability for negligence was excluded, that the words used within their ordinary meaning were sufficient to cover negligence and that no other source of liability was indicated (Lord Morton in *Canada Steamship Lines Ltd v R* [1952] AC 192). However, more recently the courts have taken a less rigid approach and acknowledged that the real test is what the intention of the parties was at the time of contracting.

CASE EXAMPLE

HIH Casualty and General Insurance v Chase Manhattan Bank [2003] UKHL 6; [2003] 2 Lloyd's Rep 61

The bank loaned money for the making of films against the security of the future receipts from the films. In order to minimise its risk, the bank contracted with the insurance company to underwrite the risk. Negotiations for the agreement had been in the hands of an intermediary party that was better informed than either of the parties. When a loss occurred the bank was able to successfully rely on an exclusion clause covering its agents.

Again, it is important to remember that exemption clauses are merely one type of term that might be included in a contract. The *contra preferentem* rule then is not limited in its application to exclusion clauses only. It can be used when construing any term in a contract where the term is in fact ambiguous. Again, the effect of the ambiguity will be to deny the party inserting the term to rely on it where it does not fit the precise circumstances of the case.

CASE EXAMPLE

Vaswani v Italian Motor Cars Ltd [1996] 1 WLR 270

In this case the principle was applied to a price variation clause in a contract for the supply of Ferrari cars. The price variation would apply only in limited circumstances. When, on a proper construction of the contract, the suppliers had increased the cost to the purchaser for a reason not falling within those limited circumstances, the supplier was unable to enforce the price variation.

It is important also to remember that while an exemption clause might excuse a party from strict liability, it will not generally relieve from negligence-based liability unless it is absolutely clear.

CASE EXAMPLE

White v John Warwick & Co Ltd [1953] 1 WLR 1285

An agreement for the hire of a cycle included a clause that 'nothing in this agreement shall render the owners liable for any personal injury'. The claimant was injured when the saddle tipped forward. While the court accepted that the words used were enough to relieve the defendants of strict liability in contract for the hire of the bicycle, they were not sufficiently clear and precise for them to avoid liability in negligence.

In fact, the principles to be applied in relation to negligence were laid down by Lord Morton in the Canadian case *Canada Steamship Lines Ltd v R* [1952] AC 192 at p 208. These have always been accepted by English courts.

JUDGMENT

'(1) If the clause contains language which expressly exempts the person … from the consequences of the negligence … effect must be given to that provision …

(2) If there is no express reference to negligence, the court must consider whether the words used are wide enough … to cover the negligence …

(3) If the words used are wide enough … the court must then consider whether [there is] some ground other than negligence [which is not] so fanciful or remote that [the defendant] cannot be supposed to have desired protection against it.'

Strict construction of standard forms

Even though the *contra preferentem* rule does not apply in the circumstances of the case, it is still possible that the judges will use a strict construction of the wording of the contract before they will allow an exclusion clause to stand. This is particularly so in standard form contracts where the clause is broad in its application and the breach is in fact a serious one.

Fundamental breach and the 'Securicor cases'

Traditionally, the courts were reluctant to allow a party to escape liability for a serious breach simply by including an exemption clause in the contract. One way in which the courts were able to control this was by a strict construction of both the clause and of the contract as a whole, as we have just seen.

One other method that the courts developed and at one time employed to combat the effectiveness of over-wide exclusion clauses was what was known as the doctrine of 'fundamental breach'. By this doctrine, if a party had committed a serious breach by breaching a central term of the contract, then judges might declare that there was a 'fundamental breach'. The effect of this applying the doctrine was that the court would find the clause rendered ineffective. In essence, the judges would treat the fundamental breach as a breach of the whole contract, and therefore the other party would be able to treat the contract as repudiated. The party inserting the exclusion clause would then be unable to rely on the clause since, because of the doctrine, he would be treated as being in breach of every term of the contract.

CASE EXAMPLE

Karsales (Harrow) Ltd v Wallis [1956] 1 WLR 936

In this case the purchaser contracted to buy a second-hand car under a hire-purchase agreement. In the written agreement was a clause stating that: 'No condition or warranty that the vehicle is roadworthy, or as to its age, condition or fitness for any purpose is given by the owner or implied herein'. Although the purchaser had previously examined the car and found it satisfactory, when it was delivered the cylinder head had been removed; valves in the engine had burnt out; two pistons were damaged; the tyres were damaged and the radio was missing. The purchaser, not surprisingly, rejected the car. When he was sued, the claimant tried to rely on the exclusion clause in the hire-purchase agreement.

The Court of Appeal rejected the argument. The court held that there had been a fundamental breach of the contract. There was such a substantial difference between the contract as formed and the contract as performed that the breach went to the root of the contract; the central purpose of the contract was defeated by the breach and the claimant was unable to rely on the exclusion clause to avoid liability.

Despite its benefits, the doctrine was not universally popular with judges. The clear argument against its application was that it undermined the basic principles of freedom of contract. Judges were also conscious of the fact that there could also be uncertainty as to what actually amounted to a fundamental breach. In consumer contracts, judges were inevitably more prepared to accept and apply the doctrine than they were in commercial contracts where bargaining strength was more equal. In consequence, the courts gradually moved to a position where they considered that the doctrine was unsustainable in the form expressed above and that the doctrine was merely a method of construction rather than a rule of law negating what the parties had freely decided between themselves.

CASE EXAMPLE

Suisse Atlantique Société d'Armement Maritime SA v NV Rotterdamsche Kolen Centrale (The Suisse Atlantique Case) [1967] 1 AC 361

The owners of a ship sought to sue the party who had chartered the vessel and were to pay them on the basis of the number of journeys made. The owners claimed, and it was accepted by the court, that breaches of the term concerning loading and unloading meant that the party chartering the vessel had made only eight voyages instead of the 14 that they might have been expected to complete. The charterparty argued that their liability was limited to a fixed amount of $1,000 per day rather than the actual loss, by virtue of a limitation clause in the contract. The ship-owners countered this and argued that there was a fundamental breach as a result of which the limitation clause could not apply. The case was decided on the basis that the clause was not a limitation clause but a genuine **liquidated damages** clause, and in any case it was felt that there was no fundamental breach. Nevertheless, the House of Lords expressed the view that the doctrine of fundamental breach was a restriction on freedom of contract. Lord Wilberforce was a little more guarded since he recognised that where a breach is so serious that it is almost the same as no performance, then it is hard to limit liability and still have a contract left.

liquidated damages

A sum of damages agreed by both parties in advance of the contract

It is useful to point to two aspects of the judgments in explaining the doctrine and the difficulties that it presents.

JUDGMENT

Lord Upjohn explained the term: 'there is no magic in the words "fundamental breach" [it] is no more than a convenient shorthand expression for saying that a particular breach or breaches of contract by one party is or are such as to go to the root of the contract which entitles the other party to treat such breach or breaches as a repudiation of the whole contract. Whether such breach or breaches do constitute a fundamental breach depends on the construction of the contract and on all the facts and circumstances of the case'.

JUDGMENT

Viscount Dilhorne identified the rule as one of construction and explained the potential consequences of the doctrine: 'it is not right to say that the law prohibits and nullifies a clause exempting or limiting liability for a fundamental breach of a fundamental term. Such a rule would involve a restriction on freedom of contract and in the older cases I can find no trace of it'.

The rules devised by the courts were originally the only means of protection for consumers against the potential harshness of exclusion clauses. The enactment of the Unfair Contract Terms Act 1977 extended greater protection to consumers against exclusion clauses. The courts have subsequently been prepared to take a more relaxed view towards exclusion and limitation clauses in commercial contracts. There is clear logic in this. In commercial contracts the parties contract on the basis of a more equal bargaining strength and have possibly had more freedom to negotiate the terms of the contract. As a result, the courts have been prepared to accept that a clause may be upheld where the parties have freely and genuinely agreed it at the time the contract was formed.

CASE EXAMPLE

Photo Productions Ltd v Securicor Transport Ltd [1980] AC 287

Securicor had contracted under its own standard terms to provide a night patrol service at Photo Productions factory. A clause in Securicor's standard terms stated that: 'Under no circumstances shall the Company be responsible for any injurious act or default by any employee of the company unless such act or default could have been foreseen and avoided by the exercise of due diligence on the part of the Company as his employer'. The duty security officer on the night in question started a fire that got out of control and as a result burnt down a large part of the factory. It was not disputed that he was suitable for the work, nor was it considered that Securicor was negligent in employing him. The trial judge accepted that the exclusion clause applied and held with Securicor. The Court of Appeal, however, applied the doctrine of fundamental breach, determined that the whole contract was effectively breached so that Securicor could not rely on the exclusion clause and found in Photo Productions' favour. The House of Lords, however, reversed the decision of the Court of Appeal. The House affirmed that parties dealing in free negotiations were entitled to include in their contracts any exclusions or limitations or modifications to their obligations that they chose by which both parties would be bound. Since the clause was clear and unambiguous there was nothing to prevent its use and it therefore protected Securicor from liability for its employee's actions. The judgments were also fairly critical of the continued use of the doctrine of fundamental breach.

JUDGMENT

In explaining the applicability of the doctrine, Lord Diplock identified that: 'In cases falling within … fundamental breach, the anticipatory secondary obligation [to pay damages] arises under contracts of all kind by implication of the common law, except to the extent that it is excluded or modified by the express words of the contract.'

The approach has since been followed. It appears that the doctrine has been abandoned in certain circumstances and in these cases it is immaterial how serious the breach is. It appears that an exclusion clause may still stand in common law if two requirements are met:

- The clause seeking to exclude or limit liability occurs in a contract in which the parties are dealing with equal bargaining strength.
- The clause seeking to exclude or limit liability is clearly and unambiguously stated in the contract itself.

In such circumstances the party inserting the clause will be able to rely on it to avoid liability for breaches of the contract.

CASE EXAMPLE

Ailsa Craig Fishing Co Ltd v Malvern Fishing Co Ltd [1983] 1 WLR 964

Securicor was under contract to the Aberdeen Fishing Vessels Owners Association Ltd, who acted on behalf of various fishing boat owners, to provide a security service in the harbour where boats moored. Following negligence by the security guard, one vessel fouled another vessel; both sank and became trapped under the quay. The contract was on Securicor's standard terms and in the ensuing action they sought to rely on a clause in the contract limiting liability 'for any loss or damage of whatever nature arising out of or connected with the provision of or failure in provision of, the services covered by this contract … to a sum … not exceeding £1,000 in respect of one claim … and … not exceeding a maximum £10,000 for the consequences of any incident involving fire, theft or any other cause of liability'. The sums are clearly very small when compared with the likely cost of the damage done to two ships. The House of Lords, however, rejected the argument that since Securicor had clearly failed to carry out the terms of its contract at all, they should be unable to rely on the limitation clause. The House of Lords stated that limitation clauses are not to be regarded with the same hostility as exclusion clauses because they relate to the risks to which the defending party is exposed, the remuneration he may receive and the opportunity of the other party to insure against loss. As a result, it held that the clause had been drafted in a sufficiently clear and unambiguous way to protect Securicor in the case. Besides this, the two parties were commercial enterprises and had contracted freely and with equal bargaining strength. (The contract was itself made before the enactment of the Unfair Contract Terms Act 1977, otherwise there may well have been a different result.)

JUDGMENT

Lord Wilberforce explained that: 'one must not strive to create ambiguities by strained construction … The relevant words must be given, if possible, their natural, plain meaning'.

These two cases, often referred to as the '*Securicor* cases', seem to suggest that the doctrine of fundamental breach can no longer apply. They also suggest that, subject now to statutory controls, where there is equality of bargaining strength and free negotiation, the parties can include terms even of the most onerous type provided that the other side freely accepts them. These terms will then bind the party who has agreed to them even if all remedies are lost as a result.

On that level it is probably the case that the statutory provisions in the Unfair Contract Terms Act 1977 may be more effective in controlling exclusion clauses than the common law is at least in inter-business dealings. One reason for this is the insertion of a test of reasonableness in the Act in the case of such contracts.

CASE EXAMPLE

George Mitchell Ltd v Finney Lock Seeds Ltd [1983] 2 AC 803

Seed merchants agreed to supply farmers with 30 lb of Dutch winter cabbage seed for £192. A limitation clause in the contract limited liability in the event of breach to the cost of the seed only or to replacement seed. The farmers planned to sow 63 acres with the seed and calculated that their return would be £63,000. The seed was the wrong sort and was not merchantable and there was no crop. The farmers sued for £63,000 in compensation for their lost production. At first instance the farmers won. The seed suppliers then appealed the case, arguing that they were protected by the limitation clause in the contract. The Court of Appeal held that the clause was not sufficiently clear or unambiguous to allow the suppliers to rely on it in excluding liability for breaches of implied terms in the Sale of Goods Act 1979. The House of Lords disagreed and held that, on a proper construction of the clause, it did cover the breach but, in any case, using the terminology of the Unfair Contract Terms Act, the House of Lords held that the clause was unreasonable and could not be relied on.

As a result of the last case, it would seem that there are limits to the application of the principles in the '*Securicor* cases'. There are situations where the courts are reluctant to intervene because the parties are of equal bargaining strength and the clause is a common one. An obvious example is in standard form contracts where the offending clause is based on long-standing, well-known and accepted trade practice.

CASE EXAMPLE

Overland Shoes Ltd v Schenkers Ltd [1998] 1 Lloyd's Rep 498

Overland shoes were importing shoes from China and Schenkers, a firm of world-wide freight carriers, were contracted to transport the shoes. The contract of carriage was based on the standard forms of the British International Freight Association. These standard forms included a 'no set-off' clause. When Schenkers claimed for their freight charges, Overland Shoes tried to set off against these sums that Schenkers owed for VAT. Schenkers objected to this particular course pointing to the no set-off clause. Overland argued that this was in effect an exclusion clause and was unreasonable under the test in the Unfair Contract Terms Act. The court held that the clause actually satisfied the statutory test of reasonableness since it was based on long-standing established custom.

7.2.3 Other limitations on the use of exemption clauses

Besides ensuring that the clause is properly incorporated into the contract, and construing the clause and the contract itself to ensure that the clause properly covers the breach, judges have used other devices to determine whether or not an exclusion clause is valid and can be relied upon by the party inserting it.

Inconsistent oral representations

A party is generally bound by a contract which he has signed (see *L'Estrange v Graucob* [1934] 2 KB 394). In some circumstances, however, the party subject to the clause may have enquired about the existence of the clause or queried the precise consequences of a clause that they have already read.

CASE EXAMPLE

Curtis v Chemical Cleaning and Dyeing Co Ltd [1951] 1 KB 805

The claimant took a wedding dress to be cleaned and was asked to sign a document that contained a clause exempting the defendants from liability for any damage 'howsoever arising'. She sensibly questioned the nature of the document that she was being asked to sign. The sales assistant then informed her that the clause only referred to the fact that the defendants would not accept liability for damage to beads or sequins attached to the dress. When the dress was returned it had a chemical stain for which Mrs Curtis tried to claim. She sued the cleaning company which countered with the exclusion clause. The defendants failed in their attempt to rely on the exclusion clause because of the oral assurances made to the claimant.

If an oral misrepresentation has then caused that party to enter the contract with confidence, the exclusion clause may be ineffective because it is the misrepresentation that has induced the other party to enter the contract.

So, as we have already seen, an oral representation made before the contract is formed can override an inconsistent express term within the written document. This principle applies to terms generally and can obviously also apply in the case of exclusion or limitation clauses.

CASE EXAMPLE

J Evans & Son (Portsmouth) Ltd v Andrea Merzario Ltd [1976] 1 WLR 1078

Here, the claimant had regularly contracted with the defendants, as carriers of machinery, on the defendants' standard forms. The machines had always been carried below decks because they were liable to rust otherwise. The carriers then changed to using containers stored on deck. The claimants were then given an oral assurance that their machinery would still be stored below decks. When one machine was put in a container and by error stored on deck, it fell overboard. The Court of Appeal accepted that the defendants were bound by the promise made by their representative to continue to carry the claimants' machinery below deck. This oral assurance overrode any inconsistent term in the contract. The standard forms did not in fact represent the actual agreement made, and the defendants were liable.

A very similar principle applies in the case of a collateral promise or undertaking which the claimant can then rely on. The effect of the collateral promise is to prevent the party who has inserted an exemption clause into a contract from relying on that clause in a subsequent dispute where the party subject to the exclusion clause has been induced to enter the contract on the basis of the collateral promise.

CASE EXAMPLE

Webster v Higgin [1948] 2 All ER 127

The defendant had negotiated to purchase a car from the claimants' garage under a hire-purchase agreement. In a hire-purchase contract, while the goods are bought under one contract, the hire-purchase agreement itself is a separate contract. Here, the garage owners promised that the car that the claimant proposed to buy was in good condition. In fact, the hire-purchase agreement contained a clause stating that: 'no warranty, condition, description or representation as to the state or quality of the vehicle is given or implied'. In fact, the car was, as the judge in the case described it, 'nothing but a mass of second hand and dilapidated ironmongery'. When the buyer refused to pay the claimant then sued for return of the car and the balance of the instalments due. The action failed. The contract was of course with the hire-purchase company but there had been a collateral promise made to the purchaser that the car was in good condition. Since the car anything but corresponded to the description applied to it by the sellers, the hire-purchase company was bound also by this collateral promise and was unable to rely on the exclusion clause in its standard forms.

The effect of exemption clauses on third parties to the contract

The doctrine of privity means that the terms of a contract are only binding on the parties to the contract themselves. We have already seen that, subject to the various exceptions to the rule whether common law or statutory, in general a party trying to enforce third party rights under a contract will fail for lack of privity. In the same way, despite the existence of an exclusion clause in a contract, it may not offer protection to parties other than the parties to the contract.

CASE EXAMPLE

Scruttons Ltd v Midland Silicones Ltd [1962] AC 446

Carriers had a contract to ship a drum of chemicals for a company, the claimants in the case. The bill of lading contained a clause limiting the liability of the carriers in the event of a breach to $500 (about £197 at the time). The defendants were stevedores who were contracted by the carriers to unload the goods. Their contract with the carriers included a term that the stevedores should also have the benefit of the limitation clause in the bill of lading. When the stevedores, through their negligence, did £583 worth of damage to the drum of chemicals they were sued by the owners and then tried to rely on the limitation clause in the contract between the claimants and the carriers. This defence failed. The court acknowledged that the stevedores were not parties to the bill of lading and their lack of privity prevented them from claiming any rights under it. They were liable for the damage that they had caused.

The fact that the doctrine of privity prevents a third party to a contract from relying on exclusion clauses contained in it may nevertheless not prevent a claimant from pursuing an action even though the other party to the contract is protected by the clause. This will apply because if the third party is responsible for the damage, and is financially worth bringing an action against, an action may be brought against that party for instance in tort.

CASE EXAMPLE

Cosgrove v Horsefell (1945) 62 TLR 140

A passenger on a bus was injured through the negligence of the driver. The contract between the passenger and the bus company contained a valid exclusion clause which thus protected the bus company from any liability. Nevertheless, this did not protect the bus driver, as a third party to the contract, from an action in negligence by the passenger.

Despite the apparent restrictions of the doctrine of privity there have still been occasions where a third party has successfully claimed the protection of an exclusion clause even though not a party to the contract in which the clause was contained. The approach has inevitably been the subject of criticism. The mechanism is to argue an agency relationship between the third party and the party inserting the exclusion clause into the contract and thus to claim that a contractual relationship is created also with the third party who is then able also to rely on the exclusion.

CASE EXAMPLE

New Zealand Shipping Co Ltd v A M Satterthwaite & Co Ltd (The Euryme-don) [1975] AC 154

Here, there was a contract between a consignor and a carrier to ship drilling equipment to New Zealand. The bill of lading contained an exclusion clause. This stated that 'it is hereby expressly agreed that no servant or Agent of the carrier (including every independent contractor from time to time employed by the carrier) shall in any circumstances whatsoever be under any liability whatsoever to the shipper, consignee or owner of the goods or to any holder of the bill of lading for any loss or damage or delay of whatsoever kind arising or resulting directly or indirectly from any neglect or default on his part'. It also stated that 'every right, exemption, limitation, condition and liberty herein contained … shall extend to protect every such servant or agent of the carrier'. In the event stevedores hired by the carriers negligently damaged the drilling equipment and were then sued by the consignors. Their attempt to claim protection under the carriers' exclusion clause succeeded. The Privy Council held that the issue centred on whether the stevedores had given consideration under the contract (see section 3.3.2). The stevedores had accepted a unilateral offer by the consignors that in return for their promise to carry out duties the consignors would in turn exempt them from any liability. The stevedores had accepted this offer by unloading the ship and could therefore rely on the exclusion clause and avoid liability for their negligence.

ACTIVITY

Quick quiz
Decide whether judges will consider that exclusion clauses notified in the following ways have been successfully incorporated into contracts:
1. a notice placed on the counter in a shop
2. a notice contained in a signed document
3. a notice contained in a delivery note, where the parties have regularly dealt on the same terms
4. a notice posted in a hotel bedroom
5. a notice contained in a receipt
6. a notice on the back of a cloakroom ticket
7. a notice posted on the machine at the entrance to a car park.

Self-assessment questions
1. For what reasons did judges develop rules to control the use of contractual terms limiting or excluding liability?
2. In what ways does a limitation clause differ from an exclusion clause?
3. In what ways can the rule in *L'Estrange v Graucob* be described as unfair?

4. What complications are created when a person uses a vending machine or a ticket machine, and how do the courts deal with these problems?
5. Why are the courts reluctant to accept that tickets or receipts can contain contractual terms that then bind the parties?
6. Why were the courts prepared to accept exclusions or limitations in the case of such extreme breaches as those in the 'Securicor cases'?
7. To what extent did the common law control of exclusion clauses make statutory intervention inevitable?
8. How does the contra preferentem rule help to control the use of exclusion clauses?

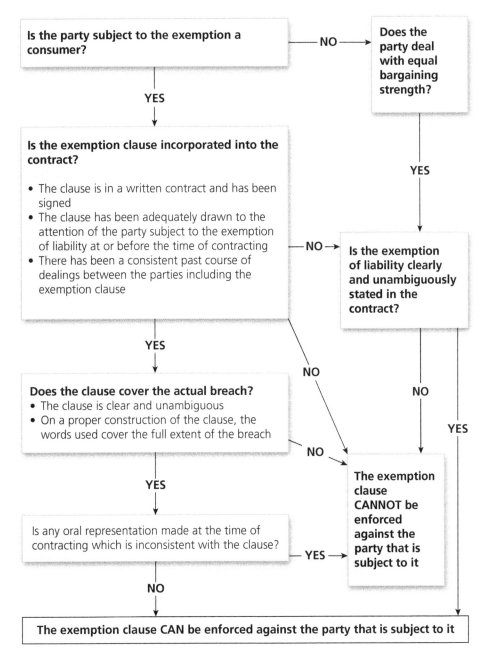

Figure 7.1 Diagram illustrating judicial controls on the use of exemption clauses

Definition	
An exclusion clause is a term of a contract that aims to avoid liability for breaches of the contract.	
A limitation clause is one which has the effect of reducing damages if there is a breach of contract.	

Common law controls	Case/statute
A party is bound by terms where he has signed an agreement.	*L'Estrange v Graucob*
An exclusion clause is not recognised unless it is incorporated – so:	
• the party subject to it must be aware of it at the time of contracting	*Olley v Marlborough Court Hotel*
• but it is possible for past dealings to be taken into account in a consistent course of dealing	*McCutcheon v MacBrayne*
• the party wishing to rely on the clause must bring it to the other party's attention effectively.	*Thornton v Shoe Lane Parking*
Oral misrepresentations about the clause may mean that the party inserting it in the contract cannot rely on it.	*Curtis v Chemical Cleaning Co*
In general, third parties to the contract cannot rely on the clause (but see also *Satterthwaite v New Zealand Shipping*).	*Scruttons v Midland Silicones*
If the clause is ambiguous, it cannot be relied upon.	*Hollier v Rambler Motors*
Where the parties contract on equal terms, the clause may be relied on.	*Photo Productions v Securicor Transport*
Providing the clause is clear and unambiguous.	*Ailsa Craig Fishing v Malvern Fishing*

7.3 Statutory control of exemption clauses

7.3.1 The scope of statutory regulation

Provisions created by statute or in regulations are clearly the most effective in controlling the operation of both exclusion and limitation clauses in contracts. This is not to say that the common law has no relevance. Quite simply, as we have seen, if an exclusion clause has not been successfully incorporated into a contract according to the normal rules then it will be inoperable anyway (see, eg, *Olley v Marlborough Court Hotel Ltd* [1949] 1 KB 532 in section 7.2.1).

There are two principal provisions provided by Parliament:

- the Unfair Contract Terms Act 1977, and
- the Unfair Terms in Consumer Contract Regulations 1999 (an adaptation of the Unfair Terms in Consumer Contract Regulations 1994) which were enacted in order to comply with EC Directive 93/13.

The Unfair Contract Terms Act 1977 is an effective brake on the operation of exemption clauses and as such can be seen as a serious inroad into the principle of freedom of contract when compared with, for instance, the 'Securicor cases'.

The 1977 Act applies to exclusions for tort damage as well as contractual breaches and so can be used even where there is no contract in place.

The 1994 Regulations are based on the EC Directive on unfair terms in consumer contracting. The Directive was obviously aimed at harmonising rules on consumer protection throughout the European Union in order to make the Single Market more effective. At the time of its introduction the rules of different member states were quite divergent.

The Regulations are in some senses much narrower than the 1977 Act. This is because existing UK law already provided many of the features of the Directive and therefore required no further enactment.

Nevertheless, in some ways the Regulations are actually much broader than the 1977 Act because the Directive was intended to apply in a much broader range of circumstances than the Act, and often imposes stricter duties.

The consequence of the above factors is that the courts, when construing specific exclusion clauses, may feel that it is appropriate to have regard to the 1977 Act, the Regulations, and the common law before determining the validity of the clause.

7.3.2 The unfair contract terms Act 1977

When passed, the 1977 Act was certainly one of the most significant areas of consumer protection, and it remains significant. However, it should be remembered that the Act does not provide a general framework to deal with every exclusion clause or indeed every unfair term.

A further limitation of the scope of the Act is identified in s 1(3) which states that the major provisions in ss 2–7 also apply only in respect of 'business liability'. Section 14 gives a loose definition of 'business' which includes professions, government and local or public authorities. It is uncertain whether certain organisations fall under this general definition. What is certain is that parties who do not fall within the definition can incorporate exclusion clauses into contracts without being subject to the controls of the Act.

What the Act does try to achieve is protection of the consumer by removing some of the inequalities in bargaining strength. It does this by achieving three specific aims:

- Making certain exclusion clauses automatically invalid.
- Drawing a distinction between consumer contracts and inter-business dealings.
- Introducing a test of reasonableness to apply in inter-business dealings and in certain other circumstances.

As a result of these, and particularly the last two, some of the problems caused by unequal bargaining strength are mitigated. It must be remembered that the Act does not apply to all classes of contract since certain contracts are specifically excluded from the operation of the Act. However, the Act will apply in some situations where no contract exists, for example where the claimant is using free car parking provided by the defendant.

Exclusions and limitations rendered void by the Act

One of the crucial ways in which the Act controls the effective use of exclusion clauses is that certain types of exclusion clauses are invalidated by the Act. The inevitable consequence is that these exclusion clauses will be unenforceable even where they have been successfully incorporated in the contract and therefore cannot be relied on by the party inserting them in order to avoid liability.

There is a definitive list of invalid exclusions. These are:

- By s 2(1), a party cannot exclude liability for death or personal injury caused by his own negligence.
- By s 5(1), in any consumer contract clauses that seek to exclude liability by reference to the terms of a guarantee will fail in respect of defects which have been caused by negligence in the manufacture or distribution of the goods.
- By s 6(1), there can be no valid exclusion of liability for breaches of the implied condition as to title in s 12 of the Sale of Goods Act 1979.
- This same provision applies in respect of Schedule 4 to the Consumer Credit Act 1974, which concerns the same type of condition, and there can be no valid exclusion of liability.
- By s 6(2), there can be no valid exclusion clause inserted in any consumer contract to avoid liability for breaches of the implied conditions in the Sale of Goods Act 1979 that:
  - the goods must correspond to any description applied to them (s 13)
  - the goods are of satisfactory quality (s 14(2))
  - the goods are fit for the purpose(s) for which they are bought (s 14(3))
  - in a sale by sample, the bulk of the goods will correspond to the sample (s 15).
- Again, the provision will invalidate breaches of the same conditions in Schedule 4 to the Consumer Credit Act 1974 so that liability for such breaches cannot be avoided.
- Under s 7(1), similar principles to those in s 6 apply in respect of goods which are transferred under the Supply of Goods and Services Act 1982.

It is also worth noting that under the Consumer Protection Act 1987 there can be no valid exclusion of liability for breaches of the basic safety standards and so liability cannot be avoided but is generally strict.

Definitions of consumer contract and inter-business dealing

The 1977 Act inevitably is designed to operate principally for the protection of consumers. As a result, the term 'consumer' has to be defined in the Act. The definition is found in s 12(1) which identifies that a party acts as a consumer in a contract when:

SECTION

'(a) he neither makes the contract in the course of a business nor holds himself out as doing so; and

(b) the other party does make the contract in the course of a business; and

(c) ... the goods passing under or in pursuance of the contract are of a type ordinarily supplied for private use or consumption.'

If the party inserting the exclusion clause in the contract wants to argue that the party subject to the clause is not a consumer then, by s 12(3), he must prove it.

Whether or not a contract involves a consumer dealing is clearly a matter of construction for the courts. There are many situations where a party might buy goods that are ordinarily for business use, or a businessman buys goods but not for business use, so that difficulties can arise. Besides which, a consumer can fall outside the definition in s 12 and thus lose the protection it entails if he holds himself out as acting in the course of a business in order to acquire a trade discount.

The standard approach adopted by the courts is potentially very broad and has been subject to some criticism.

CASE EXAMPLE

R and B Customs Brokers Co Ltd v United Dominions Trust Ltd
[1988] 1 All ER 847

The claimants were a private company operating as shipping brokers and freight forwarding agents, the company being owned and controlled by Mr and Mrs Bell. They bought a second-hand car, partly for business use and partly for their own private use. In their action the question for the Court of Appeal was whether or not the purchase had been a consumer contract and therefore whether or not it was made in the course of a business. The Court of Appeal held that the purchase was a consumer purchase since the company was not in the business of buying and selling cars.

This decision has been strongly criticised since a literal interpretation of the section would produce an entirely different result. If a purposive approach were taken, then the clear purpose of drawing a distinction between businesses and consumers is that consumers are usually the ones subjected to, rather than inserting, exclusions and so are the party needing greater protection under the Act. In an inter-business dealing the purchaser would still be protected by the requirements of reasonableness discussed below.

ACTIVITY

Quick quiz

Consider which of the following may be consumer dealings:
1. A solicitor buys 200 square yards of carpet to carpet her offices.
2. A carpet salesman sells at cost price to his brother enough carpet to carpet the whole house.
3. A private individual who owns seven large chest freezers buys enough lambs and pigs, cut into joints, to fill the freezers.
4. A young man buys a second-hand ambulance to use as a normal vehicle.

Exclusions depending for their validity on a test of reasonableness

The 1977 Act identifies a number of contractual situations in which an exclusion clause will be valid only provided that it satisfies a test of reasonableness. If it fails to satisfy these criteria then it will be invalid. Inevitably, while a number of these apply to both consumer and inter-business dealing, the provisions in general are particularly relevant to the control of exclusion clauses in an inter-business context.

- By s 2(2), a clause seeking to exclude liability for loss, other than death or personal injury, caused by the negligence of the party inserting the clause is only valid and can only be relied upon if it satisfies the test of reasonableness contained in the Act (a general category relating to avoidance of liability for negligence).

By s 3, in those contracts where one party deals as a consumer or, if not, deals on the other party's standard business forms, the party inserting an exclusion clause cannot rely on a clause excluding liability for his own breach, or for a substantially different performance, or for no performance at all, except where to do so would satisfy the test of reasonableness in the Act (particularly appropriate to inter-business dealings and may apply to variation of terms, eg, by travel agents).

By s 6(3), in inter-business dealings a party can only exclude liability for breaches of the implied conditions in:

- s 13 (description)
- s 14(2) (satisfactory quality)
- s 14(3) (fitness for the purpose), and
- s 15 (sale by sample)

of the Sale of Goods Act 1979 where the test of reasonableness is satisfied. (This is the equivalent of s 6(2) in consumer contracts – the difference being that the consumer gets the greater protection of not being bound by such a clause at all.)

This same principle operates in the case of private sellers (those not selling in the course of a business) in respect of exclusions for breaches of s 13 and s 15 of the Sale of Goods Act 1979 which are therefore subject to the test of reasonableness for validity. (There is a difference from s 14(2) and s 14(3) here because in those sections of the Sale of Goods Act there is a specific requirement that the seller is selling in the course of a business.)

By s 7(3), exactly the same requirement of reasonableness operates in respect of exclusions for breaches of the implied conditions in ss 3, 4 and 5 of the Supply of Goods and Services Act 1982.

Under s 8, any clause seeking to exclude liability for misrepresentations will be subject to the same requirement of reasonableness.

By s 4, in consumer contracts clauses requiring a party to indemnify the other against loss will be valid only where the clause satisfies the reasonableness test. (Such a clause might require the consumer to indemnify the party inserting the indemnity clause for injury, loss or damage caused to third parties.)

CASE EXAMPLE

Thompson v T Lohan (Plant Hire) Ltd & J W Hurdiss Ltd [1987] 1 WLR 649

A plant hire company hired out a JCB and driver. The contract required that the driver supplied should be competent, but the party hiring them would be liable for all claims arising from the use of the equipment or the work of the driver. On top of this, the contract required them to indemnify the plant hire company for any claims against them. When the claimant was killed as a result of the driver's negligence, the defendants claimed that the clause was a void exclusion clause under s 2(1) of the 1977 Act. The court held that it was in fact an indemnity clause covered by s 4 and thus subject to a test of reasonableness in determining its validity.

These sections, then, are a means of ensuring a proper control of the use of exclusion clauses while still protecting the principle of freedom of contract. They allow parties to use exclusion clauses in certain circumstances, provided that they satisfy the statutory definition of reasonableness explained below.

The test of reasonableness

Guidelines on what can be classed as reasonable are contained in both s 11 of and Schedule 2 to the 1977 Act. These are not absolutely definitive, so that the test is one really for judicial interpretation. However, there is only a limited amount of case law on the area.

Section 11(5) places the burden of proof on the party who inserts the clause in the contract, and thus seeks to rely on it, to show that it is reasonable in all the circumstances.

CASE EXAMPLE

Warren v Truprint Ltd [1986] BTLC 344

A contract contained a limitation clause whereby the defendants, a photo processing company, were responsible only for a replacement film and would only undertake further liability if a supplementary charge were paid. The section thus required the defendants to prove that the clause was reasonable within the meaning of the 1977 Act. They were unable to show that this clause was reasonable when they lost a couple's silver wedding snaps. Inevitably, the court held that there was a value to the photographs that went beyond the cost of a replacement film, and that the defendants should have understood this when contracting.

In fact, there is no single definition of 'reasonableness' in the 1977 Act. There are in effect three tests to be applied in measuring reasonableness.

- Firstly, under s 11(1), which applies to all exclusion clauses, there is a very general test, based on whether the insertion of the term in the contract is reasonable in the light of what was known to the parties at the time they contracted. The clause must be 'a fair and reasonable one to be included having regard to the circumstances which were, or ought reasonably to have been, known to or in the contemplation of the parties when the contract was made'.

CASE EXAMPLE

Smith v Eric S Bush [1990] 1 AC 831

Here, surveyors negligently carried out a building society valuation in advance of a house purchase, and a defect was missed which later resulted in substantial loss to the purchaser. Under the building society terms, the purchaser was obliged to pay for the valuation report even though it was commissioned on behalf of the building society. This and the mortgage application contained clauses excluding liability for the accuracy of the valuation report. The attempt to rely on the exclusion clause failed since the court was unwilling to accept that its inclusion was reasonable. It should have been obvious that the purchaser would rely on the findings of the valuation and act on them.

- Section 11(2) concerns those exclusion clauses referred to in s 6(3) and s 7(3), those involving breaches of the implied conditions in the Sale of Goods Act 1979 and the Supply of Goods and Services Act 1982 in inter-business dealings. In the case of these, the court should consider the criteria set out in Schedule 2
  - whether the bargaining strength of the two parties was comparable or equal; for instance, if the buyer could easily be supplied from another source then it is more likely that the clause would be accepted as reasonable

- whether or not the buyer received any inducement or advantage from the supplier that might make insertion of the exclusion clause reasonable, particularly if such an advantage could not be gained from any other source of supply. Such an advantage is more likely to make the exclusion reasonable
- whether the goods were manufactured, processed or adapted to the buyer's specifications. If the seller operated according to the buyer 's own set specifications then it is clearly more likely that an exclusion will be accepted as reasonable
- whether exclusions or limitations of liability were customary practice or whether the buyer ought for any other reason to have known of the existence or extent of such a clause.

CASE EXAMPLE

Watford Electronics Ltd v Sanderson CFL [2001] 1 All ER (Comm) 696

The defendants provided and integrated software into Watford's existing computer system. When Watford terminated the agreement because the system did not work satisfactorily, the cost stood at £105,000. Watford claimed damages for breach of contract for £5.5 million, or for misrepresentation and negligence of about £1.1 million. In the defendant's standard terms there was a clause excluding liability for any claims for indirect or consequential losses, whether arising from negligence or otherwise, and limiting any liability to the price of the goods as supplied. The 1977 Act was held to apply to the contract so the question for the court was whether or not the clause satisfied the test of reasonableness. The Court of Appeal was prepared to accept that it did since the parties were of equal bargaining power and the limitation clause was subject to negotiation when the contract was made.

- Section 11(4) specifically concerns limitation clauses. Here, for the clause to be considered reasonable, the party inserting the clause must show:

  '(a) the resources which [the defendant] could expect to be available to him for the purposes of meeting liability should it arise; and
  (b) how far it was open to him to cover himself by insurance.'

CASE EXAMPLE

George Mitchell Ltd v Finney Lock Seeds Ltd [1983] 2 AC 803

Here, the House of Lords considered that the clause limiting damages to the price of the seeds was unreasonable since the suppliers had often settled out of court in the past and could have insured against such loss without altering their profits substantially.

Contracts falling outside the scope of the 1977 Act

As previously stated, one of the limitations of the 1977 Act is that there are a number of contracts of specific types which will not be covered by its provisions. These are to be found in Schedule 1:

- contracts of insurance
- contracts for the creation, transfer or termination of interests in land
- contracts that involve the creation or transfer of rights under patents, copyright and other intellectual property
- contracts for the creation or dissolution of companies, partnerships or unincorporated associations

- contracts for marine salvage, charterparties, or carriage of goods by sea or air (except in the case of incidents falling within the scope of s 2(1))
- contracts for the creation or transfer of securities.

7.3.3 The unfair terms in consumer contracts Regulations 1999

The scope of the Regulations

The Regulations are straightaway significantly different in operation to the 1977 Act because they cover contractual terms in general, not just exclusion clauses. Nevertheless, they will, as their name suggests, operate only in relation to consumer contracts. By s5(1), however, they will not apply to clauses in contracts that are individually negotiated.

'Consumer dealing' is defined in terms different to those used in the Unfair Contract Terms Act 1977:

- A 'seller' or 'supplier' is defined as 'any person who sells or supplies goods or services and who in making a contract is acting for purposes related to his business'. So this is wider than in the 1977 Act.
- A 'consumer' is defined as 'any natural person who is acting for purposes which are outside his trade, business or profession'. So, this is narrower.

According to reg 5(1), the Regulations will apply only where the parties have not individually negotiated the term in question. So the Regulations operate particularly in relation to standard form contracts. In order to avoid the operation of the Regulations, therefore, the seller or supplier will need to show that the contract has been negotiated and is not in standard form.

As with the 1977 Act, the Regulations will not operate in the case of certain types of contract. These are identified in Sch 1 and include contracts relating to employment, succession, family law rights and partnerships and companies. Neither will the Regulations cover insurance contracts where the risk and the insured are clearly defined. Other than this, the scope of the Regulations seems to be much broader than the 1977 Act, though their exact scope is uncertain.

Terms falling within the scope of the Regulations

The Regulations operate in respect of 'unfair terms'. According to reg 5(1) (reg 4(1) under the 1994 Regulations), an unfair term is 'any term which contrary to good faith causes a significant imbalance in the parties' rights and obligations under the contract to the detriment of the consumer'.

As a result, the Regulations introduce a general concept of unfairness into the making of contracts, which is then subject to controls.

'Good faith' was considered in Sch 2 to the 1994 Regulations. This identified a number of factors that must be looked at in order to establish good faith:

- The relative bargaining strength of the parties to the contract.
- Whether the seller or supplier gave the consumer any inducement in order that he would agree to the term of the contract in question.
- Whether the goods sold or services supplied under the contract were to the special order of the consumer.
- The extent to which the seller or supplier has dealt fairly and equitably with the consumer.

The list has not been reproduced in the 1999 Regulations but it is likely that the courts will still continue to consider such factors in determining whether a particular clause in a consumer contract is or is not fair.

There is little case law on the issue of what falls within the scope of the Regulations. However, the courts have considered the meaning of 'good faith' under reg 5(1).

CASE EXAMPLE

Director General of Fair Trading v First National Bank plc
[2002] 1 All ER 97

Here, a fairly standard clause in a loan agreement with a bank provided that if the lender defaulted on an instalment of the loan then the full amount became payable. Connected to this clause was another provision identifying that interest on the outstanding debt would be payable even following any judgment by a court. The Director General, through the processes provided by the Regulations, challenged this clause. In the Court of Appeal it was held that this amounted to an 'unfair surprise' and therefore was contrary to the requirement of 'good faith' under reg 4(1) of the 1994 Regulations (now reg 5(1) in the 1999 Regulations). The House of Lords disagreed. Lord Bingham, for the majority, identified that the words 'significant imbalance' in the regulation referred to the substance of the agreement but that the words 'good faith' covered only procedural fairness. However, Lord Steyn did think that the words should cover both substance and procedure, in other words not just the fairness of the making of the contract but the fairness of the terms contained in it. The House held that the clause did not contravene the Regulations.

As well as these general guidelines, the Regulations, in Sch 2 (and formerly in the 1994 Regulations in Sch 3), list a great number of terms that may generally be regarded as unfair, though the list is not intended to be exhaustive:

a. terms which limit or exclude liability for the death or personal injury of the consumer arising from an act or omission of the seller or supplier
b. terms which inappropriately limit or exclude liability for a partial performance, a non-performance or an inadequate performance
c. terms that include provisions binding the consumer but which are only at the discretion of the seller or supplier
d. terms allowing the seller or supplier to retain sums already paid over by the consumer who cancels the contract where there is no reciprocal term in relation to a cancellation by the seller or supplier
e. terms requiring a consumer who is in breach of the contract to pay excessive sums in compensation to the seller or supplier
f. terms allowing the seller or supplier to dissolve the contract where the same facility is not made available to the consumer by the contract
g. terms that enable a seller or supplier to dissolve a contract that has only indeterminate duration without giving reasonable notice of the dissolution, except where there are serious grounds for doing so
h. terms which automatically allow a seller or supplier to extend a contract of fixed duration where the consumer does not indicate otherwise, when the deadline set for the consumer to indicate the contrary desire not to extend the contract is set unreasonably early
i. terms which irrevocably bind the consumer to terms with which he had no real opportunity to become acquainted prior to the formation of the contract

j. terms that allow the seller or supplier unilaterally to alter terms without any valid reason specified in the contract

k. terms allowing the seller or supplier unilaterally to alter without any valid reason the character of the goods or services supplied

l. terms enabling the price of goods to be determined at the time of delivery or which allow a seller or supplier to alter prices without the consumer having the opportunity to cancel the contract

m. terms giving the seller or supplier the right to interpret terms of the contract or otherwise to determine whether the goods or services supplied correspond to the requirements of the contract

n. terms which limit obligations or commitments made by the agents of the sellers or suppliers

o. terms requiring the consumer to comply with all obligations under the contract but not imposing a similar obligation on the sellers or suppliers

p. terms which grant the sellers or suppliers the right to transfer obligations under the contract which might then have the effect of reducing the consumer's rights under any guarantees

q. terms which would have the effect of hindering the right of the consumer to take legal action or which would restrict the availability of evidence.

It must be remembered that the Regulations cannot be used to make a bad bargain good. The purpose of the Regulations is not to protect the consumer in that sense but to police the fairness of the bargain-making process.

A further requirement under reg 7 is that the terms of a contract should be expressed in plain and intelligible language. If any term is then found to be unfair under the Regulations it will not bind the consumer and interpretation of the terminology will usually be in favour of the consumer if there is any doubt or ambiguity.

The Regulations still have certain limitations. They do not apply to any term that has been individually negotiated. This quite sensibly preserves the principle of freedom of contract, but it also has the effect in some cases of presuming an equality of bargaining strength that does not in fact exist. In introducing the Regulations, the Government construed the provisions indicated in the Directive quite narrowly. As a result of this, while the Trading Standards Department has the power to challenge the standard form contracts of companies and large corporations, the same facility has not been extended to the consumer groups who may have wished to police contracts. In consequence, the Directive may not be given full effect.

The Law Commission has proposed reforms for the area of statutory control of terms in Law Commission Report No 292 on unfair contract terms. The suggestion is to combine the 1977 Act and the 1999 Regulations and to simplify the language involved.

ACTIVITY

Self-assessment questions

1. To what extent will the Unfair Contract Terms Act 1977 prevent the exclusion or limitation of liability for negligence?

2. In what ways are a consumer dealing and an inter-business dealing different?

3. For what reasons does the Unfair Contract Terms Act 1977 make certain exclusions automatically invalid if inserted in a contract?

4. Under the Unfair Contract Terms Act 1977, what exactly does 'reasonable' mean?

5. Is there any difference between who is protected by the Unfair Contract Terms Act 1977 and by the Unfair Terms in Consumer Contracts Regulations 1999?

Statutory regulation of exclusion clauses	Case/statute
Common law controls have also been supplemented by statutory controls.	Unfair Contract Terms Act 1977
The 1977 Act draws a distinction between consumer and inter-business dealings.	
Some clauses are made void by the 1977 Act, eg:	
• exclusion of liability for death or injury caused by negligence	s 2(1)
• exclusion of liability for breaches of the implied terms in the Sale of Goods Act 1979 and Supply of Goods and Services Act 1982.	ss 6(1); 6(2); 7(2)
Others depend for validity on a test of reasonableness, eg:	
• damage caused by negligence	s 2(2)
• in standard form contracts in inter-business dealings for breaches of Sale of Goods Act 1979 and Supply of Goods and Services Act 1982 implied terms.	ss 6(3) and 7(3)
Reasonableness depends on the knowledge of the parties at the time of contracting.	s 11
And a number of factors can be taken into account, eg whether the goods were freely available elsewhere, whether the goods were made to the buyer's specification etc.	Sch 2
Recent Regulations are much wider and refer to unfair terms generally, not just exclusion clauses, but apply in consumer contracts only.	Unfair Terms in Consumer Contracts Regulations 1994 (the latter to comply with European Directive 93/13)
In general, they are aimed at remedying inequality in bargaining strength and removing unequal conditions.	

SUMMARY

- An exclusion clause is a term of a contract that aims to avoid liability for breaches of the contract or even negligence, whereas a limitation clause is one which aims to reduce the amount of damages payable on a breach of contract.
- Judges developed controls on the use of exclusion clauses because of their potential unfairness to consumers – so an exclusion clause is not recognised unless it is incorporated into the contract.
- So the party subject to it must be made aware of it before or at the time of contracting – although it is possible for past dealings to be taken into account if they are relevant and consistent. The Regulations are much wider and refer to unfair terms generally, not just exclusion clauses, but apply in consumer contracts only and remove unequal conditions. Exclusion clauses in vending machines and on tickets are usually unenforceable.
- Oral misrepresentations about the clause may prevent the party inserting the clause in the contract from relying on it.
- If the clause is ambiguous it also cannot be relied upon.

- Where the parties contract on equal terms and the clause is clear and unambiguous, then it may be enforced, however onerous.
- There are also statutory controls through the Unfair Contract Terms Act 1977 and through the Unfair Terms in Consumer Contracts Regulations 1999.
- The Act draws a distinction between consumer dealings and inter-business dealings.
- Clauses in certain types of contract are made void by the Act, eg, exclusion of liability for death or injury caused by negligence, where others depend for their validity on a test of reasonableness, eg, damage caused by negligence.
- What is reasonable depends on the knowledge of the parties at the time of contracting and a number of factors can be taken into account, eg, whether the goods were freely available elsewhere, whether the goods were made to the buyer 's specification etc.
- The Regulations are much wider and refer to unfair terms generally, not just exclusion clauses, but apply in consumer contracts only and remove unequal conditions.

SAMPLE ESSAY QUESTION

Discuss the extent to which judges have taken a restrictive view towards the use of exemption clauses in contracts.

Define exemption clauses:

- An exclusion clause is one that seeks to avoid liability for contractual breaches and even torts
- A limitation clause seeks to reduce the amount of damages payable on breach

Explain how the courts have regulated the use of exemption clauses:

- Not enforceable unless correctly incorporated
- So must bring sufficiently to the other party's attention before contract formed
- Can only assume knowledge from past dealings if a consistent course of action
- *Contra preferentum* rule
- Overriding effect of oral misrepresentations

Discuss the reasons for the judicial controls:

- Exclusion clauses and limitation clauses can be harsh on the party subject to them
- Often that party is of weaker bargaining strength
- Otherwise originally *caveat emptor* (let the buyer beware) applied
- Even the Sale of Goods Act 1893 allowed for such clauses
- Growth of consumer protection in twentieth century

Discuss whether the approach of the judges is restrictive:

- Strict controls in the ticket cases
- Lord Denning's view – the clause should be written in large red letters and with a large arrow pointing at it
- *Contra preferentum* rule operates very strictly
- Strict view has also extended to clauses that are merely onerous

Discuss the comparable treatment when the parties are of equal bargaining strength:

- Much less strict and liberal view taken where the parties are of equal bargaining strength
- Judges would allow even clauses covering a very serious and costly breach when the clause in the contract has been negotiated freely by the parties
- So this is much more like freedom of contract

Further reading

Brown, I and Chandler, A, 'Unreasonableness and the Unfair Contract Terms Act' (1993) 109LQR 41.
Collins, H, 'Good Faith in European Contract Law' (1994) 14 OJLS 229.
Rutherford, L, 'Signature of a Document' (1998) NLJ 380.

8

Void and voidable contracts

AIMS AND OBJECTIVES

After reading this chapter you should be able to:

- Understand the nature of vitiating factors
- Distinguish between void contracts and voidable contracts

8.1 The nature of vitiating factors

We have looked so far at the requirements made on parties when entering into contracts, and also at the obligations that parties may make for themselves when they have in fact contracted. If the parties have not complied with all of the necessary requirements that we looked at in Chapter 1, then there will not be a contract in existence anyway.

Nevertheless, the mere fact that all of the rules of formation have been complied with does not make a contract perfect. For instance, where a party has contracted on the basis of false information, this is a denial of freedom of contract. That party may clearly have been unprepared to enter the contract if only he had known the true facts.

Thus, even though the various requirements of formation might have been fully met, a party may still have legal rights and remedies because of other defects that are later discovered, that are to do with other 'imperfections' at the time the contract was formed. Indeed, contracts affected in such a way are often referred to as 'imperfect contracts'.

The defects in question are generally known as **vitiating factors**. A vitiating factor is one that may operate to invalidate an otherwise validly formed contract, that is a contract that conforms to all the rules of formation already identified.

To 'vitiate' basically means to impair the quality of, to corrupt or to debase. In contractual terms, this means that factors present at the time of the formation of the contract, possibly unknown to one or either party, mean that the contract lacks the essential characteristic of voluntariness, is based on misinformation or is of a type frowned on by the law.

As a result, the role of the law is to provide a remedy to the party who may not have wished to enter the contract given full knowledge of the vitiating factor at the time of formation.

There can be two effects if a contract is vitiated: it may be **void** or it may be **voidable**. Whether the contract is void or voidable in a given case depends on the type of vitiating factor that is complained of.

8.2 Void contracts

In the case of certain vitiating factors the effect of demonstrating the presence of the vitiating factor to the court's satisfaction is to render the contract void. It is as though the contract has never been.

Stating that a contract is void is in many ways the same as stating that the contract does not exist.

This is because identifying a contract as void is identifying it as having no validity and therefore no enforceability in law.

8.3 Voidable contracts

Where a contract is voidable there are different possibilities. The vitiating factor is identified and acknowledged but this does not necessarily mean that the contract is at an end.

A party who has entered a contract that is voidable for a vitiating factor can continue with the contract if that is to his benefit.

On the other hand, that party can avoid their responsibilities under the contract and in effect set the contract aside.

8.4 Classes of vitiating factors

There are essentially four classes of vitiating factors which themselves are subject to sub-divisions:

- **Misrepresentation** – where a contract has been formed but as the result of false information about its substance, the innocent contracting party who is the victim of the misrepresentation can avoid the contract.
- **Mistake** – where the contract has been formed on the basis of mistakes about contracting terms made by either party or both parties; if the mistake is operative, then the contract is void.
- **Duress and undue influence** – duress being a common law area where the contract has resulted from actual or threatened violence and the contract is void; this is now supplemented by 'economic duress' (which is improper coercion in a commercial context) and 'undue influence' (which is an equitable doctrine concerning contracts that have been made following improper coercion and where the innocent party can avoid the contract).
- **Illegality** – of which there are many types, where the type of contract will not be accepted at all, sometimes by the courts and sometimes by statute, as being legitimate and enforceable, usually for reasons of public policy.

VOID AND VOIDABLE CONTRACTS

void contract

An agreement made that is legally unenforceable

voidable contract

An equitable right to avoid obligations under a contract because of a vitiating defect

ACTIVITY

Self-assessment questions

1. What does the term 'vitiating factor' mean?
2. What are the basic consequences of a contract being declared void?
3. What are the basic consequences of a contract being declared voidable?
4. Will a contract made on the basis of a misrepresentation generally be void or voidable?
5. Will a contract made on the basis of duress generally be void or voidable?
6. Will a contract that is declared illegal be void or voidable?

The different classes of vitiating factor	The consequences of the contract being vitiated
Misrepresentation	The contract is voidable by the party who is the victim of the misrepresentation.
Mistake	The contract is void at common law if operable. The contract may be voidable in equity in certain circumstances (but see *Great Peace*).
Duress	The contract is voidable by the victim of the duress.
Undue influence	The contract is voidable by the victim of the undue influence.
Illegal contracts	The contract is void either at common law or under statute.

Figure 8.1 The different consequences on a contract of the different vitiating factors

SUMMARY

- Vitiating factors are those where, although the contract has been formed correctly, it may be declared void or avoided by a party because of some other defect.
- Contracts that can be declared void are those that had no validity when formed because of the vitiating factor, eg, the contract was formed on the basis of a mistake made by both parties.
- Contracts that are voidable and can be avoided by one party are those that are based on some coercion or misrepresentation where the party can avoid his responsibilities or continue with the contract.

9

Vitiating factors: Misrepresentation

AIMS AND OBJECTIVES

After reading this chapter you should be able to:

- Define misrepresentation
- Understand the circumstances when a misrepresentation occurs
- Understand the different classes of misrepresentation
- Understand the different remedies available
- Understand the significance of the Misrepresentation Act 1967
- Understand the role of equity in relation to misrepresentation
- Understand the circumstances where non-disclosure will amount to misrepresentation
- Critically analyse the area
- Apply the law to factual situations and reach conclusions

9.1 Introduction

We have already considered in Chapter 3 that statements made before or at the time of contracting are known as representations. These representations can, if they are incorporated into the contract, be terms of the contract and as such, may be actionable if they are breached.

Representations that are not incorporated into the contract will have no contractual significance if they are factually and accurately stated. They will have acted to induce the other party into the contract but that is where they end. Alternatively, they may be 'puffs' having no contractual significance.

A falsely made representation, however, is a 'misrepresentation' and it can have contractual significance even though it does not form part of the contract. In order to be actionable, therefore, the statement must not only be false but have acted to induce the other party to enter the contract.

'Misrepresentation' may refer to the false statement itself or it may be the action of making the false statement. The statement may be false or merely incorrect, for it is now possible to claim for an innocent misrepresentation.

The consequence of a contract having been formed on the basis of a misrepresentation is for the contract to be **voidable** at the request of the party who is the victim of the misrepresentation. It is not void because this denies that party the right to continue with the contract if that is in their interest.

Traditionally, misrepresentation was not actionable at common law. Some relief was available in equity, subject to certain qualifications, and later a remedy was available where fraud could be proved. In general, though, a party had little possibility of claiming against a misrepresentation until the passing of the Misrepresentation Act 1967. For this reason it was often critical in the past for a party to prove that a statement made to them before the contract was a term.

It may still be advantageous to a party to identify that a representation has been incorporated as a term, though this is obviously more difficult where the contract is written. Misrepresentation should still be viewed in the general context of pre-contractual statements and representations.

A final point about misrepresentation, then, is that it depends on and is interrelated with other areas of contract law also. It is inevitably connected with terms. However, for instance, it also shares some features with **common mistake** on which basis cases very often act as illustrations of both.

Cheshire, Fifoot and Furmston identify the scope of the problem:

common mistake

Where both parties forming a contract make the same mistake about the existence of the subject-matter of the contract or the true ownership of the subject-matter of the contract

QUOTATION

'Misrepresentation straddles many legal boundaries. More than other topics in the law of contract, it is an amalgam of common law and equity … The basic problem in misrepresentation is the effect of pre-contractual statements … Dissatisfaction might properly have been directed either at the rules determining when a statement is to be treated as forming part of the contract or at the sometimes strange reluctance of the courts to hold apparently serious undertakings to be terms of the contract. But in practice, it has been felt that the solution should take the form of devising remedies, which do not depend on holding such statements to be terms of the contract.'

Cheshire, Fifoot and Furmston, Law of Contract *(14th edn, Butterworths, 2001)*

9.2 When a misrepresentation occurs

Defining 'misrepresentation'

A misrepresentation occurs, as we have already said, when one party makes a false representation at or before the time that the contract is made.

Inevitably, then, there are a number of essential elements that must be satisfied in order to claim this false statement as an actionable misrepresentation. Misrepresentation can therefore be defined according to these essential elements:

- a statement of material fact
- made by one party to a contract to the other party to the contract
- during the negotiations leading up to the formation of the contract

- which was intended to operate and did operate as an inducement to the other party to enter the contract
- but which was not intended to be a binding obligation under the contract
- and which was untrue or falsely or at least incorrectly stated

This is a very precise definition and if each element above cannot be identified in the statement then it cannot be said to give rise to a misrepresentation. Each element of the definition, then, needs to be considered individually.

1. *The statement alleged to be a misrepresentation must be a statement of material fact*

- The statement cannot therefore have been offered as a mere opinion. Even though an opinion was held mistakenly, if it was a genuinely held opinion then it cannot amount to a statement of fact or a misrepresentation. However, it may well of course be a misrepresentation if the opinion was not actually held at the time of the making of the statement.

CASE EXAMPLE

Bisset v Wilkinson [1927] AC 177

A representation as to the number of sheep that land could hold was not based on any expert knowledge as this was not in the possession of the person making it. It was a mere opinion, honestly but mistakenly held, and so it could neither be relied upon nor be actionable as a misrepresentation.

According to the Court of Appeal in *Springwell Navigation Corporation v J P Morgan Chase Bank* [2010] EWCA Civ 1221 a statement is an opinion rather than an actionable misrepresentation when there is no implied representation that there are objectively reasonable grounds for the statement.

- Neither can the statement be one that is merely expressing a future intention. This would be speculation rather than fact and a misrepresentation is a false assertion of the existence of a material fact. Again, expressing a future intention could amount to a misrepresentation if the statement actually falsely represented a state of mind which did not in fact exist at the time it was made.

CASE EXAMPLE

Edgington v Fitzmaurice (1885) 29 Ch D 459

The directors of a company borrowed money, representing that they would use the loan for the improvement of the company's buildings. In fact, they had intended from the start to use the loan to pay off serious debts that were owed by the company. They had misrepresented what their actual intentions were. The court regarded this as a false statement of material fact and an actionable misrepresentation.

- Inevitably, mere 'puffs' would not be classed as statements of fact. These statements are mere boasts and they attach no weight. Courts will not accept that they are intended to be relied upon at all unless they profess to contain factual information.

CASE EXAMPLE

Carlill v The Carbolic Smoke Ball Co Ltd [1893] 1 QB 256

The company's argument that its promise to pay £100 to whoever contracted flu was only a puff failed. The maxim *simplex commendatio non obligat* could not apply because it had supported the promise by lodging £1,000 in a bank to cover possible claims.

■ It is not always necessary for the statement to be made in writing or orally. It is indeed possible that the statement could be made by conduct, in the same way that a contract could be formed by the conduct of the parties.

CASE EXAMPLE

Spice Girls Ltd v Aprilia World Service BV [2000] EMLR478

Here, the girl group had been offered a contract with a manufacturer of scooters, to promote its products through advertising. Before the contract was actually signed, the group took part in the filming of a commercial. All members of the group took part in the filming even though they all knew that one member of the group was about to leave, as she later did. In a dispute between the manufacturers and the group, the court held that the presence of all members of the group at the filming of the commercial amounted to a representation that none of them intended to leave the group and none of them was aware that one member intended to. As such, taking part in the filming of the commercial was a misrepresentation. It was a false statement of fact made by their conduct in attending.

■ Silence will generally not amount to a misrepresentation since no statement has been made. However, it is possible in certain circumstances that there is a duty on one party to inform the other party and in certain limited circumstances failing to provide that information could amount to a misrepresentation (see section 9.5, where non-disclosure amounts to misrepresentation).

2. *The statement alleged to be a misrepresentation must have been made by one party to the contract to the other party*

As a result, it will not be a misrepresentation where this false statement was made by a third party, unless that third party is the agent of the party against whom the misrepresentation is alleged.

CASE EXAMPLE

Peyman v Lanjani [1985] 2 WLR 154

The defendant took the lease of premises under an agreement requiring the landlord's permission. The defendant did not attend the meeting at which the agreement was struck but sent an agent who he thought would create a better impression with the landlord. He later decided to sell the lease on to the claimant and again this would require the landlord's permission. Once more he sent his agent. The claimant discovered the deception after he had paid over £10,000 under the agreement with the defendant. He then successfully applied to rescind the contract. Using the agent was a misrepresentation of the legitimacy of the lease which had never been agreed between the defendant and the landlord.

3. The statement alleged to be a misrepresentation must have been made before or at the time of the contract

In order to operate on the mind of the representee and induce him to enter the contract, the representation must have been made either before or at the time that the contract was formed. If the statement was made after the agreement was reached then it cannot be actionable as a misrepresentation because it had no effect on the formation of the contract.

CASE EXAMPLE

Roscorla v Thomas (1842) 3 QBD 234

After a deal had been struck for the sale and purchase of a horse, the seller then represented to the buyer that the horse was 'sound and free from vice'. In fact, the horse was unruly and also had a quite vicious character. However, the purchaser could not claim since the promise was made after the agreement.

4. The statement alleged to be a misrepresentation must be an inducement to enter the contract

An actionable misrepresentation is one that vitiates the consent of the party who relied on it in entering the contract. Therefore it must have been of material significance to the making of the contract in order to have any effect in law.

CASE EXAMPLE

JEB Fasteners Ltd v Marks Bloom & Co Ltd [1983] 1 All ER 583

Here, the claimant engaged in a take-over of another company. This was done for the purpose of obtaining the services of two of the directors of the other company, rather than for any commercial advantage in the take-over. In investigating the company prior to the take-over, the claimant relied on the company's accounts which in fact had been negligently prepared. There could be no claim of misrepresentation since the purpose of taking over the company was to secure the services of the directors. The accounts therefore could not have acted as an inducement. They were not material to the real purpose of the contract.

....

rescission

An equitable mechanism used to place the parties back in their pre-contractual position

....

However, in contrast, it will not matter that the representation would not generally be regarded as an inducement, provided that it did in fact induce the claimant to enter the contract. In that case it will be actionable.

CASE EXAMPLE

Museprime Properties Ltd v Adhill Properties Ltd [1990] EGLR 196

Three properties were sold by auction. In advance of the auction there was a misrepresentation concerning the existence of an outstanding rent review which could result in increased rents and therefore increased revenue, making it a more attractive proposition. The defendants unsuccessfully challenged the claimants' claim for **rescission**, arguing that the statement could realistically induce nobody to enter the contract. The Court of Appeal rejected their defence and applied a subjective test. It held that it was not important whether or not a reasonable bidder would have been induced by the representation; the question was merely whether or not the claimant in the case had been induced by the representation to enter the contract.

Inevitably, there cannot have been any inducement where the other party actually remained unaware of the misrepresentation.

Neither will it be a misrepresentation where the party to whom a false statement is made is already aware that the statement is false. In this case there can be no misrepresentation since the party must still have been prepared to enter the contract despite the false statement and so has not been induced to enter the contract because of it.

In the same way, it will not be a misrepresentation where the party to whom the statement was made never actually relied upon the statement in entering the contract. Again, he was not induced to enter the contract because of the false statement but would have entered the contract anyway, for whatever reason.

CASE EXAMPLE

Attwood v Small [1838] 7 ER 684

Here, a mine was purchased under a contract and certain information was given as to the remaining capacity of mineral ore. This statement as to the capacity was in fact false. The claimant could not argue a misrepresentation, however, since before buying the mine he had actually commissioned his own mineral survey. Unfortunately, in the circumstances, this survey was also inaccurate. When the error eventually came to light the purchaser was unable to argue misrepresentation since, in entering the contract, he had in effect relied on his own skill and judgment, not the false statement of the seller.

One final point identified in *Edgington v Fitzmaurice* (1885) 29 Ch D 459 is that it will not be fatal to a claim that other inducements besides the misrepresentation itself were relied upon in entering the contract.

5. *The statement alleged to be a misrepresentation must not have been intended to form part of the contract*

If the statement were intended to be contractually binding then, if anything, it would be a warranty of the contract rather than a misrepresentation. The appropriate action in this case would be for breach of contract, not for misrepresentation.

CASE EXAMPLE

Couchman v Hill [1947] KB 554

The claimant bought a heifer (a young female cow) at an auction. The heifer was described in the catalogue as being 'unserved' (in other words, that it had not mated with a bull). The printed conditions also stated that: 'The lots are sold with all faults, imperfections, and errors of descriptions, genuineness, or authenticity of, or any fault or defect in any lot, and giving no warranty whatever'. The heifer was in fact pregnant at the time of the auction and died two months later through a miscarriage. Here, the statement that the heifer was 'unserved' could not be a misrepresentation because of the significance attached to it. It was a term incorporated into the contract despite the attempted exemptions applied to it.

6. *The representation must have been falsely made*

The overriding requirement for the statement to be actionable is that it must have been falsely made, whether or not this was innocent or deliberate. Clearly, if the representation was true it would have no further contractual significance once the contract was formed. There would be no further action on it because in that sense the contract would be complete.

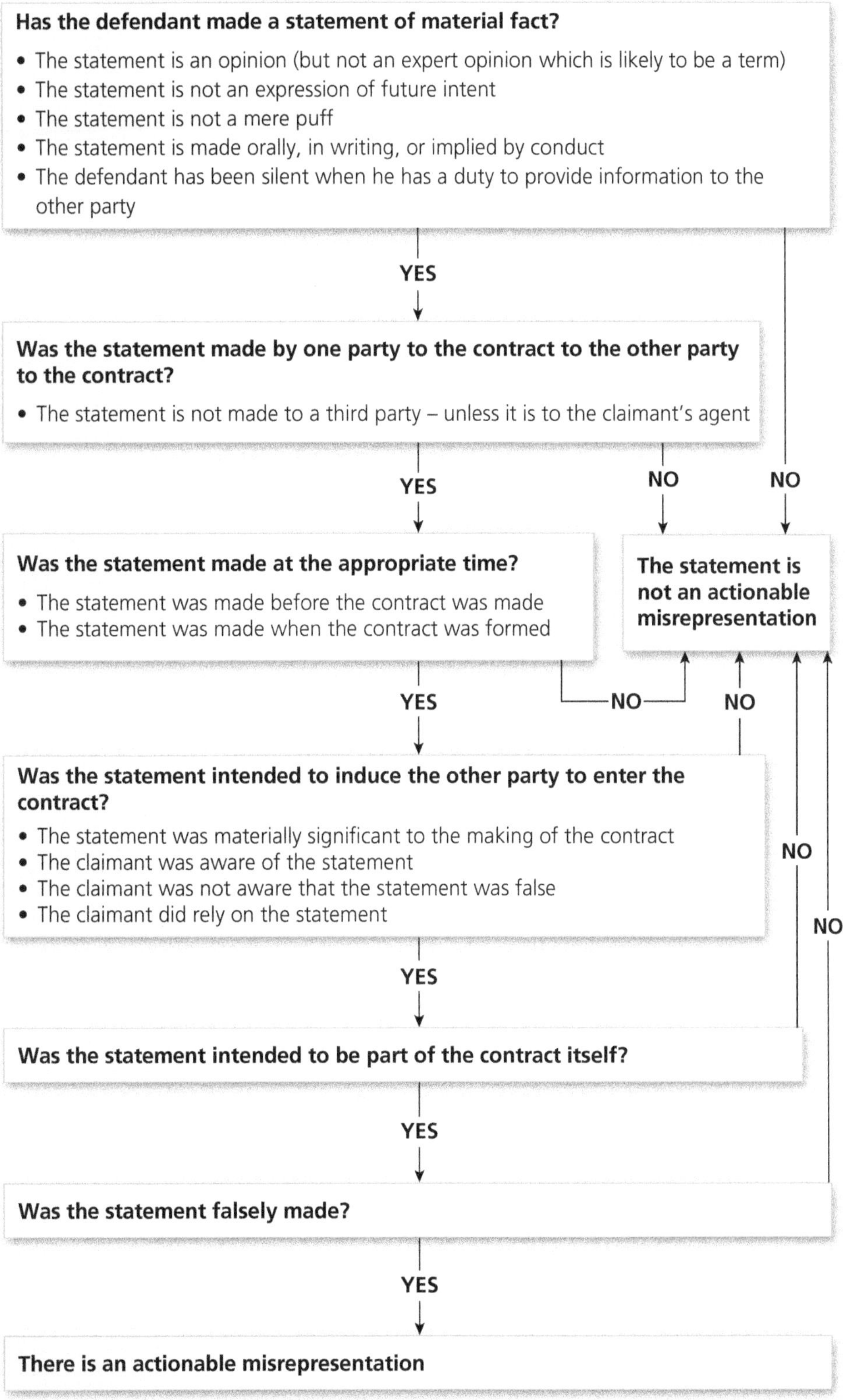

Has the defendant made a statement of material fact?

- The statement is an opinion (but not an expert opinion which is likely to be a term)
- The statement is not an expression of future intent
- The statement is not a mere puff
- The statement is made orally, in writing, or implied by conduct
- The defendant has been silent when he has a duty to provide information to the other party

YES

Was the statement made by one party to the contract to the other party to the contract?

- The statement is not made to a third party – unless it is to the claimant's agent

YES NO NO

Was the statement made at the appropriate time?

- The statement was made before the contract was made
- The statement was made when the contract was formed

The statement is not an actionable misrepresentation

YES NO NO

Was the statement intended to induce the other party to enter the contract?

- The statement was materially significant to the making of the contract
- The claimant was aware of the statement
- The claimant was not aware that the statement was false
- The claimant did rely on the statement

NO

NO

YES

Was the statement intended to be part of the contract itself?

YES

Was the statement falsely made?

YES

There is an actionable misrepresentation

Figure 9.1 Diagram illustrating when a misrepresentation has occurred

ACTIVITY

1. What is a misrepresentation?
2. How can misrepresentation be distinguished from other types of vitiating factor?
3. How can a misrepresentation be distinguished from an opinion?
4. Why does it matter whether the misrepresentation actually induces the other party to enter into the contract or not?
5. Why is it important to think of misrepresentation in the context of all pre-contractual statements?

9.3 The classes of misrepresentation and their remedies

The character of a misrepresentation

A misrepresentation can obviously occur in a number of different ways. It could be a merely inaccurate statement, made, for instance, in all innocence, the inaccuracy being unknown to the maker of the statement. This could happen where the maker of the state ment is relying on information supplied in manufacturers' specifications, for example, or oral statements made about goods by a previous owner. On the other hand, a misrepresentation can also be a quite deliberate lie, intended to deceive and stated in full knowledge that it is untrue. In between these points, a misrepresentation can also be carelessly made by assuming knowledge and failing to check on the actual details.

As a result, it is possible to class misrepresentations according to three distinct types:

- fraudulent
- negligent
- innocent

Since the passing of the Misrepresentation Act 1967, the significance of the classification, certainly between the last two, is less marked than it was. However, the classification can still be important in determining what remedy is available to a party who is the victim of the misrepresentation.

Traditionally, the character of the misrepresentation was vital since only a fraudulently made misrepresentation was actionable, and this would be under the tort of deceit rather than under contract law itself.

Originally, everything that was not a fraud was classed as an innocent misrepresentation and the only available remedy was for rescission of the contract in equity. Now it is possible to identify fraudulent, negligent and innocent misrepresentations, and there are remedies available at common law and under statute.

9.3.1 Fraudulent misrepresentation

At common law, traditionally, the only action available for a misrepresentation was where fraud could also be proved. Even this action is fairly recent, having developed only at the end of the nineteenth century. This clearly demonstrates just how vital it was for many litigants in the past to show that the statement on which they claimed to have relied had been incorporated into the contract as a term. If they could not do this then they might well be left without any remedy at all.

CASE EXAMPLE

Derry v Peek (1889) 14 App Cas 337

A tram company was licensed by Act of Parliament to operate horse-drawn trams. Under a further provision of the Act it was also possible to use mechanical power but only by gaining the certification of the Board of Trade first. The company then made an application for a licence but also issued a prospectus in order to raise further share capital in which in effect it falsely represented that it was able to use mechanical power. It did so honestly, believing that the necessary licence would be granted by the Board of Trade. However, in the event its application was actually denied and the company fell into liquidation. Peek, who had invested on the strength of the representation in the prospectus, then lost money as a result of the liquidation, and sued in the tort of deceit. His action failed since the court held that there was insufficient proof of fraud. Lord Herschell in the House of Lords defined the action as requiring actual proof that the false representation was made 'knowingly or without belief in its truth or recklessly careless whether it be true or false'.

So these are the three possibilities if an action in deceit is to be successful:

- **Knowing the statement to be false** – this is straightforward since the representor knew the inaccuracy of his statement. In other words, there is a deliberate falsehood.
- **Without belief in the truth of the statement** – if the representor acted without belief in the statement then this is also a statement that is in effect falsely made.
- **Reckless or careless as to whether the statement is true or false** – a recklessly made statement must be something more than mere carelessness.

It can also of course be deceit where an opinion is allegedly expressed which is not genuinely held because this would amount to a false statement of fact. In *Cherrilow Ltd v Richard Butler-Creagh* [2011] EWCH 2525 the court held that a party was induced into entering a contract for the purchase of a property because of a representation made as to its value of £22.5 million when in fact the more realistic market value was £10 million. There were no grounds to suppose that anyone would buy the property at the value represented and as such the representation was a false statement of fact rather than a genuine opinion.

In all cases the essence of liability is the dishonesty of the defendant in making a statement which he did not honestly know to be true. The motive for making the statement is largely irrelevant. If the claimant has suffered loss as a result, then there is a claim.

CASE EXAMPLE

Akerhielm v De Mare [1959] AC 789

In this case the directors of a company made an untrue statement that two-thirds of the capital of the company had already been subscribed. Inevitably, the reason for doing so was in order to improve the apparent standing of the company. Nevertheless the Privy Council accepted that the directors had an honest belief in the truth of the statement which was sufficient to avoid liability.

The simplest defence available in an action for fraud, then, is to show an honest belief in the truth of the statement. It would not have to be a reasonable belief, provided it was honestly held, and as a result fraud is extremely difficult to prove.

Recklessness is only evidence that a fraud may have occurred. It is not actual proof of fraud unless it can be shown to amount to a blatant disregard for the truth and therefore also, amount to dishonesty (see *Thomas Witter Ltd v TBP Industries Ltd* [1996] 2 All ER 573).

Remedies for fraudulent misrepresentation

As has already been identified, a party suffering a loss as the result of a fraudulent misrepresentation can sue for damages in the tort of deceit. Inevitably, then, the method of assessing any damages awarded will be according to the tort measure, ie, to put the claimant in the position he would have been in if the tort had not occurred, rather than the contract measure which is to put the claimant in the position that he would have been in if the contract had been properly performed. In *Clef Aquitaine SARL v Laporte Materials (Barrow) Ltd* [2000] 3 All ER 493, for instance, the claimant entered into long-term agreements as a result of fraudulent claims by the defendant. The agreements were not as profitable as they would have been if the truth had been told at the time of contracting. The claimant was able to recover damages for the loss of profit.

There are potential benefits to be gained from this since it may result in more being recovered by way of any claim for consequential loss.

JUDGMENT

Lord Denning explained this in *Doyle v Olby (Ironmongers) Ltd* [1969] 2 QB 158: 'the defendant is bound to make reparation for all the damage flowing from the fraudulent inducement'.

This point has been confirmed so that the defendant is responsible for all losses including any consequential loss, providing a causal link can be shown between the fraudulent inducement and the claimant's loss.

CASE EXAMPLE

Smith New Court Securities v Scrimgeour Vickers [1996] 4 All ER 769

The claimants had been induced to buy shares in Ferranti at 82.25p per share, as a result of a fraudulent misrepresentation that the company was a good marketing risk. The shares were actually trading at 78p per share at the time of the transaction. Unknown to either party, the shares were worth considerably less since Ferranti itself had been the victim of a major fraud. The claimants, on later discovering the fraud, chose not to rescind but to sell the shares on at prices ranging from 49p down to as low as 30p per share. The House of Lords held that the losses incurred by the claimants were a direct result of the fraud that had induced them to contract. The court held that as a result any losses awarded should be based on the figure actually paid of 82.25p rather than the 78p which was the actual value of the shares at the time that they were bought.

There are two clear consequences of the judgment:

- that heavier claims can be pursued if fraud is alleged and proved, and
- that there is therefore an encouragement to do so if proof is available.

The claimant who is a victim suffering loss as the result of a fraudulent misrepresentation, then, has two clear choices on discovering the fraud:

- he may affirm the contract and go on to sue for damages as indicated above
- but the claimant might also disaffirm the contract and refuse further performance.

If the claimant chooses the latter of the two courses of action then there are two further possible alternatives open to him:

- Firstly, if there is nothing at this point to be gained by bringing action against the other party, then the claimant can discontinue performance of his obligations and do nothing. Then if he is sued by the maker of the fraud he can then use the misrepresentation as a defence to that claim. (In this respect the claimant may refuse to return what he has already received under the contract. A good example of this would be where a party gained insurance cover as a result of a fraudulent misrepresentation. The insurance company might suspend cover on discovering this but also would be under no obligation to return the premiums already paid under the policy.)
- Alternatively, the claimant might seek rescission of the contract in equity on discovering the fraud. This would then put him back in the pre-contractual position, provided that this was possible, and none of the many bars to rescission applied in the circumstances of the case.

9.3.2 Negligent misrepresentation

Traditionally, any misrepresentation that was not identifiable as a fraud would be classed as an innocent misrepresentation for which the only possible action was for rescission of the contract in equity.

The reason there was no available action for a negligently made misrepresentation was that negligence falls short of the criteria identified by Lord Herschell in *Derry v Peek* (1889) 14 App Cas 337.

There have, however, been developments in both common law and statute, meaning that an action is now possible for a negligent misrepresentation. Any action under the common law is, again, only possible in tort rather than contract and is a much more limited action than that available under the Misrepresentation Act 1967.

Common law

The common law originally provided no remedy for negligent misrepresentations. This was not always considered to be an acceptable position. (See, for instance, the dissenting judgment of Lord Denning in *Candler v Crane Christmas & Co* [1951] 2 KB 164.) Subsequently the possibility of an action for a negligent misstatement (misrepresentation) causing a pecuniary (financial) loss to be suffered by the other party has been accepted by the House of Lords and later developed.

CASE EXAMPLE

Hedley Byrne & Co Ltd v Heller & Partners Ltd [1964] AC 465

The claimants were asked to provide advertising work worth £100,000 on credit for another company, Easipower, that was not actually known to them. They took the sensible step in the circumstances of seeking a reference as to creditworthiness from Easipower's bankers, the defendants. The bankers wrote back, confirming that Easipower were a 'respectably constituted company good for its ordinary business engagements'. The bankers also claimed to reply without any responsibility for the reference that they had given. When Easipower went into liquidation with the claimants still unpaid, the claimants brought an action in the tort of negligence against the bankers. Their action failed because the bank had validly disclaimed any liability for their reference. Nevertheless, the House of Lords, *in obiter*, considered that such an action would be possible in certain 'special relationships' where the person making the negligent statement owed a duty of care to the other party to ensure that the statement was accurately made. In reaching this conclusion, the House of Lords approved Lord Denning's dissenting judgment in *Candler v Crane Christmas & Co*, where he felt that negligently prepared company accounts should be actionable. In the case itself the House of Lords did not appear to be certain exactly what would constitute such a special relationship. It is, of course, likely to arise where advice is given in a professional capacity and ought as a result to be reliable.

Subsequent case law has both accepted and refined the *Hedley Byrne* principle. The requirements of the tort were originally threefold:

- The party negligently making the false statement must be in possession of the particular type of knowledge for which the advice is required (*Harris v Wyre Forest District Council* [1988] AC 831).
- There must be sufficient proximity between the two parties that it is reasonable to rely on the statement, and this need not be a contractual relationship (*Chaudhry v Prabhakar* [1988] 3 All ER 718).
- The party to whom the statement is made does in fact rely on the statement and the party making the statement is aware of that reliance (*Smith v Eric S Bush* [1990] 1 AC 831).

Later case law has added further requirements in order for a successful claim to be pursued:

- The party negligently making the statement must have known or ought to have known the reasons why the claimant needed the particular advice (*Caparo Industries plc v Dickman* [1990] 1 All ER 568).
- The party negligently making the statement must have assumed responsibility to give advice and information in the circumstances (*Henderson v Merrett Syndicates Ltd* [1994] 3 All ER 506).

It is also possible for the principle to apply to representations regarding a future rather than a present state of affairs.

CASE EXAMPLE

Esso Petroleum Co Ltd v Marden [1976] QB 801

Esso developed a filling station on a new site near to a busy road in Southport and under the contract leased it to Marden. During negotiations for the franchise, its representative indicated that the throughput would amount to 200,000 gallons per year. Marden queried this figure but contracted on the basis of the reassurance of the more experienced representative. In fact, the local authority then required the pumps and entrance to be at the rear of the site. This was accessible only from side streets that were away from the view of the main road and which would be unknown to any passing trade. As a result, sales of petrol were never more than 86,502 gallons per year, and the petrol station was uneconomical to run. Marden lost all his capital in the venture and eventually gave up the tenancy. Esso sued for back rent and Marden counter-claimed with two arguments, both of which were successful. Firstly, he claimed that the estimate of petrol sales was a warranty on which he was entitled to rely and for which he himself could recover damages for breach of contract. Secondly, he claimed that the relationship with Esso was a special one, creating a duty of care in the circumstances. The court accepted that Esso's failure to warn him properly of the changed circumstances and the very different throughput resulting was negligence under the *Hedley Byrne* principle which allowed a claim also for misrepresentation.

JUDGMENT

Lord Denning explained the basis of liability: 'If a man, who has or professes to have special knowledge or skill, makes a representation by virtue thereof to another … with the intention of inducing him to enter into a contract with him, he is under a duty to use reasonable care to see that the representation is correct … If he negligently gives unsound advice or misleading information or expresses an erroneous opinion, and thereby induces the other side into a contract with him, he is liable.'

Statute

The above case actually started before the Misrepresentation Act 1967 was in force; otherwise a simpler action may have been available.

The Misrepresentation Act was passed in 1967. Its benefit is that it is much broader than any of the actions previously available either in tort or in equity. It is particularly appropriate where the claimant is unable to prove fraud. It was enacted following the recommendations of the Law Reform Committee that damages should be available for losses arising from a negligent misrepresentation. However, the 1967 Act in that sense was based on the law as it existed before *Hedley Byrne* and so it takes no account of that principle but instead it operates as an alternative to fraud. Section 2(1) identifies the main means of taking action.

SECTION

'Where a person has entered into a contract after a misrepresentation has been made to him by another party thereto and as a result thereof he has suffered loss, then if the person making the misrepresentation would be liable to damages in respect thereof had the misrepresentation been made fraudulently, that person shall be so liable notwithstanding that the misrepresentation was not made fraudulently unless he proves that he had reasonable grounds to believe and did believe up to the time the contract was made that the facts represented were true.'

This sounds fairly complex. However, its effects are quite simple. All that it basically means is that a party who has been the victim of a misrepresentation has an action available even though it may be impossible for him to prove either the necessary elements of fraud or the existence of a special relationship in order to fulfil *Hedley Byrne* criteria.

There are, then, some important differences from the previous law:

- Firstly, the burden of proof is partly reversed. Where, formerly, under *Derry v Peek*, the claimant would have been required to prove fraud, under the 1967 Act it will be for the defendant to show that he in fact held a reasonable belief in the truth of the statement once it is shown to be a misrepresentation by the claimant.

- If the misrepresentation is negligently made then the claimant has the choice of whether to sue under the 1967 Act or under the *Hedley Byrne* principle.
- If the 1967 Act is the preferred means of taking action then there is no need to show the special relationship required for *Hedley Byrne*-type liability.

CASE EXAMPLE

Howard Marine Dredging Co Ltd v A Ogden & Sons (Excavating) Ltd [1978] QB 574

Contractors estimating a price for depositing excavated earth at sea sought advice from the company from whom they intended to hire barges as to the precise capacity of the barges. The Marine Manager of the hirers negligently based his answer of 1,600 tonnes on dead-weight figures from Lloyd's register, rather than checking the actual shipping register which would have shown a figure of 1,055 tonnes. Delays resulted in the work because of the differences in capacity and the contractors refused to pay the hire for the barges. When they were sued for payment they successfully counter-claimed, using s 2(1) of the Misrepresentation Act 1967. The Court of Appeal, with Lord Denning dissenting, held that there was insufficient evidence to be able to show that the Marine Manager could actually sustain his argument that he had an honest belief in the figure that he had given. He had merely quoted a capacity from his knowledge of usual dead-weight figures on the Lloyd's register but he had made no attempt to take the logical step of checking the figure he gave against the accurate payload on the actual shipping register. An action under *Hedley Byrne* may not have been quite so straightforward since the relationship here was a purely commercial one.

Remedies for negligent misrepresentation

Damages are available as a remedy both under the 1967 Act and at common law. If the *Hedley Byrne* principle is applied then damages are calculated according to the standard tort measure. This means that damages will only be awarded for a loss that is a foreseeable consequence of the negligent misrepresentation that was made.

Under the 1967 Act, damages are again calculated according to a tort measure since the Act is stated as being appropriate where fraud cannot be proved. It was at one point suggested that damages should be according to a contractual measure (see *Watts v Spence* [1976] Ch 165). However, the Court of Appeal in *Sharneyford v Edge* [1987] Ch 305 confirmed that the appropriate measure was the tort measure.

What is more arguable is whether damages will be according to the normal tort measure or whether the test applied in the tort of deceit is appropriate. The latter is more beneficial in terms of consequential loss and the court in *McNally v Welltrade International Ltd* [1978] IRLR 497 suggested awarding damages as if the misrepresentation was actually fraudulent. This principle has subsequently been the subject of further discussion in the Court of Appeal.

CASE EXAMPLE

Royscot Trust Ltd v Rogerson [1991] 3 All ER 294

Here, a person bought a car from a car dealer, financing the loan through hire-purchase. In fact, in securing the hire-purchase agreement for his client, the car dealer misrepresented to the finance company the amount of deposit that the purchaser of the car had made. The purchaser of the car then defaulted on the loan, having sold the car on to an innocent third party who, under the Hire Purchase Act 1964, gained good title to the car. The finance company made a loss as a result and sued the car dealer on the misrepresentation. It succeeded because it was able to show that it would not have been prepared to lend as much to the purchaser if it had known the true amount of the deposit paid on the car. The Court of Appeal confirmed that the measure of damages under s 2(1) should be tortious rather than contractual. Besides this, because the clear wording of the section indicates that the action is in place of an action in fraud, where damages would have been awarded if fraud could have been proved, then the damages should be the same as for the tort of deceit. The result of this is that the claimant can recover for all damages that are a consequence of the misrepresentation, rather than just those that are a reasonably foreseeable loss.

One consequence of awards of damages under the 1967 Act being calculated according to a tort measure, of course, is that they can also be reduced if it is possible to show contributory negligence too.

Traditionally, any misrepresentation that was not the result of fraud was classed as innocent misrepresentation. On this basis the only remedy originally available if the misrepresentation was negligently made would be for rescission in equity and this is still possible (see section 9.4).

9.3.3 Innocent misrepresentation

As has already been stated, any misrepresentation not made fraudulently was formerly classed as an innocent misrepresentation, regardless of how it was made – negligently or innocently. No action was therefore traditionally possible under the common law. The only action available was one for rescission of the contract in equity.

The emergence of the Hedley Byrne principle and also of s 2(1) of the Misrepresentation Act 1967 means that possibly the only misrepresentations that are likely still to be claimed to be made innocently are those where a party makes a statement with an honest belief in its truth. The obvious example of this is where the party merely repeats inaccurate information, of the truth of which he is unaware, for instance from manufacturers' specifications.

In this case an action under s 2(1) of the 1967 Act would not be possible since this can be successfully defended by showing the existence of a reasonable belief in the truth of the statement. Nevertheless, the traditional action for rescission in equity is still a possibility. There is also a possibility of claiming under s 2(2) of the 1967 Act.

Remedies for innocent misrepresentation

At common law

As we have seen, since damages were not formerly available under common law they will not be available either under s 2(1) of the 1967 Act.

Under statute

However, while there is no usual right to damages, the court has a discretion under s 2(2) of the 1967 Act to award damages as an alternative to rescission where rescission would be available if it is convinced that to do so is the appropriate remedy. Section 2(2) states:

SECTION

'Where a person has entered into a contract after a misrepresentation has been made to him otherwise than fraudulently, and he would be entitled, by reason of the misrepresentation, to rescind the contract, then, if it is claimed in any proceedings arising out of the contract that the contract ought to be or has been rescinded, the court or arbitrator may declare the contract subsisting and award damages in lieu of rescission, if of opinion that it would be equitable to do so, having regard to the nature of the misrepresentation and the loss that would be caused by it if the contract were upheld, as well as the loss that rescission would cause to the other party.'

A number of significant points need to be considered regarding s 2(2):

- There is no actual right to damages as there may be in a common law action. The award of damages is at the discretion of the court as an equitable remedy would be. In this respect the court must consider that, 'it would be equitable to do so, having regard to the nature of the misrepresentation and the loss that would be caused by it if the contract were upheld, as well as the loss that rescission would cause to the other party'. It was suggested in *Thomas Witter v TBP Industries* that damages should be independent of any right to rescind in the same way that damages under s 2(1) are freely available. However, more recent case law has cast doubt on this.

CASE EXAMPLE

Zanzibar v British Aerospace (Lancaster House) Ltd (2000) The Times, 28th March

Here, the Zanzibar Government purchased a corporate jet aeroplane from British Aerospace in 1992. The Zanzibar Government subsequently alleged that it had been induced to enter the contract on the basis of a false representation by British Aerospace as to both the type of jet and its general airworthiness. Zanzibar claimed rescission of the contract and damages as an alternative. The court denied it either, on the ground that the delay in bringing the action meant that the right to rescission had been lost and so no damages could be paid in lieu of rescission either. So the case would suggest that since s 2(2) operates in place of equitable rights, if the equitable rights are lost, so is the right to damages.

- Since damages are to be awarded as an alternative to rescission then inevitably only one remedy can be granted, not both.
- The measure of damages to be awarded is uncertain but since damages are awarded in lieu of rescission, according to the section, then it is unlikely that consequential loss could be claimed. There are some *dicta* on this point. Early cases doubted whether damages should be other than contractual and based solely on the actual loss suffered (see Lord Denning in *Jarvis v Swan Tours Ltd* [1973] 1 All ER 71 and also the first-instance judgment in *Watts v Spence*). More recently, *obiter dictum* in *William Sindall plc v Cambridgeshire County Council* [1994] 3 All ER 932 has also suggested that the measure of damages under s 2(2) should be different from that under s 2(1) since to give consequential loss would be to go beyond the rights gained by rescission for which the award of damages is an alternative. However, there is no clear authority.

In equity
Prior to the passing of the 1967 Act there was no action possible under common law and the only available remedy then was in equity for rescission.

The class of misrepresentation and its essential elements	The type of action taken	The available remedies
Fraudulent misrepresentation: • the statement was made deliberately or • without belief in its truth or • carelessly. *Derry v Peek*	The action is brought in the tort of deceit. The obvious defence is 'an honest belief' in the statement.	• Sue for damages, under tort measure. This includes all consequential loss (*Smith New Court Securities v Scrimgeour*). • Can affirm the contract; or • Can disaffirm and use the misrepresentation as a defence to a claim of breach of contract. • Can seek rescission of the contract in equity.
Negligent misrepresentation: Two types: Negligent mis-statement: • special relationship between parties • skill and knowledge of type of advice • reasonable reliance (*Hedley Byrne v Heller & Partners*) • defendant knew of reliance • defendant assumed responsibility (*Henderson v Merrett Syndicate*).	Action in Tort under *Hedley Byrne* principles. The possible defence is an absence of any of the essential elements, eg, no special relationship.	• Sue for damages under the tort measure for foreseeable damage (*Royscot Trust Ltd v Rogerson*); or • Could traditionally seek rescission in equity.
Non-fraudulent misrepresentation (statutory).	Action under s 2(1) of the Misrepresentation Act 1967. The usual defence is an honest belief in the statement.	• Sue for damages under the tort measure. • Traditionally, rescission in equity was available.
Innocent misrepresentation: • Originally, anything non-fraudulent. • Now, probably only innocently repeating false statements.	Action under s 2(2) of the Misrepresentation Act 1967.	• Damages can be awarded where rescission would be available. • Rescission traditionally available in equity.

Figure 9.2 The different classes of misrepresentation, the possible actions and the available remedies

CASE EXAMPLE

Redgrave v Hurd (1881) 20 Ch D 1

In the case, rescission was ordered in a contract between two solicitors for the sale and purchase of the one's practice. The selling solicitor had mis-stated the income from the practice and when the other solicitor backed out on learning of this, the seller tried to claim specific performance of the contract. The other solicitor successfully counter-claimed for rescission because of the misrepresentation.

Sir George Jessell explained the appropriateness of the remedy: 'no man ought to seek to take advantage of his own false statements'.

ACTIVITY

Self-assessment questions

1. Why was it traditionally so important to prove that a falsely made representation was actually incorporated into the contract?
2. How would a party traditionally prove a fraudulent misrepresentation?
3. How easy or difficult is it to prove fraud?
4. What did negligently and innocently made representations have in common?
5. Which is the more advantageous action, that under Hedley Byrne principles or tort or that under s 2(1) of the Misrepresentation Act 1967?
6. What are the major advantages of the Misrepresentation Act 1967 over other actions?
7. Are the remedies better for any particular class of misrepresentation?

Quick quiz

Suggest what type of misrepresentation is involved in the following examples:

1. Sam is selling his car to Tony, who asks the capacity of the engine. Sam, after looking at the registration documents, tells Tony that it is 1299 cc. Unknown to Sam, the documents are incorrect.
2. Sally, a saleswoman, tells Rajesh that a three-piece suite is flame-resistant, in order to gain the sale, without checking the manufacturers' specifications that would have revealed that it was not.
3. Eric, who has no qualifications at all, tells prospective employers at an interview that he has a degree in accounting and is chartered.

9.4 Equity and misrepresentation

The availability of damages for a misrepresentation varies, as we have seen, according to the nature of the misrepresentation and the nature of the action brought by the injured party. Rescission, on the other hand, may be available whatever the character of the misrepresentation.

Rescission is of course an equitable remedy and its award is subject to the discretion of the court. It must be remembered that an actionable misrepresentation makes a contract voidable rather than void, so the contract remains valid until such time as it is 'set aside' by the court for the injured party.

However, the right to rescind is not an absolute right and it may be lost in a number of circumstances. These are commonly referred to as the 'bars to rescission'.

■ *Restitutio in integrum* is vital to rescission. In essence, this means that, since the party claiming is asking to be returned to the pre-contract position, known as the *status quo ante*, this in fact must be possible to achieve. If it is not, then rescission of the contract will not be granted.

CASE EXAMPLE

Lagunas Nitrate Co v Lagunas Syndicate [1899] 2 Ch 392

A nitrate field was bought by the claimants on an innocent misrepresentation of the defendant as to the strength of the market for nitrates. They made profits for a period but were affected adversely by a general depression in prices, at which point they sought rescission. They failed because they had extracted the nitrates for some time and the field could not be restored to its pre-contract order.

- The remedy will similarly be unavailable where the party who is the victim of the misrepresentation has affirmed the contract after its formation and before seeking rescission. Any action that indicates a willingness by that party to continue with the contract will therefore defeat the claim for rescission.

CASE EXAMPLE

Long v Lloyd [1958] 1 WLR 753

A lorry was bought on the basis of a representation as to its 'exceptional condition'. Several faults were discovered on the first journey and the purchaser then allowed the seller to repair these. When the lorry again broke down through its faulty condition, the buyer's claim to rescission was unsuccessful. He had accepted the goods in a less than satisfactory condition and was unable to return them.

- Delay is said to 'defeat equity'. So a failure to claim rescission promptly may mean it is unavailable as a remedy.

CASE EXAMPLE

Leaf v International Galleries [1950] 2 KB 86

A contract for the sale of a painting of Salisbury Cathedral described it as a Constable. When the description later proved false, the purchaser's claim to rescission failed because a five-year period had elapsed by then.

- If a third party has subsequently gained rights in the goods then it would be unfair to interfere with those rights by granting rescission.

CASE EXAMPLE

White v Garden (1851) 10 CB 919

A rogue bought 50 tons of iron from the claimant, using a bill of exchange in a false name, and re-sold it to a third party who acted in good faith. When the claimant discovered that the bill of exchange was useless he seized the iron from the innocent third party. This was illicit since the third party had gained good title to the iron.

- Under s 2(2) of the Misrepresentation Act 1967, the judge has a discretion which remedy to apply. Rescission will not therefore be available if the judge has decided that damages are a more appropriate remedy.

However, it is possible to be granted rescission of a contract as well as an indemnity for other expenses incurred as a result of the misrepresentation.

CASE EXAMPLE

Whittington v Seale-Hayne (1900) 44 SJ 229

Poultry breeders took a lease of premises on the basis of an oral representation that the premises were in a sanitary condition. This was untrue. The water was contaminated and the buyer became ill and some poultry died. At the time, the claimants were not entitled to consequential loss because they could not prove fraud. However, as well as their claim to rescission of the contract, they were awarded an indemnity representing what they had spent out in terms of rent and rates and other costs.

In granting rescission the court must always take into account the seriousness of the breach and the likely consequences of rescission for both parties.

ACTIVITY

Self-assessment questions

1. Why was equity traditionally so important to a party who had entered a contract as a result of a misrepresentation?
2. How fair are the 'bars' to rescission?
3. What types of misrepresentation would be classed as innocent following the Misrepresentation Act 1967?
4. What are the advantages and disadvantages of s 2(2) of the 1967 Act?

9.5 Non-disclosure amounting to misrepresentation

There is no basic obligation at common law to volunteer information that has not been asked for. In this way, in general, merely failing to give information will not be classed as misrepresentation and no action is possible.

CASE EXAMPLE

Fletcher v Krell (1873) 42 LJQB 55

A woman who had applied for a position as a governess had not revealed that she had formerly been married. Despite the fact that single women were generally preferred, her failure to reveal her marriage was not a misrepresentation.

A logical extension of this basic principle is that silence on its own cannot generally be classed as misrepresentation.

CASE EXAMPLE

Hands v Simpson, Fawcett & Co (1928) 44 TLR 295

A commercial traveller had acquired employment without advising his new employers that he was disqualified from driving, even though this was an essential part of the work. Even so, in the case the court held that he was not obliged to volunteer the information without being asked. His silence was not a misrepresentation.

However, there are a number of situations where the supplying of information is considered to be so critical to the contract that the act of withholding or not offering information will amount to misrepresentation.

- Contracts which are *uberrimae fidei*. This principle is commonly applicable to contracts of insurance, on the basis that, with full information, the insurer may not have been prepared to accept the risk.

CASE EXAMPLE

Locker and Woolf Ltd v Western Australian Insurance Co Ltd [1936] 1 KB 408

The insured party had not revealed to the insurer when entering the contract that another company had refused him insurance. This was clearly material to the contract.

uberimmae fides

Of the utmost good faith – a requirement common in, for example, insurance contracts

Fiduciary relationships, where, again, good faith is required. These may include the relationship between trustees and beneficiaries. A failure to reveal certain information material to the contract may result in its being set aside under the doctrine of constructive fraud.

CASE EXAMPLE

Tate v Williamson (1866) LR 2 Ch App 55

A young man who was hopelessly in debt was persuaded by an adviser to sell his land in order to raise money to settle his debts. This adviser then bought the land, having not revealed full details as to its value and as a result obtaining the land at half value. The contract was set aside since the information, if revealed, would have led to the young man demanding a better price or selling to someone else.

A classic example of a fiduciary relationship is that of solicitor and client. A solicitor who acts for two opposing clients at the same time is clearly in a conflict of interest situation.

CASE EXAMPLE

Hilton v Barker Booth and Eastwood [2005] 1 All ER 651

The defendants were a firm of solicitors who acted for a property developer, the claimant and for a prospective purchaser of some of his land. The solicitors knew that the purchaser, for whom they also acted, had been in prison for fraud but did not reveal this to the claimant. The solicitors also advanced certain deposits to the purchaser. The purchaser then failed to complete. The House of Lords held that where a solicitor places himself in a position of having two irreconcilable duties, as the solicitors did here, then the solicitor is at fault and can be liable.

Where a part truth amounts to a falsehood.

CASE EXAMPLE

Dimmock v Hallett (1866) LR 2 Ch App 21

A person selling land revealed that the land was let to tenants but not that the tenants were terminating the lease and thus that the income from the land was reducing. This amounted to a misrepresentation.

Where a statement made originally in truth becomes false during the negotiations because of changed circumstances that ought really to be revealed. This will then be a misrepresentation.

CASE EXAMPLE

With v O'Flanagan [1936] Ch 575

A doctor selling his practice stated the true income at the beginning of negotiations but by the time of the sale this had dwindled to a negligible figure. Since he failed to reveal this, it was a misrepresentation.

ACTIVITY

Self-assessment questions

1. What exactly is non-disclosure?
2. In what circumstances will non-disclosure amount to an actionable misrepresentation?

KEY FACTS

Character of misrepresentation			
Must be a false statement of fact, made by one party to a contract to the other, at the time of contracting or before, and not intended to form part of the contract, but intended to induce the other party to enter the contract.			

Type of misrepresentation	Case/statute	Equity and rescission	Case/statute
Fraudulent: Must be made knowingly or deliberately; or without any belief in its truth; or recklessly as to whether it is true or not – an honest belief is a defence – remedy is in tort damages.	*Derry v Peek*	Only available if: • *restitutio in integrum* applies • the contract is not affirmed • there is no undue delay • no third party has gained rights.	*Clarke v Dickson* *Long v Lloyd* *Leaf v International Galleries*
Negligent: Based on special relationship – damages in tort.	*Hedley Byrne*	**Non-disclosure**	**Case/statute**
		Also amounts to misrepresentation:	
Or other than fraud – still based on tort damages.	s 2(1) Misrepresentation Act 1967	• in contracts *uberrimae fidei* (of utmost good faith) such as insurance	*Locker and Woolf v Western Australian Insurance*
Innocent: No remedy at common law – now can have damages in place of rescission.	s 2(2) Misrepresentation Act 1967	• where a part-truth amounts to a falsehood	*Dimmock v Hallett*
		• where a true statement later becomes false.	*With v O'Flanagan*

SUMMARY

- A misrepresentation is a false statement of fact made by one party of the contract to the other at or before the time of contracting which he intends should induce the other party to enter the contract but is not intended to form part of the contract.

- Misrepresentation allows the party to avoid his obligations under the contract and receive damages.

There are three types:
- Fraudulent misrepresentation is brought in the tort of deceit.
- Negligent misrepresentation can be brought under the *Hedley Byrne* principle in negligence or under section 2(1) Misrepresentation Act 1967.
- Innocent misrepresentation can only be brought under the Act – there is no action at common law.

Equity can sometimes be used to rescind a contract if certain conditions are met.

An action is not usually possible for non-disclosure of information except, for example, in situations involving good faith such as insurance contracts.

SAMPLE ESSAY QUESTION

Discuss the extent to which the development of a range of remedies for misrepresentation has ensured adequate protection for parties who have relied on inaccurate information when entering into a contract.

Define misrepresentation:
- A false statement of material fact but not mere opinion made by one party to the contract to the other before or at the time the contract was formed which was intended to induce the other party to enter the contract but was not intended to form part of the contract

Explain the different types of misrepresentation:
- Fraudulent – in the tort of deceit
- Negligent – before 1964 treated as innocent misrepresentation so no remedy available except in equity – now there are two types: negligent mis-statement in negligence where there is a special relationship, and an action under the Misrepresentation Act 1967 s 2(1)
- Innocent – originally only remedy was in equity – but now in Misrepresentation Act 1967 s 2(2)

Identify that there are different remedies:

- Fraudulent – damages (tort measure, including all consequential loss), can refuse performance, can seek rescission in equity

- Negligent – damages based on foreseeable loss in negligent mis-statement and on tort measure under the Misrepresentation Act 1967, and rescission available in equity

- Innocent – traditionally no remedy in common law only rescission in equity, but under Act s 2(2) judge can award damages as an alternative

Discuss the development of the area:

- No remedy before 1899 unless equity could be used

- Even then deceit was very hard to prove

- So was vital to prove representation was incorporated as a term

- No further development until 1964, which again was limited

- The Act has widened the law dramatically so that all genuine misrepresentations should be actionable

Discuss relevant criticisms of the remedies:

- Fraud hard to prove but damages measured generously

- Hedley Byrne liability very narrow and difficult to prove but damages are set on the tort measure

- The Act means action is possible for all misrepresentations and an obvious advantage is the reversal of the burden of proof and again damages are on the tort measure

- Equity always provided rescission as a remedy but it had its own limitations – the bars to rescission

Further reading

Atiyah, P S, *Essays on Contract Law* (Clarendon Press, 1990), Essay 10.
Denning, Lord, *The Discipline of Law* (Butterworths, 1979), Part 6, Chapter 5.
Treitel, G H, *The Law of Contract* (12th edn, Sweet & Maxwell, 2007).

10

Vitiating factors: Mistake

AIMS AND OBJECTIVES

After reading this chapter you should be able to:

- Understand the basic character of contracts made as a result of mistake
- Understand the different types of mistake
- Understand the consequences of the different types of mistake
- Understand the effects of equity on mistake
- Critically analyse the area
- Apply the law to factual situations and reach conclusions

10.1 Introduction

Mistake is sometimes considered to be a difficult area of law. As Cheshire, Fifoot and Furmston point out:

QUOTATION

'The first fact to appreciate in this somewhat elusive branch of the law is that the word "mistake" bears a more restricted meaning in professional than in popular speech.'

They also suggest that:

QUOTATION

'The narrow scope allowed to mistake in the English legal system is a fact to be not only noticed but welcomed … because the reaction upon third parties may be deplorable'.

Cheshire, Fifoot and Furmston, Law of Contract *(14th edn, Butterworths, 2001)*

There are certainly a number of reasons for this. It is quite closely related to the area of agreement since agreement is said to depend on a *consensus ad idem*, a voluntary arrangement mutually agreed by both parties. If a party enters a contract on the basis of a mistake, then this is said to negate the *consensus ad idem*, since any consensus could not be genuinely held in that case.

Besides this, mistake, and certainly common mistake and **unilateral mistake**, is also closely related to misrepresentation. This is because a party might claim that they are mistaken because of the misrepresentation of the other party, however innocent. In consequence, a claimant sometimes pleads both.

Where goods have passed to third parties following a contract that is made as a result of a mistake this can also have quite profound effects since one apparently innocent party is going to lack rights to the subject-matter of the contract. If a purchaser under a contract has not been given full title and then sells on to a third party then the maxim *nemo dat quod non habet* might apply. This means that a person cannot transfer title who does not already have good title himself. The result of this could be goods being reclaimed from a third party who has acquired them in innocence of the defective title. This will become apparent when considering a unilateral mistake as to the identity of the other party to the contract.

For these reasons, judges have shown unwillingness in the past to accept a mistake as operative and therefore justifying a declaration that the contract is void. The result of the courts' attitude and the common law constraints imposed on mistake has been in certain circumstances for the courts to use equitable solutions, but only in those situations where the common law rules cannot apply.

This is, then, the first distinction to make in mistake, whether it is actionable under common law or whether equity can provide a remedy. For the common law to have any effect, the mistake must have been an 'operative' one. This means that it must have been a mistake fundamental to the making of the contract such that the contract was formed only as a result of the mistake.

If the mistake is recognised by the courts as being 'operative' then the contract will be void *ab initio*. Not only will the parties be returned to their pre-contract position, but also any further rights coming out of the contract will have no effect, because the contract is treated as though it had never existed.

If the court is unable to accept that the mistake is operative, in other words the mistake was not the reason that the contract was formed, then common law rules cannot apply. However, traditionally, a solution might still be possible in equity, but this of course would be subject to the discretion of the court and application of the normal maxims of equity.

If equity can be applied then the effect is for the contract to be voidable. The contract could continue but a party to the contract who has been the victim of the mistake can avoid his obligations and the contract may be set aside. More recent case law has suggested that equity has no place at least in common mistake.

There are basically three classes of mistake:

- **common** mistake
- **mutual** mistake
- **unilateral** mistake

The three are quite different to each other both in terms of the definitions applied to them and in the circumstances in which they arise.

- A **common mistake** is one where both parties have made exactly the same mistake (the mistake is thus 'common' to both of them). The mistake can concern either

---

unilateral mistake

Where only one party is mistaken on entering a contract and the other party usually knows of and is taking advantage of the mistake

the existence of the subject-matter of the contract, or its quality, with different consequences depending on which it is. It can also involve the actual ownership of the property at the time that the contract was formed.

- A **mutual mistake** again involves both parties being mistaken. However, with a mutual mistake the parties are not making the same mistake but are at cross-purposes and have a different interpretation of the substance of the contract. If the parties are genuinely at cross-purposes then the contract is void. However, if the contract remains intact despite the mistake then the contract continues despite the mistake.

- A **unilateral mistake**, unlike the other two classes, is one where only one of the parties is entering the contract under a mistake. By implication the other party will usually know of that party's mistake and will be seeking to take advantage of it. So with unilateral mistake there is possibly an element of fraud involved. The mistake could be as to the terms of the contract or it could involve the true identity of the other party to the contract. If the mistake is material to the making of the contract then the contract may be declared void. If it is not, then the contract remains.

It is important to note, then, that, as is apparent above, these divisions themselves also sub-divide to cover more specific circumstances.

10.2 Common mistake

10.2.1 *Res extincta* (subject-matter does not exist)

res extincta

In common mistake a mistake made by both parties about the existence of the subject-matter of the contract

Here, the parties have contracted on the basis of a mistake about the existence of the subject-matter of the contract at the time that the contract was formed. In essence, for the mistake to be operative, the subject-matter will not exist at the time of contracting. If at that time the subject-matter of the contract did not indeed exist then the mistake may be regarded as an operative one, because clearly neither party to the contract would contract for something that did not exist. The contract will be declared void as a result of the mistake.

CASE EXAMPLE

Couturier v Hastie (1852) 5 HLC 673

The contract was for sale and purchase of a cargo of grain in transit and which both parties believed existed at the time of the contract. In fact, the captain of the ship had sold the cargo, as was customary practice, when it had begun to overheat. When this fact was discovered, the court declared that the contract was void and rejected the seller's argument that the buyer had accepted the risk and should pay the price. Coleridge J made no actual mention of mistake but preferred a common sense logic that since the subject-matter of the contract did not exist at the time of contracting then neither did the contract. This basic proposition is now contained in s 6 of the Sale of Goods Act 1979: 'Where there is a contract for specific goods, and the goods without the knowledge of the seller have perished at the time when the contract is made, the contract is void.'

The above case involved specific goods. However, the same principles cannot apply if the contract is of a more speculative nature. In this case, then, the consequence of the goods not existing at the time of the contract may be different, since the buyer has only bargained for a chance rather than for actual goods. An Australian case which distinguished *Couturier v Hastie* (1852) 5 HLC 673 illustrates this point:

CASE EXAMPLE

McRae v Commonwealth Disposals Commission (1950) 84 CLR 377, HC Aus

Here, the contract was for the salvage rights to a wreck. The buyer went to considerable expense to locate the wreck at the approximate position given by the Commission, but could not find it. When the buyer sued for breach of contract, the Commission tried to rely on the principle in the last case but failed. The court held that there was no operative mistake and the contract could not be declared void. The claimants had bought the salvage rights on the clear representation by the Commission that the wreck did exist, and the Commission was therefore held liable for breach of contract.

JUDGMENT

Dixon and Fullagar JJ explained the reasoning behind the decision: 'The officers of the Commission made an assumption but the plaintiffs did not make an assumption in the same sense. They knew nothing except what the Commission had told them … The only proper construction of the contract is that it included a promise by the Commission that there was a tanker in the position specified. The Commission contracted that there was a tanker there…. The Commission cannot in this case rely on any mistake as avoiding the contract, because any mistake was induced by the fault of their own servants … Since there was no tanker there has been a breach of contract.'

If the goods have 'commercially perished' at the time the contract is formed and this is unknown to either party, then this could still amount to an operative mistake, leading to the contract being declared void. 'Commercially perished' is merely a very legal way of saying that the goods no longer have the value that was attached to them in the contract.

CASE EXAMPLE

Barrow Lane and Ballard Ltd v Phillip Phillips & Co Ltd [1929] 1 KB 574

Here, the seller had bought 700 bags of groundnuts in a particular warehouse and, without ever inspecting the goods, he then sold them on. When the buyer came to inspect the goods, 109 bags had been stolen and the buyer then refused to pay. The seller was unable to sue the owner of the warehouse who had by this time become insolvent. The seller sued the buyer for the price instead but failed in his action. The court held that the goods had ceased to exist in commercial terms and the contract was void. As the court recognised, the contract was for an 'indivisible parcel' of 700 bags. This amount no longer existed and the risk for the perished goods remained with the seller.

The classical operation of the principle of *res extincta* will still apply, even in modern commercial transactions.

CASE EXAMPLE

Associated Japanese Bank (International) Ltd v Credit du Nord SA
[1988] 3 All ER 902

A sale and leaseback arrangement over four packaging machines was concluded between the bank and a man called Bennett. Credit du Nord guaranteed Bennett's obligations under the contract. The machines did not in fact exist and the bank was prevented from suing Bennett when he was declared bankrupt. It then sued on the guarantee. Steyn J held that the guarantee was subject to a condition precedent that the four machines existed at the time that the contract was formed. Applying the test from *Bell v Lever Brothers*, Steyn J held that for the mistake as to the existence of the machines to be an operative one, the subject-matter of the contract must be radically and essentially different to that expected by both parties. The guarantee was an accessory contract. The non-existence of the machines was of paramount importance to the guarantor in granting the guarantee. The *res extincta* doctrine applied and the contract of guarantee was declared void in the circumstances.

res sua

A common mistake made by both parties about the true ownership of the subject-matter under the contract

10.2.2 *Res sua* (ownership in different hands)

This principle applies to a mistake concerning the actual ownership of the goods at the time the contract was formed. If a party enters a contract as a buyer when, in fact, unknown to either party, he owns the title to the goods himself, then the contract is void. The mistake is clearly operative. The contract is only entered because the purchaser believes that ownership is in other hands. None of us would consider contracting for the purchase of something that we already owned if we knew that to be the case.

CASE EXAMPLE

Cooper v Phibbs (1867) LR 2 HL 149

Cooper took a three-year lease for a salmon fishery from Phibbs. At the time of the contract both parties believed that Phibbs owned the fishery when, in fact, it was subsequently discovered that Cooper was life tenant of the property. He was unable to dispose of the property but was effective owner at the time of contracting. Cooper then tried to have the lease set aside. The House of Lords agreed to this but also granted Phibbs a lien in respect of the considerable expense he had gone to in improving the property. Although the case was decided on equitable rather than common law principles, Lord Atkin in *Bell v Lever Brothers* refers to it as an example of *res sua*. The case is a perfect example of *res sua*. Equity was applied and the contract was declared voidable rather than void. This was because, firstly, Cooper had only an equitable interest in the property, and secondly, Phibbs had spent money on it.

10.2.3 Common mistake as to quality of the bargain

This is inevitably a more complex area than either *res extincta* or *res sua*. Generally, however, where the mistake that is common to both parties is that the subject-matter of the contract is of a quality different to that anticipated then the mistake has three consequences. The mistake will not be considered an operative one, it will have no effect in common law on the contract, and both parties are still bound by their original obligations.

CASE EXAMPLE

Bell v Lever Brothers Ltd [1932] AC 161

Lever Brothers employed Bell as Chairman of a subsidiary company, Niger Co Ltd, with the brief of rejuvenating the subsidiary. When he was successful in his task and the subsidiary was merged with another company, Lever Brothers offered a settlement of £30,000 for the termination of his existing service contract. It was later discovered that Bell was in breach of a clause of the service agreement, having entered into private dealings on his own account. Lever Brothers then sued for return of the settlement, claiming fraudulent misrepresentation, in which they failed, and breach of contract. The Court of Appeal then held that the settlement was invalid for common mistake, the mistake being that Lever were bound to pay the settlement when they could in fact have merely fired Bell. The mistake was not one affecting the consideration or that went to the root of the matter, so the contract of settlement could not be void. The mistake was not fundamental in any way to the making of the settlement agreement. Lever Brothers were merely upset because had they known of the breach before the settlement they could have fired Bell and avoided the expense. The settlement had not been given as a result of the breach or otherwise of the clause, but in recognition of the work already done by Bell. It was not an operative mistake.

JUDGMENT

In the House of Lords Lord Warrington felt that the 'mistake' could have no effect on the contract unless it was 'of such a fundamental character as to constitute an underlying assumption without which the parties would not have made the contract they in fact made'. Lord Atkin stated that: 'Mistake as to quality of the thing contracted raises more difficult questions. In such a case, a mistake will not affect assent unless it is the mistake of both parties and is as to the existence of some quality which makes the thing without the quality essentially different from the thing as it was believed to be...'.

The judgment has not been without its critics. Catherine MacMillan identifies the problems presented by the case:

QUOTATION

'The difficulty is created because Lord Atkin recognised that a sufficiently fundamental mistake as to the quality of the subject-matter can render the contract void but then he refused to find the contracts before him were void. Because it is hard to envisage a more fundamental mistake, the effect ... is to set a very strict standard. If a mistake as to quality was not sufficiently fundamental in this case, when would it ever be?'

C MacMillan, 'How temptation led to mistake: An explanation of Bell v Lever Bros Ltd (2003)' 119 LQR 623–659 at 625

The common law principle from Bell, then, is applied absolutely. Nevertheless, the fact that the mistake is not operative has not always meant that no remedy at all was available. At one point it was accepted that an action in equity to set aside the contract might still result from the mistake.

CASE EXAMPLE

Solle v Butcher [1950] 1 KB 671

In an agreement for the lease of a flat, both parties mistakenly believed that the rent was not subject to controls under the Rent Restrictions (Notices of Increase) Act 1923.

The rent was set at £250 per annum, though if subject to the Act it should have been £140. However, had the landlord realised that it was subject to those controls he might have applied to increase the rent because of considerable repairs and improvements he had made to what was otherwise war-damaged property. On discovering that the rent was subject to controls under the Act, the tenant then sued for a declaration that the rent should be £140 and for recovery of the difference already paid. On appeal, the landlord claimed that the agreement was void for mistake. The Court of Appeal held that at common law the mistake had no effect on the contract. It was merely a mistake as to quality. This did not prevent the court from setting the agreement aside in equity.

JUDGMENT

In the Court of Appeal Lord Denning explained his reasoning for setting the contract aside: 'If the mistake here had not happened, a proper notice of increase would have been given and the lease would have been executed at the full permitted rent. I think this court … should impose terms which will enable the tenant to choose either to stay on at the proper rent or to go out.'

However, the Court of Appeal has recently been called on to review the relationship between *Bell v Lever Bros* [1932] AC 161 and *Solle v Butcher* [1950] 1 KB 671. In doing so it has suggested that it is possible that the common mistake is such that the contract is neither operative, meaning that it cannot be declared void, nor, because the mistake has no effect in common law, can it then be set aside in equity.

CASE EXAMPLE

Great Peace Shipping Ltd v Tsavliris Salvage (International) Ltd [2002] EWCA Civ 1407

The defendants, who were salvors, had an interest in a ship, the *Cape Providence*, and, worried that it might sink, they approached London brokers who contacted a third party (OR), who identified the nearest vessel as the *Great Peace*, which belonged to the claimants. The defendants then agreed a charterparty contract to hire the *Great Peace*. The contract contained a clause that in the event of cancellation the party hiring the vessel would still have to pay for a minimum of five days' hire. In the event, OR was wrong, and *Great Peace* was in fact more than 400 miles away. So the charter contract was based on a common mistake.

The defendants then hired a closer vessel instead and later tried to cancel the *Great Peace* contract. The claimants claimed for five days' hire. The defendants argued that the mistake made the contract void at common law or voidable in equity. In the High Court Toulson J held that, under the principle in *Bell v Lever Bros*, since the mistake was not a mistake as to the existence of the subject-matter then the mistake was not operable and the contract could not be declared void at common law. He also went on to consider that it could not be set aside in equity either. His reasoning was that it was impossible to determine the nature of the 'fundamental' mistake that would enable the contract to be rescinded. He would not exercise any discretion to set the contract aside because the fixing of charterparties is done by professionals and is an area where certainty is important. As a result, to set aside the contract would amount to making the correctness of the information given by OR a condition of the contract and the parties themselves had included no such condition. The Court of Appeal agreed with the trial judge. The court accepted that the two parties had made a mistaken assumption that the two vessels were close enough for the *Great Peace* to be able to carry out the obligations set for it under the contract. Nevertheless, the court felt that the vessels were not sufficiently far away either that the mistake was one that would make the thing contracted for so essentially different that the mistake could be classed as operable. As a result, the contract could not be declared void for common mistake. The court also agreed with the trial judge that equity could not apply and rescission was not available. In the absence of an operative mistake, the defendants were bound to pay the fee fixed by the contract for cancellation.

The decision in *Great Peace* has some significant consequences (see sections 10.5.2 and 10.5.5). At its strictest application the principle in the case means that courts will not declare a contract void for mistake unless the common mistake makes the contract impossible to perform. In subsequent cases courts have applied this principle strictly, making successful claims on common mistake hard to achieve.

CASE EXAMPLE

Brennan v Bolt Burdon [2005] 1 QB 303

The claimant in a personal injury claim had delivered a form on a Saturday and the defendant successfully applied for proceedings to be set aside on the basis that an existing precedent meant that receipt of the form should be the following Monday, which was out of time. The defendant then agreed not to claim costs if the claimant agreed not to continue the action. Later the precedent was reversed and the claimant sought to continue his action. The defendant argued that the compromise agreement was binding and the claimant counterclaimed that the compromise agreement was void for a common mistake of law. The Court of Appeal found that the compromise agreement was not vitiated by mistake since the mistake did not make the agreement impossible to perform.

Interestingly Canadian Courts have not yet accepted *Great Peace*. The Ontario Court of Appeal in Miller Paving Ltd v B Gottardo Construction Ltd (2007) ONCA 422, 31 BLR (4th) 33, 62 CLR (3d) 161, 86 OR (3d) 161 has specifically rejected the line taken in Great Peace arguing that it was a backward step and will lead to injustice.

In some situations the parties will easily mistake the quality of the contract. This is particularly so in the case of art works or antiques or anything where the valuations of 'experts' are a matter of opinion rather than fact. In such cases the attitude taken by the court, and also therefore the apparent effect of the mistake, can vary enormously. Inevitably, the result of the case will hinge on the view taken by the court of the reliance placed on the mistaken valuation by the parties in the case.

CASE EXAMPLE

Leaf v International Galleries [1950] 2 KB 86

The contract was for the sale and purchase of an oil painting of Salisbury Cathedral that was innocently represented as being painted by Constable, a famous landscape artist of the nineteenth century. This would obviously add value to the painting if it was indeed the case. When the buyer tried to sell the painting five years later, he discovered that it was not in fact a Constable. He claimed rescission of the contract but failed and then appealed. The Court of Appeal rejected his claim, also holding that an action for damages would have been the more appropriate action, and in any case that he had also delayed too long for rescission to be an available remedy, applying the maxim 'delay defeats equity'.

The mistake voids the contract because the parties could not have contracted without subject-matter and would not have wished to if they had known the truth.

Common mistake – *res extincta*

The mistake voids the contract because B could not possibly have contracted to sell the subject-matter to A if he did not own it and they would not have contracted if they had known.

Common mistake – *res sua*

A contracts with B for something that they both think is worth more. ⟶ B contracts with A for something that they both think is worth more.

The contract cannot be void. The law will not interfere to make a bad bargain good and the only mistake was as to the quality of the bargain being made. The contract continues.

Common mistake as to the quality of the contract

Figure 10.1 The different types of common mistake and their consequences

JUDGMENT

Lord Denning made some interesting references to mistake: 'This was a contract for the sale of goods. There was a mistake about the subject matter, because both parties believed the picture to be a Constable, and the mistake was in one sense essential or fundamental. There was no mistake about the subject-matter of the sale. It was a specific picture of "Salisbury Cathedral". The parties were agreed in the same terms on the subject-matter, and that is sufficient to make a contract…' So Lord Denning suggested that the identity of the painter was irrelevant. It was a mistake only as to the quality of the contract.

This case shows unwillingness by the court here to interfere in a difficult area where the word of 'experts' is called into question. Nevertheless, precisely the opposite view has been taken in relation to the effect of a mistake as to the quality of goods where works of art are specifically concerned.

CASE EXAMPLE

Peco Arts Inc v Hazlitt Gallery Ltd [1983] 1 WLR 1315

The claimant bought from a reputable gallery a drawing that both parties mistakenly believed was an original. The contract included an express term that the work was an original inscribed by the artist. Eleven years later, the claimant then discovered that the work was in fact only a reproduction. He then tried to claim return of the purchase price paid and interest. The court distinguished *Leaf* and allowed his claim. The court held that the time lapse was no problem in allowing a remedy since it was accepted that, even without due diligence, the truth could not have been discovered at an earlier stage.

10.3 Mutual mistake

A mutual mistake occurs where the parties to the contract are at cross-purposes over the meaning of the contract. One of the problems here is that it is doubtful whether any meaningful and sustainable agreement has ever been reached.

The approach of the courts is to try to make sense of the agreement that does exist, in order that the contract may continue. To do this the courts will implement an objective test and judges will try to identify a common intent if one exists. Inevitably, if they can achieve this then they will allow the contract to continue on the terms that they believe represent the true common intention of the parties.

If, however, the promises made by the two parties so contradict one another as to render any performance of the agreement impossible, and if it is in fact impossible to make any sense of the agreement, then the court will deem that an operative mistake exists and the contract will be declared void for mistake.

CASE EXAMPLE

Raffles v Wichelhaus [1864] 159 ER 375

The contract was for the sale of cotton on board a ship named *Peerless* that was sailing out of Bombay. In fact there were two ships called Peerless sailing from Bombay, both carrying cotton, but one sailing in October and one in December. The seller was under the impression that he was selling the cargo other than the one that the buyer was intending to buy. There was no way of finding a common intention between the parties. The contract could not be completed and the court declared the contract void for mistake.

JUDGMENT

In the Exchequer Court Pollock CB identified the nature of the problem in reaching the decision: 'parol evidence may be given for the purpose of shewing that the defendant meant one "*Peerless*" and the *plaintiff* another. That being so, there was no *consensus ad idem*, and therefore no binding contract.'

Any ambiguity surrounding the subject-matter of the contract may well make a mistake operative and result in the contract being declared void.

CASE EXAMPLE

Scriven Bros & Co v Hindley & Co [1913] 3 KB 564

There are different qualities of hemp. One is called 'tow' and is generally of an inferior quality. In the case auctioneers were selling hemp that was actually 'tow', and therefore of low quality, even though this was not made absolutely clear in the auction catalogue. The purchaser bid extravagantly, under the mistaken belief that he was actually bidding for superior quality hemp. Once he discovered the mistake, he then tried to reject the goods.

The auctioneers then brought an action to enforce the contract but failed because of the mutual mistake. The court identified that there could be no reconciling the situation to the mutual satisfaction of both parties and therefore the contract was void.

However, where one party is merely mistaken as to the quality of the contract then the mistake is not mutual and indeed is not operative either. In such a case the contract can be continued, even though this is not then to the liking of the party bringing the action and the contract will not be declared void.

CASE EXAMPLE

Smith v Hughes (1871) LR 6 QB 597

Hughes was offered a consignment of oats of which he examined a sample and he then bought the consignment. On delivery, he discovered that the oats were 'new oats' rather than oats from the previous year's crop which he had actually wished to buy. He refused delivery and when the seller sued for the price claimed that the contract should be void for mistake. He believed he had been offered 'good old oats' rather than 'good oats' as the seller claimed. The court felt that it could not declare a contract void merely because one party later discovered it was less advantageous than he believed it to be. The contract stood and Hughes had to pay the price.

10.4 Unilateral mistake

10.4.1 Introduction

The cases in unilateral mistake show two distinct lines:

- the mistake concerns the **terms** of the contract or
- the mistake concerns the **identity of the other party** to the contract.

In either case the significant point is that only one of the parties to the contract is actually mistaken, hence the name 'unilateral mistake'.

The basic principle is simple. Where one party contracts on the basis of a mistake known to the other party then the contract is void because there is no *consensus ad idem* in this instance. In order for the court to declare the contract void the mistake must obviously be a fundamental or essential one. If the party who is mistaken has merely mistaken the quality of the contract then this will not suffice to make the mistake operative and the mistake will have no effect on the contract.

10.4.2 Mistaken terms

If one party to the contract makes a material mistake in expressing his intention and the other party knows, or is deemed to know, of this mistake then the mistake may be operative, with the result that the contract may be declared void.

CASE EXAMPLE

Hartog v Colin & Shields [1939] 3 All ER 566

The contract involved the sale and purchase of 30,000 Argentine hare skins. The price of the skins was stated as being 10d and 1 farthing per pound. In fact, the regular practice in the trade was to sell hare skins by the piece (or individual skin) rather than by weight. Since there were about three skins to every pound, this would reduce the cost of each piece to a third. The buyers tried to enforce the contract on the basis of the mistaken term. The sellers counter-claimed, arguing that the offer was wrongly stated, as would be common knowledge in the trade. The court declared that the mistake was a material mistake that would be known to the buyers and the contract was thus declared void for the mistake.

The test of whether or not a unilateral mistake is operative and therefore voids the contract appears to have three distinct elements:

- One party to the contract is genuinely mistaken over a material detail that, had the truth been known to him, would have meant that he would not have contracted on the terms stated. (This was clearly the position of the sellers in the above case.)
- The other party to the contract ought reasonably to have known of the mistake. (Again, the court accepted in the above case that the buyers were taking advantage of a situation of which they would have been aware because of usual custom in the trade.)
- The party making the mistake was not at fault in any other way.

CASE EXAMPLE

Sybron Corporation v Rochem Ltd [1984] Ch 112

Having opted for early retirement, a manager was awarded a discretionary pension by his employers. It was subsequently discovered that the manager, together with other employees who were subordinate to him, had engaged in a fraud on the company. The company sought to have the pension agreement set aside, and it succeeded. The Court of Appeal held that it was the manager's breach of duty that had induced the company to believe that it was obliged to grant him the pension even though there was no direct misrepresentation involved. The employers had granted the pension under a mistake of fact when in fact they could have dismissed the manager. As a result, the court accepted that the mistake was material and justified the remedy.

However, where one party contracts on the basis of a mistake of which the other party has no knowledge then this mistake cannot be operative. The other party is not taking advantage of the mistake and the result will be different.

CASE EXAMPLE

Wood v Scarth (1858) 1 F & F 293

A landlord agreed to lease premises to a tenant, mistakenly believing that his clerk had explained clearly to the tenant before the agreement that a premium of £500 (an advance payment) was expected as well as the rent. The court held that the mistake could not be operative since the tenant had contracted on terms not including the premium in good faith and without any knowledge of the landlord's mistake. The contract for rent only was therefore not affected. It was valid and enforceable against the landlord.

10.4.3 Mistaken identity

Again, the area is at first sight complex and it raises different issues to those already considered. However, the occasions when the principle arises are not straightforward. The common scenario will be when a rogue has made off with property belonging to another party after making false representations as to his identity. This, then, is the mistake made by the other party. The goods will usually have been transferred to an innocent third party from whom the original owner is trying to recover them.

The cases are distressing because the courts will have to decide between two seemingly innocent parties which to disappoint. If the contract is one covered by the Sale of Goods Act 1979 then the rogue, as a seller, has no title to pass in disposing of the goods. If the original owner identifies the title as only voidable sufficiently early then he may have rights as against a subsequent purchaser. If the third party buying the goods from the rogue does so in good faith and without notice of the defective title, then he may have a good title as against the party from whom the rogue acquired the goods.

The case law shows some confusion and contradictions. There are some basic requirements that the original owner must satisfy in order to claim that he retains ownership.

- In order to claim a mistake on the basis of a mistaken identity the party seeking to claim rights in the goods must first of all show that he intended to contract with a person other than the one with whom he did in fact contract. So there must have been another person.

CASE EXAMPLE

Kings Norton Metal Co Ltd v Edridge, Merrett & Co Ltd (The Kings Norton Metal Case) (1897) 14 TLR 98

Wallis contracted under the name 'Hallam & Co' for the purchase of expensive items of brass rivet wire. The goods were supplied but never paid for. The Metal Co sued the party who eventually purchased them from Wallis to recover the goods. The court was not prepared to void the contract for mistake. The Metal Co was not so much mistaking the identity of Wallis, since Hallam & Co did not exist, as mistaking the creditworthiness of Wallis with whom it had in fact contracted. Obviously, Wallis had disappeared by the time of the case, otherwise he could have been sued for fraudulent misrepresentation.

JUDGMENT

Smith LJ identified where the problem in such cases lies: 'The question was, with whom … did the plaintiffs contract to sell the goods? Clearly with the writer of the letters … there was a contract by the plaintiffs with the person who wrote the letters'.

- In order to claim that the mistake is operative and therefore makes the contract void, the mistake must be shown to have been material to the formation of the contract, that the contract was formed because of the mistake, otherwise the mistake is not operative and the contract will continue.

CASE EXAMPLE

Cundy v Lindsay (1878) 3 App Cas 459

Blenkarn hired a room at 37 Wood Street. In this street a highly respectable firm, Blenkiron & Co, conducted its business at number 123. Blenkarn then ordered a large number of handkerchiefs from Lindsay's, with a signature designed to be confused with that of the reputable firm, Blenkiron. The goods were supplied and billed in the name Blenkiron and, of course, the goods were not paid for. Blenkarn had sold some on to Cundy before the fraud was discovered. Lindsay then tried to recover the goods from Cundy. On appeal, the House of Lords held that the contract was void for mistake. The mistake was operable because Lindsay's were able to show that the identity of the party trading from 37 Wood Street was material to the formation of the contract. Unlike in the *Kings Norton Metal* case, there was a party here with whom the claimants wished to contract and the identity of the party was actually material to the making of the contract. The third party acquired the goods from Blenkarn without any title.

 In order for the party claiming mistake to be able to show that the mistake is to be considered material, the other party to the contract must have known of the mistake.

CASE EXAMPLE

Boulton v Jones (1857) 2 H & N 564

The defendant ordered certain goods from Brocklehurst in order to take advantage of a set-off (a legal means of keeping the goods in return for a debt already owed to the defendant). Unknown to the defendant, Brocklehurst had assigned his business to the claimant. When the goods were delivered and the defendant refused to pay, he then tried to have the contract set aside for mistake as to the identity of the party with whom he had contracted. The court held that the defendant did not have to pay the price.

10.4.4 Mistaken identity and face-to-face dealing

Where a party negotiates a contract in person then that party is deemed to be contracting with the other party who is physically present at the negotiations, whatever the identity that the other party assumes. In this way the mistake is not as to the identity but as to the creditworthiness of the other party. This is not material to the forming of the contract so the mistake is not operative and the contract cannot be declared void.

CASE EXAMPLE

Phillips v Brooks Ltd [1919] 2 KB 243

North, a rogue, selected jewellery in a shop, including a necklace worth £2,550 and a ring worth £450. He wrote a cheque for £3,000, misrepresenting himself as Sir George Bullough, whose address the jeweller found in the directory. North persuaded the jeweller to let him leave with the ring, leaving the rest of the jewels till his cheque cleared. The cheque bounced and when the jeweller later discovered the ring in a pawnshop where North had sold it, he tried to sue for its recovery. His argument, that the contract with North was based on mistaking North's identity for that of Sir George Bullough, failed. The court held that he could have only intended to contract with the party he actually met face to face. The pawnshop gained good title because it bought in good faith without notice of any defect in title.

The judgment above seems absolutely clear and sound and inevitably is followed. One later case, however, actually cast doubt on this principle and caused some confusion.

CASE EXAMPLE

Ingram v Little [1960] 3 All ER 332

Sisters jointly owned a car that they advertised for sale in a local newspaper. A man who came to buy it offered to pay by cheque. The ladies were a little wary and initially refused to accept a cheque but they were then persuaded to do so when the man passed himself off as an important local figure. One of the ladies found the name that the man used in the telephone directory and the address that the man supplied was also the same. This was then sufficient to convince the ladies that he was genuine. In fact, he was not; the cheque bounced; and when the ladies later discovered the car in the hands of an innocent third party to whom the man had sold it, they sued the third party to recover the car. The Court of Appeal, strangely, accepted that the mistake as to identity was material to the contract. The court distinguished *Phillips v Brooks* and held that the offer to accept a cheque in payment for the car was made only to the person that the ladies identified as being the important local figure. Since the man buying the car from them knew of this and the ladies initially rejected the cheque until they established his *bona fides*, they were said to have relied on the identity of the important local figure. The court held that this was a mistake which was material to the making of the contract and the court therefore declared the contract void.

JUDGMENT

Pearce LJ explained some of the reasoning of the court: 'If a man orally commissions a portrait from some unknown artist who had deliberately passed himself off … as a famous painter, the imposter could not accept the offer. For though the offer is made to him physically, it is obviously, as he knows, addressed to the famous painter. The mistake in identity in such facts is clear and the nature of the contract makes it obvious that identity was vital to the offeror.'

The inevitable result of the above case was to cause confusion with two apparently mutually exclusive lines of reasoning. The case has subsequently been seen as being either decided on the particular facts or indeed wrongly decided, and the later case law has returned to the original and more logical principle. In a face-to-face situation a person is deemed to be contracting with the person actually in front of him, irrespective of the identity which that person tries to represent himself as being.

CASE EXAMPLE

Lewis v Avery [1972] 1 QB 198

A rogue buying a car represented himself to the seller as a famous actor of the time, Richard Greene, and he also showed the seller a false studio pass after his cheque was at first refused. When the cheque was subsequently dishonoured and the seller later discovered the whereabouts of the car, he sued the new owner for recovery. His action failed. The court held that the claimant had been induced into believing that the party he contracted with was somebody different but had still in fact done no more than contract with that party. The mistake was not operative and the contract could not be declared void. In the Court of Appeal Lord Denning suggested that in such cases the mistake would render the contract voidable rather than void. This, however, is not a generally acceptable principle and Megaw LJ delivered the better judgment, returning the law to where it stood after *Phillips v Brooks*. As he stated, the claimant had not so much been concerned with the true identity of the party with whom he contracted but had rather been induced into believing that the person was somebody else. The only issue was the creditworthiness of that person, which was not a material mistake but represents a failure on the part of the claimant to ensure that he dealt with a reputable party.

JUDGMENT

Returning to the more logical reasoning of *Phillips v Brooks*, Megaw LJ said: 'I find it difficult to understand the basis, either in logic or in practical consideration, of the test laid down by the majority in *Ingram v Little*'. He then identified the better test to apply and why the claimant in the case could not succeed in a case of mistaken identity: 'at the time [the claimant] made the offer he regarded the identity of the offeree as a matter of vital importance … the mistake of Mr Lewis went no further than a mistake as to the attributes of the rogue. It was simply a mistake as to his creditworthiness.'

It naturally follows that, for a party to claim that the identity of the other party is material to the making of the contract, he must have taken adequate steps to ensure the true identity of the other party. In the cases above this was not in fact done, which is why the problems actually arose, rather than because of any mistake. The recent case law confirms this principle.

CASE EXAMPLE

Citibank NA v Brown Shipley & Co Ltd; Midland Bank v Brown Shipley & Co Ltd [1991] 2 All ER 690

A rogue passed himself off as a company officer and persuaded a bank to issue a bankers' draft to pay for large amounts of foreign currency that he was buying from another bank, and he represented that this could be recovered from the fictitious company's account. The currency was passed once the legitimacy of the bankers' draft was established. When the fraud was discovered the issuing bank tried to recover the amount of the draft from the other bank on the ground that title to the draft could never have passed because of the fraud, but it failed in its action. The bank had done insufficient to establish the *bona fides* of the rogue for his identity to be material and for its mistake to be operative. The court held that the bank should stand its own loss.

The principles associated with face-to-face dealing may also apply where the contract is made by the claimant's agent. This is because an agent binds his principal to a contract. However, if the contract is made only through a mere intermediary, lacking the authority to bind the principal, then the general principles of mistaken identity will still apply.

CASE EXAMPLE

Shogun Finance Ltd v Hudson [2003] UKHL 62

A rogue, giving a false name and address, completed hire-purchase forms to buy a car and showed a stolen driving licence in the name of D Patel to confirm his identity. The car dealer faxed a copy of the licence and draft hire-purchase agreement, signed by the rogue in Mr Patel's name, to the claimant finance company. The company then checked the credit rating of the real Patel and agreed to finance the purchase. The rogue paid 10 per cent, partly in cash and partly by cheque, and drove the car away and then sold it on to the defendant. When the finance company realised the mistake, it brought proceedings against the defendant. The rule *nemo dat quod non habet* was applied, ie a seller cannot pass on a title if he does not have one. The Court of Appeal considered the 'face-to-face' cases but decided that they did not apply. The offer of finance was made to Mr Patel, not the rogue; there was no contract between the rogue and the finance company. The situation was more like *Cundy v Lindsay* since the finance company never actually saw the rogue, dealt only with the documentation, and the salesman in the showroom was not its agent, but only an intermediary. The rogue gained no title that he could pass on, and so the innocent purchaser had to bear the loss. The House of Lords confirmed the principle.

JUDGMENT

Dyson LJ explained the point: 'The identity of the hirer was of the greatest importance to the company: the judge found that at all material times it intended to hire the car to Mr Patel.' Nevertheless, Sedley LJ, dissenting, considered that the dealer had acted as the agent of the finance company and suggested that the situation 'amounted to face-to-face dealing'.

Janet O'Sullivan prefers the dissenting judgment, for the following reasons:

QUOTATION

'Generally, the person who sells to a rogue is in a better position to check his honesty than the person who buys from a rogue, so that the rules of law should tend to protect the third party purchaser. After all, no one with any sense parts with their car unless the buyer hands over cash or any equally secure means of payment such as a banker's draft. On these facts, the claimant was even more lax, allowing the rogue to take the car away on credit terms without any means of verifying that he was the person named in the driving licence.'

J O'Sullivan, 'Case notes. Unilateral mistake as to identity – rogue fraudulently obtaining car – does title pass to innocent third party?' (2001) SL Rev, Autumn, pp 21–22

ACTIVITY

Quick quiz

Suggest what type of mistake is involved in the following scenarios:

1. I contracted with a farmer called Giles to buy his horse called Silver. He has two horses called Silver. He believes that he has sold me his brown stallion with the white flash on the nose. I believed that I was buying his grey mare.
2. A man calling himself Gordon Brown knocked on my door one evening and bought my car by cheque. I accepted the cheque because I believed he was the Prime Minister but I have now discovered that this was not the case, as his cheque has been dishonoured by the bank.
3. In the pub tonight I agreed to sell my collection of Elvis records to a man called Stan. However, when I went home and asked my wife where they were she said that she had thrown them away years ago because they were never played.

ACTIVITY

Self-assessment questions

1. In what ways is mistake close to:
   (a) agreement and
   (b) misrepresentation?
2. Why is it easy to confuse common mistake with misrepresentation?
3. Why might a party prefer to sue for a mistake rather than for misrepresentation?
4. In what circumstances will a contract be declared void in common law as a result of a mistake?
5. What must be proved for a claim of *res sua* to succeed?
6. In what sense is it possible to say that a common mistake as to quality has no effect on the contract?
7. What is the essential difference between a common mistake and a mutual mistake?
8. Under what circumstances will a contract made as a result of a mutual mistake be declared void?
9. What are the possible effects of a mutual mistake on the contract?

10. What is meant by the requirement in unilateral mistake that the mistake must be a material one?
11. Why is identity such a key factor in unilateral mistake?
12. In what ways does the case of *Ingram v Little* seem to be wrongly decided?
13. What exactly has to be proved in a unilateral mistake for the mistake to be operative and the contract declared void?

The class of mistake	The character of the mistake	The legal consequences of the mistake
Common mistake: • **res extincta** *(Couturier v Hastie)* • **res sua** *(Cooper v Phibbs)* • mistake as to **quality** *(Bell v Lever Bros)*.	The same mistake is made by both parties: • the mistake concerns the existence of the subject-matter at the time the contract is made • the mistake is about who owns the subject-matter at the time of contracting • the mistake is merely as to the quality of the bargain made.	 • The mistake is 'operative' and the contract is void • The mistake is 'operative' and the contract is void • The mistake is not 'operative'– the contract continues unless it is 'fundamental' to the contract.
Mutual mistake:	Both parties make a mistake but not the same one – they are at cross-purposes	• If performance is impossible then the contract is void *(Raffles v Wichelhaus)* • If the court can find a common intent then the contract may continue *(Smith v Hughes)*.
Unilateral mistake: • **mistake as to terms** *(Hartog v Colin & Shields)* • **mistaken identity, not face to face** *(Cundy v Lindsay)* • **mistaken identity, face to face** *(Lewis v Avery)*.	Only one party is mistaken – the other party knows and takes advantage of the first party's mistake: • (i) one party mistaken over a material detail; (ii) other party knew of mistake; (iii) mistaken party not at fault • (i) mistaken party intended to contract with someone else; (ii) mistake material to contract; (iii) mistake known to other party • party contracts in person with someone who claims to be someone else.	 • if all three then mistake is 'operative' and contract void – if not, then may be voidable in equity. • if all three then mistake is 'operative' and contract void – if not, then may be voidable in equity. • Not an 'operative' mistake – mistaken party deemed to be contracting with person in front of him.
Non est factum	• Mistake concerns nature of the document being signed • The document is (i) materially different to what it was represented to be; (ii) there is no negligence by the person signing it.	If both are present then there is an 'operative mistake' – the contract is void – but if not then there is no effect on contract. *(Saunders v Anglian Building Society)*

Figure 10.2 The different types of mistake and their legal consequences

10.5 The effects of equity

10.5.1 The intervention of equity

If a mistake has been shown to be operative then the common law applies and the contract is declared void by the court. Traditionally, if the mistake was not an operative mistake and therefore could not be declared void then an equitable solution could be sought in one of three ways:

- **Rescission** of the contract, with the contract being set aside and new terms substituted.
- A **refusal** to grant the other party's claim for **specific performance** of the contract.
- **Rectification** of a document containing a mistake which is material.

10.5.2 Rescission

At one point it was held that if the party claiming rescission could show that it was against conscience to allow the other party to take advantage of the mistake then the courts were prepared to allow rescission of the contract. It was usual at the same time to substitute more equitable terms which were more likely to represent the true interests of the parties.

CASE EXAMPLE

Solle v Butcher [1950] 1 KB 671

The mistake as to the lease being outside of the jurisdiction of the Rent Restrictions (Notices of Increase) Act 1923 was held to be a common mistake over the quality of the contract rather than a mistake as to the existence of the subject-matter, which would have allowed the contract to be declared void. At common law, then, the mistake as to the application of rent review rules had no effect. Nevertheless, the Court of Appeal was prepared to set aside the original terms that were unworkable in the circumstances and the court was prepared to allow the tenant the choice of terminating the lease or continuing it with the rent set at £250. This was the amount that would have been appropriate under the statute. Lord Denning considered that this would be appropriate since the improvements justified the increase.

Lord Denning then applied the principle in the above case in subsequent cases. He did so because he felt that rescission would often be the appropriate remedy in the contracts made as the result of an innocent misrepresentation, and where the mistake actually concerns the innocent misrepresentation.

CASE EXAMPLE

Magee v Pennine Insurance Co Ltd [1969] 2 QB 507

An insurance agent had filled out the proposal form for motor insurance for the proposer. The details as to the people driving the car were inaccurately stated as including Magee, who was stated as having a provisional licence, although he did not in fact have a licence, his eldest son, a police driver, and his youngest son possessing a provisional licence. Magee signed the proposal even though he had no idea what it contained. Only the youngest son was in fact going to drive the car. The car was then involved in an accident after which the insurance company agreed to pay £385, being the true value of the car. When the company later discovered the inaccuracies in the proposal, it refused to pay. The premiums would have inevitably been much higher had the insurance company known the true details. Magee sued to enforce the agreement to pay £385. At first instance the judge held that the insurance company could repudiate the contract for misrepresentation of the major clause, the identity and status of the drivers of the vehicle. On appeal, Lord Denning affirmed his own principle in *Solle v Butcher*, and held that the agreement to pay was made as a result of a common mistake and was voidable in equity.

It has recently been restated, however, that equity intervenes with the remedy of rescission only to allow a party to escape from an unconscionable bargain but it will not intervene to allow a party to avoid having made a bad bargain. See *Clarion Ltd v National Provident Institution* [2000] 2 All ER 265.

Even more recently, however, the case of *Great Peace Shipping v Tsavliris* [2002] EWCA Civ 1407 CA has cast doubt on whether there is a doctrine of equitable mistake justifying rescission of the contract (see sections 10.2.3 above and 10.5.5 below).

Toulson J in the High Court in *Statoil ASA v Louis Dreyfus Energy Services LP* [2008] EWHC 2257 has suggested that the effect of *Great Peace* is also that there is no equitable jurisdiction in the case of unilateral mistake either.

10.5.3 Refusal of specific performance

As an equitable remedy, specific performance depends on the discretion of the court. As a result, it can also be refused where one party entered the agreement on the basis of a mistake and in all the circumstances:

- it would be unfair or harsh to expect that party to perform the contract, or
- the mistake was actually caused by the other party's misrepresentation, or
- the other party knew of the mistake and tried to take advantage of it.

CASE EXAMPLE

Webster v Cecil [1861] 54 ER 812

Webster offered to buy land from Cecil and Cecil, who stated that the land had cost him more than that, rejected his offer of £2,000. Webster then tried to enforce a written agreement for sale of the land for £1,250. Cecil could obviously refer to these negotiations as the proof that the written document did not in fact represent the intention of the parties. The court held that Webster's claim to specific performance must fail since the written agreement was clearly inconsistent with the agreement actually reached.

The court will refuse an order of specific performance because it would be inequitable to allow it. In this way the court will not refuse an order merely because one party has made a worse bargain than he thought he had. This in itself would be inequitable.

CASE EXAMPLE

Tamplin v James (1880) 15 Ch D 215

James bought an inn at auction. He did so in the mistaken belief that the sale also included the adjoining land, since the landlord of the inn had previously owned it. James made no actual check to see that the land was in fact included. In fact, the land was not included and James tried to back out of the arrangement. The landlord sought an order of specific performance. The court granted this order. It would not refuse it. James had made no check of the plans and he could not resist an order of specific performance of the contract in the circumstances.

10.5.4 Rectification of documents

It is clearly inequitable if parties are bound to an agreement that in fact does not accurately reflect what they agreed in the first place. For this reason a court can rewrite a written document that does not conform to the actual agreement between the two parties. We have already seen how this happened in *Webster v Cecil* [1861] 54 ER 812, above.

For there to be a dispute it will usually mean that the two parties have a different view of what the agreement is. To succeed in obtaining an order for rectification, the party seeking rectification must show that a complete and certain agreement was in fact reached, and that this agreement remained unchanged up to the time of contracting but was not reflected in the written document.

CASE EXAMPLE

Craddock Bros Ltd v Hunt [1923] 2 Ch 136

Craddock agreed to sell his house to Hunt, not intending that an adjoining yard should be included in the sale. However, by mistake, the yard was included in the conveyance and so Craddock immediately sought rectification of the document and succeeded. The court accepted that the evidence showed that the written document did not reflect the actual intention of the parties in contracting.

Inevitably, it is possible that the mistake in drafting is made because at least one party's legal representatives are mistaken or not fully aware of the actual agreement. This will not prevent a court from granting rectification if the party himself is fully aware of the difference between the actual agreement and the written agreement and therefore, in effect, of the mistake.

CASE EXAMPLE

Templiss Properties Ltd v Hyams [1999] EGCS 60

In a tenancy the parties intended that the rent should not include business rates. In fact, the actual lease, when drafted, did include business rates. The tenant's solicitors were not aware of this. However, the court was prepared to grant rectification of the lease since evidence showed that the tenant himself was aware of the actual terms of the agreement.

Of course, for rectification to be allowed the claimant must show that the written agreement ran contrary to the common intention of the parties. If this cannot be shown then a request for rectification will be rejected.

CASE EXAMPLE

George Wimpey UK Ltd v VI Construction Ltd (2005) 103 Con LR 67

Wimpey bought land from VIC intending to build flats on it. It was always accepted on both sides that Wimpey would pay a basic price plus a price that reflected the difference between the actual sales price and the projected price of the flats. In draft contracts things that would increase the value of the flats were highlighted but in later contracts these were omitted by mistake. Wimpey's request for rectification was rejected by the court because the decision to enter the contract had been taken by Wimpey's board; the person negotiating for Wimpey did not have the authority to bind Wimpey; and therefore Wimpey could not show that it did not approve the contract in the form in which it was written.

ACTIVITY

Self-assessment questions

1. When, traditionally, would a party claiming a mistake be able to look for a solution in equity?
2. Why could the mistake in *Solle v Butcher* not lead to the contract being void under the common law?
3. What was Lord Denning's justification for applying equity to set the contract aside?
4. In what circumstances will the courts refuse to grant an order of specific performance?
5. What happens to the contract when rectification is applied as a remedy?

10.5.5 The effects of *Great Peace*

As we have seen already this case has cast doubts on the role of equity in common mistake (see section 10.2.3). The judge in the High Court would not rescind the contract and had difficulty in reconciling what he felt to be conflicting authorities in *Bell v Lever Bros* and *Solle v Butcher*. The judges in the Court of Appeal identified that there was no equitable doctrine of mistake and that the interpretation of the judgments in *Bell v Lever Bros* made by Lord Denning in *Solle v Butcher* was a misunderstanding. As Adam Kramer points out:

QUOTATION

'... in fact prior to *Bell*, equity did not intervene in cases in which the common law did not itself hold cases void for common mistake, the House of Lords in *Bell* would not have overlooked any such equitable doctrine, and thus *Solle* must give way in order to restore coherence to the law. The Court of Appeal was not unduly concerned by their taking the step of overruling a doctrine thought to have existed for 50 years, since it was too uncertain to be relied upon and very few cases had purported to apply it.'

A Kramer, 'Case notes. Common mistake and the abolition of the equitable doctrine' (2003) SL Rev, Spring, pp 17–19

Nevertheless, the reason for the 'misunderstanding' of the principle in *Bell v Lever Bros* can be seen in the judgments in the House of Lords in that case. The House affirmed the basic principle that where there is a common mistake as to a fundamental element in the contract, such as the existence of the subject-matter, then this renders the contract void, and this is an absolute principle. However, it also identified the possibility of a contract being void for common mistake when there was a mistake only over the quality of the contract, provided that the mistake was over a quality that makes the contract fundamentally different to that which was contracted for in the first place.

Lord Denning's reasoning in *Solle v Butcher* was to allow equity to intervene to remedy the situation. The Court of Appeal in *Great Peace* identified that the absence of this 'fundamental' mistake would mean that neither the common law nor equity would be available. Janet O'Sullivan has identified the problem facing the judges in *Great Peace* in trying to reconcile these two positions:

QUOTATION

'Toulson J [in the High Court] was therefore faced with distinguishing *Bell v Lever Bros*, which he did by concluding that the parties' mistake was not sufficiently fundamental. [He] got round the problem like most other judges have done in the past by finding that the mistake was not serious enough but that leaves the common law jurisdiction theoretically available. [And he] went on to conclude that there really is not any separate equitable jurisdiction ... This separate jurisdiction has also caused confusion in the past ... because ... Denning LJ confusingly adopted the label "fundamental" ... but presumably not quite as fundamental as required at common law.'

J O'Sullivan, 'Case notes. Common mistake – whether contract void at common law – whether contract liable to be set aside in equity' (2002) SL Rev, Summer, pp 18–19

Mark Pawloski argues that:

QUOTATION

'One only needs to compare the case of *Bell* (decided in law) with *Magee* (based on an application of equitable principles) to see that the difference in outcome is dependent solely on the choice of jurisdiction. The reality is that, despite various attempts at reconciling these two decisions, there is no material (factual) distinction between them.'

M Pawloski, 'Common mistake: law v equity', New Law Journal, 1st February 2002, p 146

The judges in the Court of Appeal in *Great Peace* clarified what the principal elements of common mistake are:

- a common assumption as to the existence of a particular state of affairs
- with neither party having made any warranty to the other party that the state of affairs does exist
- so that the mistake is not the fault of either party
- the state of affairs concerns something vital to the continuation of the contract
- and the contract is made impossible because of the mistake.

Adam Kramer argues that:

QUOTATION

'Taken as a conclusive list of requirements, the above statement is dangerously misleading.'

A Kramer, 'Case notes. Common mistake and the abolition of the equitable doctrine' (2003) SL Rev, Spring, pp 17–19

There are two problems to which he refers. Firstly, he argues that common mistake does not depend on the mistake making the contract impossible but rather that the mistake makes the essence of what the parties contracted for impossible to achieve. This is in effect the reasoning in *Bell v Lever Bros*. Secondly, he identifies also that the mistake is only an issue and the contract is only void in those circumstances where the parties themselves have not expressly or impliedly made provision for what happens if the contract becomes impossible in that way. In other words, who bears the risk of any loss. This is in effect the basis of the decision in *McRae v Commonwealth Disposals* (1950) 84 CLR 377 (see section 10.2.3). Another problem in mistake is that it is so clearly linked to other areas of the law of contract. However, this also possibly limits the problems that are identified above and has implications for the decision in *Great Peace*.

- Common mistake in most cases is linked to the requirement of *consensus ad idem* from offer and acceptance. One simple way of looking at the problem of a common mistake in the case of *res extincta* and *res sua* is that there has not in fact been a contractual agreement. This is because the parties could not and would not have contracted for subject-matter that either does not exist or is actually owned by the party contracting for its purchase. Nevertheless, even then, the judges may find the means of remedying the situation, as they did in *British Steel Corporation v Cleveland Bridge and Engineering Co* [1984] 1 All ER 504 (see section 2.4).
- Even in the case of *res extincta* and *res sua*, if the parties have an express or implied agreement on risk allocation then this may be the answer to the problem, as it may also be in the case of a mistake as to quality.
- A common mistake has much in common with **frustration**. The differences between the two are that in common mistake the false assumption was always impossible at the time the contract was made, whereas in frustration the basis of the contract becomes impossible after the contract is made.
- Common mistake as to quality also overlaps with innocent misrepresentation. The traditional difference between the two is that an operative mistake renders the contract void whereas a misrepresentation renders the contract voidable.

frustration

An event beyond the control of either party to a contract that makes the contract impossible to perform, eg the destruction of the subject-matter of the contract

The Court of Appeal has taken a bold step in *Great Peace* in declaring that there is no equitable jurisdiction to grant rescission of a contract for common mistake where the contract would be valid under common law. However, the impact of the decision might well in any case be overstated.

Firstly, it is arguable whether in fact the decision to overrule *Solle v Butcher* complies with the rules on precedent binding the Court of Appeal. In fact, this argument was raised in the case but the court felt that it had acted correctly.

Secondly, the occasions on which the issue arises are very few. As has been pointed out, in many instances the parties will have determined in the contract who bears the risk of loss. Besides this, there are actually very few cases on common mistake and where the mistake concerns a fundamental of the contract, such as the existence of the subject-matter, then the contract will be declared void.

In any case the problem only really occurs where there is a common mistake as to quality. Even then, if the mistake concerns something that fundamentally destroys the essential commercial character of the contract then the contract can still be declared void under the principle in *Bell v Lever Bros*.

Besides this, in many instances it would also be possible to deal with the issue through innocent misrepresentation, in which case under s 2(2) of the Misrepresentation Act 1967 the judges would have the discretion to rescind the contract or to award damages, whichever they felt was the more appropriate remedy.

The case has no impact on the other areas of mistake or on the other equitable remedies applied to mistake: a refusal to grant specific performance of a contract and rectification of a document drafted in error.

The case does, however, bring into focus some of the difficulties surrounding the area of common mistake. There are, of course, other possible solutions. Janet O'Sullivan offers one alternative in her conclusions:

QUOTATION

'It is suggested that the most appropriate reform of the area (a matter no doubt for Parliament) would be the abandonment, not of the equitable jurisdiction, but of the automatic, inflexible common law doctrine. This would mean that, in those rare cases where the parties really have not allocated the risk of common mistake either way and where the mistake is sufficiently serious in its impact on both parties (unlike the *Great Peace* case), the courts would be free, at their discretion, to rescind the contract and order relief on appropriate terms.'

J O'Sullivan, 'Case notes. Common mistake – whether contract void at common law – whether contract liable to be set aside in equity' (2002) SL Rev, Summer, pp 18–19

However it is done, it should not be beyond the courts to devise a cohesive doctrine of mistake. As Mark Pawloski concludes:

QUOTATION

'Clearly what is needed is a merger of the two streams of jurisdiction into one simplified, comprehensive doctrine of common mistake, which also allows for an appropriate element of discretion in determining the terms of any court order relieving the parties from their bargain.'

M Pawloski, 'Common mistake: law v equity', New Law Journal, 1st February 2002, p 146

10.6 *Non est factum*

non est factum

A mistake made about the nature of a written agreement when signing it – literally means 'this is not my deed'

This is literally translated as 'this is not my deed'. It is a doctrine that operates only in respect of written agreements. Usually the principle in *L'Estrange v Graucob* [1934] 2 KB 394 applies and a party is bound by written agreements that he has signed.

However, in some circumstances a party is able to claim that they only signed as a result of a genuine mistake as to the nature of the document signed. The doctrine is subject to strict requirements. It will only be appropriate because the party signing is subject to some weakness that has been exploited by the other party, for instance blindness or senility. Also, the other party must have represented that the document is something different than that which has been signed.

If this is so and the party signing has taken the precautions available to check on the authenticity of the document before signing, then the contract is void. However, before the court will declare the contract void it must be satisfied that the document is of a kind materially different to what it was represented to be, and that the party has not been negligent in signing it.

CASE EXAMPLE

Saunders v Anglian Building Society [1971] AC 1004

This case, which began as *Gallie v Lee*, involved an elderly widow who decided to transfer her property to her nephew on the stipulation that she could live there for the rest of her life. She did this so that he could borrow money on the property in order to start a business. The document was drawn up by Lee, a dishonest friend of the nephew, and was in fact a conveyance to him rather than a deed of gift to the nephew. Lee then borrowed against the property and defaulted on the loan. The widow, in answer to the claim for repossession, initially succeeded with a plea of *non est factum*. On a later appeal the House of Lords rejected her plea. There was insufficient difference between the documents that she did sign and had intended to sign. Both gave up her rights to the property and she had not done enough to check its nature.

- If a mistake is operative on the formation of a contract then the contract is void at common law.
- There are three types of mistake: common mistake (where both parties are making the same mistake); mutual mistake (where the parties are at cross purposes and so are both mistaken but making different mistakes); and unilateral mistake (where only one of the parties is mistaken and the other party knowingly takes advantage of this).
- A common mistake can void a contract where the mistake is as to the existence of the subject-matter of the contract or its true ownership but a mistake as to the quality of the contract has no effect on the contract.
- A mutual mistake will void the contract only where the parties are so at odds that it is impossible to make any sense of the agreement – if the mistake is only about the quality of the contract then the mistake has no effect on the contract.
- If a unilateral mistake is about the terms of the agreement then it is operative and the contract is void if the one party through no fault of his own is mistaken over a material detail and the other party knows or ought to know of the mistake. If the unilateral mistake concerns the identity of the other party then that mistake must have been material to the formation of the contract to have an effect and if the parties contract face to face then they are said to be contracting with the party in front of them, regardless of what identity they assume.
- Where the mistake is not operative equity may be used in certain circumstances.
- Where a party has some disability which is being taken advantage of and thinks that he is signing an entirely different type of document, a claim of *non est factum* (this is not my deed) is possible

SAMPLE ESSAY QUESTION

Discuss the extent to which judges have developed the law on mistake so that it is confused and lacking clarity of application rather than a coherent whole.

Explain the basic concept of mistake:
- Vitiates the contract and makes the contract void because the contract formed was not what the parties in effect agreed on

Explain the three types of mistake:
- Common mistake – both parties mistaken over either the existence of the subject-matter of the contract (*res extincta*) or the true ownership (*res sua*)
- Mutual mistake – the parties are at cross purposes
- Unilateral mistake – only one party is mistaken (either over the nature of the contract or the identity of the other party) and the other party is taking advantage of it

Discuss how judges have traditionally dealt with mistake:

- At common law the contract is void only if the mistake was operative – the contract was made because of the mistake
- Mistakes over the quality of the contract have no effect
- There were possible remedies within equity – but this is now controversial in the case of rescission

Discuss whether the law on mistake is confused and lacking in clarity:

- The problems associated with common mistake
- The links between common mistake and *consensus ad idem*
- The links between common mistake and frustration
- The similarity between common mistake as to quality and misrepresentation
- Consider the *dicta* in *Associated Japanese Bank v Credit du Nord*
- The problems associated with mutual mistake, ie establishing that the basis of the contract is in fact altered
- The problems associated with unilateral mistake – particularly face-to-face dealings
- The controversy over the application of equity in mistake – should have no impact on refusal to grant specific performance or on rectification – but rescission now subject to the rule in *Great Peace* – consider that the Court of Appeal went beyond the powers given in *Young* in overruling *Solle v Butcher*

Credit any discussion on *non est factum*

KEY FACTS

Character and effect of mistake

Three types:

Common – both parties are making the same mistake.

Mutual – parties are at cross-purposes and so are both mistaken but making different mistakes.

Unilateral – only one party is mistaken and the other party knowingly takes advantage of this.

In all cases, contract is void only if mistake is operable – the reason the contract was formed.

Common mistake	Case/statute	Equity and rescission	Case/statute
Void if as to existence of subject-matter of contract – *res extincta*.	*Couturier v Hastie*	Possible at one time that a mistake as to quality could still lead to rescission with contract set aside and new terms substituted.	*Solle v Butcher*
Void if as to true ownership of property – *res sua*.	*Cooper v Phibbs*		
But not void if mistake is only as to quality of contract unless fundamental to contract.	*Bell v Lever Bros*	But now rescission not available in common mistake because fundamental mistake would void contract.	*Great Peace v Tsavliris*
Mistake on authenticity of, for example, art work usually not void.	Compare *Leaf v International Galleries* and *Peco Arts v Hazlitt Gallery*	But rescission still possible with mutual and unilateral.	
		Court may refuse a request for specific performance of the contract.	*Webster v Cecil*
		Or rectify a document which contains a mistake.	*Craddock Bros v Hunt*

Mutual mistake	Case/statute	*Non est factum*	Case/statute
Void when parties are so at odds that it is impossible to make sense of the agreement.	*Raffles v Wichelhaus*	It is possible to claim *non est factum* (this is not my deed) in relation to a document signed, provided that:	*Saunders v Anglian Building Society*
But not if mistake is only about quality of contract.	*Smith v Hughes*	• a party has some disability which is being taken advantage of, and	

Unilateral mistake	Case/statute		
If mistake is about the **terms** then is operative and contract void if the one party through no fault of his own is mistaken over a material detail and the other party knows or ought to know of the mistake.	*Hartog v Colin & Shields*	• he thinks he is signing an entirely different type of document.	
If the mistake is the **identity** of the other party then that mistake must have been material to the formation of the contract.	*Cundy v Lindsay*		
If parties contract face-to-face they are said to contract with party in **front** of them, regardless of identity assumed.	*Lewis v Avery*		

Further reading

Cartwright, J, '*Solle v Butcher* and the Doctrine of Mistake in Contract' (1987) 103 LQR 594.

Cheshire, G, Fifoot, C, and Furmston, M, *Law of Contract* (15th edn, Oxford University Press, 2006) Chapter 8.

Pawloski, M, 'Common mistake: law v equity', *NLJ*, 1st February 2002, p 132.

11

Vitiating factors: Duress and undue influence

AIMS AND OBJECTIVES

After reading this chapter you should be able to:

- Distinguish between duress, economic duress and undue influence
- Understand the essential elements of economic duress
- Understand the essential elements of undue influence
- Understand the development of different classes of undue influence
- Understand the consequences of proving undue influence
- Understand the effect of undue influence on third parties
- Critically analyse the area
- Apply the law to factual situations and reach conclusions

duress

Threats of violence or actual violence used to make a party enter into a contract

undue influence

A form of unfair pressure used to induce another party to enter a contract

11.1 Introduction

The courts have always been keen to preserve freedom of contract. A necessary element of this freedom is that the agreement should be reached voluntarily. This means that no force or coercion should be used in order to secure the agreement. If a party does enter a contract because he has been coerced by the other party then the law recognises that the contract should be set aside and the party coerced should be relieved of their own obligations under the contract.

Traditionally, this coercion could give rise to an action either in common law or, as the law developed, in equity also. The nature of the action would depend on both the nature and the seriousness of the coercion.

- At common law, the action would be for **duress**.
- In equity, the action would be a claim of **undue influence**.

In either case, if the various elements of the action were proved then the contract would be voidable rather than void. The court would set aside the contract and the party who was the victim of the coercion would be relieved of his own obligations under the contract if that was indeed what was claimed.

If the action was at common law for duress then, provided the duress was proved, the party would have a remedy as of right and the contract could automatically be set aside.

If the claim was in equity for undue influence then a more complex process was followed. Because a court of equity was also a court of conscience, any remedies would be at the discretion of the court to award. It was not and is not sufficient merely that the claimant demonstrates the undue influence. It would also need to be demonstrated that it was equitable for the court to grant a remedy. This would inevitably mean that the claimant himself must comply with the maxims of equity or the remedy would be lost.

Where there is an element of doubt as to whether the coercion amounts to duress or undue influence then the claimant would be advised to bring the action first in duress and in the alternative under undue influence.

Both areas have been the subject of extensive development. A separate form of duress has developed, particularly applicable in commercial contracts and known as economic duress. The traditional limitations on bringing a successful claim of undue influence have proved too restrictive in a modern context and in some instances have created injustice. As a result the whole area has been subject to extensive development in recent years and particularly so where the party alleging the coercion is a wife who has been the victim of her husband's undue influence in relation to contracts with third parties, usually banks. One of the key problems here is the extent to which the third party is caught by actual or constructive notice of the husband's undue influence.

11.2 Duress

Duress is a common law area which was traditionally associated with intimidation that was real or at least sufficiently real and threatening to vitiate the consent of the other party, and mean that he was prevented in effect from acting with free will when reaching the agreement.

CASE EXAMPLE

Cumming v Ince (1847) 11 QBD 112

An inmate in a private mental asylum was coerced into signing away title to all of her property or she was threatened that the committal order would never be lifted. The judges were prepared to set the contract aside in the circumstances. It had not been made of her free will and she could not be bound by it.

The law developed along fairly strict lines to the extent that for a threat to be accepted as sufficient to vitiate the contract it must be one associated with violence to the person to whom it was made, or even death.

CASE EXAMPLE

Barton v Armstrong [1975] 2 All ER 465

A former chairman of a company threatened the current managing director that he would have him killed unless the managing director paid over a large sum of money for the former chairman's shares. It was shown in the case that the managing director was actually quite happy to buy the shares and would have done so even without any threat being made. Nevertheless threats had been made and the court held that these were therefore sufficient to amount to duress, vitiating the agreement they had reached as a result. The agreement was set aside for duress.

As can be seen above, the sorts of threats that will vitiate a contract, then, are very specific. In consequence, therefore, a threat merely to carry out a lawful action cannot amount to duress and will not act to vitiate the contract even though the threat is a very real one and if carried out could be damaging to the person threatened.

CASE EXAMPLE

Williams v Bayley (1886) LR 1 HL 200

A young man had forged his father's signature on promissory notes (IOUs) which he then gave to the bank, causing it to lose money. The bank then approached the young man's father and demanded that he should mortgage his farm to it to cover the son's debt or it would prosecute the son. The threat was for lawful action and so could not amount to duress. However, the court was disturbed by the manner of the threats and accepted that they did amount to undue influence.

The same principle can apply in other contexts. Traditionally, then, for duress to apply to allow the contract to be set aside the threat should be a threat of violence against the other party and not against their property.

CASE EXAMPLE

Skeate v Beale (1840) 11 A & E 983

A promise given in return for recovery of goods that had been unlawfully detained was not duress sufficient to vitiate the contract. The threat was not against the party and was not one of violence either. It was merely against the goods themselves. The court would not set aside the contract following this type of threat.

In this way, for a successful plea, there must be both the threat or compulsion that prevents the victim from acting with free will and that pressure must be unlawful.

CASE EXAMPLE

R v Attorney-General for England and Wales [2003] UKPC 22

The case concerns SAS soldiers who had operated behind enemy lines during the Gulf War with Iraq in 1990, two of the soldiers involved then having written books about the events. Fearing that this undermined the secrecy of the special forces, the Ministry of Defence then issued an order that the members of the SAS should sign a confidentiality agreement or alternatively they would be transferred into other units with a consequent reduction in wages and status. One of the soldiers from that mission signed without benefit of any independent advice or without being allowed to read the contract in advance. He later left the regiment and, having returned to his native New Zealand, then entered into a contract with publishers for his own account of the mission. The Attorney-General then brought an action for breach of contract. The trial judge identified that the contract with the MOD was gained through duress. The New Zealand Court of Appeal reversed this finding, holding that there was no duress or undue influence since the soldier was free to sign or to change units. The Privy Council held that there was no duress. There was indeed a compulsion of will but it was not illegitimate since the order was given to avoid the undermining of the effectiveness of the SAS and its operations. The Privy Council also identified that, while there was a relationship of influence, it did not amount to undue influence. (See section 11.4.5.)

As a result of these factors it seems that duress will be of limited availability in a modern context and undue influence is probably a better option in most instances.

11.3 Economic duress

The limitations on the scope of duress had been the subject of some criticism. As a result, a doctrine then subsequently developed in the commercial field whereby a contract could be set aside not because of threats of violence but because extreme coercion had rendered the contract otherwise commercially unviable. The possibility of such a course of action was actually first discussed in the judgments of cases but without necessarily being applied.

CASE EXAMPLE

DC Builders v Rees [1965] 3 All ER 837

In this case, as we have already seen, the Reeses forced the small firm of builders who had done extensive work for them to accept a cheque of £300 in full satisfaction of the actual bill for the work of £462. The alternative given to the builders was that they would receive nothing. They had in effect no choice in the circumstances but to accept. While the case was actually decided on application of the principle in *Pinnel's* rule, Lord Denning considered the issue of inequality of bargaining strength and felt that coercion in such circumstances justified avoidance of the agreement.

JUDGMENT

Lord Denning developed the argument further than the basic common law rule: 'It is worth noticing that the principle may be applied, not only so as to suspend strict legal rights, but also so as to preclude the enforcement of them ... The creditor is only barred from his legal rights when it would be inequitable for him to insist upon them. Where there has been a true accord, under which the creditor voluntarily agrees to accept a lesser sum in satisfaction and the debtor accepts it, then it is inequitable for the creditor afterwards to insist on the balance. But he is not bound unless there has been truly an accord between them.'

The point was then taken further and a more formal doctrine was developed, including a proper test of the circumstances in which the doctrine could be applied.

CASE EXAMPLE

Occidental Worldwide Investment Corporation v Skibs A/S Avanti (The Siboen and the Sibotre) [1976] 1 Lloyd's Rep 293

During a world recession in the shipping industry, charterers demanded a renegotiation of their contract with the shipowners. They claimed that they would otherwise go out of business (although it is unlikely that this would have actually been the case) and that as they had no assets they were not worth suing. The shipowners had no choice but to agree to the variation. Because of the recession they would have had little chance of other charters of their vessels. Kerr J suggested that the question to ask was: 'Was there such a degree of coercion that the other party was deprived of his free consent and agreement?' He also identified a two-part test to establish if economic duress had occurred:

(i) did the party alleging the coercion protest immediately, and if so

(ii) did that party accept the agreement or try to argue openly about it?

JUDGMENT

Lord Scarman then also accepted the basic doctrine *in Pao On v Lau Yiu Long* [1980] AC 614: 'there is nothing contrary to principle in recognising economic duress as a factor which may render a contract voidable provided always that the basis of such recognition is that it must always amount to a coercion of will which vitiates consent'.

Lord Scarman also outlined the test for coercion: 'whether the person alleged to have been coerced did or did not protest … did or did not have an alternative course open to him … was independently advised … took steps to avoid it'.

Lord Kerr suggested that the basic question to be asked is: 'was there such a degree of coercion that the other party was deprived of his free consent and agreement'.

The doctrine and the basic tests deriving from it have been subsequently and successfully applied in later case law.

CASE EXAMPLE

Atlas Express Ltd v Kafco (Importers and Distributors) Ltd [1989] QB 833

Atlas, a national carrier, entered into a contract with Kafco, a small manufacturer of cane goods and basketware, to deliver Kafco's basketwork to Woolworth stores. It was estimated that each load would be between 400 and 600 cartons and the parties agreed a price of £1.10 per carton for delivery. In fact the loads only amounted to about 200 cartons each and Atlas then refused to carry any more unless Kafco paid it a minimum of £440 per load. Kafco had no immediate alternative source of transport and was forced to agree to the demand in order to protect its contract with Woolworth. However, it later failed to pay the agreed new rate and Atlas sued. Tucker J held for Kafco. Kafco was coerced and had no choice in entering the agreement. Atlas was unable to enforce the new arrangement between them.

JUDGMENT

In his judgment Tucker J said: 'I find that the defendant's apparent consent to the agreement was induced by pressure which was illegitimate … In my judgment [it] can properly be described as economic duress, which is a concept recognised by English law, and which in the circumstances of the present case vitiates the defendant's apparent consent …'.

Tucker also held that there was in any case no consideration for the fresh agreement since Atlas was only doing what it was bound to do under the existing contract with Kafco. However, it is likely that since *Williams v Roffey Bros & Nicholls Contractors Ltd* [1990] 1 All ER 512 this argument could no longer be sustained.

The doctrine has been extended to apply wherever there is an intentional submission to improper pressure, although what the difference is between legitimate pressure and improper pressure is not always certain.

CASE EXAMPLE

Universe Tankships Incorporated of Monrovia v International Transport Workers Federation (The Universal Sentinel) [1983] 1 AC 366

This was one of a number of cases involving action by the International Transport Workers Federation (ITWF) in respect of a campaign to improve the conditions of crew members on ships 'flying flags of convenience'. [This expression refers to the situation where ships are registered with countries that do not operate according to established working conditions, pay very low wages, and cut corners in working practices, and therefore are more profitable and undermine reputable shipping companies.] Here, the ship was 'blacked' by the union (see next case) and forced to pay towards the ITWF welfare fund in order to secure the ship's release. The court considered that this amounted to economic duress, the pressure being illegitimate, and was sufficient to vitiate the contract. However, the court was undecided on the difference between what was legitimate pressure and what was not.

The doctrine has been applied in a number of cases involving pressure from trade unionists. There are inevitable arguments as to what amounts to legitimate industrial action and what goes beyond the law and amounts to economic duress allowing a party to avoid an agreement that they have made under pressure.

CASE EXAMPLE

Dimskal Shipping Co SA v International Transport Workers Federation (The Evia Luck) [1991] 2 AC 152

The ITWF had conducted a long campaign against ships sailing under 'flags of convenience' in an attempt to improve the conditions of workers at sea and to improve safety standards in sailing. When the *Evia Luck*, one such ship, was in port in Sweden the agents of the ITWF boarded the vessel and informed the master of the ship that it would be 'blacked'. [This means that sailors would be asked to avoid enlisting for service on it or dockers asked to avoid loading or unloading it.] He was also warned that it would not be loaded or allowed to leave port till the company that owned it and was sailing it under a Panamanian flag agreed to a number of demands in respect of extra payment for the crew and improved conditions of service. When the owners initially refused, the ship was in fact 'blacked' and so they gave in to the pressure and agreed to the demands. They later successfully claimed economic duress. The court held that the pressure applied was unlawful coercion vitiating the agreement by which they were not then bound.

The courts have recognised that there is nothing wrong as such with applying legitimate business pressure. It is the illegitimate nature of the pressure involved that distinguishes economic duress from strong business dealing. As a result it has also been held that the doctrine can be applied in the case of threats of lawful action, provided that this amounts to coercion and prevents a party acting out of his own free will.

VITIATING FACTORS: DURESS AND UNDUE INFLUENCE

CASE EXAMPLE

Alec Lobb (Garages) Ltd v Total Oil Great Britain Ltd [1983] 1 WLR 87

Here, the claimant was a company that owned a petrol filling station. It had financial problems and as a result contacted the defendants to whom it transferred ownership while retaining the petrol station under a 51-year lease. This included a leaseback arrangement under which the original directors of the company were also granted a 21-year sub-lease at a rent of £2,500 per year and which also included a solus agreement by which they were bound to buy petrol from the defendants. The use of the sub-lease was designed specifically to avoid the arrangement being classed as an unenforceable restraint of trade, as it may have been under existing law. The Court of Appeal decided that the solus clause should be severed from the sub-lease and not be enforceable against the directors.

Inevitably, the doctrine is still developing and is subject to general uncertainty. In this way, although it may be possible for a party to show that there is indeed economic duress, there is no guarantee that a remedy will actually be gained.

CASE EXAMPLE

North Ocean Shipping Co Ltd v Hyundai Construction Co Ltd (The Atlantic Baron) [1979] QB 705

A shipyard agreed to build a tanker for a shipping company for $30,950,000. Payment was to be made by five instalments. As part of the contract the shipyard opened a letter of credit for repayment of payments already made if they should fail to build the ship. After payment of the first instalment the shipyard demanded an increase of 10 per cent in the price, although there was no legal basis for this demand. The shipping company reluctantly agreed, as it needed the ship to complete other contracts. The letter of credit was increased as a result. Eventually, many months after completion of the ship, the shipping company sued for return of the excess. While the court accepted that there was economic duress, it was felt that the increase in the letter of credit amounted to sufficient consideration for the fresh promise. Besides this, the court felt that the very long delay in bringing action indicated that the buyers had affirmed the contract and were therefore bound by it.

student mentor tip

'The best way to grasp contract law is to narrow down the information into steps. For example, create a step-by-step flow chart for the formation of contracts with all the key cases beside it.'

Gayatri, University of Leicester

The case of *The Atlantic Baron (North Ocean Shipping Co Ltd v Hyundai Construction Co Ltd (the Atlantic Baron) [1979] QB 705)* has created an obvious potential disadvantage to a party trying to rely on the doctrine of economic duress in order to avoid the consequences of a contract that he has entered as the result of unfair commercial pressure. The claimant has the dilemma of steering the right course of action to achieve the best result. If that party protests too much when the original agreement is varied then he runs the risk of the other party just carrying on to breach the contract. In the *Kafco* case (*Atlas Express Ltd v Kafco (Importers and Distributors) Ltd* [1989] QB 833), for instance, this would have had disastrous consequences for the basket company which would have probably lost a lucrative contract through no fault of its own. On the other hand, if that party fails to protest with enough vigour he runs the risk that the court will consider that there has been insufficient protest and fail to declare the contract entered under pressure voidable. Even where the party does protest he must still act quickly after the contract in order to gain the support of the court.

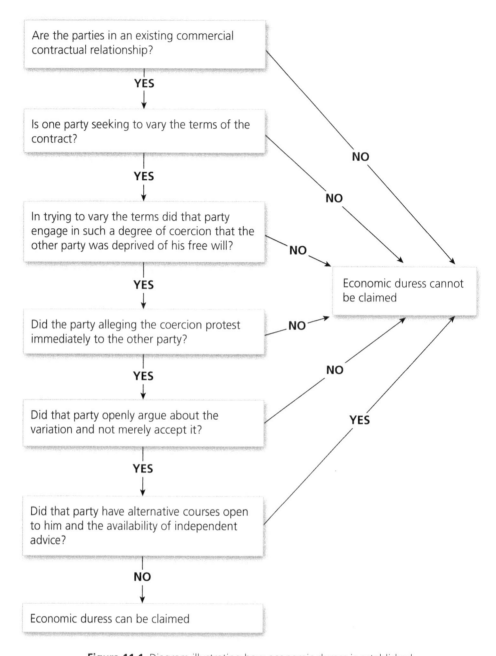

Figure 11.1 Diagram illustrating how economic duress is established

ACTIVITY

Self-assessment questions

1. What is the main limitation on a claim to duress?
2. What is the effect of:
    a) a successful claim of duress, and
    b) the alternative when duress is not available as an action?
3. Why has the doctrine of economic duress developed?

4. In what circumstances will a claim of economic duress fail and in what circumstances will it succeed?
5. Will there always be a remedy available where the court accepts that economic duress has in fact occurred?
6. What was the traditional difference between a claim of duress and a claim of undue influence?

11.4 Undue influence

11.4.1 The traditional classes

Undue influence traditionally developed under equity and so any remedy is at the court's discretion. The area developed so as to cover those areas where any form of improper pressure prevented a party from exercising their free will in entering a contract. Since equity is inevitably more flexible than common law, the doctrine could be applied whenever a party has exploited the other party to gain an unfair advantage.

Clearly, there is nothing wrong with trying to induce another person to enter a contract; this is in essence no more than basic bargaining. It is the degree of influence applied and also the context in which it occurs that the court is actually concerned with in determining what is and is not acceptable. Because of the relative vagueness of this reasoning, the courts were traditionally reluctant to give a full and precise definition of 'undue influence' in the way that they have been similarly reluctant to be too positive or precise in their definition of 'fraud'.

Traditionally, then, the doctrine developed along two distinct lines and a comparison was drawn between those situations where undue influence could be presumed from the relationship of the two parties (unless the contrary could be shown) and those where undue influence had to be proved.

Where no special relationship existed between the parties (actual undue influence)

In such circumstances the party alleging the undue influence would be required to prove the undue influence. To do this they would need to show that the other party was in a position of dominant influence over them at the time the contract was formed so that they were unable to exercise free will or choice or to behave independently in entering into the contract. This has always been referred to as **'actual undue influence'**.

CASE EXAMPLE

Williams v Bayley (1866) LR 1 HL 200

A young man had forged endorsements (signatures) on promissory notes (IOUs) and had caused a bank to lose money as a result. The bank then approached the young man's father and demanded that the father should mortgage his farm to the bank in order to cover the son's debt to it. On the face of it, there is nothing absolutely wrong in this behaviour. Where the court objected and was prepared to hold against the bank was because of the nature of the threats applied to the father. It had threatened to prosecute the son unless the father complied and, at the time of the case, this would have meant almost certain transportation, considered a very drastic punishment at that time. The House of Lords considered that it had no choice but to hold that the pressure was illegitimate and amounted to undue influence, vitiating the agreement and allowing the father to avoid his obligations under it.

Where a special relationship existed between the parties (presumed undue influence)

Where a special relationship existed between the two parties there was no need to prove undue influence. The court would be prepared to presume that a dominance existed because of the character of the relationship. This was traditionally referred to as '**presumed undue influence**'.

A special relationship could include many different relationships, some obvious and some less so. The list was neither defined nor was it exhaustive. It automatically included fiduciaries of whatever kind but also any relationship where the court could perceive that there was a natural dominance over one party by the other. The list included parents and their children; doctors and their patients; trustees and the beneficiaries that they acted for; solicitors and their clients and also the spiritual advisers of those with specific religious leanings.

In these relationships the court would presume undue influence and it would be for the party who was alleged to have exercised their influence unfairly to disprove it evidentially. In this respect it was the complete reverse of the situation where actual undue influence was concerned.

In order for the dominant party to disprove any undue influence on his part it would be necessary to show two things:

- That the other party entered the agreement with full knowledge of its character and potential effects.
- That the other party took independent and impartial advice before entering the contract.

CASE EXAMPLE

Allcard v Skinner (1887) 36 Ch D 145

A young woman belonged to a religious order and had entered as a member of a closed order. In consequence of this she took vows of poverty and chastity and significantly of obedience. She remained as a member of this order for a period of eight years and during that time she gave the order property to the value of £7,000 through the mother superior, her spiritual adviser and of course her leader in all matters to whom she owed obedience. She later left the order and eventually sued for recovery of money to the value of the property that she had handed over. In doing so she argued that the agreement to pass her property to the order had been made while she was subjected to the undue influence of the mother superior. The court accepted her argument and agreed that because of the submissive nature of the vows that she had taken and her obligation within the order to obey the mother superior, then undue influence could be presumed. Besides this, she had at no time had available to her any form of independent advice but had been guided throughout from inside the order. However, the court would not apply the doctrine to declare the contract voidable since the woman had waited for six years after leaving the order before she made her complaint. Since 'delay defeats equity' she had waited too long and her claim failed.

This traditional classification was also significant in that the relationship between husband and wife was one that was held to be expressly excluded from the presumption of undue influence. A wife would, therefore, have to show actual undue influence in order to have a remedy under the doctrine. In *Midland Bank v Shepherd* [1988] 3 All ER 17 Neill LJ stated a number of propositions:

- The relationship between husband and wife did not give rise to a presumption of undue influence.
- Even where there **was** such a presumption, for the contract to be set aside it would have to be manifestly disadvantageous to the party that was alleging undue influence.
- The court should construe this manifest disadvantage from the character of the transaction itself.
- However, the court would not enforce the arrangements in any contractual document in which the creditor secured the signature of the debtor by using a person likely to have influence over the debtor in order to obtain the signature.

Equally importantly, the relationship between banker and client was also excluded from the class, except in very limited circumstances, and again this meant that proof of actual undue influence was required in such relationships.

CASE EXAMPLE

National Westminster Bank v Morgan [1985] AC 686

Morgan's business ran into difficulties and he was unable to pay the mortgage on the home that he jointly owned with his wife. He then asked the bank to refinance his building society loan so that he might avoid repossession of the family home. The bank agreed to this in return for securing an unlimited mortgage against the house, and one that would also act as security against all of his various transactions with it. The manager of the bank arranged to meet Mrs Morgan in order to obtain her signature on the arrangement. She did express some concern that the document which she was signing would have nothing to do with her husband's ability to borrow money from the bank since she lacked confidence in his business ability and his financial management. The manager assured her, in good faith but incorrectly, that the agreement covered only the refinancing of the couple's mortgage on the home. Mrs Morgan had no independent advice at the time that she signed the agreement. The couple again fell into arrears with the mortgage and the bank tried to enforce the surety and claimed repossession of the home. Mrs Morgan counter-claimed and argued that the contract had been obtained by undue influence. In the Court of Appeal Lord Denning held that the doctrine could be applied wherever there was inequality of bargaining strength and that she could therefore succeed. The House of Lords rejected Lord Denning's very broad application. Lord Scarman explained that the relationship was not one that could give rise to a presumption of undue influence and that in any case it was insufficient merely to show the relationship. There would also have to be proof that the party alleging undue influence had also suffered a 'manifest disadvantage'. On the facts, he felt this was not the case. The Morgans had gained the advantage of being able to stay in their home on which basis there was no obligation on the bank to ensure that Mrs Morgan received independent advice.

11.4.2 The refinement of the traditional classes
Because of the inadequacies of the doctrine and because of the limitations imposed on these two classes by the courts over the years, the courts in recent times have redefined the classes and subjected them to more precise qualifications.

CASE EXAMPLE

Bank of Credit and Commerce International SA v Aboody [1990] 1 QB 923

Here, a wife had been persuaded by her husband to give a surety on jointly owned property to the bank from which he was borrowing money for his business. When the husband defaulted on the loan the wife sought to challenge the bank's action for repossession and to avoid liability. Undue influence was accepted by the court as the bank was said to have either constructive or actual notice of her husband's actions in either exercising undue influence over her or misrepresenting the amount of money that he owed the bank. Nevertheless, Mrs Aboody failed in her action because the transaction was held not to be to her 'manifest disadvantage'. The court held that in fact the loan had given the business a good chance of surviving and if it had done then the transaction would in fact have been positively advantageous.

The significance of the case is that the court redefined and drew distinctions between the two classes of undue influence:

- **Class 1 – actual undue influence** – representing the original situation where there was no special relationship between the parties and so the party alleging the undue influence is required to prove it.
- **Class 2 – presumed undue influence** – representing the traditional class where there was a special relationship and so undue influence is automatically presumed unless the contrary is actually proved.

The classifications from *Aboody (Bank of Credit and Commerce International v Aboody* [1990] 1 QB 923) have subsequently been approved in the leading cases on undue influence. They have also been subjected to some further modification and a more developed explanation.

CASE EXAMPLE

Barclays Bank plc v O'Brien [1993] 4 All ER 417

This now counts as one of the two leading cases on undue influence. The bank granted an overdraft of £135,000 to O'Brien for his failing business. The bank did so on the security of a mortgage on the jointly owned marital home. The bank's representative failed to follow the manager's instructions to ensure that both O'Brien and his wife were made fully aware of the nature of the document that they were signing and that they should seek independent advice on the transaction before signing. In fact, they both signed without reading the document. O'Brien's company then went even further into trouble and the bank then sought to enforce the surety to recover the debt. Mrs O'Brien complained that her husband had led her to believe that the loan was for only £60,000 and that it was only to last three years. In the Court of Appeal Mrs O'Brien was able to succeed in showing that she had been induced to sign as a result of her husband's undue influence and had an inaccurate picture of what she had signed. Lord Justice Scott, delivering the leading judgment, made a number of points:

- Mrs O'Brien could succeed because, as a wife, she was part of a specially protected class of persons under equity acting as surety for a debt.
- There was a presumption of undue influence against the husband.
- Such a presumption could also apply with cohabitees.
- A surety of this type could not be enforced where it had been gained by the presumed undue influence of the principal debtor.

- The bank could not enforce the surety because it had failed to take adequate steps to ensure that Mrs O'Brien had a full understanding of what she was committing herself to.
- As a result, she could only be liable for the £60,000 that she believed was the actual charge to which she had agreed.

The House of Lords took a different view. Lord Browne-Wilkinson rejected the special equity theory because this would inevitably have the effect of making lending institutions reluctant to make loans on the security of domestic residences. In any case he felt that the Court of Appeal was extending the scope of actual undue influence to include wives, for which there was no precedent. Instead the doctrine of **notice** should be applied:

- The creditor would be put on notice of possible undue influence in situations where on the face of it the transaction was disadvantageous to the wife, and there was a risk that the husband may have committed a legal or equitable wrong in getting his wife to sign.
- Unless the creditor took reasonable steps to ensure that the surety was entered into with free will and full knowledge then the creditor would be fixed with constructive notice of the undue influence.
- Constructive notice could be avoided by warning of the risks involved and advising of the need to take independent legal advice at a meeting not attended by the principal debtor.

11.4.3 The classes of undue influence after *O'Brien*

Following the reclassification of undue influence in *Aboody* and the later refinements in *O'Brien* (*Barclays Bank plc v O'Brien* [1993] 4 All ER 417), the categories of undue influence have been identified in two groups, with the second itself being divided into two distinct groups:

- **Class 1 – actual undue influence** – where the person alleging the undue influence must prove it.
- **Class 2A – presumed undue influence** – where, because of the relationship of the parties involved, the courts will presume that undue influence occurred unless the contrary is proven.
- **Class 2B – relationships of trust and confidence** – where there is no automatic presumption of undue influence but it is accepted that the relationship of the parties is one in which undue influence could arise (the most obvious relationship included in this group, because it was expressly excluded from the traditional class of presumed undue influence, but because also of the levels of trust and confidence that might be expected from it, is that of husband and wife).

Class 1 (actual undue influence)

This is the most basic form of undue influence. It applies generally where there is no special relationship between the parties that might lead to any presumption that undue influence has occurred. Because of this it is impossible to show that an abuse of confidence or trust has occurred and as a result the party alleging the undue influence must introduce evidence to show that it has in fact occurred.

To demonstrate that undue influence has indeed taken place, the claimant will need to show that there was a very real coercion. Not only this; the coercion must have amounted to a clear dominance to the extent that the claimant was in fact unable to exercise free will or act independently of the influence in entering the contract.

CASE EXAMPLE

Williams v Bayley (1866) LR 1 HL 200

Here, as we have already seen, the young man forged endorsements on promissory notes and caused loss to a bank, after which the bank approached his father and asked him to pay off the son's debts. This approach in itself was acceptable. Nevertheless the court was prepared to accept that there was undue influence because of the nature of the threat that the bank then made, reporting of the son which would lead to almost certain transportation. In these circumstances the father had no real choice but to accept the bank's terms.

Actual undue influence was originally defined in *Allcard v Skinner* (1887) 36 Ch D 145 (see above), although this was a case where the nature of the relationship involved led on to a finding of presumed undue influence. The definition given by the court was that undue influence amounts to 'some unfair and improper conduct, some coercion from outside, some overreaching, some form of cheating'. So it would be evidence of any of these that the claimant would need to introduce in order to make a successful claim.

At one point it was also considered necessary to demonstrate that the person alleging the undue influence had also suffered a manifest disadvantage as a result.

CASE EXAMPLE

Bank of Credit and Commerce International SA v Aboody [1990] 1 QB 923

Here, as we have seen above, Mrs Aboody was able to prove that she had been subject to the undue influence of her husband, or at least that he had misrepresented the truth about the loans. She could also show that the bank had constructive notice of the undue influence. However, her claim failed because there was no manifest disadvantage to her in the transaction in question. In fact, the loan could have saved the business. (See section 11.4.2.)

The court in *Aboody* here is extending the principle identified by Lord Scarman in *National Westminster Bank v Morgan* [1985] AC 686 to apply in situations of actual undue influence also. However, the House of Lords subsequently expressly rejected this requirement itself.

CASE EXAMPLE

CIBC Mortgages Ltd v Pitt [1993] 4 All ER 433

A husband and wife jointly owned their matrimonial home which was valued at £270,000. The husband then informed his wife that he wished to buy certain shares, using the house as security for a loan to be used for the purchase. The wife reluctantly agreed and they both signed, accepting the terms of a loan from CIBC Mortgages for £150,000. There was then a stock exchange crash and the husband was unable to meet the payments of the loan and the mortgage company sought possession of the matrimonial home. The wife tried to contest this, arguing that the mortgage company was caught by her husband's undue influence. The judge at first instance decided that there was actual undue influence and that the transaction was manifestly disadvantageous to the wife, although there was no special equity involved which could only be applied to sureties. The Court of Appeal disagreed and held that there was nothing manifestly disadvantageous to the wife and also that in any case CIBC had no constructive or actual knowledge of any undue influence and therefore, following *Aboody*, that the wife should fail. The House of Lords, however, held that *Aboody* was wrong on this point and that in a case of actual undue influence, where the undue influence in any case would have to be proved, there was no requirement also to prove that a manifest disadvantage had been suffered. Actual undue influence could be proved here but there was no actual knowledge on the part of the bank and there was insufficient proof of constructive knowledge since the transaction was a simple remortgage, not a surety for a debt.

JUDGMENT

Lord Browne-Wilkinson, rejecting this apparent blurring of the distinction between the two classes, identified that 'actual undue influence is a species of fraud ... a man guilty of fraud is no more entitled to argue that the transaction was beneficial to the person defrauded than a man who has procured a transaction by misrepresentation'.

This was the type of undue influence that traditionally also included the relationships of husband and wife and also banker and client as identified by Neill LJ in *Midland Bank v Shepherd*. It is specifically this triangle of relationships that has been the focus for the major developments in recent years.

Nevertheless, the class as a whole seems to be becoming more rare in its application. In a commercial sense this is as a possible result of the development and refinement of a doctrine of economic duress. Considering the types of relationship referred to above, then, the development of Class 2B has inevitably been more beneficial to wives confronted with repossession claims by lenders. This is because in these situations if the claimant can show that the circumstances of the case bring the claim within that class then the burden of proof shifts.

Class 2A (presumed undue influence)

This class applies whenever the party claiming it can show a relationship of trust and confidence with the party against whom the undue influence is alleged. The claimant need prove only the relationship, and then undue influence is presumed and it is for the other party to disprove that it has in fact occurred.

- This can only be done by showing that the party alleging the undue influence entered the contract with full knowledge of its character and effect.
- In order to achieve this the party against whom undue influence is alleged will need to show that the other party had the benefit of independent, impartial advice before entering the contract.

Traditionally, presumed undue influence applied in a number of so-called 'special' relationships. The list of these relationships is not fixed or exhaustive but there are certain obvious classes that would naturally be included because of the obvious degree of influence that the one party can exercise over the other. A parent and his child is a fairly obvious example.

CASE EXAMPLE

Lancashire Loans Co v Black [1933] 1 KB 380

An extremely domineering woman had approached a bank and asked for a loan which had in turn demanded a guarantee of her loan. She had then induced her daughter to stand as guarantor for the loan with the bank. The woman then defaulted on the loan and the bank sought to enforce the guarantee against the daughter. The daughter was successfully able to claim undue influence. The court accepted that:

- she was dominated by her mother,
- she did not properly understand the nature of the document that she was signing, and
- she had been given no independent advice, the only advice that she had received having come from her mother's solicitor.

We have already seen also that the class can be applied to very specific relationships where there is a deliberate submission to the one party by the other and where any natural form of obedience can be identified. For example, a relationship based on spiritual guidance and leadership can give rise to the presumption.

CASE EXAMPLE

Allcard v Skinner (1887) 36 Ch D 145

A woman belonging to a religious sect was persuaded to join a closed order and to give all of her property up to the order. When she later left the order she then tried to recover railway stock that she had owned. Her action failed because she waited until five years after leaving the order before claiming, and 'delay defeats equity'. Nevertheless, the court was happy to accept that a presumption of undue influence might arise in such circumstances.

Other relationships such as trustee/beneficiary (see *Benningfield v Baxter* (1886) 12 App Cas 167), doctor/patient and other fiduciary relationships have all been held to create a presumption of undue influence.

Lord Denning felt that the presumption should apply in any situation where there is any inequality in bargaining strength. In this way the presumption might cover certain transactions occurring in relationships that are actually expressly excluded from the presumption such as banker and client.

CASE EXAMPLE

Lloyds Bank v Bundy [1979] QB 326

An elderly farmer, his son, and a company that was owned by the son were all customers of the same bank. The farmer was persuaded by his son and the bank manager to use his farm, the major asset that he owned, as security for a loan to the son's company. In fact, the loan was well in excess of the actual value of the farm. When the company defaulted on the loan and the bank sought possession of the farm, the farmer successfully pleaded undue influence. Although the bank would not normally fall within the definition of 'special' relationship to be caught by undue influence, here there was a clear conflict of interest and duty because the bank represented all parties. The court identified that the proper course of action for the bank in the circumstances would have been to direct the farmer to take independent advice before allowing his farm to be used as security for the loan to the son's business.

JUDGMENT

Lord Denning felt that undue influence ought to apply wherever there was inequality of bargaining strength: 'in the vast majority of cases a customer who signs a bank guarantee or a charge cannot get out of it … Yet there are exceptions to this general rule. There are cases … in which a court will set aside a contract, or, a transfer of property, when the parties have not met on equal terms – when the one is so strong in bargaining power and the other so weak – that as a matter of common fairness, it is not right that the strong should be allowed to push the weak to the wall … I think that the time has come when we should seek to find a principle to unite them.'

However, Lord Scarman subsequently rejected this in *National Westminster Bank plc v Morgan*.

JUDGMENT

'an unequal bargain will, of course, be a relevant feature in some cases of undue influence. But it can never become an appropriate basis of principle'.

The result is that the case is another example of that type of transaction that may more appropriately now be covered by Class 2B and subject to the various requirements of that class.

Class 2B (relationship of trust and confidence)

The result of the *Aboody* classifications and their refinement and explanation in *O'Brien* is that a number of relationships are now identified as Class 2A, and it is accepted that the presumption of undue influence arises automatically, merely because of the type of the relationship. However, it is also now possible to establish a relationship where the one party proves that he has placed trust and confidence in the other where the presumption will apply even though not falling within one of the traditional categories. This is now known as Class 2B.

The most common case is that of husband and wife, which traditionally fell under the category of actual undue influence, requiring proof of the undue influence by the party alleging it, usually a wife. The court in *Bank of Credit and Commerce International SA v Aboody* rejected the proposition in *Midland Bank v Shepherd* that the wife/husband relationship gave rise only to actual undue influence, and therefore required proof of the undue influence by the husband.

It has been argued both that the party subject to undue influence in these cases is protected because the other party is seen as the agent of the creditor, or alternatively that the wife in such situations has a special protection in equity. The most common means of protecting the weaker party, however, is by application of the 'doctrine of notice'. That is the creditor, usually a bank or building society, will be unable to enforce the defaulted loan against the wife where it has actual or constructive notice of her equitable interest in the property which stands as surety for the loan.

Since *Barclays Bank plc v O'Brien*, wives are able to show a relationship of trust and confidence in their husbands and thus qualify for presumed undue influence under Class 2B. The informality of the relationship, it is accepted, means that there is a greater risk of the wife being taken advantage of in order to secure a loan based on the surety of the matrimonial property. This is then sufficient to put a creditor of the husband on notice providing that the contract is not on the face of it to the wife's advantage, and provided that there is a risk that the husband has unfairly induced the wife's acceptance. Lord Browne-Wilkinson, in the case, also suggested that the principle should apply to cohabitees where the relationship is actually known to the creditor.

So a creditor in such circumstances will be unable to enforce the surety against the loan unless he has 'taken reasonable steps to satisfy himself that the surety entered into the obligation freely and in knowledge of the true facts'. 'Reasonable steps' might include: personally interviewing the person standing surety for the loan in the absence of the principal debtor; explaining the full extent of the liability; explaining all of the risks involved; encouraging the person to seek independent legal advice before standing surety on the loan.

The creditor of course has no absolute duty to enquire what goes on when the solicitor gives this independent advice.

CASE EXAMPLE

Massey v Midland Bank [1995] 1 All ER 929

Mrs Massey was persuaded to give the bank a charge on the property she shared with Potts, the father of her children, as security for his business overdraft. The bank suggested that Mrs Massey would need independent legal advice. This was arranged with Potts' solicitor, and Potts himself attended. Potts defaulted and the bank sought to enforce the charge. The bank had notice of the relationship, and of the risk that the charge was not to Mrs Massey's advantage. However the solicitor confirmed to the bank that she had received independent advice, and it was not bound to make any further enquiries.

On this basis the creditor is generally entitled to assume that the solicitor will act honestly and competently.

CASE EXAMPLE

Banco Exterior Internacional v Mann [1994] 1 All ER 936

The husband in the case owned a company. The company took a loan from the bank which was secured, among other things, by a charge on the matrimonial home that was jointly owned by husband and wife. The bank directed that the nature of the charge should be explained to the wife by her own solicitor who should then sign a warranty to the effect that this had in fact been done. The husband passed the documents on to the company's solicitor who did as required. The company then fell into liquidation and the bank sought to enforce its charge over the matrimonial home. The wife then claimed undue influence by the husband and also that the bank had constructive notice of it. The Court of Appeal was prepared to accept that the bank had taken all necessary steps that it could have done in order to avoid constructive notice and it was thus entitled to rely on the warranty issued by the company solicitor.

JUDGMENT

As Steyn LJ put it in *Banco Exterior Internacional v Mann*: 'I do not understand Lord Browne-Wilkinson to be laying down the only steps to be taken which will avoid a bank being faced with constructive notice … rather he is pointing out best practice.'

Of course the one significant requirement that remains within the class is the need to show that the wife (or any party claiming to fall within the class) has suffered a manifest disadvantage as a result of the transaction. Although Lord Browne-Wilkinson has rejected the application of this principle to actual undue influence in *CIBC Mortgages Ltd v Pitt* [1993] 4 All ER 433, it has subsequently been reaffirmed as an essential requirement of Class 2B claims.

CASE EXAMPLE

Barclays Bank v Coleman [2000] 3 WLR 405

Here, the wife was challenging the validity of a charge placed on the jointly owned matrimonial home as security for a loan to the husband to finance investments. The case was different to *O'Brien* because the loan was not for the purposes of rescuing a failing business and also in that the charge applied to all future borrowing. The wife did receive independent legal advice before signing any agreement to the charge. The investments proved to be a bad choice, the husband could not repay the loan and the bank sought to enforce the charge. The wife claimed undue influence. The Court of Appeal, holding itself bound by the House of Lords in *National Westminster Bank v Morgan*, reaffirmed that any successful claim of undue influence under this class would require the wife to show first that she had suffered a manifest disadvantage. The court explained that this need not be a major disadvantage, just an actual disadvantage, and one where the *de minimis* principle could not be applied. In the case there was no disadvantage since by securing the loan the husband might have hoped to make a large profit from the investments. Furthermore, the bank could not be fixed with constructive notice since the wife had enjoyed the benefit of independent legal advice.

11.4.4 The position after *Etridge*

Clearly, the basic classifications of undue influence falling within Class 1 and Class 2A are still relatively straightforward. The essential differences between actual and presumed undue influence are retained, as are the basic rules on proof or shifting of the burden of proof respectively. One of the major problem areas in undue influence then still concerns a wife alleging the undue influence of her husband and trying to use this against a third party creditor. The fact that wives were not traditionally included within the special relationships giving rise to a presumption of undue influence is clearly one of the major sources of difficulty. Besides this, it is the reasoning that allows a third party creditor to be caught by the undue influence of the husband that still gives rise to difficulty and which is the subject of extensive debate in the courts.

In the case of *Royal Bank of Scotland plc v Etridge (No 2)* [2001] UKHL 44 the House of Lords actually considered the issue of whether a solicitor appointed by the bank to give the wife independent advice is an agent of the bank. Nevertheless, it reviewed all the leading authorities on undue influence, and set significant guidelines in the process. In doing so it has set out some major rules. The case also seems to suggest that the distinctions between Class 1, Class 2A and Class 2B are now in many ways less important than they were. The significant point now seems to be whether or not it can actually be shown that there was an abuse of a position of dominance or influence and whether or not a disadvantage can be said to have resulted from this abuse.

CASE EXAMPLE

Royal Bank of Scotland plc v Etridge (No 2) [2001] UKHL 44

This is in fact an appeal involving five individual cases. In *Etridge* itself a bank had taken a charge over a wife's property as a result of a loan made to a husband to use for his business overdraft. His wife had signed the charge in the presence of her husband after advice by a solicitor appointed by the bank but whom she argued later that she regarded as working for her husband. On the basis of all of these, when the bank sought to enforce the charge the wife claimed undue influence by her husband and argued that the solicitor had not explained the charge to her on her own and that the bank was therefore fixed with constructive notice of her husband's undue influence. The House of Lords reviewed all of the law on undue influence in the banking cases where a wife has stood surety for her husband's debts and applied the basic test in *O'Brien,* ie, to ask the two basic questions:

- Was the wife subject to her husband's undue influence in signing to agree to the charge?
- Was the bank put on enquiry of the potential undue influence and did it act successfully in avoiding being caught by it?

The House of Lords appears to have decided that there are not two types of undue influence. Presumed undue influence merely acts as an evidential 'lift' in helping a claimant to prove undue influence. The Lords also expressed some dislike with the words 'manifestly disadvantageous' and preferred instead to revert to the nineteenth-century language 'transactions which are not to be accounted for on terms of charity, love or affection'. They considered that it was out of touch with the way that life is now to presume that every gift from a child to a parent was secured by undue influence. The Lords also thought that most cases where a spouse guarantees a husband's business debts would be explicable and are reasonably accountable. This view might lead to fewer cases being successful. The Lords in any case issued a number of general guidelines as follows:

1. A bank should be put on enquiry whenever a wife offers to stand surety for her husband's debts or indeed *vice versa*, or even in the case of unmarried couples wherever the bank was aware of the actual nature of the relationship.
2. A bank should take reasonable steps to satisfy itself that a wife had been fully informed of the practical implications of the proposed transaction which she was entering into. This need not necessarily involve a personal meeting if a suitable alternative was available and if the bank could rely on confirmation from a solicitor acting for the wife that he had advised the wife appropriately. However, if the bank was aware that the solicitor had not properly advised the wife or ought to have realised that the wife had not received appropriate advice then the bank would be at risk of being fixed with notice of any undue influence by the husband in securing the wife's agreement to the transaction in question.
3. It would be possible for a solicitor advising the wife to act for both her and her husband (and/or the bank) unless the solicitor realised that there was a real risk of a conflict of interests, in which case the solicitor should cease acting for the wife or risk being liable.
4. The advice given by a solicitor should include explanation of the following critical issues:
   - The nature of the documents and their practical consequences for the wife.
   - The seriousness of the risks involved – ie, the extent of her financial means and whether she has other assets out of which repayment could be made.
   - That she has a choice of whether to proceed or not.
   - The solicitor should be sure that the wife does wish to proceed, and the discussion should take place at a face-to-face meeting with the wife in the absence of the husband.
5. The bank has a duty to obtain confirmation from the solicitor:
   a) *For future cases:*
   - The bank should take steps to check directly with the wife the name of the solicitor he wished to act for her.
   - This communication and response must be direct with the wife.
   - The bank should send the solicitor the necessary financial information.
   - In exceptional cases, where the bank believed or suspected that the wife was being misled by her husband, the bank should inform the solicitors of the information giving rise to that suspicion.
   - In every case the bank should obtain written confirmation from the solicitor.

b) *For past transactions*:
   - It would be sufficient if the bank obtained from a solicitor acting for the wife confirmation to the effect that he had brought home to the wife the risks she was running by standing surety.
6. *In obiter* the court also identified that the *O'Brien* principle is not confined to husband/ wife relationships but also to others who are in a sexual relationship or whenever there is a risk of undue influence (eg, parent and child). If the bank knows of the relationship, that is enough to put the bank on enquiry.

An interesting example of the guidelines from *Etridge* being applied is shown in *R v Attorney General for England and Wales* [2003] UKPC 22 (cited in *Student Law Review* Vol 40) (see section 11.2). Here, the Privy Council held that there was neither duress nor undue influence. The court accepted that there was compulsion but that the compulsion was

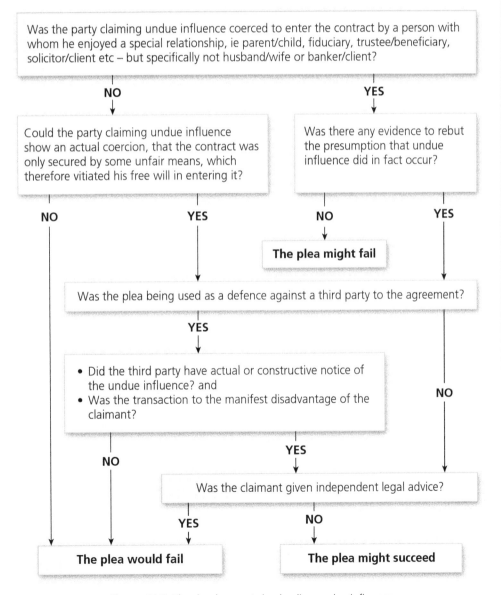

Figure 11.2 The developments in pleading undue influence

for legitimate reasons so was not duress. The court also accepted that the soldier was under the influence of his superiors within the military command. Nevertheless, there was no exploitation of the relationship and so there could be no presumption of undue influence. It was also impossible to show actual undue influence for the same reasons. Lord Scott, dissenting, did feel that the absence of independent advice was a problem.

Claiming undue influence after *O'Brien*

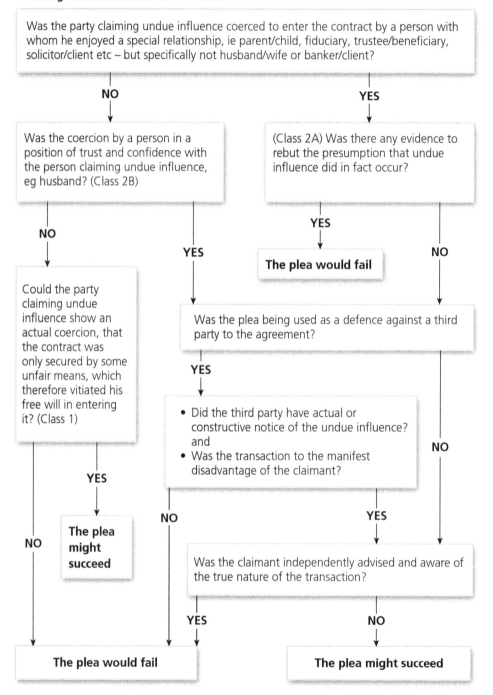

Figure 11.3 Claiming undue influence after *O'Brien*

Claiming undue influence after *Etridge*

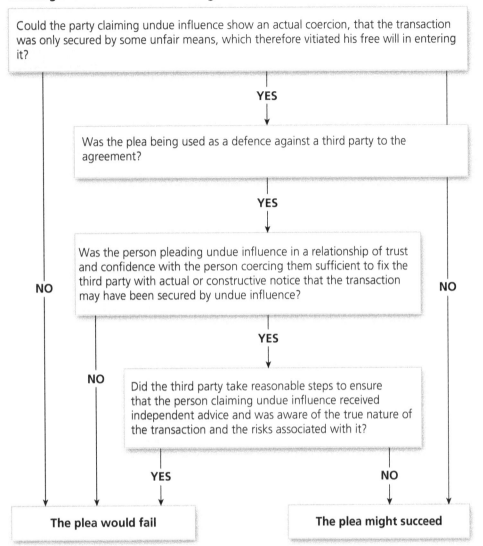

Figure 11.4 Claiming undue influence after *Etridge*

11.4.5 The effects of pleading undue influence

Where a claimant succeeds in a plea that undue influence has taken place then the contract is voidable by the party alleging the undue influence. The contract will be set aside, subject to the principle of *restitutio in integrum*.

Besides this, of course, since the area has developed out of equity then the general maxims of equity apply also. In this way the claimant in *Allcard v Skinner* failed to gain a remedy since 'delay defeats equity'. Any remedy would of course also be unavailable where it would impinge on genuine third party rights that have been gained legitimately. Where the third party is in effect also a party to the undue influence, by either constructive or actual notice, then the claimant will not be denied a remedy. Any amount of case law above has demonstrated this point, even going back to early case law and a case such as *Lancashire Loans Co v Black* [1933] 1 KB 380 where the loan company failed because it already knew of the undue influence by the mother.

The doctrine can also be applied successfully where other approaches might fail. A classic example of this is the plea of *non est factu*m.

CASE EXAMPLE

Avon Finance Ltd v Bridger [1985] 2 All ER 281

An elderly couple owned a house which was also mortgaged. The couple's son was seeking a loan from the finance company and as a result coerced his parents into signing a charge over their property to secure his loan. He actually succeeded because he falsely persuaded the couple that they were signing documents that were to do with their own mortgage on the property. The couple's claim of *non est factum* failed because the couple had done insufficient to establish the precise nature of the document that they were signing. Nevertheless, they were able to prove the undue influence of their son and the contract could then be set aside in equity.

However, there are also certain circumstances under which a party may be denied an effective remedy, even despite a successful plea of undue influence, if the actual value of the property has changed.

CASE EXAMPLE

Cheese v Thomas [1994] 1 FLR 118

Cheese, who was aged 84, contributed £43,000 to the purchase of a property costing £83,000. His nephew provided the remaining £40,000 by way of a mortgage. The property went in the nephew's sole name, but was to be solely occupied by the uncle until his death. The nephew then defaulted on the mortgage. The uncle then sought return of his £43,000, fearful of his security. The court accepted a claim of undue influence and ordered the house to be sold. However, the slump in property prices meant that the house could fetch only £55,000 and the uncle was then entitled to only a 43/83 share of the money raised.

There may, however, also be alternative remedies available, even where a plea of undue influence has failed.

CASE EXAMPLE

Cornish v Midland Bank plc [1985] 3 All ER 513

The claimant was unable to prove that the bank had unfairly taken advantage of her in getting her to sign a second mortgage of her property, and therefore she could not successfully claim undue influence. She was able to sue the bank, however, in a straightforward negligence claim, successfully arguing that the bank had breached its duty of care towards her in failing to advise her adequately of the full implications of the second charge.

11.4.6 The effect of undue influence on third parties

The traditional context for a plea of undue influence involved a direct contractual relationship between two parties where the alleged wrongdoer had by unfair means coerced the party making the plea to enter into the contract effectively against his own will. The purpose of the plea therefore was to have this contract set aside.

Many, if not most, of the modern cases, however, involve a situation where the party who has coerced the other party to enter an agreement by using undue influence has done so in order that the party coerced will enter an arrangement with a third party to the coercer's benefit. In this way the common scenario is a husband persuading his wife to enter into an agreement with a lender, usually a bank, to stand surety for a loan, with the security being offered being the matrimonial home or other jointly owned property.

This has the potential to cause great unfairness to the victim of the undue influence and is also a potentially dangerous arrangement for the lender because of the rules that have developed on undue influence. The wife in such circumstances is usually trying to avoid the enforcement of the surety following default on the loan by the husband. Three different lines of reasoning have been used over the years to try to allow the wife to claim that the lender was an actual or unwitting party to the undue influence and therefore to allow her also to avoid enforcement of the loan and the consequent loss of the matrimonial home:

- **Agency** – that the husband, or other person using undue influence to procure the arrangement, is in fact the agent of the lender.
- **Special equity** – that a special equity exists, protecting wives, and others covered by the principle, from the consequences of undue influence on which a lender is in effect relying in order to enforce agreements entered into by the wife.
- **Doctrine of notice** – that the creditor is in fact subject to the doctrine of notice and may be caught by actual or constructive notice of any undue influence by a husband in pressing his wife to enter such arrangements with the lender, unless the lender has taken certain steps to ensure that the arrangement was freely entered into by the wife.

Agency and undue influence

The logic of arguing that the husband is the agent of the bank lending money on the security of the matrimonial home is simple. The husband, who is principal debtor, could not be granted the loan without the wife's express permission. The bank could not secure the loan without the contract of surety with the wife, and of course gain the advantage of interest on the loan. The husband, therefore, according to the reasoning employed, has used undue influence for himself and on behalf of the bank making the loan.

By this simple logic, if the surety agreement has been gained through the husband's undue influence as agent of the bank, then the bank, as principal under the agency, must also be caught by the doctrine. The bank is thus unable to enforce the surety against the victim of the undue influence, in most cases the wife of the principal debtor.

CASE EXAMPLE

Kingsnorth Trust v Bell [1986] 1 All ER 423

The husband here wished to borrow £18,000 by way of a second mortgage on the matrimonial home in order to finance the expansion of a business that he owned jointly with his son and daughter-in-law. The husband knew that his second wife would not agree to this arrangement. Solicitors acting for the claimants, a finance company, drafted the necessary documents and sent them to the husband's solicitor, asking these solicitors to act as agents in the transaction. The husband's solicitors passed the documents on to him. The husband then misrepresented the contents of the documents in order to get his wife to sign. When the husband defaulted on the loan and the finance company sought to enforce the second mortgage, the Court of Appeal set aside the contract between the wife and the finance company. The court accepted that the husband was in effect acting as agent to the finance company in securing the agreement with his wife. As principal, the finance company was in effect responsible for his wrongdoing and could not take advantage of the undue influence that had obtained the wife's signature to the agreement for a second mortgage.

In fact, we have already seen how a similar line of reasoning was accepted as being sufficient to set an agreement aside and thus deny a finance company a remedy in *Avon Finance Ltd v Bridger* [1985] 2 All ER 281 (see section 11.4.5).

Nevertheless, this line of reasoning was also expressly rejected in *Barclays Bank plc v O'Brien*.

JUDGMENT

Lord Browne-Wilkinson identified that: 'the reality of the relationship is that, the creditor having required of the principal debtor that there must be a surety, the principal debtor on his own in order to raise the necessary finance seeks to procure the support of the surety. In doing so he is acting for himself, not for the creditor'.

Special equitable protection of wives

Scott LJ in the Court of Appeal in *Barclays Bank plc v O'Brien* specifically rejected the argument that an agency relationship is set up between principal debtor (husband) and lender (bank or finance company). He preferred, and argued for, a special equitable protection for particular classes of surety. Included in this class, as a matter of policy, were wives who gave surety for their husbands' debts.

The Court of Appeal considered that this special equity would mean that a surety involving a protected class would be unenforceable if certain circumstances were satisfied:

- The relationship between the surety and the principal debtor (and thus also the possibility of undue influence) was known to the creditor at the time the agreement was reached.
- Consent to the agreement had been obtained by the undue influence or misrepresentation of the principal debtor, or the surety lacked adequate understanding of the true nature and effect of the transaction entered into.
- The creditor failed to take reasonable steps to ensure that the surety gained an adequate understanding of the nature and effects of the transaction, and so any consent to the agreement was not informed and therefore cannot be relied upon.

In the case, however, the House of Lords expressly rejected this line of reasoning. It did so because, if accepted, it might lead to lending institutions becoming increasingly less willing to accept a matrimonial home as security for loans and thus defeat the aims of both borrowers and lenders.

Lord Browne-Wilkinson gave a number of specific reasons for rejecting the special equity theory:

- There could be no basis for granting protection under a special equity to wives alone.
- There was in any case insufficient support for such a proposition in the common law.

- The logical consequence of the theory would be to extend Class 2A undue influence to include husbands and wives where this relationship had always been expressly excluded from the presumption of undue influence.
- There was in any case no need to invent such a protection since there was already in existence a better means of protecting wives in these circumstances: the doctrine of notice.

The doctrine of notice and undue influence

In *Barclays Bank v O'Brien*, Lord Browne-Wilkinson suggested that the true test of whether or not a creditor can enforce the surety depends on whether the creditor had actual or constructive notice of the wife's equitable right to have the agreement set aside.

On this basis it is for the wife to show that the bank did indeed have notice of the undue influence. It is not therefore for the bank to show that it did not have notice.

CASE EXAMPLE

Barclays Bank plc v Boulter and Another [1997] 2 All ER 1002

The Boulters purchased a property by using a bank loan and granted the bank a legal charge securing all money owed by either of them. Mrs Boulter then personally covenanted to repay all such money. Mr Boulter then borrowed more money from the bank and later defaulted on the loan so that the bank sought a possession order. Mrs Boulter asked for the charge on the property to be set aside on the basis that she had trusted her husband to manage their finances properly, that he had told her that the loan was only for the purchase of the house, and that she had not been told that the covenant that she had signed covered all money owed and not just the house. She also argued that the bank could have had constructive notice, although she did not specifically argue that it did. The trial judge held that she could not claim constructive notice in her defence unless she specifically pleaded it. The Court of Appeal then reversed this and held that it was for the bank to disprove that it had constructive notice. While the House of Lords dismissed the bank's appeal on other grounds, it also held that the Court of Appeal was in error on this point. It was for Mrs Boulter to show that she was a wife living with her husband and that the transaction was manifestly disadvantageous to her, putting the bank on notice of the possibility of her husband's undue influence. In response to this, the bank would then need to show that it took the appropriate steps to ensure that her consent to the agreement was properly obtained in order for it to enforce the charge.

The reasoning for employing the doctrine of notice is straightforward. Since undue influence is a doctrine of equity then in any argument between surety and creditor the normal rule of equity that 'first in time prevails' must apply. If the latter in time has either actual or constructive notice of the other party's equitable interest then he is bound by it. This is explained in the context of wife acting as surety and lending institution in the following terms:

- Wives are usually able to show a relationship of trust and confidence in their husbands and therefore qualify under the Class 2B undue influence identified in *Aboody and O'Brien*.
- The informality in financial dealings between husbands and wives means that there is often a risk that the husband will take advantage of this trust and confidence in securing the wife's signature for the surety on the loan.

This will then be sufficient to put the lender on notice if two further conditions are met:
- the transaction is not, on the face of it, to the wife's advantage
- there is a risk that the husband, in securing the wife's signature for the surety, has committed a legal or equitable wrong.

In the House of Lords in *O'Brien*, Lord Browne-Wilkinson identified that the principle may also apply in the case of cohabitees, where this relationship is actually known to the creditor. In any case it has already been seen that the principle can apply in relationships other than husband and wife (see section 11.4.5, *Avon Finance Ltd v Bridger*).

As Lord Browne-Wilkinson identified, in these circumstances application of the doctrine of notice means that the creditor cannot enforce the surety unless he has 'taken reasonable steps to satisfy himself that the surety entered into the obligation freely and in knowledge of the true facts'. This will involve:

- personally interviewing the surety in the absence of the principal debtor
- explaining the full extent of liability
- fully explaining the actual risks of standing as surety
- encouraging the surety to seek independent legal advice
- not relying purely on written advice.

Between *O'Brien and Etridge* a number of decisions have considered some of the fine detail of this relationship between creditor, solicitor and surety, not necessarily reaching cohesive conclusions.

Where the surety has signed the agreement in the presence of a solicitor who has also advised on the issue then the creditor has no absolute duty to enquire about what went on in the interview or on the nature of the advice given by the solicitor.

CASE EXAMPLE

Massey v Midland Bank plc [1995] 1 All ER 929

Mrs Massey was persuaded by her partner and father of her two children, Mr Potts, to give a charge over property to the bank in order to secure his business overdraft. Potts actually fraudulently represented to Mrs Massey that he would pay off an outstanding charge that he had already persuaded her into. The bank told both of them that they would need to take independent legal advice, as a result of which Potts arranged an interview between Mrs Massey and his own solicitor. He also attended this interview. When Potts defaulted on the loan the bank sought to enforce the charge over the property. The court was required to answer two questions:

- Did the bank have constructive knowledge of Potts' undue influence? – The court held that it did. The bank was aware of the relationship, and of the risk of Potts' undue influence, and that the surety was potentially disadvantageous to Mrs Massey.
- Did the bank take reasonable steps to avoid being associated with the undue influence? – The court held that it had. The solicitor had informed it that Mrs Massey had received independent advice and there was therefore no need for the bank to go mechanically through the *O'Brien* test on its own account.

The bank in such circumstances then is entitled to assume that the solicitor giving the advice will act both honestly and competently.

JUDGMENT

In *Banco Exterior Internacional v Mann and Others*, Steyn LJ appraised the House of Lords test in *O'Brien* and concluded: 'I do not understand Lord Browne-Wilkinson to be laying down … the only steps to be taken which will avoid a bank being faced with constructive notice … rather he is pointing out … best practice.'

The point is that a solicitor advising a wife who is entering into a second mortgage solely for the benefit of her husband may in any case be liable for negligence. Such a claim is possible if the solicitor fails to advise her on any issue that is central to the transaction or indeed fails to consider what is in her best interests in the widest sense.

CASE EXAMPLE

Kenyon-Brown v Desmond Banks & Co (1999) 149 NLJ 1832

The Banks company was the sole principal of a firm of solicitors that had acted for Kenyon-Brown from time to time in the purchase of his home, holiday home and in other transactions. Kenyon-Brown decided to remortgage property in order to repurchase a company that he had formerly owned and sold. His wife was initially opposed to the venture but was eventually persuaded into it by her husband. The bank lending the money to finance the purchase indicated that Mrs Kenyon-Brown must have independent legal advice on the use of the existing property as security. However, the solicitor failed to point out that the transaction could benefit only her husband and not her. In this respect the test in *O'Brien* was not satisfied. In fact, Kenyon-Brown had indicated to his wife that she would be bankrupted if she would not agree to the remortgage, and thus had applied undue influence. The solicitor had failed to ask the wife why she was willing to enter the transaction but had merely established that she was prepared to go through with it. The Court of Appeal held that the solicitor could be liable in negligence for his breach of his duty to the wife.

Nevertheless, in meeting the *O'Brien* and now the *Etridge* criteria, the bank has only to act as a reasonably prudent bank would do. It has no need to show unnecessary suspicion of the husband or to make exhaustive checks on the circumstances in which the surety is gained.

CASE EXAMPLE

Woolwich plc v Gomm (1999) 78 P & CR D45

Here, Mrs Gomm was able to show that her husband had advised her in accepting a charge over property, and also that she normally placed great trust and confidence in him. When the lender sought to enforce the charge the Court of Appeal accepted that Mrs Gomm could set aside the mortgage, provided that the lender had actual or implied knowledge of the husband's undue influence. The court also held that the standard to apply to what knowledge can be implied is an objective one based on the instructions that the bank should have given, not on those that were actually given.

While *O'Brien* concerned setting aside that part of the charge of which the wife was unaware, it is also possible for the whole transaction to be set aside.

CASE EXAMPLE

TSB Bank plc v Camfield [1995] 1 All ER 951

The husband here was engaged in a car leasing partnership which approached the bank for a £30,000 loan. The bank offered the loan subject to charges on the homes of the partners while stipulating that their wives should receive independent legal advice. The bank instructed its own solicitors who confirmed that this had taken place, although the partners were present when the advice was given. Mrs Camfield only agreed to the surety because her husband had misrepresented that the charge was only for £5,000. In fact the charge was unlimited. When the partners defaulted on the loan the bank sought to enforce the charges. The Court of Appeal held for Mrs Camfield on the basis that she would not have agreed at all if she had known the true nature of the charge; the bank had failed to ensure that she had independent legal advice; and she would have been able to rescind the whole transaction against her husband so she could do so also in the case of the bank.

However, this will not be the case where there are a number of subsequent charges that have been secured by undue influence but the original transaction was legitimately voluntarily gained.

CASE EXAMPLE

Castle Phillips Finance v Piddington (1995) 70 P & CR 592

The wife here happily agreed to use a house that was her sole property as security for a loan from Lloyd's to cover the husband's business debts. The husband then misled his wife into replacing this charge with a second from Barclay's and also a third in favour of the finance company. The husband then defaulted on the loan and the finance company sought possession. The wife tried to use *Camfield* in asking for the charges to be set aside, but failed. The Court of Appeal identified that each lender was entitled to the security passed on by the previous one in taking over the debt and so the wife was liable to the full extent of the first loan.

The case law, then, has demonstrated that the courts did not perceive the *O'Brien* requirements as being exhaustive. The rules to be applied when a creditor tries to enforce a charge against a wife who claims that her consent to the arrangement has only been obtained through the undue influence of her husband are now clearly laid out in *Royal Bank of Scotland v Etridge (No 2)*:

- Where a bank instructs a solicitor in order to ensure that a wife enters a transaction voluntarily whose consent to the transaction may be procured by the undue influence of her husband, then the bank is fixed with constructive notice of the undue influence if the solicitor failed to advise the wife properly and therefore did not discharge his duty.
- The solicitor must be satisfied that the wife was free from improper influence, so it must first be established that the transaction is one that she would enter without any influence, and if not and she is still determined to go ahead with the transaction then the solicitor should cease to represent her and inform the bank of that.

It was in any case already clear from *CIBC Mortgages Ltd v Pitt* that notice is a vital factor in all types of undue influence including Class 1 or actual undue influence. As Dominic O'Sullivan comments:

QUOTATION

'In developing and rearranging the protective rules fashioned by *O'Brien* much of *Etridge* tips the scales away from the surety of wives towards creditor banks. Replacing "manifest disadvantage" with "calling for explanation" is likely to make it more difficult for wives to prove presumed undue influence ... The obligations of solicitors advising surety wives are narrowed, and it is made clear that the risk of solicitors failing to advise properly falls generally on the wife rather than the bank. At the same time, however, the new disclosure requirement imposed will probably make it more difficult for banks summarily to enforce securities in the face of an *O'Brien defence*.'

D O'Sullivan, 'Developing O'Brien' (2002) 118 LQR 337–351 at 350

ACTIVITY

Self-assessment questions

1. Why did the doctrine of undue influence develop in equity?
2. What was the traditional difference between claims made under duress and those made under undue influence?
3. What differences were there traditionally between actual undue influence and presumed undue influence?
4. Why was undue influence traditionally presumed in the case of certain relationships?
5. Were the classes of relationships covered by this principle sensible?
6. What is the difference between Classes 2A and 2B in undue influence?
7. What is the role of the 'doctrine of notice' in undue influence?
8. When will a bank have constructive notice of the undue influence, and how can it avoid this?
9. What is the basic rule in *Barclays Bank v O'Brien*?
10. What impact do cases such as Massey have on the basic rule?
11. When are banks in a special relationship with their clients?
12. How has the case of *Royal Bank of Scotland plc v Etridge (No 2)* in the House of Lords developed or helped clear up the rules on undue influence?

SUMMARY

- A contract procured by violence or threats of violence can be avoided by a claim of duress.
- Economic duress involves a party being coerced into a change of arrangements under the threat of a commercially damaging course of action in a commercial contract – the party raising it must have both protested immediately and shown reluctance to enter the arrangement to gain a remedy.
- Undue influence is an equitable area where one party has been induced by coercion to enter a contract – this can either be: actual (where the party alleging the undue influence must prove it) or presumed (in certain relationships such as parents and children where the party against whom the undue influence is alleged must disprove it).
- There is also now a type of undue influence in those situations where a wife is induced to place the family home as security for a loan made to the husband – in such situations the creditor is put on notice of the possibility of the undue influence and must take reasonable care to ensure that the wife only agrees to the arrangement after having full knowledge of the risks involved and having been given independent legal advice.

Critically analyse the circumstances in which a court will be prepared to acknowledge the application of the doctrine of economic duress.

Define economic duress:
- Contract obligations can be set aside because extreme coercion has rendered the contract otherwise commercially unviable
- Usually concerns variations to a contractual arrangement

Identify the sorts of situations in which economic duress might apply, eg:
- Commercial pressure to vary prices or conditions
- Pressure from trade unions

Explain the requirements for a successful claim of economic duress:
- There was such a degree of coercion that the party claiming economic duress was deprived of his free will
- That party protested immediately
- That party tried to argue openly about it

Discuss reasons why the doctrine developed:
- The narrowness of the common law doctrine of duress
- The fact that equity already intervened in the form of undue influence but would generally be unavailable in such circumstances
- The potential unfairness, eg, Lord Denning in *D C Builders v Rees*
- Credibility of commercial relations
- Retaining freedom of contract
- The need for a remedy in the circumstances

Discuss the circumstances in which courts are prepared to accept a plea:

- Must involve economic pressure so still operates in a fairly narrow field
- But not as narrow as duress – no need for violence or threats of violence, only economic pressure
- Same can be said in contrasting economic duress with undue influence
- It is possible to argue that uncertainty can arise because the definition is imprecise
- Application of the doctrine to trade union activity – can be argued either way
- Problem highlighted in *The Atlantic Baron*

KEY FACTS

Reasons behind duress and undue influence	
To preserve freedom of contract, the courts have traditionally invalidated a contract which has been formed as the result of any coercion.	

Duress	Case/statute
Duress is a common law action where a contract has been procured by violence or threats of violence.	*Barton v Armstrong*

Economic duress	Case/statute
Economic duress is a modern area where in a commercial contract a party is coerced into a change of arrangements under the threat of a commercially damaging course of action.	*The Siboen and the Sibotre*
The party raising it must have – (i) protested immediately, and (ii) shown a reluctance to enter the arrangement, otherwise any remedy may be lost.	*The Atlantic Baron*

Undue influence	Case/statute
Traditionally an equitable area where one party has been induced by coercion to enter a contract – it is a question of degree what level of persuasion is acceptable and what amounts to undue influence.	
There were later identified two types of undue influence – Class 1 or actual undue influence, and Class 2 or presumed undue influence.	*BCCI v Aboody*

Actual is where there is no special relationship and the party alleging the undue influence must prove it.	*CIBC Mortgages v Pitt*
Presumed undue influence occurs in certain relationships such as:	
• parents and children	*Lancashire Loans v Black*
• spiritual adviser/follower.	*Allcard v Skinner*
The party against whom the undue influence is alleged must disprove it.	
Class 2B extended this type of undue influence to those situations where a wife is induced to place the family home as security for a loan made to the husband:	*Barclays Bank v O'Brien*
• in such situations the creditor is put on notice of the possibility of the undue influence and must take reasonable care to ensure that the wife only agrees to the arrangement after having full knowledge of the risks involved, having been given independent legal advice	
• many cases concern whether or not the creditor has done sufficient to discharge their duty towards the wife to escape actual or constructive notice.	*Massey, Mann, Camfield,* and *Etridge*
Now the major rules are contained in HL judgment in *Etridge*:	
• bank should take steps to see that wife is fully informed	
• solicitor can act for both parties unless he realises that it involves a conflict of interests	
• solicitor should inform wife of nature of documents, seriousness of risk, that she has choice to back out	
• bank should get confirmation of advice from solicitor.	
O'Brien principles extend beyond husbands and wives into other similar relationships.	

Further reading

Brooman, S, 'The Creditor, the House, the Misled and her Lover' LEx, October 1995.

Doyle, L, 'Borrowing Under the Influence' (1994) 15 Bus LR 6.

O'Sullivan, D, 'Developing *O'Brien'* (2002) 118 LQR 337.

12

Vitiating factors: Illegality and unenforceable contracts

AIMS AND OBJECTIVES

After reading this chapter you should be able to:

- Understand the character of contracts declared illegal and unenforceable by the courts and by statute
- Understand the significance of policy considerations to the area
- Understand the different consequences of contracts declared illegal and unenforceable
- Critically analyse the area
- Apply the law to factual situations and reach conclusions

12.1 Introduction

Most vitiating factors represent some sort of defect in the formation of the contract. Obvious examples of this are that the agreement does not truly represent the consensus of the two parties because the agreement is based on a mistake or a misrepresentation (see Chapters 9 and 10). Illegality, on the other hand, is much more to do with the actual character of the agreement itself. It is of a type that for some reason the law frowns on and for public policy or other reasons is not prepared to accept as legitimate.

The basic principle involved is straightforward enough: the law will not enforce a contract that is tainted with illegality. However, the area is not a simple one, for a number of reasons. Firstly, the types of contract that have been declared illegal are not only numerous but also quite diverse in character. Secondly, while judges very often refer to contracts being 'illegal' or 'void' or 'unenforceable', they do not always fully distinguish between these terms. Thirdly, there is the added complication that over time both the common law and statute law have been used to render different types of contract illegal. Fourthly, the area is one that is heavily influenced by public policy.

Despite these difficulties it is still possible to identify some loose groupings in which to categorise such contracts:

- Certain contracts are said to be void and therefore unenforceable – in other words, there is nothing to prevent their creation and so long as the parties comply with the terms of their agreement they create no problems, but if one party breaches a term of the agreement, the other will have no redress in law.
- Certain other contracts are said to be illegal and therefore unenforceable – with these it is possible that they should not have been made at all; in any case other connected transactions may be tainted with their illegality.

Since contracts can be illegal both because of statutory provision or because judges have made them so through the common law, it is possible to break the area down and to classify illegality into four groups:

- Contracts **void by statute**.
- Contracts **declared illegal by statute** (with the further division between contracts that are illegal in their formation and those declared illegal because of the manner of their performance).
- Contracts that are void at common law – an area that is heavily influenced by public policy.
- Contracts that are **illegal at common la**w – again, for public policy reasons.

12.2 Contracts void by statute

12.2.1 Restrictive trade practices

These are agreements between businesses that keep prices artificially high or low or which restrict the availability of goods or services to certain areas, persons or bodies also by artificial means. The area is therefore concerned with agreements aimed at preventing or restricting proper competition.

Such agreements are against public policy and it was this that originally prevented enforceability of agreements aimed at unfairly restricting free competition. Traditionally, such agreements were regulated by statute. A number of Acts of Parliament were passed with this end in mind. These included the Resale Prices Act 1964 and the Resale Prices Act 1976, the Restrictive Trade Practices Act 1956, the Restrictive Trade Practices Act 1968 and the Restrictive Trade Practices Act 1976, and more recently the Competition Act 1980.

The Acts provide fairly rigorous procedures and machinery for regulating and controlling anti-competitive agreements. Probably the most significant of these is the role of the Director General of Fair Trading. All potentially anti-competitive agreements must be registered with his office, and there was until recently a Restrictive Trade Practices Court.

Competition law is also a central theme of EU law. All types of agreement or business practice aimed at restricting competition and that may have an effect on trade within the EU are subject to the control of the EU under Articles 101 and 102 of the Treaty on the Functioning of the European Union (TFEU).

Article 101 prohibits 'agreements between undertakings, decisions of associations of undertakings and concerted practices which may affect trade between Member States and which have as their object or effect the prevention, restriction or distortion of competition within the common market'.

- 'Agreements between undertakings' obviously refers to any contractual or other formal agreement.
- 'Decisions of … undertakings' is a clear reference to the rules of trade associations.

- 'Concerted practices' refers to any informal agreement which the parties would nevertheless feel bound by, for example a so-called 'gentleman's agreement'.

Article 101 also gives specific examples of agreements that will be considered to be anti-competitive. These are ones which:

- directly or indirectly fix purchase or selling prices or any other trading conditions
- limit or control production, markets, technical development, or investment
- share markets or sources of supply
- apply dissimilar conditions to equivalent transactions with other trading parties, thereby placing them at a competitive disadvantage
- make the conclusion of contracts subject to acceptance by the other parties of supplementary obligations which, by their nature, have no connection with the subject of such contracts.

By Article 101(2), agreements of these kinds are ordinarily void. There are mechanisms under Article 101(3) by which the EU Commission can grant exemptions and also 'negative clearance' which is a form of declaration that the agreement is not in breach of Article 101.

Article 101 is all about collusion between undertakings of an anti-competitive character. Article 102, on the other hand, involves anti-competitive actions by a single undertaking that holds a dominant position in the market and abuses that position.

Under Article 102: 'Any abuse by one or more undertakings of a dominant position within the common market or in a substantial part of it shall be prohibited as incompatible with the common market insofar as it may affect trade between Member States'.

The whole area has now been consolidated under the Competition Act 1998. This incorporates the provisions of Articles 101 and 102 into English law and requires English courts to interpret in a way that will provide consistency with EU law and the decisions of the European Court of Justice.

Section 2(1) mirrors the Article 101 prohibition and states that:

SECTION

'agreements between undertakings, decisions by associations of undertakings or concerted practices which:
(a) may affect trade within the United Kingdom; and
(b) have as their object the prevention, restriction or distortion of competition within the United Kingdom are prohibited'.

Section 18 mirrors the Article 102 prohibition and states that:

SECTION

'any conduct on the part of one or more undertakings which amounts to the abuse of a dominant position in a market is prohibited if it may affect trade within the United Kingdom'.

12.3 Contracts illegal by statute

Here, an immediate distinction can be drawn since the contract could be declared illegal by statute in either of two circumstances:

- It could be illegal to make such contracts at all – generally, this would be because, for reasons of public policy, Parliament does not wish such contracts to be made (these are known as **illegal in their formation**).

It could, on the other hand, be perfectly legal to engage in such contracts but because there are statutory requirements as to their manner of performance, the manner in which they are performed could well be illegal (these are known as **illegal on performance**).

12.3.1 Contracts illegal on formation

Clearly, where a contract is entered into which is prohibited by statute then the contract is void *ab initio* and is unenforceable as a result.

CASE EXAMPLE

Re Mahmoud and Ispahani [1921] 2 KB 716

The Seeds, Oils and Fats Order of 1919 prohibited unlicensed trading in linseed oil. One party had a licence and contracted to supply the defendant who did not but who falsely stated that he did. When the defendant backed out of the agreement the claimant sued for the failure to accept delivery. He was unsuccessful because the contract was void and unenforceable. The lack of the appropriate licence made the contract illegal in its formation.

The justification for the principle is that the contract would be, as Lord Mansfield described it, 'a transgression of the positive laws of our country'.

CASE EXAMPLE

Cope v Rowlands (1836) 2 M & W 149

An Act of Parliament made it illegal for stockbrokers to conduct certain business in London without first having obtained a licence. Cope set up business in London without obtaining a licence. As a result, when he sued Rowlands for payment for work done he failed in his action. His lack of a licence made the contract illegal and unenforceable. The purpose of the provision was to protect the public from the harm that could be caused by unregulated brokers.

It is always possible, however, that the contract will not be declared illegal because the provision in the Act is for a specific different purpose and was not enacted merely to prevent such contracts from being made.

CASE EXAMPLE

Smith v Mawhood (1845) 14 M & W 452

A tobacconist failed to get the appropriate licence to sell tobacco products, which was a set requirement of statute. The statute imposed a £200 fine in the event of a failure to comply. The licensing requirement therefore was on behalf of the Revenue and was not for the purpose of preventing tobacco sales, so the contract was not illegal or unenforceable although the penalty could still be imposed.

JUDGMENT

Baron Parke held that the contract was not illegal in its formation and explained that 'the object of the legislation was not to prohibit a contract of sale by the dealers who have not taken out a licence … but only to impose a penalty upon the party offending for the purposes of the Revenue'.

12.3.2 Contracts illegal in their performance

A contract may be created legitimately but become illegal and therefore unenforceable because the manner in which it is performed is illegal.

CASE EXAMPLE

Anderson Ltd v Daniel [1924] 1 KB 138

A statute provided that, in the sale of fertilisers, the buyer must be given an invoice listing certain chemicals contained in the product if they were included. Here, fertiliser was supplied to a buyer without the proper invoice required by statute. When the buyer failed to pay for the goods, the seller's action for the price failed. The contract itself was valid. There was nothing in law to prevent its formation. However, the absence of the invoice of the required type rendered it illegal and the seller could not then enforce it.

Clearly, the aim of the statutory requirement in the above case was the protection of consumers who, because of the requirement to list chemical products in the invoice, would be alerted to potential dangers.

It is possible that the statutory provision is aimed at another purpose rather than merely rendering the contract illegal.

CASE EXAMPLE

Shaw v Groom [1970] 2 QB 504

A landlord failed to provide his tenant with a rent book as required by statute. As a result he was guilty of an offence under the Act. However, this did not prevent him from still claiming rent from the tenant since the provision was aimed at imposing a penalty for non-compliance rather than invalidating the agreement itself.

So the mere fact that performance is not in the proscribed manner does not mean that it will be automatically unenforceable on all occasions and it is not an absolute reason for invalidating contracts.

CASE EXAMPLE

St John Shipping Corporation v Joseph Rank Ltd [1956] 3 All ER 683

The court refused to hold that a contract for the carriage of goods at sea was illegal and therefore unenforceable merely because the captain loaded his ship beyond the legal loading line. To do so would have allowed the other party to avoid payment with no justification.

The point that this last case clearly makes is that the illegality must relate to the central purpose of the contract if the contract is to be declared invalid and unenforceable.

CASE EXAMPLE

Hughes v Asset Managers plc [1995] 3 All ER 669

This case makes a similar point to that in *Cope v Rowlands*. Hughes paid £3 million to Asset Managers in order for them to purchase shares on his behalf. The market then dropped and Hughes directed the defendants to sell the shares. They did so at a loss of £1 million. Hughes then sued for the loss, arguing that under the Prevention of Fraud (Investments) Act 1958 while the defendants themselves were licensed as required by s 1(1) of the Act, the person who had actually done the deals did not possess the representative licence. Hughes failed in his action because the statute was aimed at protecting the public by imposing sanctions on those dealing with securities without a licence, but not at invalidating investment.

12.4 Contracts void at common law

The central issue here is again whether the type of contract offends public policy. Again, as void contracts there is nothing to prevent parties agreeing to their formation but the parties will be unable to enforce the terms of the contract when there is any dispute. However, there is also much uncertainty in the area.

Contracts that are void and therefore unenforceable under this heading fall into three distinct categories:

- contracts to oust the jurisdiction of the courts
- contracts that are prejudicial to family life
- contracts in restraint of trade.

12.4.1 Contracts to avoid the jurisdiction of the courts

A contract is a legally enforceable agreement between two parties and as such the courts have always been reluctant to accept that a contract can include a clause to the effect that in the event of a breach no legal action is possible. Such clauses would clearly not be in the public interest.

Generally, then, the courts have tended to reject any attempt to remove their jurisdiction through clauses in contracts to that effect. The judges have always seen the courts as the proper means of settling disputes and on this basis have argued that at the least they must reserve the right to supervisory jurisdiction over other forms of dispute resolution.

However, the courts operate on a predominantly adversarial basis. This is not always to the advantage of the parties in a dispute who may wish for compromise or a more conciliatory approach. This, together with the proliferation of tribunals and other means of dispute resolution, has meant that other areas have been recognised by the courts.

The obvious exception to the rule that the courts will not give up jurisdiction is the use of arbitration clauses. These are very often referred to as 'Scott Avery clauses' after the case *Scott v Avery* (1856) 5 HL Cas 81 in which their use was first established. Many bodies will contain a clause referring any dispute, at least initially, to a qualified arbitrator expert in the specific field. They are common in commercial disputes and among bodies such as travel companies. The area is generally now governed by the Arbitration Act 1996. One of the critical issues is the extent to which parties can bind themselves to the decision of the arbitrator as final or following which appeal is possible.

Parliament during the latter half of the twentieth century in any case identified the need to direct a greater number of disputes of a contractual nature to bodies other than the courts. An obvious example of this is employment disputes and employment tribunals.

12.4.2 Contracts prejudicial to family life

The courts traditionally have seen themselves as the defenders of moral values and marriage is seen as a sacred institution requiring the protection of the courts. Traditionally, then, any arrangement which might have the effect of harming marriage would be deemed void by the courts.

Obvious examples of this would be taking a fee not to marry or indeed procuring a marriage for a fee, or otherwise threatening a marriage.

Originally the courts would also view contracts which relinquished parental responsibility as void, as where a parent sold the child. Now this principle may be complicated by the practice of surrogacy.

12.4.3 Contracts in restraint of trade

These are undoubtedly the most important category of contracts void at common law and they are probably also the most contentious since they involve the courts in making decisions between competing interests that may appear to be legitimate in both cases.

A restraint of trade clause is quite simply a clause in a contract by which one party agrees to limit or restrict his ability to carry on his trade, business or profession.

Judges have always viewed such arrangements as *prima facie* void, for two principal reasons:

- firstly, the courts are reluctant to endorse an arrangement whereby one party effectively gives up his right to his livelihood as a requirement of the stronger party to the contract
- secondly, the judges are similarly reluctant to see the public deprived of that party's skill or expertise.

Nevertheless, the courts have always tried to protect the idea of freedom of contract and will intervene in a contractual relationship only reluctantly. As a result, while restraint clauses are *prima facie* void, the courts will allow them to stand where they are demonstrated as reasonable.

JUDGMENT

As Lord Macnaghten put it in *Nordenfelt v Maxim Nordenfelt* [1894] AC 535 HL: 'The public have an interest in every person's carrying out his trade freely: so has the individual. All interference with individual liberty of action in trading, and all restraints of trade themselves, if there is nothing more, are contrary to public policy and therefore void. That is the general rule. But there are exceptions: restraints of trade and interference with individual liberty of action may be justified by the special circumstances of a particular case. It is a sufficient justification, and indeed it is the only justification, if the restriction is reasonable.'

'Reasonable' in the context of restraint of trade clauses is measured in two ways:

- Firstly, the restraint must be reasonable as between the two parties to the contract. 'Reasonable' here means that the restraint is no wider than is needed to protect the legitimate interests of the party inserting the restraint clause into the contract. Merely preventing legitimate competition through the use of the restraint is unacceptable and the clause is void and will fail.

JUDGMENT

As Lord Parker explained in *Herbert Morris Ltd v Saxelby* [1916] 1 AC 688 HL: '[for] a restraint to be reasonable in the interests of the parties it must afford no more than adequate protection to the party in whose favour it is imposed'.

Secondly, the restraint must be reasonable in the public interest or at least not injurious to the public interest. Thus a restraint would not be considered reasonable if it deprived the public of a benefit that might otherwise be freely enjoyed or if it unduly restricted choice.

While all restraint clauses are *prima facie* void they will be upheld as reasonable in the circumstances above. Inevitably, the courts have devised a series of tests to measure reasonableness. Such clauses may be reasonable only if:

- They protect a legitimate interest of the party inserting them in the contract and do not merely prevent free competition.
- They do not cover an unnecessarily wide geographical area.
- They are not for an excessive and unnecessary duration.

Restraint clauses generally operate in one of three distinct contexts:

- **Employee restraints** – in these restraints the party inserting them is seeking to prevent employees from unfair competition on leaving the employment.
- **Vendor restraints** – these occur where the purchaser of a business seeks to prevent the seller of the business from unfairly competing after the sale of the business.
- **Agreements of mutual recognition between businesses** – these are restraints by which parties agree to regulation that restricts their trade but for a mutual benefit.

Employee restraints

These are clauses contained in the contract of employment that restrict the activities of the employee on leaving the employment. The employer seeking to rely on such a clause will succeed only where he is actually protecting a legitimate interest of his business.

An employee restraint clause will never succeed where it merely tries to prevent legitimate competition and where it has as its logical outcome therefore that the employee is effectively prevented from working.

The areas in which an employer is able to legitimately use such clauses are well defined by law. They may protect only things such as trade secrets and client connections, and sometimes serve to reduce the damage that could be done by a high-level employee leaving.

The courts use the established tests to decide what is reasonable in the circumstances of each case. In measuring what is reasonable both in the interests of the individual employee and the public they take account of a number of factors:

Whether or not the work is specialised

In cases where the work or indeed the business of the employer is highly specialised, the restraint is more likely to be seen as reasonable. Where the employee's work is commonplace then the restraint is unlikely to be seen as reasonable.

VITIATING FACTORS

CASE EXAMPLE

Forster v Suggett (1918) 35 TLR 87

A glass manufacturer included in the contracts of employees who were skilled glassblowers a clause that prevented them from working for any competitor on leaving their employment with him. The court held that the skill was so specialist at the time of the case that it amounted to a trade secret and the glass manufacturers were entitled to the protection of the clause. It was reasonable in the circumstances and was upheld.

The position held by the employee in the employer's business

The higher the position held by the employee and the more important he is to the business, then the more likely it is that inclusion of the restraint will be held to be reasonable in the circumstances.

CASE EXAMPLE

Herbert Morris Ltd v Saxelby [1916] AC 688, HL

The restraint clause in the employee's contract prevented him, on terminating his employment, from involvement with the sale or manufacture of pulley blocks, overhead runways or overhead travelling cranes for a period of seven years after leaving. In short, this covered both the whole range of the employer's business and indeed the employee's potential expertise. As such it was held to be too wide to succeed despite the key position held by the employee and despite the experience that he had gained from the employment. It would have had the effect of depriving him of any employment opportunities.

An employee may be very significant to the employer's business even without being a senior member of staff. The point, for instance, may have an interesting application in the case of sporting stars.

CASE EXAMPLE

Leeds Rugby Ltd v Harris [2005] EWHC 2290

Harris was a star rugby league player for Leeds Rhinos and was contracted to play for them until 2003. In 2001 he wanted to move to Cardiff to play rugby union so that he could also play for Wales in the rugby union World Cup. A contract and transfer was agreed including a clause requiring Harris to return to Leeds if he exercised an option to return to rugby league after three years. Harris did exercise this option and accepted an offer to play rugby league for Bradford Bulls. Leeds brought an action for breach of contract. The court held that the restraint clause was valid as it was reasonable between the parties. One reason for this was because Harris had requested the original release from Leeds and the club was entitled to protect its interests if its star player returned to rugby league.

Soliciting clients

In general, the rule is that an employer is able to protect both his trade secrets and his client contact. A clause that prevents the employee from soliciting those clients will be upheld provided that it is not too wide.

CASE EXAMPLE

Hanover Insurance Brokers Ltd and Christchurch Insurance Brokers Ltd v Schapiro [1994] IRLR 82

Here, a number of brokerages including Hanover Insurance Brokers (HIB) were sold on to Christchurch. After the sale, three directors of HIB left and set up on their own and were accused of soliciting clients. A restraint clause in their contract prevented them from soliciting the clients of Hanover Associates (of which HIB was a subsidiary) and all its other subsidiaries. The three ex-directors argued that the clause was too wide and should be declared void since they had only worked for HIB. The court accepted this, but held also that since the purpose of the restraint was to prevent soliciting of insurance clients, and only HIB engaged in this activity, then the clause could be upheld against the three directors in respect of the clients of HIB.

It may be that the restraint is declared void because the effect is to prevent the employee from future employment and goes beyond mere protection of a legitimate interest.

CASE EXAMPLE

M & S Draper v Reynolds [1957] 1 WLR 9

Here, the employee, a salesman, was restrained under the contract of employment from soliciting all clients of the firm on leaving the employment, for a period of five years. The restraint covered a great many clients that the employee had actually brought with him on entering the employment, and was declared void on this basis. The court accepted that the salesman's own client contact could also in effect be the tools of his trade and to allow the restraint would seriously damage his prospects of further work.

It might also be the case that there is no unfair competition if the employee is not known to the client contact that he later solicits. In this case the clause will be void.

CASE EXAMPLE

Austin Knight v Hinds [1994] FSR 52

The court accepted evidence to show that the employee who was the subject of the restraint could have had contact with no more than one-third of the employer's client base despite the fact that the restraint was general and prevented the soliciting of any clients of the business. The restraint clause was declared void. It was not in effect protecting a legitimate interest but was merely preventing legitimate competition on the employee leaving.

However, where it is clear that the employee may have gained an unfair advantage from his position in employment then the clause may well be reasonable and therefore valid.

CASE EXAMPLE

G W Plowman & Son Ltd v Ash [1964] 1 WLR 568

Here, a sales representative was restrained by a clause in his contract from soliciting work from any farmer or market gardener for a period of two years after terminating his employment. The clause was upheld as reasonable and therefore valid in the case because evidence showed that he had had the opportunity to solicit these clients of the business during his employment with them.

The geographical area covered by the restraint

This must not be wider than necessary to protect the legitimate interest.

CASE EXAMPLE

Fitch v Dewes [1921] 2 AC 158

Here, a solicitor's clerk was caught by a restraint clause in his contract that prevented him from operating in the same capacity within a seven-mile radius of Tamworth town hall. The restraint was upheld as reasonable by the court. At the time, Tamworth was quite a small rural community and there would only be a restricted amount of work for an individual solicitor's practice within the town. In any case the clerk was well acquainted with the employer's client contact and therefore could have been in a position to damage its business.

In comparison, where the local population is much larger, the geographical extent of the clause may have to narrow to be reasonable or the clause will be void.

CASE EXAMPLE

Fellowes v Fisher [1976] QB 122

Here, a similar restraint was incorporated into the contract of a conveyancing clerk which prevented him from taking up similar employment in the Walthamstow area of London. This was held to be unreasonable by Lord Denning since the clerk was relatively unknown and the area was quite densely populated, by contrast.

The duration of the restraint

The duration of the restraint must be no longer than is actually necessary to protect the legitimate interest of the employer. A longer period than is necessary will render the clause void and unenforceable. Inevitably, there is an element of subjectivity in determining what is a reasonable length of time and what is unreasonable.

CASE EXAMPLE

Fitch v Dewes [1921] 2 AC 158

Here, the restraint on the conveyancing clerk was actually for an unlimited duration. The restraint was still upheld as reasonable because of the rural nature of the community and the clerk's contact with the solicitor's client base.

Generally, short periods are preferred by the courts, however. Clearly, shorter periods have less chance of interfering with an employee's livelihood.

CASE EXAMPLE

Home Counties Dairies Ltd v Skilton [1970] 1 WLR 526

A milk roundsman had an employment contract containing two restraints. Clause 12 of the contract prevented him from entering any employment connected with the dairy business. The second clause, Clause 15, provided only that he should not work as a roundsman or serve any existing customer for a period of one year after leaving the employment. Clause 12 was too wide to be reasonable. Clause 15 was successful since it only protected legitimate interests and it was for only a short period of time.

The restraint must be no wider than is necessary to protect the legitimate interests of the employer

The restraint must be against only activities which would protect the employer's legitimate interests. Any attempt to widen the clause to activities not relevant to the employee's actual work will be void.

CASE EXAMPLE

Mont (JA) (UK) Ltd v Mills (1994) *The Times, 5 May*

This restraint clause was against a 43-year-old managing director in the paper tissue industry and was contained in a severance agreement. The clause prevented him from joining any company within the paper industry for a period of 12 months after ending his employment. The court decided that this was much too wide. It effectively prevented him from working in the paper industry, which was all that he knew. The clause only needed to prevent him from revealing confidential information.

The clear message is not to draft restraint clauses too widely or attempt to cover every possibility. A restraint that is drafted excessively broadly in the context of the interest that is being protected will be declared void.

CASE EXAMPLE

Home Counties Dairies Ltd v Skilton [1970] 1 WLR 526

Here, Clause 12 in the milk roundsman's employment contract restricted him from any employment at all connected with the dairy business. This clause was clearly far too wide to be reasonable. The potential areas of employment within the dairy industry were vast and the clause would have prevented the employee from taking up a wide range of employment well beyond the work he had done and with no chance of damaging his employer's interests.

Achieving restraint through other means

It is not uncommon for employers to seek other means of restraining their employees. It will also then generally be classed as unreasonable where the employer does not actually insert a restraint clause into the contract of employment but attempts to achieve the same restraint but through other means.

One way that has been tried is to use other different parts of the contract with the purpose of achieving the same end.

CASE EXAMPLE

Bull v Pitney Bowes [1966] 1 WLR 273

There was no restraint clause in the contract of employment. However, there was a clause whereby an employee would forfeit pension rights in the event of taking up work with a competitor of the employer. The court held that to all intents and purposes the provision was a part of the contract having the same purpose as a restraint. It was held to be void for public policy.

Other employers have attempted to achieve the same purpose as a restraint by agreements among themselves not to employ ex-employees. Because such agreements amount to a disguised restraint, they will still be declared void as unreasonable restraints.

CASE EXAMPLE

Kores Manufacturing Co v Kolok Manufacturing Co [1959] Ch 108

Two electronics companies reached an agreement that neither of them would hire employees of the other firm for a period of five years after their leaving. The court held that this had exactly the same effect as a restraint clause and the agreement was held to be void and unenforceable.

A further possibility is that the rules of associations are used to achieve the same purpose as a restraint. Again, this is seen as quite similar to an agreement between employers and such agreements may be unenforceable against the ex-employee.

CASE EXAMPLE

Eastham v Newcastle United FC Ltd [1964] Ch 413

Here, George Eastham, a well-known footballer of the time, challenged the rules of the Football Association on the legitimacy of the transfer system as it then existed. The FA rules meant that a club could retain a player's registration even after his contract had ended and so effectively the rules could be used to prevent him from playing again. Besides this, at the time, players could be placed on the transfer list against their will. The court determined that these rules did amount to an unlawful restraint of trade and were unenforceable. (Of course, subsequently, the whole area of the transfer market has become subject to control under Article 45 EC Treaty, following the *Bosman* ruling.)

Vendor restraints

These will occur where sellers of businesses agree under the contract of sale not to compete unfairly with the purchaser of the business. Again, such agreements are *prima facie* void. Declaring such restraints void has been justified as preventing an individual from negotiating away his livelihood, and also for preventing the public from losing a valuable benefit where the one party is prevented from trading by the other.

They are, however, more likely to be accepted as reasonable by the courts because the bargaining strength of the parties is more likely to be equal and therefore such restraints are more commonly upheld than is the case for employee restraints.

Again, to be reasonable and enforceable they must protect only legitimate interests and not merely aim to prevent legitimate competition.

CASE EXAMPLE

British Reinforced Concrete Co v Schelff [1921] 2 Ch 63

A business that specialised in the production of steel reinforcement for roads was sold. In the contract of sale a restraint clause prevented the vendors of the business from engaging in any similar business. One of the vendors then entered another business as manager of the reinforced concrete section. The clause was held to be too wide to protect legitimate interests and could not be applied.

Again, the same tests apply as for employee restraints and no clause will be enforced that is too wide in its application. Though what is too wide is a question of fact dictated by the circumstances of each case. Since businessmen are generally taken to be operating in a much more equal relationship than employers and employees, such clauses have been upheld as reasonable even though on the surface they may appear to be unusually wide both in duration and in terms of geographical extent.

CASE EXAMPLE

Nordenfelt v Maxim Nordenfelt Co [1894] AC 535

Nordenfelt had established a business manufacturing and selling guns and ammunition. Inevitably, the sales market for such products was world-wide. When he sold the business, it was subject to a clause in the contract preventing him from engaging in the armaments business anywhere in the world for a period of 25 years. This seems an unusually wide clause. However, the court was prepared to enforce the clause since the world was the appropriate market.

Mutual undertakings

Often, agreements between merchants or manufacturers or in other trades of different types will amount in effect to restraints on each party to the agreement. Similar rules apply and they may only in any case be declared reasonable and valid where both sides gain a clear benefit from the agreement. Inevitably, the fact that the parties are both businesses and usually deal on equal terms has a major impact on the outcome although, as restraints, the clauses may be *prima facie* void.

274

VITIATING FACTORS

JUDGMENT

As Lord Reid explained in Esso Petroleum Co Ltd v Harper's Garage (Stourport) Ltd [1968] AC 269 HL: 'Where two experienced traders are bargaining on equal terms and one has agreed to a restraint for reasons which seem good to him the court is in grave danger of stultifying itself if it says that he knows the trader's interests better than he does himself. But there may well be cases where, although the party to be restrained has deliberately accepted the main terms of the contract, he has been at a disadvantage as regards other terms … then the court may have greater freedom to hold them unreasonable'.

One example of restraints under this heading is where agreements are reached that are mandatory on the parties because of the rules of associations of which they are members.

CASE EXAMPLE

English Hop Growers v Dering [1928] 2 KB 124

Here, under his agreement with the association, Dering was held to be bound to deliver his entire hop crop to the association for onward sale. This arrangement was actually the way in which hop growers eliminated competition. It also ensured that any loss as well as any profit was shared equally among the members of the association in any given year. So it was a genuine protection of the members and of obvious mutual benefit to all members of the association. The agreement was reasonable and binding.

Another area where the same principles can obviously apply is in the agreements between artists and performers etc. and their various agents, particularly where there is an obvious imbalance in the bargaining strength of the parties. However, because in such arrangements the parties are usually contracting from an unequal bargaining position, they are less likely to be classed as reasonable or enforced.

CASE EXAMPLE

Schroeder Music Publishing Co Ltd v Macaulay [1974] 1 WLR 1308

An unknown composer entered into an agreement with music publishers. Under this agreement the publishers would receive world copyright on any composition that he produced, there would be no general payment for compositions and royalties were only payable on those compositions that were commercially exploited by the publishers, who gave no guarantee that any work would be published. The original five-year agreement could be extended automatically by the publishers but they could also terminate the agreement at any time with only one month's notice. The court held that this regulation of trade was plainly unreasonable and unlawful, particularly in the light of the inexperience and unequal bargaining strength of the young composer.

While the same rules generally apply, this can be contrasted with situations where, while a contract may have been originally entered into where one party may have taken advantage of the immaturity and unequal bargaining strength of the other party, subsequent compromises have been to the advantage of the other party.

CASE EXAMPLE

Panayiotou v Sony Music International (UK) Ltd [1994] 1 All ER 755

This case involved George Michael and his attempts to improve the degree of control he had over his recording contract and gain greater freedom from the restrictions it imposed on him. Originally, he and Andrew Ridgeley had a recording contract as the group 'Wham', and they had tried to get their recording contract declared void for restraint of trade. This in fact was changed in 1984 under an agreed compromise and the group moved to CBS. Michael then established himself as a solo artist and in 1988 his contract was changed to reflect his new 'superstar' status. CBS was also taken over by Sony at this time. When Michael later wanted to change his image and became dissatisfied with Sony, he sought to have this agreement declared void for restraint of trade. As the 1988 contract was based on and was an improvement on the 1984 agreement which the court accepted as a genuine compromise, it refused his claim as being contrary to public policy.

A further area where the courts have applied the principles of restraint of trade and discussed in detail the tests for determining reasonableness is in the case of the so-called 'solus agreements'. These are agreements where a retailer is restricted by a manufacturer or wholesaler in either distribution or pricing or in supply. So they very often apply to agreements to buy exclusively from one manufacturer or wholesaler.

CASE EXAMPLE

Esso Petroleum Co Ltd v Harper's Garage (Stourport) Ltd [1968] AC 269

Under the solus agreement here, Esso lent Harper's money and Harper's could sell only Esso petrol from their two garages. In the case of the first garage, known as the Corner Garage, there was a loan, the agreement was to last for 21 years, and by the same agreement Harper's were bound to pay back the loan over that 21-year period and not any shorter period. In effect, then, they were tied into the agreement to sell only Esso petrol for that 21-year period. Under the agreement for the second garage, known as the Mustow Green garage, the duration of the agreement was for only four years and five months and, unlike in the other agreement, there was no mortgage to Esso of the land on which the garage was situated. Harper's wished to change the brand of petrol that they sold and Esso sought an injunction to prevent them from doing so. In an appeal by Esso, the House of Lords discussed at length and restated the various rules for determining the validity of restraint of trade clauses. Applying these rules to the particular circumstances, it declared that the Corner Garage agreement was void on the basis of the excessive duration of the restraint. Using the same basis of duration, the House declared that the Mustow Green agreement was valid, as it was both fair and reasonable.

JUDGMENT

Lord Reid explained the reasoning: '[the appellants] are not so much concerned with any particular outlet but with maintaining a stable system of distribution throughout the country so as to enable their business to be run efficiently and economically. In my view there is sufficient material to justify a decision that ties of less than five years were insufficient, in the circumstances ... to afford adequate protection ... A tie for 21 years stretches far beyond any period for which developments are reasonably foreseeable'.

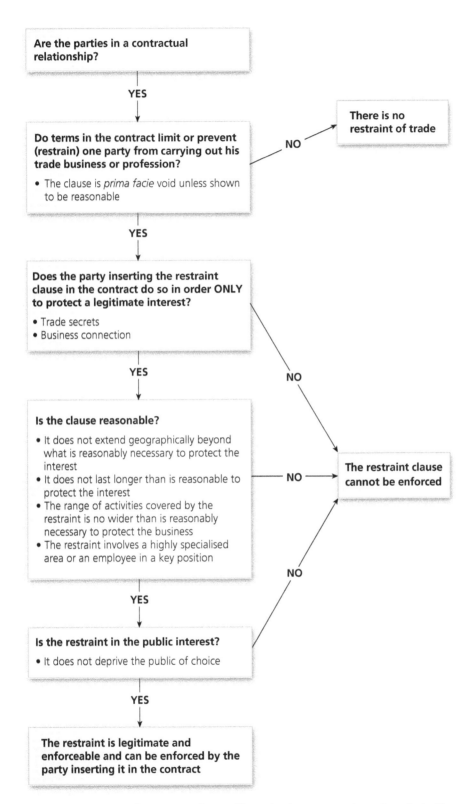

Figure 12.1 Diagram illustrating how a court determines the legitimacy of a restraint of trade clause in a contract

ACTIVITY

Applying the law

Try the following problem:

Lisa agreed to sell her hairdressing business in Wickton to Alison for £50,000, including the lease, all fixtures and fittings, and the goodwill. Lisa had planned to marry and begin a family, and thus give up hairdressing for a number of years.

In a clause in the written contract, Lisa agreed that she would not 'for a period of ten years following transfer of the business open a salon or other hairdressing establishment within a 25-mile radius' of the salon in Wickton. By a further clause in the contract Lisa was prohibited from 'approaching, soliciting for business, or contacting with a view to entering any business arrangement, for a period of five years, any client of the business'. The contract was prepared by Lisa.

Three years later, Lisa has found that she is unable to have a family, and so she plans to return to hairdressing. She has taken the lease on a hairdresser's business in Sockington which is only five miles from Wickton.

Alison is concerned that she may now lose business and seeks your advice on any remedies which may be available to her.

12.5 Contracts illegal at common law and the role of policy

This is potentially a very wide group of contracts and it includes any type of agreement that is prejudicial to the general notion of freedom of contract. The basis for judges declaring such arrangements illegal is that to allow them to stand would be harmful to the public good. So, like most aspects of illegality at common law, the reason for the illegality is public policy.

The categories of such agreements are numerous and varied. The common characteristic seems to be some form of immorality in each case. They include:

A contract to commit a wrong

The courts have never been prepared to enforce contracts that provide a payment in return for committing a legal wrong. The wrong in question might be a civil wrong such as a tort.

CASE EXAMPLE

Allen v Rescous (1676) 2 Lev 174

This is a very old case. It demonstrates the point that even from the earliest times the law would not accept contracts aimed at committing a wrong. In this case a contract was made by which one party would receive a payment in return for committing a civil assault. The contract was held to be unenforceable.

In similar fashion the courts will be unprepared to enforce a contract to commit a crime of whatever sort in return for a payment.

CASE EXAMPLE

Dann v Curzon (1910) 104 LT 66

Here, the claimant had been hired to start a riot in a theatre. When he sued for the unpaid fee of £20 he was unsuccessful. The judges, as a matter of policy, could not enforce an agreement to carry out a crime.

It could also be a contract for a fraud and it would still be unenforceable.

CASE EXAMPLE

Alexander v Rayson [1936] 1 KB 169

Here, the agreement was to defraud a local authority. Again, the contract was unenforceable, being illegal at common law.

In more recent times the courts have also identified that a contract in breach of the rules of professional bodies that have been introduced through delegated or subordinate legislation will also be unenforceable even though this relates to a breach of discipline rather than an actual legal wrong.

CASE EXAMPLE

Mohamed v Alaga [1999] 3 All ER 699

A solicitor undertook legal work on behalf of asylum seekers. The solicitor reached an agreement with a Somali national to share fees for work on behalf of asylum seekers who had been introduced by the Somali national. When the fees were not shared and an action was brought for payment, the Court of Appeal accepted the solicitor's defence that, even if such an agreement had been reached, the agreement would be illegal and unenforceable under the Solicitors' Practice Rules. Under these Rules the sharing of fees was prohibited.

A contract to benefit from the crime of another

Similarly, the courts are not prepared to enforce a contract under which a party would be able to gain a benefit from a legal wrong such as a crime.

CASE EXAMPLE

Beresford v Royal Insurance Co Ltd [1937] 2 KB 197

The question here was whether relatives of a person who had committed suicide should be able to benefit from life insurance policies of the dead person. They were prevented from benefiting from the life insurance.

JUDGMENT

In his judgment Lord Atkin explains why the courts are hostile to contracts involving the categories above: 'I think that the principle is that a man is not to be allowed to have recourse to a Court of Justice to claim a benefit from his crime whether under a contract or a gift. No doubt the rule pays regard to the fact that to hold otherwise would in some cases offer an inducement to crime or remove a restraint to crime, and that its effect is to act as a deterrent to crime.'

Contracts in breach of foreign law

Even though the contract in question may not offend English law, if it will neverthe-less breach foreign law then the courts are equally unwilling to enforce it. This again is an obvious public policy stance.

CASE EXAMPLE

Foster v Driscoll [1929] 1 KB 470

Here, a contract was formed which involved buying whisky and reselling it in the United States which at that time had laws against alcohol, commonly known at the time as 'pro-hibition'. When the shipment was not paid for, the claim to enforce the contract failed. The judges, as a matter of policy, were not prepared to allow a contract which had as its central purpose the breaching of the law of another country.

A contract to defraud the Revenue

The courts are very keen to ensure that people do not gain benefit from their own wrongdoing and they are equally eager to protect legitimate bodies such as the Inland Revenue from arrangements that might in effect amount to a fraud on the Revenue.

CASE EXAMPLE

Napier v The National Business Agency [1951] 2 All ER 264

Under his contract of employment, as well as his salary, which was set very low, the claim-ant also received expenses of £6 per week where his actual costs were no more than £1. This was a quite deliberate agreement between the two parties with the sole purpose of avoiding income tax, since expenses are not subject to taxation. When he was dismissed by his employers, Napier was owed several weeks' back pay and sued. He was unable to succeed since the contract was unenforceable. The Court of Appeal held that the whole contract was tainted with illegality and therefore unenforceable.

Contracts aimed at corruption in public life

The courts are not prepared to enforce any contract the true purpose of which is corruption, particularly in public life. Obvious examples would include bribes to officials or payments for unofficial favours.

CASE EXAMPLE

Parkinson v The College of Ambulance [1925] 2 KB 1

The claimant, who was wealthy, was asked to donate funds to a company in return for which the other party falsely represented that he would be able to gain Parkinson a knighthood. The claimant made the donation but when he was not given any honour he sued for return of his money. He failed because this was purely a corrupt practice. It was against public policy to try to secure recognition in this way and the contract was unenforceable.

Contracts to interfere with the course of justice

The courts, again as a matter of policy, will not enforce any agreement between two parties which has as its aim any interference with the course of justice. This could be an agreement not to pursue a case or to prevent a case from succeeding.

CASE EXAMPLE

Kearley v Thomson (1890) 24 QBD 742

This involved a bankruptcy hearing. Kearley had paid a solicitor £40 not to appear at the public examination and also not to oppose the order for his friend's discharge from bankruptcy. He later tried to recover the money he had paid but the court held that the agreement was against public policy and therefore he was denied.

It will also obviously include any attempt to bribe witnesses for the purpose of gaining a different result in a case.

CASE EXAMPLE

Harmony Shipping Co SA v Davis [1979] 3 All ER 177

This involved an agreement to pay money to a witness not to give evidence in a trial. The agreement was void and unenforceable.

There is also an interesting recent development of this point.

CASE EXAMPLE

Carnduff v Rock and Another (2001) The Times, 30 May

Here, the Court of Appeal held that there could be no enforceable agreement between a police informer and the police for payment for information. It would be against the public interest to allow an informer to sue for payment. Laws LJ identified that to resolve the issue fairly would involve examining the operational methods of the police in detail. This would transfer the 'difficult and delicate business of tracking and catching serious professional criminals from the confidential context of police operations to the glare of a court of justice'.

Contracts aimed at denying a legal right

In the same way, the courts are not prepared to enforce agreements whereby one party agrees to give up what would otherwise be a legal right. This again is against public policy.

CASE EXAMPLE

Cooper v Willis (1906) 22 TLR 330

This involved an agreement not to carry out divorce proceedings. The agreement could not be enforced.

CASE EXAMPLE

Hyman v Hyman [1929] AC 601

This was an agreement not to apply for maintenance, which was unenforceable.

Contracts of maintenance and contracts of champerty

There are two further areas where the judges have traditionally been hostile towards enforcing contracts that have in a sense an element of interference with justice.

The first of these is referred to as a contract of maintenance. This is an agreement by one party financially to support litigation in which he has no personal interest. This is against public policy because it clearly has the potential to be unfair to the other party in the case.

CASE EXAMPLE

Martell v Consett Iron Co Ltd [1955] Ch 363

This involved an agreement by a fishing club financially to support a person who was taking action against a company over pollution that it was causing. This was not classed as maintenance and so the agreement was not held to be illegal and could be relied upon.

The second, champerty, is an old word referring to financial support though purely for a share of damages awarded. This, again, was traditionally held to offend public policy and was not accepted for the same reasons.

CASE EXAMPLE

Picton Jones & Co v Arcadia Developments [1989] 3 EG 85

Here, the claimants, who were chartered surveyors, acted for the defendant in an attempt to acquire amusement arcades by making planning applications for both planning permission and licences. The defendant then failed to pay according to the agreement and, when the claimants sued, argued that the contract was illegal for champerty. However, the court rejected his argument because champerty only applied to litigation, not to legal proceedings in general.

Contracts to promote sexual immorality

Judges have always seen themselves as guardians of morality and as a result will not accept agreements that are based on sexual immorality.

CASE EXAMPLE

Pearce v Brooks (1866) LR 1 Ex 213

A prostitute hit on the idea of conducting her trade from hired carriages. She engaged in this activity with the full knowledge of the party from whom she hired the carriage. When she then failed to pay the fee owed, the owner's action for the price failed. The contract was for immoral sexual purposes and was known to be so by both parties. As a result, it was against public policy and was unenforceable.

Soliciting itself is unlawful and therefore there is some logic to the case. The courts will, however, extend the principle, even where the agreement concerns purely private arrangements.

CASE EXAMPLE

Benyon v Nettleford (1850) 3 Mac & G 94

Here, an arrangement was made for a woman to become a man's mistress. The court declared the arrangement illegal and unenforceable.

Of course, this last principle may differ somewhat in modern times where cohabitees reach agreements on distribution of property. Since sexual morality inevitably changes over time, the more recent application of the principle in *Pearce v Brooks* (1886) LR 1 Ex 213 is possibly only now in situations where there is at least a crime involved.

CASE EXAMPLE

Armhouse Lee Ltd v Chappell (1996) *The Times*, 7th August

The case concerned magazines that included advertisements for sex lines and sex dating. The defendant failed to pay for the advertisements and the magazine sued for payment. The claimant won at first instance on the basis that the contract was illegal and unenforceable because of public policy. The defendants appealed successfully. The Court of Appeal held that it would be 'undesirable in such a case, involving an area regarded as the province of the criminal law, for individual judges exercising a civil jurisdiction to impose their own moral attitudes'.

In conclusion, the area of contracts declared illegal by the courts is very broad, based on ideas of morality and corruption, and above all the reasoning for failing to enforce such contracts is entirely based on public policy.

12.6 The consequences of a contract being declared void

Where the contract is declared void the significant difference in consequences may depend on whether the contract is declared void under the **common law** or whether it is declared void because of **statute**.

12.6.1 At common law

Where the contract is declared void by the courts, as may be the case with, for example, a contract in restraint of trade, then there are a number of possible consequences.

▨ Firstly, depending on the wording of the contract itself, the whole contract is not necessarily declared void, although the offending clause may well be.

CASE EXAMPLE

Home Counties Dairies Ltd v Skilton [1970] 1 WLR 526

In the milk roundsman's contract the court determined that Clause 15, which in effect only protected the employer's existing client contact, was reasonable and enforceable. However, Clause 12, which prevented him from entering any employment connected with the dairy business, was too wide to be reasonable and so the court declared that clause void and unenforceable.

▨ Secondly, money that has been paid over under the contract may be recoverable as a result of the contract being declared void, as in *Hermann v Charlesworth* [1905] 2 KB 123 where the procurement of a marriage for a fee was declared void.

▨ It also seems that subsequent and dependent terms will only be void if they are also actually based on the void term in the contract.

▨ Finally, it is possible to sever the clause that is void from the rest of the contract to avoid voiding the whole contract.

severance

Splitting aspects of a contract to remove illegal aspects and retain legitimate aspects

Severance could take one of two forms:

▨ By deleting the void term from the contract in its entirety.

CASE EXAMPLE

Attwood v Lamont [1920] 3 KB 571

A tailor's cutter was restrained, on leaving his employment, from taking up any work as 'tailor, dressmaker, general draper, milliner, hatter, haberdasher, gentleman's, ladies' or children's outfitter at any place within a ten-mile radius' of his employer's business. One argument was that it was within the power of the court to apply the clause only to the work of tailor's cutter since that was the role of the employee, rather than to declare the clause void. The court felt that there was no way of reducing or changing the list in the clause. It was not so much as a list but a comprehensive description of the employer's whole business and as such severance was not possible, the restraint was too wide and was void and unenforceable.

▨ By reducing the scope of the clause so that it accurately represents the protection of a legitimate interest.

CASE EXAMPLE

Goldsoll v Goldman [1915] 1 Ch 292

Here, there was a restraint clause in a contract for the sale of a jewellery business. The restraint prevented the vendor from selling real or imitation jewellery both in the UK and also in the Isle of Man, France, the United States of America, Russia, Spain and within a 25-mile radius of specific locations in Berlin or Vienna. When the purchaser tried to enforce the clause it was shown that the business only specialised in the sale of imitation jewellery and that it had never enjoyed an export market. The court severed the word 'real' from the contract, because it was unnecessary to the protection of the business, and also those elements relating to the areas outside of the UK. The rest of the clause was upheld.

JUDGMENT

As Lord Cozens-Hardy commented: 'It is admitted that the business of a dealer in real jewellery is not the same as that of a dealer in imitation jewellery. That being so it is difficult to support the whole of this provision, for the covenant must be limited to what is reasonably necessary for the protection of the covenantee's business.'

However, the court will not sever parts of a contract where to do so would alter the whole character of the agreement. This was indeed the case in *Attwood v Lamont* [1920] 3 KB 571.

Neither will the court employ severance if to do so would interfere with public policy when it was this that rendered the contract void in the first place.

CASE EXAMPLE

Napier v The National Business Agency [1951] 2 All ER 264

Here, because of the tax avoidance mechanism, the agreement between the two parties was void and the claimant was unable to recover any of the money owed to him.

However, courts are more willing to 'rewrite' a clause to give it commercial sense in a commercial contract than they would be in the case of an employee restraint.

CASE EXAMPLE

Chipsaway International Ltd v Errol Kerr [2009] EWCA 320

The claimant had rights to a system under the trade name 'Chipsaway' for filling and restoring damaged car bodywork. The claimant also supplied paints to be used with the system. The claimant granted a car care franchise to Kerr under an agreement for an initial 5 year period. Kerr, a sole trader, complied with terms in the agreement under which he was bound to display the 'Chipsaway' name and logos. At the end of the term Kerr renewed his franchise but then changed his mind and wrote to the claimant to that effect and continued the same work but without using Chipsaway paint and other products. The claimant then argued that Kerr was in breach of a restrictive covenant in the franchise agreement. The issue for the court was what in fact the clause meant since it is was badly drafted. The clause provided that 'for a period of twelve months following termination of this agreement for whatever reason…the franchisee will not without Chipsaway's prior written consent be engaged in any capacity in any business which competes with the Business'. 'Business' was defined in the agreement as 'the provision by the Franchisee of a service to the customers'. On the face of it this seems pointless since it appeared to identify that Kerr should not engage in a business which would compete with Kerr providing a service to repair damage to car paintwork. The first instance judge held that because this made no sense the clause should be interpreted to mean Kerr was restricted from engaging with any business which competed with any business which is a successor to the franchise after termination of Kerr's franchise arrangement. So Kerr could not carry out the same activity within the territory covered by the original franchise. On which basis he was not in breach of the restrictive covenant since no new franchisee had been appointed to cover that area. The Court of Appeal disagreed because the result would not be sensible commercially. The commercial purpose of such a clause was to prevent the franchisee from competing for a period of time after the end of the franchise to protect the goodwill of the franchisor and to give it time to find a new franchisee. As a result Kerr was in breach of the restrictive covenant.

12.6.2 By statute

The effects, if the contract is void because of a statutory provision, may obviously vary and will depend on the wording of the Act itself. Very often the statute will identify what will occur as a result of the contract being declared void.

However, where the statute itself is silent on the effects of the contract being declared void then the common law effects above will apply.

12.7 The consequences of a contract being declared illegal

Here, the principal difference is not between the common law and statute but between contracts that are illegal **as formed**, and therefore cannot be legally made, and those contracts which, although they are legally formed, only become illegal because of the manner in which they are **performed**.

12.7.1 Illegal on formation

Where either statute or the common law has declared that a particular class of contract will be illegal if it is made, then such a contract can never be either legally formed or performed and it will be illegal from the moment of formation. There are, then, a number of consequences for such agreements:

- Since the agreement is illegal from the time that it is actually made, it can never result in a valid contract. It is therefore also unenforceable by either party.

CASE EXAMPLE

Dann v Curzon (1910) 104 LT 66

The agreement to start the riot was criminal and therefore illegal. As a result, there was no legal way of enforcing payment, the point being that nobody should be allowed to profit from his own crime.

- Since the contract itself is illegal, property or money that is transferred in advance of the agreement cannot generally be recovered either.

CASE EXAMPLE

Parkinson v The College of Ambulance [1925] 2 KB 1

Here, the court could not accept as a matter of public policy that a contract could be formed that was in essence based on corruption. In consequence, neither could it permit recovery of the donation that in any case should have been given freely, without thought of return.

The same principle will apply even in those situations where the parties are unaware of the illegality of their agreement.

CASE EXAMPLE

J W Allan (Merchandising) Ltd v Cloke [1960] 2 All ER 258

Here, fees were charged for the hire of a roulette wheel. What neither party knew was that the activity and therefore the transaction would be illegal under the Betting and Gaming Act 1960. In consequence, the fee paid could not be recovered despite the parties' lack of awareness of the illegality.

However, there are certain exceptions to this basic rule where property that has been transferred may be recoverable:

■ Where not to allow recovery would be against 'public conscience'.

CASE EXAMPLE

Howard v Shirlstar Container Transport Ltd [1990] 3 All ER 366

The contract was to recover an aircraft that had been impounded in Nigeria, so the effect of the contract was stealing the aircraft for the owner. When it was completed and the aircraft owner refused to pay, claiming that the arrangement was void for illegality, the court held that the claimant could recover in the circumstances.

■ Where the illegality is not vital to the cause.

CASE EXAMPLE

Tinsley v Milligan [1993] 3 WLR 126

The two parties to the action jointly bought a house, putting it in the first party's name so that the second party could make fraudulent claims for state benefits. The agreement inevitably had the appearance of illegality. The second party later tried to claim a share of the property under a resulting trust arising out of her contribution to the purchase of the house. The first party argued that the agreement was void for illegality and thus was also unenforceable. However, the House of Lords accepted that the second party was not merely trying to enforce an illegal contract but was in fact asserting a property right that arose out of a trust. The agreement was therefore enforceable. In this way the House of Lords rejected the idea that the contract should be void because it was against public conscience (as in the previous case) but preferred to find that the potential illegality of the agreement had no bearing on the case in hand. Lord Goff dissented, believing that to enforce a trust would require the party seeking to do so to come to court with clean hands, and he believed that the party seeking to enforce the agreement here was behaving inequitably.

■ Where the party seeking to enforce the agreement is not *in pari delicto*, ie that party is not as responsible for the illegal nature of the contract as the other party.

CASE EXAMPLE

Kiriri Cotton Co Ltd v Dewani [1960] AC 192

A landlord demanded a premium (an up-front payment) from a tenant even though the legislation regulating such tenancies did not recognise premiums. The tenant was able to recover the cost because the court felt that he was not a party to the illegality but had had no choice but to go along with the illegal arrangement.

▨ Where the agreement has been induced by a fraud.

CASE EXAMPLE

Hughes v Liverpool and Victoria Legal Friendly Society [1916] 2 KB 482

The claimant was induced by the fraudulent representations of an insurance agent to take out insurance on parties who were not insurable by her. When the fraud was discovered she was entitled to return of the premiums paid. She had not been a willing party to the illegal arrangement but had indeed herself been the victim of fraud.

▨ Where the one party repents before the contract is performed.

In *Kearley v Thomson* (1890) 24 QBD 742, for instance, the court identified that if the contract ultimately did not take place because of one party's voluntary decision to withdraw, that party might claim back any money handed over in advance of the contract. The court also recognised that recovery is impossible once the illegal purpose is carried out.

More recently, since the passing of the Human Rights Act 1998, the courts have had to consider whether or not the basic rule preventing the recovery of money or property passed in advance of an illegal contract offends basic human rights principles.

CASE EXAMPLE

Al-Kishtaini v Shansal [2001] 2 All ER Comm 601

The contracts here were with Iraqi citizens and the illegality in question resulted from regulations passed to comply with United Nations sanctions preventing trade with Iraqi concerns, put in place following the Iraq invasion and occupation of Kuwait and the Gulf War that liberated Kuwait in 1990. The argument in favour of recovery of property passed under the contracts was that the general rule infringed Article 1 of the First Protocol to the European Convention on Human Rights. This states that: 'No one shall be deprived of his possessions except in the public interest and subject to conditions provided for by law and by the general principles of international law'. Obviously, one of the consequences of the Human Rights Act 1998 is that courts must interpret English law so as to comply with the basic rights under the Convention. The Court of Appeal rejected the argument. On the one hand it felt that Article 1 of the First Protocol did not in any case apply. If it did, the court felt that in any case prevention of recovery for the illegality could still be justified because this was in the public interest.

288

VITIATING FACTORS

12.7.2 Illegal on performance

If both parties are equally responsible for the illegal performance then the rules are basically the same as for contracts that are illegal in their formation:

* the contract is void and unenforceable
* money paid over in advance of the contract cannot be recovered (although there are exceptions, as above (see section 12.7.1).

However, if one party is unaware of the illegality then he may have remedies available, including recovery of any money that was handed over in advance of the contract.

CASE EXAMPLE

Marles v Trant [1954] 1 QB 29

A seed supplier sold seed to Trant, describing it as 'spring wheat' seed which in fact it was not. Trant then sold the seed on to Marles, but without giving him also an invoice which was required in such transfers by statute. When Marles discovered that the seed was in fact 'winter wheat' seed he was able to sue for recovery of the price despite the illegality of the contract.

The appropriate test to determine whether or not a party can recover damages is whether he would actually need to rely on the illegality in order to bring the claim. If that were the case then damages would not be available. The party would quite naturally be tainted with the illegality of the agreement. However, if the illegality is only ancillary to the subject of the claim itself then that party may well be able to recover damages.

CASE EXAMPLE

Hall v Woolston Hall Leisure Ltd [2000] 4 All ER 787

The claimant had been dismissed from employment when she became pregnant and was claiming that this was for reasons of sex discrimination and therefore contrary to the Employment Rights Act 1996. The employer was trying to defend by claiming that the contract of employment was itself illegal and therefore unenforceable. This was because the woman was aware that the employer was paying and recording her wages in a way that would defraud the Inland Revenue of tax. While the woman was indeed aware of the arrangement, this was done for the benefit of the employer and she had no control over it. The Court of Appeal held that the illegality was specifically the cause of the employer and in any case had nothing to do with the precise claim being made by the woman. In these circumstances there was nothing to prevent it from awarding her compensation for her unfair dismissal.

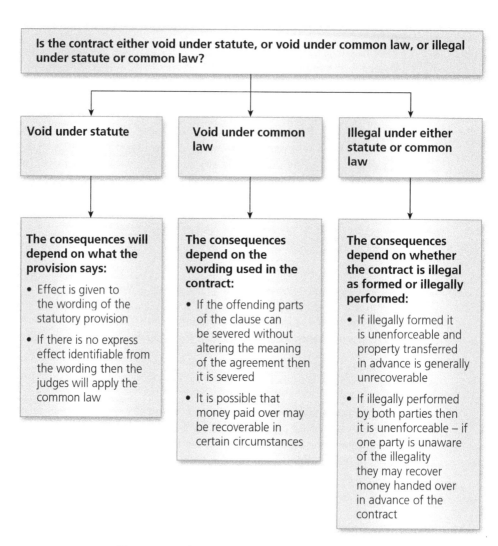

Figure 12.2 Diagram illustrating the consequences of a contract being tainted with illegality

ACTIVITY

Self-assessment questions

1. In what ways does illegality differ from other vitiating factors?
2. How are restrictive trade practices regulated in modern times?
3. What is the difference between a contract illegally formed and a contract illegally performed?
4. How important do you think control of contracts prejudicial to marriage is in the present day?
5. Why are contracts in restraint of trade *prima facie* void?
6. When will a restraint clause be upheld?
7. How is reasonableness measured in restraint of trade?
8. What are the common characteristics of contracts declared illegal by the common law?
9. In what circumstances can a party recover money or property handed over under an illegal contract?
10. What are the purposes of severing a contract?

SUMMARY

- Illegality covers contracts that are illegal, void and unenforceable.
- It divides into four possibilities: void by statute, illegal by statute, void in common law and illegal in common law.
- Contracts void by statute include restrictive trade practices.
- Contracts illegal by statute include contracts that are illegal in their formation and contracts that are legally formed but are illegal in the manner of performance.
- Contracts void at common law include: contracts to oust the jurisdiction of the court, some contracts harmful to family life and contracts in restraint of trade (the latter are prima facie void but may be enforced if they are accepted as reasonable as between the parties, and in the public interest – reasonableness is measured against the geographical extent and the duration of the restraint and a party is only allowed to protect legitimate interests).
- Contracts illegal at common law are all for reasons of public policy and include: contracts to commit a wrong or a crime or to defraud the Inland Revenue, contracts aimed at corruption, contracts to interfere with justice and contracts to promote immorality.
- Where a contract is void by statute the effect depends on what the statute says.
- Where a contract is void at common law then money paid over may be recovered and sometimes the offending clause can be severed to save the rest of the agreement.
- A contract that is illegally formed is unenforceable and money paid over is generally unrecoverable though there are exceptions.
- A contract that is legally formed but illegally performed will have remedies available to a party who is unaware of the illegality.

SAMPLE ESSAY QUESTION

Discuss the extent to which the rules created by judges for declaring illegal a restraint of trade clause in a contract are an unnecessary interference with freedom of contract.

Explain the general area of illegality of contracts:

- Hard to define – but there are some broad categories
- Can be divided into void by statute, illegal by common law, void by common law and illegal by common law
- Identify in each case that the effect is that the contract is unenforceable

Explain the term restraint of trade:

- Comes under contracts void at common law
- Is a clause in a contract preventing one party to the contract from doing something once the contract is terminated

Explain the basic rules on restraint of trade:

- *Prima facie* void for public policy
- Can be upheld if reasonable
- Must be reasonable as between the parties and in the public interest
- To be reasonable must do no more than is necessary to protect a legitimate interest – could be a trade secret or client connection
- Must also be no longer in duration than is necessary and the geographical extent must not be too wide

Discuss the context in which restraint clauses operate:

- Vendor restraints – protect against unfair competition when a business has been sold
- Employee restraints – protect a business from unfair competition after the employee has left the employment
- In either case the fact that such clauses are *prima facie* void is technically an interference with freedom of contract

Discuss whether the judge-made rules are necessary:

- Ex-employees could otherwise use knowledge gained in employment for unfair competition
- Businesses could otherwise take advantage of a client connection in a business just sold
- The protections operate within strict limits

KEY FACTS

Illegality and reasons for lack of enforceability	
Illegality is a difficult area because judges refer to contracts being 'illegal', 'void' and 'unenforceable', and also because a contract can be invalidated by statute or by the common law.	
Void by statute	
Include restrictive trade practices.	
Illegal by statute	**Case/statute**
Can be in formation, in which case it is unenforceable.	*Re Mahmoud and Ispahani*
Or a legally formed contract can be illegal in its performance.	*Anderson Ltd v Daniel*

Void at common law	Case/statute
Contracts to oust the jurisdiction of the court.	
Contracts harmful to family life.	
Contracts in restraint of trade	
• *prima facie* void but may be enforced if they are accepted as reasonable as between the parties, and in the public interest	
• reasonableness depends on:	
• geographical extent	*Fitch v Dewes*
• duration of the restraint	*Home Counties Dairies v Skilton*
• a party is only able to protect legitimate interests.	*British Concrete v Schelff*
• A vendor restraint is more likely to be held reasonable than an employee restraint.	*Nordenfelt v Maxim Nordenfelt*
• A party cannot either try to use other means to effect a restraint.	*Bull v Pitney Bowes*

Contracts illegal at common law	Case/statute
All declared unenforceable for policy reasons:	
• a contract to commit a wrong	*Dann v Curzon*
• a contract to commit a crime	*Beresford v Royal Insurance Co*
• a contract to defraud the Revenue	*Napier v The National Business Agency*
• contracts aimed at corruption	*Parkinson v The College of Ambulance*
• contracts to interfere with justice	*Harmony Shipping Co v Davis*
• contracts promoting immorality	*Pearce v Brooks*

The effects of illegality	Case/statute
• If a contract is void by statute, the effect depends on what the statute says.	
• If a contract is void at common law then money paid over may be recovered and sometimes the offending clause can be severed to save the rest of the agreement.	*Hermann v Charlesworth* *Goldsoll v Goldman*
• A contract illegal as formed is unenforceable and money paid over is generally unrecoverable, though there are exceptions.	
• A contract legally formed but illegally performed will have remedies available to a party who is unaware of the illegality.	*Marles v Trant*

Further reading

Grodeski, 'In Pari Delicto' (1955) 71 LQR 54.

Marsh, N, 'The Severance of Illegality in Contract' (1948) 64 LQR 230.

Wynn-Evans, 'Restrictive Covenants and Confidential Information' (1977) 18 Bus LR 247.

13

Third party rights and the doctrine of privity

AIMS AND OBJECTIVES

After reading this chapter you should be able to:

- Understand the basis of the doctrine of privity
- Understand the effect of the doctrine on third parties to contracts
- Understand the exceptions to the doctrine developed by the courts
- Understand the effects of the Contracts (Rights of Third Parties) Act 1999 on third party rights
- Critically analyse the area
- Apply the law to factual situations and reach conclusions

13.1 The doctrine of privity of contract

13.1.1 The basic rule

This is possibly the most contentious of all the rules that remain from the basic definitions of contract law. The rule works in conjunction with aspects of the rules on consideration, particularly that in *Tweddle v Atkinson* [1861] 121 ER 762, that nobody can sue or be sued on a contract who has not provided consideration under the contract. The doctrine, simply stated, is that any person who is not a party to the contract can neither sue on it nor can they be sued under it.

We have already seen this in operation in *Tweddle v Atkinson* (see section 3.2.2). Here, even though the claimant was named in a written agreement he was unable to claim an enforceable third party right as he had provided no consideration for the original agreement. Put in the context of privity, he could not seek to enforce a contract to which he was not an actual party even though he was named in the contract as a potential beneficiary of the agreement.

A number of justifications have been made for the rule but none of them is entirely satisfactory:

- Since contract law concerns bargains it is said that it would be unfair to allow a person to gain under a bargain when he has actually provided nothing in return for the benefit gained from the arrangement.
- Another way of putting this is that it would be unfair to impose an obligation on a party who has played no part in the agreement; for example, if A and B agree that A will pay B a certain price if C performs some service for A then why should C be bound when he has not been a party to the agreement in the first place?
- It is also said that it is unfair to allow somebody the right to sue on a contract when he cannot be sued.
- Finally, it is a common characteristic of contract law, that it cannot be used to enforce purely gratuitous promises and this would be possible without the operation of the doctrine.

Like many basic principles of contract law, the doctrine is actually quite old and certainly was given definition and application during the period of *laissez-faire* economics in the nineteenth century.

CASE EXAMPLE

Price v Easton [1833] 110 ER 518

Here, Easton had agreed with another party that if that party did specified work for him he would pay £19 to Price, a third party to the contract. While the work was completed by the other party, Easton nevertheless failed to pay Price who then sued to try to enforce the contract. Price's claim was unsuccessful. He had given no consideration for the arrangement and was not therefore a party to the contract either and gained no enforceable rights under it.

The modern statement of the rule demonstrates the point that, even with quite closely connected commercial arrangements that appear almost as a sequence, there is still a need to maintain the independence of the individual contracts and to comply with the rules of contract at all times. The statement of the law is found in Lord Haldane's judgment in the case below.

CASE EXAMPLE

Dunlop Pneumatic Tyre Co Ltd v Selfridge & Co Ltd [1915] AC 847

In a contract dated 12th October 1911 Dew & Co, who were wholesalers, agreed to buy tyres from Dunlop, who were tyre manufacturers. They did so on an express undertaking in the contract that they would not sell the tyres below certain prices fixed by the manufacturers. Dew & Co also undertook to obtain the same price-fixing agreements from clients to whom they sold on. Dew then sold tyres on to Selfridge on these terms. However, Selfridge broke the agreement and sold tyres at discount prices. Dunlop sued Selfridge, the third party, and sought an injunction. It failed for lack of privity. (The case would of course now be subject to the Competition Act 1998 or EU Law.)

JUDGMENT

In the House of Lords Lord Haldane explained the principle briefly and clearly: 'only a person who is a party to a contract can sue on it. Our law knows nothing of a *jus quaesitum tertio* arising by way of contract. Such a right may be conferred by way of property, as, for example, under a trust, but it cannot be conferred on a stranger to a contract as a right to enforce the contract *in personam*'.

JUDGMENT

Lord Dunedin, while feeling forced by virtue of the doctrine to find against Dunlop because of its lack of privity, nevertheless commented on the unfairness of the doctrine: 'the effect of that doctrine in the present case is to make it possible for a person to snap his fingers at a bargain deliberately made, a bargain not unfair in itself, and which the person seeking to enforce it has a legitimate interest to enforce'.

In diagram form, the rule can be shown very easily, as follows:

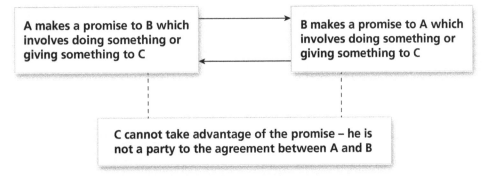

Figure 13.1 The basic operation of the doctrine of privity of contract

13.1.2 Consequences and problems associated with the rule

The rule clearly has very obvious purposes. Nevertheless the rule can also be seen as both unpractical and unfair and has a number of specific consequences:

- A person who receives goods as a gift will be unable to sue personally where the goods are defective.
- In such a case it may prove embarrassing to that person to try to enlist the help of the actual purchaser of the goods and as a result he may lose the value of the gift.
- Even if the purchaser is approached and does sue, he will in most cases only be able to recover for his own loss, the price of the goods, and not necessarily for the loss suffered by the person receiving the gift.
- The rule may well prevent enforcement of services that have already been paid for. This was indeed the case in *Price v Easton* [1833] 110 ER 518, meaning that a person who has acted in good faith has nevertheless lost out.
- The rule may also mean that a benefactor's express wishes are denied, as was the case in *Tweddle v Atkinson*.

student mentor tip

"Contract law can be difficult but if you read in advance of lectures and seminars it will help you in the long run."

Adil, Queen Mary University

- More dramatically, in commercial contracts, as Lord Dunedin identified in *Dunlop v Selfridge* [1915] AC 847, the rule may actually enable a party to accept the specific terms of an agreement and yet have no intention of carrying them out or operating according to the terms to which they have agreed.
- In any case the doctrine does not sit comfortably with the reality of modern commercial contracting.

As a result, the rule has been widely criticised and there have been consistent calls for its reform until eventually this was partly achieved through statute in the form of the Contracts (Rights of Third Parties) Act 1999. Even this was late in coming. As early as 1937, the Law Revision Committee, in its report on the doctrine, expressed dissatisfaction with the rule. It recommended that where third party benefits were expressly stipulated in a contractual agreement, they should be enforceable by the third party in the same way that other rights were enforceable by the actual parties to the agreement.

Judges have also been critical of the rule and over time have created a number of exceptions where it would not apply.

13.2 The Exceptions to the basic rule

13.2.1 Introduction

Not surprisingly, the rule is unpopular and many attempts have been made to avoid the harsh effects of the rule on enforcing third party rights in a contract. The courts have achieved this by using a variety of means or simple case law principles. However, most of these have no foundation in contract law and none of them has really affected the basic rule.

13.2.2 Statutory exceptions

Parliament, as the supreme law-maker, is inevitably not bound by the strict rules of contract law when enacting new provisions. The result is that there are a number of statutory inroads into the rule.

One example comes under s 148(7) of the Road Traffic Act 1988. This obliges a motorist to take out third party liability insurance. Another motorist who is involved in an accident with this motorist can then rely upon the statutory provision for recovery of compensation for damage or any loss. The insurance is enforceable despite the fact that the other motorist lacks any privity in the insurance contract.

Another example, again concerning insurance, arises under the Married Women's Property Act 1882. Under this Act a husband can take out insurance in his own name but identify it as being for the benefit of his wife and children. They can then enforce the terms of the insurance despite not having been parties to the contract between the husband/father and the insurance company.

There have, of course, been attempts made to use statute out of context in order to avoid the effects of the rule. In such cases, however, the courts have not been prepared to allow an Act to be used for an entirely incorrect purpose and such attempts have failed.

CASE EXAMPLE

Beswick v Beswick [1968] AC 58

A coal merchant, Peter Beswick, sold his business to his nephew, John Beswick. The contract contained two specific undertakings required of the nephew. The first was that the nephew should provide Peter with an income of £6, 10s (50p) for the rest of Peter's life.

The second was that after Peter's death John should provide Peter's widow with a weekly annuity of £5. Peter Beswick then died intestate and John Beswick made only one payment of £5 to Peter's widow. The widow then sued both as administratrix of her dead husband's estate and on her own behalf in trying to enforce the agreement for the weekly annuity. The agreement was clearly a condition in the sale of her husband's business to the nephew, but the widow also clearly lacked privity to the agreement and had provided no consideration for it. In pursuing her own action she attempted to use a provision in s 56(1) of the Law of Property Act 1925 stating that: 'A person may take an immediate interest or other interest in land or other property ... although he may not be named as a party to the conveyance or other instrument'. In the Court of Appeal she succeeded in her claim for specific performance of her dead husband's contract with John. In respect of her own claim using s 56, Lord Denning and Dankwerts LJ held that since the 1925 Act at s 205 also provided that: 'unless the context otherwise requires ... Property includes ... real or personal property' and thus accepted her claim that s 56 exempted the widow from the application of the doctrine of privity and that she could, as a result, succeed. The effect of the Court of Appeal decision was to create another major exception to the doctrine of privity. In John's appeal to the House of Lords the court upheld the right to specific performance of the husband's contract with John. However, it rejected the reasoning and the decision of the Court of Appeal in respect of the wife's claim under s 56. The court held that since the Act referred only to real property (land or interests in land) it could not appropriately be applied to purely personal property in this manner.

JUDGMENT

Lord Hodson commented: 'I am of the opinion that s 56 ... does not have the revolutionary effect claimed for it ... that the context does require a limited meaning to be given to the word "property" in the section.'

13.2.3 Trust law

Despite lacking privity, a party identifying third party rights under a contract may be able to show that a trust of the rights is created in his favour. Trust law, for example, can be used in the case of enforcing the rights of beneficiaries under wills or indeed even where no will is made. It is also useful where ownership of or interests in land is in question. The simple point is that a party gains a right in equity that is legally enforceable. The simple distinction from contract law is that there is no requirement that the party has provided some form of consideration in return for the right or that he is party to any actual agreement. Inevitably, what must be proved is that the right alleged does in fact create a trust in favour of that party by which another party is bound.

CASE EXAMPLE

Gregory & Parker v Williams (1817) 3 Mer 582

Parker owed money to both Gregory and Williams. Since he could see no way of organising settlement of his debts himself, he assigned all of his property to Williams on the understanding that Williams would then pay off the debt to Gregory. Williams failed to pay over the money to Gregory. Gregory, of course, was not a party to the agreement between Parker and Williams and as a result was unable to sue on it in contract law. However, the court was nevertheless prepared to accept Gregory's argument that a trust of the money had been created in Gregory's favour, which was then enforceable against

Williams. There was never any intention that Williams should keep all of the money; a beneficial interest was created in Gregory's favour; and Williams held the sum of the debt owed to Gregory by Parker only as a trustee. Williams was therefore bound to return this money to Gregory.

Trust law operates because a clear intention can be shown for the holder of certain property to pass it on to the person entitled to it. It is this express or implied intention that a person who is not party to a contractual agreement should benefit under it that allows equity to intervene. In this way the court will not accept that a trust is created unless the claimant can show an intention that he should receive the benefit.

CASE EXAMPLE

Les Affreteurs Reunis SA v Walford (Walford's Case) [1919] AC 801

Walford was a broker who negotiated an agreement between a charterparty and the owner of the vessel, but was obviously not a party to the agreement. The agreement was between the owners of the vessel and the charterparty only. The agreement contained a stipulation that Walford should receive a 3 per cent commission from the shipowners for securing the agreement. They failed to pay and Walford sued for his commission. The court was prepared to accept that a trust was created only because he was named as receiving a benefit under the agreement.

The courts will not in any case accept that a trust is created unless there is a clear intention to create one. So it will not automatically follow that a person who is not a party to a contract but appears to gain an interest under it can automatically claim that a trust exists. Before the court will accept and enforce the benefit it must be satisfied that the interest claimed conforms to the general character of a trust.

CASE EXAMPLE

Green v Russell [1959] 2 QB 226

Here, an employer had insurance in his own name that also covered certain employees including Green and was expressed as being for the benefit of dependent relatives. There was, however, no such requirement in the contract of employment. When both men were killed in a fire, the insurance company would not pay Green's wife, who then sued. The Court of Appeal concluded that there was no trust in favour of Green since the employer could have surrendered the policy at any time. In contrast, in a trust the beneficiary would be bound by the terms of the trust which could not be changed so readily.

In this way the cases in which a claimant might claim that a trust is created are probably quite limited in their application in avoiding the doctrine of privity. In any case use of the trust is not a means of a third party enforcing the contract through contract law itself but rather looks to a different area of law for a remedy.

13.2.4 Restrictive covenants

This is another device created by equity by which a party selling land retains certain rights over the use of the land. The covenant is obviously enforceable between the original vendor and original purchaser because they are in a straightforward contractual relationship. However, even though the original seller is not a party to any subsequent sales of the land, as a result of the device he might nevertheless still enforce the original agreement against new owners.

Because equity rather than common law created the device and because equity will not impose unfair burdens, the restriction created in the covenant must be a negative one. Obvious examples are preventing use of the land for business purposes or preventing building on the land.

The covenant is said to run with the land. So, if properly created, it will bind subsequent purchasers of the land even though there is no privity between them and the original seller. This will apply even if the land retained by the original seller has also been sold on.

CASE EXAMPLE

Tulk v Moxhay [1848] 41 ER 1143

Tulk owned certain land in London that he sold with an express undertaking that it would never be used to build property on. The land was then re-sold on numerous occasions, each time subject to the same undertaking, until Moxhay eventually bought it. Moxhay bought it knowing of the limitation but nevertheless intended to build on it. Tulk sought an injunction to prevent this building from taking place and was successful. The court accepted that it would be against conscience for Moxhay to buy, knowing of the restriction, and it was prepared to grant the injunction and enforce the original agreement even though Moxhay had never been a party to it.

It must be remembered, though, that the device will generally operate only in respect of land. The courts have usually resisted attempts to extend the principle to cover other property. In this way it is not possible to claim the mechanism merely as a method of enforcing an agreement controlling the pricing of goods.

CASE EXAMPLE

Taddy v Sterious [1904] 1 Ch 354

Tobacco manufacturers sold tobacco to wholesalers with an express condition in the contract requiring that retailers should not sell below fixed prices. When this agreement was breached, one argument that the manufacturer tried to use in an attempt to enforce the condition was that *Tulk v Moxhay* could be applied. In other words, they were suggesting that, even though there was no contractual relationship between manufacturers and the retailers who had breached the condition, the contractual provision in the contract with the wholesalers should run with the goods in the same way that the restrictive covenant runs with the land. The court rejected this argument out of hand and held that restrictive covenants were a mechanism that applied only to rights in land.

Nevertheless, the principle has subsequently been applied in other contexts even though this was by the Privy Council. However, the use of the principle outside of the context of rights in land has also been heavily criticised.

CASE EXAMPLE

Lord Strathcona Steamship Co v Dominion Coal Co [1926] AC 108

Dominion Coal had a long-term charter of a ship. The ship was actually sold on many times during the course of the charter and eventually to the Lord Strathcona Steamship Co. These new owners knew of the charter when they bought the ship from its previous owners with whom they had agreed that they would abide by the charter after the purchase. Nevertheless, they refused to hand the ship over to Dominion Coal for the charter, which then sued. The steamship company defended its actions by arguing that, since it had never been a party to the charter, it could not be bound by it. Quite uniquely, the Privy Council chose to apply *Tulk v Moxhay* principles in the case and held that the new owners were bound by the charter even though they had not been a party to the agreement.

While this application of the principle has been criticised, it has also more recently been reviewed. The question considered by the court was whether where a person acquires property from another person who has entered into a binding agreement with a third party to use that property for a specific purpose, the person acquiring the property is bound to use the property for the agreed purpose and not for any purpose which would be inconsistent with the agreement.

CASE EXAMPLE

Law Debenture Trust Corporation plc v Ural Caspian Corporation Ltd [1993] 2 All ER 355

Shareholders of companies which traded in Russia prior to the 1917 Revolution and whose assets were later confiscated by the Soviet Government without compensation agreed to sell their shareholdings to another company, Leisure Investments (Overseas) Ltd. A condition of the agreement was that if the Soviet authorities ever did pay compensation for the confiscation that it should be used for the benefit of the existing shareholders. All parties later covenanted for the same with the claimants, who were acting as the trustees of the shareholders. The shareholdings were then sold on to another company and finally to the defendants but in neither case were these sales subjected to the same covenants originally agreed and that should have been inserted in these contracts of sale, although in each case there was knowledge of the covenant. When compensation was paid but was not passed on to the claimants as required by the original agreement, they sued. Hoffmann J concluded that there was no arguable claim since there was no actual contractual agreement between the claimants and the defendants.

13.2.5 Privity of estate in leases

Where an owner of land creates a lease in favour of another person, the terms of the lease are in effect contractual obligations. These terms are more usually known as the 'covenants' of the lease and are enforceable by both parties because there is privity between them.

The principle of 'privity of estate' means that the landowner will be able to enforce the covenants also against anybody to whom the holder of the lease then assigns their lease. By ss 141 and 142 of the Law of Property Act 1925, a tenant will also be able to enforce covenants of the lease against a new owner of the freehold. In the same way the new landlord will be able to enforce the covenants against the tenant.

However, the landlord will not have privity with a sub-tenant, although the sub-tenant may be sued by the lessee for breach of covenants.

13.2.6 The rule in *Dunlop v Lambert*

There is a common law rule of commercial law origins which states that a remedy can be granted to a party notwithstanding the absence of privity of contract. The rule will allow a remedy to be awarded 'where no other would be available to a person sustaining loss which under a rational legal system ought to be compensated by the person who caused it'. This is the rule from the case of *Dunlop v Lambert* [1839] 6 Cl & F 600. It operates where the parties to a contract have contemplated that a breach of the contract would lead to a loss to an identifiable third party who, though not a party to the contract, might depend on its completion.

The origins of the rule were in contracts for the carriage of goods. It allowed the consignor of goods to sue for damages caused by the carrier where the goods had become the property of the consignee before transit but the consignee had no rights to sue under the contract of carriage. It ensured that there was an action for damages where otherwise lack of privity would mean that no action was possible despite an obvious loss resulting from a breach of contract.

More recently, the rule has been considered and has been both approved and applied.

CASE EXAMPLE

Darlington BC v Wiltshier Northern Ltd [1995] 1 WLR 68

The council wanted a new recreation centre. In order to avoid certain financial restraints it was under, it hired Morgan Grenfell who in turn hired the builders of the new centre. A collateral agreement provided for Morgan Grenfell to pay the builders, Wiltshier Northern Ltd, and for the council to reimburse Morgan Grenfell and for Morgan Grenfell to assign all rights it might have against Wiltshier to the council. When £2 million worth of defects were discovered in the building, the council obviously wished to sue. Morgan Grenfell would be unable to recover in tort, having no proprietary interest in the building. The council would normally be prevented from suing because of its lack of privity in the building contract. However, Lord Diplock applied the principle in *Dunlop v Lambert* and allowed the action. The justification was that Morgan Grenfell was the fiduciary of the council and had assigned its rights in the building contract over to the council.

But there is also a proviso that the rule will not be applied where the parties to the original contract, the consignor and the carrier had contemplated that there would be a separate contract between carrier and consignee to regulate liability between them. This proviso has also been considered recently.

CASE EXAMPLE

Alfred McAlpine Construction Ltd v Panatown Ltd (1998) 88 BLR 67

McAlpine was employed by Panatown to design and build a multi-storey car park. When this contract was formed, McAlpine also entered into a 'duty of care deed' with Unex Investment Properties Ltd (UIPL) who were the actual owners of the site. When Panatown sued McAlpine, claiming that the building was so defective that it would need to be rebuilt, McAlpine countered that Panatown had never been the owner of the site and it was UIPL that had suffered the loss, not them – so that Panatown could claim only nominal damages and UIPL nothing at all since they were not parties to the contract. The Court of Appeal held that the rule in *Dunlop v Lambert* was relevant (that a contracting party could recover damages even though it was a third party who suffered the actual loss). The issue then was whether the proviso applied to prevent recovery by Panatown. The Court of Appeal accepted that the deed with UIPL indicated that contractual rights had been given to the third party but that on the facts since all accounts were bound to be settled between Panatown and McAlpine then Panatown must have the right to sue on behalf of the third party. (However, the House of Lords took a different view (see section 13.2.8).)

The rule in *Dunlop v Lambert* of course still has limitations despite the fact that it has now been extended to operate in a broader context than merely contracts for the carriage of goods. It will only operate in situations where damage has been caused to property which has been transferred to a third party by one of the parties to the contract. Therefore it cannot be used as a general means of avoiding the restraints caused by the doctrine of privity of contract. Brian Coote makes the following comment on the development of the doctrine:

QUOTATION

'The Panatown case raised questions fundamental to the nature of contractual damages. They include questions about which differing views have been long held and it would be asking too much to hope that they could have been resolved in a single case.'

B Coote 'Performance Interest' (2001) 117 LQR 95

13.2.7 Procedural rules

In very rare instances, rules of procedure have been used to get round the effects of the doctrine of privity. Such a course has only succeeded because to do so has corresponded to the actual promise made, and because all of the parties are present in the court.

injunction

An equitable remedy which prevents one party from doing something

Where the contractual term that has been breached is a promise to refrain from a particular course of action, then the appropriate remedy would be an **injunction**. In this way, if the promise is one not to sue the other party then the correct procedure may be to ask the court to stay proceedings rather than to seek an injunction. The courts on at least one occasion have shown a willingness to get round the restrictions of the doctrine of privity by use of this device.

CASE EXAMPLE

Snelling v John G Snelling Ltd [1973] 1 QB 87

Three brothers were all directors of their own company, John G Snelling Ltd. The company was financed by loans from the three brothers. When the company borrowed money from a finance company, the three brothers entered into an agreement with one another. The nature of the agreement was such that until such time as the finance company loan was repaid, if any of them resigned their directorship in the company they would forfeit the amount of their own loan to the company. The company itself was not a party to this agreement. One brother later did leave the company and resign his directorship and he sued the company for return of his loan. The remaining two brothers applied to join the company as defendants and counter-claimed, on the basis of the agreement reached between the three brothers, that the forfeiture agreement should apply. The court upheld their argument. Even though the company was not a party to the agreement, the brothers and the company were in many ways the same and thus all parties to the action were in effect present in the court. The court held that a stay of execution of the brother's claim was the appropriate order in the particular circumstances of the case.

13.2.8 Actions on behalf of a third party beneficiary and the so-called 'holiday cases'

The issue of recovery for mental distress and the 'holiday cases' is also a relevant topic of discussion in the context of damages and is discussed later (see section 16.1.6). However, significant development was also made in these cases in respect of third party rights.

The doctrine of privity makes it inevitable that a person may only sue in his own name on a contract to which he is actually a party. Nevertheless, at times it has appeared possible that, in certain fairly limited circumstances, a party may sue not only on his own behalf but on behalf of other people who would have benefited from the contract and who would have suffered a loss as the result of its breach.

CASE EXAMPLE

Jackson v Horizon Holidays [1975] 1 WLR 1468

Jackson had booked a 'family holiday' from Horizon Holidays, the booking being in his sole name. The holiday was a complete disaster and fell far short of the contract description. Jackson sued the holiday company not only on his own behalf but on behalf of his family also. The company, while accepting liability, disputed that it should pay damages awarded by the trial judge in respect of the family since there was no privity of contract. In the Court of Appeal it was held that the loss of enjoyment suffered by the family was in effect a loss to the contracting party himself. He had paid for a 'family holiday' but not received it. Damages were awarded on this basis. This would appear to be straining the law a long way, albeit in order to achieve a just result.

JUDGMENT

In upholding the claim Lord Denning quoted from the judgment of Lush LJ in *Lloyd's v Harper* (1880) 16 Ch D 290 at p 321: 'I consider it to be an established rule of law that where a contract is made with A for the benefit of B, A can sue on the contract for the benefit of B and recover all that B could have recovered if the contract had been made with B himself.' As a result Lord Denning felt that the claimant was able to recover 'for the discomfort, vexation and upset which the whole party have suffered by reason of the breach of contract'. As he explained: 'People look forward to a holiday. They expect the promises to be fulfilled. When it fails, they are greatly disappointed and upset. It is difficult to assess in terms of money; but it is the task of the judges to do the best they can.'

Lord Denning took a simplistic view that an action is acceptable generally to recover damages in respect of third party beneficiaries. The House of Lords, however, has indicated that this method of getting round the doctrine of privity is not generally applicable and is confined only to 'holiday contracts'.

CASE EXAMPLE

Woodar Investment Development Ltd v Wimpey Construction (UK) Ltd [1980] 1 WLR 277

The contract involved the sale of 14 acres of land to the defendants for £850,000, completion to be two months after granting of certain planning permission or a set date, whichever came earlier. Under the contract a third party was also to be paid £150,000 on completion. The market then fell and so the defendants unlawfully repudiated the contract. The House of Lords had to decide whether damages should include the sum payable to the third party. The House, while not expressly overruling the *Jackson* case, held that there was no general principle allowing a party to a contract to sue on behalf of third parties injured by a breach of the contract. Lord Wilberforce's view was that *Jackson* fell into a specialist group of contracts involving families where it was intended that the benefit of the contract should be shared between the members of the family. The House also rejected Lord Denning's interpretation of the judgment of Lush LJ in *Lloyd's v Harper* and identified that this referred specifically to the relationship between agents and their principals and could not be applied generally as Lord Denning had suggested.

JUDGMENT

Lord Wilberforce explained the difficulty: 'The extract on which [Lord Denning] relied from the judgment of Lush LJ in *Lloyd's v Harper* … is no authority for the proposition required in Jackson's case, still less for the proposition required here, that, if Woodar made a contract for a sum of money to be paid to Transworld, Woodar can, without showing that it has itself suffered loss or that Woodar was agent or trustee for Transworld, sue for damages for non-payment of that sum. Assuming that *Jackson's* case was correctly decided, it does not carry the present case, where the factual situation is quite different.'

Nevertheless, the Law Lords have at a later stage appeared to relax their attitudes to using this means to avoid the limitations of the doctrine. In doing so they appear to have created yet another exception.

CASE EXAMPLE

Linden Gardens Ltd v Lenesta Sludge Disposals Ltd [1994] AC 85

Property developers and a building company contracted for the construction of shops, offices and flats. Before the building work was complete the property company assigned its interest over to a third party who was to use the completed buildings. However, it did so without gaining the permission of the builders so that there was no contractual relationship between the builders and the third party. At a later stage defects were discovered in the building work which had occurred after the assignment had taken place. The property company sued the builders who counter-claimed with the argument that at the time of the defective work, the property had passed to the third party and so no loss had been suffered by the property company. The basic rule on privity would mean that it could not sue on the behalf of the third party. The House of Lords rejected this argument and applied the rule in *Dunlop v Lambert*, extending its application from carriage of goods to property. The House held that, since the builders knew that the property company would inevitably transfer the property to another party, the whole purpose of the development in the first place, then the builders would have known that in the case of any defective work amounting to a breach of the original building contract, it would be this third party that would suffer loss.

The law is not static in this area and the House of Lords has considered the various applications of and exceptions to the rule more recently, although without particularly clarifying the law.

Alfred McAlpine Construction Ltd v Panatown Ltd [2000] 4 All ER 97

McAlpine was employed by Panatown to design and build a multi-storey car park but had also entered into a 'duty of care deed' with Unex Investment Properties Ltd (UIPL), the actual owners of the site. When the building work was defective and Panatown sued, the Court of Appeal accepted that the 'duty of care deed' with UIPL gave contractual rights to it but also accepted that Panatown must have the right to sue. The House of Lords was split three to two on this issue. Panatown argued that it could recover as a result of both the narrower principle from *Dunlop v Lambert* and the broader principle from the *Linden Gardens* case. The House of Lords held that the existence of the 'duty of care deed' with UIPL prevented Panatown from suing. The deed meant that the third party was given a specific remedy by the contract even though this remedy was more limited than that which would have been available under Panatown's breach of contract action. The judges in the majority accepted the narrow principle from *Dunlop v Lambert* as a recognised exception but felt that its application was inappropriate and unnecessary in the case because of the 'duty of care deed'. They were more sceptical about the legitimacy of the broader principle from *Linden Gardens*. The two judges dissenting, Lord Goff and Lord Millett, would have been prepared to allow Panatown to recover under either principle.

The law is still rather unclear on this area, then. Inevitably, parties may find an alternative course of action under the Contracts (Rights of Third Parties) Act 1999 (see section 13.4). A lot depends on how contracts are drafted.

13.2.9 Protecting third parties in exclusion clauses

A party to a contract can include an exclusion clause or a limitation clause in a contract relieving or reducing the extent of liability in the case of a breach. Because of the potential unfairness on the other party, such clauses themselves have been subject to rigorous scrutiny by the courts and also statutory controls. (See Chapter 7.)

While such clauses may be relied upon by the parties to the contract, the traditional view, however, was that they would offer no protection to third parties so that a sub-contractor would be unable to claim the benefit of the exclusion clause, even if he had been named under it.

Scruttons Ltd v Midland Silicones Ltd [1962] AC 446

A shipping company was carrying a drum of chemicals for the claimants under a contract containing a clause limiting damages in the event of breach to $500. Stevedores were sub-contracted to the shipping company and then did $1,800 worth of damage. The stevedores attempted to rely on the limitation clause but failed because of their lack of privity. The court held that as the stevedores were not parties to the contract they could not enforce or take the benefit of clauses within the major contract.

JUDGMENT

However, Lord Reid did feel that there could be 'success in agency if the bill of lading makes it clear that the stevedore is intended to be protected by the provisions'.

Despite this, there have been exceptional situations in which third parties have been able to claim cover under an exclusion or limitation clause despite lacking any privity with the major contract.

CASE EXAMPLE

New Zealand Shipping Co Ltd v A M Satterthwaite & Co Ltd (The Euryme- don) [1974] AC 154

Carriers contracted with the consignors of goods to ship drilling equipment. The carriers hired stevedores to unload the equipment, and through the stevedores' negligence, substantial damage was caused to the equipment. The contract between the consignors and the carriers included a limitation clause. This clause also identified that the limitation extended to any servant or agent of the carriers. The stevedores sought to rely on this clause to limit their liability. The Privy Council accepted that there was a contractual relationship based on agency. The Privy Council held that the stevedores could succeed and rely on the limitation clause. The reasoning given by Lord Wilberforce was that the stevedores were identified as agents in the contract. The stevedores were also able to succeed because of the very strained view of consideration taken by the court. (See section 3.3.)

13.2.10 Collateral contracts

In its simplest form a collateral contract is one where in effect one party is induced into entering a contract as a result of a promise made by a party who is not a party to the contract.

As a result it can sometimes be used as a means of avoiding the doctrine of privity by allowing the person entering the contract to sue the third party on the basis of the promise made. The mechanism might succeed therefore when the claimant complains that he has only entered the contract because of the reliance on the collateral promise made by the third party to the contract.

CASE EXAMPLE

Shanklin Pier v Detel Products Ltd [1951] 2 KB 854

The claimants owned a pier and were assured by the representatives of the defendants, paint manufacturers, that their paint was suitable to paint the pier in that it was durable and weather resistant. They had also been promised that the paint would not flake or peel and would last a minimum of seven years. Relying on this assurance, the pier owners then contracted with painting contractors to paint the pier and instructed them to use Detel's paint. The paint was in fact unsuitable and very quickly peeled, in fact within three months. The pier owners were unable to sue the painters who had completed the painting professionally and there was no question of their workmanship being at fault: the sole fault was the quality of the paint. The pier owners were not a party to the contract between the painters and Detel for the purchase of the paint and so would normally be unable to sue. Nevertheless, in the pier owners' action against Detel, the court held that Detel was liable on the promise despite any apparent lack of privity in the painting contract. Detel had made a collateral promise on which the pier owners were able to rely and sue when the promise was broken.

Of course, it is arguable whether collateral contracts can technically be seen as an exception to the privity rule. The whole point is that the court is in fact identifying a contract between the two parties based on the collateral promise even though the relationship seems somewhat more indirect. The party making the promise gains the benefit of selling their goods because their promise has induced the other party to enter into a quite separate contract with another party. As a result they must be bound by their promise. Therefore, the device can be quite useful in modern contracting.

13.3 Agency, assignment and negotiable instruments

13.3.1 Introduction

All of the exceptions to privity that have been considered so far are enforceable either because of principles contained in individual cases, whether these have been later developed or not, or because they rely on areas of law other than contract, such as trust law.

There are, however, some major exceptions to the doctrine of privity, which operate within contract law, where the precise nature of the contractual relationship itself is that it must inevitably involve three parties rather than the two that we would normally expect.

There are three main situations in which this will occur:

- **agency**
- **assignment of interests**
- **negotiable instruments**

13.3.2 Agency

An agency situation involves three very specific parties:

- The **principal** – this is the person on whose behalf the contract is made. There are a number of reasons why the principal is not the actual person making the contract, but in all cases it is the principal that is taking the benefit from the contract rather than the agent.
- The **agent** – this is the party who is actually a party to the formation of the contract with a third party with whom he has a direct relationship, but the agent merely makes the contract on behalf of the principal and not on his own behalf.
- The **third party** – this is the party with whom the agent contracts on behalf of the principal and who as a result of the very special rules enjoys a series of mutual rights and obligations with the principal, but there is no contractual relationship with the agent.

The agency relationship is an essential feature of business and indeed a 'commercial agent' is a specific type of agent, now covered by very specific rules as a result of EU legislation. Nevertheless the agency relationship can arise in a less formal manner. In this way agency situations can be many and varied. Just a few examples are:

- Employees on behalf of their employers, eg, the shop assistant who enters into contracts of sale on behalf of the business.
- Company officers on behalf of the company, eg, the director who enters into contracts on behalf of the company.
- A family member on behalf of another family member, eg, the child sent to the shops on an errand for his parents.

Where one party acts as an agent for another, the principal, then the agent can make and carry out contracts with a third party on the principal's behalf. The significance of this is that the agent can make agreements by which the principal is bound despite the apparent lack of privity. Where all of the appropriate rules are complied with then the principal and the third party are able to sue and be sued by each other under the contract made by the agent. At all times it should be remembered that, even where a person is employed to act as an agent, the term refers to a relationship, not a job.

In diagram form, the nature of the agency relationship can be compared very easily with the standard situation in privity, as follows:

The relationship between agent, principal and third party

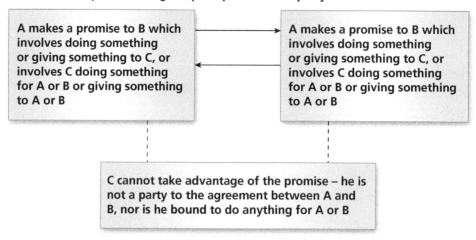

The strict application of the doctrine of privity

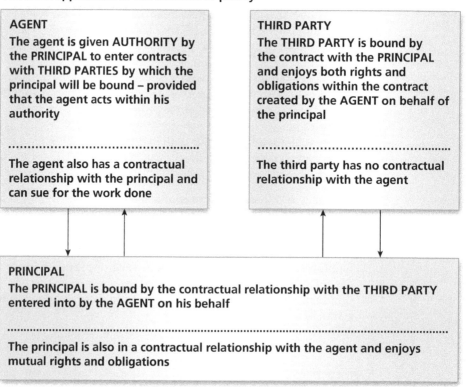

Figure 13.2 The comparison between the simple rule on privity of contract and the agency relationship

The creation of agency

The agency relationship is significant because the rules on agency allow the agent to form contracts with third parties on behalf of a principal which then binds those last two parties. Agency arises in different ways and the extent of the authority that the agent has depends on how the agency relationship arises.

Express agreement between agent and principal

Here, inevitably, the extent of the authority given to the agent is identified in the express agreement between the parties. This is generally referred to as 'express authority'.

Implied agreement between agent and principal

Here, the authority of the agent to bind the principal to a contract is identified by an objective test of the intention of the parties, and the agent will have the authority to carry out all such acts as are incidental to the performance of his duties.

One way that the authority arises is because of the conduct of the parties.

CASE EXAMPLE

Hely-Hutchinson v Brayhead Ltd [1967] 3 All ER 98

Here, the directors of a company allowed the chairman to act as though he was in fact the managing director, although he had never been appointed to that role and so had no express authority to bind the company. The company was held to be bound by transactions entered into by the chairman as a result.

The agent also has implied authority to act in any way that is incidental to the performance of his duties, even where there is no express authority given for the act in question.

CASE EXAMPLE

Mullens v Miller (1822) 2 Ch D 194

An estate agent was held to have implied authority to give details and make warranties in respect of properties that he was selling.

Sometimes the agent is given what is known as customary authority (sometimes referred to as usual authority). This means that the agent can perform acts and enter transactions that are customary with a particular trade.

CASE EXAMPLE

Watteau v Fenwick [1893] 1 QB 346

Here, the agent was the manager of a public house and had express authority to buy goods for the business. His principal had instructed that the manager should not, however, purchase cigars which the owner would be supplying himself. The manager then bought cigars from the claimant who then sued the principal for the price. The court held with the claimant since he was unaware of the instruction to the manager and it was customary in the trade for managers to buy in all stock.

Even where the agent has no express or implied authority for the particular transaction he may still bind the principal if the latter ratifies the contract. For ratification to have effect:

- the agent must have actually entered the contract on the principal's behalf (so an undisclosed principal cannot ratify the agreement)
- the principal must exist at the time the agreement between third party and agent was reached
- the principal must have known of the transaction made by the agent
- the transaction must not be void or unenforceable.

CASE EXAMPLE

Kelner v Baxter (1866) LR 2 CP 174

Here, a number of people joined together to form a company and before it was in fact formed they ordered wine. The company then ratified the agreement but went into liquidation before it paid for the wine. The seller sued the purchasers who claimed that the company was liable rather than they were because it had ratified the purchase. They were held personally liable because the company did not exist at the time of the contract.

Operation of law

Here, the agent's authority to bind the principal comes from a number of possible sources:

- from a specific **Act of Parliament**, eg, under the Consumer Credit Act 1974 where the dealer setting up a transaction on credit is deemed to be the agent of the finance company; or
- out of **necessity**, eg, in shipping contracts where a ship's captain will be identified as having the authority to sell the cargo in certain circumstances; or
- from a **presumption** in a particular type of relationship, eg, in cohabitation.

In such circumstances the agent may act with what is referred to as apparent authority, sometimes called ostensible authority, and sometimes the situation is referred to as agency by estoppel, because the circumstances mean that the principal is 'estopped' or prevented from denying the agent's authority to bind him.

CASE EXAMPLE

Spiro v Lintern [1973] 3 All ER 319

Here, a wife instructed estate agents on her husband's behalf to sell his house. The estate agents found a purchaser and a contract of sale was passed to the purchaser, although with no authority from the husband. However, the husband then allowed builders to work on the property for the purchaser. The husband then sold the house to another party and the original purchaser sued, claiming that the wife was the husband's agent and that a contract therefore existed. The court held that the husband by his acquiescence had represented that his wife was indeed acting for him and was thus estopped from denying that the wife had been given the authority to sell the house on his behalf.

In this way in order for apparent authority to apply the principal must have represented expressly or by conduct that a person was acting for him as agent who in fact had no such authority so that a third party relied on the representation in the transaction.

CASE EXAMPLE

Freeman & Lockyer v Buckhurst Park Properties (Mangal) Ltd
[1964] 2 QB 480

A company allowed one of its officers to act as managing director even though he had never been appointed to the role. The company then tried to avoid liability under a contract made by this officer. The Court of Appeal held that the officer bound the company to the transaction. While he had no express actual authority, the company directors had held him out as having authority and there was apparent authority for the transaction.

In commercial situations the courts will often find that authority arises through necessity. This will be because:

- The agent controlled the principal's property at the time in question.
- It was impossible for the agent to obtain instructions from the principal in the circumstances.
- The agent acted out of a genuine emergency.
- The agent also acted in good faith.

In such circumstances the actions of the agent are binding on the principal.

CASE EXAMPLE

Great Northern Railway Co v Swaffield (1874) LR Exch 132

A horse was delivered by train to the defendant who failed to collect the horse immediately. The railway company was bound to take the horse off the train. It could not contact the defendant and so had the horse fed and stabled. When the owner did collect the horse he refused to pay the costs of this. The court held that the railway company acted reasonably in the circumstances and the defendant was liable to pay for the stabling.

The relationship between principals and third parties

Generally, where the principal is **disclosed**, that is the third party **knows** that he is dealing through an agent, then the agent in effect has no further part in the contract once it is made. The principal and third party can of course sue each other under the normal principles of contract law.

Where the principal is **undisclosed**, that is the agent has **not** told the principal that he has acted only as an agent, then, provided that the agent acted with authority, the principal and third party can sue each other. This is obviously a major exception to the doctrine of privity. The third party can also of course sue the agent.

However, the situation is different in the case of an undisclosed principal where the terms of the contract are inconsistent with an agency relationship; where there is in any case an express clause in the contract that the agent is acting as a sole principal; and where the identity of the principal was of material significance to the third party in entering the contract.

Said v Butt [1920] 3 KB 497

A theatre critic knew that he was not welcome in a particular theatre because of poor reviews that he had given in the past. He wanted to go to the first night of a new play and so he got a friend to buy a ticket for him in the friend's name. He was refused admittance on the night and sued. The court held that his identity was critical to the willingness of the theatre to contract; he was an undisclosed principal; and his action failed.

The relationship between agents and their principals

The terms of the agency will ordinarily be determined by the agency agreement. The agent has two key duties to the principal: to carry out all instructions given, and to act with care and skill. The agent is also in a fiduciary relationship with the principal so he must avoid any conflict of interest and duty, must not take any bribe or secret profit and must account for all property belonging to the principal.

The agent also has certain rights. He can expect a full indemnity from the principal for all necessary expenses. He may also receive remuneration which is expressed or implied by the agency agreement. The agent in certain circumstances will also be able to exercise a lien over the principal's property in respect of debts arising out of the agency relationship.

The relationship between agents and third parties

In general, an agent incurs no liability to the third party. However, where the principal is undisclosed the agent may be liable to the third party. Even if the principal later becomes disclosed, the third party will have the choice of which to sue.

An agent can also be personally liable to the third party where he has made a misrepresentation. He may also be personally liable where he has acted in breach of his authority.

CASE EXAMPLE

Yonge v Toynbee [1910] 1 KB 215

A solicitor was instructed to act for a defendant in a case. Because the client then became insane, the solicitor's authority to act was then in effect terminated. As a result of this, all proceedings carried out by the solicitor after that date were struck out by the court and the solicitor was obliged to pay the other party's costs.

The termination of agency

The agency relationship can be ended either by the parties themselves or by operation of law. In the case of the latter this automatically terminates the agent's authority.

Termination by the parties

- The agency may end because it is for a **fixed time** and that time has lapsed.
- The agency may end because of an **express agreement** between the parties.
- If **one party** unilaterally ends the agency then that party may be in breach of contract.

Termination by operation of law

- The agency may be **frustrated** in the same way that other contracts are, eg, it becomes impossible.
- The agency may terminate because of the **death** of either party.
- The agency may be ended because of the **insanity** of either party.
- The agency may end because of the **bankruptcy** of either party.

The EU law on commercial agents

New law on commercial agents was introduced by the Commercial Agents (Council Directive) Regulations 1993. The Directive was obviously aimed at harmonising the law on commercial agents throughout the EU.

The Regulations set out the rights and duties of commercial agents and make express provision for remuneration and commission. They also cover minimum periods of notice and regulate termination of the agency relationship.

13.3.3 Assignment

Assignment is a specific system devised for the transfer of property rights. This may be appropriate, for instance, with debts and other 'choses in action'. If the assignment of the debt conforms to the proper rules of assignment then the party to whom the debt is assigned can sue the debtor, despite the apparent lack of privity between them. There are two methods of enforcing these rights:

- through **statutory provisions**
- through **equity**.

Assignment under s 136 of the Law of Property Act 1925

The section gives a general power of assignment which allows a party to assign or pass all of the rights under the debt or other choses in action as follows:

SECTION

'(a) the legal right to such debt or thing in action; (b) all legal and other remedies for the same; and (c) the power to give a good discharge for the same without the concurrence of the assignor.'

There are three further requirements within the section:

- The assignment must be **absolute** – if the assignment of the right is conditional or if only part of the right is being transferred, then equitable assignment would be needed for the transfer of right to be valid.
- The assignment must be **in writing** and **signed** by the assignor with the instruction to the debtor to pay instead to the assignee.
- As a natural consequence of the assignment of rights, the transfer must be given to the debtor which has effect when it is actually received.

However, one clear advantage of an assignment conforming to the statutory rules above is that there is no need for consideration by the assignee.

Assignment in equity

The precise rules on assignment in equity depend on whether the right assigned is legal or equitable. The latter is really much more to do with trust law. The right to enforce a contract is a legal right.

The assignment may be **absolute**, in which case the assignor gives up all rights in the thing in action. Alternatively it may be **non-absolute**. In this case the assignment takes the form of a charge which only entitles the assignee to payment from the total fund of the amount actually assigned to him.

CASE EXAMPLE

Jones v Humphreys [1902] 1 KB 10

A school teacher, in return for a £15 loan, assigned the necessary part of his salary that would pay the debt together with interest, as well as for any sums that he might in future owe the claimant. The court held that this merely amounted to a charge on his salary, not an assignment of his salary.

The general rules relating to equitable assignment are slightly different to those under s 136 of the Law of Property Act 1925.

- Generally, no specific form is required for an equitable assignment of a legal chose in action of purely personal property. However, if the assignment is of an equitable interest then the provisions in s 53(1)(c) of the Law of Property Act 1925 must be complied with. This means that it must be in writing and signed by the assignor.
- Notice need not be given to the debtor, although in most cases it would be advisable.
- There is an issue of consideration because of the maxim 'equity will not assist a volunteer ', meaning equity will not enforce something on behalf of someone who has not provided consideration. There are three different consequences:
  - Where there is an assignment of an **equitable** chose in action, provided that the assignor has done everything that he can to effect the transfer, then this is classed as an actual transfer and is enforceable by the assignee.
  - In the case of an assignment of a **legal** chose in action the same principle will apply.
  - However, where there is only an **agreement** to assign a chose in action this is to take place in the future and so must be supported by consideration in order to be enforceable.

General rules on assignment

Where the debtor has made more than one assignment of the same chose in action and his funds are insufficient to meet the claims of the different assignees, then the assignees must give notice of their interest. Priority is then given in order of the date of giving notice.

Assignees also take the risk of any defences that may be available to the assignor. This is known as taking the assignment 'subject to the equities of the assignor'.

Certain rights in any case cannot be assigned. These include where the contract entered into by the original parties expressly provides against this; a right to sue for damages, since this conflicts with the rules on champerty and maintenance; where the contract is based on personal performance; and also on certain policy grounds.

13.3.4 Negotiable instruments

Negotiable instruments were originally a device of merchant traders. The rules devised by the merchants were eventually given statutory force in the Bills of Exchange Act 1882. Possibly the most common form of negotiable instrument with which we are familiar in modern times is the cheque. By various processes it is then possible to transfer ownership of the property identified in the instrument: in the case of a cheque, a sum of money.

In the case of a cheque the three parties are the drawer, the drawee and the payee:

- The **drawer** is the person holding the bank account and who has been issued with the cheque book with which to pay for goods or services.
- The **payee** is the party to whom the cheque is made out, in other words the person receiving the cheque, the negotiable instrument, from the drawer as payment for the goods or services.
- The **drawee** is the drawer 's bank. Because the drawer has funds in the bank or even an overdraft or borrowing facility, the bank undertakes to pay the sum of money identified on the cheque to the payee when it is presented.

As can be seen, there is a contractual relationship generally between the drawer and the payee. There is also a debtor/creditor relationship between the drawer and the drawee. The bank is able to reduce the drawer's account by the amount of the cheque. However, there is no contractual relationship between the payee and the drawee, although in general the rules explained in very simple terms above indicate that the payee generally has the means to enforce payment of the value of the cheque presented to the bank.

13.4 Statutory intervention and the contracts (rights of third parties) act 1999

We have already seen at the beginning of this section some of the harsh effects that the doctrine of privity can have in preventing third parties from enforcing rights which appear to have been granted to them in contracts.

The fact that judges have been prepared to allow so many exceptions to the basic rule is a fair indication of a general dissatisfaction with the operation of the doctrine. In many cases, indeed, judges have themselves called for legislative reform, particularly because of the complexities that are caused by there being so many different exceptions.

This is not a new feeling and as early as 1937 the Law Revision Committee was recommending reforms. In simple terms, it suggested that third parties should be able to enforce provisions in a contract which 'by its express terms purport to confer a benefit on a third party'.

The Law Commission in its Consultation Paper No 121 argued that there should be a 'third party rule' in privity. Nevertheless, it rejected various proposed courses of action:

- Extending the number of exceptions – rejected because there were already too many.
- Leaving enforcement of third party rights to promisees under the contract – rejected as too onerous a burden and no guarantee it would happen.
- Introducing a general rule preventing privity from denying any third party rights – rejected as too vague, and might 'open the floodgates' to claims.

So the Law Commission favoured a more precise rule whereby third parties would only be able to enforce rights identified in the terms of the contract as intending to confer a legally enforceable benefit on the third party.

Even here the Law Commission felt that parties to the contract should be able to vary such terms where the contract specifically allowed for such variation.

The Law Commission subsequently prepared a draft Bill in a further report (No 242). Its major provision is contained in s 1(1) by which: 'a person who is not a party to a contract (in this Act referred to as a third party) may in his own right enforce the contract if: (a) the contract contains an express term to that effect; or (b) subject to subsection (2) the contract purports to confer a benefit on the third party'.

The first ground under subsection (a) is self-explanatory. The second ground is subject to subsection (2). It states that ground (b) will be unavailable to a third party where, 'on the proper construction of the contract it appears that the parties did not intend the contract to be enforceable by a third party'. In consequence, it seems only those rights actually conferred by the contract can be enforced.

One final recommendation of the Law Commission here was the abolition of the rule that consideration must move from the promisee that would otherwise defeat the reform. The reforms were presented to Parliament in a draft Bill in January 1999. This has subsequently been enacted as the Contracts (Rights of Third Parties) Act 1999.

The 1999 Act identifies that third parties can gain rights in limited circumstances where there is an intention that a benefit was in fact to be conferred on that party. This third party right is also subject to a rebuttable presumption which will depend on the construction given to the contract by the courts. The main third party right is identified in s 1.

SECTION

's1(1) ... a person who is not a party to a contract may in his own right enforce a contract term if:

(a) the contract expressly provides that he may; or

(b) subject to subsection (2), the term purports to confer a benefit on him.

(2) Subsection (1)(b) does not apply if on a proper construction of the contract it appears that the parties did not intend the term to be enforceable by the third party.'

By s 1(3) the 1999 Act will apply if a third party is identified in the contract either by name or even as a member of a class. The third party does not have to exist at the time the contract was formed as long as he is identifiable as part of the class.

CASE EXAMPLE

Nisshin Shipping Co v Cleaves & Co Ltd [2003] EWHC 2602; [2004] 1 All ER (Comm) 481

In a contract between ship owners and charterers of the vessel a clause was included for payment of commission to the broker who had negotiated the agreement between the two parties, but who was not a party to the contract. When the commission was not paid and the broker sued, the court held that he could enforce his rights under the 1999 Act. He was identifiable from the contract so that s 1(3) applied and the contract clearly conferred a benefit on him so that s 1(1)(b) was also satisfied.

This is a fairly straightforward situation and straightforward application of the Act. It has obvious similarities with cases such as *Walford's Case* (see section 13.2.3) and shows how certain of the exceptions to the privity rule may have been in effect replaced by the Act. It also demonstrates the importance of parties declaring their intentions clearly in their contracts. The court in *Nisshin* recognised that the effect of s 1(2) of the Act is to place the burden on the party claiming that s 1(1)(b) does not apply to prove it.

However, without express mention of at least a class of persons from whom the claimant is recognisable s 1(3) has no application.

CASE EXAMPLE

Avraamides and Another v Colwill and Another [2006] EWCA Civ 1533

The claimants had brought an action against the defendants in respect of defective work by a company, BTC Ltd, which the defendants had bought. The agreement for the transfer of the business, while it agreed to 'settle the current liabilities' of BTC Ltd and to 'complete outstanding customer orders', did not at any point identify by name or class any third parties. As a result the Court of Appeal felt that it could not confer rights on the claimants.

The 1999 Act contains some amendments from the Law Commission's draft Bill. Certain types of contract are excluded, notably those contracts where other legislation already applies. Another inclusion is a rule preventing a third party from suing an employee who is in breach of his contract of employment. This is to protect workers where they take legitimate industrial action. Another exception is the 'statutory contract' under s 33 of the Companies Act 2006, which gives shareholders the right to sue officers of the company on issues arising from the memorandum and articles of association.

The 1999 Act has a number of important consequences:

- A wide range of third party rights will be enforceable under the Act.
- A number of the exceptions to the basic privity doctrine become unnecessary; eg the claimant in *Tweddle v Atkinson* would have an enforceable right, as would the family members in *Jackson v Horizon Holidays*.
- Where a third party comes within the scope of an exclusion clause, it will be much easier to enforce in their favour.
- Many exceptions will still apply as the Act will have no impact on them, eg collateral warranties.
- The Act can still prove ineffective as its provisions can be expressly excluded in a contract.

The Act obviously remedies some of the harsher aspects of the doctrine of privity and answers some of the criticisms. Nevertheless, while it does indeed simplify certain issues of third party rights and must be seen as a major reform, there is obvious uncertainty as to how s 1(2) will be construed and it is likely that in many contracts it will simply be excluded. The 1999 Act itself, then, is subject to criticism also. Jeff de Rhune identifies some of the problems:

QUOTATION

'The real danger will come where contracting parties are unaware of the provisions of the Act and the possible consequences. Where the Act has not been expressly excluded, the contracting parties may unknowingly end up owing obligations to a host of third parties and those third parties may well seek enforcement, resulting in some interesting times ahead for the litigators.'

J de Rhune, 'Contracts (Rights of Third Parties) Act 1999'
The Legal Executive, *April 2000, p 22*

ACTIVITY

Self-assessment questions

1. What are the major justifications for the rule on privity of contract?
2. What is the connection between the doctrine of privity and the requirement of consideration in a contract?
3. In what ways is the doctrine of privity unfair?
4. Why is it not possible to argue that whenever a third party right is identified in a contract it automatically creates a trust?
5. Is it possible to use the mechanism of a restrictive covenant to protect third party rights in cases that involve things other than land?
6. To what extent are the judgments in *Scruttons v Midland* Silicones and *The Eurymedon* consistent with one another?
7. Other than where Parliament grants enforceable third party rights by statute, what are the most effective exceptions to the basic rule on privity?
8. To what extent does the Contracts (Rights of Third Parties) Act 1999 address the problems of all third parties affected by the doctrine of privity?

KEY FACTS

The basis of the doctrine	Case/statute
Nobody can sue or be sued under a contract who is not a party to the contract.	*Dunlop v Selfridge*
Put another way, nobody can enforce a contract who has not provided consideration under the contract.	*Tweddle v Atkinson*
The exceptions to the basic rule	**Case/statute**
Since the rule unfairly prevents third parties identified as gaining rights under a contract from enforcing those rights a number of exceptions to the strict rule have developed:	
• statutory exceptions as with third party insurance under the Road Traffic Acts	
• stating that a trust is created in favour of the third party	*Gregory & Parker v Williams*
• but only so long as the interest conforms to the character of a trust	*Green v Russell*
• restrictive covenants	*Tulk v Moxhay*
• but only in relation to land, not other interests	*Taddy v Sterious*
• the rule in *Dunlop v Lambert*	*Darlington BC v Wiltshier Northern Ltd*
• privity of estate in leases	*Snelling v John G Snelling Ltd*
• procedural rules	
• the 'holiday cases'	*Jackson v Horizon Holidays*
• protection given to third parties in exclusion clauses	*New Zealand Shipping Co v Satterthwaite*
• collateral contracts	*Shanklin Pier v Detel*
• agency, assignment and negotiable instruments.	*Products Ltd*

The Contracts (Rights of Third Parties) Act 1999	Case/statute
Now Parliament has passed to enable third parties to enforce rights that they are given under a contract – so a third party can enforce provisions in a contract if:	
• the contract expressly states that he can	s 1(1)
• the contract purports to confer a benefit on the third party.	s 1(2)

SUMMARY

- By the doctrine of privity nobody can sue on or be sued under a contract who is not a party to the contract.
- This is the other side of the rule of consideration that nobody can enforce a contract who has not provided consideration under it.
- Because of the potential unfairness of the rule to third parties who are identified as gaining rights under a contract but cannot enforce those rights, a number of exceptions to the strict rule have developed which include:
  - Statutory exceptions, eg third party insurance under Road Traffic Acts
  - Trusts – as long as the interest conforms to the character of a trust
  - Restrictive covenants – in relation to land not other interests
  - The rule in *Dunlop v Lambert*
  - Privity of estate in leases
  - Procedural rules
  - The 'holiday cases'
  - Collateral contracts
- But the major exceptions are agency, assignment and negotiable instruments.
- The Contract (Rights of Third Parties) Act 1999 enables third parties to enforce rights that they are given under a contract – so a third party can enforce provisions in a contract if the contract expressly states that he can or the contract purports to confer a benefit on the third party.

SAMPLE ESSAY QUESTION

'The rule that only a party to a contract can sue under it was always unfair to third parties who might expect to acquire rights under the contract. However, this unfairness is now removed by the Contract (Rights of Third Parties) Act 1999.'
Discuss the accuracy of this statement.

Explain the doctrine of privity of contract:

- A person who is not a party to a contract can neither sue nor be sued under the contract
- Similarly a person who has not provided consideration can neither sue nor be sued

Discuss the unfairness of the privity rule:

- A person receiving defective goods as a gift may not sue
- The purchaser in that case would only be able to claim based on the defect not for any consequential loss
- May prevent enforcement of a contract already paid for
- A benefactor's express wishes may be thwarted
- Lord Dunedin said in *Dunlop v Selfridge* it allows a party to behave unconscionably and shamelessly avoid the consequences of an agreement he has freely made
- The courts simply would not have accepted so many exceptions to a rule that was not unfair, eg a trust in favour of the third party, restrictive covenants allowing a third party to enforce rights over land but not personal property, the rule in *Dunlop v Lambert*, privity of estate in the case of leases, procedural rules where all parties are represented in court, the so-called 'holiday cases', collateral contracts – where a promise made by a third party may be relied upon

Explain the basic provisions under the Act:

- Third party rights are enforceable: where the contract provides for enforceability by the third party; or where the contract purports to confer benefits on a third party
- No need for the third party to be named in the contract as long as he fits a class of person described in the agreement

Discuss whether the unfairness is indeed removed by the Act:

- Gives rights to a third party who is named or who expressly or impliedly is intended to benefit from a contract
- But does not apply to all contracts
- And contract may show that it is not intended to be enforceable by a third party so most professionally drafted agreements are likely to exclude the Act
- Difficult for parties who are unaware of the provisions in the Act
- Impact on exceptions to the privity rule is inconsistent
- And the exceptions to the privity rule are not expressly repealed – so it does not actually replace them and possibly they are still needed

Further reading

Hudson, 'Abolition of Privity' NLJ, January 1999, p 22. Stone, R, 'Privity: The New Legislation' (1999) 22 SL Rev 19.

Treitel, G H, 'Damages in Respect of Third Party Loss' (1998) 114 LQR 527.

14

Capacity

After reading this chapter you should be able to:

- Understand the nature and purpose of rules on capacity
- Understand how contracts made by minors, people under the influence of drink, people suffering from mental illnesses are regulated
- Understand the special rules applying to contracts entered into by corporations
- Understand the consequences of incapacity or limitations on capacity
- Critically analyse the area
- Apply the law to factual situations and reach conclusions

14.1 The nature and purpose of capacity

capacity

The legal status to be able to enter contracts

It would probably make more sense to refer in this section to incapacity rather than **capacity** since it involves limitations to the general assumption that all parties to a contract have the power to enter into it.

The law ultimately is concerned with promoting freedom of contract. In this way, the logic of rules on capacity is aimed at protecting certain types of person who may enter a contract either for their own protection or for the protection of the party who contracts with them. It will do so to avoid an unfair advantage being taken by a party in a superior position. The law does not necessarily prevent such people from entering contracts, but the consequences both for the party who lacks full capacity and the party with whom they deal may be different.

The law sensibly distinguishes between **natural** persons and **artificial** persons, the latter being corporations of whatever type.

In the case of **natural** persons, there are three classes who may be affected by capacity:

- **minors** (those under the age of 18 when the contract is formed)
- people who are **drunk** (when the contract is formed)
- **mental patients** (those suffering from a mental illness when the contract is formed).

14.2 Capacity and minors' contracts

14.2.1 The basic principle of minority

The Family Law Reform Act 1969 made some significant changes to the law on minority. Firstly, prior to the Act this group of people was referred to as 'infants' rather than 'minors'. Secondly, before that Act the group comprised all those under the age of 21 whereas now it comprises all those under the age of 18.

One effect of the 1969 Act may have been temporarily to reduce the significance of the rules relating to minors since they now applied to a much smaller group of young people. However, since 1969 time has moved on again. Young people are more mobile, many more are probably now living away from their parents, and the range of contracts that they may enter into has probably also changed. As a result, the area of minors' contracts may be important once more.

14.2.2 The character and purpose of rules on minority

Inevitably, young people do enter contracts and need to have the ability to make contracts as much as adults. The law on capacity in relation to minors is in no way seeking to prevent young people from making contracts or even to restrict or limit their ability to enter into contracts.

The law may be seen as somewhat patronising or paternalistic but what it is essentially trying to achieve is the protection of the minor from unscrupulous businessmen and others seeking to enforce a contract against the minor. These persons might otherwise take advantage of the minor or exploit the minor to his own advantage by tying him to contractual arrangements that are really against the minor's better interests.

Minors' contracts are divided into three categories. The different categories in essence represent different consequences for the parties to the contract in each case. The three categories are:

- Contracts that are **valid** and therefore **enforceable** against the minor.
- Contracts that the minor may enter but can also back out of if required and which are therefore **voidable**.
- Contracts that are **unenforceable** against the minor and which in practical terms therefore may be difficult for him or her to make.

The nature of these categories means that they can and should serve as much as a guide for the adults who contract with minors as for the protection of the minors themselves.

14.2.3 Contracts valid or enforceable against minors

Those contracts that a party may feel secure in making with minors themselves divide into two further categories. This is so because, provided the contract is validly

necessaries

Goods which a minor needs and which are appropriate to his station in life so that the seller can enforce a reasonable payment for the goods

formed, it can be enforced against the minor in the event of a breach of contract by the minor.

Contracts for necessaries

The law does not intervene to prevent minors from entering contracts. This would be unworkable. The common law, then, traditionally accepted that minors should pay for those goods and services that are actually supplied to them and that are classed as '**necessaries**' both according to their station in life and according to their present need.

CASE EXAMPLE

Chapple v Cooper (1844) 3 M & W 252

A minor whose husband had recently died contracted with the undertakers for his funeral. She later refused to pay the cost of the funeral, claiming her incapacity to contract. The court held that she was liable to pay the bill. The funeral was for her private benefit and was necessary as she had an obvious obligation to bury her dead husband.

The purpose and effect of such a rule is clear. It will allow minors to enter into contracts that are beneficial to them. However, at the same time, it prevents unscrupulous businesses from taking advantage of their youth and inexperience.

'Necessary' in this context is a very specific legal term. It does not have to mean the same as 'necessity'.

JUDGMENT

As Baron Alderson said in *Chapple v Cooper*: 'the proper cultivation of the mind is as expedient as the support of the body'.

In this way the term need not be so limited as to include only things such as food and clothing. The consequence of this is that what is accepted as being a necessary can differ according to the needs of the particular minor.

The courts have established a two-part test for determining what is a necessary and therefore what will be enforceable against the minor in the individual case:

- The goods or services must be necessary according to the '**station in life**' of the particular minor.
- The goods or services must also suit the **actual requirements** of the minor at the time when the contract is formed.

CASE EXAMPLE

Nash v Inman [1908] 2 KB 1

A Cambridge undergraduate, the son of an architect, was supplied with clothes to the value of £122 by a Savile Row tailor. These included 11 'fancy waistcoats' priced at 2 guineas each (the equivalent of £2.10 now). While the court was prepared to accept that the supply of such clothing could be appropriate to the station in life of the undergraduate, the contract was still held to be enforceable because facts showed that the minor was already adequately supplied with clothes. Therefore those that the tailor supplied could not be classed as necessaries.

Of course, decisions of this kind appear to be far more relevant to society in the nineteenth century than conditions today. As Treitel explains:

QUOTATION

'Such "quaint examples of a bygone age" have no counterpart in modern litigation. But the question whether minors are bound by contracts can still arise today: for example out of employment contracts, out of contracts of young professional athletes and entertainers, and out of contracts made by minors who pretend to be of age.'

G H Treitel, An Outline of the Law of Contract (5th edn, Butterworths 1995)

Clearly, then, what is necessary varies according to the minor's background. Thus, what is a 'necessary' for the son of the managing director of a large public company may not be a 'necessary' for the son of the car park attendant in the same company.

But, of course, the supplier will have to demonstrate not only that the goods supplied are 'necessaries' in relation to the particular minor, but also that the minor has need of them at the time of the contract. Section 3 of the Sale of Goods Act 1979 states:

SECTION

'Where necessaries are sold and delivered to a minor, or to a person who by reason of mental incapacity or drunkenness is incompetent to contract, he must pay a reasonable price therefor.'

This then leads to two further points concerning 'necessaries':

- The minor is only liable to pay for goods that are actually supplied. This may mean that executory contracts are unenforceable.
- The minor is even then only obliged to pay 'a reasonable price'. Therefore, even though the supplier is able to enforce the contract he may be unable to recover the actual contract price.

One final point concerns contracts that contain harsh or onerous terms. Even though a minor has been supplied with 'necessaries' according to the established tests, the contract may still be unenforceable if the terms of the contract are actually prejudicial to the minor's interests.

CASE EXAMPLE

Fawcett v Smethurst [1914] 84 KB 473

The minor hired a car in order to transport luggage. This, on the face of it, could easily be classed as a 'necessary'. Nevertheless, under a term in the contract the minor was to be held absolutely liable for any damage to the car regardless of how that damage was caused. On this basis, the court felt the contract to be too onerous and therefore unenforceable against the minor.

Beneficial contracts of service

The common law again sensibly concludes that the minor may need to support himself financially, and therefore must have the capacity to enter contracts of employment. School-leaving age is 16 and this is two years below the age of majority. To hold otherwise would not be sensible and would be unfair on the minor.

Such a contract would be *prima facie* valid and therefore enforceable. However, from an early time the courts accepted that the contract would be binding on the minor only if, on balance, the terms of the contract were substantially to the benefit of the minor.

The court will have to look at the whole contract. The fact that some of the terms act to the minor's detriment will not automatically invalidate the contract of service providing that it still operates mostly for the minor's benefit.

CASE EXAMPLE

Clements v London and North Western Railway Company [1894] 2 QB 482

The minor had taken up employment as a porter with the railway company. He agreed to join the company's insurance scheme as a result of which he would relinquish any rights he might have under the Employers' Liability Act 1880. In the event of an accident the statutory scheme would be of greater benefit to the minor since it covered a wider range of accidents for which compensation could be claimed, although the levels of compensation were lower. When the minor tried to claim that he was not bound by the employer's scheme he failed. Viewing the whole contract, on balance, it was generally to his benefit.

By comparison, where the contract is made up of terms, which are predominantly detrimental to the minor, then the court will have no choice but to invalidate the contract as a whole.

CASE EXAMPLE

De Francesco v Barnum [1890] 45 Ch 430

Here, a 14-year-old girl entered into a seven-year apprenticeship with De Francesco, to be taught stage dancing. By the apprenticeship deed the girl agreed that she would be at De Francesco's total disposal during the seven years, and that she would accept no professional engagements except with his express approval. He was under no obligation to maintain her or to employ her. In the event that he did employ her, the scales of pay were set extremely low. She was also obliged not to marry except with his permission. Finally, De Francesco was able to terminate their arrangement without notice whenever he wished. When the girl was set to accept other work, De Francesco's action to prevent it failed. The provisions of the apprenticeship deed were held to be unfair by the court and therefore unenforceable against her. They were not substantially for her benefit.

As can be seen from the last case, the principle has not been limited in its application to contracts of service only but has been extended in its application to cover contracts of apprenticeship, education and training, since it is to the general advantage of a minor that he should secure the means of acquiring a livelihood. During the last century the courts took an even more progressive view of those circumstances which can be classed as a beneficial contract of service.

CASE EXAMPLE

Doyle v White City Stadium Ltd [1935] 1 KB 110

Here, the principle was extended to cover a contract between a minor who was a professional boxer and the British Boxing Board of Control. Under the agreement the minor would lose his 'purse' (the payment for the fight) if he were disqualified. The agreement was held to be binding on the minor since it was to encourage not only clean fighting but also proficiency in boxing, and was therefore for the benefit of the minor.

The principle can be applied to a contract for services as well as to a contract of service.

CASE EXAMPLE

Chaplin v Leslie Frewin (Publishers) Ltd [1966] Ch 71

In this case the principle was extended to a contract to write an autobiography. This was held to be similar to a contract for services and was beneficial to the minor, and so was binding on him.

It follows that, since contracts for necessaries and beneficial contracts of service are enforceable against the minor, if the goods or service are not necessaries or if the contract of service is not beneficial then these contracts are voidable by the minor.

CASE EXAMPLE

Proform Sports Management Ltd v Proactive Sports Management Ltd and *Another* [2006] All ER (D) 38

Wayne Rooney, a famous England footballer, had signed a management and agency agreement with the claimant when he was 15, lasting for two years. He did so without any legal advice. Rooney was already contracted to Everton at this point. Rooney was approached by another agent and six months before the agreement was due to end, he wrote to the claimant giving notice of his intention not to renew the agreement when it expired. After taking legal advice Rooney then terminated the arrangement. The claimant argued that the other agent had induced a breach of its contract with Rooney. The defendant argued that it was not illegal to induce termination of a contract that was voidable by a minor. The agreement between Rooney and the claimant was so that the claimant could represent him in future transfer deals. The court held that the contract with the claimant was not a contract of apprenticeship, education and service substantially to Rooney's benefit and therefore he was entitled to avoid it. Therefore the defendant was not liable.

14.2.4 Contracts voidable by minors

This category of contracts made by minors refers to those contracts which, though the minor might enter with perfect validity, he may nevertheless avoid by repudiating his obligations under the contract while still a minor or within a reasonable time after reaching the age of 18.

The common feature of such contracts is that they involve subject-matter of some permanency. So they are otherwise known as contracts of continuous or recurring obligations. They involve long-term interests and the law sensibly considers that, while a minor should be able to enter such contracts, he should also be in a position to repudiate all obligations and avoid further liability if that is more appropriate, providing that the repudiation occurs sufficiently early.

There are four principal classes of contracts falling within this category. They are:

- contracts to **lease property**
- contracts to **purchase shares** in a company
- contracts to enter a **partnership**
- contracts of **marriage settlement**.

It is clearly the case that such contracts are voidable by the minor because of their potentially onerous nature. Nevertheless, if the minor chooses not to repudiate the contract then he will obviously be bound by all of the obligations falling under the contract, eg, a minor will be bound by the usual covenants in a lease, and will be bound also by outstanding amounts owed on shares.

Whether the minor has repudiated in sufficient time to avoid the contract is a question of fact to be determined by the court in each case.

CASE EXAMPLE

Edwards v Carter [1893] AC 360

Here, a minor sought to repudiate an agreement under a marriage settlement by which he agreed to transfer the money he would inherit from his father's will to the trustees under the settlement. He tried to repudiate more than a year after his father's death and four-and-a-half years after actually reaching the age of majority. His argument that he was incapable of repudiating until he knew the full extent of his interest under his father's estate failed. The court held that his repudiation was too late in time to be reasonable.

JUDGMENT

The point was actually explained by Lord Watson in the case: 'If he chooses to be inactive, his opportunity passes away; if he chooses to be active the law comes to his assistance.'

Where the minor repudiates the contract before any obligations under it have arisen, then no particular problems arise and the contract is simply at an end. The minor cannot be sued on any obligation that would have arisen after this point.

However, where obligations have already arisen before this point then the position is not so clear-cut. Academic opinion seems to favour the view that the minor is bound by debts arising from the contract prior to the date of repudiation.

Where the minor has transferred money under the contract then it would appear that this is not recoverable unless there is a complete failure of consideration.

CASE EXAMPLE

Steinberg v Scala (Leeds) Ltd [1923] 2 Ch 452

A minor was allotted company shares for which she had made the payment due for the allotment and for the first call. Since she was unable to meet the payments for the further calls she sought to repudiate the contract and also to recover the money which she had already paid over to the company. The court was happy to accept the repudiation. This meant that her name could be removed from the register of shareholders and she would bear no further liability for the company. However, the court was not prepared to grant return of her money. There was no failure of consideration. Even though she had received no dividends or attended any meetings of shareholders, she had received everything she was bound to under the contract. She had been registered as a shareholder.

In contrast, the minor may succeed in recovering money paid over if he can prove that he has not received what was promised under the contract.

CASE EXAMPLE

Corpe v Overton (1833) 10 Bing 252

Here, the minor reached an agreement to enter a partnership in three months' time, and to pay £1,000 on signing the partnership deed. The minor paid a deposit of £100. When he repudiated the agreement on reaching majority the court accepted that he should be able to recover the deposit since he had received no benefits under the agreement. There was a failure of consideration.

14.2.5 Contracts void and unenforceable against minors

At one time, much of the law governing minors' contracts was contained in the Infants Relief Act 1874. After much call for change in what was a very complex piece of legislation, its provisions were eventually repealed in the Minors' Contracts Act 1987. This Act took the unusual step of restoring the common law as it was before the prior Act, although with some modification. As a result, the law is not without its complexities.

The basic position is that, with the exception of those classes of contracts we have already discussed, a contract made by a minor will not bind him and is therefore unenforceable against him. To the sensible party contemplating entering into a contract with a minor, what this means is that the range of contracts open to a minor is necessarily more limited than that available to an adult. There are therefore situations where it is prudent not to contract with a minor.

What it does not mean is that in the case of contracts other than those already considered they are devoid of legal consequences. For example:

- Even though the minor is not bound by the contract, the other party still will be if such a contract is entered.
- If the minor has paid over money under the contract he may be able to recover that money if there is a total failure of consideration.
- If the minor ratifies such a contract on reaching the age of 18, then the ratification will bind the minor. It is not necessary for the contract to be expressly ratified; continuing with the contract may be sufficient for ratification to be implied.

Section 1 of the Infants Relief Act 1874 listed the classes of contract that would be void and unenforceable against the minor. These were:

- contracts for the repayment of money lent or to be lent
- contracts for goods supplied or to be supplied other than necessaries
- accounts stated, ie, IOUs.

The law has now been somewhat modified by the Minors' Contracts Act 1987. Clearly, in modern circumstances many minors might wish to take advantage of the credit and loan facilities now freely available. Such contracts would have been formerly unenforceable against the minor. Furthermore, by the Infants Relief Act 1874 even a guarantee for a loan given by an adult close to the minor would have been unenforceable since a guarantor is said to 'stand in the shoes of the principal debtor'. If the contract could not be enforced against the minor then neither could it be enforced against the guarantor. In this way it is understandable that there would be a reluctance to offer loans or to contract to supply things other than necessaries to minors. The consequence of this was that the capacity of minors to enter certain contracts was restricted.

Now, under s 2 of the Minors' Contracts Act 1987 a guarantee can be enforced and minors therefore have perhaps gained greater access to credit facilities.

SECTION

's 2(1) Where
  (a) a guarantee is given in respect of an obligation of a party to a contract made after the commencement of this Act, and
  (b) the obligation is unenforceable against him (or he repudiates the contract) because he was a minor when the contract was made, the guarantee shall not for that reason alone be unenforceable against the guarantor.'

Of course, the provision still depends on the minor being able to find a guarantor for the debt.

14.2.6 Minors' contracts and the role of equity

We have seen that the aims of the law governing minors' contracts is not so much to restrict or limit the ability of a minor to enter contracts but rather to protect the minor from those who might exploit him and take advantage of his youth and inexperience.

Just as the law protects minors against unscrupulous people who would take unfair advantage of their age, logic dictates also that the other party to the contract might in certain circumstances require protection from an unscrupulous minor who tries to take full advantage of his contractual incapacity.

Traditionally, while the common law would fail such a party where the contract was unenforceable against the minor, equity could intervene with the remedy of restitution to prevent the minor's 'unjust enrichment'.

CASE EXAMPLE

R Leslie Ltd v Sheill [1914] 3 KB 607

Here, a minor fraudulently misrepresented his age in order to get a loan from the claimant. The court held that at common law the claimant could not recover the amount of the loan since this would have the effect of enforcing an unenforceable contract. However, the court also identified that had the contract involved goods then the minor would have been obliged in equity to return them. Restitution would not apply in the same way to the money lent unless the very coins or notes lent were still identifiable in the hands of the minor.

JUDGMENT

Sumner LJ explained the reasoning behind the decision: 'the whole current of decisions down to 1913, apart from dicta which are inconclusive, went to shew (show) that, when an infant obtained an advantage by falsely stating himself to be of full age, the equity required him to restore his ill-gotten gains, or to release the party deceived from obligations or acts in law induced by the fraud, but scrupulously stopped short of enforcing against him a contractual obligation, entered into while he was an infant, even by means of fraud. Restitution stopped where repayment began.'

So the doctrine of restitution would still have limited application in preventing the minor's unjust enrichment.

Now, the role of equity in the way applied above has been superseded by s 3 of the Minors' Contracts Act 1987. Now under this provision:

SECTION

'3(1) Where –
  (a) a person ("the claimant") has after the commencement of this Act entered into a contract with another ("the defendant"), and
  (b) the contract is unenforceable against the defendant (or he repudiates it) because he was a minor when the contract was made, the court may, if it is just and equitable to do so, require the defendant to transfer to the claimant any property acquired by the defendant under the contract, or any property representing it.'

This provision means that it will no longer be vital to prove fraud against the minor in order to be able to recover from him provided that the court can identify an unjust enrichment and it is equitable for the property to be recovered.

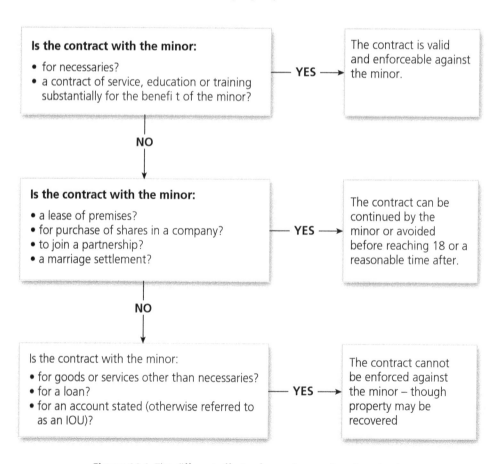

Figure 14.1 The different effects of capacity on minors' contracts

ACTIVITY

Multiple choice questions

1. From the following choices, select the situation which most accurately describes a contract which is enforceable against a minor:
   a) Jennifer agrees to lend Margaret, aged 17, £5,000 with which Margaret is to buy a car.
   b) Gurdeep, aged 17, is hoping in the future to become a chef. He has agreed to sign up for a catering course at his local Further Education college that will cost him £300 a term in registration and tuition fees.
   c) Satnam, who is 17, has signed an agreement to lease a flat from George.
   d) Chan, aged 17, has borrowed £50,000 from Archie in order to spend a year touring around the world.

2. From the following choices, select the situation which most accurately describes a contract which is void and unenforceable against a minor:
   a) Aaron, who is aged 17, has ordered a suit from Top Toff Tailors. He has recently been accepted for employment in a sales department and he is required to wear a suit and tie.
   b) Thelma, aged 17, has just formed a business partnership with her best friend Louise under which they are each contributing £500 to start the business.
   c) Victoria is 17 and she got married to Noel when she was only 16. Noel recently died in a car crash and Victoria has contracted with local funeral directors for Noel's funeral arrangements.
   d) Craig, an unemployed 17-year-old, has agreed to buy a small aeroplane, priced at £200,000.

Self-assessment questions

1. Why does the law apply different rules to contracts made by minors?
2. What exactly is a 'necessary', and how does that differ from a necessity?
3. What is the common feature between necessaries and contracts of service or of apprenticeship, education or training?
4. Why does the law allow a minor to 'avoid' the effects of a contract of continuing or recurrent obligations?
5. Why were there different results in *Steinberg v Scala (Leeds) Ltd* and in *Corpe v Overton*?
6. Where a contract has been declared unenforceable against a minor, are there any consequences of the contract having been made at all?
7. Is it always the minor that the law is seeking to protect?
8. In what circumstances will equity act against a minor?
9. How different is the provision under s 3 of the Minors' Contracts Act 1987?

14.3 Capacity and mentally disordered persons

'Mental patient' and 'mental disorder' have become the subject of widespread definition in modern times, and the administration of the property of mental patients subject to numerous rules. However, the contractual capacity of such people is still predominantly the subject of common law rules, as with minors.

In considering the capacity of such a party to contract, the first question for the court to determine is whether at the time of contracting that party was actually suffering from a mental disability to the extent that he was incapable of understanding the nature of his act when forming the contract.

If this is the case then the contract will be voidable by the party with the mental disorder rather than void, provided also that the other party to the agreement was aware of the disability at the time at which the contract was formed: *Imperial Loan Co v Stone* [1892] 1 QB 599.

A contract that has been formed during a period of lucidity, however, will be binding upon the mentally incapacitated person even if they lapse back into mental illness. This is because there was full capacity at the time of contracting.

Where necessaries are supplied to a person who is suffering from a mental illness then s 3 of the Sale of Goods Act 1979 applies once again. The person will be obliged, as usual, to pay a reasonable price for the goods and it will not matter whether the other party is aware of the disability or not.

Under Part VII of the Mental Health Act 1983 the property of a mental patient now falls under the control and jurisdiction of the courts to determine what contracts will bind the individual concerned.

14.4 Capacity and drunkenness

When a party who is also drunk enters into a contract he is given certain protections. Provided that he does not know the quality of his actions at the time that the contract is formed, and provided also that his drunkenness is also evident to the other party to the contract, then the contract is voidable by the drunken person on his return to a sober state (see *Gore v Gibson* (1845) 13 M & W 623).

However, the party making it may later ratify such a contract: *Matthews v Baxter* (1873) LR 8 Exch 132.

It follows that a contract made with a party who is so drunk as not to know the quality of their act will almost always be voidable since it seems very unlikely that this would then be unknown by the other party.

The same provision concerning necessaries under s 3 of the Sale of Goods Act 1979 that applies to both minors' contracts and to mental patients applies also to those who are incapacitated through drunkenness.

ACTIVITY

Self-assessment questions

1. Why are there special rules on capacity when dealing with people who are drunk or who are mental patients?
2. What common features are shared between all three groups?
3. In what circumstances will people who were drunk at the time of the contract or people suffering from mental illnesses be bound by the contract?

14.5 The capacity of corporations

corporation

A body (rather than a person) with legal capacity to contract, e g a company

A **corporation** is a body which is accepted in law as having its own separate legal personality. In this way a corporation can form contracts and sue or be sued in its own name.

A corporation inevitably is made up of a variety of people, whether employees or officers. However, while it is these individuals who run the business of the corporation and make contracts on the behalf of the corporation, they can neither sue nor be sued. An obvious example of a corporation would be a company registered under the Companies Acts. This should be contrasted with something like a local darts club. The club might represent the interests of the members and act on their behalf, but it would be an unincorporated association. Any legal liability would be on the members themselves. They would be held accountable on any contracts, and the club as such could not sue or be sued.

Incorporation inevitably creates only an artificial legal personality. A company is not a person and therefore will have more limited capacity than would an actual person. So the capacity of a corporation will depend on the way in which it has been formed.

14.5.1 The different types of corporation

A corporation can be formed in one of three ways:

- By **Royal Charter** – these charters were commonly given to the original trading companies such as the East India Company. The capacity was determined by the terms of the charter, though it was usually wide.
- By **statute** – many of the old nationalised industries and bodies such as the BBC gained their status by Act of Parliament. Their capacity to contract was obviously identified in the statute itself or possibly in regulations made under the statute.
- By **registration as a company** under the Companies Acts – this would be the most common form of incorporation. Each company on formation has to register certain documents for public inspection. One of these documents is the memorandum of association that includes one important part called the objects clause. The objects clause is in effect the constitution of the company and the company may then do anything legal in furtherance of these objects or anything reasonably incidental to them provided it has granted itself the appropriate power. Going beyond the objects is known as acting ultra vires and such actions will be illegal.

14.5.2 The *ultra vires* doctrine

When a corporation goes beyond its capacity to act in making transactions then it is said to act *ultra vires* (beyond its powers). This could traditionally be unfair on a party contracting with a company that was deemed by company law rules to know of the company's capacity to contract. Now, to comply with EU law, the Companies Acts have introduced provisions to protect such a party from the company pleading its own *ultra vires* to avoid the consequences of the contract.

In the case of companies incorporated and registered under the Companies Acts, the doctrine was the traditional means of preventing the company from doing anything that was not empowered by its objects clause. Any *ultra vires* act would be void and therefore unenforceable by either party to the transaction.

The doctrine in essence sought to protect three classes of people: the investors (share- holders), creditors of the company and any third parties entering transactions with the company.

The means of protection arose from the requirement of publicity. The memorandum of association and the articles of association of the company (in effect, the constitution of the company) must be registered and lodged with the Registrar of Companies and would also be available for public inspection, so that the public would have notice of the limited liability of the company. The problem with this for people who dealt with companies is that irrespective of whether or not they had inspected the company documents, they were fixed with constructive notice of the company's objects clause. In this way the company could plead its own *ultra vires* in a transaction to defeat a claim by a legitimate creditor.

CASE EXAMPLE

Ashbury Railway Carriage Co Ltd v Riche (1875) LR 7 HL 653

The company was formed to carry out the building of railway stock and was an engineering company. The directors contracted to assign a concession that they had bought to build a railway in Belgium to a Belgian company. When they failed to honour their agreement, the Belgian company brought an action to enforce the agreement. The court held that there was nothing in Ashbury's objects clause allowing it to build railways so the agreement was *ultra vires* and therefore void.

Before the Companies Act 1989 an *ultra vires* act could never be ratified by the shareholders. Nor could such an act be enforced by third parties who dealt with the company, even where they could prove that they were unaware of the *ultra vires* nature of the transaction.

CASE EXAMPLE

Re Jon Beauforte Ltd [1953] Ch 131

The objects clause authorised the making of clothing. The company started making veneered panels and ordered coke on headed notepaper describing itself as manufacturers of veneer panels. When the company failed and fell into liquidation, the coke suppliers' action for the price of the coke failed. The court held that they were caught by constructive notice of the company's objects clause despite the letter heading to the contrary.

Ancillary powers under an objects clause can also cause problems since they could be used for either a legitimate purpose lawfully or unlawfully for purposes that are not within the objects clause. Traditionally, the view was that use of a power in the latter way would be caught by the *ultra vires* doctrine.

CASE EXAMPLE

Introductions Ltd v National Provincial Bank Ltd [1970] Ch 199

The company was formed to provide entertainment and accommodation during the Festival of Britain. It was later bought 'off the shelf' (a simpler alternative to first registration) and was used for pig breeding. The company later borrowed money, a power available to it under the objects clause, and failed to repay. When the bank sued for return of the money it failed in its action. This was because the court held that the company had used a legitimate power but for an illegitimate purpose.

However, even common law began to doubt this principle and complicated the rules.

CASE EXAMPLE

Rolled Steel Products (Holdings) Ltd v British Steel Corporation [1985] 2 WLR 908

Rolled Steel was owned by a family that also owned a company called Scottish Sheet Steel which was owed £400,000 worth of debentures by Rolled Steel. Scottish Sheet Steel was a steel stockholder and bought from BSC which it owed £800,000. Rolled Steel owned certain land which BSC suggested a charge should be put on to guarantee the debts of Scottish Sheet Steel. Rolled Steel did this but still failed to pay the debts. In liquidation the land was sold for £1.2 million but this money was used for costs etc. The liquidator challenged the validity of the debenture and the guarantee since Rolled Steel, while it had the ancillary power to give security for debts and to give guarantees, was actually doing it here on behalf of another company and thus for an unlawful purpose. Nevertheless the House of Lords held that the transaction was lawful.

JUDGMENT

Lord Justice Slade said: 'if the transaction is entered into in pursuance of a power which is capable of being exercised for purposes within the objects, then it will not become *ultra vires* merely because the transaction is entered into for purposes outside the objects'. The judgment seems to be quite contrary to the previous law.

14.5.3 Statutory controls

While the original purpose of the *ultra vires* doctrine was to protect various parties from the effects of unlawful dealing, the nature of the doctrine, particularly constructive notice of the memorandum, meant that companies were able to use it to defeat claims by legitimate creditors. At the same time, the effect of the doctrine was to limit the ability of companies to expand their operation in response to current trading trends, with the result that objects clauses were often drafted over-widely.

Harmonisation of company law as required by EU law led to insertion of new provisions in s 35 of the Companies Act 1985. The section states that:

SECTION

'(1) in favour of a person dealing with a company in good faith, any transaction decided on by the directors shall be deemed to be one which is within the capacity of the company to enter into, and the power of the directors to bind the company shall be deemed to be free of any limitations under the memorandum.

(2) a party to a transaction so decided is not bound to enquire as to the capacity of the company to enter into it or as to any such limitations on the powers of the directors and is presumed to have acted in good faith unless the contrary is proved.'

This provision had two positive effects:

- The company was unable any longer to raise its **own** *ultra vires* as a defence to a claim.
- Registration of the memorandum no longer acted as **constructive notice** of the objects clause and therefore of the incapacity of the company to act – so **positive notice** was now required.

However, the lawfulness of the transaction was now also dependent on the good faith of the third party dealing with the company. Also, the company could no longer enforce its own *ultra vires* contracts, and the directors of the company could still be liable to the shareholders.

Section 35 was amended by s 108 of the Companies Act 1989 in three specific ways:

- by providing that an act cannot be invalidated merely because it falls outside of the company's capacity
- so third parties are protected and can enforce agreements
- as can the company as against third parties.

But shareholders can prevent directors from entering an *ultra vires* contract by use of an injunction:

- and as a result, construction of objects clauses is also relaxed so that under s 110 the objects clause may state that the company is to 'carry on business as a general commercial company'.

Now under s 40(2) Companies Act 2006 enquiries as to the powers of directors to bind the company and as to whether a transaction is permitted in the objects in the memorandum are no longer required.

SUMMARY

- There are four distinct categories where capacity is an issue: minors, mentally incapacitated, drunkards, corporations.
- Contracts made with minors are of three types: those that are enforceable against the minor; those that are voidable by the minor and those that are unenforceable against the minor.
- Contracts enforceable against a minor include contracts for necessaries – which are measured against the minor's station in life and current needs; and by s 3 Sale of Goods Act 1979 – a minor only has to pay a 'reasonable price' for goods that are actually delivered; and also contracts of employment, training and apprenticeship, but only those that are substantially to the minor's benefit.
- Contracts voidable by a minor include long-term arrangements such as leases, purchase of shares, agreements to enter partnerships – any money paid over is only recoverable if there is a total failure of consideration.
- Contracts unenforceable against a minor include loans and goods other than necessaries – but s 2 Minors Contracts Act 1987 allows that guarantees of such contracts can be enforced – and s 3 allows the other party to recover goods handed over to the minor in an unenforceable contract if it is just and equitable.
- Rules on incapacity also apply in the case of drunkards and mental patients and contracts made during periods of such incapacity will be unenforceable.
- Corporations are also limited in the type of contracts that they can make – the limitation depending on the type of corporation.

SAMPLE ESSAY QUESTION

'The rules developed by both the courts and in statutory provisions regarding the capacity of certain groups in society to contract are aimed predominantly at protecting those groups from unscrupulous trading practices.' Discuss the accuracy of the above statement.

Identify the groups that are affected by rules on contractual capacity:

- Minors, those temporarily incapacitated by drunkenness or by mental illness, and corporations

Explain the rules on the capacity of minors:

- Enforceable include necessaries and contracts of employment, training and apprenticeship substantially to the minor's benefit
- Voidable include long-term arrangements, eg leases, purchase of shares, agreements to enter partnerships
- Unenforceable are goods other than necessaries
- S 2 Minors Contracts Act 1987 allows that guarantees of such contracts can be enforced and s 3 allows the other party to recover goods handed over to the minor in an unenforceable contract if it is just and equitable

Explain the rules on capacity while drunk:

- A contract made while drunk is not binding if the person does not know the quality of his actions when the contract is formed and his drunkenness is evident to the other party, but he may later ratify the contract

Explain the capacity of the mentally ill:

- Any contract will be voidable rather than void if the other party was aware of the disability when the contract was formed

Explain the capacity of corporations:

- Capacity limited by method of incorporation
- *Ultra vires* transactions with corporations were traditionally void
- Now a third party is protected as long as he dealt with the corporation in good faith

Discuss the protections created by the rules:

- Minors are protected because of their inexperience and youth but are given opportunity to enter contracts to their benefit – businesses in some cases are also protected against unscrupulous minors
- Drunkards are given the benefit of the doubt during periods of unawareness
- Those with mental illness have similar protection
- Shareholders are protected from improper dealing by the officers of companies but those dealing with corporations may have more limited protection

KEY FACTS

The nature of capacity in contract law	
Nobody can sue or be sued on a contract if they lack the capacity to enter it.	

Minors' contracts	Case/statute
Contracts made with minors are of three types: (i) those that are enforceable against the minor; (ii) those that are voidable by the minor; (iii) those that are unenforceable against the minor.	
Contracts enforceable against the minor include those for necessaries – which are measured against the minor's station in life and current needs	*Nash v Inman*
• by s 3 of the Sale of Goods Act 1979 the minor is only obliged to pay a 'reasonable price' for goods actually delivered.	
Enforceable contracts also include contracts of employment, training and apprenticeship, but only if they are substantially to the minor's benefit.	*De Francesco v Barnum*
Voidable contracts are long-term arrangements and include leases, purchase of shares, agreements to enter partnerships etc:	
• any money paid over is only recoverable if there is a total failure of consideration	*Steinberg v Scala Leeds)*
• unenforceable contracts include loans and goods other than necessaries.	*Leslie v Shiell*
Section 2 of the Minors' Contracts Act 1987 allows that guarantees of such contracts can be enforced.	
Section 3 allows the other party to recover goods handed over to the minor in an unenforceable contract if it is just and equitable.	

Contracts with the mentally ill	Case/statute
Any contract will be voidable rather than void if the other party to the contract was aware of the disability when the contract was formed.	*Imperial Loan Co v Stone*
A contract formed when the mentally ill person is lucid will be binding even if he lapses back.	
Where necessaries are supplied, the person must pay a reasonable price for the goods and it will not matter whether the other party is aware of the disability or not.	s 3 Sale of Goods Act
Property of a mental patient now falls under control and jurisdiction of the courts to determine what will bind.	Part VII Mental Health Act 1983

Contracts with drunkards	Case/statute
A person making a contract while drunk is not bound if he does not know the quality of his actions at the time that the contract is formed and his drunkenness is evident to the other party to the contract.	*Gore v Gibson*
However, the party making it may later ratify such a contract.	*Matthews v Baxter*

Corporations	Case/statute
Corporations can be created by Royal Charter, by statute, and under the Companies Acts.	
Their capacity to contract is limited by the method of their incorporation. *Ultra vires* transactions with corporations were traditionally void.	*Ashbury Railway Carriage v Riche*
Now people who deal with companies do not have to make enquiries	s40 Companies Act 2006

Further reading

Cheshire, G, Fifoot, C and Furmston, M, *Law of Contract* (15th edn, Oxford University Press, 2006) Chapter 13.

Hudson, A, 'Mental Incapacity Revisited' (1986) Conv 178.

Kronman, A, 'Paternalism and the Law of Contracts' (1983) 92 Yale LJ 736.

15

Discharge of a contract

AIMS AND OBJECTIVES

After reading this chapter you should be able to:

- Understand how contractual obligations may be discharged by performance and the effects of partial and substantial performance
- Understand how contractual obligations are discharged by agreement
- Understand the different consequences of bilateral agreements and unilateral agreements
- Understand how contractual obligations are discharged by frustration of the contract
- Understand the consequences of a contract becoming frustrated
- Understand how contractual obligations may be discharged through a breach of contract
- Understand the different types of breach
- Understand the consequences of different types of breach
- Critically analyse the area
- Apply the law to factual situations and reach conclusions

15.1 Introduction

Discharge of the contract refers to the ending of the obligations under the contract, so that where we have thought of formation being the beginning of the contract, discharge represents the end or possibly the completion of the contract. At the very least, it will represent the point at which one party is no longer bound by his obligations under the contract.

In its simplest form, discharge will be the point at which either:

- all of the primary obligations created by the contract have been met in a satisfactory manner; or
- one party has failed to complete some or all of their primary obligations.

If it is the first of these then the contract is generally complete and there are no further consequences of the contractual relationship.

If the second applies, however, then the situation is not always that simple or straightforward and there are times when we refer to the contract being discharged even though the obligations under the contract remain uncompleted. In this case there is the possibility that further obligations (sometimes referred to as secondary obligations) will be created by this failure to complete the contract as required.

The obvious example of this latter point is where the contract has been breached. Secondary obligations in this case may be substituted for the primary obligations, and a party not carrying out his obligations under the contract may be required, for instance, to pay damages, a quite different obligation and one set by the court in order to ensure that the other party is not cheated of the bargain that he made.

Where all of the obligations under the contract have been carried out, this is referred to as performance of the contract. The contract is discharged, but even then the area can be complicated by one party completing some but not all of the obligations.

There are four ways in which a contract can be discharged:

- By **performance** – in which case the terms of the contract have been met and all obligations under the contract have been performed and the contract is complete.
- By **agreement** – since both parties enter a contract as the result of a mutual agreement then pure logic dictates that the parties should be able to release each other from any or further performance as a result of reaching another agreement.
- By **frustration** – which occurs when, after the contract is formed, factors beyond the control of the parties to the contract make performance impossible, at which point the parties may be released from their obligation to perform.
- By **breach of contract** – it is only fair that if one party fails to perform their side of the bargain and breaches their contract, then the other party, who is the victim of the breach, should not necessarily be expected to perform their obligations under the contract and may indeed have the right actually to repudiate – but it will be the case also that while the party in breach may be given the opportunity to fulfil their primary obligations under the contract, these will usually be substituted for secondary obligations arising from the legal action on the breach.

15.2 Discharge by performance

15.2.1 The strict rule of performance and its application

The rule in Cutter v Powell

The starting point for performance of the contract, sometimes known as the 'perfect tender' rule, is that there should be complete performance of all of the obligations under the contract. If this is the case then the contract is in effect complete and discharged.

On the other hand, the strictness of the rule also means that if there is any deviation from complete performance where a party fails to meet all of his obligations then the contract is not discharged but breached and this may require the other party to be remedied.

The bare and potentially unjust simplicity of the rule can be seen in a very early case from which this basic principle emerges.

CASE EXAMPLE

Cutter v Powell (1795) 6 Term Rep 320

Cutter was the second mate on a ship, *The Governor Parry*, sailing from Jamaica to Liverpool. The boat set sail on 2nd August and reached Liverpool on 9th October. Cutter died during the voyage, on 20th September. When his widow received no wages for his work on the voyage she then sued on a *quantum meruit* basis (meaning for the amount owed – in other words, she tried to recover for the amount appropriate to the work that he had done before he died). Her action failed because, according to the terms of his contract, her husband had signed on for the complete voyage. The significant wording in the contract read: 'provided he proceeds, continues, and does his duty as second mate in the said ship, from hence to the port of Liverpool'. The fact that he died during the voyage meant that he had, strictly speaking, failed to complete his contract. Since it was an entire contract, in other words complete performance was a condition precedent of the contract, the court held that there was no obligation on the shipowners to pay. The situation appears unfair on the face of it. However, as Lord Kenyon CJ explained in his judgment, for signing on and committing himself to the whole voyage, Cutter stood to earn nearly four times what he would have done on the normal monthly rate for the time he actually served.

JUDGMENT

Ashhurst J explained it in the following terms: 'as [the contract] is entire, and as the defendant's promise depends on a condition precedent to be performed by the other party, the condition must be performed before the other party is entitled to receive any thing under it … the [party] did not perform the contract on his part; he was not indeed to blame for not doing it; but still as this was a condition precedent, and as he did not perform it, his representative is not entitled to recover'.

An entire contract, then, is one where all of the obligations are seen as a single transaction that cannot be broken down in any way. The case illustrates the effect of failing to perform such a contract. It also shows how it can create injustice since Cutter could hardly be said to have defaulted by dying, an event that was beyond his control.

The application of the strict rule

Application of the strict rule can be commonly seen in sale of goods contracts where the description applied to the contract may mean that all rather than part is essential for completion of the contract.

CASE EXAMPLE

Arcos Ltd v E A Ronaasen & Son [1933] AC 470

Under the contract one party bought wooden staves which were described in the contract as half an inch thick. Those delivered were a sixteenth of an inch narrower and so did not correspond exactly to the contract description. The buyer then rejected the goods and the seller sued for the loss of profit. The court accepted that in law the buyer was entitled to reject the consignment sent to him, applying the strict rule on performance of entire contracts from *Cutter v Powell*. The absolute strictness of the rule is shown in the case because the precise width of the staves did not matter to the purchaser, who could still have used them for the purpose for which he had wanted them.

JUDGMENT

Lord Atkin illustrated the principle very effectively in his judgment when he said: 'a ton does not mean about a ton, or a yard about a yard. If a seller wants a margin he must, and in my experience does, stipulate for it'.

The nature of the strict rule is such that it has even been possible to apply it in respect of ancillary obligations under the contract such as packaging.

CASE EXAMPLE

Re Moore & Co and Landauer & Co's Arbitration [1921] 2 KB 519

The terms of the contract required the seller to deliver a consignment of a specific quantity of tinned fruit to the buyer. In the contract the goods were described as being packed in cases of 30 tins. When the consignment was delivered some of the cases were smaller than others and contained only 24 tins, although the overall total number of tins ordered was actually correct. The contract was complete in all respects except a minor descriptive difference in the outer packaging. The buyer intended to resell the goods so the difference would have had no impact on him in any case. Nevertheless, the Court of Appeal, applying the strict rule, held that packaging could be included in description and that the buyer was correct in rejecting the goods and repudiating the contract.

It is of course always possible that a judge in a case may reject the strict rule and apply instead the maxim *de minimis non curat lex* (this means in effect that the law will not grant a remedy for something that is too trivial).

CASE EXAMPLE

Reardon Smith Line Ltd v Hansen-Tangen [1976] 1 WLR 989

We have already seen in this case, using innominate terms, how the judges were not prepared to accept a repudiation of obligations where the term was a mere technicality describing the shipyard and job number. Although the terms were stated as conditions of the contract, their breach would have no impact on the contract at all.

This principle that a buyer should not be allowed to reject goods delivered when there is a slight shortfall or excess has actually now been incorporated into the Sale of Goods Act 1979 as s 30(2A), by s 4(2) of the Sale and Supply of Goods Act 1994.

Despite the restraints and injustices of the strict rule, there is nevertheless acceptance by judges that there is never any obligation on a party to extend beyond the standard of performance that is specifically required by the contract itself.

CASE EXAMPLE

Ateni Maritime Corporation v Great Marine (1991) The Times, 13th February

A contract for the sale and purchase of a ship was based on what were known in the trade as 'Norwegian Standard Scales' requiring registration of the vessel. The contract contained a clause that if, on delivery, there were any defects which would affect this registration of the vessel, then the seller would be obliged to make good the defects. On the ship in question the propeller was actually damaged. The sellers at first instance were found to be liable for an amount of damages far in excess of the amount needed to secure registration. On appeal this was found to be imposing too high a standard on the sellers and damages were reduced accordingly.

However, it is still clear that a natural consequence of the strict rule, when applied, is that it may lead to injustice.

15.2.2 The exceptions to the strict rule

It is almost inevitable that the potential injustice caused by application of the strict rule, as seen in *Cutter v Powell*, has led to judges identifying and accepting exceptions when the rule does not operate. There are a number of these.

Divisible contracts

Divisible contracts are ones where the contract can be seen as being made up of various parts or as a series of quite separate obligations rather than a single obligation. If each part can be discharged separately then it might also be enforced separately, and the strict rule need not apply. The rule here can be particularly appropriate, for instance, where there is a sale of goods by delivery in separate instalments, except where the seller has included an express stipulation in the contract for a single payment following the final delivery.

CASE EXAMPLE

Taylor v Webb [1937] 2 QB 283

Premises were leased to a tenant for rent. A term in the lease required the landlord to keep the premises in good repair. In the event the landlord in fact failed to maintain the premises and the tenant then refused to pay the rent. In the landlord's action the court held that the contract had divisible obligations: to lease the premises, and to repair and maintain. The contract was thus not entire and the tenant could not legitimately refuse payment.

Acceptance of part-performance

Where one of the parties has performed the contract partly but not completely then, if the other party has shown willingness to accept the part performed, the strict rule will usually not apply and he may be sued if he fails to pay or to honour his own obligations under the contract. Part-performance may occur either where there is a shortfall on delivery of goods or where a service has not been fully carried out. Nevertheless, this exception to the rule will only apply when the party who has received only partperformance has a genuine choice of whether or not to accept whatever benefit he has in fact received under the contract.

CASE EXAMPLE

Sumpter v Hedges [1898] 1 QB 673

A builder was hired to build two houses and stables. The builder had completed some of the work when he then ran out of money and was unable to complete the work. The landowner then had the work completed, using materials that the builder had left on the land. The builder then sued for the price of the work. While the builder was awarded the value of the materials that he had provided and which had been used, his argument that part-performance had been accepted by the landowner was rejected. The landowner had no choice but to find an alternative way of completing the work. His only alternative would have been to leave the partly completed buildings as an eyesore on his land. He had not accepted part-performance and the court would not accept the builder's claim for payment.

JUDGMENT

In the Court of Appeal, Collins LJ explained the point that in a building contract the contract is treated as entire so that no payment is due until the contract is actually completed: 'If the plaintiff had merely broken his contract in some way so as not to give the defendant the right to treat him as having abandoned the contract, and the defendant had then proceeded to finish the work himself, the plaintiff might perhaps have been entitled to sue on a **quantum meruit** on the ground that the defendant had taken the benefit of the work done. But that is not the present case. [The defendant] is not bound to keep unfinished a building which in an incomplete state would be a nuisance on his land.'

Substantial performance

Part-performance can obviously range from almost nothing to a substantial part of the work. If a party has done substantially what was required under the contract then the doctrine of substantial performance can apply. The doctrine means that a party who has substantially performed what was required under the contract can then sue and recover an amount that is appropriate to what has been done under the contract, providing that the contract is not an entire contract.

CASE EXAMPLE

H Dakin & Co v Lee [1916] 1 KB 566

Here, under the terms of a contract a builder was bound to complete major repair work to a building. He did in fact complete all of the work that was required under the contract. However, some of it was carried out so carelessly that the owner of the building refused to pay, on the ground that performance was in effect incomplete. The builder then sued for payment. The court held that he was able to recover the price of the work less an amount representing the value of the defective work which obviously would have to be put right, causing extra expense to the other party.

The price is thus often payable in such circumstances and the sum deducted will generally represent the cost of repairing the defective workmanship.

CASE EXAMPLE

Hoenig v Isaacs [1952] 2 All ER 176

A decorator was hired to decorate and furnish a flat for £750. He completed the work. The owner had moved into the flat and paid £400 by three instalments while the work was under way. Then, because of defects to a bookcase and a wardrobe that would cost about £55 to put right, he refused to pay the remaining £350. The Court of Appeal held that the contract was substantially performed and differed from the terms of the contract only in some minor respects. The court ordered that the balance of the price should be paid to the decorator, less the amount representing the defects in the work.

It is also possible that where the defective work has little impact on the contract and the cost of putting it right would be out of all proportion, then the court might take an alternative approach. In this case it may deduct a sum that represents what the party responsible for the defective work saved by contrast to carrying out the work properly.

CASE EXAMPLE

Young v Thames Properties Ltd [1999] EWCA Civ 629

The contract was for the building of a car park. On completion, the limestone base was only 30mm deep when it should have been 100 mm and it was surfaced with the wrong grade of tarmac. The party commissioning the work then failed to pay and the builder sued for payment. It was accepted that the failure to match the exact terms of the contract would actually make little difference while the cost of digging up and re-laying the whole car park would have been excessive. The court held that the builders should be paid the contract price less the amount that they had saved by completing the work defectively.

■ However, what a court is prepared to accept as representing substantial performance is a question of fact to be decided in each case. It will largely depend on what remains undone and its value in comparison with the value of the contract as a whole.

CASE EXAMPLE

Bolton v Mahadeva [1972] 1 WLR 1009

An electrical contractor was hired to install a central heating system. When it was installed the system gave off fumes and did not work properly. When payment was refused as a result, the contractor sued for the price. The Court of Appeal rejected his claim on the ground that there was not substantial performance. The reasoning of the court lay in the costs involved. On completion of the work there was £174 worth of defects which required repair. The system itself cost £560. The cost of repair was too great a proportion of the original cost of installation to accept that the work had been substantially performed or the contract complied with.

Prevention of performance

Where a party to a contract prevents the other party from carrying out his obligations under the contract because of some act or omission then the strict rule cannot apply. In these circumstances the party trying to perform may have an action for damages.

CASE EXAMPLE

Planche v Colburn (1831) 8 Bing 14

A publisher was planning to produce a series of books on a particular theme. The publisher then hired an author, the claimant, to write one of the books in the series. When the publisher decided to abandon the whole series, the author was prevented from completing the work through no fault of his own and despite the fact that he had already done a lot of work for the book. The court held that the author was entitled to recover half his fee for his wasted work, on a *quantum meruit* basis. (He might also have been able to consider the abandoning of the series by the publisher as an anticipatory breach and pursued a claim that way). (See sections 15.5.2 and 15.5.3.)

Tender of performance

This refers to a similar situation to the above but with slightly different consequences. It occurs where a party has offered to complete all of his obligations under the contract but the other party has unreasonably refused to accept performance.

In situations like this the party 'tendering' performance is entitled to sue and to recover under the contract. He may also consider his own obligations discharged even though there has been no performance.

CASE EXAMPLE

Startup v Macdonald (1843) 6 Man & G 593

The contract was for 10 tons of linseed oil to be delivered by the end of March. The seller in fact delivered at 8.30 pm on 31st March, which was a Saturday, and the buyer refused to accept delivery. The court held that the seller was able to claim that he had tendered performance and to recover damages as a result. (The answer might be different now under the Sale of Goods Act 1979 since delivery should be at a 'reasonable hour' and this would be a question for the court to decide in the individual case.)

However, where it is money that is owed and this is tendered but refused, while the debtor may be released from making further offers of payment, the debt will still exist and as a result can still be sued on.

15.2.3 Stipulations as to time of performance

It is generally a rule that a failure to perform a contract on time, while it does give a right to an action for damages, will not give the victim of the breach the right to repudiate the contract.

While under the common law it was accepted that time of performance could be 'of the essence' (essential to the contract), this principle was not generally accepted in equity, and this is now the general assumption.

Despite these general principles, there are nevertheless three principal occasions when time of performance will be considered to be 'of the essence' and when a repudiation of the contract will therefore be available as a remedy for the breach of contract:

- Where the parties themselves have made an **express stipulation** in the contract that time is of the essence.
- Where the **surrounding circumstances** show that time of performance is critical, as would be the case with delivery of perishable goods where delivery on time is obviously critical.
- Where **one party has already failed to perform** his obligations under the contract. In this case the other party is able to confirm that unless performance is then complete within a stated period, repudiation will occur.

ACTIVITY

Self-assessment questions

1. In what circumstances is a contract considered to be 'entire'?
2. How can the strict rule cause injustice?
3. What is a 'divisible contract'?
4. In what way can the *de minimis* rule be applied to performance?
5. What is the effect of a contract being only partly performed?
6. How is it possible to measure 'substantial performance'?
7. What are the basic differences between *Hoenig v Isaacs* and *Bolton v Mahadeva* that caused them to be decided differently?
8. What effect will it have when one party to the contract prevents the other from performing his obligations under the contract?

9. What effect does failing to perform on time have on a contract?
10. When is time of performance 'of the essence'?

Quick quiz

In the following situations, suggest which is an entire contract, which is a divisible contract, which involves substantial performance and which involves only part-performance that would not justify any claim to payment by the party providing the service. Suggest also what the probable outcome would be in each case.

1. Dan was contracted to build a swimming pool in Tom and Margot's back garden. Dan has dug out the pool and partly lined it with concrete. He has not moved any of the earth and rubble that he dug out and the garden is also full of various building rubble such as empty cement bags. He has now gone out of business and Tom has had to get other contractors in to finish the work.

2. Midshires University has a contract with Heatitup for supply of central heating oil for a year. Under the terms of the contract, Heatitup deliver on a monthly basis and each delivery is invoiced and paid for separately. Heatitup failed to deliver in November and Midshires University now wishes to refuse any further deliveries.

3. David is a semi-professional footballer for a non-league team. He has signed a contract under which he agrees to play all 40 games in the season for a fee of £2,000. Other players, who are paid by the games they play, receive only £25 per game. David missed two important games because he went on holiday and the club is refusing to pay him.

4. Alex has contracted with Sukhy to erect a fence around the back garden of Sukhy's house and to supply the fencing panels. There are 30 panels in all. Alex is charging Sukhy £5 per panel, £150 in all, and £250 for the labour. Two of the panels are broken and Sukhy is refusing to pay the bill.

KEY FACTS

The strict rule on performance	Case/statute
The strict rule on performance is that in an 'entire contract' all obligations must be performed – so there can be no payment for part-performance.	Cutter v Powell
The strict rule can even be applied in the case of descriptions applied rather than the goods or services themselves.	Re Moore & Landauer
The exceptions to the strict rule	Case/statute
If obligations are 'divisible' then payment should be made for the part performed.	Taylor v Webb
Where a party has accepted part-performance then this should be paid for.	Sumpter v Hedges
Where there has been substantial performance then the full price will be paid, less the sum appropriate to what has not been done.	Hoenig v Isaacs
But it will not be classed as substantial performance if too much remains to be done under the contract.	Bolton v Mahadeva
A party can sue for damages where his performance has been prevented by the other party.	Planche v Colburn
And also where he has offered to perform but this has been refused.	Startup v Macdonald

> **Time of performance**
>
> Generally, where the contract is not performed on time only an action for damages is possible. Repudiation of the contract may be possible if time is of the essence.
>
> Time of performance is 'of the essence' when:
>
> (i)   it says so in the contract
>
> (ii) the circumstances make it so
>
> (iii) one party has already failed to perform.

15.3 Discharge by agreement

If a contract is formed following an agreement then it seems almost pure logic to suggest that the contract can also be ended by agreement without it necessarily having been performed. Inevitably, what is required is mutuality.

There are in fact two ways in which the contract could be discharged by agreement:

▨ A **bilateral** discharge – this results in a completely new agreement between the two parties in replacement of the original agreement; the clear assumption is that both parties are to gain a fresh but different benefit from the new agreement.

▨ A **unilateral** discharge – this amounts to one party releasing the other party from his obligations under the original agreement; as a result, the benefit is probably only to be gained by one party, who is therefore trying to convince the other party to let him off the obligations arising under the original agreement; lack of consideration is an inevitable problem if one party is merely promising to release the other from existing obligations.

So two possible problems are immediately apparent whenever a contract is discharged by agreement:

▨ There is a distinct possibility that there is no consideration for the fresh agreement – and therefore in the strictest sense it could not be seen as contractual or enforceable.

▨ In the case of speciality contracts there is also the possibility that the new agreement has not been reached according to the proper formalities for speciality contracts – and again although the agreement has been reached there may be a problem in enforcing it.

15.3.1 Bilateral agreements

Wholly executory arrangements

A wholly executory agreement would be one that is based on mutual promises. The agreement has been reached but the property has yet to be passed or the service has yet to be performed under the contract.

If neither side has yet performed any obligations under the contract then it is possible that there is no real problem at all. Each side can release the other from performance and there is in fact new consideration for the new promise in each case. A party being released from the contract and not having to perform the obligations under the original agreement is the consideration in return for agreeing to release the other party from his obligations. The fresh agreement discharges the original contract.

student mentor tip

"Always read topics more than once and break it down – make sure you fully understand it in your own words"

Pelena, University of Surrey

A further possibility occurs where the parties wish to continue the contractual arrangement but to substitute new terms for the old ones. In this case it is possible for the parties to 'waive' their rights under the old agreement and to substitute the new agreement. Agreeing to abandon the original obligations and to substitute new ones in their place in each case is the consideration for the new binding agreement that can then be enforced.

Arrangements which are partly executory and partly executed

In this situation one of the parties wishes to give less than full performance and, since there is an agreement, then this part-performance is in fact acceptable to the other party. This would clearly contrast with the situation in, for instance, *Sumpter v Hedges* [1898] 1 QB 673 (see section 15.2.2 above) where the claimant was being asked to accept a part-performance that was not in fact acceptable.

In such circumstances it is possible for the other party to waive his rights under the original agreement. Inevitably, however, there is an obvious problem with this situation: there is an apparent absence of consideration for the fresh agreement. Nevertheless judges have been prepared to give effect to the doctrine of waiver, on the basis that enforcement of a mutual agreement is better than to allow the breaking of a clear promise by one side. This is an example of where waiver has been used to follow what already amounted to common business practice.

Where form is an issue

Form can inevitably be an issue in discharge where the original agreement was required to conform with specific formalities, usually some form of writing. Traditionally, this would have been dealt with subject to the rule in s 40 of the Law Property Act 1925 and the doctrine of part-performance. However, these provisions no longer apply.

Now, an agreement to vary the terms in a contract that requires specific form may be invalid unless it is evidenced in writing. If a new agreement is to be substituted for an existing agreement then again this change will be unenforceable unless evidenced in writing.

15.3.2 Unilateral agreements

Where the contract is left unperformed by one party despite the willingness of the other party to reach a fresh agreement, there are a number of possible consequences.

Release

Firstly, the party not in default might release the other from performing, but this would require a deed for validity otherwise it would fail for lack of consideration.

However, as we have already seen in relation to consideration (see section 3.3.4), the principle in *Williams v Roffey Bros & Nicholls Contractors Ltd* [1990] 1 All ER 512 may be sufficient to discharge the other party's obligations in circumstances where there is an extra benefit gained. The extra benefit gained by the one party is identified as the consideration given by the other party in exchange for being released from existing obligations of the original contract.

Accord and satisfaction

It is also possible to discharge the party in default from full performance where there is 'accord and satisfaction'. This can be achieved in a number of ways. Some of these were indicated in the rule in *Pinnel's case* (1602) 5 Co Rep 117a; 77 ER 237. The significant feature of the process is that the original agreement is changed by the introduction of some new element.

There are a number of different means by which accord and satisfaction can be reached and the obligations thus discharged:

- In *Pinnel's case* itself the court identified that payment of a lesser sum but at a date earlier than set for payment would release the debtor from further obligations if the creditor had accepted that arrangement. Clearly, there might be big advantages in doing so.

JUDGMENT

The judge explained the reasoning behind the principle in the following terms: 'The payment and acceptance of parcel [part] before the day in satisfaction of the whole would be a good satisfaction in regard to circumstance of time, for parcel of it before the day would be more beneficial to [the claimant] than the whole at the day, and the value of the satisfaction is not material.'

- The judges in *Pinnel's case* also recognised the possibility that introducing some new element into the bargain in place of the agreed consideration could discharge the contract even if the new element ultimately lacked the overall value of the original consideration, provided that the creditor agreed to the change.

JUDGMENT

Again, in *Pinnel* the judges explained this point even though it was not appropriate to the circumstances of the case: 'the gift of a horse, hawk or robe, etc in satisfaction is good. For it shall be intended that a horse, hawk, or robe, etc might be more beneficial to the plaintiff than the money in some circumstance, or otherwise the plaintiff would not have accepted it in satisfaction'.

CASE EXAMPLE

British Russian Gazette Ltd v Associated Newspapers Ltd [1933] 2 KB 616

The claimant offered to give up two libel actions that he was bringing against the *Daily Mail* newspaper, in return for 1,000 guineas (a guinea is the same as £1.05). The payment would be in full satisfaction of any settlement and costs that he would receive. Before payment had actually been made, he went ahead with the actions and in the case the court ignored his argument that there could be no accord and satisfaction until payment was actually made. The letter offering to withdraw the actions and the response was good consideration, a promise in return for a promise, and he was bound by it.

- It is possible in the case of the latter that the changed element could be given in replacement of part of the sum or even the whole sum, as long as the change is accepted by the creditor.

Promissory estoppel

Finally, by the equitable doctrine of promissory estoppel, where the party waiting for performance has agreed to waive rights under the contract, knowing that the other party is relying on this promise to forgo performance, then the party making the promise may be prevented from going back on the promise.

Of course, in order for estoppel to discharge the debtor's obligations under the contract, the requirements identified by Lord Denning in *Combe v Combe* [1951] 2 KB 215 must be satisfied:

- There must be an existing contractual relationship between the claimant and the defendant.
- The claimant must have agreed to waive (give up) some of his rights under that contract (the amount of the debt that has been left unpaid).
- The claimant has waived these rights knowing that the defendant would rely on the promise in determining his future conduct.
- The defendant has in fact acted in reliance on the promise to forgo some of the debt.

This is because estoppel operates as a defence to the creditor's claim for full payment because equity will not allow him to go back on an agreement that he has reached knowing that the other party's actions will be altered because of the genuine reliance on the promise.

ACTIVITY

Self-assessment questions

1. Why should parties to a contract be able to discharge their obligations by agreement without actually performing them?
2. What is the difference between a bilateral discharge and a unilateral discharge?
3. In what way is form a problem in discharge by agreement?
4. In what ways is lack of consideration a problem in discharge by agreement?
5. When is it easiest to discharge a contract by agreement?
6. What is the easiest way of discharging a contract in a unilateral discharge?
7. What exactly is 'accord and satisfaction'?

KEY FACTS

Since a contract can be formed by agreement it can also be discharged without performance, by agreement of both parties.

Bilateral agreements	Case/statute

Bilateral discharge is simple where the contract is executory – the waiving of rights is given by the one party in return for the waiving of rights by the other:
 	
 • Where form is an issue, the discharge will need evidence in writing
 • Where only one party wants to back out of the contract then that party will need to give some consideration, as in accord and satisfaction, unless estoppel applies
 • If consideration is partly or wholly executed at new agreement:
   • a party may 'waive' rights (an example of where waiver has followed business practice)
   • the clear problem is the absence of consideration – judges will allow waiver to avoid broken promises
 • If form is an issue:
   • traditionally, there was no problem with an oral agreement to discharge where s 40 LPA 1925 was complied with
 • But agreements to vary terms are invalid unless evidenced in writing
 • If a new agreement is to be substituted for an existing agreement then it is unenforceable except in writing	

Unilateral agreements	Case/statute
A unilateral discharge is more difficult because one party fails to perform so there is a lack of consideration.	
There are three possibilities:	
• release by deed (although see now *Williams v Roffey* where the consideration is the 'extra benefit' gained by the party releasing the other from his obligations)	
• accord and satisfaction – which can be introducing a new element; or part-payment at an earlier stage (*Pinnel's case*)	*British Russian Gazette v Associated Newspapers Ltd*
• estoppel – when equity will not allow the party waiving rights to break the promise.	*Central London Properties Trust Co v High Trees House*

15.4 Discharge by frustration

15.4.1 The purpose and development of the doctrine

In the strictest sense, effective discharge of a contract, as we have seen, requires performance of all of the obligations under a contract. Inevitably, also, there will be times when the requirement for strict performance will lead to injustice.

This can be the case particularly where there is a factor preventing a party or parties from performing which is beyond the control of either party to the contract. It is because of this potential injustice that the doctrine of frustration developed in the nineteenth century.

The original common law rule was that a party was bound to perform his obligations under the contract regardless of the effect of any intervening events that might make it more difficult or even impossible to perform the contract. Under this strict rule, then, a party could not be discharged from contractual obligations even though the factors preventing him from performing were entirely unforeseeable and beyond his control.

CASE EXAMPLE

Paradine v Jane (1647) Aleyn 26

Paradine sued Jane for the rent that was due under a lease. Jane's defence was that he had been forced off the land by an invading army for a period of three years during the lifetime of the lease. The court held that he still had a contractual duty to pay the rent due under the lease, which was not discharged by any intervening event. The court considered that if he had wished to reduce his liability to take account of intervening events preventing his performance then he should have made express provision for that in the lease.

This was the strict rule and it would override any circumstances. The clear injustice of the strict rule above inevitably led on to the creation of exceptions. In the nineteenth century a doctrine was developed by which a party who was bound by contractual promises, in circumstances where he was prevented from keeping those promises because of an unforeseeable, intervening event, could then be relieved of the strict obligation to perform in all circumstances. As a result, that party would not be held liable for a breach of contract and both parties' obligations would be discharged at that point.

This is said to be the origin of the doctrine of frustration. It applies where, because of some external event, the fundamental purpose of the contract becomes 'frustrated' or made impossible to perform so that any attempt at performance would amount to something quite different from what was in the contemplation of the parties at the time the contract was formed.

CASE EXAMPLE

Taylor v Caldwell (1863) 32 LJ QB 164

Caldwell had agreed to rent the Surrey Garden and Music Hall to Taylor for four days for a series of concerts and fêtes. After the contract date, but before the concerts were due to start, the music hall burnt to the ground and performance of the contract was therefore impossible. The contract contained no stipulations as to what should happen in the event of fire. Since Taylor had spent money on advertising the concerts and other general preparations, he sued Caldwell for damages under the principle in *Paradine v Jane*. The court held, however, that the commercial purpose of the contract had ceased to exist, performance was impossible, and so both sides were excused from further performance of their obligations under the contract.

JUDGMENT

Blackburn J identified how judges could achieve the desired result by the fiction of implying into the contract a term that:

'in contracts in which performance depends on the continued existence of a given person or thing, a condition is implied that the impossibility of performance arising from the perishing of the person or thing shall excuse the performance … that excuse is by law implied, because from the nature of the contract it is apparent that the parties contracted on the basis of the continued existence of the particular person or chattel'.

Cheshire, Fifoot and Furmston comment that:

QUOTATION

'The precise legal theory upon which this doctrine of frustration is based has aroused much controversy. No fewer than five theories have been advanced at one time or another; but the essential question is whether the courts strive to give effect to the supposed intention of the parties or whether they act independently and impose the solution that seems reasonable and just. The former method was preferred by Blackburn J in *Taylor v Caldwell*.'

Cheshire, Fifoot and Furmston, Law of Contract *(14th edn, Butterworths, 2001)*

The doctrine has subsequently developed to cover those situations where the frustrating event has meant that performance as envisaged in the contract was impossible.

CASE EXAMPLE

Davis Contractors Ltd v Fareham UDC [1956] AC 696

A building firm contracted to build houses for a local council for £92,450 over a period of eight months. In fact, because of a shortage of skilled labour, the work took some

22 months to complete and the builders wanted an extra £17,651. The council paid the contract price. The builders claimed that the contract was frustrated in order to claim the extra amount on a *quantum meruit* basis. The House of Lords held that the contract was not in fact frustrated.

JUDGMENT

Lord Radcliffe did explain those factors that would justify the doctrine when used: 'without default of either party, a contractual obligation has become incapable of being performed because the circumstances in which performance is called for would render it a thing radically different from that which was undertaken by the contract'.

The immediate consequence of application of the doctrine, then, is that both parties are relieved of the burden of further performance, and of any liability for not performing. This will inevitably not remove every possible injustice since the one party to the contract is still being denied the performance of the other party through no fault of his own, and may still have incurred costs in anticipation of the contract being performed.

As a result, operation of the doctrine is subject to a number of limitations, and parties may provide in their contracts for what happens if there are intervening frustrating events: the so-called *force majeure* clauses.

15.4.2 The classifications of frustrating events

The doctrine has developed largely out of the case law, and it operates in many different circumstances. However, these can generally be grouped into three broad categories:

- Where the intervening event makes performance of the contract **impossible**.
- Where the intervening event means that performance of the contract becomes **illegal**.
- Where the intervening event means that the contract is in effect **commercially sterilised**.

Impossibility

The contract may be frustrated because of the destruction of the subject-matter. There would be little point in continuing with a contract where the subject of the contract no longer exists. If the thing to be exchanged no longer exists or the service can no longer be offered then the contract is impossible to perform and it would be unfair to hold the parties to their agreement.

CASE EXAMPLE

Taylor v Caldwell (1863) 32 LJ QB 164

Here, the destruction of the music hall was the cause of the impossibility. Since, under the contract, the concerts were to take place in the music hall, its destruction was central to preventing performance from taking place and hence the contract was frustrated for impossibility.

It may alternatively be the case that, even though the subject-matter exists, it may nevertheless become unavailable at the time when the contract is to be performed. This still makes the contract impossible to perform and it is frustrated in that sense.

CASE EXAMPLE

Jackson v Union Marine Insurance Co Ltd (1874) LR 10 CP 125

A ship was chartered to sail from Liverpool to Newport and then to sail on from there to San Francisco with a cargo of iron rails. The ship ran aground off the Welsh coast and could not be loaded for some time. The court accepted that a term should be implied into the contract that the ship should be available for loading in a reasonable time. The long delay in loading amounted to a frustration of the contract. It was impossible to perform the contract within a reasonable time.

Where a contract is for services, the frustrating event may be the unavailability because of illness of the party who is to render the service under the contract. Again, this makes the contract impossible to perform as expected in the contract.

CASE EXAMPLE

Robinson v Davidson (1871) LR 6 Ex 269

The defendant, while acting as agent for his wife, a celebrated pianist, contracted for her to perform. A few hours before her performance was due to begin, she became ill and the husband contacted the claimant to inform him that she would be unable to attend. The claimant then sued for a breach of contract but the court held that the contract was conditional on the woman being well enough to perform and because of her illness this was impossible. The contract was frustrated and she was excused performance in the circumstances.

This principle of impossibility because of the unavailability of a party who is central to performance of the contract may apply even where there is only a risk that the party will be unavailable.

CASE EXAMPLE

Condor v The Baron Knights [1966] 1 WLR 87

A contract entered into by a pop music group allowed that the group should be available to perform for seven evenings a week if necessary. One member of the group became ill and was advised to rest and work fewer hours. Though he actually ignored this advice, the court still held that the contract was frustrated since it was necessary to have a stand-in musician in case he fell ill.

Illness is merely one reason making it impossible for a person to perform his obligations under the contract, and long-term illness is certainly a common frustrating factor in the case of employment contracts. However, it is not the only possible reason – in fact, any good reason that will mean that a party is unavailable to perform his obligations may lead to a frustration of the contract.

CASE EXAMPLE

Morgan v Manser [1948] 1 KB 184

A music hall artiste was contracted to his manager for a 10-year period commencing in 1938. Between 1940 and 1946 he was in fact conscripted into the armed forces for most of the period of the Second World War. He was obviously unavailable to take up his usual commitments. His absence undermined the central purpose of the contract with his manager and both parties were thus excused performance.

We have already seen above the effect of delay on performance of a contract. In general, any excessive and unavoidable delay in performing has the potential to be classed as impossibility, since performance is expected to be in a reasonable time. This will usually mean that the contract is frustrated and the parties are relieved of further performance.

CASE EXAMPLE

Pioneer Shipping Ltd v BTP Tioxide Ltd (The Nema) [1981] 2 All ER 1030

The contract was for a time charter of nine months' duration. At the time of the agreement it was anticipated that seven voyages were possible within the time of the charter. In fact, because of strikes at the port where the vessel was loaded, the number of actual voyages was reduced to two. The excessive delays made it impossible to perform in the manner originally expected and the contract was held to be frustrated for impossibility.

Often, war and the obvious dangers of war can make it impossible to continue with contracts, particularly those involving shipping of cargoes through or near areas where there is active military engagement. A number of cases concerning ships that were left stranded and unable to move during the first Gulf War between Iraq and Iran illustrate this point. See *The Evia* [1983] 1 AC 736; *The Agathon* [1983] 2 Lloyd's Rep 211; *The Wenjiang* [1983] 1 Lloyd's Rep 400; and *Finelvet AG v Vinava Shipping Co Ltd* [1983] 2 All ER 658.

Outbreak of war is in any case, for the reasons stated above, a common frustrating event. The dangers presented by war will commonly make it unsafe and therefore impossible to perform the contract and so the courts will release the parties from their obligations. However, there are other factors during wartime that may make the contract impossible to perform.

CASE EXAMPLE

Metropolitan Water Board v Dick Kerr & Co Ltd [1918] AC 119

In July 1914 a contract was formed for the construction of a reservoir and a water works. The contract allowed that the work should be completed within a six-year period. In 1916 a government order stopped the work and also requisitioned most of the plant. It was held that the contract was frustrated at the time of the government order. It was impossible for the parties to continue performance after that point.

Subsequent illegality

The law will not enforce any contract that is illegal or tainted with illegality. In this respect a contract may become frustrated because of a change in the law after the time when the contract is formed that makes the contract illegal to perform in the manner anticipated in the contract. The courts would not expect parties to be bound to continue with contracts that could not be performed legally.

CASE EXAMPLE

Denny, Mott & Dickson Ltd v James B Fraser & Co Ltd [1944] 1 All ER 678

Here, the agreement was for the sale and purchase of timber. The contract was to continue over a number of years and under it the buyer was also bound to let a timber yard to the seller and provide him with an option to purchase it. In 1939 it became illegal to continue with the timber sales. The House of Lords held that since the contract for the sale of timber had been frustrated by the change in the law then the whole agreement had been radically altered and as a result it was prepared to consider that the option to purchase the yard had also been frustrated.

JUDGMENT

Lord Macmillan stated that: 'It is plain that a contract to do what it has become illegal to do cannot be legally enforceable.'

As was seen in the previous sub-section, the outbreak of war is an obvious time when laws may change rapidly in order to meet the needs of the current circumstances and as a result may cause a contract to be frustrated.

CASE EXAMPLE

Re Shipton Anderson & Co and Harrison Bros & Co [1915] 3 KB 676

Here, the contract was for the sale and purchase of a cargo of grain. Before the cargo could be delivered, war broke out. The government requisitioned the cargo for its own needs and the contract was frustrated as a result.

Commercial sterility

In those circumstances where, even though the contract is not impossible to perform, the commercial purpose of the contract has disappeared as a result of the intervening event or an event which is fundamental to the contract cannot or does not occur, then the contract might still be held to be frustrated. This is sometimes also known as 'frustration of the common venture', and it is commonly claimed when the essence of the bargain has in fact been lost.

CASE EXAMPLE

Krell v Henry [1903] 2 KB 740

A contract was reached for the hire of a room overlooking the procession route for the coronation of King Edward VII for two days in 1902. There was no specific mention of the purpose of the hire in the written agreement. However, when the coronation did not take place because of the king's illness and the defendant refused to pay for the room, the court, applying the principle from *Taylor v Caldwell*, accepted that the contract was frustrated. Watching the coronation procession was the 'foundation of the contract'; the defendant was relieved further performance and in other words was not bound to pay for the room.

However, for the contract to be considered frustrated, all commercial purpose must have been destroyed by the frustrating event. If some purpose can still be found in the contract then it will not be held to be frustrated and the obligations under the contract are not discharged and will continue.

CASE EXAMPLE

Herne Bay Steamboat Co v Hutton [1903] 2 KB 683

This was another case arising from the delayed coronation of the King. Part of the coronation celebrations was to be a review of the fleet by the newly crowned King. The defendant hired a boat from which to see the review of the fleet by the King but also, significantly, to sail round the Solent and see the fleet which was rarely all together in port at one time. His claim that the contract was frustrated failed. One purpose had disappeared, but it was still possible to use the boat and to see the fleet. The court would not accept that the commercial value of the contract had disappeared completely.

JUDGMENT

Vaughan Williams LJ drew an interesting comparison to explain the point: 'I see nothing to differentiate this contract from a contract by which some person engaged a cab to take him on each of three days to Epsom to see the races, and for some reason, such as the spread of an infectious disease or an anticipation of a riot, the races are prohibited. In such a case it could not be said that he would be relieved of his bargain.'

The leasing of land is always done with an ulterior purpose. Traditionally, however, when the purpose for which the lease was taken on was destroyed there was some doubt as to whether this would frustrate the contract and so the parties could still be bound by their obligations under the terms of the lease. The logic of this position is that the tenant still gains the benefit of owning a legal estate in land. So even though the house or premises that the tenant leased may be destroyed, eg by fire, and therefore unusable for the normal purpose, the rent would still be payable.

CASE EXAMPLE

Cricklewood Property and Investment Trust Ltd v Leighton's Investment Trust Ltd [1945] AC 221

A 99-year lease was taken out on land on which the lessee intended to build a number of shops. After the contract for the lease but before building started, the Second World War began. The government then introduced regulations preventing building developments of the type intended. The lessee attempted to claim frustration of the lease. The House of Lords rejected this claim, part of the reasoning being that the lease was a long one while the war would be only a short-term interference. The House was split on whether the doctrine of frustration could be applied to leases.

The case appears both unfair and irrational since obvious comparisons can be drawn with *Taylor v Caldwell* and the doctrine has been applied in the case of licences. The House of Lords at a later stage accepted that frustration could be applied to leases of land in limited circumstances where the purpose of the lease envisaged by both parties has become impossible and there is no longer any purpose to the lease.

CASE EXAMPLE

National Carriers Ltd v Panalpina (Northern) Ltd [1981] AC 675

Here, a party entered a 10-year lease of a warehouse. After the lease had been in operation for five years, the local authority then closed the street in which the warehouse was situated because of problems with another building in the street, thus obviously preventing access to the premises. The street was not due to be re-opened for 18 months. The tenant stopped paying rent and when the landlord brought an action for the rent, the tenant argued that the lease had been frustrated. Since there was still more than three years of the lease left to run after the street re-opened, the House of Lords felt that there was insufficient interruption with the purpose of the lease over its 10-year duration to amount to frustration. Nevertheless, with only Lord Russell dissenting, the House did accept that it would be illogical not to accept that a lease could be frustrated where the whole purpose of the lease as identified in the lease and contemplated by the parties to it became impossible following the intervening event.

JUDGMENT

Lord Wilberforce commented: 'A man may desire possession and use of land or buildings for, and only for, some purpose in view and mutually contemplated. Why is it an answer, when he claims that this purpose is "frustrated" to say that he has an estate if that estate is unusable and unsaleable? In such a case the lease, or the conferring of an estate, is a subsidiary means to an end, not an aim or end of itself.'

15.4.3 The limitations on the doctrine of frustration

The doctrine developed in *Taylor v Caldwell* (1863) 32 LJ QB 164 mitigates some of the harshness of the traditional common law rule on performance from *Paradine v Jane* (1647) Aleyn 26. However, while the doctrine removes the pressure to perform in circumstances where performance has become impossible, it still has the potential to act unfairly on the other party who may be ready and willing to complete his side of the bargain.

In an attempt to ensure that the doctrine applies as fairly as possible, the courts have identified a number of situations where they have stated that the doctrine **cannot** apply:

- Where the frustration is **self-induced**.
- Where the contract is merely **more difficult** or more onerous to perform rather than impossible to perform.
- Where there is a **foreseeable risk** of the frustrating event at the time when the contract is made.
- Where the parties have made **provisions** for the frustrating event in the contract itself.
- Where the contract in any case includes an **absolute undertaking** to perform.

Self-induced frustration

The nature of the doctrine of frustration demands that the parties are prevented from performing their obligations by an event which is beyond the control of either party. As a matter of logic, if one party has caused the event or it is within the control of that party, then the doctrine will not be applied to relieve further performance.

CASE EXAMPLE

Maritime National Fish Ltd v Ocean Trawlers Ltd [1935] AC 524

A fishing company had four trawlers but wished to fish with five trawlers. As a result, it chartered a trawler. All five trawlers were fitted with a specific type of fishing equipment and each vessel required a licence from the Canadian Government before it could be used. The company applied to the Canadian Government for five licences but in the event was granted only three. It was required to name the trawlers to which the licences applied and used three of its own. It then claimed that the charter had been frustrated and refused to pay for the hire of the trawler. The Privy Council rejected the company's claim and held that the contract was not discharged. The company could have used one of the three licences for the chartered vessel but instead had chosen to apply the licences to its own vessels. It had not been prevented from completing its obligations by an intervening event but was actually in control. The contract was not frustrated and the court held that the company was bound to pay for the hire of the vessel.

In the last case the court rejected the claim that the contract was frustrated because the party alleging it breached the contract by choice. Any frustration, therefore, was self-induced and it was only fair to hold that party to the contract. However, there are circumstances in which the intervening event forces that party into choosing between two contractual obligations and breaching one. In such circumstances, self-induced frustration may still be applied but the outcome may appear less fair in the circumstances.

CASE EXAMPLE

J Lauritzen AS v Wijsmuller BV (The Super Servant Two) [1990] 1 Lloyd's Rep 1

The contract was to transport an oilrig from Japan to its moorings at sea. Both parties were aware that the rig could only be transported by one of two ships owned by the defendant, called the *Super Servant One* and the *Super Servant Two*, although the contract did not actually specify which of the two vessels would be used for the contract. The owners of the two ships had intended to use *Super Servant Two* and on that basis, contracted the other ship for other work. Unfortunately, the *Super Servant Two* then sank, so that it was unavailable. The defendants almost inevitably claimed that the contract was frustrated and wished to be discharged from their obligations under it. The Court of Appeal rejected this claim and held that any impossibility arose not from an intervening event but from the defendants' own choice. Even though the destruction of the vessel was not the fault of the defendants, the contract was in effect made impossible as a result of their own choice and the doctrine of frustration could not be applied to relieve them of their liability to perform.

Contract more onerous to perform

The courts will not declare a contract frustrated and release the parties from their obligations merely because the contract has become more difficult to perform or because the contract has become less beneficial to one party as a result of the intervening event.

CASE EXAMPLE

Davis Contractors Ltd v Fareham UDC [1956] AC 696

Here, the builders wanted to claim that the contract was frustrated in order to avoid the contract merely because the shortages of building supplies meant that they would take much longer to complete the work than they had envisaged and therefore would lose profit they wished to make. The court was not prepared to accept that mere hardship or inconvenience was sufficient grounds to justify declaring the contract frustrated.

This may even be the case where, as a result of a change in the law, the contract has merely become less advantageous than it might otherwise have been.

CASE EXAMPLE

Bormarin AB v IBM Investments Ltd [1999] STC 301

The contract was for the purchase of share capital. The major purpose of the contract was for the purchaser to be able to set losses off against gains. Under the law at the time of the contract, this was legal but, under a change in the law, losses could not then be set off in this way. The Court of Appeal refused to accept the claim of frustration since the contract had merely become less advantageous to the purchaser.

It will also be the case where the contract is made impossible to perform in a manner which was contemplated by only one of the parties.

CASE EXAMPLE

CTI Group v Transclear SA (The Mary Nour) [2008] EWCA Civ 856

A seller of cement intended to break a cartel operated by a Mexican company by buying up a large amount of cement from a supplier and storing it in a ship moored off Mexico where it could be re-bagged and then sold on to a buyer in the Mexican market. Unfortunately the supplier then failed to deliver the cement when it was put under pressure by the Mexican cartel. The court accepted that the doctrine of frustration might apply to a sale by description of unascertained goods. However, it also held that in the circumstances of the case there was no intervening act that was not the fault of either party. The fact that the supplier had chosen not to supply the cement making it impossible for the seller to perform the contract was not sufficient on its own to frustrate the contract.

Foreseeable risk

If, at the time when the contract was formed, the event claimed as frustrating the contract was a risk that was already in the contemplation of the parties, that might carry with it the possibility that the contract might not be completed, then the plea of frustration will be rejected. The court will not accept that the event is one that intervenes beyond the control of either party when the parties already contemplated or should have contemplated that it might occur.

CASE EXAMPLE

Amalgamated Investment & Property Co Ltd v John Walker & Sons Ltd [1977] 1 WLR 164

The defendants contracted to sell a building to the Investment Company who wanted it for redevelopment. Indeed, the building was stated in the contract as being suitable for development. The claimants never made any enquiries as to whether or not the building was of historic or architectural interest and the defendants were not aware at the time of the contract that it was. Unknown to either party, the Department of the Environment then listed the building, meaning that it was of historical or architectural interest and as a result it could not be used for property development. In consequence, the value of the building dropped by £1.5 million from the contract price of £1.71 million. The court rejected the claimant's argument that the contract was frustrated as a result of the listing. The court held that listing was a common risk associated with all old buildings of which the developers, being specialists in the property market, should have been aware. The case was also argued on the basis of a common mistake that should have rendered the contract void. The court also rejected this argument since the mistake would not have been operative at the time the contract was made.

Provisions made in the contract for the frustrating event

If the parties have contemplated the possibility of a frustrating event and catered for that possibility within the contract, then a plea of frustration will fail and there can be no release from contractual obligations.

CASE EXAMPLE

Fibrosa Spolka Akcyjna v Fairbairn Lawson Combe Barbour Ltd (The Fibrosa case) [1943] AC 32

A contract was formed for the sale of machinery to a Polish company. Before the contract could actually be performed, delivery was made impossible because of the German invasion of Poland before the start of the Second World War. In fact, the contract actually contained what was referred to as a 'war clause' and the argument was raised that there was no frustration because the clause covered the event in question. However, the House of Lords in this instance was prepared to accept that the contract was still frustrated in the event because the clause only provided for delays in delivery and inconvenience caused by war, but not for the more dramatic and far-reaching consequences of invasion.

So-called *force majeure* clauses are commonly used in contracts as a means of determining what happens if a frustrating event, the possibility of which is foreseen at the time the contract is formed, actually occurs. Such clauses will identify who bears any consequential losses. However, if the clause does not specifically cover the event in question then frustration of the contract may inevitably still be claimed.

CASE EXAMPLE

Jackson v Union Marine Insurance Ltd (1874) LR 10 CP 125

Here, the ship chartered to sail from Liverpool to Newport and then to San Francisco with a cargo of iron rails ran aground and could not be loaded for some time. The contract included the words 'damages and accidents of navigation excepted'. Because the charterparty was asked if it would continue with the contract the shipowners then tried to claim that their initial agreement to some delay was an affirmation of the contract. The Court of Appeal would not accept that the clause covered the event; the contract was therefore frustrated; and there could be no affirmation in these circumstances.

Absolute undertaking to perform

Where the contract contains an undertaking that performance should occur in any circumstances then a frustrating event will not affect the obligations. This inevitably binds the parties to the contract and the intervening event is irrelevant in the context of the contract. The principle is also, of course, the basic original common law rule.

CASE EXAMPLE

Paradine v Jane (1647) Aleyn 26

The principle originally operated quite strictly in relation to land. In this case the court took the view that, despite the loss of the practical benefits of possession of the land, since the parties had made no express provision for what should happen in the case of an intervening event, they were bound absolutely by the terms of the lease.

ACTIVITY

Quick quiz

Which of the following involve frustrating events and which do not?

1. A famous comedian dies just before he is due to appear on stage.
2. A plumber is contracted to fit central heating in a house. He underestimates the days needed to complete the work and as a result he will lose profit on the price agreed.
3. A car I had contracted to buy is destroyed when an explosion sets fire to it.
4. As a lecturer, I have contracted personally to take 15 students on a trip to court. An Act is passed requiring teaching and lecturing staff to take no more than 10 students per one member of staff on educational visits.
5. In a contract to supply a Far Eastern state with machinery, one clause stipulates what happens in the event of war. In fact, war is declared after the making of the contract.

15.4.4 The common law effects of frustration

The traditional common law principles operated fairly harshly on one party to the contract. This was the reason behind the development of a doctrine of frustration. However, even under the doctrine the effects of frustration could still prove harsh, but usually on the other party.

By the doctrine, the contract terminates at the actual point of the frustration. The result of this is that the parties are released from their obligation to perform from the point when the contract is frustrated. However, they would still be bound by any obligations that have arisen before the frustrating event occurred.

CASE EXAMPLE

Chandler v Webster [1904] 1 KB 493

This was another of the cases arising from the delayed coronation of Edward VII. The facts are similar to *Krell v Henry*. Again, a party hired a room in a position along the route of the procession in order to watch it. In this instance, however, and unlike in *Krell v Henry*, where the room was to be paid for on the day of the procession, in this case the room was actually paid for in advance. While the court was prepared to accept that the contract was indeed frustrated, it would not allow recovery of the money already paid.

This is clearly an unsatisfactory situation because the effective outcome depends entirely on the point reached in the contract when the frustrating event occurs. So the same frustrating event can lead to entirely different outcomes for the parties.

The House of Lords recognised the harshness of the principle in the *Fibrosa* case ([1943] AC 32) and devised rules to modify the harshness created by the rule.

CASE EXAMPLE

Fibrosa Spolka Akcyjna v Fairbairn Lawson Combe Barbour Ltd
(The Fibrosa case) [1943] AC 32

The contract for the manufacture and delivery of machinery to a Polish company was frustrated by the invasion of Poland prior to the start of the Second World War. Under the contract, the Polish company had been required to make an advance payment of £1,000 for the machinery. The House of Lords held that a party could recover payments made prior to a frustrating event provided that there was a total failure of consideration. This is an improvement on the basic position in frustration, but of course it may still mean that one party, in this case the manufacturer of the machines, will lose out and will receive no payment for work that has already been done in advance of a contract.

JUDGMENT

Lord Macmillan explained the position in the *Fibrosa* case: 'Owing to circumstances arising out of present hostilities the contract has become impossible of fulfilment according to its terms. Neither party is to blame. In return for their money the plaintiffs have received nothing whatever from the defendants by way of fulfilment of any part of the contract. It is thus a typical case of a total failure of consideration. The money paid must be repaid.'

15.4.5 Statutory effects under the law reform (Frustrated Contracts) Act 1943

Frustration is a common law doctrine originally developed to avoid some of the harshness of the existing common law rules. Nevertheless, as has been shown, it can still lead to injustice itself. As a result, Parliament, following the *Fibrosa* case, passed the Law Reform (Frustrated Contracts) Act 1943 specifically to deal with the consequences of frustrating events and to provide a fairer means of identifying who should bear loss and who should be entitled to recover and in what circumstances.

The 1943 Act covers three main areas:

- recovery of **money paid in advance** of a contract
- recovery for **work already completed** under the contract
- financial reward where a **valuable benefit** has been conferred.

Money paid in advance

Section 1(2) of the 1943 Act confirms and expands on the principle already established in the *Fibrosa* case: that money already paid over in advance of performance of the contract can be recovered despite the apparent lack of consideration. Of course, it is also the case that money due under the contract also ceases to be payable.

This must be read in conjunction with s 1(3) that covers those situations where a party has gained a valuable benefit under the contract and which may in that case limit the right to recover money paid over.

Nevertheless, the section means that it is possible to recover sums paid over even in certain cases where a partial performance has occurred and therefore there is not in fact a complete absence of consideration.

Recovery for work already undertaken

Section 1(2) of the 1943 Act also tries to reduce the potential unfairness both under the original common law rule and under *Fibrosa*. It does so by giving the court some

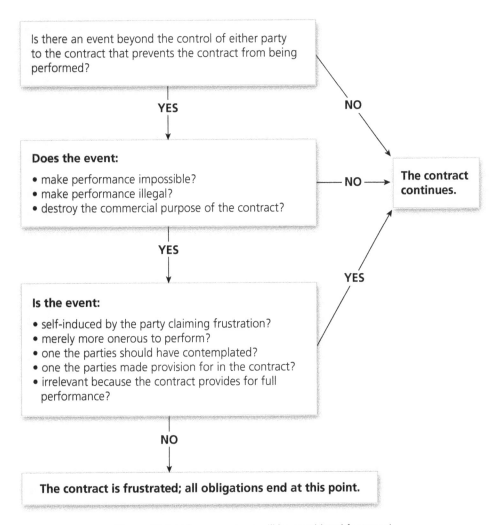

Figure 15.1 When a contract will be considered frustrated

discretion to provide some form of reward for a party who has carried out work under or in preparation for the contract.

While having the potential to mitigate the harshness of the rule, the section nevertheless has two important limitations:

- The sum awarded is discretionary and is what the court believes to be a fair amount in the circumstances, not what a party has actually incurred in the way of expenses. So it is not a guarantee of recovery of all expenses incurred.

CASE EXAMPLE

Gamerco SA v ICM/Fair Warning Agency [1995] 1 WLR 1226

The case involved the cancellation of a pop concert after the government, for safety reasons, closed the venue for the concert. The claimant had paid over $412,500 in advance and had suffered an overall loss of around $450,000. The defendants had incurred expenses of around $50,000. The court held that the discretion could be exercised in the case and that, in all the circumstances and taking both things into consideration, a fair solution was recovery of $412,500 by the claimants.

> Besides this, the court will only apportion the loss in this way where there was also an obligation to pay money over in advance of the contract.

Recovery for a benefit gained through partial performance

Finally, under s 1(3) of the 1943 Act, a party is able to recover for a partial performance which has conferred a valuable benefit on the other party before the contract was discharged by the frustrating event. Again, application of the principle is at the discretion of the court.

The principle is not particularly straightforward but has been explained in subsequent case law. In applying s 1(3), the court has to engage in a two-part process:

> Firstly, it must be satisfied of the existence of a valuable benefit gained by one party.
> Secondly, once this is established then the court must identify what is the appropriate or 'just' sum to award in the circumstances of the case. (In this respect the section identifies that the sum must not exceed the value of the actual benefit gained by the other party.)

CASE EXAMPLE

BP Exploration Co (Libya) Ltd v Hunt (No 2) [1979] 1 WLR 783

By the contract between them, Hunt was granted a concession by BP to explore for oil in Libya and then also drill for any oil that was found. BP agreed to finance the project in return for a half-share of the concession. Its expenses would be three-eighths of the oil found until it had recovered 125 per cent of its outlay. Hunt did in fact discover quite a large oil field and began drilling operations but the Libyan Government then claimed all rights to the oil field, meaning that the contract between Hunt and BP was in effect frustrated. At this point BP had actually recovered only a small proportion of its expenses and consequently sued under s 1(3) of the 1943 Act since Hunt had gained a valuable benefit in terms of the oil that he had already drilled and compensation from the Libyan Government. Applying the principles above, the court identified that any sum awarded should be based not on the sum that BP had spent in financing the arrangement but on the benefit already enjoyed by Hunt. BP had already spent $87 million on development and Hunt had also received £10 million. Under the terms of the agreement, BP had recovered so far only £62 million. On this basis it was awarded $35 million by the court, the difference between the two amounts, since this did not exceed the benefit gained by Hunt.

This application of the provision appears to be based on preventing the unjust enrichment of one party. The provision obviously does help to prevent some of the unfairness in the previous law but it also has obvious limitations. The section can only be used where a party has obtained a valuable benefit before the frustrating event discharges the contract. If any benefit would not be gained by the other party before this time and neither was any money payable before this time, then neither s 1(2) nor s 1(3) could be used to recover for work already completed.

Limitations of the 1943 Act

The effectiveness of the 1943 Act is also limited further because it does not apply in certain circumstances identified in the Act itself. These include:

> By s 2(4), the Act will not apply in the case of severable or divisible contracts where one part of the contract has been completely performed before the frustrating event. This is not a problem if that part of the contract is paid for separately.
> By s 2(5), the Act will not apply to contracts for the carriage of goods by sea, except time charterparties.

- Also by s 2(5), the Act does not apply to insurance contracts. However, such contracts in any case concern accepting the risk of specific events occurring, eg a house burning down for which a sum of money is then payable, so this exclusion is perfectly logical.
- By s 2(5)(c), the Act will not apply in the case of the perishing of goods under s 7 of the Sale of Goods Act 1979.
- Finally, it is possible by s 2(3) for the parties to exclude the provisions of the Act where they have already arranged in the contract for what happens if a frustrating event occurs.

ACTIVITY

Self-assessment questions

1. What was unfair about the rule in *Paradine v Jane*?
2. What exactly is 'a frustrating event'?
3. How did *Taylor v Caldwell* help to modify the harshness in the law?
4. What are the differences between 'impossibility' and 'commercial sterility'?
5. In what ways is the doctrine still unfair on at least one party?
6. Is there really a frustrating event where the frustration is self-induced?
7. How does the *Fibrosa* case modify the principle?
8. How does the Law Reform (Frustrated Contracts) Act 1943 modify the principle?

KEY FACTS

The background to frustration and the basic rule	Case/statute
A frustrating event is one that prevents performance of the contract but is beyond the control of either party.	
The original rule on frustrating events was that a party was still bound by all obligations under the contract.	*Paradine v Jane*
A doctrine was developed in the nineteenth century so that in such cases obligations finished at the point of the frustrating event.	*Taylor v Caldwell*

Frustrating events	Case/statute
Impossibility:	
• because of the destruction of the subject-matter	*Taylor v Caldwell*
• because of the unavailability of the other party	*Robinson v Davidson*
• because of the outbreak of war	*Metropolitan Water Board v Dick Kerr & Co*
• because of excessive, unavoidable delay.	*The Evia*
Subsequent illegality:	
• because the law of another country changes	*Denny, Mott & Dickinson v James B Fraser*
• because of outbreak of war.	*Re ShiptonAnderson*
Commercial sterilisation:	
• because the commercial purpose in the contract is lost	*Krell v Henry*
• but not if some commercial purpose remains.	*Herne Bay Steamboat Co v Hutton*

Frustration will not include	Case/statute
Where it is self-induced.	*Maritime National Fish Ltd v Ocean Trawlers Ltd*
Where the contract is merely more burdensome to perform.	*Davis Ltd Contractors v Fareham UDC*
Where the risk is foreseeable.	*Amalgamated Investment & Property Co Ltd v John Walker & Sons Ltd*
Where the risk of the event has been provided for in the contract.	*the Fibrosa case*
The common law effects of frustration	**Case/statute**
At common law, all obligations finish at the point of frustration.	*Chandler v Webster*
The common law principle was changed so that payments made before the frustrating event could be recovered.	*Fibrosa*
Law Reform (Frustrated Contracts) Act 1943	**Case/statute**
Money ceases to be payable from the point of frustration (as in *Taylor v Caldwell*).	s 1(2)
Also, money paid in advance of the contract can be recovered.	s 1(2)
Also, the court has discretion to reward a party who has done work under the contract.	s 1(2)
The court can allow recovery for partial performance that has conferred a valuable benefit on the other party.	s 1(3)
But it is for the court to determine what is reasonable in the circumstances.	*BP Exploration (Libya) v Hunt (No 2)*
The Act does not apply to carriage of goods by sea, contracts of insurance, and perishing of goods under Sale of Goods Act 1979.	

15.5 Discharge by breach

15.5.1 The fundamental nature of breach of contract

Whenever a party fails to perform an obligation arising under a contract then that party can be said to be in breach of contract.

A breach of the contract can actually occur in one of two ways:

- By **failing to perform obligations** – this situation itself can occur in one of two ways:
  - either the contract is not performed at all; or
  - the contract is not performed to the standard required under the contract, eg by providing goods that are not of satisfactory quality.
- By **repudiating the contract**, or obligations under it, without any lawful justification.

Breach is always described as a method of discharge although this actually seems slightly illogical since by definition a breach means that the obligations under the contract have not been discharged.

Lord Diplock explained this position in *Photo Productions Ltd v Securicor Transport Ltd* [1980] AC 827. He suggested that the terms of a contract, whether express or implied, are primary obligations. If a party fails to perform what he has promised to do then this is a breach of a primary obligation. The consequence of the breach of this primary obligation is that it is then replaced by a secondary obligation, the most common one obviously being the requirement to pay damages. Seen in this way, breach is not so much a discharge of the contract but a replacing of one set of obligations with a different set.

Lord Diplock also saw there being two basic exceptions to his proposition:

- The doctrine of **fundamental breach** – whereby if a breach of a term deprives the other party of substantially the benefit they were to receive under the contract then the whole contract is said to be breached. (It is unlikely, of course, that this doctrine has actually survived the Securicor cases.)
- Breach of a **condition** – where the term is so central to the contract that its breach renders the contract meaningless and thus entitles the other party to repudiate their obligations under the contract instead of or as well as a claim for damages.

One of the most important traditional differences between the two would have been the effect on exclusion clauses. While exclusion clauses would be rendered ineffective where a fundamental breach of the contract was recognised, under the second it would still be possible successfully to rely on an exclusion clause despite there being a breach of a condition. This is precisely the point that the *Securicor* cases demonstrate.

15.5.2 The different types of breach

Based on the above, it is possible to identify three particular forms of breach. The consequences of the breach depend on the nature of the breach. They are:

- breach of any **term**
- breach of a **condition**, going to the root of the contract
- an **anticipatory breach**, where performance of the contract is not yet due, but the claimant is aware that a breach will occur.

Breach of an ordinary term

Here, in effect, the character of a term is unimportant. Regardless of whether it is a condition or a warranty, if a term is breached there will always be available an action for damages.

Breach of a condition

A condition is a term going to the root of the contract. This means that if it is breached it would render the contract meaningless. A condition can either be expressed by the parties themselves or indeed it can be implied by law, as in the case of the implied conditions in the Sale of Goods Act 1979 (see section 6.3.4). However if it is identified as being a condition, it must of course conform to the nature of a condition or it will not attract the range of remedies associated with that. Damages may be available as a remedy but the victim of the breach will not be able lawfully to repudiate his obligations under the contract.

CASE EXAMPLE

Schuler (L) AG v Wickman Machine Tools Sales Ltd [1974] AC 235

Here (as we have seen in section 6.5), the claimants were not able to rely on the term regarding the required frequency of visits by the defendants to the motor manufacturers in order to repudiate their obligations. They had accepted numerous similar breaches in the past. The term obviously did not go to the root of the contract. Despite the fact that the term had been stated in the contract as a condition, because it did not demonstrate the actual characteristics of a condition, the court was unable to accept that the repudiation of the party was lawful. As a result, the court held that, despite the classification of the term in the contract, the only available remedy would have been damages, as for breaches of terms generally.

JUDGMENT

Lord Reid identifies the reasoning of the court: 'we must remember that we are seeking to discover intention as disclosed by the contract as a whole. Use of the word "condition" is an indication – even a strong indication – of such an intention but it is by no means conclusive. The fact that a particular construction leads to a very unreasonable result must be a relevant consideration. The more unreasonable the result, the more unlikely it is that the parties can have intended it, and if they do intend it, the more necessary it is that they shall make themselves abundantly clear.'

A breach of a condition could also in effect include a breach of an innominate term where the effect of the breach was so serious as to justify repudiation by the other party.

CASE EXAMPLE

Bunge Corporation v Tradax Export SA [1981] 1 WLR 711

Here, where the buyer was required under the contract to give at least 15 days' notice of readiness to load the vessel and gave only 13 days' notice, the House of Lords held that there was a breach justifying repudiation. Lord Wilberforce explained that since the sellers' obligation to ship was a condition then obligation to give notice to load in proper time should be a condition also. The consequences of the breach were irrelevant to the issue. In the event, they were minor, which was why the first-instance judge had felt that the breach did not justify repudiation. Nevertheless, Lord Wilberforce felt that stipulations as to time in mercantile contracts should usually be viewed as conditions.

At a time when the doctrine was still operative, then the principle might also have included a fundamental breach.

Anticipatory breach

An anticipatory breach is one that occurs before the date for performance of the contract. It is accepted as a breach because one party to the contract either expressly gives notice to the other party that he will not complete his obligations, or alternatively his conduct is such that it can be implied from that conduct that he will not complete his obligations under the contract and that there will therefore be a breach of contract.

Again, this does not necessarily have to mean that all of the party's obligations will remain unperformed. It could, of course, be the case that some, or even all, of the obligations will be performed but not according to the manner described in the contract. An obvious example of the latter would be late performance, where the delivery of the goods will not occur until after the due date in the contract.

In effect, then, the doctrine of anticipatory breach can probably be described more correctly as a breach as a result of an anticipatory repudiation of the contract, as this is in effect what is usually taking place.

CASE EXAMPLE

Hochster v De la Tour (1853) 2 E & B 678

The claimant was hired to begin work as a courier two months after the contract date. One month later, the defendants wrote to him and cancelled the contract. The defendants then tried to answer his claim by arguing that he could not sue unless he could actually show that on the due date he was ready to perform. The court would not accept this defence. The court held that there was no requirement that the victim of a breach of contract should be obliged to wait until the contract was in fact breached before being able to sue. It was sufficient that the claimant was aware that a breach would occur and he could sue accordingly.

JUDGMENT

Lord Campbell CJ explained why: 'it is surely much more rational, and more for the benefit of both parties, that, after the renunciation of the agreement by the defendant, the plaintiff should be at liberty to consider himself absolved from any further performance of it, retaining his right to sue for any damage he has suffered by the breach of it. Thus, instead of remaining idle and laying out money in preparations which must be useless, he is at liberty to seek service under another employer, which would go to **mitigation** of the damages to which he would otherwise be entitled.'

---

mitigation

A party who is the victim of a breach of contract ensuring that they do not unreasonably add to the damages payable to them by the other party

---

15.5.3 The different consequences of breach of contract

It is a natural consequence of there being different types of breach that the effects of the breach will also differ. The consequences for the party who is the victim of a breach of contract and the remedies available will vary according to the categories of breach that we have already considered.

Breach of an ordinary term

Wherever there is a breach of a term, an action for damages is always available, regardless of how the term is classified. If the term is only a warranty or, where a court determines that the terms in question are innominate but the breach is not a serious one and therefore does not justify repudiation of the contract by that party, then only an action for damages is available. In these particular circumstances the victim of the breach needs to exercise some caution because any attempt to repudiate the contract will itself amount to a breach of contract. The other party then has an action for the unlawful repudiation.

Breach of a condition

Where, on the other hand, a condition is breached or the court has declared that the term is innominate and the breach is sufficiently serious to justify repudiation of obligations, the party who is the victim of the breach has more choice. He may continue with the contract and sue for damages, or repudiate his own obligations under the contract, or indeed both repudiate his own obligations and sue for damages as well.

Before repudiating, of course, a party should be certain that the term is in fact a condition that would entitle him to repudiate his obligations or that where terms are classed as innominate the breach by the other party is so serious as to justify repudiation. Again, the problem for the victim of the breach is that his own repudiation might be identified as a breach, giving the other party a right to a remedy for the unlawful repudiation.

CASE EXAMPLE

Cehave NV v Bremer Handelsgesselschaft mbH (The Hansa Nord)
[1976] QB 44

Here, the court identified that the buyer's refusal to accept the animal feed was an unlawful repudiation. By classing the term as innominate it could then be shown that, since the buyer went on to buy the goods and still use them for the original purpose, the effects of the breach could not have been sufficiently serious to justify repudiation.

The intention of the parties at the time the contract was formed is clearly significant in determining the outcome of a breach. However, the manner in which the parties describe the term may be less important to the court in determining the outcome than whether or not the term was in fact a significant and central term and thus whether in fact the breach was a significant breach.

CASE EXAMPLE

Rice v Great Yarmouth Borough Council (2000) *The Times*, 30th June

The claimant had contracted with the council to provide leisure management and grounds maintenance services for a four-year period. One clause of the contract, Clause 23, identified that if any obligation under the contract were breached then the council would be entitled to consider the contract terminated. The council then sought to rely on this clause to terminate the contract. The Court of Appeal rejected the use of such a wide-ranging clause and held that there could only be a right to repudiate the contract where there was a breach of a term that was sufficiently serious to justify repudiation. It also held that a common-sense approach should be taken in interpreting Clause 23. The clause, if literally interpreted, would give the right to repudiate in the case of any breach of any term, even where the term was of minor significance to the overall performance of the contract, and this was not acceptable.

Anticipatory breach

Here again, the party who is victim of the breach has choices available once having discovered that the contract will be breached. This is largely because that party should not be made to suffer by having to wait for the breach, but it may well be advantageous to that party to wait for the breach before deciding how to react.

As a result of this, one course of action open to the victim of the breach is immediately to consider the contract at an end and sue for damages.

CASE EXAMPLE

Frost v Knight (1872) LR 7 Exch 111

At one time a broken promise to marry was actionable in law, although this has since been repealed. Here, the defendant had promised to marry his fiancée when his father died. Before his father did die, however, he broke off his engagement with his fiancée. The fiancée then sued successfully for the breach of promise even though the date of the actual beach had not yet arrived since the father was still alive.

An alternative to suing immediately is to continue with the contract, to wait for the due date of performance and, if the contract is not then performed, to sue instead at that point. This can of course be advantageous to the claimant, and the claimant might consider that there is still a possibility that the contract could be completed. However, it can also be disadvantageous if conditions change before the actual breach.

CASE EXAMPLE

Avery v Bowden (1855) 5 E & B 714

Bowden was contracted to load cargo onto a ship for Avery. At one point before the due date it became clear that Bowden would be unable to meet his obligations. At this point, as we have seen, Avery could obviously have sued. He waited, however, in the hope that the contract would be completed, but intending to sue if it was not completed. This actually turned out to be a mistaken strategy since the Crimean War then broke out, frustrating the contract, so that the court inevitably held that obligations ceased at the point of frustration and Avery was in consequence left without a remedy for the breach.

It is always a danger for a party to take this latter course of action. The contract remains in force and as a result it is always possible for the party who is the victim of the breach not only to lose his remedy but also to become liable for a breach.

CASE EXAMPLE

Fercometal SARL v Mediterranean Shipping Co SA (The Simona) [1989] 2 All ER 742

A charterparty contained an 'expected readiness to load' clause, entitling the charterers to repudiate if the ship was not loaded by 9th June. The shipowners asked for an extension on 2nd June and the charterers then chartered another ship. The shipowners, instead of repudiating at this point for the breach by the charterers, gave notice of readiness to load instead. In fact, this was not the case and they were unable to. The charterers continued to use the other vessel. The shipowners' action eventually failed in the House of Lords. The House held that since the victims of the breach had elected to affirm the contract they were in fact still bound by their own original terms. The court held that they were in breach of these terms because they were not ready to load on 9th June.

It is also possible that the fact of the innocent party having the right to affirm the contract can itself cause apparent injustice to the other party.

CASE EXAMPLE

White and Carter Ltd v McGregor [1962] AC 413

Under a contract, one party was to supply litter bins for a local council. The bins were to be paid for from advertising revenue from businesses that would have advertisements placed on the bins for a three-year period. One such business backed out of the arrangement before the bins had actually been prepared. The supplier of the bins nevertheless prepared the advertising and continued to use it for the whole period of the contract. He then sued successfully for the full price. The court accepted that he was not bound to end his own obligations merely because the other party's had been breached.

Where the innocent party decides to accept the repudiatory breach of the other party then he is entitled to recover for the loss of any benefits that would have resulted from performance of the contract. The party in breach cannot then try to reduce damages because of a subsequent act of the innocent party that might have the effect of reducing the overall loss.

CASE EXAMPLE

Chiemgauer Membrand und Zeltbau (formerly Koch Hightex GmbH) v New Millennium Experience Co Ltd (formerly Millennium Central Ltd) (No 2) (2001) The Times, 16th January

The claimant was given the contract to build the roof of the Millennium Dome in London. Under the contract the defendants could terminate provided they paid a sum of compensation identified in the contract as 'direct loss and damage'. The claimant then became insolvent. In its claim against the defendants it argued that 'direct loss' should include its loss of profits and the court, applying the first limb of *Hadley v Baxendale*, agreed. The defendants argued that the claimant would have been unable to complete the contract even without their termination and that its subsequent insolvency meant that they should not be fixed with the claimant's loss of profits. The Court of Appeal disagreed, and considered that the facts could be compared with those cases where an innocent party accepts the other party's repudiatory breach and is still entitled to all benefits arising naturally under the contract.

Another issue concerns whether an innocent party who is the victim of a repudiatory breach of a contract including a right to terminate and a clause for liquidated damages is also able to elect to treat the contract as repudiated and claim also for loss of bargain.

CASE EXAMPLE

Stocznia Gdynia SA v Gearbulk Holdings Ltd [2009] EWCA Civ 75

Under a contract Stocznia Gdynia were to construct three ships for Gearbulk Holdings. Article 10 of the contract identified that the price would reduce by way of liquidated damages if the case of excessive delay in supplying the vessels or for other named deficiencies and Gearbulk could terminate the contract in the event of a major breach in failing to proceed with the construction of the vessels. In this event under Clause 10 Gearbulk would be entitled to return of all money already paid in advance of the contract together with interest. In fact none of the three vessels was completed although some minimal work was done on the hull of one. Gearbulk then terminated the contract and wrote to Stocznia asking not only for the return of money already paid together with interests but also for a sum representing the loss of the bargain, in other words for the difference between the contract price and what it would now have to pay in the open market. Stocznia argued that Gearbulk was only entitled to return of the money already paid plus interest as under clause 10 and this then went to arbitration. In the Court of Appeal it was held that the fact that Gearbulk was able to benefit under clause 10 by terminating the contract and gaining liquidated damages did not mean that it had no right in common law to repudiate and receive damages also for loss of bargain.

JUDGMENT

Moore-Bick LJ identified: "... [Stocznia] *had repudiated each of the contracts by the time Gearbulk sent its letter of termination ... It must be borne in mind that all that is required for acceptance of a repudiation at common law is for the injured party to communicate clearly and unequivocally his intention to treat the contract as discharged ... In the present case ...* [the breaches by Stocznia] *which entitled Gearbulk to terminate the contracts were in each case sufficient to amount to a repudiation ...* [although] *Gearbulk purported to terminate the contract pursuant to Article 10 ... and not under the general law, ... each of the letters made it clear that it was treating the contract as discharged and in those circumstances each was sufficient to amount to an acceptance of* [Stocznia's] *repudiation.*

The case law shows up many of the difficulties of the area.

Michael Whincup comments on the difficulties for claimants confronted by anticipatory breach:

QUOTATION

'This whole area of law is evidently far more problematic than one might at first imagine, particularly in the light of its commercial significance. Up to a point, of course, uncertainty is inherent and inevitable, but it does not seem too much to ask that the law should give some clearer guidance to innocent parties on identifying and acting upon anticipatory breaches. While every case turns largely on its own facts, litigants still need to know which facts are likely to be important, and what are the probable legal consequences.'

M Whincup, 'Reacting to Repudiation' New Law Journal, 17 May 1996, p 729

ACTIVITY

Self-assessment questions

1. In what way does a breach of contract discharge the obligations under it?
2. Identify precisely what Lord Diplock means when he refers to 'primary obligations' and 'secondary obligations'.
3. How limited are the remedies available to a party who has suffered only a breach of warranty?
4. What reasons are there for there being a difference between the remedies available for a breach of a condition and those available for a breach of a warranty?
5. What effect does breach of an innominate term have?
6. Exactly what is an anticipatory breach?
7. Why does a claimant have a choice of possible courses of action when there is an anticipatory breach?
8. What possible problems are there in waiting till the actual breach when there is an anticipatory breach?

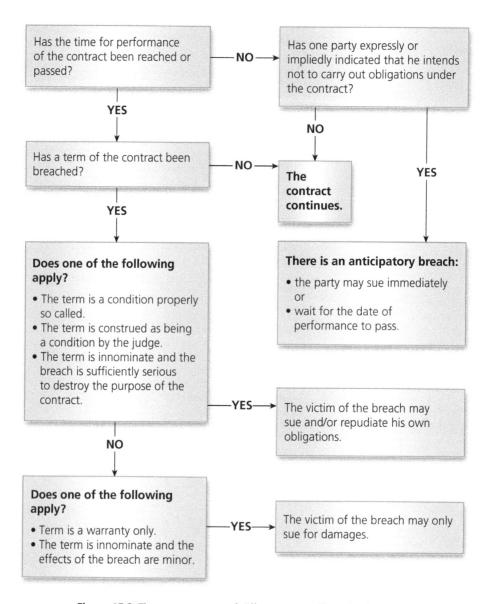

Figure 15.2 The consequences of different types of breach of contract

SUMMARY

Discharge is the ending of obligations under a contract – it can occur in one of four ways: performance, agreement, frustration and breach.

Performance

- The strict rule on performance is that in an 'entire contract' all obligations must be performed or there will be no payment – but 'divisible' obligations give rise to payment for the part performed, and if a party accepts part performance then this should be paid for, and where performance is substantial then the full price will be paid less the sum appropriate to what has not been done unless too much remains to be done under the contract.

- A party can sue for damages where his performance has been prevented by the other party and also where he has offered to perform but this has been refused.
- Time of performance is only 'of the essence' when: it says so in the contract; the circumstances make it so or where one party has already failed to perform.

Agreement

- Since a contract can be formed by agreement it can also be discharged by agreement of both parties.
- This can be: a bilateral arrangement (where both parties wish to back out of the arrangement) and a unilateral arrangement (where only one does).
- In an executory contract, bilateral discharge is simple – the waiving of rights by one party is given in return for the waiving of rights by the other.
- If form is required then discharge needs to be evidenced in writing.
- If only one party wants to back out of the contract, then that party needs to give consideration, as in accord and satisfaction, unless estoppel applies.

Frustration

- Frustration is an event that is beyond the control of either party which prevents performance of the contract.
- Frustrating events include: impossibility (because of destruction of the subject-matter, unavailability of the other party, or outbreak of war); subsequent illegality; commercial sterilisation.
- The contract will not end where: the frustration is self-induced; the contract is merely more onerous to perform; the risk is foreseeable or has been provided for in the contract.
- The Law Reform (Frustrated Contracts) Act makes provisions for determining where the loss lies.

Breach

- A breach occurs when one party fails to perform at all, or does less than is required under the contract, does not perform satisfactorily, or wrongly repudiates his obligations under the contract.
- Breach of a warranty gives rise to an action for damages.
- Breach of a condition gives rise to a right to repudiate as well as an action for damages.
- With innominate terms the remedy depends on the seriousness of the breach.
- Anticipatory breach occurs where a party makes known before performance is due that the contract will not be performed.
- The victim of an anticipatory breach can treat the contract at an end and sue immediately or wait until performance is due and then sue for the breach.

KEY FACTS

Nature of breach
A breach of contract occurs when one party fails to perform at all, or does less than is required under the contract, or does not perform satisfactorily: • Lord Diplock explained that a breach replaces 'primary obligations' (to perform the contract) with 'secondary obligations' (eg, to pay damages to remedy the breach). • It will also be a breach where one party wrongly repudiates his own obligations.

The effects of breaches of different types of term	Case/statute
Breach of a warranty allows only an action for damages.	
Breach of a condition allows for action for damages and/or repudiation, but only if the term is really a condition going to the root of the contract.	*Schuler v Wickman Machine Tool Sales Ltd*
The same choice applies where the effect of breach of an innominate term is sufficiently serious	*The Hansa Nord*
Anticipatory breach	**Case/statute**
An anticipatory breach occurs where a party makes it known before performance is due that the contract will not be performed.	*Hochster v De la Tour*
The victim of an anticipatory breach has the right to treat the contract at an end and sue immediately.	*Frost v Knight*
But he also has the right to wait until performance is due and then sue for the breach.	*Avery v Bowden*
The latter course can be unfair to the party in breach.	*White & Carter Ltd v McGregor*
Waiting for the actual breach can also mean losing the remedy.	*Fercometal v Mediterranean Shipping Co*

SAMPLE ESSAY QUESTION

Critically discuss the circumstances in which courts will accept that a contract has been discharged for frustration.

Explain the original rule on performance and the nature of the doctrine of frustration:

- The original rule was that complete performance was required
- The doctrine of frustration developed so that when performance is impossible because of an event that is no fault of either party, the parties are excused further performance and obligations end at the point of frustration

Describe the circumstances in which a contract is discharged for frustration:

- Impossibility because of destruction of the subject-matter or unavailability of a party
- Subsequent illegality
- Commercial sterilisation of the contract – all purpose lost

Describe the limitations on frustration where a contract is not discharged:
- Self-induced frustration
- The contract is merely more onerous or costly to perform
- The frustrating event could have been foreseen by the parties
- The frustrating event was provided for in the contract
- There is an absolute undertaking to perform

Discuss the reasons for the doctrine:
- The unfairness of the original rule in *Paradine v Jane*
- Why should a party be bound by obligations which become impossible to perform and which is not his fault?

Discuss the issues associated with the doctrine:
- Doctrine simply applied in early case
- But a party may still suffer unfairly depending on when the frustrating event occurs – hence the need for statutory reform – although the provisions in the Act can still work unfairly
- The doctrine generally acts fairly because it only applies where neither party is at fault – so if one party bears some responsibility for the frustrating event, the contract continues
- The doctrine only operates where the frustrating event destroys 'the very basis of the contract'
- It is usually simple to establish impossibility or subsequent illegality – but more difficult to establish that some purpose remains when commercial sterilisation is claimed
- In self-induced frustration, one party created the frustrating event and so is at fault; if merely more onerous to perform, then may be because one party prepared inadequately for the contract – either way not to allow frustration is fair

Further reading

Denning, Lord, *The Discipline of Law* (Butterworths, 1979), Part 1, Ch 4.
Hall, C, 'Frustration and the Question of Foresight' (1984) 4 LS 300.
Whincup, M, 'Reacting to Repudiation' NLJ, 17th May 1996, p 675.

16

Remedies in contract law

AIMS AND OBJECTIVES

After reading this chapter you should be able to:

- Understand the difference between common law remedies and equitable remedies
- Understand the rules on causation in unliquidated damages
- Understand the bases of assessment of awards of unliquidated damages
- Understand rules regarding liquidated damages
- Understand the rules relating to the main equitable remedies
- Critically analyse the area
- Apply the law to factual situations and reach conclusions

16.1 Common law remedies

16.1.1 Introduction

Limitation periods

All actions in contract law, as in tort, are subject to limitation periods outside of which an action cannot be brought. There are a variety of reasons why a claimant should be limited in the time that he can wait before bringing an action for the damage suffered. Even in equity, we can see the maxim 'delay defeats equity' operating so that a claimant who delays too long in bringing a claim will be prevented from succeeding. See eg *Allcard v Skinner* (1887) 36 ChD 145 in undue influence or *Leaf v International Galleries* [1950] 2 KB 86 in misrepresentation and common mistake as to quality.

Firstly, if there is a valid case to be fought then the claimant is to be encouraged to bring the action as soon as possible. If the evidence for the claim can be gathered, there is no purpose in delaying.

Secondly, there is the difficulty of actually preserving evidence intact if a claim is delayed for too long. Certainly, the scene will be disturbed over time, forensic evidence may deteriorate, but also the memory of witnesses can only fade.

Finally, it is only fair on a defendant to bring the claim as early as possible if it is indeed actionable. Although many claims are settled out of insurance, a defendant may be damaged by the uncertainty of his budget when contemplating the possible costs of a successful action against him. This may in turn prevent the potential defendant from planning effectively for the future.

Basic limitation periods

The majority of contract and tort actions are subject to the same basic limitation period of six years from the date on which the action accrues. In the case of contract the period is identified in s 5: 'An action founded on simple contract shall not be brought after the expiration of six years from the date on which the action accrued.'

There are also a number of different periods applying in more particular instances, for example in the case of speciality contracts, in respect of defective products under the Consumer Protection Act 1987.

The range of available remedies

There are a number of possible remedies that may be awarded in the event of a breach of contract or in the event of an actionable vitiating factor such as mistake, misrepresentation or undue influence.

The most usual remedy to be awarded, of course, will be a sum of money compensation in the form of unliquidated damages. However, there are a number of other remedies that may be appropriate according to the circumstances of the particular case. In any case, a claimant must state in his pleadings the specific remedy that he is seeking though there is nothing to prevent a claimant from seeking different remedies in the alternative.

Remedies may be either under the **common law** or may be **equitable** in character, with certain differing consequences:

- In the case of common law remedies, provided that the breach is proved, the remedy should follow and be available as of right.
- In the case of equitable remedies, these are discretionary and are granted only subject to the requirement that it is equitable to grant them. They will be granted by reference to the maxims of equity.

Common law remedies are of four main types:

- **Unliquidated damages** – these are assessed by the court according to the breach itself and the losses arising from it.
- **Liquidated damages** – these are set sums identified by the parties prior to formation of the contract.
- **Restitution of payments made in advance of a contract** – recovery is possible where there is a complete failure of consideration or where there is a mistake of law (considered in Chapter 17).
- *Quantum meruit* – recovery for an amount of work already done (again, this area is considered in Chapter 17).

Equitable remedies are usually of four main kinds in contract law:

- **Specific performance** – where in certain circumstances the terms of the contract are enforced.
- **Injunctions** – where in certain circumstances parties are prevented from enforcing the contract.
- **Rescission** – where parties are allowed, if it is possible in the circumstances, to return to their pre-contractual position.
- **Rectification** – where a written contract is altered on order of the court in order to reflect the actual agreement accurately.

The purpose of damages in contract

Damages is a sum of money paid by the defendant to the claimant once liability is established, in compensation for the harm suffered by the claimant.

In the case of damages awarded for a breach of contract, the purpose of the award is to compensate the claimant for the losses suffered as a result of the breach.

JUDGMENT

As Baron Parke put it in *Robinson v Harman* [1848] 154 ER 363: 'the purpose is to put the victim of the breach, so far as is possible and so far as the law allows, into the same position he would have been in if the contract had not been broken but had been performed in the manner and at the time intended by the parties'.

In this way, damages in contract law are aimed to put the victim in the position he would have enjoyed if the contract had been properly completed and performed by the defendant.

This contrasts with damages in tort where the purpose of damages is, as far as is possible to do so, to put the claimant in the position he would have been in had the tort never occurred. So tort damages, by contrast with contract damages, represent a very artificial remedy. Inevitably, there is a large measure of speculation involved in awarding damages in tort since it involves predicting what would have happened if the tort had not occurred, whereas, in contract, damages will represent an actual financial loss, and are rarely speculative.

16.1.2 Unliquidated damages

There are in effect two tests used in assessing an award for an unliquidated sum of damages in contract:

- The first test concerns the **loss** in respect of which the claimant can recover (simply stated, the question can be seen as 'For what can the claimant recover?').
- The second test concerns the **quantity of damages** available (again, simply stated, the question is 'How much can the claimant recover?').

The first of these two questions actually concerns causation. There must be a causal link between the defendant's breach of the contract and the damage suffered by the claimant. Moreover, there is a general principle that damages will never be awarded in respect of a loss that is too remote a consequence of the defendant's breach.

16.1.3 Tests of causation and remoteness of damage
Causation is measured, then, both according to fact and according to law, remoteness of damage, is measured in a similar way to tort.

Causation in fact
Causation is a question of fact in each case. The court will decide whether or not the breach is the predominant reason for the loss suffered by the claimant.

CASE EXAMPLE

London Joint Stock Bank v MacMillan [1918] AC 777

A customer of a bank owes a contractual obligation not to draw cheques in such a way that they are easily alterable. Here, the client who breached his duty by making his cheque easily alterable was liable when a third party fraudulently altered the cheque and caused a consequent loss to the bank.

As the Court of Appeal identified in *Galoo Ltd and Others v Bright Grahame Murray* [1995] 1 All ER 16, in doing so the court will have to consider on a common-sense basis whether the breach was in fact the cause of the loss or was merely the occasion for the loss.

It is possible that the loss may arise as a result of the nature of the contract itself rather than as the result of the breach.

CASE EXAMPLE

C & P Haulage v Middleton [1993] 3 All ER 94

The claimant hired a garage from the defendant under six-monthly contracts. During one six-month period, the claimant equipped the garage for his own particular needs. The defendant then breached his contract and terminated the agreement 10 weeks earlier than he should have done. The claimant sued for the loss of the cost of equipping the garage for his own needs. The claim failed because the defendant could have legitimately terminated the agreement 10 weeks later and the claimant would still have suffered the loss at that time. The court would not accept that the loss was the cause of the breach.

If the loss arises partly from the breach and partly as the result of intervening events, then the party in breach may still be liable, provided that the chain of causation is not broken.

CASE EXAMPLE

Stansbie v Troman [1948] 2 KB 48

A decorator was entrusted with keys to the premises in which he was contracted to work. When he left the premises unlocked, a thief entered and stole property. The decorator was liable for the loss that was the result of his failure to comply with his contractual duty to secure the premises properly on leaving. The thief was the direct cause of the loss but the theft could not have occurred but for the breach of duty by the decorator.

Problems connected with causation will usually arise only where there is intervention by some third party or some external force. However, such an intervention will not necessarily break the chain of causation, provided that it is a reasonably foreseeable event.

CASE EXAMPLE

De La Bere v Pearson Ltd [1908] 1 KB 280

A newspaper offered to give advice on financial matters to persons writing to it. One person who did write for advice was given the name of a stockbroker with whom to invest money. Unknown to the newspaper, the stockbroker was actually an undischarged bankrupt and he used the claimant's money for his own purposes. The newspaper was still held to be liable for the loss because it had breached its duty to the claimant to offer sound advice.

Similarly, where the loss has been brought about as the result of two different causes, only one of which is the breach of contract, then the breach may still be considered to be the cause of the loss and liability may result.

CASE EXAMPLE

Smith, Hogg & Co v Black Sea Insurance [1939] 2 All ER 855

A ship sank not just because of the prevailing conditions while it was out at sea but also because it was generally not seaworthy. It was still held that the loss was the result of sending the ship out to sea not properly serviceable for the voyage. Without the poor condition of the ship, the loss may not have occurred.

Remoteness of damage

The general principle is that damages will never be awarded for a loss that is too remote a consequence of the breach.

The test of remoteness is in two parts, remains largely unchanged to the present day and was originally derived in the nineteenth century by Baron Alderson in the Court of Exchequer.

CASE EXAMPLE

Hadley v Baxendale (1854) 9 Exch 341

In the case, a mill owner contracted with a carrier to deliver a crankshaft for his mill. The mill was actually not operating at the time because the existing crankshaft was broken. The carrier did not know at the time the contract was formed that the mill owner did not have a spare crankshaft. The carrier was then late with delivery by several days, during which time the mill was of course unable to grind corn and thus supply its customers with corn. The mill owner sued for loss of profit. He was unsuccessful because the carrier was unaware of the importance of prompt delivery.

JUDGMENT

Alderson B identified that: 'Where the parties have made a contract which one of them has broken the damages which the other party ought to receive in respect of such breach of contract should be such as may fairly and reasonably be considered arising either naturally, ie according to the usual course of things, for such breach of contract itself, or such as may be reasonably supposed to have been in the contemplation of both parties at the time they made the contract as the probable result of the breach.'

So in essence the test of remoteness of damage is in two parts:

■ one is measured **objectively**, according to what loss is a natural consequence of the breach
■ the second is measured **subjectively** and based on the specific knowledge of potential losses that is in the minds of both parties at the time the contract is formed.

The test remains largely unchanged to this day, although it has been modified on occasions and put into more modern terms.

CASE EXAMPLE

Victoria Laundry Ltd v Newman Industries Ltd [1949] 2 KB 528

Here, the defendants had been contracted to deliver a boiler to the laundry company and failed to deliver until five months after the contract date. The laundry sued for the loss of its usual profits of £16 per week from the date of the breach. It succeeded since this was a natural consequence of the loss. It also sued in respect of lost profits of £262 per week from a government contract that it had been unable to fulfil as a result of being without the new boiler. It succeeded in respect of the usual profits since the court accepted that the claimants had made it clear to the defendants that they were particularly anxious that the boiler should be fitted by the due date. It failed in the latter action since the government contract was unknown to the defendants at the time the contract was formed.

It was noted that the two heads of *Hadley v Baxendale* (1854) 9 Exch 341 possibly represent only a single principle of remoteness based on different tests of what is foreseeable. Asquith LJ made a number of vital points on the issue of remoteness:

■ To give the claimant a complete indemnity for any loss suffered by the claimant, no matter how remote, is too harsh a test to apply to the defendant.
■ As a result, recoverable loss should be measured against a test of reasonable foreseeability – so the loss should be one which at the time the contract was formed would be reasonably foreseeable to result from the breach.
■ Foreseeability of loss is itself dependent on the knowledge that is possessed at the time of formation of the contract.
■ Knowledge possessed at the time of formation can be of two types:
  (i) **common knowledge** – that knowledge which any reasonable person would be expected to have of loss that would naturally arise from the breach (representing the first head in *Hadley v Baxendale*); and
  (ii) **actual knowledge** enjoyed by the defendant – knowledge which was particular to the parties at the time that the contract was formed (representing the second head in *Hadley v Baxendale*).

- But liability for loss need not be based on actual knowledge but can also be implied on the basis of what a reasonable man may have contemplated in the circumstances would be a loss arising from the breach.
- On this final point, for loss to be established it need not be based on what a reasonable man **must** have contemplated would have arisen from the breach in the circumstances – it is sufficient that a reasonable man **may** have contemplated such a loss.

Clearly, it is ultimately a question of fact in each case precisely what loss is recoverable under either test. Clearly, also, the test of reasonable foreseeability is one which has the potential to create confusion and difficulties of interpretation and be made unnecessarily complex.

CASE EXAMPLE

Koufos v C Czarnikow Ltd (The Heron II) [1969] 1 AC 350

A vessel was chartered to carry sugar to Basrah, a known sugar market. Because of the carrier's breach, the vessel arrived nine days late, during which time the price of sugar had fallen considerably. The claimant had intended to re-sell the sugar immediately on its arrival in port, a fact that was unknown to the defendant carrier at the time of contracting. The claimant sued for his consequent reduction in profits following the fall in the price of sugar. The Court of Appeal held that this was too remote a consequence of the breach. The House of Lords, however, held that the claimant could recover under the first head of *Hadley v Baxendale*, and suggested that in certain circumstances, the reasonable man ought to contemplate that a particular loss was a natural consequence of a breach (despite the fact that this actually seems more like implied knowledge, which is more appropriate to the second head). The judges in the House of Lords also suggested that the definition of 'foreseeability' differed between contract and tort. However, different judges gave different definitions:

- Lord Reid described it as, 'not unlikely … considerably less than an even chance but nevertheless not very unusual and easily foreseeable'.
- Lord Morris as, 'not unlikely to occur … liable to result'.
- Lord Hodson as, 'liable to result'.
- Lords Pearce and Upjohn as, 'a real danger … a serious possibility'.

The reasoning of the House of Lords is somewhat confusing and possibly what it shows is that on the issue of remoteness, commercial contracts may well be treated differently from those made by ordinary citizens. However, this in itself creates further difficulties in establishing what reasonable man in particular the courts have in mind when applying the test of foreseeability.

However, Lord Scarman has subsequently rejected the view that there are different tests of foreseeability and held that the test of remoteness depends not on contemplation of the level of injury but merely on proof that the loss could have been anticipated.

CASE EXAMPLE

H Parsons (Livestock) Ltd v Uttley Ingham [1978] QB 791

The contract was for the sale and installation of an animal feed hopper with a ventilated cover. The ventilation hatch was sealed during transit but the installers then forgot to open it. As a result, the feed became mouldy, the pigs contracted an intestinal disease and 254 died. The judge at first instance considered the loss was too remote and not within the contemplation of the defendants but this was later reversed by the Court of Appeal. Lord Denning drew the distinction between loss of profit, such as in the three cases above, where he felt that a test of remoteness based on contract should apply, and property damage, such as the present case, where he felt the test should be the same test of foreseeability as in tort. Lord Scarman rejected such a distinction and held that the loss was merely an example of what should be in the contemplation of the parties when the contract was formed. Both views cause their own difficulties.

As Cheshire, Fifoot and Furmston suggest:

QUOTATION

'None of the judgments explains why, if any illness to the pigs were contemplatable, the plaintiffs were not at fault in continuing to feed the nuts to the pigs.'

Cheshire, Fifoot and Furmston, Law of Contract (Butterworths, 1996), p 616

It must be remembered that in determining remoteness it is what was in the contemplation of the parties at the time that the contract was made which determines the outcome.

CASE EXAMPLE

Jackson v Royal Bank of Scotland plc [2005] UKHL 3; [2005] 2 All ER 71

The claimant imported dog chews from a company in Thailand and sold them on to a firm called Easy Bag. The chews were already packaged and ready for sale according to Easy Bag's instructions. The firm was happy to act through an intermediary and made good profits from the goods. Both the claimant and Easy Bag banked with the Royal Bank of Scotland. Payment was by letters of credit on invoices that included the claimant's mark-up but did not indicate the price that he was paying the Thai company. In fact he was making 19 per cent. The bank, in breach of its requirement of confidentiality to the claimant, then mistakenly revealed the size of the mark-up to Easy Bag which then stopped dealing with the claimant. The House of Lords held that the termination of the relationship was a clear consequence of the breach of contract by the bank. This is obviously an example of the first head of *Hadley v Baxendale*; the bank should have contemplated the result of breaching the claimant's confidentiality.

It has also been suggested that the test is not merely based on what was foreseeable to the parties at the time of contracting but also whether the damages is of a type that the defendant ought reasonably to have accepted responsibility for.

CASE EXAMPLE

Transfield Shipping Inc. v Mercador Shipping Inc. (The Achilleas) [2008] UKHL 48

Mercator chartered the vessel Achilleas to Transfield initially for about five to seven months at a daily rate of $13,500 and then by a further addendum for a further five to seven months at a daily rate of $16,750 with the agreed final date for redelivery of the vessel being 2 May 2004. Mercator also agreed with another party to charter the vessel to it for four to six months at a daily rate of $39,000 with the latest date for delivery being 8 May 2004 after which the new charterers were entitled to cancel under the agreement. The market rate by this time had increased significantly. By 5 May 2004 the vessel had been delayed and it was obvious that it would not be available to the new charterers before the cancelling date of 8 May and in fact it was not redelivered until 11 May. By 8 May market rates had fallen and in return for an extension of the cancellation date to 11 May Mercator agreed to a reduced rate of $31,500 a day. Mercator then claimed damages from Transfield for the loss of the difference between the original rate and the reduced rate with the new charterers which at $8,000 a day amounted to $1,364,584.37. Transfield argued that Mercator were not entitled to damages calculated by reference to its dealings with the new charterers but only the difference between the market rate and their charter rate between 2 May and 11 May, amounting to only $158,301.17. The arbitrators hearing the dispute held that Transfield should pay the higher figure on the basis that, under the first rule in *Hadley v Baxendale*, it would have foreseen that Mercator would be likely to enter into another charter agreement after its and that would risk losing it in the event of late return of the vessel. The then House of Lords (now the Supreme Court) allowed Transfield's appeal holding that it would place an undue burden on Transfield to expect it to accept responsibility for any loss resulting from its late delivery even though it had no knowledge of or no control over the new charter. This would be completely inconsistent with the reasoning in *Victoria Laundries v Newman Industries*.

16.1.4 The bases of assessment

Once the tests of causation and remoteness of damage have established that there is indeed liability for the loss claimed, then the court has to determine precisely how much the claimant can recover.

Nominal damages

The purpose of contract damages is to put the claimant in the position financially that he would have been in had the contract been properly performed. If no loss is actually suffered but the breach has been established, it would usually follow that no damages would be available. However, proof of damage has never been an essential of contract law as it is in many areas of tort. It is possible, then, for the court to award 'nominal damages'.

The likely motive of the claimant in suing is to ensure that there is a declaration by the court that the contract is at an end.

CASE EXAMPLE

Staniforth v Lyall (1830) 7 Bing 169

Lyall was under a duty to load his cargo onto the claimant's boat by a certain date. He failed and the boat owner sued for breach. He had actually hired his boat out to another party immediately following the breach and for a greater profit than he would have made had the contract been properly performed. He succeeded in having the contract declared terminated and, even though he suffered no actual loss, he was awarded a nominal sum.

The three bases of assessment

There are normally said to be three bases for assessing awards of damages in contract claims even though these themselves can be broken down into more specific areas:

- **loss of a bargain**
- **reliance loss**
- **restitution** (recovery of payments made).

Loss of a bargain

The idea here is to place the claimant in the same financial position as if the contract had been properly performed. This may represent a number of situations for which the claimant may recover:

- **Defective goods or services** – the difference in value between the goods or services of the quality indicated in the contract and those actually delivered where they are of inferior value. This sum can be assessed according to the diminution in value or the cost of bringing them up to the contract quality.

CASE EXAMPLE

Bence Graphics International Ltd v Fasson UK Ltd (1996) *The Times,* 24th October

The defendant supplied vinyl film on which the claimant printed decals to put on bulk containers. In the claimant's contract with the container company, there was an implied term that the decals would survive in a readable form for five years. In fact, they lasted only two years. The claimant sued for the whole purchase price or an indemnity against its customer's claim. This was rejected by the judge at first instance who, applying s 53(3) of the Sale of Goods Act 1979, held that the claimant could only recover for the difference in the value of the goods. However, the Court of Appeal held that the claimant could recover the actual loss suffered.

- **Failure to deliver goods or provide services or to accept delivery** – damages will ordinarily be based on the difference between the contract price and the price obtained in an 'available market'. This can apply where there is either a failure to deliver the goods or services and an alternative supply has to be found, or where there is a failure to accept delivery and an alternative market has to be found.
- If the **claimant's ability to buy or sell the goods at the same price remains** despite the breach then there is no entitlement to damages.

CASE EXAMPLE

Charter v Sullivan [1957] 2 QB 117

Here, the defendant contracted for the purchase of a car but then, in breach of the contract, refused to take delivery of it. Because demand for the particular model of car at the time easily outstripped supply, there was no interference in the seller's ability to sell the car at the time when the contract was breached. In consequence, the claimant was able to recover only nominal damages.

- However, if there is **no available market** then the claimant will be able to recover the full loss.

CASE EXAMPLE

W L Thompson Ltd v Robinson Gunmakers Ltd [1955] Ch 177

Here, in another contract for the sale and purchase of a car, the buyer, again in breach of contract, refused to take delivery of the car. There was in this case, however, excess in supply of the type of car ordered under the contract. As a result, because there was a much smaller available market and the goods would have been more difficult to sell, the seller was able to recover full damages. In fact the seller had been able to mitigate the loss by finding an alternative buyer but this is no bar to a successful action.

However, the **'available market' rule** is no longer as rigidly applied as it once was:

CASE EXAMPLE

Shearson Lehman Hutton Inc v Maclaine Watson & Co Ltd (No 2) [1990] 3 All ER 732

The defendants contracted to buy large quantities of tin from the claimants and in breach of contract then refused to accept delivery of the goods. It was shown in the case that there would have been an 'available market' if the claimants had tried to sell the goods at the time of the breach. However, they did not immediately try to sell the tin and the market later dropped. In assessing damages the court was asked to make a judgment on the basis of a hypothetical market in which the goods could have been sold: in other words, whether there were potential buyers. In fact, there would have been potential buyers but they would be only for a single large quantity rather than for many individual transactions. The judge imposed a heavy duty to mitigate and refused the higher level of damages.

- **Loss of profit** – a claimant may recover for the profit on contracts that he would have been able to complete but for the breach of contract. This will only be the case where the loss is not too remote a consequence of the breach.
- **Loss of a** chance – in rare circumstances the courts have allowed a claimant to recover a loss that is entirely speculative in the circumstances, although generally in contract law a speculative loss is not recoverable.

CASE EXAMPLE

Chaplin v Hicks [1911] 2 KB 786

An actress had a contractual right to attend an audition. At this audition 12 actresses would be chosen out of the 50 invited to attend. When she was wrongly prevented from attending, the court awarded her £100 in compensation even though she had only a 50:12 chance of gaining work from the audition. The court stated that the mere fact that damages were difficult to calculate should not prevent her recovering.

Reliance loss

A claimant is entitled also to recover for expenses he has been required to spend in advance of a contract that has been breached. This will normally be based on the defendant's knowledge, either actual or imputed, that expenses would be incurred in advance of or in preparation for performance of the contract by the other party.

A claim for reliance loss will normally be made where the amount of any loss of profit in the circumstances is too speculative to be able to calculate effectively.

CASE EXAMPLE

Anglia Television Ltd v Reed [1972] 1 QB 60

Anglia paid out a large sum of money in preparing to make a film, including paying script-writers, hiring production and technical staff and other necessary expenses. The actor contracted to take the starring role in the film then backed out, in breach of his contract, and the company was forced to abandon the production, since there was no appropriate substitute. It sued for its loss of profit but this in itself was highly speculative and of course if the project had flopped it may well have been nil. Its reliance loss was much easier to account for in the circumstances than any loss of profit.

Generally, it is not possible to claim for both loss of profit and reliance loss since it is said to be compensating twice for the same loss. However, it is possible where the claim for lost profit concerns only net rather than gross profit which would include the reliance loss.

CASE EXAMPLE

Western Web Offset Printers Ltd v Independent Media Ltd (1995)
The Times, 10th October

The defendant wrongly repudiated a contract under which the claimant was to print 48 issues of a weekly newspaper. The claimant sued for gross profits of £176,903, having deducted the costs of direct expenses such as printing, ink and paper from the contract price. The defendant argued that the claimant should only be entitled to net profits and that labour costs and other overheads amounting to £38,245 should also be deducted from the claim. The Court of Appeal held that since the claimant had no alternative work for the workforce following the breach of contract, the whole claim could be recovered.

But it may also on occasions be possible to recover damages for the loss of a valuable amenity that in effect is lost as a result of the breach.

CASE EXAMPLE

Farley v Skinner [2001] 3 WLR 899

The claimant hired a surveyor before buying a house and asked the surveyor to report specifically on whether the property was affected by aircraft noise. The report stated that it would not be substantially affected by aircraft noise but this was wrong and also negligent as the house was near a beacon for stacking aircraft at busy times. The claimant paid £490,000 for the house and spent £125,000 on it before moving in. When he moved in and discovered the noise, he decided not to move but sued the surveyor for damages for loss of amenity. The House of Lords held that, for loss of amenity to succeed, it was not essential for the contract to be one the object of which was to provide pleasure, relaxation etc. The claimant did not forfeit his right to non-pecuniary damages by not moving and he was awarded £10,000. The House of Lords also approved the reasoning in *Ruxley Electronics v Forsyth* [1995] 3 All ER 268 (see section 16.1.6).

Restitution

Restitution in the context of a breach of contract is simply a repayment to the claimant of any money or other benefits that he has passed to the defendant in advance of the contract that has been breached.

Restitution is a massive area of law in its own right and full explanations are only to be found in books dealing specifically with the subject. (Certain aspects of the area are more fully covered in Chapter 17.)

Inevitably, restitution in contract law has to do with consideration and the presence or absence of consideration may determine the appropriateness of the remedy.

CASE EXAMPLE

Stocznia Gdanska SA v Latvian Shipping Co [1998] 1 WLR 574

Here, a shipyard entered into a contract under which it was bound to both design and build a ship for the buyers. The shipyard later rescinded the contract before any ownership in the goods had passed to the buyers. The buyers claimed for return of an instalment of the contract price, on the basis that there was a failure of consideration. The shipyard successfully resisted this claim. The House of Lords held that the true test of whether there was a failure of consideration was not based on whether the buyer had received nothing under the contract but on whether the seller had done nothing under the contract.

....

quasi contract

A means of gaining a remedy for a loss not generally recoverable under strict rules of contract

....

One other way in which restitution may possibly be used is a means of preventing the unjust enrichment of the other party. This is more commonly associated with restitution in the context of **quasi-contract** (see Chapter 17). Recovery of damages in contract law has not generally been accepted under this principle. However, in one recent case it has been the subject of extensive discussion. The normal reason for awarding damages in contract law is to compensate for the claimant's loss. Where restitution is used to prevent unjust enrichment, on the other hand, the purpose of the award is to prevent the defendant gaining unfairly. This is a principle that has traditionally been expressly rejected in contract law.

CASE EXAMPLE

Attorney General v Blake [2001] 1 AC 268

This involved a notorious spy of the 1950s who was a member of the British Secret Service and who had passed secrets to the Russians during the time of the Cold War. He was convicted but then escaped to Russia where he has been ever since. In 1990 he wrote an autobiography for which he was to be paid £150,000, some of which he had already received in advances. In the book he gave various details of his work in the Secret Service, which was illegal because he was still bound by the Official Secrets Act 1989 and was also as a result a breach of his employment contract. The Attorney-General brought an action to prevent Blake from claiming the money that was still owed him. The Court of Appeal allowed an injunction against Blake and also considered the position on damages. Without the Attorney-General being able to show a loss by the Government, damages could be only nominal. Nevertheless, the court clearly did not want the defendant to profit from his crimes and breach of contract and held that restitution could be used in the context because it was an exceptional case. It gave two justifications. Firstly, the defendant had failed to provide the full service that he had contracted to give and for which he had been paid. Secondly, the defendant had obtained a profit, the payment for the book, for doing the very thing that he had contracted not to do: breaching his promise of secrecy. The House of Lords accepted the reasoning of the Court of Appeal and allowed the Attorney-General a full account of the profits made by Blake. The House concluded that there was no reason in principle why such an award could not be made in exceptional circumstances such as existed in the case. However, the House was quite vague as to when exceptional circumstances might arise and there is an obvious danger if the principle is applied in a commercial context.

While *Blake* may appear to be very much a policy decision it has been followed in subsequent cases where substantial damages have been awarded in circumstances where traditionally it might have been thought that only nominal damages might be appropriate.

Experience Hendrix LLC v PPX Enterprises Inc [2003] EWCA Civ 323

Jimi Hendrix was a famous rock guitarist of the 1960s. The defendant music publisher had been suing Hendrix before his death and after Hendrix's death a compromise settlement was reached. By this agreement the defendant was to gain entitlement to various listed recordings from master tapes in return for payment of royalties to the heir to Hendrix's estate, the claimant. The defendant, in breach of the settlement, later granted licences to recordings that were not listed in the settlement agreement and the claimant sued. The Court of Appeal held that the defendant should pay a reasonable sum to the claimant. The defendant had clearly gained a benefit from the breach even though the claimant had not suffered actual loss.

16.1.5 The duty to mitigate

There is a clear principle of English law that the party injured by a breach of contract must take reasonable steps to minimise the effects of the breach. This is commonly referred to as the 'duty to mitigate'. To hold otherwise may well prove unfair to the defendant. The principle is as appropriate to tort as it is to contract law, and a failure to mitigate may be taken into account in awarding damages.

CASE EXAMPLE

British Westinghouse Electric and Manufacturing Co Ltd v Underground Electric Railways Co of London Ltd [1912] AC 673

British Westinghouse had contracted for the supply of turbines to Underground Electric Railways. When the goods were delivered they did not match the specifications in the contract. As a result, the buyers had to replace them with turbines which they bought from another supplier. In the event the alternative turbines were so efficient that they soon paid for the difference between contract price and the actual value of the equipment under the first contract. Therefore this could not be claimed for but those losses that had been sustained before the original turbines were replaced were recoverable.

JUDGMENT

Lord Haldane LC said that a claimant has 'the duty of taking all reasonable steps to mitigate the loss consequent on the breach [which] debars him from claiming in respect of any part of the damage which is due to his neglect to take such steps'.

However, while a claimant is bound to try to keep the loss to an acceptable minimum or not to deliberately increase the loss, he will not be bound to go to extraordinary lengths in order to mitigate the loss. The claimant is only expected to do whatever is reasonable in the circumstances.

CASE EXAMPLE

Pilkington v Wood [1953] 2 All ER 810

As the result of a solicitor's negligence, the claimant bought a house with defective title, and was thus unable to take up residence for some time while the issue was being resolved. He therefore incurred the extra costs of hotel bills and travelling to and from his old house until the dispute as to title was settled. He also telephoned his wife daily and ran up many other bills, all of which he claimed for in his action against the solicitor. The solicitor's argument, that the claimant could instead have brought his action against the vendor and thus mitigated the loss in his action against the solicitor, was rejected.

Similarly, in the case of an anticipatory breach, the claimant is not bound to sue immediately that he knows of the possibility of the breach but can wait till the actual time of the breach, even though this may increase the loss suffered.

CASE EXAMPLE

White and Carter v McGregor [1962] AC 413

A firm had contracted to buy advertising space on litter bins to be fitted to lamp-posts by the claimants. When they backed out in breach of their agreement the claimants nevertheless continued to produce the bins. The argument that the claimants might have mitigated the loss by not continuing to fit the bins failed.

What is certainly true is that the claimant must not take any unreasonable steps which would actually increase the amount of the loss.

In *Reichman v Beveridge* [2006] EWCA Civ 1659 the principle was also followed in the case of leases in respect of rent arrears where tenants quit the premises before the end of the lease.

CASE EXAMPLE

The Borag [1981] 1 WLR 274

Here, a ship was detained in breach of contract. The owners of the vessel then borrowed large sums of money at excessive interest rates in order to secure its release. The Court of Appeal would not allow recovery in respect of the interest since it held that there was no real justification in incurring them.

16.1.6 The 'mental distress' cases

In contract law we have already seen that the courts have been careful to avoid granting damages of a speculative nature since damages in contract are awarded in respect of a specific loss. Of course, there have been rare exceptions such as that in *Chaplin v Hicks* [1911] 2 KB 786 where damages were awarded for the loss of a chance in an audition.

The courts have always been careful to separate contract and tort. In the case of tort there is clear evidence of this for instance in the reluctance of judges to allow a remedy for a pure economic loss in negligence, which they see as being more appropriate to principles of contract law. The judges have been equally careful in traditionally avoiding allowing recovery in contract law for a claim seen as being more appropriate to principles in tort.

CASE EXAMPLE

Addis v The Gramophone Company [1909] AC 488

The claimant was wrongly dismissed from his post as the defendants' manager and they had replaced him with a new manager even before he left. The House of Lords refused his claim for damages for injury to his reputation caused by the improper dismissal and also for the mental distress caused by the humiliating manner of his dismissal, the proper place for this according to Lord Atkin being under the tort of defamation. The court held that he could recover only for the loss of salary and commission owed.

In similar fashion, the courts refused actions claiming damages for indignity and humiliation resulting from the breach.

CASE EXAMPLE

Hurst v Picture Theatres [1915] 1 KB 1

Here, the claimant was roughly thrown out of a cinema to which he had paid the admission fee. The court accepted his claim that he had been wrongly ejected and he was able to recover substantial damages in tort for the wrongful arrest and the false imprisonment but the court would not accept his claim to recover any damages in contract law.

However, an exceptional group of cases has developed in contract law in recent times despite the strict principle in *Addis* [1909] AC 488 allowing recovery of damages of a highly speculative nature in relation to what has become known as 'mental distress'. The principle will not apply generally and as a result the cases are generally known as the 'holiday cases'.

The reason for this is that the principle of awarding damages for mental distress was first accepted in relation to a spoiled holiday.

CASE EXAMPLE

Jarvis v Swan Tours Ltd [1973] 1 QB 233

The claimant contracted for a Tyrolean holiday, advertised as a 'house party' with the tour company. In fact, he was on his own for the second week, and the holiday was inferior to most aspects advertised in the brochure. The judge at first instance awarded him £31.72 for the difference between the quality of the holiday as described in the brochure and the quality of the actual holiday. However, the Court of Appeal upheld his claims for disappointment and mental distress and awarded him damages of £125.

In fact, this was not a unique judgment at the time. The courts had actually previously created an exception to the rule in *Addis*, again in a case involving a holiday.

CASE EXAMPLE

Cook v Spanish Holidays (1960) *The Times*, 6th February

Travel agents were held to have failed in their contractual duty when a double booking meant that a honeymoon couple were left without a room on their wedding night, and the couple were awarded damages for loss of enjoyment.

In fact, the principle has been effectively extended also as an exception to the doctrine of privity where the claimant has recovered not only for his own mental distress but for the distress suffered by his family too.

CASE EXAMPLE

Jackson v Horizon Holidays [1975] 1 WLR 1468

Here, the pattern was fairly predictable in the light of the previous cases. The hotel was dirty; there was an absence of the promised facilities and poor food, among other breaches of the description applied to the holiday. The significant difference from the previous cases was that the claimant was allowed to recover damages not only for his own mental distress but for that suffered by his family too. The apparent logic employed by the Court of Appeal was that the distress suffered by the family was in itself a loss to the overall contract. As such, the claimant had received much less than he had bargained for.

The reason for allowing the claims is that in holiday contracts, 'the provision of comfort, pleasure and "peace of mind" was a central feature of the contract'.

The focus of the principle, as the title 'holiday cases' suggests, is fairly narrow. There have been some fairly limited extensions to the principle. For instance, it has been extended to include certain problems caused by solicitors.

CASE EXAMPLE

Heywood v Wellers [1976] QB 446

The claimant was awarded damages for mental distress where her solicitors, in breach of their contractual obligations, failed to obtain an injunction to prevent her former boyfriend from molesting her.

More recently, damages for 'loss of amenity' have been allowed where the sole purpose of the contract was for 'the provision of a pleasurable amenity'.

CASE EXAMPLE

Ruxley Electronics and Construction Ltd v Forsyth; Laddingford Enclosures Ltd v Forsyth [1995] 3 All ER 268

Here, there was a contract for the construction of a swimming pool. The purchaser stipulated in the contract for a maximum depth of 7 feet 6 inches. In fact, the pool when completed was only 6 feet 9 inches and the area which was for diving was only 6 feet. Since this might prevent the purchaser from safely enjoying the pleasure of diving into the pool, damages were awarded for loss of amenity by the House of Lords, reversing the decision of the Court of Appeal.

Nevertheless, the courts are still reluctant to allow the principle to develop too far or to apply in too many different areas.

CASE EXAMPLE

Hayes v James and Charles Dodd [1990] 2 All ER 815

The claimant here was successful in his claim to recover for anger and annoyance caused by his solicitor's failure to ensure that there was a right of way to the business premises that he was purchasing and without which he would be unable to run the business. Nevertheless, the court identified that the principle must have limitations.

JUDGMENT

Staughten LJ stated that recovery for mental distress should not include: 'any case where the object of the contract was not pleasure or comfort or the relief of discomfort, but simply carrying on a commercial contract with a view to profit'.

Similarly, the courts have shown that they are very reluctant to allow the principle to be applied in the case of commercial transactions: *Woodar Investment Development Ltd v Wimpey Construction UK Ltd* [1980] 1 All ER 571.

16.1.7 Liquidated damage clauses

A sum of liquidated damages may be available where the parties have fixed the amount in the contract that will be available in the event of a breach. However, the courts will only accept this sum and deny the victim of the breach a claim for an unliquidated sum where the sum identified in the contract represents an accurate and proper assessment of loss.

Providing that the figure set in the contract represents a genuine assessment of the loss that is likely to arise from the breach, it will be binding on both parties and no further action for unliquidated damages will be allowed.

Where, however, the sum identified in the contract bears no relationship to the loss at all, this is seen as a 'penalty', a punishment for the breach, and it will be unenforceable. Penalty clauses are void in law and in the event of a breach of contract the court will disregard a **penalty clause** and the injured party may then still bring an action for unliquidated damages.

Any clause that provides for payment of a greater sum than the actual loss is *prima facie* a penalty clause and therefore void. It is for the party seeking to rely on the clause to prove that it is indeed a genuine pre-contract assessment of loss and therefore an acceptable means of settling the dispute in advance and thus avoiding protracted litigation.

penalty clauses

Clauses in a contract usually to pay large sums of compensation for fairly minor breaches

CASE EXAMPLE

Bridge v Campbell Discount Co [1962] AC 600

A depreciation clause in a hire-purchase agreement for a car bore no relation to actual depreciation in value. It was actually only designed to guarantee a certain financial return to the owner. The clause was declared void as a penalty.

The courts have developed a series of rules for determining the difference between genuine liquidated damages and a penalty clause. These were first established in a judgment of Lord Dunedin.

CASE EXAMPLE

Dunlop Pneumatic Tyre Co v New Garage and Motor Co [1914] AC 79

Dunlop supplied tyres to the garage owners. Under its contract with Dunlop, the garage was bound to pay £5 in respect of breaches such as tampering with the manufacturers' mark or selling at under the manufacturers' recommended prices. The garage did sell tyres under price, in breach of its agreement. In this case the House of Lords accepted that the sum identified in the contract represented a genuine assessment of possible loss and so was a genuine liquidated damages clause and not a penalty. Lord Dunedin's test included a number of points:

- An extravagant sum in view of the possible consequences of a breach will always be regarded as a penalty (nevertheless it is always possible that a breach worth only a few pounds itself could lead to loss of a great amount – for example where a tradesman fails to fit a lock properly and there is a subsequent theft from the premises – so each case must be viewed entirely on its own merits).

- Payment of a large sum for a failure to settle a much smaller debt will usually be seen as a penalty (this is clearly based on the logic that the true measure of damages in relation to a debt is the debt itself – nevertheless it has been the practice in recent times, particularly in the area of bridging loans, to add substantial damages to unpaid debts).
- A single sum operating in respect of a variety of different breaches, particularly where they each result in minor losses, is likely to be considered as a penalty.
- The wording used by the parties is not necessarily conclusive (thus the courts are unwilling to accept that damages are liquidated merely because the parties describe them as such in the contract – they prefer to look at all of the circumstances of the clause and the breach itself and then construe accordingly).
- It is not necessarily a bar to recovering a liquidated sum that actual assessment of the loss was impossible before the contract (this is providing that the sum fixed can be seen as a genuine attempt to avoid unnecessary litigation and is not out of all proportion to the actual value of the breach).

The rules appear to be used flexibly and the common feature is that the courts will not allow a party to hide behind a so-called liquidated damages clause which in fact is out of all proportion to the legitimate expectations of any actual loss arising out of the breach.

CASE EXAMPLE

Duffen v Fra Bo Spa [2000] Lloyd's Rep 180

This involved an agency agreement under which a 'liquidated damages' clause identified that in the event of termination the principal should pay the agent the sum of £10,000. The Court of Appeal identified this clause as a penalty clause. The court could find no actual attempt to gauge potential loss; it merely gave the agent a large sum of money in the event of a breach.

In *Alfred McAlpine Capital Projects Ltd v Tilebox Ltd* (2005) 104 Con LR 39, the judge identified that in determining whether or not there is a genuine pre-contract estimate of damages, the fact that the amount is reasonable in relation to the likely loss is more important than the way in which the amount has been worked out.

On this basis the liquidated damages clause must accurately reflect the position of both parties to the agreement.

CASE EXAMPLE

Cine Bes Filmcilik ve Yapimcilik v United International Pictures [2003] EWCA Civ 1669

A clause in a licensing agreement for films provided for payment by the licensee to the licensor in the event of termination of the agreement. However, the clause took no account of payment to the licensee for any benefits gained by the licensor. As a result the clause could be seen as a penalty clause since it failed to take account of the position of both parties.

ACTIVITY

Self-assessment questions

1. What is a court trying to achieve when it makes an award of damages in contract law?
2. When will it be possible to recover damages even though the injured party has suffered no loss?
3. How does a court decide whether the defendant's breach of contract caused the actual damage suffered?
4. What are the basic differences between the judgments in *Hadley v Baxendale* and *Victoria Laundry v Newman Industries*?
5. In what ways is the judgment in *The Heron* not a sensible one?
6. Why was the case rejected in *Parsons v Uttley Ingham*?
7. How does the 'available market' rule affect an award of damages?
8. When is reliance loss awarded rather than loss of a bargain?
9. Is it possible to recover both?
10. What effect does an anticipatory breach have on an award of damages?
11. What restrictions exist in the case of recovering damages for mental distress?
12. In what ways is a penalty different to liquidated damages?
13. How do the courts determine whether an amount of damages indicated in the contract is genuine liquidated damages or merely a penalty?

KEY FACTS

Key facts on contract damages	
The purpose of contract damages	**Case/statute**
To put a party in the position he would have been in if the contract had been properly performed.	*Robinson v Harman*
Causation and remoteness of damage	**Case/statute**
Factual causation means that the breach must be the main reason for the claimant's loss.	*London Joint Stock Bank v MacMillan*
Remoteness of damage limits the recoverable damage – there are two types of recoverable loss for which the claimant can recover:	*Hadley v Baxendale*
• loss that is a natural consequence of the breach	
• loss in the contemplation of the parties when the contract is formed.	*Victoria Laundry v Newman Industries*
This is based on what is foreseeable.	
Bases of assessment	**Case/statute**
There are three normal bases:	
• loss of a bargain – eg loss of profit, or failure to deliver – can be subject to the 'available market' rule	*Charter v Sullivan*
• reliance loss, ie necessary expenses made in advance of contract	*Anglia TV v Reed*
• restitution, ie a price already paid under the contract.	
But it is now possible to claim for loss of a valuable amenity.	*Farley v Skinner*

Nominal loss or speculative loss	Case/statute
If no real loss, then nominal damages are available.	*Staniforth v Lyall*
It is possible to claim for loss of a chance.	*Chaplin v Hicks*
It is possible to claim for mental distress in holiday cases.	*Jarvis v Swan*
And also for loss of an amenity where provision of a 'pleasurable amenity' was the purpose of the contract.	*Ruxley Electronics and Construction Ltd v Forsyth*

Liquidated damages	Case/statute
These are identified in the contract itself.	*Dunlop v New Garage*
They must not amount to a penalty:	
• an extravagant sum is a penalty	
• payment of a large sum for a small debt is a penalty	
• one sum for a variety of breaches is a penalty; a sum for one breach is not	
• the wording used by the parties is not conclusive; it depends on construction by the court	
• a claim for liquidated damages will not fail because the potential loss was impossible to calculate at the time of formation.	

16.2 Equitable remedies

16.2.1 Introduction

There may well be cases where a sum of money damages is an inadequate remedy in the circumstances of the case and justice would not be served. There are obvious examples:

- where the subject-matter of the contract is unique and no adequate alternative could be purchased elsewhere
- where damages are too difficult to assess
- where the defendant would be unable to pay damages
- where a party's trade is being damaged
- where one party would not have entered the contract except for a mistake or a misrepresentation
- where a written contract is not an accurate reflection of the actual agreement reached by the parties.

In such instances, equitable remedies may be available.

Equitable remedies are available in both contract and tort, although equity is much more closely associated with contract law. The whole purpose of equitable remedies is that they should operate where an award of damages is an inadequate remedy and justice is not served.

Equitable remedies are at the discretion of the court, unlike an award of damages, which is an automatic consequence of liability being established. Because the remedies are discretionary they are awarded subject to compliance with the various 'maxims of equity' such as 'he who comes to equity must come with clean hands', 'delay defeats equity', 'equity looks to the intention not to the form' etc.

On that basis there are a number of different remedies available to the court, particularly in contract law, which more adequately reflect the need of the claimant. There are four that are particularly relevant:

- **specific performance**.
- **injunctions**.
- **rescission**.
- **rectification**.

16.2.2 Specific performance

This is an order of the court for the party in default to carry out his obligations under the contract. An example would be an order of the court that property should be handed over or title to the property should be transferred. As a remedy it is rarely granted because of the difficulty of overseeing it. Specific performance, then, will only be granted subject to certain well-established principles:

Not available where damages are an appropriate remedy

It will never be awarded where damages are an adequate remedy and therefore the more appropriate remedy.

CASE EXAMPLE

Fothergill v Rowland (1873) LR 17 Eq 132

Here, Jessell MR rejected the argument that specific performance should be awarded in a contract where damages would be difficult to assess because the contract involved production and delivery of goods over a specified period.

Available only if the subject-matter of the contract is unique

Usually, it will be the unique quality of the subject-matter of the contract that makes damages an inadequate remedy.

Land is always seen as being unique property (see *Adderly v Dixon* [1824] 57 ER 239). Other property can be seen as unique for the purposes of awarding the remedy but there is a much less clear pattern. Valuable antiques or works of art, for instance, will generally be seen as unique and thus within the remedy (see *Falcke v Gray* (1859) 4 Drew 651).

Available only where the remedy is capable of enforcement by the court

One maxim of equity is that 'equity will do nothing in vain'. As a result, the courts will never grant specific performance unless the judges are sure that they are capable of supervising performance and ensuring that the order can be carried out.

CASE EXAMPLE

Ryan v Mutual Tontine Westminster Chambers Association [1893] 1 Ch 116

Under a tenancy agreement the landlord was obliged to provide a hall porter to take care of the common areas. The person employed failed to properly do the work. An order for specific performance was refused because the court could not supervise the work.

This contrasts with the situation where no particular supervision is required and the order in itself is sufficient because of the consequences of not complying with the order.

CASE EXAMPLE

Posner v Scott-Lewis [1987] 3 WLR 53

Here, the landlord of flats was in breach of his obligation to provide a hall porter. The landlord argued that the remedy was inappropriate since he had in fact employed a non-resident porter. The court had no problem in awarding specific performance since the tenancy agreement specifically required a resident porter. Had the landlord not complied with the order of the court, he would then have been in contempt of court.

Not generally available in employment contracts (contracts for personal services)

This is simply an extension of the previous principle. In a contract of employment it would be very difficult for the court to oversee an order of specific performance and therefore it will generally not be awarded.

CASE EXAMPLE

De Francesco v Barnum [1890] 45 Ch 430

Here, a contract of apprenticeship was very disadvantageous to the young dancer who was bound by it. She got no payment under the contract and one clause prevented her from taking up any paid employment without express approval. When the girl was set to accept other work, the claimant's action to prevent it failed. The provisions of the apprenticeship deed were held to be unfair and unenforceable against her. Neither an injunction nor specific performance of the contract would have been available to the claimant.

However, this will not always be the case and it is possible for an employee, for instance, to use the remedy to prevent an employer from using incorrect procedure. (See *Robb v Hammersmith and Fulham LBC* [1991] IRLR 72.)

Not available if the claimant delays too long in seeking the remedy

'Delay defeats equity' and it was traditionally felt that a delay of more than 12 months might prevent the court from awarding the remedy. However, in *Lazard Bros & Co Ltd v Fairfield Properties (Mayfair) Ltd* (1977) 121 SJ 793, it was held that the mere fact of a delay in itself was insufficient reason to deny the remedy without the delay also being based on other unconscionable behaviour.

Not available where granting the remedy would cause undue hardship

In awarding any equitable remedy the court has to be certain that the remedy is only remedying what the claimant suffered. The remedy should not go so far that it harms the defendant.

CASE EXAMPLE

Hope v Walter [1900] 1 Ch 257

Specific performance was refused in a contract for the sale and purchase of a property that neither party to the sale knew was being used at the time as a brothel.

Not available unless the claimant can show that he has performed or is ready and willing to perform his obligations under the contract

The claimant is seeking an order from the court to make the defendant carry out his side of the bargain. It would be inequitable to award such an order unless the claimant is actually still prepared to complete his side of the bargain.

CASE EXAMPLE

Dyster v Randall & Sons [1926] Ch 932

Here, the purchaser of property under a contract was denied a remedy of specific performance. The reasoning of the court was simple. The claimant had been made bankrupt and there was therefore no means by which he could pay the seller in the event of the contract being enforced.

Not available unless mutuality is possible

The courts will not because of equity award the remedy unless mutuality between the parties can be achieved. In this way the remedy will not be awarded against the one party where it would be unavailable against the other party in the same circumstances.

CASE EXAMPLE

Flight v Bolland (1828) 4 Russ 298

Here, the party making the application for the remedy was a minor. The court would not award it since the other party could not have succeeded in obtaining the same remedy against the minor who obviously lacked capacity.

Not available if the claimant's actions are inequitable

Since the remedy is discretionary under equity, it will not be awarded where the claimant's actions in seeking the order are unconscionable, from the maxim 'he who comes to equity must come with clean hands'. This would in fact be the case with all equitable remedies.

CASE EXAMPLE

Webster v Cecil [1861] 54 ER 812

The claimant was trying to enforce a written document for the sale and purchase of land that he knew contained an inaccurate statement of price. Since there was evidence to show what the actual price should be, his action failed and the document of sale was rectified accurately to reflect the price actually agreed.

16.2.3 Injunctions

Injunctions are of two main types:

- **mandatory** – where the order of the court is for the party actually to do something positive
- **prohibitory** – where the order is for the party to refrain from doing something.

Prohibitory injunctions must be distinguished from mandatory:

- prohibitory – these prevent the breach of a legal or equitable right
- mandatory – these are rarely granted as they impose positive obligations and they are hard for the court to enforce but prohibitory injunctions with a positive effect have on occasions been granted.

Injunctions may also vary as to the relief that they offer. They can be:

- **perpetual** (known as final, prior to the Woolf reforms) – the remedy in itself is a final remedy
- **interim** (known as interlocutory, prior to the Woolf reforms) – these are granted in advance of any trial of the issue to retain the *status quo*.

Perpetual injunctions (final relief) should be distinguished from interim:

- Perpetual injunctions would settle the dispute – so they are granted only where damages in any case would be an inadequate remedy.
- Interim injunctions are granted where the claimant might suffer irreparable harm if forced to wait for the main action and so they are granted to prevent the breach continuing until the wider issue is resolved at trial, but only subject to stringent safeguards since the defendant also needs protection.

In contract law, injunctions are rarely mandatory among other reasons for the same reason as with orders of specific performance: the difficulty of overseeing and enforcing them. As a result, they are usually negative restrictions on the defendant.

There are three common instances where an injunction may be claimed in respect of a dispute over contract law issues:

- to enforce a restraint of trade by which one party is bound
- to restrain a breach of confidence by one party to the contract
- to encourage performance of a contract of personal services

Enforcing a contract in restraint of trade

Such contractual clauses are *prima facie* void, and so an injunction will be granted only if the restraint is reasonable as between the parties and in the public interest, and only if they protect a legitimate interest.

CASE EXAMPLE

Fitch v Dewes [1921] 2 AC 158

Here, a very long restraint on a solicitor's clerk from taking up the same employment within a seven-mile radius of Tamworth Town Hall was held to be reasonable. The court accepted that it went no further than protecting a legitimate interest. As well as this, in all the circumstances of the case, particularly the location, a small rural town at the time, it was accepted that the tests of reasonableness in terms of duration of the restraint and the area covered by it were also satisfied. This was because of the influence on the employer's business that was possible in the event of the restraint being breached by the employee.

However, these tests of duration and geographical extent still play a major part in determining the outcome of a request for an injunction.

CASE EXAMPLE

Fellowes v Fisher [1976] QB 122

Here, a five-year restraint on a conveyancing clerk from taking similar employment in Walthamstow was held to be unreasonable by Lord Denning. The major difference from the last case is that the clerk was actually relatively unknown in what was a densely populated area. The employer could not be said to be genuinely protecting a legitimate interest. The effect was more to prevent the employee from taking up work.

One of the areas with less clear definition is the requirement that the restraint should be in the public interest, or at least that it should not be contrary to the public interest. The lack of clarity can be shown in case law.

CASE EXAMPLE

Deacons v Bridge [1984] AC 705

Here, a clause in a solicitor's contract restraining him from practising in Hong Kong for a period of five years was upheld as in the public interest.

CASE EXAMPLE

Kerr v Morris [1987] Ch 90

In contrast to the last case, a clause in the partnership agreement of a doctor working for the National Health Service restraining him from practising within a certain area was held to be contrary to the public interest.

Interim injunctions are very often sought in respect of enforcement of covenants in restraint of trade. They will not be granted if to do so would prejudice the final outcome at trial or might permanently damage the position of either party.

They were originally granted only where it was possible to show a strong *prima facie* case of an infringement of rights, and that damages were an inadequate remedy, and also that the balance of convenience favoured granting the remedy.

The rules on granting interim injunctions are generally now those identified in Lord Diplock's test in *American Cyanamid Co v Ethicon Ltd* (1975) 8 Sydney LR 207:

- the court is satisfied that the claim is neither frivolous nor vexatious; and
- the court is satisfied that there is a serious issue to be tried; and
- the balance of convenience test favours awarding the remedy; and
- as a last resort only the court may consider the relative strength of each party's case.

Lord Denning preferred to use the previous test based on being able to show a strong *prima facie* case and he argued for this approach in *Fellowes v Fisher* [1976] QB 122. Inevitably, what the courts do not wish to do is to become involved in a full review of all of the evidence in advance of the case itself since that creates the possibility of the injunction being used as the means of obtaining final relief without the issue itself being properly heard.

Restraining a breach of confidence

Injunctions are used in this context as a means of enforcing a provision protecting legitimate trade secrets or specialist information. Very often a contract will contain an express provision preventing an employee from disclosing trade secrets or other specialised information to which the employee has become a party only by virtue of his employment.

Even where there is no such express stipulation, the courts at times have been willing to imply such a term into the contract where the circumstances demand it.

Such a restriction can be drafted to cover a variety of protections of an employer's legitimate business interests:

■ Restraints to prevent the soliciting of the employer's existing customers.

CASE EXAMPLE

Home Counties Dairies Ltd v Skilton [1970] 1 WLR 526

A clause in a milk roundsman's contract of employment provided that he should not work as a roundsman or serve any existing customer for a period of one year after leaving the employment. It was upheld as it only protected legitimate interests.

■ Restraints to prevent the disclosure of trade secrets, manufacturing processes etc (see *Faccenda Chicken v Fowler* [1986] 1 All ER 617 below).
■ Restraints to prevent the improper use or disclosure of lists of the employer's client contacts (see *Home Counties Dairies Ltd v Skilton* [1970] 1 WLR 526 above and *Faccenda Chicken v Fowler* below).
■ Restraints to prevent the improper use or disclosure of lists of charges, delivery routes, delivery dates etc.

CASE EXAMPLE

Faccenda Chicken v Fowler [1986] 1 All ER 617

Fowler was employed as the sales manager of a company selling fresh chickens. He developed a new sales strategy based on door-to-door sales from refrigerated vans. An injunction was sought by his employer to prevent competition. The action was unsuccessful because the termination was reasonable and there was no express provision in the contract restraining Fowler from engaging in such a venture.

Encouraging compliance with a contract of personal service

Where a clause is entered into a contract of personal service, attempts to enforce its use by means of an injunction will inevitably depend for their success on the nature of the contract and the character of the clause.

The courts have devised certain tests with which the applicant must comply before the injunction will be granted:

■ Since the remedy in these circumstances appears to have all the characteristics of a mandatory injunction, then it will only be awarded where there is actually an express negative restriction in the contract and it will not be awarded where it amounts in effect to only a mandatory injunction.

CASE EXAMPLE

Warner Bros Pictures Inc v Nelson [1937] 1 KB 209

A young film actress, Bette Davis, was contracted to work in films exclusively for the claimants for a one-year period that could be extended by the claimants for a further seven years. The actress then at one point came to England and, in breach of her contract, agreed to act in a film for a rival company. It would have been impossible for the claimants to secure an order of specific performance, which could not in any case have been effectively enforced by the court. However, the court was prepared to allow the claimants an injunction since the order was to restrain her from taking up the alternative employment.

> The injunction will not be granted if it is excessively broad in its scope and where it would have the effect of preventing the employee from earning a living without the express permission of the claimant.

CASE EXAMPLE

Lumley v Wagner [1852] 42 ER 687

An opera singer, Joanna Wagner, had entered into a contract that contained an express stipulation that during the three months for which she was contracted she would not take up work with any other theatre. When she did enter another contract that would run simultaneously with her contract with Lumley, she was successfully restrained from doing so by grant of the injunction. Bearing in mind the brief duration of the contract, it in no way interfered with her general ability to earn a living and was reasonable and enforceable in all the circumstances.

> The court will not be prepared to grant an injunction where the order itself would be futile or where to do so would actually be unreasonable on the party restrained under the contract.

CASE EXAMPLE

Page One Records v Britton [1968] 1 WLR 157

'The Troggs' were a well-known pop group in the 1960s. By their contract they were bound indefinitely to their manager through a clause that they would not at any time appoint anybody else to act as their manager. The terms of the contract were also extremely unfavourable. When they became disillusioned and found a new manager, the existing manager tried to enforce the contract by means of an injunction, but failed. The court would not grant such an order because it felt that its effect would be to tie the group to their manager indefinitely and against their will or otherwise to prevent them from working as musicians.

16.2.4 Rescission

The remedy of rescission is an order of the court that seeks to put the parties back into their pre-contractual position if that is in fact possible in the circumstances. As such, it is about setting the contract aside on the application of one of the parties who has the right to 'avoid' the contract because of some defect in it.

Rescission, then, is particularly common in all classes of misrepresentation and also in mistake and is awarded on the basis that the party may not have been prepared to enter the contract if aware of the defect when the contract was formed.

Rescission is obviously a very precise remedy, granted once again at the discretion of the court, and so it will only be granted where certain precise conditions are met (the so-called 'bars to rescission').

It will only be granted where *restitutio in integrum* is possible

Restitutio in integrum must apply in order for a claim for rescission of a contract to be successful. This means that it must actually be possible to return the parties to the positions that they were in before the contract was formed. One obvious example of this is that the subject-matter of the contract must not have been substantially altered in any way.

CASE EXAMPLE

Clarke v Dickson [1858] 120 ER 463

Clarke was persuaded to buy shares in a partnership as a result of misrepresentations made to him prior to the agreement. Four years later, the partnership became a limited company. When the company failed and was wound up, Clarke then discovered the misrepresentation. Clarke then sought rescission and return of the money he had paid to enter the partnership. He was unable to rescind because the nature of the shares had changed from partnership shares to company shares. The judge in the case gave an excellent example of how *restitutio in integrum* applies. He said that if a butcher bought live cattle and then slaughtered them and then discovered a defect in the contract and wished to rescind, this would be denied. The state of the subject-matter of the agreement, the cattle, would have changed so dramatically that it would actually prove impossible in reality to put the parties back into their pre-contract position.

Restitutio in integrum is clearly also impossible where the value of the goods has disappeared following the contract.

CASE EXAMPLE

Lagunas Nitrate Co v Lagunas Syndicate [1899] 2 Ch 392

The claimants bought a nitrate field because of an innocent misrepresentation made by the defendant as to the strength of the market for nitrates. The claimants made profits for a certain period but were then affected adversely by a general depression in prices. At this point they sought rescission. They failed because they had extracted the nitrates for some time and the field could not be restored to its pre-contract order. The amount and value of the remaining minerals was considerably less than it was prior to the formation of the contract.

However, this is not to say that rescission will always be denied because the precise pre-contract conditions cannot fully be met. Case law has in the past demonstrated some leeway for the judges on this point.

CASE EXAMPLE

Armstrong v Jackson [1917] 2 KB 822

Here, a contract for the sale and purchase of shares was rescinded. This was despite the fact that by the time the case was heard, the share price had dropped from £3 per share to 5 shillings (25p) per share. Rescission was possible because a stockbroker had sold his own shares to his client and it therefore involved a conflict of interests.

CASE EXAMPLE

Head v Tattersall (1871) LR 7 Exch 7

A contract for the sale and purchase of a horse was rescinded even though at the time of the case the horse was injured. This was possible because the injury was not the fault of the claimant.

It will not be granted where the party seeking it has already affirmed the contract

Another important requirement for rescission is that the party seeking it must genuinely wish to be removed from his contractual obligations. If that party by his conduct has actually acted in a way that shows approval (or affirmation) of the contract then the court will not be prepared to award the remedy.

CASE EXAMPLE

Long v Lloyd [1958] 1 WLR 753

Here, the claimant bought from the defendant a lorry that proved to be defective, contrary to the contract description. Defects were immediately apparent but the purchaser twice allowed the seller to make repairs to the lorry. He had thus affirmed the contract and as a result lost the right to rescission.

The remedy will be unavailable if there is an excessive delay in seeking it

'Delay defeats equity' is a maxim of equity. In the same way that the Limitation Act 1980 prevents recovery of damage after certain set periods of time, equitable remedies are lost if there is too great a time span between the formation of the contract and the application for the remedy. This applies equally to rescission as to other equitable remedies.

CASE EXAMPLE

Leaf v International Galleries [1950] 2 KB 86

This involved a contract for the sale and purchase of a painting falsely represented as being an original Constable. Rescission was not possible because the claim did not occur until five years after the contract was made.

The remedy is not available where an innocent third party has gained rights in the property

Rescission is an equitable order and it would be unfair to impose the remedy on a party who is blameless in respect of the defect in the original contract. As a result, where a third party has obtained the property in good faith and for value, the remedy will generally be denied.

CASE EXAMPLE

Oakes v Turquand and Harding (1867) LR 2 HL 325

Here, the claimant was fraudulently induced to sell goods to a rogue and as a result was not paid. The goods had been sold on to an innocent third party, the defendant, before the claimant could try to exercise a claim for rescission. At this point the remedy could not be granted.

The remedy may be unavailable because of s 2(2) of the Misrepresentation Act 1967

Section 2(2) of the 1967 Act gives judges the discretion to award damages in place of rescission. If the court is of the opinion that damages are the appropriate remedy then the right to rescind will be lost.

16.2.5 Rectification of a document

This is an order of the court to rectify a mistake in a written contract where the written document does not accurately reflect the real agreement reached by the parties. Again, the remedy is at the discretion of the court and it will only be granted where it can be shown that the written agreement differs to that reached by the parties and it would be unconscionable to allow the existing written document to stand.

CASE EXAMPLE

Craddock Bros Ltd v Hunt [1923] 2 Ch 136

Craddock agreed to sell his house to Hunt, not intending an adjoining yard to be included in the sale. However, by mistake, the yard was included in the conveyance so Craddock immediately sought rectification of the document and succeeded.

Type of remedy	Purpose of remedy	Limitations on remedy	Where appropriate
Common law			
Unliquidated damages	To place the party in the same position he would be in if the contract had been properly carried out	Breach must be the cause of the claimant's loss Can only recover for a loss that is a natural consequence of the breach, or that was in the contemplation of both parties at the time the contract was formed	Breach of contract
Liquidated damages	To identify in advance of the contract an agreed amount of compensation	Must not be a penalty But a claim for liquidated damages will not fail because potential loss was impossible to calculate at the time of formation	Breach of contract
Quantum meruit	To provide payment for services rendered	The parties must be in a contractual relationship	Part performance or prevention of performance Price not stated Implied fresh agreement

Equitable			
Specific performance	To make a party in default carry out his contractual obligations	Only granted if: • Damages would be inadequate • Subject-matter is unique • Claimant acts equitably • No excessive delay • Not a contract of personal service • Would not cause hardship • Claimant has performed or will do so • Mutuality is possible • Court can oversee order	Breach of contract
Rescission	To return the parties to their pre-contractual position	Only available if: • *Restitutio in integrum* possible • Contract is not affirmed • No excessive delay • No third party has gained rights • Damages are not a better remedy under s 2(2) Misrepresentation Act	Vitiated contract for, eg misrepresentation, duress, undue influence
Injunction	To restrain a party from breaching contractual obligations	In a restraint of trade clause which protects a legitimate interest, is reasonable between the parties and in the public interest; and is not unreasonable in duration and geographical extent Protects confidentiality Enforces compliance with a contract of personal service – containing an express negative provision; and does not merely prevent the person from working; and is not futile	Anticipatory breach
Rectification	To rewrite a contractual document drafted in error	Court must accept that it is inequitable to allow the document to stand	Written agreement inaccurately reflects real agreement

Figure 16.1 Chart illustrating the differences between the different remedies available in contract law

ACTIVITY

Self-assessment questions

1. What are the common features of property that can be the subject of an order for specific performance?
2. In what circumstances will an order for specific performance be denied?
3. Why are the courts reluctant to award mandatory injunctions?
4. When, if ever, is an injunction possible in a contract of employment?
5. In rescission, why is the rule relating to *restitutio in integrum* necessary?
6. What other bars to rescission are there?
7. What has gone wrong when rectification of a document is ordered?

Applying the law

Consider which equitable remedy might be appropriate in the following circumstances:

1. Charnjit has bought a dental practice from Ali. Before the contract, Ali told Charnjit that it had a very stable client base. At the time of forming the contract this was 2,000. In fact, by the time of the transfer of the business, the client base has reduced to a few hundred because Ali is quite old and infirm and has been hurting some of the patients.
2. Sally and James agreed by phone conversations and exchange of letters that Sally would buy a set of DJ equipment and records from James and his goodwill for £5,300. In fact, a written agreement drafted for James and signed by both parties has the price as only £3,500 and Sally is now refusing to pay more.
3. Andre was employed as a stylist with 'Luscious Locks' salon. By his contract he agreed not to act as a stylist within a three-mile radius of the salon or to solicit its customers for a period of six months after leaving. Andre left the salon last week and has opened his own salon across the road from 'Luscious Locks', having accepted bookings from many of his former customers.
4. Sukhy agreed to buy a 50-acre site in the city centre from Chris for £5 million, and intended to develop luxury apartments on it. After exchange of contracts, Chris informed Sukhy that he was not going to go through with the sale because he had found a buyer who would pay £6 million for the site.

KEY FACTS

Specific performance	Case/statute
An order for the party in default to carry out obligations under the contract	
The remedy is only granted if:	
• damages would be inadequate	*Fothergill v Rowland*
• subject-matter is unique	*Adderly v Dixon*
• claimant acts with conscience	*Webster v Cecil*
• no excessive delay in seeking it	
• not a contract of personal service	*De Francesco v Barnum*
• would not cause hardship to defendant	*Hope v Walter*
• claimant has performed or is ready to do so	*Dyster v Randall*
• mutuality is possible	*Flight v Bolland*
• court can oversee order.	*Posner v Scott-Lewis*

Injunctions	Case/statute
An order to restrain a party from breaching contractual obligations. Covers three situations:	
• enforcing restraint of trade clauses – in which case must (i) protect a legitimate interest; (ii) be reasonable between the parties and in the public interest; (iii) be reasonable in duration and geographical extent	*Fitch v Dewe*
• to protect confidentiality	*Faccenda Chicken v Fowler*
• to enforce compliance with a contract of personal service	
• contract must contain express negative provision to that effect	*Warner Bros v Nelson*
• provision must not merely prevent the person from working	*Lumley v Wagner*
• the provision must not be futile or unreasonable.	*Page One Records v Britton*

Rescission	Case/statute
An order returning the parties to their pre-contractual position. So available only if:	
• *restitutio in integrum* is possible	*Clarke v Dickson*
• contract is not affirmed	*Long v Lloyd*
• there is no excessive delay in claiming	*Leaf v International Galleries*
• no third party has gained rights	*Oakes v Turquand*
• in misrepresentation the judge has not declared damages to be a better remedy.	s 2(2) Misrepresentation Act 1967

Rectification of a document	Case/statute
An order to redraft a written contract which inaccurately represents the actual agreement.	*Craddock Bros v Hunt*

SUMMARY

Damages

▨ A claimant can only recover for damage that is the natural consequence of the breach, and damage that was in the contemplation of both parties at the time when the contract was formed.

▨ There are three normal bases of assessment of damages: loss of a bargain (eg, loss of profit, failure to deliver), reliance loss (ie, necessary expenses made in advance of the contract), and restitution (recovery of a price already paid under the contract).

Liquidated damages

▨ This is a sum identified in the contract itself which must not be a penalty.

Equitable remedies

▨ **Specific performance**: An order for the party in default to carry out obligations under the contract only granted if certain conditions are met.

- **Injunction**: An order to restrain a party from breaching contractual obligations – usually either to enforce restraint of trade clauses, to protect confidentiality, or to enforce compliance with a contract of personal service.
- **Rescission**: An order putting the parties back to their pre-contractual position providing certain conditions are met.
- **Rectification**: An order to redraft a written contract which inaccurately represents the actual agreement.

Further reading

Bishop, W D, 'The Choice of Remedy for Breach of Contract' (1985) 14 LS 299.

Danzig, R, '*Hadley v Baxendale*: A Study in the Industrialisation of Law' (1975) 4 LS 279.

Spry, I, *The Principles of Equitable Remedies* (8th edn, Sweet & Maxwell, 2009).

17
Quasi-contract

AIMS AND OBJECTIVES

After reading this chapter you should be able to:

- Understand the basic character of quasi-contract
- Understand where actions can be made to recover payments made
- Understand where parties can recover on a *quantum meruit*
- Critically analyse the area
- Apply the law to factual situations and reach conclusions

17.1 Introduction

'Quasi-contract' is a term used in relation to an area where a party is seeking a remedy for a loss suffered but the loss cannot strictly be recovered under the general rules of contract law and the usual remedies in contract law are unavailable. There are many reasons why this situation may arise:

- Firstly, because the loss has not resulted from an actual breach of contract.
- Because the agreement itself is not actually a contract, eg in circumstances where a vitiating factor renders the agreement void – mistake being the obvious example.
- Because the courts are of the opinion that the classic ingredients for formation of a contract have not been satisfied although some property has actually passed under the agreement. An example of this would be the situation in *British Steel Corporation v Cleveland Bridge and Engineering Co* [1984] 1 All ER 504 (see section 2.4).
- Because work has been completed under an agreement where there is no specific agreement in relation to payment.

The area has some relationship with contract law, then, but the normal rules concerning contractual remedies cannot apply. This is why it is known as quasi-contract, 'quasi' meaning 'near' or 'in a certain sense' or 'to a degree'.

In fact, the area is part of a much broader area known as restitution. This has its roots in the old forms of action and the law of obligations. There are clear historical connections with both contract and tort although this method of remedying a loss operates independently of either contract or tort. In fact, the basis of such an action is in equity and its purpose is different to the purposes for awarding either tort or contract damages.

There are a number of situations in which the principle might apply but there are also common features as identified by the judges.

JUDGMENT

As Lord Mansfield stated in *Moses v Macferlan* (1760) 2 Burr 1005: 'This kind of equitable action, to recover back money, which ought not in justice to be kept, is very beneficial, and therefore much encouraged … it lies for money paid by mistake; or for money got through imposition (express or implied); or extortion; or an undue advantage taken of the plaintiff's situation, contrary to laws made for the protection of persons under those circumstances. In one word, the gist of this kind of action is, that the defendant upon the circumstances of the case, is obliged by the ties of natural justice and equity to refund the money.'

So the common feature in all of the various areas is that the money or property is returned because it would be unfair if it were not. Because such a means of recovery for loss fell strictly outside of the rules of contract, it was originally justified as being based on contracts implied by law. However, this mechanism was rather artificial and was subject to a lot of criticism and more recently judges have accepted that the area is based on the idea of unjust enrichment.

JUDGMENT

In *Fibrosa Spolka Akcyjna v Fairbairn Lawson Combe Barbour Ltd* [1943] AC 32 (the *Fibrosa case*), Lord Wright explained the justification for this means of recovering loss: 'It is clear that any civilised system of law is bound to provide remedies for what has been called unjust enrichment or unjust benefit, that is to prevent a man retaining the money of or some benefit derived from, another which it is against his conscience he should keep.' He also recognised the distinction of the area from other remedies: 'Such remedies in English law are generically different from remedies in contract and tort, and are now recognised to fall within the third category of the common law which has been called quasi-contract or restitution.'

There are two principal situations in which this type of claim is appropriate:

- **Actions to recover money paid over** (this could either be because there is a total failure of consideration or because the money was passed under a mistake of fact or law).
- **Actions to recover a payment for work done** (known as *quantum meruit*, meaning 'for the amount done').

17.2 Actions to recover payments made

17.2.1 Actions to recover payments where there is a total failure of consideration

This use of the principles of restitution applies in circumstances where a party, acting in full reliance that the other party will perform his contractual obligations, has transferred money in advance of the contract but there has been a total failure of consideration by the other party.

A total failure of consideration in this context would mean that the party has received nothing of what he was expecting or entitled to under the contract. The claimant has the choice of recovering the money under a claim for breach of contract or alternatively seeking restitution. The significance here is that restitution allows the party to recover the payment made even though there is not a breach of contract.

Where, on the other hand, there is only a partial failure of consideration, and the claimant has received part of the benefit that he should have received under the contract, then usually the appropriate action would be for a breach of contract and the remedy would be for damages appropriate to the breach (see section 15.2.2).

CASE EXAMPLE

Whincup v Hughes (1871) LR 6 CP 78

The claimant had paid a premium of £25 to a watchmaker in an agreement under which the claimant's son would serve as an apprentice of the watchmaker for a period of six years' training. The watchmaker then died after only one year of the apprenticeship. The claimant sued the executrix of the watchmaker for recovery of all or part of the premium, but failed. The court held that there was not a complete failure of consideration allowing restitution but only a partial failure.

JUDGMENT

Brett J explained the position: 'Where a sum of money has been paid for an entire consideration, and there is only a partial failure of consideration, neither the whole or part of any such sum can be recovered.'

It is nevertheless possible for partial restitution to be granted in situations where it is easy to apportion. The obvious example of this would be in the case of divisible contracts.

The classic example of where restitution will be allowed for a total failure of consideration is frustration. Here there cannot be said to be a breach because the contract is discharged because of a factor beyond the control of either party making it impossible to continue.

CASE EXAMPLE

Fibrosa Spolka Akcyjna v Fairbairn Lawson Combe Barbour Ltd (the Fibrosa case) [1943] AC 32

Here, the contract to build and deliver machinery to a Polish company was frustrated because of the German invasion and occupation of Poland prior to the start of the Second

World War. The contract required the Polish company to make an advance payment of £1,000. The House of Lords held that it was possible to recover payments made prior to a frustrating event provided that there was a total failure of consideration, that the party had received nothing of what he contracted for. This rule itself mitigates some of the potential injustice of the basic rule on frustration that discharges the parties at the time of the frustrating event, and therefore can lead to a party losing what he has already given by the pure chance of when the frustrating event occurs. The Law Reform (Frustrated Contracts) Act 1943 attempts to introduce a more fair distribution of losses (see section 15.4.5).

There are, however, some strange situations in which the courts have allowed restitution on the basis of a total failure of consideration even though the party recovering has clearly gained a benefit under the contract.

CASE EXAMPLE

Rowland v Divall [1923] 2 KB 500

Here, the claimant had bought a car that turned out to be stolen and for which therefore the seller was unable to pass good title in breach of s 12 of the Sale of Goods Act 1979. When the proper owner took the car back, the claimant was able to recover the full purchase price from the seller even though by this stage the buyer had enjoyed four months' use of the car. The court held that the central purpose of the contract was to pass ownership of the car to the buyer. This was impossible in the circumstances and so the court was prepared to accept what appears on the face of it to be a partial failure of consideration as a total failure of consideration. The other interesting feature of the case is that restitution applies to prevent the unjust enrichment of a party and yet it is difficult to see how the seller could have been unjustly enriched in these circumstances.

Generally, however, the fact that a party has received a benefit under the contract will defeat any claim that there is a total failure of consideration. The appropriate action in that case is for breach of contract.

CASE EXAMPLE

Hunt v Silk (1804) 5 East 449

This involved a contract for the creation of a lease. Under the contract the tenant was to pay a £10 premium in advance and the landlord was obliged to make certain repairs, to execute the lease within 10 days and give immediate possession of the property. In fact, while the tenant did pay the £10 and take immediate possession, the landlord failed to carry out the agreed repairs or to execute the lease within the agreed time. The tenant left and tried to claim the premium, arguing a total failure of consideration. The court would not accept this argument. The tenant had enjoyed brief occupation of the property and therefore had gained a benefit deriving from the contract. It was wrong to say that there was a total failure of consideration in the circumstances and the action failed, even though there might have been a more suitable action for breach of contract.

17.2.2 Actions to recover payments made under a mistake of fact

It has long been accepted that a party who has paid money over on the basis of a mistake of fact is entitled to recover under principles of restitution.

CASE EXAMPLE

Kelly v Solari (1841) 9 M & W 54

Here, money was paid out under a life insurance policy. In fact, at the time of payment the last premium under the policy had not been paid. As a result of this, the policy should have lapsed. The insurance company forgot to take this into account and paid out under the policy. When the company sought restitution, the court allowed recovery of the money because of the mistake of fact.

JUDGMENT

As Baron Parke explained at p 58: 'Where money is paid to another under the influence of a mistake, that is, upon the supposition that a specific fact is true which would entitle the other to the money, but which in fact is untrue, and the money would not have been paid if it had been known to the payer that the fact was untrue, an action will lie to recover it back.'

The principle operates quite simply because it would be inequitable for one party to be unjustly enriched as a result of another paying over money when that party would not have done so but for the mistake of fact.

CASE EXAMPLE

Norwich Union Fire Insurance Society Ltd v Price Ltd [1934] AC 455

Here, a cargo of lemons was shipped from Messina to Sydney. The cargo was insured against loss under a policy of marine insurance. The insurance company paid the policy-holder when it believed that the cargo had been destroyed through sea damage. In fact, the cargo had been sold during the voyage when the fruit was found to be ripening too fast to reach its intended destination. The court acknowledged that the payment had been made under a mistake of fact and the insurance company was entitled to restitution of the payment made.

There are a number of considerations that may be taken into account when allowing recovery of money paid over as a result of the mistake of fact:

- Traditionally, recovery could only be for a mistake of fact so recovery was not possible in the case of a mistake of law (but see now section 17.2.3).
- The mistake does not need to have arisen in the context of a contract.
- The mistake need not be one between payer and payee.
- The person seeking recovery is not entitled if he knew that the payment was not due.
- The claimant may be estopped from relying on the mistake and recovering the payment if in fact the claimant has represented to the defendant that the payment was due and the defendant, acting in reliance on this statement, has spent the money.
- The party paying money may be mistaken that they have a legal duty to pay the money over but they may still recover money that they have given voluntarily under the mistake, provided that the mistake is sufficiently serious in character.

Larner v LCC [1949] 2 KB 683

The claimant was an employee of the defendants who was called up for service in the Royal Air Force. The defendants had a policy at the time of making up the difference between service pay and normal pay in their employment and they paid the claimant according to this policy. The claimant was required in return to notify the employee of any changes in his RAF pay. However, he failed to do this and as a result he was overpaid. When he returned to work from service in the RAF, his employers then made regular deductions from his pay to recover the overpayment. The claimant then sued for the sums deducted and the employers counter-claimed, demanding return of the overpayment. The Court of Appeal rejected the claimant's argument that, although the overpayment was a mistake of fact, since the arrangement with the employer was a voluntary one, there could be no recovery. The court recognised that since the claimant was under a legal duty to undertake military service in the RAF there was no actual consideration for the defendant's promise to pay. The court held that a voluntary payment could be recovered only if it was made as the result of a sufficiently serious mistake of fact.

17.2.3 Actions to recover payments made under a mistake of law

Traditionally, it was impossible to recover money paid over under a mistake of law. This results from the simple principle that ignorance of the law is no excuse.

The rule has a lengthy history. Lord Ellenborough distinguished mistakes of fact and mistakes of law in *Bilbie v Lumley* (1802) 2 East 469, identifying that there could be no recovery for money paid over under a mistake of law. The principle in this case was later affirmed in *Brisbane v Dacres* (1813) 5 Taunt 143. It has also been affirmed in more recent times in *Westdeutsche Landesbank Girozentrale v Islington London Borough Council* [1996] AC 669.

However, the rule seems particularly harsh and it has not been without criticism.

Kiriri Cotton Co Ltd v Dewani [1960] AC 192

Here, a tenant was required to pay a premium even though this was illegal under Ugandan law. The Privy Council held that the tenant was entitled to recover the premium because he was not *in pari delicto* (he was not responsible for the illegality).

Lord Denning explained that: 'if as between the two of them the duty of observing the law is placed on the shoulders of one rather than the other – it being imposed on him specially for the protection of the other – then they are not *in pari delicto* and the money can be recovered'.

More recently, the House of Lords has actually overruled the original rule and held that in certain circumstances money paid over under a mistake of law can be recovered. The House of Lords has done this because of developments elsewhere in other common law jurisdictions and also as a result of the recommendations of the Law Commission in its Report No 227 in 1994.

CASE EXAMPLE

Kleinwort Benson Ltd v Lincoln City Council [1999] 2 AC 349

During the 1980s, local authorities were under quite severe restrictions on spending because of government policy. A number of local authorities got round the difficulty by entering into loan arrangements with banks in order to raise funds known at the time as 'loan swaps'. Under one such agreement the bank lent money to Lincoln City Council and both parties were subject to mutual payment of interest, with one side paying a fixed rate and the other paying at a market rate. In essence, the arrangement was highly speculative as to what market rates would be and was therefore almost a gamble. In 1992 in *Hazell v Hammersmith and Fulham London Borough Council* [1992] 2 AC 1, the House of Lords then declared such arrangements *ultra vires* (beyond the power of) the local authorities and therefore void. Kleinwort had entered the arrangement believing it to be legal and after the *Hazell* decision, tried to recover money, claiming that it had passed the money over under a mistake. The case was also complicated because, since the bank had made the arrangements more than six years previously, issues of limitation were also involved. Nevertheless, on the point of whether or not the bank was entitled to claim on the basis of a mistake of law, the House of Lords was unanimous in deciding that the traditional rule should be abolished. The reasoning given by Lord Goff in the leading judgment for changing the rule was that to do otherwise would allow a situation to continue where one party could be unjustly enriched as a result of the mistake, and also because to allow a contract to stand that was *ultra vires* would ignore the fact that contracts that were contrary to public policy were also illegal and void. Lord Goff also acknowledged the fact that defences would very quickly appear, an example being that the money could not be recovered from a party who had received the money in good faith and then spent it.

The position taken by the House of Lords on mistake of law has subsequently been followed.

CASE EXAMPLE

Nurdin and Peacock plc v D B Ramsden & Co Ltd (No 2)
[1999] 1 All ER 941

Under the terms of a 25-year lease, rent was set at £207,000 and in years 4 and 5 an extra £59,000 was due, at which point there was to be a rent review. In fact, the review never occurred and according to the lease the rent should have reverted to the original sum. The tenant was unaware of this and carried on paying at the higher rate for a few years. On discovering the mistake, the tenant wanted to set off the overpayments against the rent. The tenant's solicitor, however, advised the tenant to pay the higher sum until arbitration, at which point a full refund would be possible. The original overpayments were made under a mistake of fact and so were recoverable. However, the payment that was made after the tenant discovered the mistake and took legal advice was not made under a mistake of fact. The defendants argued that this was a mistake of law and recovery was possible only if the claimant mistakenly believed that he was liable to pay. The court accepted that recovery was possible for a mistake of law and rejected the defendant's argument. The court held that it was sufficient that the mistake was directly related to the overpayment and that the claimant would not have paid the money over but for the mistake.

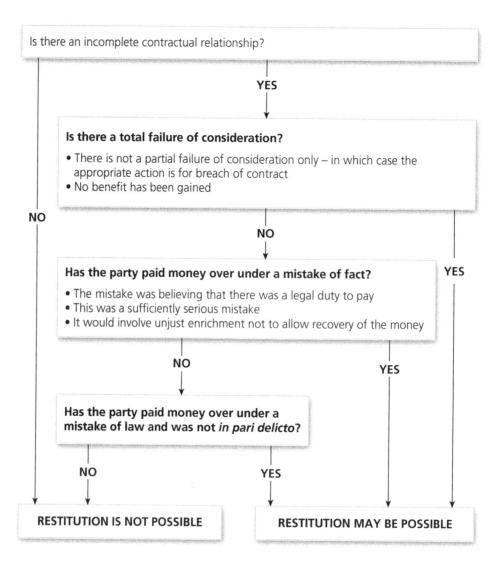

Is there an incomplete contractual relationship?

YES

Is there a total failure of consideration?
- There is not a partial failure of consideration only – in which case the appropriate action is for breach of contract
- No benefit has been gained

NO

NO

Has the party paid money over under a mistake of fact?
- The mistake was believing that there was a legal duty to pay
- This was a sufficiently serious mistake
- It would involve unjust enrichment not to allow recovery of the money

YES

NO

YES

Has the party paid money over under a mistake of law and was not *in pari delicto*?

NO

YES

RESTITUTION IS NOT POSSIBLE

RESTITUTION MAY BE POSSIBLE

Figure 17.1 Diagram illustrating a claim for restitution

17.3 Actions to recover on a *quantum meruit* basis

So far, we have looked at money paid over by one party and the equitable means of recovering the money. In some instances, rather than having paid money over, a party will have completed work or given some other benefit. In these circumstances recovery may be on the basis of *quantum meruit*. *Quantum meruit*, meaning 'for the part earned', is merely recovery of an unqualified sum in respect of services already rendered.

We have, for instance, already seen its operation in relation to part-performance. A party will seek money under this principle in circumstances where at least part of a contract has been carried out and the money sought represents an appropriate price for the part completed.

CASE EXAMPLE

Planche v Colburn (1831) 8 Bing 14

A publisher was planning to produce a series of books on a particular theme and hired the claimant to write one of the books in the series. When the whole series was abandoned, the author was prevented from completing the work through no fault of his own and despite having already done a lot of work for the book. The court held that the author was entitled to recover half his fee for his wasted work on the basis of *quantum meruit*. (He might also have been able to consider the abandoning of the series by the publisher as an anticipatory breach and pursued a claim that way. See sections 15.5.2. and 15.5.3.)

Quantum meruit is accepted by the courts as a remedy in circumstances where either:
- the party it is being claimed against requested the service
- the party against whom the claim is made has freely accepted the service.

There are a number of other specific common circumstances in which the courts are prepared to make such an award.
- Where it is accepted that a contract for services in fact existed but that the contract was silent on the issue of remuneration. In such circumstances the court will allow recovery of a sum which is appropriate to the actual service rendered.

CASE EXAMPLE

Upton RDC v Powell [1942] 1 All ER 220

The case involved provision of services, namely firefighting, by a retained fireman. (Retained firemen are part-time employees of the fire service, often in rural areas, who attend only when there is a fire or other reason for the call out.) The man had provided services even though there was no fixed agreement as to what wages would be payable when he attended fires. The court awarded a sum that it considered reasonable in the circumstances on the basis of *quantum meruit*.

- Another application of the principle occurs in circumstances where events mean that the original agreement cannot operate in the manner envisaged. In these circumstances if it can be shown that a fresh agreement can be implied in place of the original one and that an increase in the amount of payment is also due, then the court will allow an extra payment to reflect those changed circumstances based on *quantum meruit*.

CASE EXAMPLE

Steven v Bromley [1919] 2 KB 722

Under the original contract, Steven had agreed to carry steel for Bromley at a fixed rate. When the consignment of steel was delivered to Steven, it in fact also contained extra goods not considered under the original agreement. Steven was able to claim an extra payment for carrying the extra goods under *quantum meruit*.

In circumstances where one party has elected to consider the contract discharged by the other's breach or where a party has been prevented from performing by the other party, then in either case the party might claim damages under the breach of contract. As an alternative, that party can also claim for the work already completed under the contract under *quantum meruit*. The application of the principle is particularly useful in this context since it allows the party to consider himself discharged from further obligations and in effect cut losses and get out of the contract.

CASE EXAMPLE

De Barnady v Harding (1853) 8 Exch 822

In an agency relationship, the principal wrongly revoked his agent's authority to act on his behalf. The agent was then entitled to claim for the work that he had already done as agent and also for all expenses necessarily incurred in the course of acting for the principal.

It is also possible to recover on a *quantum meruit* basis for work done under a contract which has subsequently been declared void.

CASE EXAMPLE

Craven-Ellis v Canons Ltd [1936] 2 KB 403

The claimant was employed as managing director of the defendant company. However, the correct procedures had not been carried out in appointing the claimant, as a result of which the agreement between the two parties was void and the claimant could not lawfully act for the company. He had in fact already carried out work for the company arising from his office. In contract law he could not have recovered payment for this work since the contract was void and therefore unenforceable. However, the court was prepared to allow him recovery for the work done on the basis of *quantum meruit*.

In the same way it is also possible to recover on *quantum meruit* for work done in expectation of a contract that in fact is then not formed.

CASE EXAMPLE

British Steel Corporation v Cleveland Bridge and Engineering Co [1984] 1 All ER 504

Here, the engineering company had wanted to acquire specific steel nodes from BSC. In fact the parties were constantly in such disagreement over the specifics of the contract that the judge in the case was unable to identify that any contract existed at all. Nevertheless, the steel nodes had been provided by BSC and had been fitted by the engineering company. Without an actual contract, an action for breach was impossible but the court was prepared to accept that, since the central purpose of the contract had been fulfilled, there was an entitlement to payment for the service actually rendered.

One final example of the same sort of principle operating arises in s 1(3) of the Law Reform (Frustrated Contracts) Act 1943. According to this provision, even though a contract has been frustrated, a party is entitled to recover a sum that the court considers just in the circumstances of the case, provided that the other party has obtained a valuable benefit before the frustrating event put an end to obligations under the contract.

ACTIVITY

Self-assessment questions

1. What is the principal reason for granting restitution?
2. What are the different effects of a total failure of consideration and a partial failure of consideration?
3. Why in the past did courts not grant restitution of money paid under a mistake of law?
4. What is the common characteristic of all claims for *quantum meruit*?

KEY FACTS

Key facts on quasi contracts	
The basis of restitution	
Generally applies where there is not a contract or a complete contract. Allows for recovery of money paid over to prevent unjust enrichment.	
Types of claim	**Case/statute**
Available where there is a total failure of consideration	*The Fibrosa case*
• but not for a partial failure, where damages for breach should be claimed	*Whincup v Hughes*
• nor generally if a benefit has been gained.	*Hunt v Silk*
Can recover payments made under a mistake of fact:	*Kelly v Solari*
• this is to avoid unjust enrichment	*Norwich Union v Price Ltd*
• can be a mistake that there was a legal duty to pay if mistake sufficiently serious.	*Larner v LCC*
Traditionally, there was no recovery for money paid under a mistake of law:	*Brisbane v Dacres*
• this could be harsh – so exceptions, eg where the party was not *in pari delicto* in an illegal contract	*Kiriri Cotton v Dewani*
• but the House of Lords has recently accepted that it is possible to recover money paid under a mistake of law.	*Kleinwort Benson Ltd v Lincoln City Council*
***Quantum meruit* – nature of**	
Means 'the part earned' – so is an unqualified sum for services already rendered.	
Types of claim	**Case/statute**
Can apply in a contract for services which is silent on remuneration.	*Upton RDC v Powell*
Or where the manner of performance of a contract has had to change.	*Steven v Bromley*
Or where a party has been prevented from completing performance.	*De Barnady v Harding*
Or where the contract has later been declared void.	*Craven-Ellis v Canons Ltd*
Or where work has been done in expectation that a contract will be formed.	*BSC v Cleveland Bridge and Engineering Co*

SUMMARY

Involves losses that cannot be recovered under the usual rules of contract, eg because the loss has not arisen from a breach or work has been completed without a specific payment agreed to etc.

There are two main situations where a claim is appropriate:

- an action to recover money paid over
- an action for work done (*quantum meruit*).

An action to recover money paid over could be because of:

- a total failure of consideration
- a mistake of fact
- a mistake of law.

An action to recover for work done can be when the other party requested the service or freely accepted the service and either:

- the contract existed but was silent on remuneration
- the agreement can no longer operate in the manner envisaged
- following breach or prevention of performance for work already done under the contract
- for work done under a contract that has subsequently been declared void
- for work done in expectation of a contract that is not then formed
- under s1(3) Law Reform (Frustrated Contracts) Act 1943.

Further reading

Friedmann, D, 'The Efficient Breach Fallacy' (1989) 18 LS 1.
Goff, R and Jones, G, *The Law of Restitution* (7th edn, Sweet & Maxwell, 2009).

Appendix 1

Legal essay writing

Below is a sample essay title and a guide to how to prepare to answer it.

It has been said that, 'Judicial rhetoric still clings to the remnants of the exchange mode, of benefit being derived in return for the promise. However, the driving force behind the recent decisions on the existing duty question quite clearly has been a mixture of consideration of fairness and commercial utility.'

(Adams and Brownsword, 'Contract, consideration and the critical path' (1990) 53 MLR 536 at 540.)

In the light of the above, critically consider the extent to which the courts will allow performance of an existing duty to be accepted as providing consideration for an entirely fresh agreement.

Answering the question

There are usually four key elements to answering essays in law:

- **identifying** the point of the discussion in the question
- **engaging** in a discussion relevant to the question
- **supporting** the discussion with appropriate law
- **reaching** appropriate conclusions.

Of course, in essence, what you are trying to achieve is two things:

- Firstly, you are required to reproduce certain factual information on a particular area of law and this is usually identified for you in the question
- Secondly, you are required to answer the specific question set, which usually is in the form of some sort of critical element: ie you are likely to see the words 'discuss' or 'analyse' or 'comment on' or 'critically consider' or 'evaluate', or even 'compare and contrast', if two areas are involved.

Students for the most part seem quite capable of doing the first, but also generally seem less skilled at the second. The important points in any case are to ensure that you deal with only relevant legal material in your answer and that you do answer the question set, rather than one you have made up yourself, or indeed the one that was on last year's paper.

For instance, in the case of the first, in this essay you are likely to provide detail on the following:

- definitions of consideration itself
- explanations of the rules relating to performance of existing duties
- some specific references to the case law on performance of existing duties, both those identifying that it is not consideration and those representing exceptions to the simple rule.

This is not, then, the opportunity to write all that you know about consideration. In fact, it is essential that you are selective in the information that you give. Aspects of adequacy and sufficiency, past consideration, movement from the promisee and the rules on part-payment of debts are irrelevant to the question set. So you should focus on only a very limited range of information from your total knowledge on consideration.

In the case of the second, the essay title asks you in effect to analyse the extent to which there are exceptions to a basic rule of contract, the rule on performance of existing obligations. So in this essay, again, you have to be really selective with the subject of your discussion as well as with the base of knowledge from which it is drawn.

Relevant law

The appropriate law appears to be:

- A brief explanation of the nature of consideration (consideration being the *quid pro quo* – the proof of the existence of a bargain enforceable in law) and an appropriate definition of consideration such as that in *Dunlop v Selfridge* ('an act of forbearance or the promise thereof is the price for which the promise of the other is bought, and the promise thus given for value is enforceable').
- An explanation of the basic rule on performance of existing duties as consideration – that this is not allowable because it is in effect no consideration – *Stilk v Myrick*.
- An explanation that this principle applies not merely in the case of contractual duties but in the case of performance of statutory or other legal duties also – *Collins v Godefroy* and *Ward v Byham*.
- Explain the various exceptions to the basic rule that the courts have accepted over time, namely:
  - Where something more is given over and above that required under the contract – *Hartley v Ponsonby*.
  - Where extra is provided over and above that required by the statutory or other legal duty – *Ward v Byham* and *Glassbrook Brothers v Glamorgan CC*.
  - Where the promise is made to a third party – *Scotson v Pegg* – or where third party rights would inevitably be affected – *Pao On v Lau Yiu Long*.
  - Where not to enforce the arrangement might threaten the integrity of a commercial agreement – *New Zealand Shipping Co v A M Satterthwaite & Co (The Eurymedon)*.
  - Where a party gains an extra benefit from the performance of the existing duty.
  - Use any other relevant cases as examples, eg, *Shadwell v Shadwell*.

Discussion and evaluation

The essay title asks for a 'critical discussion' of the circumstances in which the courts will allow exceptions to the basic rule on using performance of existing duties as consideration for fresh agreements to stand.

On this basis it is not sufficient merely to rely on a purely narrative approach, listing the basic rule and the exceptions, as we have done for the knowledge element. Something more must be done to appraise the rule itself and the exceptions to it.

On the basic rule itself, certain comments can be made:

- The rule is obviously a necessary one since it protects against the situation where a party gains more out of the original agreement than he was entitled to without giving anything extra himself.
- In advance of a doctrine of economic duress, it could operate to prevent a party from trying to extract more from the agreement after the event by threatening not to perform.
- In the context of *Stilk v Myrick*, it may still be seen as unfair – and clearly one of the points in *Williams v Roffey* was to prevent the breaking of a later promise made in a commercial context on which the other party had relied, to his possible detriment.

On the exceptions to the basic rule, relevant comments might include:

- That it is perfectly logical and legitimate where something is added to the original consideration to enforce the later agreement which in effect is a new agreement supported by its own consideration.
- That nevertheless very often the reasoning behind the decision to enforce the fresh agreement can be strained or at least somewhat doubtful, for example:
  - In *Shadwell v Shadwell* and in *Ward v Byham* there is the obvious contradiction that the agreements, being domestic, may be seen as lacking an intention to create a legally enforceable relationship.
  - In *Williams v Roffey* the defendants had the opportunity to sue anyway – in effect, although the extra benefit is taken to be the avoidance of penalties, a party could extend the reasoning to avoid bringing an action themselves where the other party may not complete and make an empty promise merely to save themselves the expense of suing on the breach.
- That very often what the court accepts as consideration is difficult if not impossible to identify in terms of being 'real, and tangible' even if it might tenuously be described as having some 'value', for example *Scotson v Pegg, Ward v Byham, Williams v Roffey*.
- That many of the cases actually involve third parties so may be conflicting with the basic rules of privity, for example *Scotson v Pegg, Pao On v Lau Yiu Long, The Eurymedon*.
- That certain of the cases are in any case Privy Council decisions so are persuasive only, for example *Pao On v Lau Yiu Long*.
- That the courts have in any case chosen to restrict the development of these exceptions to the extent, for example, that they will not allow the principle in *Williams v Roffey* to be used in the case of part-payment of debts in full satisfaction of the whole debt – *Re Selectmove*.
- It may also be discussed whether or not the law on the area is a demonstration of the courts' willingness to protect free bargaining by parties and how much cases like *Williams v Roffey* demonstrate a willingness to intervene to ensure that commercial agreements can be relied upon and respected.
- Any sensible conclusion would do – but it is probably appropriate to conclude by stating that while the basic rule has some logic, the exceptions seem often to be contradictory to the basic principles behind the requirement of consideration.

Of course, it will usually be required of you in producing a discussion that you make references also to the arguments of academic commentators either in leading texts or in journal articles.

You should also take care to follow whatever system for citation and use of tables and bibliography you have been given.

Appendix 2

ACTIVITY

Legal problem solving

Below is a very simple problem question and a guide on how to answer it.

There are four essential ingredients to answering problem questions:

- Firstly, you must be able to identify the important facts in the problem, the ones on which the answer may depend.
- Secondly, you will need to know and understand the law which is likely to apply in the situation.
- Thirdly, you will need to be able to apply the law to the facts.
- Fourthly, you will need to be able to draw conclusions from that process. This is particularly so where the problem asks you to 'advise'. If you are advising then your client is depending on you to say what to do in the circumstances.

Consider the following situation:

Problem

On 29th September, Noel wrote to his friend Liam, offering to sell Liam for £50 a ticket to a concert in which Robbie, one of his favourite artists, was starring.

Liam then wrote to Noel, posting the letter on the same day and writing:

> *Dear Noel*
> *Thanks for the offer of a ticket for Robbie's concert. I would like to go*
> *but £50 seems a bit on the dear side. I would be happier paying £35.*
> *Alternatively, could I pay you £35 now and pay you the other £15 when*
> *I get paid at the end of October?*
>
> *Yours,*
>
> *Liam*

Later on the same day, Liam wrote a second letter, again posting it on the same day. In this letter he wrote:

> *Dear Noel*
> *I have thought over your offer and decided that I really do want to see*
> *the concert and it is likely to be sold out soon so I will buy the ticket*
> *from you for £50.*
>
> *Yours truly,*
>
> *Liam*

Noel received Liam's first letter on the morning of 1st October and immediately sold the ticket to his friend Gary. When Noel returned home on the evening of 1st October, Liam's second letter had arrived.

Liam never got to see Robbie in concert and seeks your advice.

Answering the question

The facts

Unlike in real life, when a tutor or an examiner makes up a problem it is common for nearly all of the facts to be relevant in some way. Even so, they may still need to be put into some logical order to connect them to the law you need to use.

Here, the key facts seem to be:

- On 29th September Noel made an offer to Liam by post of a concert ticket for £50.
- On 29th September Liam replied by post that he would prefer to pay £35, and alternatively asked if he might pay £50 in two instalments.
- Later on 29th September, Liam sent a straightforward letter of acceptance.
- Noel sold the ticket to Gary on the morning of 1st October, after receiving Liam's first letter.
- Noel received the second letter later in the day on 1st October.
- Liam missed the concert.

The law

We know, because the problem is all about whether Noel is obliged to sell the ticket to Liam or not, that it concerns formation, and particularly offer and acceptance – indeed the word 'offer' is used in the situation.

From this and other facts we can deduce what particular rules are important to solving the problem.

The appropriate law would appear to be:

- A contract can only be formed if there is an agreement, which is a valid offer followed by a valid acceptance.
- An offer must be communicated – *Taylor v Laird*.
- An offer can be withdrawn any time before acceptance – *Routledge v Grant*.
- But this must be communicated to the offeree – *Byrne v Van Tienhoven*.
- A contract is formed once the offer is accepted.
- The acceptance must be communicated to the offeree – *Felthouse v Bindley*.
- Where the post is the normal, anticipated method of accepting then the contract is formed when the letter is posted, not when it is received – *Adams v Lindsell*.
- A counter-offer is a rejection of the offer that is no longer open to acceptance – *Hyde v Wrench*.
- But a mere enquiry has no such effect – *Stevenson v McLean*.

Applying law to fact

It is tempting to look at Liam's first letter and see it as a counter-offer. Of course, if we do that, there is nothing left to answer about. This should be a pointer in itself, but really in any problem where a particular act can be seen as one thing or the other, we need to look at both or all possibilities.

On the other hand, if we do not see it as a counter-offer, it means Liam's second letter could be an acceptance ('I will buy the ticket for £50'). We need to examine the first letter, then, to decide whether we think the first part is a definite rejection of the offer, and if not, whether the second part is only an enquiry.

If we accept that it is, then our next real concern is that Noel has sold the ticket. Can he do this? Well, if there was a counter-offer he can, with no thought to Liam. If not, then he needs to tell Liam before he sells it.

The final part of the problem is whether the postal rule applies or not. Noel has not sold the ticket until after he receives Liam's first letter. If the letter has no contractual significance then Noel has in effect withdrawn the offer without informing Liam.

Liam, on the other hand, has accepted in his second letter. If the postal rule applies (which appears possible here because all the communications are by letter) then the acceptance takes place when the letter is posted, not when Noel receives it after he has sold the ticket. The contract is formed at the time the letter is posted and Noel would be in breach of contract by selling the ticket to Gary.

Conclusions

It just remains now to make a judgment, based on our analysis above, whether to advise Liam to sue Noel or not.

Just as in real life, there might not be a definite or straightforward answer. The point is to reach a logical conclusion by using the law correctly.

You should remember to use references and citations and tables and bibliography in the way that you have been told.

Glossary of terms

Acceptance
an unconditional positive response to an offer

Accord and satisfaction
a method of replacing existing contractual terms with new ones

Adequacy
a non-legal term referring to the market value of consideration given (consideration does not have to be adequate)

Affirm
an indication of a willingness to continue with a contract

Agent
a person who has authority to act for another in forming contracts etc

Agreement
the first requirement for a validly formed contract which involves a valid offer by one party being followed by a valid acceptance by the other

Assumpsit
an old form of enforcing an undertaking to carry out a promise

Bilateral contract
a contract where both parties have negotiated the terms

Bona fide
done in good faith

Breach
a failure to honour the obligations under the contract

Capacity
the legal status to be able to enter contracts

Caveat emptor
means 'let the buyer beware' – so is a principle of freedom of contract

Charterparty
a contract for the hire of a ship

Collateral warranty
a promise made by a third party to a contract on which a contracting party may rely

Common mistake
where both parties forming a contract make the same mistake about the existence of the subject-matter of the contract or the true ownership of the subject-matter of the contract

Condition
an important term of a contract which is said to 'go to the root of the contract' allowing the victim of the breach of the term to repudiate his own obligations under the contract as well as to sue for damages

Consensus ad idem
the agreement between the parties – literally a meeting of minds

Consideration
the thing (or promise) given by a party to a contract in exchange for what the other party gives (promises to give)

Contra preferentum
a rule meaning that any ambiguity in a clause in a contract works against the party inserting the clause

Corporation
a body (rather than a person) with legal capacity to contract, eg a company

Damages
a common remedy for a breach of contract – a sum of money compensation aiming to put the injured party in the position he would have been in had the contract been properly performed

Detinue
in early contract law an action for delivery of a chattel

Discharge
how a contract comes to an end

Duress
threats of violence or actual violence used to make a party enter into a contract

Economic duress
coercion or commercial pressure used by one party in an existing commercial contract to force a variation of the contract

Exclusion clause
a term of a contract inserted by a party to exclude liability for their contractual breaches or possibly their negligence

Express term
a term of the contract agreed by the parties in advance

Frustration
an event beyond the control of either party to a contract that makes the contract impossible to perform, eg the destruction of the subject-matter of the contract

Honour pledge clause
a clause in a contract stating that the contract is not legally enforceable

Implied term
a term that is implied into a contract rather than being included by either party

Injunction
an equitable remedy which prevents one party from doing something

Innominate term
a term the remedy for breach of which depends on the consequences of the breach rather than on any prior classification

Invitation to treat
an invitation to a party to make an offer to buy as distinct from an offer

Limitation clause
a clause in a contract limiting the amount payable in damages to a set sum

Liquidated damages
a sum of damages agreed by both parties in advance of the contract

Minor
a person under the age of eighteen

Misrepresentation
a false statement of fact made by one party of the contract to the other at or before the time of contracting which he intends should induce the other party to enter the contract but which is not intended to form part of the contract

Mistake
a wrong assumption made by one or more parties to a contract on entering the contract

Mitigation
a party who is the victim of a breach of contract ensuring that they do not unreasonably add to the damages payable to them by the other party

Mutual mistake
where the two parties to a contract are at cross purposes in what they believe they are contracting on

Necessaries
goods which a minor needs and which are appropriate to his station in life so that the seller can enforce a reasonable payment for the goods

Non est factum
a mistake made about the nature of a written agreement when signing it – literally means 'this is not my deed'

Offer
an expression of willingness to be bound by certain terms

Offeree
a person to whom an offer is made

Offeror
the person making an offer

Parol evidence rule
a rule preventing the variation of a written contract by oral evidence

Penalty clauses
clauses in a contract usually to pay large sums of compensation for fairly minor breaches

Privity of contract
the requirement that to be capable of suing or being sued under a contract a person must actually be a party (privy) to that contract

Puffs
advertising boasts that are not to be relied upon

Quantum meruit
an alternative to contractual damages – a payment for work already done – literally means 'for as much as is deserved'

Quasi contract
a means of gaining a remedy for a loss not generally recoverable under strict rules of contract

Representation
a statement made in the negotiating stages of a contract

Repudiation
declaring contractual obligations at an end – could be unlawful or could be a remedy

Res extincta
in common mistake a mistake made by both parties about the existence of the subject-matter of the contract

Rescission
an equitable mechanism used to place the parties back in their pre-contractual position

Res sua
a common mistake made by both parties about the true ownership of the subject-matter under the contract

Severance
splitting aspects of a contract to remove illegal aspects and retain legitimate aspects

Sufficiency
a legal term referring to consideration provided by a party to a contract that is considered valid, ie is real, tangible and of value in the eyes of the law

Term
an obligation under a contract

Uberimmae fidei
of the utmost good faith – a requirement common in, for example, insurance contracts

Undue influence
a form of unfair pressure used to induce another party to enter a contract

Unilateral contract
a contract formed where one party performs as required by the other party's unilateral offer

Unilateral mistake
    where only one party is mistaken on entering a
    contract and the other party usually knows of and
    is taking advantage of the mistake
Unilateral offer
    an offer which demands performance rather than
    acceptance, eg reward
Unliquidated damages
    damages assessed by the court after the breach
    rather than by the parties in advance of the
    contract

Vitiating factor
    a defect that renders an otherwise validly formed
    contract void or voidable
Void contract
    an agreement made that is legally unenforceable
Voidable contract
    an equitable right to avoid obligations under a
    contract because of a vitiating defect
Warranty
    a minor term of a contract which only gives rise to
    an action for damages

Index

INDEX

459

INDEX